Fifth Edition

Handbook for
GEORGIA COUNTY
COMMISSIONERS

Fifth Edition

Handbook for
GEORGIA COUNTY
COMMISSIONERS

Edited by Betty J. Hudson and Paul T. Hardy
Published in cooperation with the
Association County Commissioners of Georgia

Carl Vinson | Institute of Government

Handbook for Georgia County Commissioners
Fifth Edition

ISBN 978-0-89854-230-1

Library of Congress Cataloging-in-Publication Data

Handbook for Georgia county commissioners / edited by Betty J. Hudson and Paul T. Hardy.—5th ed.

p. cm.

ISBN 978-0-89854-230-1

1. County government—Law and legislation—Georgia. 2. County officials and employees—Georgia—Handbooks, manuals, etc. I. Hudson, Betty J., 1955- II. Hardy, Paul T., 1953- III. Title.

KFG432.H36 2010

342.758'09—dc22

Contents

Part 2. Management of County Government

Part 3. **County Services**

Preface

For almost 85 years, the Carl Vinson Institute of Government of the University of Georgia has worked to extend the resources of the university to state and local public officials. Through training, research, policy analysis, and technical assistance, the Institute has brought the latest techniques, practices, and legal requirements to the attention of Georgia public officials. These efforts have also provided the Institute's faculty and staff with the opportunity to learn the practical problems facing county officials across the state.

The *Handbook for Georgia County Commissioners*, the first edition of which appeared in 1978, is published in cooperation with the Association County Commissioners of Georgia (ACCG). The handbook consolidates the experiences of Vinson Institute personnel, county officials, ACCG staff, and others, bringing together in one volume the fundamental principles of county government in Georgia.

Greater demands for services, considerable federal and state regulation, the need for additional county revenues, and the rapid influx of numerous technological innovations have made governing a county far more difficult than in past years. Recognizing the increasing complexity and scope of providing and funding county government services, the editors and authors of this fifth edition of the handbook have significantly revised the material to address the most relevant issues and problems that today's local governments face, including those to do with economic development and budgetary constraints.

Credit for this publication is due to many people, including the elected and appointed county officials in Georgia who have invited Vinson Institute staff to their communities and have shared with them their knowledge and understanding of local government. It is designed primarily for new or first-term Georgia county commissioners who need an introduction to county government. It is also for the experienced county commissioner who

- desires to refresh or enlarge his or her concept of county government,
- wants a brief summary of current state and federal law pertaining to counties, or
- needs a concise description of new ways to solve county problems.

The book also will also be useful to other county officials and employees and to citizens and students who desire a greater understanding of Georgia county government and its relationship to the state and other local governments.

Now as never before, Georgia county commissioners need solid grounding in the fundamentals of county government, the numerous and diverse services it does or can provide, and the various state and federal mandates under which counties must operate. Moreover, commissioners must be knowledgeable about a broad range of subjects and be informed sufficiently in order to effectively engage specialists and help them solve county problems. This book is intended to assist in meeting these needs.

Acknowledgments

The editors of the handbook, Paul T. Hardy and Betty J. Hudson, also made major contributions to the publication as authors. Mr. Hardy retired from the Governmental Services and Research Division of the Vinson Institute in 2010. Ms. Hudson is a public service associate in the Governmental Services and Research Division.

Other current or former Vinson Institute faculty and staff who wrote all or portions of chapters or who served as reviewers include the following:

David N. Ammons
Richard W. Campbell
Sabrina Wiley Cape
Don Christy
Wes Clarke
Stephen E. Condrey
Paul E. Glick
Harry W. Hayes
Dan Hope
Rob McDowell
Margaret Myszewski
John A. O'Looney
Paula S. Sanford
Jerry A. Singer
Charles R. Swanson Jr.
J. Devereux Weeks

ACCG contributors who wrote all or portions of chapters include the following:

Kathleen Bowen
Elizabeth Bradley
Beth Brown
Todd Edwards
James F. Grubiak
Randy Hartmann
Matthew Hicks
Ross King
Clint Mueller
Michele NeSmith
Kelly J. L. Pridgen
Dave Wills

The editors also thank ACCG legal intern Stefanie Mueller for her work in verifying legal citations throughout the handbook.

Other contributors who wrote all or portions of chapters include the following:

Melissa Carter, Office of the Child Advocate
Donald Cronin, O'Quinn and Cronin LLC
Kevin Doran, Holland & Knight LLP
Richard M. Gold, Holland & Knight LLP
R. Terry Hadaway, The Media Trainers LLC
Kelly Joiner, Medical Center of Central Georgia
James Monacell, Smith, Gambrell & Russell LLP
Virgil Moon, Cobb County Government
Michael O'Quinn, O'Quinn and Cronin LLC
Michael Sherberger, Johnson, Maples, and Associates Inc.
Saralyn Stafford, Georgia Academy for Economic Development
Charlie Walters, Department of Behavioral Health and
    Developmental Disabilities
Annaka Woodruff, Georgia Department of Community Affairs

Introduction

Public service calls individuals to work on behalf of their nation, state, or community. It draws people who are willing to dedicate their time and talents to make a difference in the lives of others. The challenges and complexities of governing today require leaders with vision, compassion, creativity, and commitment. Throughout Georgia, men and women from all walks of life are addressing the challenges and responsibilities of their local communities by serving their constituents.

The effect of a successful leader is not always recognized while he or she is in office but instead may be reflected in the legacy of accomplishments that span far beyond an official's tenure. Developing a clear vision for a community—together with strategies and benchmarks—can greatly aid county commissioners in reaching specific goals. Whether that vision calls for increasing economic development, preserving the local culture, addressing critical infrastructure, improving the efficiency of local government, or a combination of these objectives, greater success comes from having a clear understanding of a vision and being able to articulate and implement it.

In addition to having a clear vision, great leaders have compassion for those whom they govern. The many diverse services offered by local governments touch the lives of constituents every day. Whether they work in the criminal justice system or the local health department, county officials interact with people who are dependent upon or need services from their local government. In many cases, local governments quietly provide services throughout a community that citizens often overlook but that are necessary for the maintenance of health, welfare, and public safety.

In today's economy, county commissioners must make difficult decisions that affect service delivery for not only required services but also services that are expected by a community such as parks and recreation, libraries, and facilities for senior citizens. In making such decisions, they must carefully assess the information at hand, recognizing that each action will have a direct consequence on the people they were elected to serve. Recognizing the responsibility to represent the diverse interests of the constituents who make up a community requires understanding all aspects of an issue before making a decision. By communicating compassion toward their respective constituencies, even in the face of tough times, commissioners can help people understand that their concerns are appreciated.

Another outstanding trait of successful leaders is innovation. The ability to examine a problem and develop creative solutions can redefine how long-standing government services function. One of the most readily available resources a commissioner has is county staff. Many of these employees (including county managers, administrators, clerks, county attorneys, finance directors, and road superintendents) can offer both experience and insight into particular problems. Constitutional officers can also be solicited to provide solutions, especially if the county commission has fostered a good working relationship with them. Questioning why or how local government functions or services are provided while soliciting input from more experienced county officials or county staff from within a jurisdiction or across county lines can help commissioners make better-informed decisions.

Local government does not function in isolation. The Georgia Constitution establishes counties as extensions of state government for service delivery. Counties are legally required to provide many services such as jails, the courts system, indigent defense, and elections. This interconnected nature of governing means that county commissions do not always have flexibility in managing budgets. For this reason, it is imperative that county commissioners establish strong working relationships with state legislators. They should be able to make the connections between the needs of county governments and their roles and responsibilities, thereby ensuring that changes made at the state level do not negatively affect service delivery at the local level.

Likewise, county commissioners should get to know federal legislators representing their area. The federal government is passing more and more funding from federal programs directly to local governments. Commissioners should recognize that federal legislators can and do serve as advocates for needs within their jurisdiction.

Public service is a commitment that is not without its complexities. As local government leaders, county commissioners celebrate the successes of their respective communities and their citizens. At the same time, they understand the challenges that stand before them.

Having an overview of county government processes is necessary before an official can make a real contribution to his or her community. This handbook, published by the Carl Vinson Institute of Government in cooperation with the Association County Commissioners of Georgia (ACCG), serves as a reference guide for newly elected and experienced commissioners alike. It consolidates the expertise of Vinson Institute personnel, ACCG staff, county officials, and others, bringing together in one volume the fundamental principles of county government in Georgia. The handbook explains how county government works, provides a summary of the current state and federal laws pertaining to counties, and highlights options to consider for specific situations. Other citizens who wish to have a greater understanding of county government will also find this book useful.

Local government leadership may seem like a daunting task, but county commissioners are not in it alone. The organizations that have produced this handbook are ready to serve county officials. For nearly 100 years, ACCG has brought county officials together and provided leadership development, cost-efficient services, and public policy development and advocacy. ACCG's professional staff assists local government through an ever-growing variety of programs and services including technical assistance, legislative action, civic engagement, communications and education initiatives, pooled risk management, insurance and retirement programs, and other services offering savings for county operations.

By becoming involved with ACCG, officials are able to keep current with trends in county government, cost-saving initiatives, legislative issues, professional training, and successful strategies employed by other counties across the state. Members are able to tap into the collective knowledge and experience of the organization, which will assist them in their roles as elected officials.

County commissioners can further their understanding of local government by participating in the Vinson Institute's professional training and certification programs offered in partnership with ACCG. Through training, research, policy analysis, technical assistance, and other educational programs, the Institute offers the latest techniques, practices, and legal requirements to Georgia public officials. These nationally recognized programs, offered for more than two decades, provide training in specialized areas from leading experts in local government. Furthermore, the peer-to-peer interaction gained through these training opportunities helps local leaders bring effective solutions back to their communities.

As you absorb the material in this handbook and become active in the organizations that have produced it, bear in mind that public service provides an incredible means by which to influence government programs and services and increase civic engagement. Leaders in the public arena are able to leave a lasting legacy for Georgia's communities and create a true sense of community along with meaningful opportunities for the next generation.

PART 1

Organization and Structure

1

Richard W. Campbell, David N. Ammons, and Dave Wills

County Government Structure

A county government's structure—also known as its form of government—allocates formal authority among key officials. In so doing, the structure assigns primary policy-making and executive responsibilities and influences the way county officials interact.

Over the last two to three decades, in response to increasing citizen demands and federal and state mandates, counties have been called upon to provide a wider range and higher level of services. Moreover, scholars such as David Osborne and Ted Gaebler have called upon government officials to pay greater attention to efficiency, productivity improvements, and results-oriented management practices.[1] Consequently, officials in a large number of U.S. counties have adopted structures that provide for professional management.[2] In Georgia, the percentage of counties having a professional manager or administrator with extensive executive authority grew from 34 percent in 1993 to almost 74 percent (117 counties) in 2009. Of the remaining 42 counties, 29 have full-time management via a sole commissioner, elected chief executive officer, or full-time commission chairperson, leaving just 13 counties with no formal, full-time management.[3]

This chapter examines the policy-making and executive roles involved in the five primary structural forms of government, some of the variations in forms, the arguments generally offered in support of professional management, and the legal requirements associated with structural change in Georgia.

POLICY-MAKING AND EXECUTIVE ROLES

A county government's leaders perform the policy-making role when they decide important issues, establish priorities, plan the county's future, or declare what values will be emphasized by the county government.

The most obvious examples of county policy are the ordinances, resolutions, and formally adopted motions of the duly elected governing body. Additionally, the adoption of the annual county budget may be construed as a component of establishing policy since it allocates funding for services. These forms of policy making represent the exercise of legislative responsibility.

In contrast, the executive role typically is depicted in terms of administrative duties. The most obvious aspect of executive responsibility is the management of county government operations. Implementing county policies and delivering county services are primarily executive responsibilities.

In some counties, policy-making and executive roles are merged, and a single official or body of officials is charged with both. In others, the formal structure of county government divides executive and policy-making roles—typically to achieve separation of powers or as an attempt to insulate the administrative side of county government (e.g., selecting contractors, purchasing supplies, hiring employees, and responding to service requests) from political considerations.

On the surface, the distinction between policy-making and executive functions appears to be clear-cut. In the world of county government, however, that distinction is rarely so clear. Executive actions, for example, sometimes define county policies when the governing body has been silent. Furthermore, the advice of executive officials on various issues may influence the thinking of official policymakers. In such cases, executives are drawn into the policy-making process. In turn, policymakers often become involved in the oversight of a particular operation that interests them or their constituents, and their interest may influence management actions to a degree beyond that normally associated with the policy-making role. Beneath the surface of apparent separation of duties in many governments, then, is a cooperative arrangement in which formal role assignments designate primary or ultimate responsibility rather than exclusive prerogatives.

ALTERNATIVE FORMS OF GOVERNMENT

County governments in Georgia generally fit into one of five structural categories: traditional commission, sole commissioner, elected executive, commission-administrator, or commission-manager form of government. Although variations occur, most county structures generally conform to one of the five forms. Each may be distinguished from the other four by its formal assignment of primary policy-making and executive roles

(Table 1-1). The existence of a full-time chairperson is a significant variation on these categories, one that may affect the allocation of roles and responsibilities between the chairperson and the board and, if one exists, the manager or administrator. A full-time chairperson is most commonly found in traditional commissions but may also be found in commission-manager and commission-administrator forms of government.

Traditional Commission

Throughout most of the twentieth century, the most common county government structure in Georgia, and across the nation, was the traditional commission form in which primary policy-making and executive responsibilities are combined and held by a board of commissioners

Table 1-1. *Assignment of Primary Policy-Making and Executive Roles in County Government*

Form of Government	Primary Policy-Making Role*	Primary Executive Role*
Traditional commission	Board of commissioners	Board of commissioners (as a whole, individually or as committees—perhaps with the assistance of an appointed administrator). Sometimes provides additional administrative authority to the chairperson.
Sole commissioner	Single commissioner	Single commissioner.
Elected executive	Shared by board of commissioners and elected executive	Elected executive (perhaps with the assistance of an appointed administrator).
Commission-administrator	Board of commissioners	Typically shared by commission and appointed administrator—and sometimes involves special administrative authority for the chairperson.
Commission-manager	Board of commissioners	Appointed manager held accountable for executive functions by board of commissioners. In "pure" form, manager reports to full commission rather than primarily to the chairperson.

*Limited by the existence of separately elected "constitutional officers."

(Figure 1-1). However, with the movement toward professional management in the 1990s and early 2000s, only slightly more than one-fifth of Georgia's counties (34) continued to have this form as of 2009 (Figure 1-2). Of these counties, 21 have full-time chairpersons.[4] Although the traditional commission form is distinguished by the merging of primary policy-making and executive responsibility in the hands of the governing authority, governments using this form vary in their approach to handling executive duties. While the most overt policy-making (or legislative) functions are performed by the board of commissioners deliberating as a collective body, the board's handling of executive functions usually follows one of four patterns:

- *Functional assignments for individual commissioners.* The "pure" commission form designates each commissioner as the administrative head of a given function, department, or set of departments. A variation involves the hiring of a department head for a given function who reports to the designated commissioner.

- *Executive supervision by committee.* Under this approach, a county supervises its various functions through a committee system. Committees made up of members of the board of commissioners are responsible for the supervision of assigned functions or departments.

- *Supervision by "committee of the whole."* A county commission that supervises departmental operations and addresses executive matters as a collective body operates under this system.

- *Primary executive role for commission chairperson.* Under this approach, the board of commissioners retains ultimate executive responsibility, but day-to-day executive duties are performed by the chairperson of the board of commissioners.

Boards of commissioners operating under the traditional commission form in Georgia generally have three to seven members, with a five-member board being most common. In nearly three-quarters of the Georgia counties operating with this structure, the commission chairperson is selected directly by the voters in a general election; in the remainder, the commission chooses its own chairperson from among its members.

Sole Commissioner

Some jurisdictions in Georgia have a form of county government rarely found outside the state. They operate under a structure that resembles the traditional commission with one major difference: the "board of commissioners" consists of only one individual. The sole commissioner possesses the full policy-making and executive responsibilities assigned to boards of commissioners in counties operating under the traditional commission form. Considerable authority, therefore, is concentrated in the hands of a single official.

During the early 1990s, Georgia's unique sole commissioner form of government came under the scrutiny of the federal courts. Lawsuits under the Voting Rights Act were brought against Bleckley, Wheeler, and Pulaski Counties. In 1992, in *Hall v. Holder*, the 11th Circuit Court of Appeals ruled that single-commissioner county commissions violated Section 2 of the Voting Rights Act.[5] Based on this ruling, Wheeler County changed to a three-member commission under a court order in May 1993. Subsequently, the voting rights case involving Bleckley County reached the U.S. Supreme Court. In this case, the court reversed the 11th Circuit's decision and held that the single-commissioner form of government was not subject to a vote dilution challenge under Section 2 of the Voting Rights Act.[6] This decision effectively ended the litigation involving Pulaski County. Currently, Bleckley and Pulaski still retain the single-member county commission.

As of October 2009, nine Georgia counties, seven of which are located in the northern portion of the state, were operating with a sole commissioner.[7]

Elected Executive

The elected executive form of county government most closely resembles the separation-of-powers structure of national and state governments in the United States. Under this structure, the board of commissioners—like Congress at the national level—is elected to perform the legislative functions of government, and the executive (the county executive or chief executive officer), like the president, heads the executive branch.

Like state governors, elected county executives may be granted extensive or very limited formal authority. When formal authority is extensive, the "strong" county executive may enjoy unfettered power to appoint or remove department heads and to develop the county's proposed budget and may have authority to veto acts of the board of commissioners. When formal authority is more limited, the "weak" county executive may be required to seek concurrence of the board of commissioners for appointment or removal of department heads, may simply coordinate the receipt of departmental budget requests for development of a budget by the board of commissioners, and may possess no veto power.[8] In Georgia, as of October 2009, only DeKalb County was operating under the elected executive structure.[9]

Figure 1-1. *The Five Forms of Georgia County Government (Hypothetical Organization Charts)*

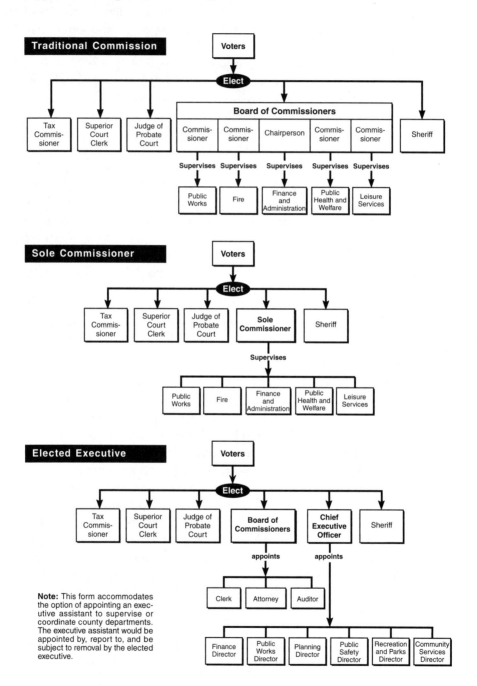

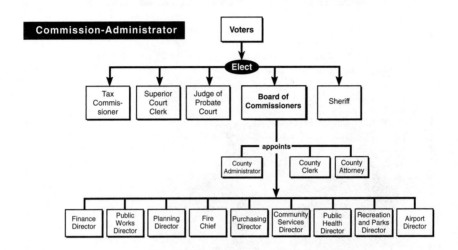

Note: As drawn in this hypothetical organization chart, the county administrator would coordinate the efforts of various departments headed by directors appointed by the board of commissioners. An alternative commission-administrator structure would place the county administrator directly beneath the board of commissioners in the path leading to most department heads, indicating greater supervisory responsibility, and could give the county administrator the authority to appoint and remove most department heads with the concurrence of the commission.

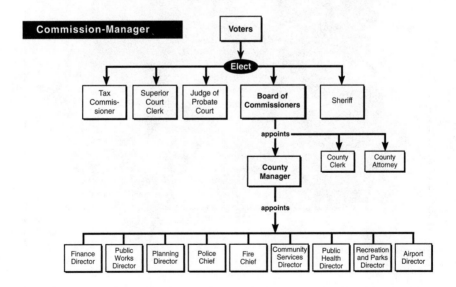

Figure 1-2. *Forms of County Government in Georgia*

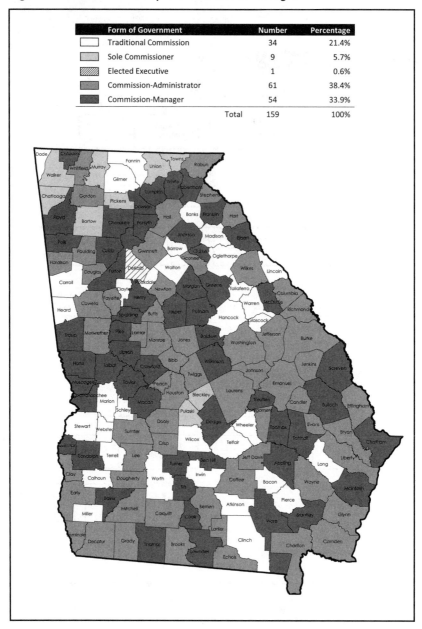

Form of Government	Number	Percentage
Traditional Commission	34	21.4%
Sole Commissioner	9	5.7%
Elected Executive	1	0.6%
Commission-Administrator	61	38.4%
Commission-Manager	54	33.9%
Total	159	100%

Source: Data compiled from *Characteristics of County Government* (Atlanta: Association County Commissioners of Georgia, 2009).

Commission-Administrator

Under the commission-administrator form, the board of commissioners bears ultimate responsibility for the policy-making and executive functions of county government but secures advisory assistance in the policy role and substantial administrative assistance in the executive role through its appointment of a county administrator. In Georgia, 55 percent of the commission-administrator counties select the commission chairperson from among the members of the commission. By contrast, 71 percent of traditional commission counties and 60 percent of commission-manager counties select the chairperson by vote in a general election.

Formal authority granted to the county administrator differs from one county to another but normally is more limited than that granted to appointed executives having the title "county manager." Typically, the county administrator's authority over department heads and over the preparation of the proposed budget is limited, with a substantial role reserved for the commission. The board of commissioners customarily has the power to appoint or remove the county administrator—although in some cases the chairperson may have extraordinary authority in that regard. As of October 2009, almost 39 percent (61) of Georgia's counties were operating under the commission-administrator form of government.

Commission-Manager

The commission-manager form of county government corresponds to the council-manager form of municipal government. Under this structure, the board of commissioners fills the primary policy-making role and oversees the executive functions of the county but assigns the day-to-day duties of the executive role to an expert manager whom the board selects based on administrative qualifications and experience. Ultimate control over operations of county government is retained through the board's authority to remove the manager at any time it deems necessary or appropriate.

Although clearly subordinate to the board of commissioners, the county manager is granted substantial executive authority commensurate with primary (though not ultimate) executive responsibility. In the "pure" commission-manager structure, the manager has authority to appoint and remove most department heads, is responsible for preparing the proposed budget for submission to the board of commissioners, and reports directly to the full board of commissioners rather than to a single officeholder. Just over one-third of Georgia's counties (54) were operating under the commission-manager structure as of October 2009.

PROFESSIONALISM IN RELATION TO COUNTY GOVERNMENT STRUCTURE

County governments vary in the emphasis they place on professionalism, and that emphasis is often supported by the form of government in use. A desire for increased efficiency, effectiveness, and equity in service delivery typically underlies decisions to enhance professionalism. Modern county governments increasingly draw on professional expertise to tackle difficult issues and manage day-to-day operations. Some counties retain traditional structures but nevertheless tap professional expertise by hiring consultants or employing professionally trained staff assistants and department heads. Other counties have chosen to fundamentally alter their administrative structures to reduce political pressures on executive functions and thereby allow professional management considerations to weigh more heavily in service delivery decisions.

Appointing a professional manager as the county's chief executive is generally regarded as the highest preference for professionalism in service delivery. The structure that embodies that strategy—the commission-manager form—has been endorsed by the National Civic League since 1930.[10] The formal allocation of executive authority to a qualified manager ensures that professional expertise will be brought to bear on local operations and problems, increases the likelihood that other professionals (e.g., planners, finance officers, and personnel experts) will be brought on board in subordinate capacities, and enhances the county's recruiting edge over traditional structures in the pursuit of talented professionals.

A county manager's authority over departmental operations, personnel, and budget development is extensive under the commission-manager structure, but the commission's ultimate control over the manager is absolute. Modified versions with more limited executive authority for the appointed administrator—including the commission-administrator form—provide some of the benefits of increased professionalism associated with the commission-manager plan but typically retain a more political flavor and in some instances may even reduce the role of the county administrator to performing the functions of a coordinator or administrative assistant. Such structures often make the county administrator responsible to the commission chairperson first and the commission second and frequently establish direct relationships between departments and commission members for matters of budget, personnel, and operations. Understandably, arrangements tying the administrator primarily to the chairperson tend to tie the administrator's future to the political fortunes of that individual and may lead to distortions of the management recommendations that might be provided to the board of commissioners under a more direct reporting arrangement. Establishing direct linkages between commission members and departments for budget, personnel, and operations tends to undermine the administrator's ability to control the county bureaucracy. Such arrangements may, then, attract a pool of management candidates that differs from that drawn to more fully empowered county manager opportunities.

It is important to note that the terms "county manager" and "county administrator" are not legally defined terms. Thus, a county administrator in Georgia may have powers consistent with those of a county manager. In other words, one must look at the actual duties assigned to the county manager or administrator rather than the title of the position.

Many counties claim to be professionally managed. The label has a very positive connotation, and those counties may feel that it is an entirely accurate description of their government's management. Many base their assessment on the fact that they employ an individual who earns a substantial salary and performs administrative duties on a full-time basis. However, professional management goes beyond those criteria.

Under a more stringent view of professional management, a highly trained and experienced administrator is hired to serve as chief executive and is granted extensive executive authority commensurate with that responsibility. Among professional local government managers, formal training increasingly includes graduate education—often a Master of Public Administration degree—and professional experience increasingly means responsible administrative experience in local government. Many elements are included in such a grant of extensive formal executive authority, but the three most crucial are

- authority to appoint and remove most department heads,
- authority to develop the proposed budget for consideration by the board of commissioners, and
- direct responsibility to the full board of commissioners.[11]

The authority to appoint and remove department heads is a key element of executive control. To the extent that the board of commissioners retains control of such decisions, personnel decisions—and, as a consequence, many operational decisions—remain political. Similarly, the manager's responsibility for preparing the proposed budget increases the likelihood that management considerations will weigh more heavily in initial budget preparation, with such considerations tempered by political judgments at the stage of commission review. Under such a format, departments are forced to submit budget requests that are managerially sound rather than rely primarily on their ability to "play politics."

The third element of executive empowerment for a professionally managed county is a direct reporting relationship between the manager and the full board of commissioners. Alternative arrangements—perhaps requiring the manager to report through the chairperson on budgetary and other key matters or granting the chairperson extraordinary authority in the selection or removal of the manager—may, by setting the stage for the filtering of managerial recommendations by the chairperson, deprive the full board of commissioners of the professional advice it desires and, by tying the manager to a single political official, tend to politicize rather than professionalize county management.

Perhaps the most stringent registry of professional management among Georgia counties is compiled by the International City/County Management Association (ICMA) in its list of counties recognized as having council-manager (e.g., commission-manager) government. In that form, the manager (1) is appointed by a majority of the council or commission, (2) has an advisory role in policy formulation and direct responsibility in policy implementation, (3) is designated as having responsibility for preparation and implementation of the budget, and (4) has authority to appoint and remove at least most department heads. Among Georgia counties, 25 have been recognized by ICMA as having council-manager government; 5 others have been identified as complying with the somewhat relaxed standards of "general management" government.[12] All of these counties assign substantial budgetary authority to their appointed administrator. The grant of personnel management authority to an administrator varies, however, with full authority more common among council-manager counties than among those recognized by ICMA as having general management government.

In Georgia, the commission-manager form of government tends to be found among more populous counties with higher per capita incomes. The traditional commission and sole commissioner forms tend to be found most often among smaller counties with lower per capita incomes.

CHANGING A COUNTY'S FORM OF GOVERNMENT

A county's form of government may be changed by local legislation adopted by the Georgia General Assembly. Local legislation changing a county's structure generally amends those laws that create the county governing authority and defines its operations, powers, and limitations.[13] The office of the county manager may also be created by an ordinance of the county governing authority. In creating the office of county manager through the adoption of an ordinance, the governing body is authorized by state law to vest in that office powers, duties, and responsibilities of an administrative nature and to define the qualifications, method of selection, appointment, and compensation.[14] Since a local ordinance can be altered or repealed at any meeting of the governing authority, creation of the office of county manager through the passage of an ordinance rather than through local legislation could result in a less stable organizational structure.

Commonly Asked Questions about Form of Government

Does form of government really make any difference?

Yes, it does. Form of government sets the fundamental rules of county governance. It declares whether the county's major policy decisions will be in the hands of a governing body acting collectively, a single elected official, or some combination through separation of powers. It also declares whether a government's executive functions will be managed by committee, by a single elected official, or by a professional manager.

Are different orientations or values associated with particular forms of government?

Yes, they are—although those associations are more aptly described as general tendencies than as absolute relationships. The commission-manager form emphasizes a management orientation. Its proponents have likened that form to the corporate model of organization, with the board of commissioners, chairperson, and county manager being analogous to the board of directors, chairperson, and corporate president, respectively. Other forms of government are more politicized than the commission-manager form and tend to emphasize political leadership.

The commission-administrator form of government seems to be a blend of the traditional commission and the commission-manager forms of government. Is that blend an effective way to secure the best characteristics of each model?

That is precisely what commission-administrator proponents claim for that form. It is important to recognize, however, that the "blend" is in many respects a compromise and that several of the characteristics are usually diluted in the hybrid. Typically, the county administrator's executive authority is more limited than that of a county manager in important functions such as personnel and budget, with the board of commissioners retaining a larger role in these functions than would a board of directors in the corporate model. Furthermore, if the county administrator's employment is tied to the chairperson, he or she may not have the privilege of a direct relationship with the full board of commissioners. Primary affiliation with a single elected official rather than with the governing body as a whole may link the administrator's fortunes to those of the chairperson and restrict the administrator's ability to function as an objective professional.

In short, the commission-administrator form may differ rather sharply from the commission-manager form in terms of managerial authority and professionalism. These factors are likely to affect the pool of candidates for the post of administrator and are almost certain to influence government operations in the long run.

Why are budgetary and personnel authorities considered important elements of professional management?

A professional manager expects to have the opportunity to present objective budgetary recommendations to the governing body and to assemble a professional staff that will abide by the manager's directives. Without the authority to prepare the proposed budget or to appoint and remove subordinates, "end runs" to the commission will be common, and the manager's ability to truly manage county operations will be limited.

Can the county manager become too powerful?

It is true that the county manager possesses extensive executive authority and that many managers become trusted and influential advisors to county commissions on policy matters. But county managers serve at the pleasure of the commission. They may be removed at any time by a vote of the commission. Most long-tenured managers have demonstrated an adeptness at gauging the role expectations their commissions hold for the manager and a willingness to limit their initiative and accept a background role when that is the commission's wish.

How can a particular county know which form of government is best for it?

It is difficult to provide a simple answer. However, if the county believes that the most likely avenue to solving its problems or realizing its opportunities is through improved management, the commission-manager form or perhaps the commission-administrator form is worth a careful look. If, on the other hand, the most likely avenue is through political means (e.g., bargaining among groups and individuals), one of the more traditional forms may be preferable.

Which forms of government are considered "strong" executive forms? Which are "weak" executive forms? Are those characteristics relevant to the ability of the board of commissioners to influence the executive function?

The "strong" and "weak" labels pertain to the degree to which executive authority is concentrated or diffused and not to the characteristics or capabilities of the individual or individuals serving in the executive post. When executive authority is concentrated in the hands of a single official—as in the elected executive form, the sole commissioner form, and the commission-manager form—the "strong" executive has greater ability to coordinate departmental operations and command the smooth operation of county functions. When executive authority is diffused, coordination and control by "weak" executives is often very difficult. The principal ramification for the board of commissioners lies in the degree to which that body has influence over the executive function. Commissioners share control of the executive function in the "weak" executive forms but, as the label implies, executive authority is fragmented and disjointed. Among the "strong" executive options, only the commission-manager form offers a multimember commission ultimate authority over the executive.

What are the pros and cons of concentrated executive authority in a single office (strong executive) versus executive authority diffused among several office holders (weak executive)?

The rationale for concentrated executive authority rests on the desire to establish clear lines of accountability, to establish an effective means of executive control over operations, and to provide to the executive substantial authority commensurate with significant responsibilities and high performance expectations for that office. Those counties that have opted instead for more limited or more broadly diffused executive authority have generally done so in order to minimize potential for abuse of power—even at the cost of limited executive coordination and control. Those counties adopting the commission-manager form typically have perceived that structure as a means of securing the advantages of a strong executive while simultaneously minimizing the potential for abuse of power. The commission-manager structure features strong executive coordination and control in a professional manager but places that manager under the ultimate authority of a representative governing body.

Why do some counties choose to separate the primary policy-making and executive roles while others grant greater authority for both to the board of commissioners?

The rationale for separation—either fully and formally (e.g., elected executive form) or through separation of duties and authority while retaining ultimate control by the commission (e.g., commission-manager form)—usually emphasizes the desirability of checks and balances through role separation, the desirability of legislative scrutiny over a separate executive branch in the budget approval process, and, in the case of the commission-manager form, a preference for appointment rather than election as the means of securing expert administrative officials for the county government.

Does the existence of "constitutional officers" restrict the extent to which executive control can be fully concentrated?

Yes, it does. The status of specially elected officials called constitutional officers—sheriff, superior court clerk, judge of probate court, and tax commissioner—relative to other officials formally charged with policy-making and executive responsibility can be a serious issue. The direct election of other county officials is often used by the framers of state constitutions to limit the concentration of executive authority. It may also have the effect of removing such officials from effective legislative or executive control of the county commission. Many of these elected officials choose to comply with policy decisions and executive directives of the county commission, but because they are directly elected by the citizens and protected by the constitution, a county commission often has little recourse against those who do not cooperate. In such instances, those officials formally designated as having primary policy-making or executive roles may discover that their ability to fulfill those prescribed roles is more limited than they might have imagined.

NOTES

1. David Osborne and Ted Gaebler, *Reinventing Government* (Reading, MA: Addison-Wesley, 1992).
2. *Local Government Longitudinal Statistics* (Washington, DC: ICMA, 1984–2009).
3. *Characteristics of Georgia County Government* (Atlanta: Association County Commissioners of Georgia, 2009).
4. Ibid.
5. Hall v. Holder, 955 F.2d 1563 (1992).
6. Holder v. Hall, 512 U.S. 874 (1994). Bartow, Bleckly, Chattooga, Murray, Pickens, Pulaski, Towns, Union, and Walker Counties have a sole commissioner.
7. *Characteristics of Georgia County Government.*
8. The "weak" and "strong" labels attached to various government structures refer to the concentration and strength of formal authorities granted to the executive. When formal executive authority is modest and diffused, the government is said to have a weak executive structure. When formal executive authority is extensive and concentrated in a single office, the government has a strong executive.
9. Dade County's enabling law provides for a chairperson/county executive, but this position does not have the authority typically attributed to an elected executive.
10. *Model County Charter* (Denver: National Civic League, 1990). Previous endorsements by the league, then known as the National Municipal League, include the Model County Manager Law, published in 1930, and the first Model County Charter, published in 1956.
11. For a more complete discussion of the granting of executive authority to professional managers in Georgia counties, see David N. Ammons and Richard W. Campbell, "Does Your County Have Professional Management or Just Limited Professional Assistance?" *Georgia County Government* 44 (July 1992): 24–27. Also see James H. Svara, "Leadership and Professionalism in County Government," in *The American County: Frontiers of Knowledge*, ed. Donald Menzel (Tuscaloosa: University of Alabama Press, 1996).
12. *Who's Who in Local Government Management* (Washington, DC: International City/County Management Association, 2009).
13. Ga. Const. art. IX, §2, ¶1.
14. Official Code of Georgia Annotated §36-5-22.

2

James F. Grubiak and Kelly J. L. Pridgen

Counties: Sources and Limits of Power

The State of Georgia is subdivided into 159 counties. Georgia counties derive their powers from the Georgia Constitution, federal and state statutes, local legislation, county ordinances, and resolutions. Conversely, counties' powers are limited by these same sources, as well as by the U.S. Constitution.[1]

A county is a political subdivision of the State of Georgia and exists, in large measure, to administer locally the general powers and policies of the state.[2] A county acts by and through its local county governing authority. The county governing authority is the elected board of commissioners, sole commissioner, chief executive officer (CEO) and commissioners, or mayor/chairperson and council/commissioners of a consolidated government.[3] The local governing authority may only take those actions and exercise those powers that are expressly stated in law[4] (i.e., express powers) or those powers that are necessarily implied from these express powers[5] (implied powers). Stated in another way, county commissioners may not take any action, enter into any contract, or incur any liability unless it is expressly authorized by law.[6]

GEORGIA CONSTITUTION AND STATE STATUTES

The highest level of state law governing counties is the Georgia Constitution of 1983 and subsequent amendments. It is supreme to all general and local acts of the General Assembly, as well as to county ordinances and resolutions. Any state law that is inconsistent with the constitution is void.[7]

The next level of laws governing counties includes general statutes and local legislation enacted by the General Assembly. General statutes are codified in the Official Code of Georgia Annotated (O.C.G.A.) and generally apply to counties on a statewide basis. A category of general statutes, known as population acts, applies to counties falling within certain population categories—oftentimes, only one county is affected due to a narrow gap between the upper and lower populations specified. While numerous population acts are currently in effect, enactment of new population acts has been effectively eliminated by the 1983 Constitution and subsequent legislation.[8] The practical effect has been that the General Assembly now passes new population acts for only one purpose: to adjust the population categories of existing population acts after each decennial census in order to allow for the statutes to continue to affect the same county or counties they were originally intended to affect.[9]

In addition to general state statutes and local legislation (described in more detail later), county officials need to be aware of any local constitutional amendments that apply to their county. Local constitutional amendments can no longer be enacted under the current constitution. As with population acts, many local constitutional amendments are still in effect. Existing constitutional amendments can be repealed, but they cannot be amended.[10]

Local constitutional amendments and population acts were enacted to authorize or require certain counties to do something that counties were not generally allowed or empowered to do. County officials should periodically review any local constitutional amendments and population acts pertinent to their county to ensure that they are in compliance with these special laws and ensure that these special laws are still appropriate or necessary—particularly after each census.

LOCAL LEGISLATION

Local legislation is generally adopted by the General Assembly for individual counties. Local legislation is often referred to as enabling legislation when it dictates the organizational structure or form of government of the county governing authority (e.g., whether it has a sole commissioner, full-time or part-time chairperson) and much of what it may and may not do.[11] All county commissioners, managers, and attorneys should be familiar with their county's local legislation in order to determine the limits of their power and authority as well as be aware of certain actions that they are required by law to take. For all practical purposes, local legislation passes the General Assembly by "local courtesy," which means that as long as the county's legislative delegation (i.e., the state senators and state representatives who represent the county) agrees to the local legislation, the rest of the members of the General Assembly will vote to approve the local legislation without debate.

Form of Government

A county's local legislation establishes the form or structure of the county governing authority. For example, local legislation typically establishes the governing authority as a traditional commission, sole commissioner, elected executive, commission-administrator, commission-manager or consolidated county structure.[12] See Chapter 1 for descriptions of the alternative forms of government. The local act also designates the number of commissioners, establishes the geographical boundaries of each commissioner's district, sets the length of terms of office, specifies whether the commissioners serve staggered or concurrent terms, and states whether the chairperson serves full time or part time. In addition, the local act specifies whether the chairperson is elected by the citizens or the members of the board or whether the position rotates among board members. Local legislation also specifies whether commissioners run in single-member, at-large districts, or a combination of the two.

Compensation

Although local legislation may address compensation and expense reimbursement for county commissioners, commissioners also have home rule authority to establish their own salaries and expense reimbursement policies.[13] See Chapter 3 for details.

Other Matters

Local legislation may list the powers and duties of the chairperson as well as other county officials and employees such as the county attorney, manager, clerk, or finance officer. It may also include requirements regarding commission meetings such as dates and locations or specify use of certain meetings procedures such as *Robert's Rules of Order*. A local act may also include thresholds and procedures for purchasing. In some counties, the commissioners have been given power regarding the compensation of other county officers and their employees through local legislation. While local legislation to change the form of government is often made subject to a referendum, a referendum is not required by the constitution.

Codification

A county's local legislation must be codified and included with the rest of its ordinances.[14]

HOME RULE AUTHORITY

The Georgia Constitution gives counties "home rule" authority to manage the county rather than merely executing decisions made at the state level. County commissioners have legislative power to adopt clearly reasonable ordinances, resolutions, or regulations relating to the property and affairs of the county in cases for which no other provision has been made by general law, so long as these actions are not inconsistent with the constitution or any applicable local or general law.[15]

Pursuant to the county's home rule authority, commissioners may also amend local legislation enacted by the General Assembly applicable to the county except regarding certain matters that are preempted by general law or reserved to the General Assembly.[16] For example, county commissioners may change the timing or frequency of their regular meetings through a home rule amendment to their local legislation.

In order for a county to amend its local legislation through home rule, the commissioners must adopt a resolution or ordinance at two consecutive regular meetings that are no less than 7 or more than 60 days apart. A notice of the amendment must be published once per week for three weeks within the 60 days prior to the final adoption of the amendment. The notice must specify that a copy of the amendment is available in the superior court clerk's office. The amendment, with an affidavit from the newspaper stating the notice publication dates, must be filed with the secretary of state before the amendment may be effective.[17] The General Assembly may not repeal, modify, or supersede a home rule amendment lawfully enacted by a county commission under its home rule powers.[18]

However, home rule power does not extend to subjects that are within the exclusive control of the General Assembly.[19] Commissioners may not amend their local legislation or adopt ordinances in order to do the following:

- Change the composition or form of the county governing authority (i.e., commissioners cannot change the number of commissioners or the structure of the local governing authority)[20]
- Change the procedure for the election or fill a vacancy on the local governing authority[21]
- Change the compensation of the county officers (i.e., sheriff, tax commissioner, superior court clerk, and probate judge)[22] or of the courts[23] or their employees[24]
- Define any new criminal offense or provide for criminal punishment.[25] However, the General Assembly has provided a pro-

cedure for the prosecution of and maximum punishment for county ordinance violations.[26]

- Create any new forms of taxation beyond those taxes authorized by statute or the Georgia Constitution[27]
- Regulate businesses that are regulated by the Public Service Commission unless otherwise authorized by local legislation adopted by the General Assembly, general law, or the Georgia Constitution[28]
- Change the way that property is condemned.[29] However, a county commission may use condemnation procedures established by general statute.[30]
- Affect any public school system[31]

In other words, while the General Assembly may authorize a county to act in the these matters, the commissioners may not use their home rule powers to do so in the absence of a legislative enactment by the General Assembly.

ORDINANCES

In order to perform its various functions, a county governing authority enacts its own legislation, usually in the form of an ordinance. An ordinance is a permanent rule of conduct.[32] It is more formal than a resolution. It is a law or legislative act of the commissioners.

As has been discussed, commissioners may adopt clearly reasonable ordinances, resolutions, or regulations relating to county property, affairs, and government.[33] Counties may adopt ordinances to protect and preserve the public health, safety, and welfare in the unincorporated areas of the county so long as they are not "preempted" by the state.[34] Counties are preempted when the statute expressly states that they may not act on a particular matter or in an implied manner when the state provides regulation and does not also provide for local regulation. For example, where the state regulates the application of sludge to land, the county cannot adopt and enforce an ordinance that also regulates the application of sludge.[35]

Some areas in which counties have been expressly given the authority to regulate through ordinance include zoning;[36] historic preservation;[37] building codes;[38] signs;[39] adult bookstores and movie houses;[40] dangerous dogs;[41] rabies, by licensing of animals;[42] shore protection;[43] drainage basins;[44] soil erosion and sedimentation control;[45] solid waste handling and disposal;[46] repairing, closing, and demolishing unfit buildings;[47] litter;[48] removal of junk vehicles;[49] cable television;[50] alcoholic beverages;[51] fortune-telling;[52] auctioneering;[53] billiard rooms;[54] precious metal and gem dealers;[55] used vehicle and used vehicle parts sales;[56] traffic regulation;[57] off-road vehicles;[58] public indecency;[59] loitering;[60] disorderly conduct;[61] public drunkenness;[62] smoking in public places;[63] sale of model glue to minors;[64] street gangs;[65] and inspection of meats, poultry, and dairy products.[66]

Format

There is no required format for a county ordinance, but there are some basic elements to a well-drafted ordinance that may allow a county to avoid challenges to its validity and meaning:

- *Identifying Number:* In order to codify and make ordinances easier to find, they should be given a number. For instance, some counties use the year of the ordinance followed by a hyphen, the initials "ORD," and a three-digit identifying number (e.g., 2010-ORD-001, 2010-ORD-002).

- *Title:* In order to make it easier to identify ordinances, they should have an identifying name at the top of the ordinance (e.g., ORDINANCE REGULATING THE PURCHASE OF GOODS AND SERVICES BY _____ COUNTY).

- *Preamble:* A preamble is used to briefly explain the purpose of the ordinance and the objectives to be accomplished by it.

- *Enactment Clause:* This clause formally declares the passing or adoption of an ordinance and identifies the enacting legislative body (e.g., the _____ County Board of Commissioners hereby ordains that . . .).

- *Definition Section:* Any words or phrases that have special meaning in the ordinance should be identified and defined in this section.

- *Body:* The body is the basic act itself, organized and divided into identifiable numbered sections.

- *Severability Clause:* This clause stipulates that if any portion of the ordinance is held invalid, the remaining provisions continue in full force and effect.

- *Repealer Clause:* This clause abolishes previous ordinances that the county governing authority no longer wishes to be operative. A repealer clause that specifically identifies provisions to be abolished is far preferable to a general clause simply stating that "all conflicting enactments are hereby repealed." The latter type can lead to much confusion concerning which resolutions or ordinances or parts thereof have been repealed.

- *Violation and Enforcement Clause:* This portion of the ordinance identifies the county officer authorized to enforce the ordinance and explains the consequences of a violation of the ordinance.

- *Effective Date:* The ordinance should specify the date on which it becomes effective.

The ordinance should be authenticated or certified by the signature of the chairperson (or the entire board) and attested by the county clerk.

Codification

Counties are required to codify their current ordinances and resolutions that have the effect of law into one code.[67] Amendments to existing ordinances and newly adopted ordinances must be incorporated into the code at least once every year.[68] A copy of the code must be posted on the Internet and submitted to the county's law library, if it has one.[69] Additionally, the code and updates must be available for sale to the public at a reasonable price.[70]

County commissioners should be familiar with their code of ordinances. They should also ensure that other county officials and employees have access to the code and are familiar with its requirements.

Commissioners have the discretion to use law library fees to pay for the costs of codification. The fees are collected by the trustees of the county law library on all civil and criminal cases filed in the superior, state, probate, or magistrate court.[71] If a county does not have a county law library, the commissioners have the discretionary power to cause the levy of a fee on filings for codification purposes.[72]

Ordinance Violations

In general, violations of county ordinances are under the jurisdiction of the magistrate court and punishable by a fine of up to $1,000 and/or 60 days in jail.[73] However, violations of ordinances imposing the uniform rules of the road[74] must be heard in state court, if there is one, or probate court.[75] The commissioners may designate the county attorney or some other attorney to prosecute violations of county ordinances in magistrate court.[76]

Code Enforcement Boards

A county may also establish one or more code enforcement boards to bring properties into compliance with ordinances such as zoning, subdivision, litter control, junk vehicles, and other ordinances regulating the development of property.[77] Code enforcement boards have civil rather than criminal enforcement powers. Unlike the magistrate court, code enforcement boards may order a property owner to bring his or her property into compliance.[78] Failure to comply with an order of a code enforcement board may be punishable by an administrative fine.[79]

Federal Limitations

Federal law imposes limits on a county's power to implement or enforce some ordinances. All county officials should be aware of the possible application of federal law to proposed and existing legislation and to county practices. For instance, the First Amendment prohibits counties from implementing ordinances that unconstitutionally regulate expression (e.g., ordinances regulating adult entertainment facilities, signs).[80] The Cable Act of 1992 and subsequent regulation by the Federal Communications Commission limit how counties regulate cable television provider's rates and customer service.[81] Individuals may argue that zoning ordinances, subdivision regulations, shore protection ordinances, drainage basin ordinances, and other regulatory ordinances may be a "taking" of private property for governmental use for which the county may be liable[82] or may unreasonably infringe on use of land for religious purposes.[83] In order to prevent a Fourteenth Amendment to the U.S. Constitution due process claim, counties revoking an alcoholic beverage license must provide notice and a meaningful opportunity to respond.[84] Additionally, ordinances that are vague or overly broad may be struck down.[85]

RESOLUTIONS

Although some people use the terms "resolution" and "ordinance" interchangeably, a resolution is typically a formal written motion expressing the sense, will, opinion, or action of the governing body, while an ordinance is a law enacted by the county. A resolution is generally temporary in nature and is made in a ministerial or administrative capacity, for a special purpose, or for the disposition of a particular item of the administrative business of the county.[86] For example, while some counties may approve a contract or take some other action on a motion approved by the governing authority entered on the minutes, other counties use a resolution to do so.

There is no required format for a resolution, but there are some basic elements to a well-drafted resolution.

- *Identifying Number:* Some counties use the year of the resolution, a hyphen, the initials "RES," another hyphen, and a three-digit identifying number in sequential order (e.g., 2010-RES-001, 2010-RES-002) in order to make it easier to keep track of resolutions.

- *Title:* As with ordinances, providing a name for the resolution makes it easier to identify (e.g., RESOLUTION OF THE _____ COUNTY BOARD OF COMMISSIONERS COMMENDING").

- *Purpose and Authority:* This element consists of an unnumbered introductory statement or statements establishing the purpose or authority of the resolution, each beginning with "WHEREAS . . . ."

- *Body:* The action or will of the commission is contained in the body of the resolution. It is usually introduced by a phrase such as "NOW THEREFORE BE IT RESOLVED by the _____ County Board of Commissioners that . . . ," followed by the provisions of the resolution.

- *Effective Date:* This specifies the date on which the resolution becomes effective.

The resolution should be authenticated or certified by the signature of the chairperson (or the entire board) and attested by the county clerk.

CLAIMS AND LAWSUITS AGAINST THE COUNTY

Unless otherwise provided by law, the county commission must audit all claims for money or damages against the county.[87] The commissioners have not only the right but also the duty to examine, audit, and approve such claims when the evidence shows that the county is responsible for payment to avoid unnecessary litigation.[88] This duty cannot be delegated.[89]

All claims against the county must be in writing.[90] In general, claims must be presented to the county commission within 12 months after they accrue or become payable. If the claim is not made to the commissioners within this 12-month period, any lawsuit filed against the county on the claim should be dismissed, as the claim is barred.[91]

Defending and Insuring the County

As the fiscal authority, a county commission may purchase insurance, hire attorneys, purchase bonds, and otherwise protect the taxpayers from judgments against the county. However, the commission is required to insure all volumes of public laws and appellate court decisions furnished to the probate judge and the clerk of the superior court.[92]

Bonding County Officials

State law requires the sheriff, sheriff's deputies, jailers, clerk of superior court, deputy clerk, probate judge, tax commissioner, magistrate, coroner, child support receiver and employees, clerk of state court, county administrator for the probate court, board of trustees of the county law library, county library board, county police officers, county surveyor, county treasurer, jailers, and the warden of a county correctional institution to be bonded.[93] These bonds protect the county and its taxpayers in case these officials fail to faithfully perform their duties. In general, the amount of the bond is set by state statute and may only be increased by local legislation. The premium of the bonds must be paid by the county governing authority out of county funds. Rather than purchase several individual bonds, the county may purchase a "blanket bond" to cover all of its officials.[94]

Insuring County Officials, Employees, and Property

County commissioners are authorized but not required to purchase liability insurance for the elected and appointed officials as well as the employees of the county in case they are sued in their official capacity. The commissioners may also purchase insurance against damages involving county property. The amount of the coverage, if purchased, is also at the discretion of the commissioners.[95] The commissioners may also purchase general liability coverage from an interlocal risk management agency composed of county members rather than from a commercial insurer.[96] There is no statutory authority empowering a county officer or employee to procure liability insurance with county funds independent of the county commission. Like other employers, counties must provide workers compensation benefits to cover county employees injured on the job.[97] As with general liability insurance, the commissioners may purchase commercial insurance to cover the county's liability or may purchase coverage from a workers' compensation group self insurance fund composed of county members.[98]

Defending County Officials

Similarly, it is up to each county commission to hire an attorney to represent the county or any county official or employee.[99] Except as outlined later in this chapter, it is in the discretion of the commissioners to provide a legal "defense" for civil, criminal (other than theft, embezzlement, etc., of county property),[100] or quasi-criminal actions brought against any county official or employee.[101] There is one situation in which a "county officer" (i.e., sheriff, probate judge, clerk of superior court, tax commissioner, tax collector, or tax receiver) may retain the services of an outside attorney at the expense of the county.[102] If the county officer is involved in a civil case in which the county attorney has a conflict of interest preventing him or her from representing both the county and the county officer, the county officer must first make a written request to the county commission to use outside counsel. If the commission denies the request or fails to respond to the request, then the chief judge of the superior court determines whether the county attorney has a conflict of interest ethically preventing him or her from representing both the county and the county officer.[103] If the chief judge determines that such a conflict exists, then the county is obligated to pay the county officer's attorney "reasonable fees" that may not be any more than the rate paid to the county attorney or more than a schedule of rates for outside counsel adopted by the commissioners. Such fees are subject to approval by the chief judge. In addition, the Georgia Supreme Court has determined that if a county officer sues the county, that constitutes a conflict for the county attorney, and the commissioners will be obligated to pay the county officer's attorney fees whether or not the county officer prevails in court.

COUNTY TAXATION AND SPENDING

Power to Tax

The taxing power belongs to the state and not the county.[105] Unless prohibited by the constitution, the General Assembly may authorize or require a county to levy taxes for local purposes.[106] The county may exercise the power of taxation only as authorized by the constitution or by general law.[107] Authorization for a county to tax must be clear. Any doubt as to this power is resolved against the county (i.e., the court will strike down the tax).[108] These general principles cannot be overcome by a county's constitutional home rule authority.[109]

Purposes of Taxation

County taxes (including those taxes levied for the school board) may be levied and collected for the following specific purposes:

1. To pay the expenses of administration of the county government
2. To cover the cost of the collection and preservation of records of vital statistics
3. To pay the principal and interest of any debt of the county
4. To provide a sinking fund for any debt of the county
5. To provide reasonable reserves for public improvements as may be fixed by law
6. To pay for litigation
7. To pay the expenses of courts
8. To pay for the maintenance and support of inmates
9. To pay sheriffs and coroners
10. To pay county police
11. To provide for fire protection of forest lands
12. To provide for the conservation of natural resources
13. To build and repair public buildings
14. To build and maintain a system of county roads
15. To build and repair bridges
16. To acquire, improve, and maintain airports
17. To acquire, improve, and maintain public parks
18. To provide ambulance services within the county
19. To provide for public health purposes in the county
20. To provide sanitation, water pollution control projects, sewage treatment facilities, and storm and sanitary sewer and water supply facilities
21. To provide hospitalization and medical or other care for the indigent sick people of the county
22. To support indigent individuals
23. To provide for the payment of assistance to aged persons in need, to the needy blind, and to dependent children
24. To pay for other welfare benefits
25. To pay county agricultural and home demonstration agents
26. To provide financial assistance to county or joint county and municipal development authorities to develop trade, commerce, industry, and employment opportunities, provided, however, the tax does not exceed one mill per dollar upon the assessed value of the taxable property in the county

27. To provide for workers' compensation and retirement or pension funds for officers and employees
28. To pay pensions and other benefits and costs under a teacher retirement system or systems
29. To pay for school lunch programs on property located outside of independent school systems
30. To pay for educational purposes upon property located outside the areas of independent school systems
31. To provide for financial assistance to county children and youth commissions providing children and youth services to study the needs, issues, and problems relating to children and youth
32. To pay for the dissemination of information relating to issues of children and youth[110]

General Tax Levies

As a general rule, taxes are levied to meet the needs of the county for the year in which the levy is made.[111] In levying taxes, county commissioners have broad discretion. The courts do not interfere with the commissioners' decision unless that discretion is abused.[112] According to the Georgia Supreme Court, "it [is] beyond the province of the trial court to require the county authorities to justify the wisdom (as opposed to the legality) of proposed county expenditures."[113]

Tax Assessment and Collection

The assessment and collection of taxes, including determination of exemptions and property subject to taxation, are primarily the functions of county tax assessing and collecting officers, discussed in Chapter 4. County commissioners do, however, have certain powers in this area. For example, a commissioner may, by resolution or ordinance, provide for the collection and payment of ad valorem taxes on tangible property (other than motor vehicles) in two installments.[114]

Tax Refunds

When a taxpayer claims for any reason that taxes should be refunded, the commissioners may hear and determine if the taxpayer was, in fact, overtaxed and authorize a refund or credit, and under certain circumstances, penalties may also be waived.[115] The commissioners can also refund to a taxpayer all taxes and license fees that may have been erroneously or illegally assessed and collected.[116]

Spending Tax Funds

An expenditure of public money must be authorized by law; otherwise, the payment is prohibited.[117] Funds may be expended for any public service or function. No levy of taxes need state the particular purpose for which the levy is made unless required by the court or by law.[118] However, the surplus of a fund raised for a specific purpose, after all demands and indebtedness chargeable against it have been paid, becomes part of the general fund and may be used for payment of any other liability against the county.[119]

Spending Nontax Funds

If not required to be spent for a particular purpose, funds derived from sources other than taxation (i.e., fees) may be applied to any purpose for which the county has authority to spend public funds.[120]

Gratuities

The Georgia Constitution limits the power of counties to make contributions of public funds or property. A county may not donate money or property or lend its credit to any private person or nonpublic entity unless it is a purely charitable organization and the General Assembly has authorized it.[121] A county cannot make a gift that gives government property to a private party. For example, local government donations to a chamber of commerce, freight bureau, and a convention and tourist bureau have been held to violate the Georgia Constitution.[122] However, a county may pay money or provide property to a private party pursuant to a contract for services. It is not considered a gratuity or donation when the county receives substantial benefits in return for the private use of its property.[123] Counties with a population over 400,000 are expressly authorized by general law to donate county funds or property to purely charitable purposes pursuant to a contract for services, so long as the charitable activities occur within that county.[124] In sum, counties may not make contributions even to nonprofit organizations unless they qualify as a charity and the contribution has been expressly authorized by an act of the General Assembly.[125] Examples may be donations to support a symphony orchestra or arts or welfare organizations.

SERVICES

The Georgia Constitution expressly gives counties what are known as "supplementary powers." The General Assembly may regulate or restrict how a county provides services through the county's supplementary powers, but it may not totally withdraw these powers from the county.[126] Additionally, unless otherwise provided by general or local law, the county may provide these services only in the unincorporated area of the county, unless it has a contract with the city.[127] The supplementary powers include the following:

- Police protection.[128] Counties may establish a police department to service only the unincorporated area of the county, if approved by the voters in a referendum.[129] In contrast, the sheriff has the power to provide law enforcement services inside incorporated areas, just as he or she does in the unincorporated areas,[130] although counties may contract with the city to provide additional law enforcement[131] and with the city or other counties to provide mutual aid.[132]

- Fire protection.[133] In addition to providing fire protection services to cities through contract, counties may enter into mutual aid agreements with cities and other counties.[134]

- Garbage and solid waste collection and disposal[135]

- Public health facilities and services.[136] This includes hospitals,[137] ambulance,[138] emergency rescue services, and animal control.[139]

- Road construction and maintenance.[140] The Georgia Department of Transportation promulgates uniform regulations for the erection and maintenance of signs, signals, markings, and other traffic control devices to regulate, warn, and guide traffic for all public roads.[141] Even though a county road extends into a municipality, it remains a county road, unless it is removed from the county road system.[142] The county may contract with the city to maintain the county's roads that extend into the city.[143] However, the city regulates and controls the use of those portions of the county road that are located within the city (e.g., traffic signals, parking meters).[144] When a city annexes portions of the county, the city may be liable for maintaining those roads.[145] Counties may only regulate the installation, construction, maintenance, renewal, removal, and relocation of pipes, mains, cables, wires, poles, towers, and traffic and other signals on the portion of the county road right-of-way in the unincorporated area.[146] Although counties have the right to control their right-of-way, federal law requires that they do so with regard to telecommunications companies on a competitively neutral and nondiscriminatory basis.[147]

- Parks, recreational areas, programs, and facilities[148]

- Storm water collection and disposal systems[149]

- Sewage collection and disposal systems[150]
- Water treatment and distribution[151]
- Public housing[152]
- Public transportation[153]
- Libraries[154]
- Archives[155]
- Arts and sciences programs and facilities[156]
- Terminal, dock, and parking facilities[157]
- Building, housing, plumbing, and electrical codes[158]
- Air quality control[159]

Regardless of the source of the authority to provide a service, federal law requires that all services and programs provided by a county must be accessible and may not discriminate against disabled people.[160] Counties must provide an equal opportunity for disabled individuals to participate in the programs, services, and activities in the most integrated setting appropriate.[161]

PLANNING AND ZONING

The Georgia Constitution reserves to counties (as well as municipalities) the authority to adopt plans and exercise the power of zoning. The constitution does, however, allow the General Assembly to enact general laws establishing procedures for the exercise of that power, which it has done (see Chapter 9).[162] It also expressly authorizes the General Assembly to impose restrictions upon land use in order to protect and preserve the natural resources, environment, and vital areas of this state.[163]

State law also requires counties to prepare comprehensive plans[164] and further provides that counties and cities are to develop nonconflicting or single countywide land-use plans as part of a service delivery strategy agreement.[165] In addition, the Service Delivery Strategies Act says that the provision of water and sewer services by a city or a county outside its boundaries must be consistent with the land-use plan of the adjoining local government.[166] Furthermore, where a county has a bona fide land-use objection to an annexation proposed by a city, the objection is to be resolved through a dispute resolution process spelled out in general law.[167]

Federal law restricts counties from making zoning decisions that discriminate against any religious assembly or institution on the basis of religion; that place unreasonable limits on religious assemblies, institutions, or structures; or that completely exclude religious assemblies from a jurisdiction.[168] Additionally, any land-use regulation of a religious institution must be in furtherance of a compelling governmental interest and must be the least restrictive means of furthering that compelling governmental interest.[169]

Federal law also prohibits counties from enacting regulations that prohibit (or have the effect of prohibiting) the ability of a telecommunications company from providing service.[170] Although counties may not regulate the placement of telecommunications facilities (i.e., cell towers) based on environmental effects of radio frequency emissions,[171] counties retain their zoning authority regarding such placement, so long as the regulations do not unreasonably discriminate among telecommunication providers and do not prohibit the provision of personal wireless services.[172] Any decision denying a request to locate a facility must be in writing.[173]

There are special requirements in the case of collocation or modifications to existing equipment or towers. Companies are not required to go through an entire rezoning or to acquire an additional special land-use permit so long as the collocation neither increases the height or width of the tower or the footprint of the accessory equipment nor exceeds applicable weight limits of the tower. Wireless companies still have to comply with any applicable site plan and building permit requirements for the existing tower and would have to comply with zoning and land-use requirements generally, including any conditions placed on the use when initially approved and any subsequently adopted amendments to such conditions of approval. Decisions must be made within 90 days. The county must determine whether an application is complete within the first 30 days of its receipt. If it is not complete, the 90-day "shot clock" stops until all enumerated documentation is submitted to the county.[174]

SPECIAL SERVICE DISTRICTS

The Georgia Constitution also authorizes counties to create special districts for the provision of county services. The services offered through a special district may be paid for in whole or in part by special fees, assessments, or additional mills levied only within the district.[175] For instance, counties that do not provide fire services throughout the county may create special tax districts to do so for a smaller geographical area in which the service is provided. A service district may consist of the entire unincorporated area of a county or a portion of the county. Property owners within a special district pay additional fees or taxes to fund the service beyond what they would pay in general county taxes. In sum, special service districts provide a means by which some citizens of a county may be provided and charged for a service above and beyond what citizens of the county generally receive. Conversely, citizens outside a special district who are not receiving the service otherwise provided through a special service district would not be taxed to pay for that service since they are not getting the benefit of the service being offered. Special districts may be created by general law or by adoption of an ordinance or resolution of the commissioners. Although special districts generally include less than the entire county, a countywide service district for the provision of hospital services has been approved by the courts while such a district has not been approved for a sheriff.[176] Counties have used special districts to provide street lighting, road paving, and waste collection among other county services. The creation by the county of a special district may be made contingent upon approval of the referendum, but a referendum is not required by the constitution or by general law.

NOTES

1. See U.S. CONST. art. VI, cl. 2.
2. Hines v. Etheridge, 173 Ga. 870 (1931); Troup County Electric Membership Corporation v. Georgia Power Company, 229 Ga. 348 (1972); Thomas v. Ragsdale, 188 Ga. 238 (1939); Barton v. Harden, 204 Ga. 108 (1948).
3. OFFICIAL CODE OF GEORGIA ANNOTATED (O.C.G.A.) §1-3-3(7).
4. Forsyth County v. White, 272 Ga. 619 (2000); Twiggs County v. Atlanta Gas Light Company, 262 Ga. 276 (1992); Stephenson v. Board of Commissioners of Cobb County, 261 Ga. 399 (1991); DeKalb County v. Atlanta Gas Light Company, 228 Ga. 512 (1972); Forsyth County v. Childers, 240 Ga. App. 819 (1999).
5. DeKalb County v. Atlanta Gas Light Company, 228 Ga. 512 (1972); Decatur County v. Roberts, 159 Ga. 528 (1924); Bowers v. Hanks, 152 Ga. 659 (1922).
6. Twiggs County v. Atlanta Gas Light Company, 262 Ga. 276 (1992); Mobley v. Polk County, 242 Ga. 798 (1979); Brock v. Chappell, 196 Ga. 567 (1943); McCrory Company of Georgia v. Board of Commissioners of Fulton County, 177 Ga. 242 (1933); Decatur County v. Roberts, 159 Ga. 528 (1924); Bowers v. Hanks, 152 Ga. 659 (1922); Forsyth County v. Childers, 240 Ga. App. 819 (1999).
7. Jones v. McCaskill, 112 Ga. 453 (1900); Christian v. Moreland, 203 Ga. 20 (1947); Commissioner of Roads and Revenues of Fulton County v. Davis, 213 Ga. 792 (1958). However, see Building Authority of Fulton County v. State of Georgia, 253 Ga. 242 (1984).
8. GA. CONST. art. III, §6, ¶4(b).
9. O.C.G.A. §28-1-15.

10. GA. CONST. art. XI, §1, ¶4(a), (b), (c).

11. An index of current local legislation for a particular county may be found in Vol. 42 of O.G.G.A. The actual text may be found in Georgia Laws, which is published after each session of the General Assembly.

12. However, a county may create the office of county manager without local legislation pursuant to O.C.G.A. §36-5-22.

13. O.C.G.A. §36-5-24. The decision to increase compensation of the governing authority must be made before the qualifying date of the general election. Notice of any proposed salary increase must be posted in the legal organ of the county once a week for three consecutive weeks prior to any action on a salary increase. The notice must specify the fiscal impact of the compensation increase. Any increase in compensation may not take effect until January 1 following the next general election.

14. O.C.G.A. § 36-80-19(b)(1).

15. GA. CONST. art. IX, §2, ¶1(a).

16. GA. CONST. art. IX, §2, ¶1(b). See Forbes v. Lovett, 227 Ga. 772 (1971).

17. GA. CONST. art. IX, §2, ¶1(b)(1).

18. GA. CONST. art. IX, §2, ¶1(a).

19. GA. CONST. art. IX, §2, ¶1(c).

20. GA. CONST. art. IX, §2, ¶1(c)(2).

21. Ibid.

22. GA. CONST. art. IX, §1, ¶3.

23. GA. CONST. art. IX, §2, ¶1(c)(7).

24. GA. CONST. art. IX, §2, ¶1(c)(1), (7); Boswell v. Bramlett, 274 Ga. 50 (2001) and Warren v. Walton, 231 Ga. 495 (1973).

25. GA. CONST. art. IX, §2, ¶1(c)(3); Richmond County v. Richmond County Business Association, Inc., 225 Ga. 568 (1969).

26. See O.C.G.A. §15-10-60 et seq.

27. GA. CONST. art. IX, §2, ¶1(c)(4); Richmond County v. Richmond County Business Association, Inc., 224 Ga. 854 (1968); Cotton States Mutual Insurance Company v. DeKalb County, 251 Ga. 309 (1983). See also DeKalb County v. Brown Builders Company, Inc., 227 Ga. 777 (1971).

28. GA. CONST. art. IX, §2, ¶1(c)(5).

29. GA. CONST. art. IX, §2, ¶1(c)(6).

30. See O.C.G.A. §§22-1-2 et seq., 32-3-1 et seq.

31. GA. CONST. art. IX, §2, ¶1(c)(8).

32. Allen v. Wise, 204 Ga. 415 (1948). See also City of Ludowici v. Brown, 249 Ga. 857 (1982); Campbell v. City of Columbus, 224 Ga. 279 (1968).

33. GA. CONST. art. IX, §2, ¶1(a).

34. O.C.G.A. §36-1-20(a).

35. Franklin County v. Fieldale Farms Corporation, 270 Ga. 272 (1998).

36. GA. CONST. art. IX, §2, ¶4; O.C.G.A. §36-66-1 et seq.

37. O.C.G.A. §44-10-20 et seq.

38. GA. CONST. art. IX, §2, ¶3(a)(12); O.C.G.A. §§8-2-25, 36-13-1 et seq.

39. O.C.G.A. §36-13-6.
40. O.C.G.A. §36-60-3.
41. See O.C.G.A. §4-8-29. See also Ga. Const. art. IX, §2, ¶3(a)(3).
42. O.C.G.A. §31-19-3. See also Ga. Const. art. IX, §2, ¶3(a)(3).
43. O.C.G.A. §12-5-243.
44. O.C.G.A. §12-5-453.
45. O.C.G.A. §12-7-1 et seq.
46. See O.C.G.A. §12-8-30.9.
47. O.C.G.A. §41-2-7 et seq.
48. O.C.G.A. §§36-1-20(a), 16-7-48.
49. O.C.G.A. §36-60-4.
50. O.C.G.A. §36-18-1 et seq. For restrictions on a county providing cable service, see O.C.G.A. §36-90-1 et seq.
51. See O.C.G.A. §§3-3-2, 3-4-49, 3-4-90, 3-5-40 et seq., 3-6-40, 3-7-40.
52. O.C.G.A. §36-1-15.
53. O.C.G.A. §43-6-25.1.
54. O.C.G.A. §43-8-2.
55. See O.C.G.A. §43-37-5.
56. O.C.G.A. §43-47-13.
57. O.C.G.A. §§36-1-20(a), 40-6-371, 40-6-372, 40-6-374.
58. O.C.G.A. §40-7-5.
59. See O.C.G.A. §16-6-8(e).
60. See O.C.G.A. §16-11-36(d).
61. See O.C.G.A. §16-11-39(c).
62. See O.C.G.A. §16-11-41(b).
63. See O.C.G.A. §16-12-2.
64. See O.C.G.A. §16-13-95.
65. See O.C.G.A. §16-15-6.
66. O.C.G.A. §26-2-212.
67. O.C.G.A. §36-80-19.
68. O.C.G.A. §36-80-19(b)(1).
69. O.C.G.A. §36-80-19(d).
70. O.C.G.A. §36-80-19(b)(3).
71. O.C.G.A. §§36-15-7, 36-15-9.
72. O.C.G.A. §36-15-9(g).
73. O.C.G.A. §§36-1-20, 15-10-60 et seq.
74. See O.C.G.A. §40-6-372.
75. See O.C.G.A. §§40-13-21, 40-13-29.
76. O.C.G.A. §§15-10-62, 15-10-63.
77. O.C.G.A. §36-74-1 et seq.

78. O.C.G.A. §§36-74-25, 36-74-45.

79. O.C.G.A. §§36-74-26, 36-74-46.

80. City of Erie v. Pap's A.M., 529 U.S. 446 (2000); Hill v. Colorado, 530 U.S. 703 (2000); Flanigan's Enterprises, Inc. of Georgia v. Fulton County, 242 F.3d 976 (2001), cert. denied, 122 S.Ct. 2356 (2002); David Vincent, Inc. v. Broward County, 200 F.3d 1325 (11th Cir. 2000); Wise Enterprises, Inc. v. Unified Government of Athens-Clarke County, 217 F.3d 1360 (2000); International Eateries of America, Inc. v. Broward County, Florida, 941 F.2d 1157 (11th Cir. 1991). See also Chambers v. Peach County, 268 Ga. 672 (1997), Quetgles v. City of Columbus, 268 Ga. 619 (1997); Goldrush II v. City of Marietta, 267 Ga. 683 (1997); Chambers v. Peach County, 266 Ga. 318 (1996); Harris v. Entertainment Systems, Inc., 259 Ga. 701 (1989); Paramount Pictures Corporation v. Busbee, 250 Ga. 252 (1989).

81. 47 UNITED STATES CODE ANNOTATED (U.S.C.A.) §541 et seq. See 47 C.F.R. §§76.309, 76.910, 76.922, 76.933, 76.1602, 76.1603.

82. Fifth and Fourteenth Amendments to the U.S. Constitution; Palazzolo v. Rhode Island, 533 U.S. 606, 121 S.Ct. 2448 (2001); City of Monterey v. Del Monte Dunes at Monterey, Ltd., 119 S.Ct. 1624 (1999); Dolan v. City of Tigard, 512 U.S. 374 (1994); Lucas v. South Carolina Coastal Council, 505 U.S. 1003 (1992); Nollan v. California Coastal Commission, 483 U.S. 825 (1987); Penn Central Transportation Company v. New York City, 438 U.S. 104 (1978); Agins v. Tiburon, 447 U.S. 255 (1980).

83. Religious Land Use and Institutionalized Persons Act, 42 U.S.C.A. §2000cc et seq.

84. See O.C.G.A. §3-3-2(b).

85. See City of Chicago v. Morales, 523, 527 U.S. 41 (1999).

86. Allen v. Wise, 204 Ga. 415 (1948). See also Wayne County v. Herrin, 210 Ga. App. 747 (1993); City of Ludowici v. Brown, 249 Ga. 857 (1982); Campbell v. City of Columbus, 224 Ga. 279 (1968).

87. O.C.G.A. §36-11-2.

88. Armistead v. MacNeill, 203 Ga. 204, 45 S.E.2d 652 (1947).

89. McGinty v. Pickering, 180 Ga. 447, 179 S.E. 358 (1935).

90. O.C.G.A. §36-11-1; Powell v. The County of Muscogee, 71 Ga. 587 (1883); Williams v. Lowndes County, 120 Ga. App. 429 (1969); Meadows v. Houston County, 295 Ga. App. 183 (2008).

91. O.C.G.A. §36-11-1; Griffin Realty and Construction Company v. Chatham County, 47 Ga. App. 545, 171 S.E. 237 (1933); Doyal v. Department of Transportation, 142 Ga. App. 79, 234 S.E.2d 858 (1977); Christensen v. Floyd County, 158 Ga. App. 274, 279 S.E.2d 723 (1981); Puckett v. Gwinnett County, 200 Ga. App. 53, 406 S.E.2d 561 (1991); Burton v. DeKalb County, 202 Ga. App. 676, 415 S.E.2d 647 (1992).

92. O.C.G.A. §36-9-4.

93. O.C.G.A. §§15-6-59, 15-10-20(h), 15-9-7, 15-15-3, 15-16-5, 15-16-23, 20-5-50, 36-6-4, 36-7-5, 36-8-3, 36-15-3, 42-4-2, 42-5-32, 45-16-4, 48-5-122(b), 53-6-41.

94. O.C.G.A. §45-4-11.

95. O.C.G.A. §45-9-20.

96. O.C.G.A. §36-83-1 et seq.

97. O.C.G.A. §34-9-1 et seq.

98. O.C.G.A. §34-9-150 et seq.

99. Stephenson v. Board of Commissioners of Cobb County, 261 Ga. 399 (1991).

100. O.C.G.A. §45-9-21(b).

101. O.C.G.A. §45-9-21(a).

102. O.C.G.A. §45-9-21(e).

103. See Haralson County v. Kimball, 243 Ga. App. 559 (2000).

104. Gwinnett County v. Yates, 265 Ga. 504 (1995); Board of Commissioners of Dougherty County v. Saba, 278 Ga. 176 (2004).

105. Albany Bottling Company v. Watson, 103 Ga. 503, 30 S.E. 270 (1898).

106. Wright v. Fulton County, 169 Ga. 354, 150 S.E. 262 (1929); Blackman v. Golia, 231 Ga. 381, 202 S.E.2d 186 (1973); Chanin v. Bibb County, 234 Ga. 282, 216 S.E.2d 250 (1975).

107. GA. CONST. art. IX, §4, ¶1.

108. Richmond County Business Association Inc. v. Richmond County, 224 Ga. 854, 165 S.E.2d 293 (1968); Chanin v. Bibb County, 234 Ga. 282, 216 S.E.2d 250 (1975).

109. Ibid.

110. O.C.G.A. §48-5-220.

111. Spain v. Hall County, 175 Ga. 600, 165 S.E. 612 (1932).

112. McMillan v. Tucker, 154 Ga. 154, 113 S.E. 391 (1922).

113. Board of Commissioners of Fulton County v. 1991 Tax Digest of Fulton County, 261 Ga. 702, 410 S.E.2d 721 (1991).

114. O.C.G.A. §48-5-23.

115. O.C.G.A. §§48-5-241, 48-5-242.

116. O.C.G.A. §48-5-380.

117. Nelson v. Wainwright, 224 Ga. 693, 164 S.E.2d 147 (1968); Humber v. Dixon, Ga. 480, 94 S.E. 565 (1917).

118. GA. CONST. art. IX, §4, ¶2, 3.

119. Butts County v. Jackson Banking Company, 136 Ga. 719, 71 S.E. 1065 (1911); Spain v. Hall County, 175 Ga. 600, 165 S.E. 612 (1932).

120. Stewart v. Davis, 175 Ga. 545, 165 S.E. 598 (1932); Harrison v. May, 228 Ga. 684, 187 S.E.2d 673 (1972).

121. GA. CONST. art. III, §6, ¶6; art. IX, §2, ¶8; Grand Lodge of Georgia. I.O.O.F. v. City of Thomasville, 226 Ga. 4 (1970). See 1983 Op. Att'y Gen. No. U83-7, regarding development authority.

122. Grand Lodge of Georgia. I.O.O.F. v. City of Thomasville, 226 Ga. 4 (1970).

123. Smith v. Board of Commissioners of Hall County, 244 Ga. 133 (1979).

124. GA. CONST. art. IX, §2, ¶8; O.C.G.A. §36-1-19.1.

125. GA. CONST. art. IX, §2, ¶8.

126. GA. CONST. art. IX, §2, ¶3(c).

127. GA. CONST. art. IX, §2, ¶3(b).

128. Ga. Const. art. IX, §2, ¶3(a)(1).

129. O.C.G.A. §36-8-1 et seq.

130. O.C.G.A. §15-16-10(a)(9).

131. O.C.G.A. §15-16-13.

132. O.C.G.A. §36-69-1 et seq.

133. Ga. Const. art. IX, §2, ¶3(a)(1); O.C.G.A. §25-3-1 et seq.

134. O.C.G.A. §§25-6-1 et seq., 36-69-1 et seq.

135. Ga. Const. art. IX, §2, ¶3(a)(2). See also O.C.G.A. §12-8-20 et seq.

136. Ga. Const. art. IX, §2, ¶3(a)(3). However, most public health services are provided by county boards of health (see O.C.G.A. §31-3-1 et seq.), which receive funding from the county and the state.

137. However, hospital services are typically provided at the county level by hospital authorities pursuant to O.C.G.A. §31-7-70 et seq.

138. See O.C.G.A. §31-11-1 et seq.

139. See O.C.G.A. §§4-8-29, 31-19-3.

140. Ga. Const. art. IX, §2, ¶3(a)(4). See O.C.G.A. §32-4-40 et seq.

141. O.C.G.A. §32-6-50.

142. See O.C.G.A. §32-4-1(2).

143. O.C.G.A. §32-4-41(1).

144. O.C.G.A. §§32-4-92(a)(7), 32-6-2.

145. See O.C.G.A. §36-36-7(c); Bush v. City of Gainesville, 105 Ga. App. 381 (1962); 1976 Op. Att'y Gen. U76-21.

146. O.C.G.A. §§32-4-42(6), 32-4-92(a)(10).

147. 47 U.S.C.A. §253(c).

148. Ga. Const. art. IX, §2, ¶3(a)(5). See O.C.G.A. §36-64-1 et seq.

149. Ga. Const. art. IX, §2, ¶3(a)(6).

150. Ibid.

151. Ga. Const. art. IX, §2, ¶3(a)(7). See also O.C.G.A. §§36-60-2, 36-60-15.1.

152. Ga. Const. art. IX, §2, ¶3(a)(8). However, public housing services are typically provided at the county level by local authorities pursuant to O.C.G.A. §8-3-1 et seq.

153. Ga. Const. art. IX, §2, ¶3(a)(9). See also O.C.G.A. §32-9-1 et seq.

154. Ga. Const. art. IX, §2, ¶3(a)(10). See O.C.G.A. §20-5-40 et seq.

155. Ibid.

156. Ibid.

157. Ga. Const. art. IX, §2, ¶3(a)(11).

158. Ga. Const. art. IX, §2, ¶3(a)(12); O.C.G.A. §36-13-1 et seq.

159. Ga. Const. art. IX, §2, ¶3(a)(13).

160. 42 U.S.C.A. §12131 et seq.; 28 C.F.R. §35.102.

161. 28 C.F.R. §35.130.

162. Ga. Const. art. IX, §2, ¶4; O.C.G.A. §§36-66-1 et seq., 36-67A-1 et seq.

163. Ga. Const. art. III, §6, ¶2(a)(1).

164. O.C.G.A. §36-70-1 et seq.
165. O.C.G.A. §36-70-24(4)(A).
166. O.C.G.A. §36-70-24(4)(B).
167. O.C.G.A. §36-36-11.
168. 42 U.S.C.A. §2000cc(b).
169. 42 U.S.C.A. §2000cc(a)(1).
170. 47 U.S.C.A. §253(a).
171. 47 U.S.C.A. §332(c)(7)(A),(B)(iv).
172. 47 U.S.C.A. §332(c)(7)(B)(i).
173. 47 U.S.C.A. §332(c)(7)(B)(iii).
174. O.C.G.A. §36-66B-1 et seq.
175. GA. CONST. art. IX, §2, ¶6.
176. Higdon v. Greene County Board of Commissioners, 277 Ga. App. 350 (2006); Houston v. Channell, 2010 Ga.Lexis 559 (July 12, 2010).

3

James F. Grubiak and Kelly J. L. Pridgen

County Commissioners: Powers and Duties

The governing authority in all counties except those that are consolidated is a board of commissioners or a sole commissioner. These county governing authorities are created by local act of the General Assembly, as provided for in the Georgia Constitution.[1] A board of commissioners is commonly referred to as a county commission. The elected officials who make up the governing authority are referred to as commissioners or county commissioners. For consolidated governments, the governing authority may be a chairman or mayor and commission or a chairman or mayor and council.

POWERS

Under previous constitutions, the powers and duties of county governing authorities did not have to be uniform.[2] The Georgia Supreme Court had ruled that the General Assembly was authorized to pass local acts dealing with the powers and duties of county commissions even when those local acts conflicted with general law.[3] Under the current constitution, however, the General Assembly no longer has the power to pass local acts pertaining to county commissions that conflict with general law. These local acts still exist and are presumed valid, but because they are so varied and their legal status is unclear, this chapter will deal only with the basic powers granted to county commissioners by the current constitution and general laws of Georgia.

Oath of Office

Commissioners are not to embark on the duties of their office without first taking and filing an oath of office swearing, among other things, that they are qualified to hold the office, will support the constitutions of the United States and Georgia, and meet the residency requirements of the office. The oath may be taken before any officer authorized to administer an oath, including a superior court judge, the probate judge, or magistrate. The oath is to be filed in the Office of the Probate Judge and entered on the minutes of the court.[4] Commissions of county commissioners are issued under the seal of the Office of the Governor and signed by the governor.[5]

Original and Exclusive Jurisdiction

In order to determine its powers and duties, each county commission must be aware of the local acts that pertain to it. The powers of county commissioners are strictly limited by law.[6] Where such powers exist, the commission, absent clear abuse, has wide discretion in the administration of county affairs.[7]

Under general law, the county commission has "original and exclusive jurisdiction" to

1. direct and control all county property;
2. levy a general tax for general county purposes;
3. levy a special tax for particular county purposes;
4. establish, alter, or abolish roads, bridges, or ferries;
5. fill vacancies in county offices by appointment;
6. order elections;
7. examine, settle, or pay claims against the county;
8. examine, audit, and settle the accounts of all officers who care for, manage, keep, collect, or disburse money belonging to the county or appropriated for its upkeep;
9. make such rules and regulations for the support of the poor of the county;
10. make rules and regulations for the county police and patrol;
11. make rules and regulations for the promotion of health and for quarantine; and
12. regulate peddling and fix the cost of peddling licenses.[8]

TRUSTEE/FISCAL AUTHORITY

County commissioners are trustees with a fiduciary relationship to their citizens [9] and have "the exclusive authority to control the fiscal affairs of the county. . . ."[10]

Budgeting and Spending County Funds

As the fiscal authority, county commissioners are given the authority and responsibility for preparing and administering the budget (see Chapter 19 for more information on county budgets). A county commission must provide a reasonable budget that allows the other county elected officials (i.e., sheriff, tax commissioner, superior court clerk, probate judge, magistrate judge, and coroner) to perform their statutory duties. While the commissioners may not dictate to a county officer how to perform his or her statutory duties, the commission's decision to set a budget will only be overturned by the court if the court determines that the commission "abused its discretion."[11] "The budget is under the control of the county commission, which, subject to some limitations, has authority to amend or change estimates or required expenditures presented by another officer acting under his or her statutory duty."[12] However, once the budget is adopted, a county commission does not have the unilateral authority to refuse to fund expenditures by a county officer—even if it believes that a county officer's purchases were not made in the exercise of his or her duties. Instead, the board should seek relief from a court by way of a mandamus or declaratory judgment action.[13]

Contracts

County commissioners are empowered to make contracts on behalf of the county (see Chapter 8). All contracts entered into by the commission on behalf of the county must be in writing and entered on the minutes of the county commission,[14] and the power to do so cannot be delegated to an employee.[15]

AUDITS AND ACCOUNTS

The commissioners of any county with a population in excess of 1,500 persons or annual expenditures of $300,000 or more shall provide for an annual audit of the financial affairs of the county. Counties with populations of fewer than 1,500 persons or annual expenditures of less than $300,000 are required to have audits every two years. State agencies are prohibited from making or transmitting any state grant to a county that has failed to provide all the audits required in the preceding five years.[16] (See Chapter 16 for further discussion.)The commissioners may employ an accountant to aid in examining and auditing the books, vouchers, and accounts of any county officer who handles county funds.[17] None of these provisions, however, diminish the power of the grand jury to investigate, inspect, and examine the books and records of county officers or, when necessary, to appoint one or more citizens of the county to do so.[18]

COUNTY PROPERTY

Control

Control of all property belonging to the county is vested in the county commission,[19] which has "original and exclusive jurisdiction" over the control of county property.[20] Its members are required to exercise the utmost good faith, fidelity, and integrity in dealing with that property as trustees and servants of the people.[21] Because of the county commission's fiscal power and responsibility, the commissioners have the right to deny the use of county property to any county officer who uses it in a wasteful, negligent, or ineffective manner.[22] While the jail is "placed in the keeping of the sheriff" for purposes of protection, this power is "subject to the order of the board of commissioners"[23] and is funded through the commissioners.

A county's control over its property is also affected and limited by federal law. For instance, the Americans with Disabilities Act requires that all county programs and services be readily accessible to and usable by disabled people.[24] Compliance may mean alterations to existing county buildings (e.g., widening doorways, installing ramps, providing elevator access) and redesigning county equipment (e.g., telecommunication devices for the deaf).[25] New construction must also be accessible,[26] including roads and sidewalks, which must have curb ramps or sloped areas at their intersection.[27]

Another example of federal law impacting how commissioners control property is the Eighth Amendment to the U.S. Constitution's requirement that an inmate be free from cruel and unusual punishment. If a jail is not properly funded and maintained to ensure that inmates are not deprived of a basic need,[28] the county could incur a great deal of liability and be forced to pay to board their inmates at another jail outside the county. The U.S. Department of Justice may find significant deficiencies in bed space, medical care, fire safety, supervision, and sanitation to be unconstitutional conditions. Some counties have had to pay to board their inmates in other counties while building new jails.

County Buildings

County buildings, including jails and courthouses, are erected, repaired, maintained, and furnished at the expense of the county under the direction of the commissioners, which is authorized to make all necessary contracts for such purposes.[29] There is no general law mandating when public buildings in the county are to be erected, what types are to be built, or what their cost is to be.[30] Buildings constructed with public funds, however, are required to be made accessible to persons with disabilities.[31] Furthermore, if the cost is more than $100,000, then the commissioners must follow the Georgia Local Government Public Works Construction Law to bid out the contract as discussed in more detail in Chapter 8.

The courthouse must be located at the county site that is commonly referred to as the county seat.[32] The commissioners can, however, locate administrative facilities and services, such as jails, correctional camps, health clinics, and hospitals, outside the boundaries of the county seat so long as the location is not inconsistent with the terms of the county's local legislation.[33]

In any county in which the county seat is located in an unincorporated part of the county, the county commission is authorized to construct one or more permanent satellite courthouses within the county and designate each structure as a courthouse annex or an additional courthouse. Any business of the superior court, state court, probate court, or grand jury may be conducted at the satellite courthouse, and all actions taken at the satellite courthouse are fully valid and binding. However, at least one superior court judge must hold at least one session of superior court in the courthouse at the county site each year.[34]

Planning, constructing, and equipping the courthouse is the responsibility of the county commission. The details of exercising this power are within its discretion but must be performed with the view of serving public interest and convenience.[35] Selecting the courthouse site, within the county seat, is also within the discretion of the county commissioners.[36]

The commissioners are responsible for designating the rooms in the courthouse to be used by each county officer. These room assignments must be entered in the county commission's minutes and may be changed at its pleasure.[37] All utilities, furniture, stationery, records, and general office supplies for the various county offices located in the courthouse are to be provided at county expense.[38] The courthouse must be kept open for business during normal working hours—a minimum of 40 working hours during each calendar week, except for those during which public and legal holidays designated by state law or the county commission are observed.[39] However, the law provides some flexibility in hours of operation for the clerk of court and probate judge.

The county jail must be of sufficient size and strength to keep prisoners securely confined. Each jail must contain at least two properly ventilated apartments, one for males and one for females.[40] The Georgia Supreme Court has held that it is the duty of the commissioners to provide sufficient funds for feeding prisoners.[41] (See Chapter 14 for further discussion of jail standards.)

Protection

Public grounds and all county property are placed in the safekeeping of the sheriff, subject to the order of the commissioners. It is the duty of both the county commission and the sheriff to preserve them from injury or waste and to prevent intrusions upon them.[42]

Courthouse Security

Sheriffs also have the responsibility to develop and implement a comprehensive plan for the security of the county courthouse and any courthouse annex.[43] After the security plan is initially developed by the sheriff, it is submitted to the chief judge of the superior court, who has 30 days to review and make modifications to the security plan. The sheriff must provide the estimated cost of the security plan and a schedule for implementation to the commissioners 30 days before it is adopted. However, note that the security plan and all related technologies are subject to the annual budget approval by the county commission.[44] The security plan is considered a confidential matter of public security. As such, the commissioners may review the proposed security plan in executive session. The sheriff is the official custodian of the security plan and determines who has access to it. The sheriff must let the commissioners review it, although he or she can require that the review take place in his or her office or in an executive session. The sheriff must review the security plan at least every four years.

Inventory

On or before January 15 of each year, all commissioners and other county officers are required to make a complete inventory of public property in their charge and to enter it in an inventory book.[45]

Acquisition and Disposal

Deeds, conveyances, grants, or other documents transferring property for the use and benefit of the county vest title in the county. The county commission may, after following specific procedures, sell or dispose of county real property through bid or at public auction to the highest bidder.[46] However, when the commission has failed to place the order of authorization of sale of property on its minutes as required by law, it may ratify the deed and place the authorization on the minutes at a subsequent meeting. Procedures for disposing of county personal property are not directly addressed in general law. However, by law, commissioners have control of county property and may exercise discretion in disposing of the county's personal property. Personal public property (i.e., property that is not real property) that becomes unserviceable may be sold or disposed of by an order of the commissioners. This action must be recorded in the commission's minutes.[47] (See Chapter 8 for further discussion.)

Demolition of Historic Courthouses

A county commission does not have the authority to demolish a county courthouse that was constructed prior to January 1, 1905, and that is listed in the National Register of Historic Places without first posing the question to the qualified voters of the county for approval or rejection.[48]

COUNTY ROADS AND TRAFFIC

County commissions are required to provide an adequate county road system. In order to accomplish this, commissioners have control of, and are responsible for, construction and maintenance of all county roads.[49] The commission is also responsible for maintaining traffic control signs and signals on county roads and has a major role in transportation planning. (See Chapter 12 for further discussion of county roads.)

COMMISSIONERS' COMPENSATION

County commissioners' salary, reimbursable expenses, and expenses in the nature of compensation (e.g., per diems) may be set by local legislation of the General Assembly or by the county commissioners through their home rule authority. Commissioners may increase their compensation so long as the notice of any proposed salary increase is posted in the county legal organ and the decision to increase the salary (or expense reimbursements) is made before the qualifying date of the general election. The notice in the legal organ must specify the fiscal impact of the compensation increase. It must run in the county legal organ once a week for three consecutive weeks prior to any action on a salary increase. Any increase in compensation may not take effect until January 1 following the next general election.[50] Note, however, that the General Assembly may change any such salary set by the county commission or take the power to set salary away from the commissioners if it so chooses.[51]

Commissioners who have completed certified county commissioner training are entitled to a supplement of $100 per month in addition to whatever other compensation they receive.[52] All salaries of county commissioners are entitled to annual cost-of-living adjustments. Additionally, commissioners may receive group health and other employment benefits.[53]

RESIGNATIONS, VACANCIES, AND TERMS OF OFFICE

Vacancies may occur as a result of, among other circumstances, a commissioner resigning from office; dying in office; ceasing to be a resident of the state, county, or district to which he or she was elected; abandoning the office; ceasing to carry out duties of the office; or being convicted of a felony.[54] Resignations are made to the governor.[55] Oftentimes, the procedure to fill a vacancy on the county commission is established in local legislation. However, when the local act does not provide such a procedure and the unexpired term exceeds six months, the probate judge must call a special election. If the unexpired term is for less than six months, the judge of the superior court is to appoint a successor for the unexpired term. Unless otherwise provided by local law, when a special election is required, the remaining members of the board constitute the county governing authority during the interim. If a vacancy or combination of vacancies results in there being no commissioner in office, the probate judge serves as the county governing authority until the election and qualification of all successors to office.[56] Election expenses are subject to the control of the county commission.[57] Note that no office to which a person has been elected can be abolished, nor can the terms of the office be shortened or lengthened by local act of the General Assembly, unless approved by the voters in a referendum.[58]

RELATIONSHIP TO OTHER COUNTY OFFICIALS

In the administration of county affairs, and particularly with regard to financing other county offices, the commissioners are given broad discretion. (See Chapter 4 for discussion of other county officials.) Disputes between a county's constitutional officers (i.e., sheriff, probate judge, tax commissioner, and clerk of superior court) and the commissioners and issues regarding the administration of county affairs are reviewable by the superior court. This reviewing power is exercised with caution, and the courts will not interfere with actions of the commissioners except in cases of clear and manifest abuse of discretion.[59]

One exception to this general rule concerns the responsibility of the county to pay any contingent expenses incurred in holding any session of superior court upon the issuance of a certificate of the judge of superior court approving the expenses.[60] The supreme court has ruled that the certificate is presumed valid and that the burden of proof to establish that the expense is not valid rests with the county.[61]

In another decision, the Georgia Supreme Court held that when a county constitutional officer, acting in his or her official capacity, is required to hire outside counsel to assert a legal position that the county cannot or will not assert and the officer is successful, the county must pay the officer's attorney fees.[62]

COUNTY COMMISSIONERS AS EMPLOYERS

Employees' Compensation

Pursuant to home rule authority, county commissioners may provide salaries, compensation, and expense reimbursement for the employees of the commissioners.[63] However, the Georgia Constitution prohibits the provision of extra compensation to any employee after the service has been rendered.[64]

Other County Officials and Their Employees' Compensation

While commissioners are charged with approving the budget that appropriates county funds to compensate county officers and their employees, commissioners are not authorized to set the salaries of the county officers or their employees,[65] absent local legislation to the contrary. County officers, magistrate judges, and some coroners are either paid according to the state minimum salary based on population[66] or by local legislation, whichever provides the greater compensation.[67] A base salary is established by statute, which is increased by supplements for additional duties that may be performed by the county official,[68] by longevity,[69] and by cost-of-living adjustments determined by the legislature.[70] A county commission may, but is not required to, supplement a county officer's salary.[71] However, once a supplement is given by the commissioners, it may not be reduced or eliminated during the officer's term of office. A county commission has the authority, but is not required, to provide a monthly expense allowance to county officers based upon population.[72] If a county officer is paid according to general law, rather than pursuant to local legislation, he or she must be paid in equal monthly installments.[73] Coroners have the option of being paid a salary or a death investigation fee.[74]

Benefits

Pursuant to its home rule authority, a county commission may provide retirement benefits, insurance, workers' compensation, and hospitalization benefits for the employees of the commission,[75] as well as retirement benefits, pension benefits, group health insurance coverage, life insurance coverage, disability insurance coverage, social security coverage, and employment security coverage for the county officers and their employees.[76] Retirement benefits may be in the form of a traditional defined benefit pension plan, a defined contribution (401) plan, a deferred compensation (475) plan, or a combination of such plans.

Merit System

A county commission may establish a merit or civil service system for its employees.[77] The employees of the sheriff, probate judge, clerk of court, and tax commissioner may be included in the system created for the employees of the commissioners, but only if the county officer makes a written request to the commissioners to include his or her employees in the county's civil service system.[78] (See Chapter 7 for further details.)

Office Hours

The county commissioners must keep the county courthouse and county offices open for a minimum of 40 hours during normal working hours each week, except those weeks during which there are public and legal holidays recognized and designated by law or the commissioners.[79] A state statute dictates minimum office hours for the clerk of superior court and the probate judge. In the case of a clerk of superior court with at least one employee, the office must be open Monday through Friday from 9:00 a.m. until 5:00 p.m., unless the office is open on Saturdays.[80] The clerk may close the office for inclement weather if other county offices are closed. In counties with a population of fewer than 10,000, the clerk may close the office for lunch if all other county offices are closed for lunch. The probate judge is authorized to establish his or her own hours so long as the office is closed on Sundays. Additionally, the probate judge may close the office for one other day each week.[81]

Federal Law and County Employees

Several federal laws limit a county's authority over its employees, as well as the employees of the county officers. (See Chapter 7 for discussion of the Fair Labor Standards Act, the Americans with Disabilities Act, the Family Medical Leave Act, the Age Discrimination in Employment Act, limitations on political activity of employees, and other related matters.)

Due Process

The Fourteenth Amendment to the U.S. Constitution protects county employees from being deprived of their liberty or property without due process of law. All county employees have a "liberty interest" that gives them the right to a "name clearing hearing" when they are terminated and a county official makes what the employee believes is a false statement of a stigmatizing nature about the employee's discharge.[82]

Where granted by the personnel plan established by the commissioners, some county employees who have an expectation of continued employment have a "property interest" in their job with the county (e.g., those employees who may only be terminated for cause). Due process requires that they be provided notice and a meaningful opportunity to respond to a proposed termination of employment.[83] (See Chapter 7 for more information regarding due process requirements.)

NOTES

1. GA. CONST. art. IX, §1, ¶1.
2. See 1976 GA. CONST. art IX, §1, ¶6, 7.
3. Bradford v. Hammond, 179 Ga. 40, 175 S.E. 18 (1934); Williams v. Richmond County, 241 Ga. 89, 243 S.E.2d 55 (1978).
4. OFFICIAL CODE OF GEORGIA ANNOTATED (O.C.G.A.) §§45-3-1 et seq.
5. O.C.G.A. §45-3-31.
6. Beasley v. DeKalb County, 210 Ga. 41, 77 S.E.2d 740 (1953); Nelson v. Wainwright, 224 Ga. 693, 164 S.E.2d 147 (1968); DeKalb County v. Atlanta Gas Light Company, 228 Ga. 512, 186 S.E.2d 732 (1972); Warren v. Walton, 231 Ga. 495, 202 S.E.2d 405 (1973); Boswell v. Bramlett, 274 Ga. 50, 549 S.E.2d 100 (2001).

7. Terry v. Wade, 149 Ga. 580, 101 S.E. 539 (1919); McCrory Company of Georgia v. Board of Commissioners of Fulton County, 177 Ga. 242, 170 S.E. 18 (1933); Smith v. Board of Commissioners of Roads and Revenues of Hall County, 244 Ga. 133, 259 S.E.2d 74 (1979); Wheeler v. DeKalb County, 249 Ga. 678, 292 S.E.2d 855 (1982); Woodard v. Smith, 254 Ga. 39, 325 S.E.2d 377 (1985); Forsyth County v. White, 272 Ga. 619, 532 S.E.2d 392 (2000).

8. O.C.G.A. §36-5-22.1. See Armistead v. MacNeill, 203 Ga. 204, 45 S.E.2d 652 (1947).

9. GA. CONST. art. I, §2, ¶1; Malcolm v. Webb, 211 Ga. 449, 459 (1955).

10. Stephenson v. Board of Commissioners of Cobb County, 261 Ga. 399 (1991).

11. See Griffies v. Coweta County, 272 Ga. 506 (2000), Chaffin v. Calhoun, 262 Ga. 202 (1992); Board of Commissioners of Randolph County v. Wilson, 260 Ga. 482 (1990); Lovett v. Bussell, 242 Ga. 405 (1978).

12. Board of Commissioners of Randolph County v. Wilson, 260 Ga. 482 (1990).

13. See Griffies v. Coweta County, 272 Ga. 506 (2000).

14. O.C.G.A. §§36-10-1, 36-91-20. But see Board of Commissioners of Spalding County v. Stewart, 284 Ga. 573, 668 S.E.2d 644 (2008).

15. Floyd v. Thomas, 211 Ga. 656 (1955).

16. O.C.G.A. §§36-60-8, 36-81-7.

17. O.C.G.A. §§36-1-10, 36-81-7.

18. McLarty v. Fulton County, 52 Ga. App. 445, 183 S.E. 646 (1936); O.C.G.A. §15-12-70.

19. O.C.G.A. tit. 36, ch. 9.

20. O.C.G.A. §§36-5-22.1(a)(1), 36-9-2.

21. Timbs v. Straub, 216 Ga. 451, 117 S.E.2d 462 (1960); Smith v. Board of Commissioners of Roads and Revenues, 244 Ga. 133, 259 S.E.2d 74 (1979).

22. Wolfe v. Huff, 232 Ga. 44, 205 S.E.2d 254 (1974); Wheeler v. DeKalb County, 249 Ga. 678, 292 S.E.2d 855 (1982).

23. O.C.G.A. §36-9-8.

24. 28 C.F.R. §35.149.

25. 28 C.F.R. §35.150(b)(1).

26. 28 C.F.R. §35.151(c). See also O.C.G.A. §30-3-3 et seq.

27. 28 C.F.R. §35.151(e).

28. See Farmer v. Brennan, 511 U.S. 825 (1994); Wilson v. Seiter, 501 U.S. 294 (1991); Rhodes v. Chapman, 452 U.S. 337 (1981); Alabama v. Pubh, 438 U.S. 781 (1978); Estelle v. Gamble, 429 U.S. 97 (1976); Hamm v. DeKalb County, 774 F.2d 1567 (11th Cir. 1985).

29. O.C.G.A. §36-9-5. See *In re* DeKalb County Courthouse Fire Sprinkler System, 265 Ga. 96, 454 S.E.2d 126 (1995), where the supreme court upheld the right of the county commission to deny a superior court judge's order that a sprinkler system be installed in the courthouse.

30. Commissioners of Habersham County v. Porter Manufacturing Company, 103 Ga. 613, 30 S.E. 547 (1898).

31. O.C.G.A. tit. 30, ch. 3.

32. Jackson v. Gasses, 230 Ga. 712, 198 S.E.2d 657 (1973).

33. GA. CONST. art. IX, §2, ¶1(a); Jackson v. Gasses, 230 Ga. 712, 198 S.E.2d 657 (1973); Brewster v. Houston County, 235 Ga. 68, 218 S.E.2d 748 (1975); Dozier v. Norris, 241 Ga. 230, 244 S.E.2d 853 (1978).

34. O.C.G.A. §§15-6-17(b), 15-6-18.

35. Turner v. Johnson, 183 Ga. 176, 187 S.E. 864 (1936).

36. Trapnall v. Candler County, 146 Ga. 617, 91 S.E. 771 (1917).

37. O.C.G.A. §36-9-6; Graham v. Merritt, 165 Ga. 489, 141 S.E. 298 (1928); 1978 Op. Att'y Gen. No. 78-15.

38. O.C.G.A. §36-9-7; Floyd County v. Graham, 24 Ga. App. 294, 100 S.E. 728 (1919).

39. O.C.G.A. §36-1-12; Mobley v. Polk County, 242 Ga. 798, 251 S.E.2d 538 (1979); O.C.G.A. §§15-6-93, 15-9-83.

40. O.C.G.A. §36-9-9.

41. Board of Commissioners of Jasper County v. Persons, 155 Ga. 277, 116 S.E. 538 (1923); Lumpkin County v. Davis, 185 Ga. 393, 195 S.E. 169 (1938).

42. O.C.G.A. §36-9-8.

43. O.C.G.A. §15-16-10(a)(10).

44. O.C.G.A. §36-81-11.

45. O.C.G.A. §§50-16-140, 50-16-141.

46. O.C.G.A. §§36-9-1, 36-9-2, 36-9-3; Head v. Lee, 203 Ga. 191, 45 S.E.2d 666 (1947); West v. Fulton County, 267 Ga. 456, 479 S.E.2d 722 (1997).

47. Braswell v. Palmer, 191 Ga. 262, 11 S.E.2d 889 (1940); O.C.G.A. §§36-9-3, 50-14-3(4); Building Authority of Fulton County v. State, 253 Ga. 242, 321 S.E.2d 97 (1984).

48. O.C.G.A. §36-9-2.1.

49. O.C.G.A. §32-4-41; Ledbetter Bros. v. Floyd County, 237 Ga. 22, 226 S.E.2d 730 (1976).

50. O.C.G.A. §36-5-24.

51. O.C.G.A. §36-5-24(c).

52. O.C.G.A. §36-5-27.

53. O.C.G.A. §§36-5-28, 36-1-11.1.

54. O.C.G.A. §§45-5-1, 45-5-6.1.

55. O.C.G.A. §45-5-5.

56. O.C.G.A. §36-5-21.

57. O.C.G.A. §21-2-71.

58. O.C.G.A. §1-3-11.

59. McCrory Company of Georgia v. Board of Commissioners of Fulton County, 177 Ga. 242, 170 S.E. 18 (1933); Moore v. Baldwin County, 209 Ga. 541, 74 S.E.2d 449 (1953); Lovett v. Bussell, 242 Ga. 405, 249 S.E.2d 86 (1978); Board of Commissioners of Randolph County v. Wilson, 260 Ga. 482, 396 S.E.2d 903 (1990); Chaffin v. Calhoun, 262 Ga. 202, 415 S.E.2d 906 (1992); Griffies v. Coweta County, 272 Ga. 506, 530 S.E.2d 718 (2000); Boswell v. Bramlett, 274 Ga. 50, 549 S.E.2d 100 (2001).

60. O.C.G.A. §15-6-24.

61. McCorkle v. Judges of Superior Court of Chatham County, 260 Ga. 315, 392 S.E.2d 707 (1990). In addition, see McCorkle v. Bignault, 260 Ga. 758, 399 S.E.2d 916 (1991).

62. Griffies v. Coweta County, 272 Ga. 506, 530 S.E.2d 718 (2000).

63. GA. CONST. art. IX, §2, ¶1(f). See Richmond County v. Pierce, 234 Ga. 274, 215 S.E.2d 665 (1975), holding that this paragraph vested in the county governing

authority sole power over compensation, retirement, etc., of employees of the county governing authority and divested the General Assembly of the power to enact a retirement act for Richmond County.

64. See Ga. Const. art. III, §6, ¶6. As applied to counties, see Grand Lodge, I.O.O.F. v. City of Thomasville, 226 Ga. 4, 172 S.E.2d 612 (1970).

65. Ga. Const. art. IX, §2, ¶1(c)(1); Boswell v. Bramlett, 274 Ga. 50, 549 S.E.2d 100 (2001).

66. O.C.G.A. §§15-6-88, 15-9-63, 15-10-23, 15-16-20, 45-16-11, 48-5-183.

67. O.C.G.A. §§15-16-20(d), 48-5-183(g), 15-6-91, 15-9-65, 15-10-23(e), 45-16-11(e).

68. O.C.G.A. §§15-16-20.1, 48-5-137(g), 21-2-213(c), 15-6-89, 15-9-63.1, 15-9-64, 15-10-105.

69. O.C.G.A. §§45-16-11(b), 15-10-23(b), 15-9-65, 15-9-63.1(c), 15-6-90, 48-5-183(b), 15-6-20(b).

70. O.C.G.A. §§15-16-20(a)(2), 48-5-183(b)(2), 15-6-88(b), 15-9-63(a)(2), 15-10-23(c), 45-16-11(a)(2).

71. O.C.G.A. §§15-6-88(d), 15-9-63(a)(3), 15-10-23(d), 15-16-20(a)(3), 45-16-11(a)(3), 48-5-183(b)(3).

72. O.C.G.A. §§15-6-88.2, 15-9-64.1, 15-10-23.1, 15-10-105.2, 15-16-20.2, 45-16-11.2, 48-5-183.1.

73. O.C.G.A. §§15-6-88(a), 15-9-63(a)(1), 15-10-23(a)(6), 15-16-20(a)(1), 45-16-11(a)(1), 48-5-137(g), 48-5-183(b)(1).

74. O.C.G.A. §§45-16-27(b), (b.1).

75. Ga. Const. art. IX, §2, ¶1(f). See Richmond County v. Pierce, 234 Ga. 274, 215 S.E.2d 665 (1975).

76. Ga. Const. art. IX, §2, ¶3(a)(14); O.C.G.A. §36-1-11.1(a).

77. O.C.G.A. §36-1-21.

78. Ga. Const. art. IX, §1, ¶4; O.C.G.A. §36-1-21; Gwinnett County v. Yates, 265 Ga. 504, 458 S.E.2d 791 (1995).

79. O.C.G.A. §36-1-12; Mobley v. Polk County, 242 Ga. 798, 251 S.E.2d 538 (1979).

80. O.C.G.A. §15-6-93.

81. O.C.G.A. §15-9-83.

82. Cannon v. City of West Palm Beach, 250 F.3d 1299 (11th Cir. 2001); Maxwell v. Mayor and Aldermen of the City of Savannah, 226 Ga.App. 705, 487 S.E.2d 478 (1997). See also Brewer v. Schacht, 235 Ga.App. 313, 509 S.E.2d 378 (1998); Sykes v. City of Atlanta, 235 Ga.App. 345, 509 S.E.2d 395 (1998).

83. DeClue v. City of Clayton, 246 Ga.App. 487, 540 S.E.2d 675 (2000).

4

Paul T. Hardy and Dave Wills

Other County Officials, Officers, Boards, Authorities, and Regional Commissions

Understanding the relationship of the county governing authority to other county officials, officers, boards, and authorities is important in conducting county affairs because in many cases, these other offices have legal power to act independently of the governing authority. This chapter briefly describes the powers and duties, selection, terms of office, compensation, and expenses of these officials, officers, boards, and authorities.[1]

The first part of the chapter describes other county officials who work directly with the county's governing authority in the daily administration of the county. The second part describes the four county constitutional officers: the sheriff, clerk of superior court, judge of probate court, and the tax commissioner. The following sections describe locally elected state judicial officers, other elected and appointed county officers, the county police and grand jury, and county boards and authorities. Because of their close involvement with county planning and development, regional commissions are also included in the final section.

COUNTY ADMINISTRATIVE OFFICIALS

Clerk of the County Governing Authority (The County Clerk)

The authority to employ a clerk is generally derived from local acts of the General Assembly—although no special authority is needed to hire a county clerk. The clerk is responsible for recording the board of commissioners' official actions, preparing correspondence and reports, maintaining county records, and any other responsibilities and duties as provided in the local act that created the position. The clerk is ordinarily appointed to and removed from office by the governing authority, and specific statutory qualifications may be imposed as well. The clerk is paid a salary determined by the governing authority or prescribed by local law.[2]

County Manager/Administrator

In a number of counties, a manager or administrator is the chief administrative official of the county and is responsible for the day-to-day operations of the county. The duties of this official, whether he or she is called a manager or administrator, are usually numerous and varied. In some counties, these duties include the appointment and removal of county employees.[3] Additional duties include

- supervising the conduct of county employees;

- administering county laws, ordinances, and resolutions;

- exercising control over county departments and agencies;

- preparing an annual budget;

- informing the governing authority about the financial conditions and needs of the county and maintaining accurate records reflecting its financial affairs;

- examining the accounts and records of county departments;

- supervising the performance of contracts;

- regulating purchases of county supplies and materials; and

- performing all other duties delegated by the governing authority.[4]

The manager or administrator is usually chosen on the basis of his or her general executive and administrative qualifications. Specific statutory qualifications may be imposed as well. Unless otherwise provided in local legislation, the county governing authority appoints and may suspend or remove the manager or administrator. Members of the governing authority are ineligible to serve as the county manager or administrator. In some counties, an individual is not eligible to run for office as a member of the commission until a year after leaving office, and the terms of office and compensation are generally determined either by the county governing authority or by local statute.[5]

The governing authority of any county is authorized by state law to create the office of county manager, which may be granted any powers, duties, and responsibilities that are administrative in nature. The qualifications, method of selection, appointment, compensation, tenure, and any other matters related to the office of county manager are provided for by the governing authority of the county.[6] For more information, see Chapter 1.

County Attorney

The primary functions of the county attorney are to advise the governing authority and other county officers on their powers and duties under the law, to prepare ordinances and legal documents, to review proposed contracts, and to represent the county in court. The governing authority appoints and removes the county attorney and in so doing, is free to appoint the attorney it pleases and to fix the duties, term of office, and compensation of the office.[7]

CONSTITUTIONAL OFFICERS

There are four constitutional officers in each county: the sheriff, clerk of superior court, judge of probate court, and tax commissioner. They are independently elected county officers.[8] The board of commissioners has authority to establish the budgets of the constitutional officers, but its actions in making such appropriations are subject to review by the courts for an abuse of discretion. In addition, after appropriations have been approved for the constitutional officers, the board of commissioners does not have any authority to dictate how such budget will be spent. Employees of the constitutional officers are considered employees of the elected officers and not employees of the county.[9] However, Georgia law provides specific steps by which such employees may be placed under the county's merit system.[10] For a brief discussion of the relationship between the county governing authority and these four officials, see Chapter 3.

Sheriff and Deputies

Sheriff

In general, it is the duty of the office of the sheriff

- to execute and return the processes and orders of the courts;
- to attend all sessions of the superior court and all sessions of the probate court whenever required by the judge;
- to be present on election days at all election locations from the opening to the closing of the polls;

- to publish sales, citations, and other proceedings as required by law and to keep a file of all newspapers in which the official advertisements appear;

- to keep an execution docket for entering a description of all executions received, the dates of their delivery, and the actions taken on them;

- to keep a book which contains a record of all sales made by process of the court or by agreement under the sanction of the court and which describes the property and the process under which sold, the date of the levy and sale, the purchaser, and the price;

- to receive from the preceding sheriff all unexecuted writs and processes and proceed to execute them and to complete other unfinished duties;

- to serve as the county jailor;

- to develop and implement a comprehensive plan for security of the courthouse and annex subject to budget approved by the commissioners;[11] and

- to perform all other duties imposed on that office by law.[12]

The courts have held that the office of sheriff carries with it all the powers and duties historically exercised by the sheriff except as modified by statute. In exercising these powers and duties, and acting as "a conservator of the peace within the county," the sheriff has the right and duty to enforce the laws enacted for the protection of the lives, persons, property, health, and morals of the people.[13] With the written consent of the county governing authority, the sheriff is authorized to contract with any city located within the county for the purpose of providing law enforcement services to the city.[14]

The office of the sheriff must be kept at the county seat and at the courthouse. However, the sheriff may also operate administrative facilities in areas of the county located outside the county seat.[15]

The sheriff is elected for a term of four years. When a vacancy occurs in the sheriff's office, the probate judge must appoint some qualified person to act as the sheriff until an election can be held. If the probate judge fails to appoint someone, then the coroner acts as the sheriff until the probate judge appoints someone or an election is held. If there is no coroner, the sheriff of any adjoining county is authorized to act as sheriff until the probate judge makes an appointment or an election is held.[16]

If the duties of the office are not faithfully performed, the sheriff may be fined for contempt and is subject to imprisonment or removal from office. The sheriff can be removed from office by the superior court judge for sufficient cause, including incapacity or misbehavior in office, upon written charges and a trial by jury.[17]

The General Assembly is responsible for setting the compensation of the sheriff. No fee-based compensation is allowed for sheriffs. The county home rule provision of the constitution prohibits local governing authority action affecting elective county officers and personnel and provides that such must be done by a general or local act of the General Assembly. Thus the governing authority cannot alter the salaries or expenses of the sheriff or deputies, except to supplement their compensation or provide for a monthly expense allowance as authorized by state law.[18]

The following rules concerning the sheriff's relationship with the county governing authority are particularly noteworthy:

1. While the governing authority cannot divest the power and duty of the sheriff to enforce the laws and preserve the peace by establishing a county police force, the board of commissioners may transfer funds and equipment from the sheriff's office to the county police department.[19]

2. By virtue of its fiscal authority and responsibility, the governing authority has the right to deny the use of county property to any county officer, including the sheriff, if it is used in a wasteful, negligent, or ineffective manner.[20]

3. The governing authority is required to adopt a budget for the sheriff that provides funding and equipment necessary for the sheriff to perform the duties of the office.[21]

Local laws detailing the governing authority's responsibilities toward the sheriff's office are in effect in many counties and, where they exist, must be consulted to determine more fully the governing authority's powers and duties with respect to the sheriff.[22]

Deputies

A deputy sheriff is an agent of the sheriff and has no powers other than those possessed by the sheriff. The sheriff is authorized to appoint one or more deputies to assist in carrying out the duties of the office. Unless a sheriff has agreed to participate in the county's civil service system, deputy sheriffs are considered employees of the sheriff, not of the county and are appointed and removed by the sheriff. The sheriff has the power to set the salaries of deputies within constraints of the county budget.[23]

Clerk of the Superior Court

The powers and duties of the clerk of superior court are almost entirely ministerial and include the maintenance of court records, the registration of property transactions, oversight of the board of equalization,[24] and the recording of subdivision plats. To help perform duties of the office, the clerk may appoint deputy clerks.[25]

The clerk of the superior court is elected for a term of four years, with vacancies in this office filled by election. When a vacancy occurs, the probate judge appoints some qualified person to discharge the clerk's duties until a new clerk is elected. The clerk is subject to removal by the judge of the superior court for sufficient cause, upon written charges and trial by jury.[26]

Clerks are compensated by a salary based on population as provided by general law, and counties are authorized to supplement the salaries of clerks in such amount as the county governing authority determines from time to time, but such supplements cannot be reduced during the clerk's term of office. In addition to their salaries, counties are authorized to pay clerks contingent expenses for the operation of their office in an amount based on the county's population.[27]

The office of the clerk must be kept at the county seat and courthouse. If there is inadequate space in the courthouse, the clerk may, subject to certain conditions, request that the governing authority move the office to some other designated place not more than 500 feet from the courthouse. The county must furnish the clerk with office supplies, equipment, furniture, record books, and other items necessary to maintain the office in a modern, up-to-date manner.[28]

In any county where the governing authority constructs a permanent satellite courthouse and designates that courthouse as a courthouse annex, the office of the clerk may be located at that satellite courthouse.[29]

Judge of the Probate Court

The judge of the probate court is charged with the performance of judicial, ministerial, and clerical duties and has original, exclusive, and general jurisdiction over

1. the probate of wills;
2. the granting of letters testamentary and of administration and the repeal or revocation of the same;
3. all controversies in relation to the right of executorship or administration;

4. the sale and disposition of the property belonging to, and the distribution of, deceased persons' estates;

5. the appointment and removal of guardians of minors, conservators of minors, guardians of incapacitated adults, and conservators of persons who are incompetent because of mental illness or mental retardation;

6. all controversies as to the right of guardianship, except that the probate court is not an appropriate court to take action under O.C.G.A. §19-7-4 (loss of parental custody);

7. the auditing and passing of returns of all executors, administrators, guardians of property, conservators, and guardians;

8. the discharge of former sureties and the requiring of new sureties from administrators, guardians of property, conservators, and guardians;

9. all matters as may be conferred on them by O.C.G.A. Chapter 3 of Title 37 (Examinations and Treatment for Mental Illness);

10. all other matters and things that pertain or relate to estates of deceased persons and to persons who are incompetent because of mental illness or mental retardation; and

11. all matters as may be conferred on them by the constitution and laws.[30]

In addition and unless otherwise provided by law, judges of probate courts have the power to

1. perform county governmental administration duties;

2. perform duties relating to elections;

3. fill vacancies in public offices by appointment;

4. administer oaths to public officers;

5. accept, file, approve, and record bonds of public officers;

6. register and permit certain enterprises;

7. issue marriage licenses;

8. hear traffic cases;

9. conduct trials, receive pleas of guilty, and impose sentences in cases of violations of game and fish laws;

10. hold criminal commitment hearings; and

11. perform such other judicial and ministerial functions as may be provided by law.[31]

Probate judges also have jurisdiction over all cases involving the removal of obstructions from roads; the authority to approve all official bonds that are received by the judge from the governor; the authority to conduct trials, receive guilty pleas, and impose sentences for certain misdemeanors, including violations of state rules and regulations regarding parks, historic sites, and recreational areas; violations of the "Georgia Boat Safety Act"; possession of less than an ounce of marijuana; the purchase or possession of alcohol by a minor; and cases involving littering on public and private property.[32]

The probate judge is elected for a term of four years.[33] When a vacancy occurs in this office, it is filled, in consecutive order, by the chief judge (if any) of the state or city court, as the case may be; the clerk of the superior court (if able to serve); or some person appointed by the superior court judge until the vacancy is filled by special election.[34]

Probate judges' compensation consists of population-based minimum salaries, cost-of-living increases, supplements, and expenses for the operation of their offices as provided in state law.[35]

The probate judge's office must be kept at the county seat and at the courthouse unless doing so is impracticable. In any county where the county seat is located in an unincorporated area of the county and the governing authority constructs a permanent satellite courthouse, the probate judge's office may be located at the satellite courthouse. The county governing authority must furnish the probate judge with office supplies, equipment, and furniture necessary to carry out the duties of the office.[36]

Tax Commissioner

The state constitution authorizes the General Assembly to consolidate the offices of tax receiver and tax collector into the office of tax commissioner, and every county in Georgia has consolidated the positions. The tax commissioner exercises the duties of the combined offices, including receiving all tax returns, maintaining county tax digests, receiving property tax exemption applications, collecting and paying over tax funds to state and local units of government, and issuing executions against delinquent taxpayers.[37]

The tax commissioner is elected to a four-year term. When a vacancy occurs, the probate judge appoints someone to discharge the tax commissioner's duties until the vacancy is filled.[38]

Depending on general and local statutes applicable to a particular county, a tax commissioner may be compensated entirely from commissions based on a percentage of taxes collected. However, most are paid a minimum salary, supplement, and expense allowance based on the population of the county. The county is generally responsible for expenses incurred in operating the office and discharging the duties of the tax commissioner.[39]

With respect to the interaction between the tax commissioner and the governing authority, the following responsibilities should be noted:

1. In counties of 30,000 or more population, the tax commissioner must each week pay over county taxes to the proper county officers. In counties of less than 30,000 population, the tax commissioner must pay over all county taxes at least once every two weeks.[40]

2. The tax commissioner is required to keep a cashbook in which all items of cash collected for taxes, as well as disbursements of such funds to the proper state and local authorities, are recorded. Generally, this book must be balanced and filed by April 20 of each year with the governing authority, which has the power to audit it.[41]

3. The tax commissioner is required to appear annually before the governing authority to render an account of official actions and to exhibit books, vouchers, and accounts. If there is a failure or refusal to do so after being notified by the governing authority, the governing authority must suspend the tax commissioner from office pending a decision from the courts on whether he or she should be removed from office.[42]

4. If the tax commissioner fails to make proper reports, payments, or final settlements of taxes, the governing authority must report such to the governor who, after following certain procedures, can remove the tax commissioner from office.[43]

LOCAL ELECTED JUDICIAL OFFICERS

Judge of the Superior Court

The superior courts are the highest-ranking courts in the state with original and general trial jurisdiction. They have original, exclusive, or concurrent jurisdiction of all civil and criminal cases granted to them by the constitution and laws. Superior courts have exclusive jurisdiction in cases of divorce, felonies, the trial of any minor between the ages of 13 and 17 who is accused of any of seven designated felonies, cases concerning title to land, and equity cases. They also have exclusive jurisdiction in adoption cases, except for such authority granted to juvenile courts. Superior courts possess appellate jurisdiction from judgments of the probate or magistrate courts, and they are empowered to exercise general supervision over all inferior courts and to review and correct their judgments.[44]

The state is divided into 49 judicial circuits, each of which must consist of at least one county. Superior court judges are elected on a nonpartisan basis and hold office for four years. Vacancies in the office of judge of superior court are filled by appointment of the governor until they can be filled by election.[45]

Counties and the state share the funding of the superior court, with the state paying the base salary for the superior court judges and for one secretary and one law clerk for each circuit. In addition, the state pays the travel expenses of superior court judges and court reporters for travel outside their home county, plus a contingent expense allowance. Counties may supplement the salaries and fringe benefits of these state employees.[46] However, counties may only supplement the salaries of superior court judges if authorized by general law or by local legislation.[47] Expenses of the superior court, such as lights, fuel, stationery, rent, and publication of grand jury presentments, are paid out of the county treasury.[48]

Sessions of superior court must be held at the county seat and the courthouse, if any, of each county in the circuit not less than twice a year at such times as set by the General Assembly. However, in any county where the county seat is located in an unincorporated area of the county and the governing authority constructs a permanent satellite courthouse and designates that courthouse as a courthouse annex, the superior court may be located in the satellite courthouse, subject to certain restrictions.[49]

District Attorney

The district attorney represents the state in all criminal cases in superior court and in all cases taken up from the superior courts to the court of appeals and the supreme court.[50] Specific duties of the district attorney include advising grand juries in relation to matters of law, drawing up indictments or presentments when requested by the grand jury, prosecuting all indictable offenses, prosecuting or defending any civil action in which the state is interested, arguing criminal cases on appeal, and assisting the attorney general when certain prosecutions are moved to a U.S. District Court.[51]

The district attorney is elected to a four-year term by the voters of the judicial circuit that he or she serves. Vacancies in this office are filled by appointment of the governor.[52]

The state and counties share the funding of the district attorney's office, with the state paying the base salaries for the district attorneys, their secretaries, and assistant district attorneys. In addition, the state pays the travel expenses of district attorneys for travel outside their home county, plus a contingent expense allowance. Counties may supplement these salaries and expenses either in the discretion of the board of commissioners or by a local legislative act.[53] The county or counties that make up the judicial circuit must provide all offices, utilities, telephone expenses, materials, and supplies necessary to equip, maintain, and furnish the district attorney's office in an orderly and efficient manner.[54]

Judge of the State Court

State courts are created by local acts of the General Assembly.[55] While referred to as state courts, these are essentially county courts that enforce state law. Within the boundaries of the county or counties for which they are created, state courts have jurisdiction over

1. the trial of nonfelony criminal cases;
2. the trial of civil cases regardless of the amount in controversy, except for those actions in which exclusive jurisdiction is vested in the superior courts;
3. the hearing of applications for and the issuance of arrest and search warrants;
4. the holding of courts of inquiry;
5. the punishments of contempts of court by fines not exceeding $500 or by imprisonment not exceeding 20 days or both; and
6. the review of decisions of other courts as provided by law.[56]

In addition, state courts have concurrent jurisdiction with other courts over offenses involving possession of one ounce or less of marijuana.[57]

The General Assembly establishes by local law the number of judges for each state court and whether or not they are full-time or part-time judges. State court judges are elected on a nonpartisan basis and hold office for four years. Vacancies are filled by appointment of the governor until they can be filled by election. State court judges are compensated from county funds as provided by local law, and the county governing authority is authorized to supplement the compensation to be paid.[58]

Solicitor-General of the State Court

In those counties with a state court, the solicitor-general represents the state in all criminal cases in that court unless there is a local law designating the district attorney to do so. Specific duties of the solicitor-general include the filing of accusations and prosecution of all criminal cases triable in state court and arguing any criminal cases on appeal from the state court. A solicitor-general may be authorized by local law to represent the state in more than one county within a judicial circuit.[59]

The solicitor-general is elected to a four-year term by the voters of the county or counties in which he or she serves. Vacancies in this office are filled by appointment of the governor. Solicitors-general are compensated from county funds, and the county governing authority may not decrease the salary of the solicitor-general below the amount set by local law. The county must reimburse all actual expenses of the solicitor-general and any personnel of his or her office and must provide all offices, utilities, equipment, telephone expenses, legal costs, transcripts, materials, and supplies necessary for the solicitor-general to perform the duties and obligations of the office in an orderly and efficient manner.[60]

Chief Magistrate

There is one magistrate court in each county, and each magistrate court and each magistrate has jurisdiction and power over

1. the hearing of applications for and the issuance of arrest and search warrants;
2. the issuance of warrants and related proceedings as provided in O.C.G.A. Article 4 of Chapter 6 of Title 17, relating to bonds for good behavior and bonds to keep the peace;
3. the holding of courts of inquiry;
4. the trial of charges of violations of county ordinances and penal ordinances of state authorities;
5. the trial of civil claims including garnishment and attachment in which exclusive jurisdiction is not vested in the superior court and the amount demanded or the value of the property claimed does not exceed $15,000 provided that no prejudgment attachment may be granted;
6. the issuance of summons, trial of issues, and issuance of writs and judgments in dispossessory proceedings and distress warrant proceedings as provided in O.C.G.A. Articles 3 and 4 of Chapter 7 of Title 44;
7. the punishment of contempts of court by fine not exceeding $200 or by imprisonment not exceeding 10 days or both;

8. the administration of any oath that is not required by law to be administered by some other officer;

9. the granting of bail in all cases for which the granting of bail is not exclusively committed to some other court or officer;

10. the issuing of subpoenas to compel attendance of witnesses in the magistrate court and subpoenas for the production of documentary evidence before the magistrate court;

11. the trial and sentencing of misdemeanor violations of O.C.G.A. §16-9-20, relating to the criminal issuance of bad checks;

12. the execution or subscription and the acceptance of written waivers of extradition as provided in O.C.G.A. §17-13-46;

13. the trial and sentencing of other specified misdemeanor violations; and

14. such other matters as are committed to their jurisdiction by other general laws.[61]

Each magistrate court has a chief magistrate and may have one or more other magistrates. Generally, the chief magistrate is elected by the voters for a four-year term. Other magistrates are appointed by the chief magistrate with the consent of the superior court judges, and the term of the other magistrates runs concurrently with the term of the chief magistrate who made the appointment. A vacancy in the office of chief magistrate is filled by an appointment of the judges of superior court of that county for the remainder of the unexpired term, and a vacancy in the office of any other magistrate is filled by an appointment of the chief magistrate with the consent of the superior court judges for the remainder of the unexpired term. The General Assembly may, by local law, provide for the number of magistrates in a particular county and for different methods of selecting magistrates and filling vacancies.[62] Magistrates are subject to discipline, removal, and involuntary retirement by the Judicial Qualifications Commission.[63]

Magistrates are compensated solely on a salary basis. General law provides for minimum salaries based on population that may be supplemented by the county, and the General Assembly may by local law set the compensation of any or all of a county's magistrates. The county may also provide an expense allowance, based on the county's population, for the operation of the magistrate court.[64]

The county governing authority must provide suitable offices and courtrooms for the use of the magistrate court and must supply all fixtures, supplies, and equipment necessary for the proper functioning of the magistrate court.[65]

OTHER ELECTED AND APPOINTED OFFICERS

Circuit Public Defender

The federal and state constitutions guarantee legal representation for individuals accused of a crime. If an accused person cannot afford to hire an attorney, one must be provided.[66] These services are provided through the office of the circuit public defender. With the exception of 6 single-county circuits that are not included in the statewide system, each of the other 43 judicial circuits has a chief public defender. While the state is primarily responsible for indigent defense services in superior and juvenile courts, counties are required to provide office space, utilities, materials, and supplies to support the office of the circuit public defender.[67] In addition, counties are obligated to pay a share of the costs of attorneys' services in any death penalty case when the costs exceed $150,000.[68] Counties are also authorized to supplement the pay of the circuit's public defenders and to pay the salaries of additional assistant public defenders. Circuit public defenders are appointed by their own circuit's Public Defender Supervisory Panel, which includes at least two county commissioners appointed by the governor. In addition to appointing the circuit public defender, the panels may recommend removal of a circuit public defender to the Georgia Public Defenders Standards Council.[69] Counties are also obligated to provide and pay for the full cost of any legal defense services required in state, magistrate, and probate court and may do so by setting up a county legal defense program or by contracting with the Georgia Public Defenders Standards Council through the local circuit defender program.[70]

Coroner

The coroner is responsible for holding an inquest into the cause of death in cases in which a person dies (1) as a result of violence, suicide, or casualty; (2) suddenly when in apparent good health; (3) when unattended by a physician; or (4) in any suspicious or unusual manner.[71]

Upon receiving notice of death under any of the above circumstances, the coroner is to take charge of the body immediately and summon a medical examiner and peace officer. Together, they must make an inquiry into the cause and manner of death. The medical examiner performs a postmortem examination or an autopsy and reports the findings to the director of the division of forensic sciences of the Georgia Bureau of Investigation. Unless there has been a finding of foul play, a dead body must be released to the next of kin within 24 hours of demand.[72]

Coroners are required to take 16 hours of training per year at the Georgia Police Academy.[73]

The coroner is elected for a four-year term. Whenever the office is vacant, the probate judge appoints someone to serve as coroner until the vacancy is filled by election.[74] The coroner is subject to removal by the judge of the superior court for sufficient cause, upon written charges and trial by jury.[75]

State law provides for minimum salaries for coroners in counties that have a population of fewer than 35,000. Coroners have the option of being paid either an investigative fee of $175 whenever no jury is impaneled or $250 if a jury is impaneled or a salary set by local legislation.[76] When performing the duties of a sheriff, the coroner's fees are the same as the sheriff's.[77] In any county in which there is more than one state correctional facility or prison, the state must pay the coroner $110 for each state inmate death in the county.

Coroners must have at least one deputy coroner who is appointed by and serves at the pleasure of the coroner. A deputy coroner has the same powers and is entitled to the same fees as the coroner, but the deputy coroner can only act when the coroner is unable to act.[78]

Medical Examiner

In three counties—Fulton, Cobb, and DeKalb—the coroner's office has been abolished by local constitutional amendment, and the office of medical examiner has been created.[79] General law provides for the abolishment of the office of coroner and the establishment of the office of medical examiner by local law.[80] The law also provides for the qualifications, powers, and duties of anyone appointed as medical examiner and the compensation and expenses due the medical examiner. Generally, the medical examiner possesses the same powers, duties, liabilities, and obligations formerly possessed by the coroner in these counties. The governing authority appoints the medical examiner and fixes the compensation.[81]

Surveyor

The county surveyor's duties include surveying county and district lines, conducting other surveys for the county, and maintaining plats of all surveys made. The law requires that there be one surveyor for each county, but in a number of counties this office is vacant. The General Assembly may by local law abolish the office of elected county surveyor and authorize the governing authority to appoint a county surveyor. When there is no county surveyor, any Georgia resident who is a duly licensed land surveyor may be appointed to perform the duties of county surveyor.[82]

The surveyor is elected for a term of four years. Whenever an election fails to fill this office, or a vacancy occurs, the probate judge appoints someone to serve as surveyor until the vacancy is filled. The county surveyor is subject to removal by the probate judge for incapacity.[83]

The surveyor is allowed to establish a fee for services. When a survey is ordered by the county, the fee is paid out of county funds, and it must be reasonably equivalent to that charged by a private surveyor. When surveys are made for private or corporate benefit, the surveyor's services may be contracted. In these cases, the fees are paid by the person or corporation requesting the survey. When the survey is made by court order, the fees are taxed in the bill of costs unless otherwise agreed upon. The office may be kept at the residence of the county surveyor if it is within the county limits; the county is not required to furnish the surveyor with an office or facilities.[84]

Treasurer

The county treasurer, an elected officer, is responsible for collecting all money due the county and for depositing, disbursing, and accounting for all county funds. In addition, some specific duties are imposed by law, including appearing before the county governing authority at least twice a year to render an account of official acts and to exhibit records.[85]

The office of county treasurer may be abolished by local act of the legislature; a large number of counties have abolished it.[86] Many of these acts authorize the county commissioners to designate a county employee, some other person, or a bank to perform the duties of county treasurer. In any county in which such an act is applicable, it must be looked to for the powers, duties, and responsibilities of the depositories created and the method for handling county funds.[87]

Where the office of treasurer still exists, the term of office is four years, and vacancies are filled by appointment of the probate judge until a special election can be called or the next regular election of county treasurer is held. The treasurer's commissions for receiving and disbursing funds are prescribed by statute. In most counties, the fee system of compensation has been abolished, and the treasurer is paid a salary.[88]

Emergency Management Director

The governing authority is authorized to establish a local organization for emergency management in accordance with the state emergency plan and program. The executive officer of the governing authority nominates a local director to the state emergency management director who has authority to make the appointment. A local director must be at least 21 years of age, not have been convicted of a felony, have completed a high school education or its equivalent, be capable of writing emergency management plans, and not be self-employed or have any other occupation in the private sector that conflicts with his or her duties as a local director. The local director is responsible for the organization, administration, and operation of the county emergency management unit, subject to the direction and control of the governing authority.[89]

A county has broad authority in matters of emergency management, including the power to appropriate and expend funds; make contracts; obtain and distribute equipment, materials, and supplies for emergency management purposes; provide for the health and safety of persons and property; and appoint and employ various emergency management workers. Any county that has not established a local organization for emergency management in accordance with the state emergency plan is ineligible for state disaster relief funds. In addition, the National Incident Management Systems (NIMS) was created by presidential directive to the Secretary of Homeland Security of the Federal Emergency Management Agency to serve as a structured network for federal, state, and local emergency agencies to respond to natural disasters and terrorist attacks. A county must have adopted NIMS in order to be eligible for federal preparedness assistance.[90]

OTHERS

County Police

The governing authority has the power to appoint county police, but the creation of a county police department must be approved by the voters. If an attempt to create a county police force is rejected, the issue may not again be submitted to the voters within 48 months of the failed referendum.[91]

When a county police force has been created, the law requires that the county governing authority make rules and regulations for its conduct, management, and control; this power may not be delegated. In its discretion, the county governing authority may enlarge, modify, or change such rules and regulations.[92] The governing authority, and not the sheriff, is responsible for the direction and control of the county police force, but it cannot prevent the county police force from cooperating with the sheriff in the enforcement of laws and preservation of the peace.

County police possess the same law enforcement powers as the sheriff in the county of their appointment and may make arrests and execute and return criminal warrants.[93]

The governing authority is responsible for setting the terms of office and salaries of the county police and can remove them from office. In order to provide funds to meet county police expenses, the governing authority can levy a tax.[94]

Grand Jury

Under the American system of jurisprudence, a grand jury usually functions only as an informing or accusing body. Georgia grand juries, however, are also empowered by various general laws to carry out numerous civil duties, most of which can, if exercised, affect or involve county officials. In performing its duties, the grand jury is advised on matters of law by the district attorney but has no authority to employ attorneys for this purpose at county expense.[95]

Under Georgia law, the grand jury's civil powers include the following:

1. Examining returns submitted to it by the probate judge, treasurer, superior court clerk, and sheriff specifying the amount and sources of money received by them belonging to the county, as well as expenditures made by their offices[96]

2. Inspecting the county jail and making recommendations necessary for providing proper sanitation, ventilation and heating, and treatment of inmates[97]

3. Examining the sheriff's jail book containing certain information on all persons committed to jail and reporting to the appropriate court the failure to keep or the improper keeping of this record[98]

4. Fixing the compensation of court bailiffs and grand and trial jurors[99]

5. Appointing county boards of equalization[100]

6. In addition, when deemed necessary by eight or more of its members, appointing a committee of its members to inspect or investigate any county office, building, authority, court, or school[101]

A grand jury consists of no fewer than 16 nor more than 23 persons randomly selected by superior court judges under specific statutory procedures. All Georgia citizens above the age of 18 who have resided in the county for six months are qualified and liable to serve as grand jurors except those who

- are incompetent because of mental illness or mental retardation,

- hold any elective office in state or local government or who have held any such office within a period of two years preceding the time of service as a grand juror, and

- have been convicted of a felony and have not been pardoned or had their civil rights restored.[102]

The first grand jury impaneled at the fall term of superior court shall set the compensation of all jurors, including grand jurors, and increases in such amounts must be approved by the county governing authority.[103]

COUNTY BOARDS AND AUTHORITIES

Board of Tax Assessors, Equalization Board, Appraisers

Board of Tax Assessors

The board of tax assessors is responsible for determining what property in the county is subject to taxation and for requiring its proper return. It examines and corrects errors in all real and personal property county tax returns. The board must see that all property in the county is returned for taxes at fair valuation, and that valuation between individual taxpayers is fairly equalized so that each pays, as nearly as possible, only his or her proportionate share of taxes.[104]

There is a county board of tax assessors in each county consisting of no fewer than three nor more than five members appointed by the county governing authority. Each county governing authority must establish by resolution the term of office of members of its county board of tax assessors within the range of not less than three years and not more than six years. Thereafter, all assessors are to be appointed for terms as set by the county governing authority. This change in the length of terms does not affect the terms of assessors in office at that time. No person may be appointed or reappointed to a county board of tax assessors if the individual is related to a member of the county governing authority as a

- mother or mother-in-law,
- father or father-in-law,
- sister or sister-in-law,
- brother or brother-in-law,
- grandmother or grandmother by marriage,
- grandfather or grandfather by marriage,

- son or son-in-law, or
- daughter or daughter-in-law.[105]

Board members can be removed by the governing authority only for cause shown, for failure to perform the duties or to meet the qualifications imposed by law, or by the superior court judge upon petition by 100 or more real property owners of the county. Assessors must possess certain qualifications specified by statute and successfully pass an examination administered by the state revenue commissioner.[106]

The compensation of members of the board of tax assessors is fixed by the county governing authority within limits set by statute.[107] With county governing authority approval, the board of tax assessors may contract with individuals and firms for staff assistance in performing its duties, the cost of which is paid out of county funds.[108] The state revenue commissioner is authorized to make loans or contract with counties to aid them in financing personnel to assist the board of tax assessors in carrying out survey, valuation, and equalization programs.[109]

The county governing authority may, upon adoption of a resolution, request that a performance review of the county board of tax assessors be conducted. Upon receipt of the request, the state revenue commissioner appoints three persons to serve as members of the performance review board: one member must be an employee of the state revenue department, and the other two must be assessors who are not members of the board under review. It is the duty of the review board to conduct a thorough and complete investigation of all actions of the tax assessors and appraisal staff regarding the technical competency of appraisal techniques and compliance with state law. The review board issues a written report of its findings, including evaluations, judgments, and recommendations. The county governing authority is required to reimburse the members of the review board for reasonable expenses incurred in the performance of their duties. The findings of the review board can be used as grounds for the removal of one or more of the members of the board of tax assessors.[110]

Board of Equalization

The board of equalization hears taxpayers' appeals from assessments made by the board of tax assessors. If it believes an assessment is not uniform with other assessments in the tax digest, it can order the board of tax assessors to take action necessary to obtain uniformity. Board of equalization decisions may be appealed to the superior court of the county by the taxpayer or the board of tax assessors.[111] At the option of the taxpayer, when certain requirements are met, an appeal may be made to a hearing officer or to binding arbitration in lieu of the board of equalization.[112] The use of arbitration precludes a later appeal of the arbitrators' decision to the superior court.

The board of equalization consists of three members and three alternate members who are property owners in the county selected from the current grand jury list by the grand jury. Multicounty regional boards may also be formed by intergovernmental agreement.[113] No member of the governing authority, county board of education, board of tax assessors, employee of the county board of tax assessors, or chief appraiser is eligible to serve as a member or alternate member of the county board of equalization.[114] Management of the boards of equalization is the responsibility of the clerk of superior court of the county.[115]

In counties with more than 10,000 parcels of real estate, the governing authority may elect to have one additional member of the board of equalization for each additional 10,000 parcels of real estate or any part thereof. Members and alternate members serve terms of three years. If a vacancy occurs on the board of equalization, an alternate member fills it for the remainder of the term, and the grand jury selects another person to serve as alternate. When considering appeals and when attending required appraisal courses, board members are compensated by the county on a per diem basis at a rate of not less than $25 per day, to be determined by the county governing authority. Facilities and clerical help necessary to carry out the duties of the board of equalization are furnished by the county governing authority to the superior court clerk.[116]

County Appraisal Staff

In general, the county property tax appraisal staff appraises taxable property, maintains county tax records, prepares annual assessments, and assists both the tax assessors and equalization board.[117] The chief appraiser, who heads the appraisal staff, is designated by the board of tax assessors and may be a member of that board.[118] In counties with a population of 100,000 or more, no member of a county property appraisal staff is eligible to serve as a member of the county board of tax assessors. In those counties in which a chief appraiser or member of the county appraisal staff is permitted to serve as a member of the county board of tax assessors, the membership on such board ends automatically upon such person ceasing to serve as an appraiser.[119] Members of the appraisal staff may go onto property outside of buildings, posted or otherwise, to carry out their duties, provided they display sufficient identification. Such members of the appraisal staff may not enter upon the property unless the owner and occupant of the property have been provided reasonable notice regarding the purpose for which such person is entering the property.[120]

Counties are classified on the basis of the number of parcels of real property located within their boundaries for the purpose of determining minimum staff requirements under the law. When a county employs the required minimum staff and maintains proper tax records, the state is authorized to assist in financing the county tax equalization system.[121] Qualifications and minimum compensation for appraisers are determined by the state revenue commissioner, with state merit system approval. Appraisers are paid from county funds and before being employed, must pass an examination prepared by the state merit system. They may also be required to take courses of instruction administered by the state revenue department.[122] The commissioners are authorized to provide that staff and employees of the county board of tax assessors be positions of employment covered by the county personnel system.[123]

Board of Health and Health Districts

There is a county board of health in each county in the state that determines the county's health needs and resources and develops programs to meet these needs. In general, responsibility for all public health matters within the county (such as the placement of septic tanks, the abatement of public nuisances, disease prevention, vaccinations against contagious diseases, and such other matters to prevent the spread of infectious matter, and rabies control) is vested in the board of health. This responsibility includes the enforcement of health laws and regulations.[124]

The county board of health is composed of seven members. They are

1. the chief executive officer of the county governing authority or some other person designated by said officer;
2. the county superintendent of schools or a school system employee designated by the superintendent;
3. a physician actively practicing medicine in the county;
4. a person appointed by the county governing authority who is a consumer or a person from an advocacy group who will represent the county's consumers of health services;
5. a person appointed by the governing authority of the largest municipality in the county who is a consumer, interested in promoting public health, or a registered professional nurse or a licensed practical nurse;

6. a person appointed by the county governing authority who is a consumer and who will represent the county's needy, underprivileged, or elderly community; and

7. the chief executive officer of the largest municipality in the county or some other person designated by said officer.[125]

The terms of members of the board of health appointed by the governing authority of either the county or largest municipality in the county are six years. Vacancies in the appointed positions are filled for the unexpired term in the same manner as the original appointment, and no employee of the state Department of Human Services or the county board of health shall be a member of the board.[126] Members of the board are paid an amount governed by statute, if funds for that purpose have been provided by the county.[127] The board appoints a director, who must be a physician licensed to practice medicine in Georgia, to act as its chief executive officer. While the director is subject to the policies and directives of the board of health, the director is a state employee who reports to the director of environmental health of the state Department of Community Health. The director of the board may, subject to the board's approved budget, designate additional aides and assistants to carry out the responsibilities of the board. Normally, such aides and assistants are state employees.[128]

The county governing authority is authorized to fund the reasonable expenses of the board of health through property taxes, with office facilities and equipment for the board also supplied by the county.[129] In addition, the board receives federal and state financial assistance. To assist it in performing its duties, the board of health may utilize the services of the county attorney or employ other counsel.[130]

With the consent of the boards of health and the county governing authorities, the Department of Community Health may establish a health district comprising one or more counties with the same powers and duties as the individual health boards.[131] For further discussion of health and human services, see Chapter 15.

Board of Family and Children Services

Georgia law requires the state Department of Human Services to provide public assistance services to those in need in each of the counties, including the organization and supervision of a county Department of Family and Children Services (DFACS) to administer public assistance functions and compile public assistance information. The county DFACS is the state agency charged with the administration of all forms of public assistance at the county level.[132]

DFACS consists of a board, a director, and such additional employees as necessary.[133] The board is made up of five members appointed to five-year overlapping terms by the county governing authority. No elected official of the state or any political subdivision can be appointed, and vacancies are filled for the remainder of the term in the same manner as are original appointments. Members of the board serve without compensation except that they shall be paid, subject to county budget limits, a per diem as provided in state law and shall be reimbursed for travel and other expenses incurred in the performance of their official duties.[134] The county director is the executive and administrative officer and secretary to the board and is a state employee appointed, from a list of qualified candidates provided by the board, by the commissioner of the Department of Human Services. The county DFACS staff members are state employees subject to the approval of the Department of Human Services Commissioner.[135] For further discussion of family and children services, see Chapter 15.

Regional Planning Boards for Mental Health/Community Service Boards

Regional planning boards and community service boards are instrumentalities of the state created to plan for, coordinate, and provide mental health, developmental disabilities, and addictive disease services to the community. Boards are governed by a board of directors appointed by the county commissioners of the participating counties based on criteria specified in state law. Service areas are designated by the Department of Behavioral Health and Developmental Disabilities. A regional coordinator is appointed by the commissioner of the department to operate the regional planning board while the community service board is responsible for employing an executive director to direct the day-to-day operations of the community service board.[136] See Chapter 15 for additional information.

Planning Commission and Board of Zoning Appeals and Variances

Planning Commission

There is no general law establishing a planning commission in each county. However, many counties have created by ordinance or local legislation a board known as a planning commission or a planning and zoning commission. These boards may not make planning and zoning decisions for commissioners. They may serve to evaluate and conduct public hearings on rezoning requests, zoning text changes, comprehensive plan updates, and future land-use map changes, for example. They may make recommendations to the county governing authority, which is the ultimate decision maker on these issues. The jurisdiction, make up, appointment, terms, and compensation of this board are entirely within the discretion of the county governing authority so long as the laws governing planning, zoning, and open meetings are observed.[137]

Board of Zoning Appeals and Variances

Although there is no statutory authorization, some counties have created boards of zoning appeals and variances to provide relief from administrative decisions of county staff, address alleged errors in enforcement of the zoning ordinance, and grant variances to the zoning ordinance. A variance is an exception allowed in a zoning ordinance, granted on a case-by-case basis, when strict enforcement of the ordinance would result in a hardship on the property owner (i.e., failure to grant the variance would result in the property being totally useless) due to specific site conditions (e.g., property configuration, topography, soil conditions). Oftentimes, these variance ordinances relate to physical or dimensional requirements such as required road frontage, setbacks, building height, and floor space. The board of zoning appeals and variance would consider these factors, along with whether or not the granting of the variance would result in a hazard to the public health or safety or in granting a special privilege to the property owner. Any type of variance or appeal must be clearly spelled out in the ordinance. The jurisdiction, make up, appointment, terms, and compensation of this board are entirely within the discretion of the county governing authority so long as the laws governing planning, zoning, and open meetings are observed.[138] For further discussion of planning and zoning, see Chapter 9.

Public and Law Library Boards

Public Library Board

A board of library trustees, which approves the constitution of the library system, is entrusted with the general supervision of county public libraries. It also has the duty and responsibility to (1) make rules and regulations for the operation of libraries, (2) appoint a library director who satisfies state certification requirements, (3) approve budgets prepared by the library director, (4) determine the number and kind of library

personnel employed and appoint or dismiss them upon recommendation of the library director, and (5) present financial reports to governing
officials and to the public.[139]

The board consists of at least one member appointed from each
governmental agency financially supporting the library. The appointment
must be in writing, stating the length and expiration date of the term,
and sent to the appointee and the library. Vacancies are filled in the same
manner as the appointments. Members of the board do not receive any
compensation except that they can be reimbursed for reasonable expenses
incurred in the performance of their duties.[140]

Board of Trustees of the County Law Library

The board of trustees of the county law library is empowered to select
publications for the law library, make all rules and regulations governing its
use, and exercise all other powers necessary for its proper administration.[141]

The board consists of the chief superior court judge; the probate
judge; the senior state court judge, if any; the solicitor-general, if any;
the superior court clerk; and two practicing attorneys of the county
selected by the other trustees. The superior court judge is chairman of
the board, and all trustees serve without pay. The board can appoint a
secretary-treasurer and may designate the probate judge, a deputy clerk
of the superior court, or some other person to act as librarian.[142]

The board controls all county law library funds, which must be
spent for library publications, equipment, and supplies, as well as for
maintenance and operation expenses and librarian services. If the board
of trustees determines in its discretion that it has excess law library funds,
the board may grant such excess funds to charitable tax-exempt organizations that provide civil legal representation for low-income people. Any
remaining excess funds shall be turned over to the county governing authority for the purchase of fixtures and furnishings for the
courthouse.[143]

To provide revenue for the library, a maximum $5 fee may be charged
in civil and criminal cases filed in the superior, state, probate, and other
courts of record except county recorders' or municipal courts. This fee
is set by the chief superior court judge. At the discretion of the county
governing authority, law library fees may be used for codification of
county ordinances, but the amount shall not exceed the cost of
establishing or maintaining the codification. If a county does not
have a law library and the county governing authority so requests, the
chief superior court judge may direct that law library fees be collected

and used for codification of county ordinances. The board may receive gifts or grants of money or property and hold or invest such for the use of the library.[144]

If a county has a law library, the county governing authority must furnish necessary space, lights, heat, and water for its maintenance. All law books, reports, texts, and periodicals purchased by the board of trustees become the property of the county.[145]

Park or Recreation Boards

The county governing authority may establish a system of supervised recreation and vest in the board of education, a park or recreation board, or some other existing body the power to provide county recreational activities and facilities. The governing authority can also furnish recreational facilities jointly with other local units of government. The board, so vested, has the power to develop, maintain, operate, and equip all types of recreational facilities and programs and may employ recreation directors, supervisors, or other personnel.[146]

If a park or recreation board is created, the membership consists of no fewer than five nor more than nine persons appointed to five-year overlapping terms by the presiding officer of the county governing authority. Members serve without pay. Vacancies are filled for the unexpired term by the presiding officer of the governing authority.[147]

The board designated to furnish recreational facilities has exclusive control of all recreation funds. It may accept grants, gifts, or donations to the recreation system, but those that will subject the county to additional expense must be approved by the county governing authority. The governing authority may levy a tax and issue bonds to fund the recreation program. If a county has adopted a minimum, maximum, or a minimum and maximum recreation tax, the governing authority may adopt a resolution to remove the tax upon voter approval. Once the tax has been removed, the county governing authority determines the funding level.[148] See Chapter 13 for a more detailed discussion of county park and recreation programs.

Development Authority

There is a county development authority in each county in the state in order to promote trade, commerce, industry, and employment. A joint development authority may be established with another county or counties or with one or more municipalities.[149]

The powers of a development authority are all those necessary or convenient to carry out its purposes, including the power to make contracts; receive and administer grants and gifts; dispose of as well as lease or exchange real and personal property; appoint and employ agents and employees; construct, repair, and maintain projects such as agricultural, manufacturing, and mining structures, air and water pollution control projects, and air transportation facilities; and expend excess funds for the promotion of industry, agriculture, and trade. No project may be operated by an authority or the county but must be leased or sold to private firms or individuals.[150] In addition, a development authority may issue revenue bonds and obligations to provide funds for carrying out its purposes and projects. Bonds, obligations, and other indebtedness of an authority are not debts of the county.[151]

Generally, an authority is exempt from paying state or local taxes or assessments on any property that is acquired by it, under its control or supervision, or leased by it to others.[152]

Development authorities have been created in a number of counties by local constitutional amendments and local laws. In such counties, pertinent local legislation should be consulted to determine the powers and duties of those development authorities.[153]

A development authority consists of a board of no fewer than seven nor more than nine directors appointed by the county governing authority for staggered four-year terms. Each director must be a taxpayer and county resident. No more than one county commissioner may be appointed as a director. Except for a director who is also a member of the governing authority, each director or member of the development authority must attend and complete at least eight hours of training on development and redevelopment programs within 12 months of the director's or member's appointment to the development authority. This training requirement does not apply to any director or member who was in office on January 1, 2000. Directors receive no compensation other than reimbursement for actual expenses incurred in performing their duties.[154]

Hospital Authority

The county governing authority is authorized by general law to create a hospital authority to establish and operate hospital facilities within and beyond county boundaries. A county can also set up a hospital authority jointly with municipalities and other counties. A hospital authority has all powers necessary or convenient to carry out its purposes, including the authority to make contracts; acquire real and personal property by purchase, lease, grant, or otherwise; appoint officers, agents, and employees; and operate, construct, improve, and repair hospital projects.[155] In addition, an authority fixes the rates and charges for use of its facilities. It cannot, however, operate any project for profit. An authority may also borrow money and issue revenue certificates, which are not debts of the county.[156]

The board must file an annual activity report with the governing authority containing the budget adopted by the board. In addition, the authority must annually prepare a community benefit report that discloses the cost of indigent and charity care provided by the authority. The report must be filed with the superior court clerk and the county governing authority within 90 days of the end of the fiscal or calendar year. It must also have an annual audit made of the financial affairs of the authority, and if it fails to do so, the governing authority or any county taxpayer may petition the superior court to require the audit.[157]

A hospital authority itself has no power to tax. However, the county governing authority may contract with the authority to pay for services rendered to indigent sick and others and levy a property tax, not exceeding seven mills, to pay for such services. A hospital authority has the same tax exemptions and exclusions as do cities and counties operating similar facilities.[158]

A hospital authority consists of a board of trustees of no fewer than five nor more than nine county residents appointed by the governing authority for staggered terms as specified by the county. By resolution, the number of members of any hospital authority may be increased by not more than two additional members. Where a joint authority exists, the number of trustees can be no larger than 15. Vacancies are generally filled by the board itself from a list of three eligible persons submitted by the county governing authority. Board members receive no compensation other than reimbursement for actual expenses incurred in performing their duties, or they may elect to be reimbursed for such expenses on a per diem basis in an amount as set by state law per meeting or a total amount as set by state law per month.[159]

Housing Authority

Under general law, a housing authority can be established at any time by the county governing authority or upon the filing of a petition signed by 25 residents of the county. The law requires that a housing authority be created if the governing authority finds that unsanitary or unsafe dwellings exist in the county or that there is a shortage of safe or sanitary dwelling accommodations available to persons of low income at rentals they can afford.[160]

A housing authority has all powers necessary and convenient to carry out its purposes, including the power to make contracts; acquire, prepare, lease, and operate housing projects; provide for their construction, repair, and furnishings; borrow money or accept grants or other financial assistance from the federal government; and issue bonds. Bonds and other obligations of the authority are not debts of the county.[161] Housing authorities are authorized to enter into contracts with for-profit entities for the ownership of a housing project and are authorized to incorporate nonprofit corporations as subsidiaries of the authority.[162]

A housing authority is headed by five commissioners appointed by the governing authority for staggered five-year terms. All vacancies are filled for the unexpired term only. Commissioners cannot be officers or employees of the county, and they receive no compensation other than reimbursement for necessary expenses. The authority shall select from its commissioners a vice-chairman and may employ a secretary (who is the executive director of the authority) and other personnel as well as determine their qualifications, duties, and compensation. It may utilize the services of the county attorney or employ other counsel and legal staff. All vacancies are filled for the unexpired term only. Commissioners cannot be officers or employees of the county, and they receive no compensation other than reimbursement for necessary expenses.[163]

The property and the authority are exempt from all county and state taxes and special assessments. In lieu of these taxes, however, the authority may agree to make payments to the county for improvements, services, and facilities furnished by the county for the benefit of any housing project. An authority is prohibited from constructing or operating a housing project for profit or as a revenue source for the county. Moreover, it must fix rentals at no higher rates than necessary, and it is obligated to comply with certain statutory requirements concerning rentals and tenant selection. When a housing authority is created, the county governing authority must donate an amount of money necessary to cover the administrative and overhead expenses of the authority for the first year. The county may also, from time to time, lend or donate money to the authority.[164]

Any two or more housing authorities may cooperate with one another in exercising their powers with respect to housing projects. In addition, the governing authorities of two or more contiguous counties can create a regional housing authority if it would be a more efficient and economical administrative unit. In such cases, each county housing authority involved ceases to exist after completing all business and shall deed all of its property and obligations to the regional housing authority.[165]

When two or more counties create a regional housing authority, the counties establish, by resolution, the composition and size of the housing authority provided that each county has at least one commissioner on the board of the authority and that at least one of the commissioners is a recipient of direct assistance of a public housing authority within the region.[166] State law provides for the addition to and the exclusion and detachment of counties from regional housing authorities.[167]

Airports/Airport Authority

By general law, Georgia counties are authorized, separately or jointly, to acquire, establish, own, and operate airports and landing fields inside or outside the county. The governing authority can construct, maintain, and operate airports or landing fields; adopt regulations and establish fees for their use; fix penalties for violations of these regulations; and lease airport facilities to private parties. The governing authority may provide funds for airports or landing fields, acquire easements for lights and markers, and police all airport facilities.[168]

A number of airport authorities have been created by local constitutional amendment or local legislation. These authorities are usually permitted to make contracts, obtain and dispose of property, fix and collect charges and tolls, issue revenue bonds, and accept loans and grants.[169]

9-1-1 Authority

By resolution, county governing bodies are authorized to create and activate, with other counties and municipalities, multi-jurisdictional authorities to operate emergency 9-1-1 systems. The resolutions that create and activate these authorities must specify the number of members of the authority, the number to be appointed by each participating county and municipality, their terms of office, and their residency requirements. Such authorities are required to elect a chairperson and any other officers as deemed necessary. The authority selects a director, who is responsible for establishing operating standards and procedures and overseeing the operations of the emergency 9-1-1 system. It is responsible for hiring, training, supervising, and disciplining employees. The authority must submit its annual budget and a report of its financial records to the local governing bodies that created the authority.[170]

County School Board and Superintendent

Board of Education

In Georgia, the responsibility for the administration and financial support of the public school system is divided between the state and the county (or city) board of education. Except for levying the property tax certified by the board of education, the county has virtually no role in the provision of education. The state Board of Education has authority to formulate educational and administrative policies and standards for the improvement of public education within the state.[171] Management and control of the public schools within each county are the responsibilities of the county's board of education.[172]

The county board of education possesses broad authority. It is the tribunal for hearing and determining all local controversies relating to school law and is given wide discretionary powers in this area. It establishes and makes regulations for the various county schools, including elementary and high school, and it administers kindergarten programs, special education services for students with special needs, vocational programs, early intervention programs for students at risk of not reaching or maintaining an academic grade level, alternative education programs, and summer school programs.[173] The board of education has extensive authority over school property and facilities, including the complete ownership of and the right to buy and sell school property.[174] It also has authority, within certain limitations, to borrow sufficient amounts of money for the operation of the public school system and may issue bonds for building and equipping schoolhouses and purchasing school sites.[175] Teachers, principals, other certified professional personnel, and all other school employees are appointed by the board of education upon the recommendation of the county superintendent of schools.[176]

In order to receive state funds, the county board of education raises money to operate the schools, primarily through taxation. The constitution requires the county governing authority to levy an annual school tax certified to it by the board of education (not exceeding 20 mills per dollar) upon all taxable property in the territory served by the school system, but there are a few school systems that are exempt from the 20 mill cap. The amount of the levy is recommended by the board of education, but the levy is actually made by the county governing authority and collected by the tax commissioner.[177]

The local school system must submit to the state Board of Education an annual budget that must conform to a uniform budgeting and accounting system established by the board, and the state board may either accept or reject the budget.[178]

The Georgia Constitution and general law provide that members of a county board of education are to be elected by the voters of the school district that the board member represents. The General Assembly may provide by local law for nonpartisan elections. A member is required to reside in the district that he or she represents. No person who is a member of the state Board of Education, who is employed by the state board or a county board of education, or who is employed by or who serves on the governing body of a private school is eligible to serve as a member of a county board of education. No person who has an immediate family member (spouse, child, sibling, or parent or spouse thereof) sitting on a local board of education or serving as a local school superintendant, principal, assistant principal, or member of the system's administrative staff is eligible to serve as a member of the local board of education. No person who is on the National Sex Offender Registry or the state sexual offender registry shall be eligible for election to or service on a local board of education.[179]

Members are elected for terms of four years unless their terms are otherwise provided by local act or constitutional amendment. Vacancies for the remainder of an unexpired term are filled by appointment of the remaining members of the board if the vacancy occurs less than 90 days prior to the general election. However, if the vacancy occurs more than 90 days before the general election, it must be filled by a special election to be held on the date of the next general election.[180]

Board members of any local system for which no local act exists receive a per diem as provided in state law per day for attendance at board meetings, plus reimbursement of actual expenses. General law also authorizes provision of group medical and dental insurance for members of the board of education.[181]

Superintendent of Schools

The county superintendent of schools, who is the communication link between the state superintendent of schools and subordinate school officers, is the executive officer of the board of education as well as the agent in procuring such school equipment and materials as might be ordered. The superintendent ensures that prescribed textbooks are used and keeps a record of all official acts. It is the duty of the county superintendent to enforce all regulations, rules, and instructions of the state superintendent of schools and the county board of education.[182]

Under the constitution and general law, the superintendent is appointed by the board of education. Superintendents are employed under written contracts for terms of not less than one year and not more than three years. Vacancies are filled by appointment by the board.[183]

Regional Commissions

Regional commissions, which are successors to regional development centers, are directly involved in local intergovernmental relations. They have been established in order to

- develop, promote, and assist in establishing coordinated and comprehensive planning in the state;

- assist local governments in participating in an orderly process for coordinated and comprehensive land-use, environmental, transportation, and historic preservation planning in the state;

- assist local governments in preparing and implementing comprehensive plans that will develop and promote the essential public interest of the state and its citizens;

- assist local governments in participating in an orderly process for coordinated and comprehensive planning;

- assist local governments in preparing and implementing comprehensive regional plans that will develop and promote the essential public interest of the state and its citizens;

- advance positive government relations among the state, regional, and local levels; and

- prepare and implement comprehensive regional plans that will develop and promote the essential public interests of the state and its citizens.[184]

All Georgia counties are members of a regional commission.[185] Counties in the Atlanta metropolitan area are members of the metropolitan area planning and development commission, the Atlanta Regional Commission, which has enhanced planning and review powers.[186]

There are 12 regional commissions in Georgia (see Figure 4-1), and each one is governed by a council consisting of the following:

- the chief elected official of each county in the region for a period of time concurrent with the elected official's term of office;

- one elected official from one municipality in each county for a time period concurrent with the elected official's term of office (in the case of a consolidated government in which there is not another municipality within the county, a second member of the consolidated government shall be appointed to the council);

- three residents of the region appointed by the Governor, one of whom shall be a member of a school board located in the region or a superintendant of schools located within the region and two nonpublic council members, each for terms of two years;

- one nonpublic council member appointed by the Lieutenant Governor for a term of two years;

- one nonpublic council member appointed by the Speaker of the House of Representatives for a term of two years; and

- any additional members determined to be necessary by the Board of Community Affairs for the purposes of complying with laws or otherwise for a term of one year.

Figure 4-1. *Regional Commissions, State of Georgia*

The council elects from its members a chairperson, vice chairperson, and secretary or treasurer who serve for terms of two years and until their successors are elected and qualified.[187] In addition, the council of each regional commission is responsible for such things as the appointment and removal of a full-time executive director of the regional commission, the exercise of its statutory powers, the establishment of such committees as it deems appropriate, the adoption of an annual budget to support the annual work program, and the determination of the policies and programs to be implemented and operated by the regional commission.[188]

Each county and municipality is required to pay annual dues for membership in its regional commission. If a county pays dues only on behalf of residents of the unincorporated areas of the county, the dues must come only from revenues obtained from the county's unincorporated areas.[189] Each regional commission must collect annual dues in the amount of 25 cents for every resident of its member counties. However, in order to be eligible for any minimum funding from state-appropriated funds, each regional commission must assess and collect annual dues in the aggregate, averaging a minimum amount of $1 for each resident of each county within the regional commission.[190]

Regional commissions are authorized to engage in the delivery of direct governmental services for local governments, provided a resolution requesting the same has been approved by the local government and the council of the regional commission. The provision of such services must be on a not-for-profit basis.[191]

Authorities and Intergovernmental Contracts

Counties are authorized by a number of general and local statutes to create or activate various public authorities for the provision of public services. In addition, under Article IX, Section IV, ¶1 of the Georgia Constitution, counties may enter into intergovernmental contracts with other governments for up to 50 years. The following list contains examples of such authorities and agreements:

- O.C.G.A. §8-3-100—Regional Housing Authority
- O.C.G.A. §12-8-50—Regional Solid Waste Authority
- O.C.G.A. §25-6-1—Mutual Aid Resource Pact (Fire)
- O.C.G.A. §3-7-72—Hospital Authorities
- O.C.G.A. §36-60-2—Wastewater Treatment Service
- O.C.G.A. §36-69-1—Mutual Aid Act (Law Enforcement)

- O.C.G.A. §36-73-1—Regional Facilities

- O.C.G.A. §42-4-90—Regional Jail Authority

- O.C.G.A. §49-3-1—District Departments of Family and Children Services

Regional cooperation portends benefits as local governments join together to provide services that they otherwise might not be able to offer or to achieve a lower cost of delivery than when operating independently.

NOTES

1. Portions of this chapter are drawn from the section on other county officials in *Handbook for Georgia County Commissioners*, 4th ed., ed. Betty J. Hudson and Paul T. Hardy (Athens: Carl Vinson Institute of Government, University of Georgia, 2002).
2. Ga. Laws 2005, 3785; 2004, 4552; 2003, 4492.
3. Ga. Laws 2008, 3605; 2004, 4571; 2004, 4027.
4. Ibid.
5. Variations in the powers and duties of the administrator, manager, or controller may occur from county to county due to differences in the language of the local acts authorizing the appointment. To determine more precisely the powers and duties of this officer in a particular county, reference must be made to the applicable local acts.
6. OFFICIAL CODE OF GEORGIA ANNOTATED (O.C.G.A.) §36-5-22; Ga. Laws 1999, 4345.
7. Ga. Laws 2004, 3679; 2004, 4571; 2004, 4552; 1997, 4136. In regard to tenure and appointment of county attorney, see Madden v. Bellew, 260 Ga. 530, 397 S.E.2d 687 (1990); Brennan v. Chatham County Commissioners, 209 Ga. App. 177, 433 S.E.2d 597 (1993).
8. The Office of Tax Commissioner was abolished and merged with the Board of Tax Assessors in Dougherty County by local constitutional amendment, Ga. Laws 1974, 1654.
9. Hill v. Clayton County Board of Commissioners, 283 Ga. App. 15, 640 S.E.2d 638 (2006); Brown v. Dorsey, 276 Ga. App. 851, 625 S.E.2d 16 (2005); Griffies v. Coweta County, 272 Ga. 506, 530 S.E.2d 718 (2000); Boswell v. Bramlett, 274 Ga. 50, 549 S.E.2d 100 (2001); Chaffin et al. v Calhoun et al., 262 Ga. 202, 415 S.E. 2d 906 (1992).
10. O.C.G.A. §36-1-21; Board of Commissioners of Spalding County v. Stewart, 668 S.E.2d 644 (2008); Wayne County v. Herrin, 210 Ga. App. 747, 437 S.E.2d 793 (1993); Gwinnett County v. Yates, 265 Ga. 504, 458 S.E.2d 791 (1995).
11. O.C.G.A. §36-81-11.
12. O.C.G.A. §§15-16-10(a), 42-4-1(a).
13. Elder v. Camp, 193 Ga. 320, 18 S.E.2d 622 (1942); Veit v. State, 182 Ga. App. 753, 357 S.E.2d 113 (1987).

14. O.C.G.A. §15-16-13.

15. O.C.G.A. §§15-16-9, 15-6-61(a)(1), 15-6-86; Brewster v. Houston County, 235 Ga. 68, 218 S.E.2d 748 (1975).

16. GA. CONST. art. IX, §1, ¶3(a); O.C.G.A. §§15-16-1(b), 15-6-50(a), 15-16-8, 15-6-54.

17. O.C.G.A. §§15-16-14, 15-16-10(b), 15-6-82, 42-4-4(c); Adamson v. Leather, 60 Ga. App. 382, 3 S.E.2d 871 (1939).

18. GA. CONST. art. IX, §1, ¶3(b); art. IX, §2, ¶1. A minimum annual salary based on the county population and an addition to the minimum salary are provided by general law, O.C.G.A. §§15-16-19, 15-16-20, 15-16-20.1, 15-16-20.2. Otherwise, the sheriff's salary is set by local law, and such salary may be greater than that set by general law. Lawson v. Lincoln County, 292 Ga. App. 527, 664 S.E.2d 900 (2008); Houlihan v. Saussy, 206 Ga. 1, 55 S.E.2d 557 (1949); Warren v. Walton, 231 Ga. 495, 202 S.E.2d 405 (1973).

19. Wolfe v. Huff, 232 Ga. 44, 205 S.E.2d 254 (1974). See Chaffin et al. v. Calhoun et al., 262 Ga. 202, 415 S.E.2d 906 (1992), in regard to the reduction of a sheriff's budget and the transfer of equipment from the sheriff to the county police. For the state law governing the creation of a county police force, see O.C.G.A. tit. 36, ch. 8.

20. Wolfe v. Huff, 232 Ga. 44, 205 S.E.2d 254 (1974). Compare Clayton v. Taylor, 223 Ga. 346, 155 S.E.2d 387 (1967).

21. Wolfe v. Huff, 233 Ga. 162, 210 S.E.2d 699 (1974); Chaffin et al. v. Calhoun et al., 262 Ga. 202, 415 S.E.2d 906 (1992). See Board of Commissioners of Randolph County v. Wilson, 260 Ga. 482, 396 S.E.2d 903 (1990), in which the court upheld the board's refusal to budget funds necessary for the sheriff to have five deputies and ruled that the board is only responsible for budgeting a lump sum that was not an abuse of discretion for the sheriff's office and not a specific amount that would provide the sheriff with sufficient funds to have five deputies.

22. See O.C.G.A. vol. 42, *Index to Local and Special Laws and General Laws of Local Application.*

23. O.C.G.A. §15-16-23; Freeman v Barnes, 282 Ga. App. 611, 640 S.E.2d 611 (2006); Wayne County v. Herrin, 210 Ga. App. 747, 437 S.E.2d 793 (1993); Employees Retirement System v. Lewis, 109 Ga. App. 476, 136 S.E.2d 518 (1964); Drost v. Robinson, 194 Ga. 703, 22 S.E.2d 475 (1942). Compare Board of Commissioners of Randolph County v. Wilson, 260 Ga. 482, 396 S.E.2d 903 (1990), which holds that a county commission may decrease "lump sum" budget appropriations for the sheriff's office in a manner that foreseeably leads to a dismissal of deputies. See Chaffin et al. v. Calhoun et al., 262 Ga. 202, 415 S.E.2d 906 (1992); Boswell v. Bramlett, 274 Ga. 50, 549 S.E.2d 100 (2001).

24. O.C.G.A. §48-5-311(d)(4).

25. O.C.G.A. §§15-6-59–15-6-74.

26. GA. CONST. art. IX, §1, ¶3(a); O.C.G.A. §§15-6-54, 15-6-56, 15-6-82; Wallace v. State, 34 Ga. App. 281, 129 S.E. 299 (1925); Adams v. Leather, 60 Ga. App. 382, 3 S.E.2d 871 (1939).

27. O.C.G.A. §§15-6-88, 15-6-88.2.

28. O.C.G.A. §§15-6-61(a), 15-6-86, 36-9-7. See also Floyd County v. Graham, 24 Ga. App. 294, 100 S.E. 728 (1919).

29. O.C.G.A. §§15-1-10, 15-6-86, 36-9-5.

30. O.C.G.A. §15-9-30(a).
31. O.C.G.A. §15-9-30(b).
32. O.C.G.A. §§15-9-30.1–15-9-30.7.
33. GA. CONST. art. 9, §1, ¶3(a).
34. O.C.G.A. §15-9-10.
35. O.C.G.A. §15-9-63.
36. O.C.G.A. §§15-9-80, 15-9-81, 36-9-7.
37. GA. CONST. art. IX, §1, ¶3(c); O.C.G.A. §§48-5-21, 48-5-103, 48-5-127.
38. GA. CONST. art. IX, §1, ¶3(a); O.C.G.A. §§48-5-210, 48-5-211.
39. O.C.G.A. §§48-5-180, 48-5-183.
40. O.C.G.A. §§48-5-141, 48-5-142.
41. O.C.G.A. §§48-5-138, 48-5-139, 48-5-154.
42. O.C.G.A. §48-5-140.
43. O.C.G.A. §48-5-145.
44. GA. CONST. art. VI, §1, ¶1; art. VI, §4, ¶1; O.C.G.A. §§15-6-8, 15-11-5, 15-11-28, 19-8-2.
45. GA. CONST. art. VI, §1, ¶6; art. VI, §7, ¶1; art. VI, §7, ¶3; art. VI, §7, ¶4; O.C.G.A. §§15-6-1, 15-6-4.1.
46. GA. CONST. art. VI, §7, ¶5; O.C.G.A. §§15-6-25–15-6-32.
47. GA. CONST. art. VI, §7, ¶5; O.C.G.A. §§15-6-29(c), 45-7-4(a)(20).
48. O.C.G.A. §15-6-24. See Fulton County v. State, 282 Ga. 570, 151 S.E.2d 679 (2007); Chatham County v. Gaundry, 120 Ga. 121, 47 S.E. 634 (1904).
49. O.C.G.A. §15-6-17.
50. GA. CONST. art. VI, §8, ¶1(d).
51. O.C.G.A. §§15-18-6, 15-18-7.
52. GA. CONST. art. VI, §8, ¶1 (a).
53. GA. CONST. art. VI, §8, ¶1(c); O.C.G.A. §§15-18-10–15-18-12, 15-18-14, 15-18-17–15-18-20.
54. O.C.G.A. §15-18-23. See Wilson v. Southerland, 258 Ga. 479, 371 S.E.2d 382 (1988), which held that because the counties of a judicial circuit had consented to the employment of an assistant district attorney in previous years, they were not thereafter obligated to continue to compensate additional district attorneys. In support, see Cramer v. Spalding County, 261 Ga. 570, 409 S.E.3d 30 (1991).
55. O.C.G.A. §15-7-2.
56. O.C.G.A. §15-7-4(a).
57. O.C.G.A. §15-7-4(b).
58. O.C.G.A. §§15-7-20, 15-7-22, 15-7-23.
59. O.C.G.A. §§15-18-60–15-18-74.
60. Ibid.
61. GA. CONST. art. VI, §10, ¶1(6). The county court of Echols County shall be classified as a magistrate court. The county courts of Baldwin County and Putnam County shall be classified as state courts. O.C.G.A. §§15-10-1, 15-10-2, 36-1-20.
62. O.C.G.A. §15-10-20.
63. O.C.G.A. §15-10-24.

64. O.C.G.A. §§15-10-23, 15-10-23.1; Rowland v. Tattnall County, 260 Ga. 109, 390 S.E.2d 217 (1990).

65. O.C.G.A. §15-10-5.

66. GA. CONST. art. I, §1, ¶14.

67. O.C.G.A. §§17-12-23 (a), 17-12-34.

68. O.C.G.A. §17-12-12.1.

69. O.C.G.A. §17-12-20.

70. O.C.G.A. §17-12-23(d).

71. O.C.G.A. §§45-16-24, 45-16-27, 45-16-27.1.

72. O.C.G.A. §§45-16-25, 45-16-25.1, 45-16-32. See O.C.G.A. §45-16-22, which authorizes the county governing authority, after consulting with the coroner, to appoint one or more local medical examiners who shall be licensed physicians or pathologists.

73. O.C.G.A. §§45-16-6, 45-16-66.

74. O.C.G.A. §§45-16-1, 45-16-2.

75. O.C.G.A. §§15-6-82, 45-16-1(a).

76. O.C.G.A. §§45-16-11, 45-16-27(b).

77. O.C.G.A. §§45-16-9, 15-16-21.

78. O.C.G.A. §§45-16-7, 45-16-11.

79. Ga. Laws 1980, 3827; 1966, 3406; 1965, 2497.

80. O.C.G.A. §45-16-80.

81. Ibid.

82. O.C.G.A. tit. 36, ch. 7.

83. Ibid.

84. Ibid.

85. O.C.G.A. §§36-6-14, 36-6-15, 36-6-16, 36-6-22.

86. O.C.G.A. §36-6-1(b).

87. See, for example, Ga. Laws 1991, 3588, 4460; 1986, 5294; 1985, 4768.

88. O.C.G.A. §§15-6-54, 36-6-25, 36-6-12, 36-6-1; 1981 Op. Att'y Gen. No. 81-87. The General Assembly may fix compensation by local law. See O.C.G.A. vol. 42, *Index to Local and Special Laws and General Laws of Local Application.*

89. O.C.G.A. §38-3-27.

90. Ibid.; Homeland Security Presidential Directive (HSPD)-5 (2004).

91. O.C.G.A. §36-8-1. Authority for the county to provide police protection is also provided by GA. CONST. art. IX, §2, ¶3(a)(1); Thompson v. Hornsby, 235 Ga. 561, 221 S.E.2d 192 (1975).

92. O.C.G.A. §36-8-7.

93. O.C.G.A. §36-8-5; Wolfe v. Huff, 232 Ga. 44, 205 S.E.2d 254 (1974).

94. O.C.G.A. §§36-8-2, 36-8-4; Wolfe v. Huff, 232 Ga. 44, 205 S.E.2d 254 (1974).

95. O.C.G.A. §§15-12-71–15-12-80, 15-18-6(2). *In re* Grand Jury Gwinnett County, 284 Ga. 510, 668 S.E.2d 682 (2008); Daniel v. Yow, 226 Ga. 544, 176 S.E.2d 67 (1970).

96. O.C.G.A. §36-1-7.

97. O.C.G.A. §15-12-78.

98. O.C.G.A. §§42-4-7, 42-4-8.

99. O.C.G.A. §15-12-7.
100. O.C.G.A. §48-5-311(c).
101. O.C.G.A. §15-12-71(b)(2).
102. O.C.G.A. §§15-12-60–15-12-62. In regard to exemptions from jury duty, see O.C.G.A. §15-12-1.
103. O.C.G.A. §15-12-7.
104. O.C.G.A. §§48-5-299, 48-5-306(a); Smith v. Elbert County Board of Tax Assessors, 292 Ga. App. 417, 664 S.E.2d 786 (2008); Rogers v. DeKalb County Board of Tax Assessors, 269 Ga. 31, 495 S.E.2d 33 (1998).
105. O.C.G.A. §§48-5-290, 48-5-295(a).
106. O.C.G.A. §§48-5-291, 48-5-295(b)–(d), 48-5-296.
107. O.C.G.A. §48-5-294.
108. O.C.G.A. §48-5-298. For limitations on this right to contract, see Sears, Roebuck and Company v. Parsons, 260 Ga. 824, 401 S.E.2d 4 (1991), in which the contingent fee provision of the contract to seek out and appraise unreturned property was held to violate public property.
109. O.C.G.A. §48-5-330. See also Ga. Const. art. IX, §5, ¶4, which exempts from the constitutional debt limitation debt to pay in whole or in part the cost of property valuation and equalization programs for ad valorem tax purposes.
110. O.C.G.A. §48-5-295.1.
111. O.C.G.A. §48-5-311; DeKalb County Board of Tax Assessors v. Kendall, Inc., 164 Ga. App. 374, 295 S.E.2d 345 (1982); Interstate North Sporting Club v. Cobb County Board of Tax Assessors, 250 Ga. App, 221, 551 S.E.2d 91 (2001).
112. O.C.G.A. §48-5-311(e).
113. O.C.G.A. §48-5-311(a)(4).
114. O.C.G.A. §48-5-311.
115. O.C.G.A. §48-5-311(d)(4).
116. O.C.G.A. §48-5-311.
117. O.C.G.A. §48-5-263(b).
118. O.C.G.A. §48-5-264.
119. O.C.G.A. §48-5-292.
120. O.C.G.A. §48-5-264.1(a).
121. O.C.G.A. §§48-5-261, 48-5-262, 48-5-267.
122. O.C.G.A. §§48-5-263(a), (c), 48-5-268.
123. O.C.G.A. §48-5-262(d).
124. O.C.G.A. §§31-3-1, 31-3-4, 31-3-5, 31-3-5.1, 31-5-9, 31-12-1, 31-12-3, 31-14-10, 31-17-3, 31-19-1, 31-26-2, 31-28-6.
125. O.C.G.A. §31-3-2.
126. Ibid.
127. O.C.G.A. §§31-3-7, 31-3-14.
128. O.C.G.A. §§31-3-11, 31-3-12.
129. Ga. Const. art. IX, §4, ¶¶1–3; O.C.G.A. §§31-3-9, 31-3-14.
130. O.C.G.A. §31-3-10.
131. O.C.G.A. §31-3-15.
132. O.C.G.A. §§49-2-6, 49-3-6.

133. O.C.G.A. §49-3-1. With the approval of the state Department of Human Services, two or more counties may form a district department of family and children services.

134. O.C.G.A. §49-3-2.

135. O.C.G.A. §§49-3-3–49-3-5. See O.C.G.A. §49-3-3.1 for reporting requirements regarding the care and custody of children.

136. O.C.G.A. tit. 37, ch. 2.

137. See O.C.G.A. §§ 36-66, 36-67, 36-67A, 50-14.

138. Ibid.

139. O.C.G.A. §§20-5-41, 20-5-43, 20-5-45, 20-5-47.

140. O.C.G.A. §§20-5-42, 20-5-44.

141. O.C.G.A. §36-15-4.

142. O.C.G.A. §§36-15-1, 36-15-2.

143. O.C.G.A. §§36-15-5, 36-15-7, 36-15-9.

144. O.C.G.A. §§36-15-6, 36-15-7.

145. O.C.G.A. §§36-15-7, 36-15-8.

146. O.C.G.A. §§36-64-3, 36-64-4.

147. O.C.G.A. §36-64-5.

148. O.C.G.A. §§36-64-6–36-64-11, 36-64-15.

149. GA. CONST. art. IX, §6, ¶3; O.C.G.A. §§36-62-3, 36-62-4, 36-62-5.1, 36-62-7.

150. O.C.G.A. §36-62-6, 36-62-7. For the definition of project, see O.C.G.A. §36-62-2(6).

151. O.C.G.A. §§36-62-6(a)(13), 36-62-9, 36-62-10.

152. O.C.G.A. §36-62-3. This exemption, however, does not apply to sales and use tax on property purchased by the authority or for its use. It also does not apply to property leased for certain types of projects. See O.C.G.A. §36-62-2.

153. O.C.G.A. vol. 42, *Index to Local and Special Laws and General Laws of Local Application.*

154. O.C.G.A. §§36-62-4, 36-62-5, 36-62A-21.

155. O.C.G.A. §§31-7-72, 31-7-75 31-7-85; Richmond County Hospital Authority v. Richmond County, 255 Ga. 183, 336 S.E. 2d 562 (1985); Tift County Hospital Authority v. MRS of Tifton, Ga., Inc., 255 Ga. 164, 335 S.E.2d 546 (1985).

156. O.C.G.A. §§31-7-77, 31-7-78–31-7-83, 31-7-88.

157. O.C.G.A. §§31-7-90, 31-7-90.1, 31-7-91, 31-7-92, 31-7-93.

158. O.C.G.A. §§31-7-84, 31-7-72(e)(1). For exemption of certificates and other obligations of a hospital authority, see O.C.G.A. §31-7-79.

159. O.C.G.A. §§31-7-72, 31-7-74. The board should consider a licensed doctor or registered nurse to fill a vacancy if no member of either profession is represented on the board.

160. O.C.G.A. §§8-3-4, 8-3-5. The supreme court has ruled that this law does not violate the constitution. Telford v. City of Gainesville, 208 Ga. 56, 65 S.E.2d 246 (1951).

161. O.C.G.A. §§8-3-30, 8-3-32, 8-3-70, 8-3-71, 8-3-72.

162. O.C.G.A. §§8-3-3, 8-3-8, 8-3-11, 8-3-30.

163. O.C.G.A. §§8-3-50, 8-3-51.

164. O.C.G.A. §§8-3-11, 8-3-12, 8-3-155. Exemption of property of the housing authority from taxation is constitutional. Culbreth v. Southwest Georgia Regional Housing Authority, 199 Ga. 183, 33 S.E.2d 684 (1945).

165. O.C.G.A. §§8-3-13, 8-3-100, 8-3-102.

166. O.C.G.A. §8-3-106. Some local acts provide for additional commissioners in certain counties.

167. O.C.G.A. §§ 8-3-111–8-3-116.

168. O.C.G.A. §§6-3-20, 6-3-24, 6-3-25, 6-3-26.

169. O.C.G.A. vol. 42, *Index to Local and Special Laws and General Laws of Local Application*; Ga. Laws 1984, 4935; 2000, 4082.

170. O.C.G.A. §46-5-138.

171. O.C.G.A. §20-2-240. With respect to regional educational service agencies, see O.C.G.A. §§20-2-270–20-2-274.

172. Ga. Const. art. VIII, §5, ¶2; O.C.G.A. §§20-2-50–20-2-71; Banks County School District v. Blackwell, 191 Ga. App. 790, 383 S.E.2d 159 (1989); Payne v. Blackwell, 259 Ga. 483, 384 S.E.2d 393 (1989).

173. Ga. Const. art. VIII, §5, ¶2; O.C.G.A. §§20-2-150–20-2-156, 20-2-59; Bacon v. Brewer, 196 Ga. App. 130, 395 S.E.2d 383 (1990); Banks County School District v. Blackwell, 191 Ga. App. 790, 383 S.E.2d 159 (1989); Payne v. Blackwell, 259 Ga. 483, 384 S.E.2d 393 (1989).

174. O.C.G.A. §20-2-520; Bailey v. County Board of Education of Elbert County, 213 Ga. 308, 99 S.E.2d 124 (1957); Ingram v. Doss, 217 Ga. 645, 124 S.E.2d 87 (1962).

175. Ga. Const. art. IX, §5, ¶¶1, 4; O.C.G.A. §§20-2-390, 20-2-430.

176. O.C.G.A. §20-2-211(a).

177. Ga. Const. art. VIII, §6, ¶1. See Ga. Const. art. VIII, §6, ¶2 concerning raising the millage rate; O.C.G.A. §§20-2-160–20-2-168, 48-5-400–48-5-404; Board of Commissioners of Newton County v. Allgood, 234 Ga. 9, 214 S.E.2d 522 (1975).

178. O.C.G.A. §20-2-167(c).

179. Ga. Const. art. VIII, §5, ¶2; O.C.G.A. §§20-2-51, 21-2-139(a).

180. O.C.G.A. §§20-2-52, 20-2-54.1.

181. O.C.G.A. §20-2-55.

182. Ga. Const. art. VIII, §5, ¶3; O.C.G.A. §20-2-109.

183. Ga. Const. art. VIII, §5, ¶3; O.C.G.A. §20-2-101.

184. O.C.G.A. §50-8-30.

185. O.C.G.A. §50-8-32.

186. O.C.G.A. §§50-8-80–50-8-103.

187. O.C.G.A. §50-8-34(e).

188. O.C.G.A. §50-8-34(f).

189. O.C.G.A. §50-8-33(b)(1).

190. O.C.G.A. §50-8-33(b)(2).

191. O.C.G.A. §50-8-35(a)(11).

5

Michael O'Quinn, J. Devereux Weeks, and Donald Cronin

Liability of Public Officials and the County

The role of county government has expanded into many different areas and touches the lives of individuals and businesses in many different ways. Local governments are providing an increasing number of services to the public. Associated with this increased interaction between local officials and the community are liability issues. Like individuals and corporations, counties are legal entities that are subject to lawsuits. However, because a county can only act through its elected officials and employees, there is an individual or a group responsible for every controversial decision, accident, failure to act, or error in judgment. Thus, elected officials and county employees can be sued for events that arise out of the performance of their duties, and while not a common occurrence, they may be personally liable or be forced to pay a judgment out of their personal assets. This chapter explains some of the liability rules that are unique to counties.

Lawsuits against counties and county officials fall into three broad categories: (1) federal civil rights and employment claims, (2) state law tort claims, and (3) state law claims that ask a judge to change or overrule a decision made by a board of commissioners. The subject matter or event being litigated determines the type of lawsuit. In all cases, the plaintiff (i.e., the person who filed the suit) almost always claims damages for which he or she seeks compensation in the form of money. A jury, rather than a judge, most often determines the amount of money to which a plaintiff is entitled. In some types of cases, there may be caps or limits on the amount awarded, but usually it is any amount that a jury deems fair. The county, individual county officers or employees, or both the county and its officials and employees may be liable. However, there is a group of cases in which the county is immune to liability and only individual county officers can be liable.

If all of this seems confusing, do not be discouraged; it is confusing, even to lawyers and judges, particularly when one lawsuit attempts to combine two, or even all three, categories of claims into alternative theories of relief. The best advice is to accept the rules of liability and damages at face value. Do not try to find a rational basis for the distinctions or assume that there is any logical or coherent pattern or reason for the differences in the rules. These rules were established by different bodies: Congress, in conjunction with the federal courts, in the case of federal claims and the Georgia General Assembly in the case of state law claims. They have evolved over hundreds of years, starting with English common law. At the end of the Civil War, civil rights legislation was passed by Congress. More civil rights legislation was passed one hundred years later, during the 1960s, with significant revisions and additions during the 1990s. State legislation has a similarly complex history.[1] The rules of liability and damages have developed piecemeal, as a result of the political process, which is heavily influenced by changing events and is often the result of compromises struck between competing interest groups. Add to this mix the decades of judicial interpretations of these rules and it becomes apparent why there is no rhyme or reason to the complex set of liability rules faced by county government. This chapter describes the rules of liability for counties and their officials and employees, using the three categories of cases you are likely to encounter.

FEDERAL CIVIL RIGHTS AND EMPLOYMENT CLAIMS

Congress has enacted legislation authorizing suits for damages against counties and county officials when a person claims his or her rights, as guaranteed by the United States Constitution, have been violated. This statute is found at Title 42 of the United States Code (U.S.C.), Section 1983,[2] and these cases often are referred to as 1983 actions. Congress has also enacted statutes prohibiting unlawful discrimination in employment, and because counties are employers, they can be sued for these violations as well. A statute commonly referred to as Title VII[3] prohibits employment discrimination on the basis of race, sex, religion, or national origin. There are also federal statutes that prohibit age discrimination (protection for workers aged 40 and over)[4] and discrimination against the disabled.[5] The Family and Medical Leave Act[6] sets forth mandatory rules regarding time off from work, and the Fair Labor Standards Act[7] governs the payment of overtime compensation to employees. A violation of any of these statutes by a county can result in a lawsuit being filed in federal court.[8] One particular disadvantage of being sued in federal court (as opposed to state court) is that few, if any, of the jurors who are impaneled to hear the case are residents of the county being sued. Those who live outside the county may therefore find it easier to return a verdict against the county when they do not have to pay taxes in that county. Moreover, a successful plaintiff in a federal suit is almost always entitled to a separate award of attorney fees[9] (which can often run in the hundreds of thousands of dollars), in addition to damages, whereas plaintiffs filing state law claims generally are not allowed to recover attorney fees. Because a plaintiff who prevails in federal court is generally entitled to attorney fees, plaintiffs understandably attempt to seek redress under federal law whenever possible. The rules of who can be sued, and for what, are different for each type of federal claim.

Claims under 42 U.S.C. §1983

The Bill of Rights of the Constitution guarantees each citizen the right of free speech (First Amendment), the right to be free from unreasonable searches and seizures (Fourth Amendment), the right not to have one's property taken without just compensation (Fifth Amendment), the right to be free from cruel and unusual punishment (Eighth Amendment), and the right to due process and equal protection of the laws (Fourteenth Amendment). These rights have been interpreted by the courts to cover a broad range of activities that may be infringed upon by the actions of counties and their officials.[10] For example, a county employee who believes she has been turned down for a promotion because she spoke in her capacity as a citizen concerning a matter of concern to the general public can file suit against the commissioners under §1983 for a violation of her right to free speech under the First Amendment.[11] Alternatively, a §1983 claim for an unlawful seizure under the Fourth Amendment may be justified if a person is arrested for "disorderly conduct" upon being unable to produce identification at the request of a county sheriff's deputy.[12] Inmates at county jails routinely file suits under §1983, alleging that jail conditions (e.g., food, lack of exercise, poor medical attention, etc.) constitute cruel and unusual punishment under the Eighth Amendment.[13] The due process and equal protection clauses of the Fourteenth Amendment have been used to challenge myriad decisions by local governments as arbitrary and capricious (a violation of "substantive" due process),[14] imposed without notice and an opportunity to respond (a violation of "procedural" due process),[15] or discriminatory (a violation of equal protection).[16]

Regardless of the factual basis underlying a §1983 suit, the county itself and the county officials actually involved in the conduct in question can be sued, although the rules of liability are very different. A third group—supervisors and officials who were not directly involved but who are alleged to have failed to intervene to prevent a violation or who are sued simply because they are in the chain of command—are sometimes drawn into §1983 suits. In general terms, the rules of liability depend on the class of defendant.

The Person Who Actually Committed the Violation

The individual county official or employee who actually violated the plaintiff's constitutional rights can be sued and held personally liable under 42 U.S.C. §1983. There is no limit or cap on the amount of damages the jury can award, and the jury can even award punitive damages in order to punish the county official.[17] As noted, attorney fees are added to the verdict.[18] Accused county officials, however, can assert a defense known as qualified immunity. The test for qualified immunity is whether a reasonable official who possesses the same knowledge as the official who is on trial would have known that his or her conduct violated the "clearly established" rights of the plaintiff.[19] Many claims do not involve clearly established rights, and qualified immunity can therefore be a powerful defense. In fact, it usually leads to the dismissal of the individual defendants in First Amendment cases[20] and in some Fourth Amendment cases.[21] Additionally, there can be no liability under §1983 when the deprivation was the result of simple negligence on the part of a county official.[22] Instead, there must be proof of an intentional act or at least gross negligence or recklessness.[23]

The County

Under §1983, a county is not held liable simply because one of its employees caused an injury while acting within the scope and course of his or her employment (referred to as vicarious liability or *respondeat superior*). In other words, counties are not automatically liable simply because a county employee violated someone's rights.[24] Rather, the county itself can be held liable only if the violation was the result of an official policy or custom adopted or followed by the county.[25] Official county policy, in most cases, can only be established by a majority vote of the county commissioners. A "custom" can be proved without any official action by the board of commissioners, but it generally takes more than a single or isolated event to prove a custom.[26] A single incident, if not undertaken by someone who has final decision-making authority on behalf of the county, will not be enough to prove a custom or policy.[27] Argued correctly, this defense frequently will lead to the dismissal of the county from the lawsuit. If the defense is unsuccessful, qualified immunity is not available to the county itself.[28] In other words, the county cannot escape liability by arguing that the plaintiff's rights were not clearly established, as can the individual county official. However, counties (unlike individuals) cannot be held liable for punitive damages.[29] Attorney fees, however, are awarded against the county if the plaintiff wins the case.

Section 1983 liability is complicated regarding the law enforcement actions of sheriffs. Under Georgia law, sheriffs are "county officers,"[30] and courts historically have held counties liable for the actions of their sheriffs. Sheriffs do not answer to the board of commissioners, however, and the board is largely powerless to control the sheriff's law enforcement activities. Moreover, the sheriff generally enforces state law, not county ordinances, and in that sense the sheriff acts as an agent of the state, not the county. A 2002 federal decision[31] indicates that there may be a movement toward counties not being held responsible under §1983 for the sheriffs' acts.

Supervisors and "Chain-of-Command" Officials

Assuming that a county employee has violated a plaintiff's civil rights, the employee's supervisors, up to and perhaps including the county manager and the members of the board of commissioners, may be sued under §1983 for failing to train and supervise the guilty employee or for failing to have adopted adequate policies and procedures that might have prevented the injury. Just as a county cannot be held automatically liable for employing an individual who violates a citizen's civil rights, a supervisor cannot be held automatically liable merely because a subordinate violated a citizen's civil rights. Additionally, liability under §1983 will not be imposed if the plaintiff can show nothing more than negligence or poor planning on the part of supervisors.[32] In order for supervisors to be liable, there must be a "causal connection" between the supervisory deficiency and the deprivation, and the lack of supervision or training must be so severe and pervasive as to amount to "deliberate indifference."[33] In other words, there must be more than inadequate or incomplete training. For §1983 liability based upon negligent supervision, the plaintiff must prove that the negligence was so pervasive that a violation was inevitable. If the supervisor is found to be personally liable, punitive damages and attorney fees may be awarded, with no cap or limit on the amount of the award that can be imposed. To avoid liability, counties should adopt appropriate policies and procedures regarding the activities of their employees and establish appropriate training and supervisory practices.

Legislative Immunity

Legislative immunity is available to county commissioners who are sued in their individual capacities for civil rights violations, and it provides an absolute bar to both suit and liability. The defense applies to comments or actions taken during a commission meeting while debating the merits of a resolution or ordinance.[34] The act of passing resolutions and ordinances is a legislative function, and commissioners cannot be held liable for anything they might say during the heat of discussion on an issue during a meeting. However, if a commissioner uses defamatory or disparaging remarks while discussing an issue outside of a regular or called meeting (such as at a restaurant, the golf course, or the commissioner's place of business), then legislative immunity does not apply because the setting is not part of the legislative process. There is a statutory defense for defamatory comments made outside of a meeting,[35] but it is not as broad or strong as legislative immunity; the statutory defense can be defeated with proof of malice or evidence that the commissioner knew his or her statements were not entirely factually accurate.[36] Thus, commissioners are well advised to reserve comments or statements of a controversial nature for meetings of the board.

The defense also applies to the actual votes cast by commissioners in favor of or against resolutions and ordinances as long as the resolutions and ordinances involve "policy-making."[37] In other words, the vote has to relate to the public at large. If the vote only addresses a particular entity or individual, the commissioner will not be entitled to legislative immunity.[38] For example, when a commissioner votes to deny a specific person a building or zoning permit, the defense of legislative immunity does not apply because such votes are not considered to be legislative in nature.[39]

Federal Employment Law

Even if a county is an "at will" employer under Georgia law, counties must nevertheless comply with federal employment law. The major statutes include Title VII,[40] the Age Discrimination in Employment Act,[41] and the Fair Labor Standards Act.[42]

Title VII prohibits discrimination based on race, sex, religion, and national origin. It covers all aspects of the employer-employee relationship, including hiring, pay rates, promotion, discipline, and termination. Among the main prohibitions, an employer cannot discriminate on the basis of race or gender. Also prohibited is sexual harassment, including overt behavior such as pressuring an employee to have sex in exchange for a job benefit as well as more subtle forms of unwelcome, offensive behavior (i.e., offensive jokes, pictures, or office talk about sex) that constitutes a "hostile environment."[43] Counties should ensure that they have up-to-date policies against sexual harassment.[44]

Title VII claims that are perhaps less obvious but equally serious are retaliation and discrimination against nonminorities. It is a violation of Title VII to punish an employee because he or she either filed an unsuccessful charge of discrimination or testified on behalf of someone who filed a charge.[45] Many groundless Title VII claims are actually made stronger by employers who make the mistake of retaliating against the person who filed a frivolous allegation. Discrimination suits brought by nonminority individuals are becoming more frequent because of affirmative action or minority preferences adopted by some counties. Although well intentioned, any employment practice that takes race or gender into consideration is probably illegal and a violation of Title VII. Do not assume that helping minorities is legal; discrimination against a majority group can also be a violation of Title VII.[46]

Because Title VII suits may be filed only against the employer, not individuals such as department heads or county managers,[47] the county itself is the only properly named defendant. Since 1991, Title VII cases have been tried by a jury.[48] There is a cap on damages, depending on the number of people employed by the county.[49] Punitive damages are not allowed, but attorney fees may be recovered.[50]

The Age Discrimination in Employment Act protects workers over the age of 40.[51] Employment decisions should not be made on the basis of age. Older workers who have tenure tend to earn more, and their benefits package is usually higher than that of a newer, younger employee. When looking to reduce costs, it may be tempting to terminate older workers and to replace them with younger, "cheaper" employees, but this practice is a violation of the Age Discrimination in Employment Act. A county may lawfully impose a reduction in force in order to cut expenses, but the jobs that are cut must be consolidated or remain unfilled.[52] If the county instead intends to fill the same position with a younger employee who is willing to accept a lower salary, the older employee should be offered a generous severance package in exchange for a release that complies with the special procedural safeguards that protect older workers,[53] and the county must not retaliate if this offer is rejected. Age discrimination cases may be filed against the county.[54] The case will be decided by a jury.[55] Recoverable damages include lost wages and benefits.[56] Punitive damages are not recoverable,[57] but attorney fees are.[58]

The Fair Labor Standards Act[59] governs overtime pay requirements for county employees and prohibits gender discrimination in the compensation of county employees. There are very specific, different rules for police, fire, and emergency medical personnel. Each county should periodically check its compliance with the Fair Labor Standards Act because even unintentional violations may result in extremely large awards or back pay to large groups of employees that typically are not covered by insurance. Only the county and certain employees in their official capacities can be sued under the Fair Labor Standards Act,[60] and punitive damages are not allowed.[61] Attorney fees are typically awarded to a successful plaintiff.[62] Fair Labor Standards Act cases may be tried by a jury.[63] For more information on federal employment laws, see Chapter 7.

STATE LAW CLAIMS

A tort claim usually involves an accidental injury, although there are intentional torts such as assault and battery and slander. The typical case arises when someone is hurt because a county official performed an act in a negligent manner or failed to act in a reasonable manner. Automobile accidents involving county vehicles and injuries that occur on county property or because of street and road defects are the most common reasons why counties are sued in the state court system. If a county employee operating a county vehicle while on county business causes a collision, a tort claim based on negligent operation of the vehicle can be filed in superior court or, where available, in state court. For example, there are a number of wrecks and lawsuits each year involving the operation of emergency vehicles. Additionally, plaintiffs may cite negligent roadway design, maintenance, or signage as the cause of an accident involving a single vehicle or only private vehicles. In these cases, the county road superintendent or public works director is sued under the theory that the accident was caused by a defect on the county road on which the accident occurred.

In every tort case, the defenses of sovereign immunity and official immunity come into play.[64] Sovereign immunity is a defense that belongs to the county itself.[65] Official immunity is a defense that can be asserted by a county official or employee who is sued in his or her individual capacity.[66] Although both defenses are derived from the same provision of the Georgia Constitution, Article I, Section II, Paragraph IX, they are not identical. Sovereign immunity, when available to a county, is an absolute defense that bars any recovery. Whether or not sovereign immunity is available is a legal issue for the judge to decide; it is never a jury question.[67] Official immunity, however, is not an absolute defense; it is available only for discretionary duties performed in a nonmalicious manner.[68] If the duty did not require a discretionary judgment call but instead required the county official to act in a clear, direct, and readily apparent manner, it is called a ministerial duty, and there is no immunity from liability if a jury determines that the act or omission was performed in a negligent way.[69] Because official immunity is not as strong as sovereign immunity, it is not uncommon for the county itself to be dismissed from a lawsuit, whereas the county official or employee must remain a party until judgment.

Sovereign Immunity

A county is entitled to sovereign immunity in response to any tort claim except for claims involving the negligent operation of an insured county vehicle.[70] For example, in cases in which the injury was caused because county property was negligently maintained (e.g., broken playground equipment, road defects, a drowning in a county-owned swimming pool, etc.), the county itself is entitled to absolute sovereign immunity from suit because no insured county vehicle caused the injury. The discretionary versus ministerial distinction is irrelevant and inapplicable in determining a county's entitlement to sovereign immunity. Only one question must be answered: Did an insured county vehicle cause the injury? If not, then sovereign immunity applies. If so, then the county itself can be sued. There can be no recovery against the county in excess of the insurance policy limits,[71] and punitive damages are not allowed.[72]

Official Immunity

Regardless of the type of tort suit (e.g., automobile accident, road or park maintenance, public safety claims, etc.), every county official or employee, when sued in his or her individual capacity, can assert the defense of official immunity. The defense will succeed, however, only if the duty in question is ruled to be a discretionary function, and only if the act was performed without malice.[73] If the duty was ministerial (i.e., nondiscretionary), then official immunity does not apply, and it will be up to a jury to decide if the official or employee acted negligently. There is no limit on the amount of the verdict that can be returned against the county official or employee if the jury determines that there has been negligence. If insurance coverage is unavailable or exhausted, then the judgment can be enforced against the personal assets of the official or employee. Punitive damages are recoverable in cases involving intentional torts.

Two examples from actual cases help explain these immunity provisions. In *Lincoln County v. Edmond*,[74] the county and the county road superintendent were sued for negligence when a felled tree caused a serious accident prior to the arrival of the work crew. The fallen tree had been reported early in the morning, before the workday began, but the superintendent did not go directly to the site as soon as he learned the road was blocked. The county was dismissed based on sovereign immunity because the accident involved only privately owned vehicles, no insured county vehicles. The road superintendent asserted official immunity, claiming he was performing a discretionary function, but his claim to immunity was denied. The court ruled that once the road superintendent knew that the downed tree created a road hazard, he had a ministerial duty to remove it. It was up to a jury to decide if he acted negligently. He therefore faced unlimited exposure, and the case was settled.

In *Cameron v. Lang*,[75] a county sheriff's deputy was pursuing a fleeing felon at a high rate of speed. The felon crossed the centerline and struck a third party's car head on, killing the driver. The deceased driver's widow sued the deputy and the sheriff in his official capacity, which was the equivalent of suing the county government. The deputy was granted official immunity because his actions in pursuing the fleeing felon, in the heat of an emergency, were held to be discretionary. Because, in his official capacity, the sheriff represented the county, he claimed sovereign immunity. However, because the deputy's patrol car was insured by the county, sovereign immunity had been waived, and his immunity defense was rejected. If a jury were to determine that the deputy acted negligently in starting or continuing the chase, then even though the deputy is immune, the sheriff would be liable because sovereign immunity had been waived. The sheriff's liability is limited, however, by the amount of insurance covering the patrol car.

These cases reveal that there are two key questions to be answered in every tort case against a county and its officials and employees: (1) Was there an insured county vehicle involved in causing the injury? (2) Was the official or employee performing a discretionary or ministerial function? If no insured county vehicle was involved, then the county will be dismissed, and the county official or employee will have to stand trial individually. If the county official or employee negligently performed a ministerial function, then there is no limit to his or her personal liability.

During the 2002 legislative session, the Georgia General Assembly decided that counties should not be able to avoid responsibility for accidents involving their county vehicles simply by choosing not to insure those vehicles.[76] Since 2005, counties have been liable for the negligent operation of county vehicles, whether they are insured or not. The limits of liability are $500,000 per person and $700,000 per occurrence.[77] The county employee who negligently operates the vehicle will not be subject to suit or personal liability.[78] Although the legislation did not require counties to insure their vehicles,[79] there is no longer a financial incentive for being uninsured. This legislation applies only to motor vehicle claims; the law of sovereign and official immunity remains the same for cases not involving the operation of county vehicles.

STATE LAW CHALLENGES TO THE DECISIONS OF THE BOARD OF COMMISSIONERS

There are some situations in which an aggrieved party is more interested in overruling a board of commissioners' decision than in suing for damages. The most common examples are zoning and land use decisions and denials or revocations of licenses and permits. In these instances, a person who files suit asks a judge to overrule the commissioners' decision and requests a particular permit or license or that an order be issued giving the property owner the right to use the land as desired. These types of cases seek remedies known as an injunction,[80] a writ of mandamus,[81] or a declaratory judgment.[82] An injunction is a court order to stop a certain type of conduct. For example, a nightclub owner may seek an injunction asking the court to stop the board of commissioners from enforcing an adult entertainment ordinance. The request may also be for an order to change the status quo, such as an order to the commissioners to stop tabling a request to rezone a piece of property. A writ of mandamus is an order from the court requiring that certain actions or decisions be made. For example, an unsuccessful applicant for a beer and wine license may ask the court for a writ of mandamus ordering the commissioners to grant the license. A declaratory judgment action is a request that the court declare the rights and obligations of the parties when there is an actual and present controversy about an issue. A person who believes an ordinance is illegal or unconstitutional can seek a declaratory judgment to have the ordinance stricken.

In each of these cases, commissioners will frequently be sued in their individual capacities because the order that is being sought is designed to change or overrule the commissioners' conduct or decisions. Monetary compensation for damages allegedly caused by the decision may also be sought in a separate count or claim within the lawsuit, but these specific claims pertain to the correctness of the decision itself and are an effort to get the decision changed. Attorney fees are routinely sought and sometimes awarded if the court agrees with the person seeking the change.

There are a number of defenses that make these claims difficult to win. For example, an injunction will not be issued unless the plaintiff can show irreparable harm and that no other adequate remedy exists except for an injunction.[83] A writ of mandamus will not be issued except in cases in which the plaintiff has a clear, absolute, and nondiscretionary legal right to the relief being sought.[84] A declaratory judgment will not be entered if there is only a hypothetical or speculative dispute, as opposed to an actual controversy.[85] All of these defenses are the result of the judiciary's reluctance to second-guess legislative or executive decisions or to intervene in the day-to-day administration of government.

If the decision at issue is discretionary and involves the weighing or balancing of competing interests, and if there is a record (usually recorded in the minutes) that shows a careful and thoughtful decision was made based on rational factors, then the courts generally will not overturn a board of commissioners' actions. On the other hand, if the county's own ordinance is clear that if certain conditions are met, the rezoning, license, or permit must be issued, and if these conditions are met but the requested action was denied, then the courts will require a county to follow its own ordinance.[86] Similarly, even if the ordinance allows for discretion, if the record is devoid of any articulated reason for the decision or if improper or illegal factors were relied upon, then even discretionary decisions will be overturned. To avoid this type of litigation, therefore, county commissioners should know what their county ordinances say. Further, commissioners should be able to distinguish between ordinances that clearly require a specific decision from those that do allow for discretion and record in their minutes that all relevant factors were considered and no improper or illegal reasons were offered in support of the decision.

Citizens may use improper or illegal reasoning when voicing their opposition to a measure. During a public hearing session of a rezoning request, for example, citizens may state, "we don't need another auto parts store" or "we already have too many starter home subdivisions." The presiding officer needs to be able to tactfully note for the record that these are not appropriate reasons to deny a request. If the request is denied, then proper reasons, as expressed in the ordinance, need to be recited as the board's (not the public's) reasons for the decision.

RISK MANAGEMENT, INSURANCE, AND INDEMNIFICATION AGREEMENTS

Risk management is a deliberate, proactive process designed to identify areas of potential liability exposure, to reduce the risk of losses, and to provide for the funding of liability losses that do occur. Identification of potential risks is particularly important in the areas of county law enforcement, personnel practices, road construction and maintenance, and land use regulations. A proactive process means identifying a potential problem and taking steps to prevent it rather than simply reacting to problems after they surface. A county risk management program should

- designate an appropriate official to be responsible for overseeing all liability prevention activities;
- increase awareness of liability exposure on the part of county officials and employees through training and seminars;
- monitor legal developments in the area of liability;
- monitor and update administrative policies and procedures, which should be in writing, in compliance with current law, and enforced;
- review personnel polices and practices and institute procedures for responding promptly and equitably to employee problems;
- respond to and record citizen complaints;
- monitor local media to help assess public opinion;
- obtain adequate and comprehensive insurance coverage (whether through commercial insurance, participation in an intercounty insurance pool, or through a self-insured fund); and
- adopt a policy to protect county officials and employees from personal liability for job-related claims.

Risk management has become a recognized discipline taught at colleges and universities, and specialists in this field, working in conjunction with the county attorney and department heads, often make up a county's risk management team. Some counties are able to hire individuals with risk management training or education as part of their permanent staff. Other counties contract for these services privately. Local Government

Risk Management Services, which operates under the direction of the ACCG and GMA, provides free or low-cost risk management services to counties that are insured by the interlocal risk management agency operated by ACCG known as ACCG-IRMA.

By continually assessing the county's risks and being proactive in taking steps to avoid losses, a county not only will avoid liability issues but also will be in a much better position to evaluate its insurance needs and coverage.

When it comes to covering the financial risk of loss, counties have three options: (1) purchase comprehensive general liability insurance from a private carrier, (2) participate in ACCG-IRMA, an entity created by state law[87] and authorized to administer a program of self-insurance for counties who pool together, or (3) self-insure by setting aside funds for contingent liabilities, or reserves, for losses as they occur. Careful consideration should be given to specific coverage provisions: Is there coverage for punitive damages and attorney fees? What role will the county play in settlement negotiations? Do defense costs erode the coverage limits? Will threats of litigation be covered, or will coverage apply only when suit is actually filed? Is there any risk management or loss prevention service that comes with this coverage? What acts or claims are excluded from coverage, rendering the county uninsured? These are some of the factors that good risk management practices must address.

Even if insurance coverage of $1 million or more is procured, an adverse verdict that exceeds the amount covered by insurance may nevertheless be returned against a county official or employee. In other words, there could be a loss that exceeds the county's insurance limits, and the personal assets of the county official or employee may be jeopardized. Some counties have elected to pass indemnification ordinances or resolutions, which basically say that the county will pay an excess verdict in order to protect its employees from personal financial disaster. Obviously, certain terms need to be considered, such as how much the county will pay and what type of conduct by an official or employee should be excluded from protection. Although these agreements are not legally required, there are at least two good reasons to have them: (1) it gives county officials and employees an added level of security, knowing that they will not lose their home or life savings as the result of a lawsuit, which should enable the county to attract and retain better personnel; and (2) without such an agreement, a county official or employee will often demand that cases with large verdict potential (e.g., involving death or paralysis) but with questionable liability be settled in order to eliminate their personal exposure, resulting in the settlement of some cases that ought to be tried. As an alternative to an indemnification agreement, counties also have the option of buying either higher coverage limits ($3–$5 million is not unreasonable) or buying an excess or umbrella policy for the rare but catastrophic claim. These issues should be considered proactively by the county's risk management team before a multimillion-dollar loss occurs.

NOTES

1. OFFICIAL CODE OF GEORGIA ANNOTATED (O.C.G.A.) §36-92-1 et seq. See section on state law claims in this article.
2. The statute states, "Every person who, under color of any statute, ordinance, regulation, custom, or usage, of any State or Territory or the District of Columbia, subjects, or causes to be subjected, any citizen of the United States or other person within the jurisdiction thereof to the deprivation of any rights, privileges, or immunities secured by the Constitution and laws, shall be liable to the party injured in an action at law, suit in equity, or other proper proceeding for redress. . . ."
3. 42 UNITED STATES CODE ANNOTATED (U.S.C.A.) §2000e.
4. 42 U.S.C.A. §623.
5. 29 U.S.C.A. §12101 et seq.
6. 29 U.S.C.A. §2601 et seq.
7. 29 U.S.C.A. §201 et seq.
8. 28 U.S.C.A. §§1331, 1343. Because enforcement of a federal statute is involved, there is no requirement of diversity of citizenship.
9. 42 U.S.C.A. §1988.
10. The United States Supreme Court ruled that counties could be sued as persons under Section 1983 in Monell v. Department of Social Services of City of New York, 436 U.S. 658 (1978).
11. In 2006, the Supreme Court significantly curtailed First Amendment retaliation suits by ruling that a governmental employee who speaks in his employment capacity cannot successfully sue for retaliation under the First Amendment (Garcetti v. Ceballos, 547 U.S. 410 (2006)). In other words, if the employee's speech is linked to the employee's job duties, the employee cannot successfully maintain a First Amendment claim (547 U.S. at 421).
12. See generally Ortega v. Christian, 85 F.3d 1521, 1525 (11th Cir. 1996).
13. Fambro v. Fulton County, Ga., 713 F.Supp. 1426 (N.D. Ga. 1989).
14. McKinney v. Pate, 20 F.3d 1550 (11th Cir. 1994).
15. Cleveland Board of Education v. Loudermill, 470 U.S. 532 (1985).
16. Johnson v. City of Fort Lauderdale, 148 F.3d 1228 (11th Cir. 1998).
17. Smith v. Wade, 461 U.S. 30 (1983).
18. 42 U.S.C.A. §1988.
19. Lassiter v. Alabama A & M University, Bd. of Trustees, 28 F.3d 1146 (11th Cir. 1994). The U.S. Supreme Court has recently clarified the doctrine of qualified immunity. See Hope v. Pelzer, 536 U.S. 730 (2002).
20. Maggio v. Sipple, 211 F.3d 1346 (11th Cir. 2000).
21. Jones v. City of Dothan, 121 F.3d 1456, 1460 (11th Cir. 1997).
22. Daniels v. Williams, 474 U.S. 327 (1986).

23. County of Sacramento v. Lewis, 523 U.S. 833 (1998).
24. Monell v. Department of Social Services of City of New York, 436 U.S. 658 (1978).
25. Ibid. at 690.
26. City of Oklahoma City v. Tuttle, 471 U.S. 808 (1985).
27. Pembaur v. Cincinnati, 475 U.S. 469 (1986).
28. Moore v. Morgan, 922 F.2d 1553, 1556 (11th Cir. 1991).
29. City of Newport v. Fact Concerts, 453 U.S. 247 (1981).
30. GA. CONST. art. IX, §1, ¶3.
31. Manders v. Lee, 338 F.3d 1304 (11th Cir. 2003).
32. Greason v. Kemp, 891 F.2d 829 (11th Cir. 1990). Of course, if the supervisor personally participated in the event causing the injury, or if he or she was physically present and failed to intervene, then personal liability can be established on this basis alone. Dean v. Barber, 951 F.2d 1210 (11th Cir. 1992).
33. Brown v. Crawford, 906 F.2d 667 (11th Cir. 1990).
34. Bogan v. Scott-Harris, 523 U.S. 44 (1998).
35. O.C.G.A. §51-5-7(9).
36. O.C.G.A. §51-5-9.
37. Crymes v. DeKalb County, 923 F.2d 1482, 1485 (11th Cir. 1991).
38. Corn v. City of Lauderdale Lake, 997 F.2d 1369, 1393 (11th Cir. 1993).
39. Corn, 997 F.2d at 1393; Crymes, 923 F.2d at 1486.
40. 42 U.S.C.A. §2000e.
41. 29 U.S.C.A. §621 et seq.
42. 29 U.S.C.A. §201 et seq.
43. Faragher v. City of Boca Raton, 524 U.S. 775 (1998).
44. In order for a county to avail itself of the defense recognized by the U.S. Supreme Court in Burlington Indus., Inc. v. Ellerth 524 U.S. 742, 118 S. Ct. 2257, 141 L. Ed. 2d 633 (1998) and Faragher v. City of Boca Raton, 524 U.S. 775, 118 S.Ct. 2275, 141 L.Ed. 2d 662 (1998), these policies should require employees who witness or experience sexual harassment to report the harassment in writing to the human resources manager of some other high-ranking official who did not participate in the harassment at issue.
45. 42 U.S.C.A. §2000e-3(a).
46. "Discrimination is discrimination no matter what the race, color, religion, sex, or national origin of the victim." Bass v. Board of County Commissioners, 256 F.3d 1095, 1102-03 (11th Cir. 2001).
47. Smith v. Lomax, 45 F.3d 402 (11th Cir. 1995).
48. 42 U.S.C.A. §1981a(c).
49. 42 U.S.C.A. §1981a(b)(3)(A)–(D), as follows: (A) in the case of a respondent who has more than 14 and fewer than 101 employees in each of 20 or more calendar weeks in the current or preceding calendar year, $50,000; and (B) in the case of a respondent who has more than 100 and fewer than 201 employees in each of 20 or more calendar weeks in the current or preceding calendar year, $100,000; and (C) in the case of a respondent who has more than 200 and fewer than 501 employees in each of 20 or more calendar weeks in the current or preceding calendar year, $200,000; and (D) in the case of a respondent who has more than 500 employees in each of 20 or more calendar weeks in the current or preceding calendar year, $300,000.

50. 42 U.S.C.A. §§1981a(b)(1), 2000e-5(k).

51. 29 U.S.C.A. §631(a).

52. Jameson v. Arrow Co., 75 F.3d 1528 (11th Cir. 1996).

53. In order for a settlement with an older worker to effectively protect the county from suit under the Age Discrimination in Employment Act, the release agreement must satisfy specific procedural requirements imposed under the Older Workers Benefit Protection Act, 29 U.S.C.A. §626 (f)(1)(F)(i).

54. Smith v. Lomax, 45 F.3d 402 (11th Cir. 1995).

55. 29 U.S.C.A. §626(c)(2).

56. Goldstein v. Manhattan Industries, Inc., 758 F.2d 1435 (11th Cir.), *cert. denied*, 474 U.S. 1005, 106 S.Ct. 525, 88 L.Ed.2d 457 (1985).

57. Ibid.

58. McKennon v. Nashville Banner Pub. Co., 513 U.S. 352 (1995) (citing 29 U.S.C.A. §626(b)).

59. 29 U.S.C.A. §201 et seq.

60. Welch v. Laney, 57 F.3d 1004, 1011 (11th Cir. 1995).

61. Snapp v. Unlimited Concepts, Inc., 208 F.3d 928 (11th Cir. 2000).

62. 29 U.S.C.A. §216(b).

63. Lorillard v. Pons, 434 U.S. 575 (1978).

64. GA. CONST. art. I, §2, ¶4.

65. Norris v. Emanuel County, 254 Ga. App. 114 (2002).

66. Ibid.

67. Cameron v. Lang, 274 Ga. 122 (2001).

68. GA. CONST. art. I, §2, ¶4(d).

69. Ross v. Taylor County, 231 Ga. App. 473 (1998).

70. Woodard v. Laurens County, 265 Ga. 404 (1995).

71. Ibid.; O.C.G.A. §33-24-51(d).

72. Martin v. Hospital Authority of Clarke County, 264 Ga. 626, 626–27, 449 S.E.2d 827, 828 (1994).

73. Stone v. Taylor, 233 Ga. App. 886 (1998).

74. Lincoln County v. Edmond, 231 Ga. App. 871 (1998).

75. Cameron v. Lang, 274 Ga. 122 (2001).

76. O.C.G.A. §36-92-1 et seq.

77. Ibid.; O.C.G.A. §36-92-2.

78. Ibid.; O.C.G.A. §36-92-3(a), (b).

79. Ibid.; O.C.G.A. §36-92-4(a).

80. O.C.G.A. §9-5-1 et seq.

81. O.C.G.A. §9-6-20 et seq.

82. O.C.G.A. §9-4-1 et seq.

83. Thomas v. Mayor of Savannah, 209 Ga. 866 (1953).

84. Torbett v. Butts County, 271 Ga. 521 (1999).

85. Baker v. City of Marietta, 271 Ga. 210 (1999); Johnson v. Fulton County, 216 Ga. 498 (1960).

86. Cain v. Town of Sparks, 256 Ga. 310 (1986); Hernandez v. Board of Commissioners, 242 Ga. 76 (1978).

87. O.C.G.A. §36-85-1 et seq.

6

James F. Grubiak

Ethics, Conflicts of Interest, and Abuse of Office

According to Webster's dictionary, the word "ethics" is derived from the Greek word ethos, meaning custom, disposition, or character. It is defined as "the principles of morality . . . or right conduct"—not exactly a precise definition for guiding the conduct of public officials. The issue of ethics and conflicts of interest is not a new one. Organized societies have established rules of conduct or ethical standards to guide citizens and public officials since the beginning of recorded history. Ethics was a concern to the Greek philosophers, including Socrates, who has been called the Father of Ethics. In the United States, concern about unethical behavior of public officials has been evident since colonial times, when bribery, embezzlement of public funds, and nepotism were all identified as problems of the day. Creating conflict of interest laws, codes of ethics, financial disclosure acts, public meeting laws, freedom of information laws, and privacy acts are all actions that government has taken to raise and maintain ethical standards in public service.[1]

In Georgia, several statutory provisions and a substantial body of case law provide a basis for ethical behavior by public officials. Many pitfalls, including criminal sanctions for abuse of office, await the unwary public servant or the one who ignores the law in this area.

STANDARDS EXPRESSED IN THE GEORGIA CONSTITUTION

A public office is a trust created in the interest and for the benefit of the people.[2] All public officials, at whatever level of government and regardless of their private vocations, are trustees. Accordingly, they are subject to every limitation imposed by law upon trustees generally—including those limiting personal financial gain from the discharge of their duties.[3]

This concept is expressed in the Georgia Constitution and provides the foundation for the requirement that public officials be held to a very high standard. Article I, Section II, Paragraph I, of the constitution describes the origin and foundation of government in Georgia: "All Government, of right, originates with the people, is founded upon their will only, and is instituted solely for the good of the whole. Public officers are trustees and servants of the people and are at all times amenable to them."

In declaring them to be trustees, the constitution establishes the fiduciary relationship between public officials and the citizens of the state. A fiduciary relationship demands that trustees carry out their duties with the sole intent and purpose of benefiting the object of the trust—in this case, the citizens of Georgia. Consequently, a public officer's actions must be devoted to promoting the public good, not his or her personal good. The constitution further solidifies the relationship of public officials to the citizenry by expressly declaring that public officers are "servants" of the people. Since the existence of a servant implies a master, the public is necessarily the master, and the public servant is charged with the duty of tending to the interests of the citizens. While this constitutional provision does not refer specifically to county officials, the Georgia Supreme Court has confirmed that county commissioners are indeed trustees, and as a consequence their actions—like those of other public officials—are to be governed by fiduciary standards.[4] Stated another way, public officials have a duty to disclose material facts and owe an obligation of loyalty to their principals, the citizenry. Essentially, they are obliged to do the people's business for the people's benefit. Public officials are required to exercise their discretion and judgment free from the taint of self-interest, bias, or undisclosed conflicts of interest.[5]

CODES OF ETHICS

State Code

In 1968, the General Assembly enacted a Code of Ethics for Government Service.[6] According to the attorney general, it is a "comprehensive statutory statement as to desired ethics and avoidance of conflicts of interest of public officials and employees."[7] The code sets forth guidelines for carrying out public duties. The following excerpt declares that public officials, including county commissioners, should undertake the following:

1. Put loyalty to the highest moral principles and to country above loyalty to persons, party, or government department.

2. Uphold the Constitution, laws, and legal regulations of the United States and the State of Georgia and of all governments therein and never be a party to their evasion.

3. Give a full day's labor for a full day's pay and give to the performance of his duties his earnest effort and best thought.

4. Seek to find and employ more efficient and economical ways of getting tasks accomplished.

5. Never discriminate unfairly by the dispensing of special favors or privileges to anyone, whether for remuneration or not, and never accept, for himself or his family, favors or benefits under circumstances which might be construed by reasonable persons as influencing the performance of his governmental duties.

6. Make no private promises of any kind binding upon the duties of office, since a government employee has no private word which can be binding on public duty.

7. Engage in no business with the government, either directly or indirectly, which is inconsistent with the conscientious performance of his governmental duties.

8. Never use any information coming to him confidentially in the performance of governmental duties as a means for making private profit.

9. Expose corruption wherever discovered.

10. Uphold these principles, ever conscious that public office is a public trust.

While it may be comprehensive, the Code of Ethics has been criticized for not being mandatory and for lacking penalties as an enforcement mechanism. Compliance is essentially left up to the conscience of the public official.[8] As in other matters of conduct and behavior, those who abide by the provisions of the code would probably have done so even if it had never been enacted or adopted.[9] Nonetheless, despite being essentially advisory, the Georgia Supreme Court has invoked the Code of Ethics in ruling that a county employee had violated the code by using his position as building inspector and threatening to require expensive home repairs to pressure an elderly homeowner to sell her house to him at a below-market price. The court said that profiting from his knowledge of the condition of the homeowner's property amounted to a violation of the inspector's duty as a public officer as expressed in the Code of Ethics.[10]

Special Rules for Members of Boards, Commissions, and Authorities

In addition to the advisory code of ethics for all persons in government service, there is a second similar set of special rules that is mandatory for members of boards, commissions, and authorities that are created by general law. These mandatory rules do not apply to county commissioners, however. As with the code of ethics, these rules include a bar against members of a board, commission, or authority engaging in any business with the government that is inconsistent with the conscientious performance of their duties. The rules also require that the members expose corruption, never engage in conduct unbecoming to the office, never engage in conduct that would constitute a breach of trust, never accept gifts or gratuities in exchange for influence, and never take official action in which they have a direct or indirect monetary interest.[11] A member of a board, commission, or authority who violates the ethics provisions of the law may be removed by the governor following a hearing on the charges upon their being filed with the governor.[12]

Local Codes

Many counties have adopted local codes of ethics. These vary greatly in scope, procedure, and approach, although typically they are more stringent than the state code of ethics. Some of the variations between county codes of ethics pertain to penalties, enforcement proceedings, and creation of independent ethics review panels. The courts will enforce county ethics codes and have affirmed that local governments may adopt ethical standards that are higher than what the state requires. When ethical standards are established locally, local officials are bound by them.[13]

CONFLICTS OF INTEREST GENERALLY

Whereas ethics is generally viewed as a broad set of moral principles, conflicts of interest tend to be viewed in a more transactional manner. For example, a conflict of interest inquiry may focus on whether personal benefits flow to a public official as a consequence of a contract between a county and a vendor or a request for a rezoning by a developer. When a conflict has affected a particular transaction, the law considers the public to have been deprived of true value for the expenditure of public money as much as if it were stolen outright. In most instances, a potential conflict of interest may be obvious to a public official. In others, however, there may be a subtle line dividing a public official's legitimate personal interest and a conflict with his or her public duties. To complicate things, a public official can run afoul of these proscriptions by acting on matters for which there is a mere appearance of a conflict or the potential to profit from his or her official duties. Furthermore, the supreme court has made it clear that no public official should even be presented with the opportunity or be led into temptation to make a profit out of the public's business.[14] Clearly, a public official cannot profit from his or her public position. The broader question, however, is whether there is an opportunity for the public officer or employee to derive a profit from a transaction involving his or her office or employment. If there is such an opportunity—or even the appearance of one—then there is a conflict of interest.[15]

Litigation involving conflict of interest charges has been before the Georgia courts for many years. As early as 1850, the Georgia Supreme Court applied the "no personal profit" rule in order to prevent "temptation to infidelity" when it ruled that a sheriff could not purchase anything from one of his own sheriff's sales either for himself or on behalf of anyone else.[16] In 1925, the supreme court held that a board of commissioners could not issue a cemetery permit to one of its own members or to a company in which one of its members was financially involved. Since the board member had a potential for profit from issuance of the license, he consequently was faced with a conflict of interest between personal gain and his public responsibilities.[17] More recently, Georgia's attorney general addressed a similar situation in which a newly elected commissioner had, for many years prior to his election, supplied groceries to the county jail. He wanted to continue doing so after being elected and asked whether a competitive sealed bid process would negate any conflict of interest concern. The attorney general ruled that a conflict would still exist. Even if he were awarded the contract through competitive bidding, he would inevitably be called upon to examine matters such as timely delivery, quality of the goods, and other issues in regard to contract performance. As a member of the board of commissioners, he would be judging his own company's performance of the contract—an impermissible conflict.[18]

Other examples of conflicts of interest involving elected public officers and employees follow:

- County officer buys and places vending machines he or she owns in a county building.

- Commissioner is a concessionaire overseeing flight operations at an airport owned by the county.

- Commissioner is a major stockholder in a privately held corporation that has bid on a county contract. In contrast, stock ownership in a large corporation probably would not present a conflict of interest unless the public official would benefit from the transaction beyond what he or she would as a stockholder generally.[19]

- City councilman leases land he owns to the city for use as a county park—even though the lease provides substantial benefits to the city.[20]

- County official owns a building in which the county leases office space.[21]

- City votes to swap land with the state for a state road project. A councilmember's firm has a subcontract with the state to provide hauling services for the road project.[22]

- County rejects a landfill site where a county commissioner owns land adjoining the site in favor of an alternative where the commissioner would not be adversely affected by the landfill.[23]

- Chairman of a board of commissioners is named county road superintendent and is compensated for those duties as an employee of the county.[24]

- County commissioner serves as county coroner.[25]

- Building inspector has an interest in a general contracting firm subject to being inspected by the county.

- County commissioner's son, an attorney, represents property owner in a rezoning application before the board of commissioners.[26]

Zoning and Conflicts of Interest

In 1986, the General Assembly enacted legislation specifically addressing conflicts of interest relative to zoning decisions. The law requires county commissioners to disclose any property interest or financial interest they or their family members may have in any property that may be before the board for a rezoning decision. Further, applicants for rezoning who have made campaign contributions of $250 or more to one of the commissioners must disclose that fact. For the purposes of this statute, the term "family member" includes a spouse, mother, father, brother, sister, son, or daughter of an elected official. Disclosure is not enough, however, since the law further requires commissioners to disqualify themselves from voting on the matter and prohibits any other attempts to influence the decisions of other board members. Note also that counties may establish more stringent standards regarding conflicts in zoning than required by the state.[27] A commissioner who knowingly fails to comply with the requirements of the law would be guilty of a misdemeanor.[28]

Holding Conflicting Governmental Positions

An impermissible conflict of interest may arise out of the simultaneous holding of governmental positions. Such conflicts stem from the common law doctrine of incompatibility of offices or the express prohibition in state law against any person holding more than one county office at a time.[29] The underlying public policy concern is that an officeholder's performance should not be influenced by divided loyalties. A conflict exists when one office is subordinate to another or is subject to its supervision or when duties conflict leading the official to prefer one obligation over another.[30] If the official in one capacity supervises or reviews his or her functions or performance in another capacity, common law incompatibility exists even if there is no direct supervision or control of one position over the other. For example, a member of the county board of elections cannot serve as the clerk to the board,[31] a deputy sheriff cannot serve as a school board member or coroner,[32] and a county road superintendent cannot serve as county commissioner.[33] Nonetheless, while certain elected county officials may have to resign when qualifying for a different elected position (depending on the time left in their present term), other county officials and staff are not required to resign unless elected.[34]

ABUSE OF OFFICE

When a transaction—such as a contract or zoning decision—is tainted by a public official's ethical violation or a conflict of interest, the transaction in question is usually voided to protect the public from the wrong that would otherwise have been carried out.[35] The public official may suffer more severe consequences, however, in the form of criminal penalties. Several state statutes prohibit bribery, extortion, and other acts classified as abuse of office and provide severe penalties for the public official who ignores their intent.

Acts of Abuse of Office

Bribery

Bribery is committed by a public official when he or she directly or indirectly solicits, receives, or agrees to receive a "thing of value" while implying that doing so will influence his or her performance on some official action. Bribery is likewise committed when persons offer public officials any benefit to which they are not entitled with the purpose of influencing them in the performance of their duties. The law, however, does acknowledge that a public official may be reimbursed for certain expenses and may accept certain promotional, honorary, and other token gifts without committing bribery. According to the state bribery statute, accepting one or more of the following items does not in and of itself constitute bribery:

- Food or beverage consumed at a single meal or event
- Legitimate salary, benefits, fees, commissions, or expenses associated with a public official's nonpublic business
- An award, plaque, certificate, memento, or similar item given in recognition of the public official's civic, charitable, political, professional, or public service
- Food, beverages, and registration at group events to which all members of the governing authority are invited
- Actual and reasonable expenses for food, beverages, travel, lodging, and registration for a meeting that are provided to a public official so that he or she may participate or speak at the meeting
- A commercially reasonable loan made in the ordinary course of business
- Any gift with a value less than $100
- Promotional items generally distributed to the general public or to public officials
- A gift from a member of the public official's immediate family
- Food, beverage, or expenses afforded public officials, members of the immediate families, or others that are associated with normal and customary business or social functions or activities[36]

Any person convicted of bribery is subject to a fine of not more than $5,000 or imprisonment for not less than 1 nor more than 20 years, or both.[37] In sum, other than those benefits of public office that are expressly authorized and established by law, no public official is entitled to request or receive—from any source, directly or indirectly—anything of value in exchange for the performance of any of his or her duties of office. A bribe or payoff, for example, given to a public official under the guise of a campaign contribution is still a bribe. The mere fact that a contribution has been reported as a campaign contribution would not change its character as a bribe.[38]

Selling Influence

State law also defines two additional and more targeted forms of bribery related to selling influence as a felony: when a public officer or employee asks for or receives something of value in return for (1) procuring or attempting to procure passage or defeat of an ordinance, resolution, or other county legislation[39] or (2) attempting to influence official action of any other public officer or employee of the county. Upon conviction, the officer or employee is to be punished by imprisonment for not less than one nor more than five years, fined up to $100,000, or both.[40]

Extortion

Public officials are guilty of extortion when they demand or receive, under color of office, money, fees, or other things of value that they are not entitled to or which represent more value than is due them. A public officer found guilty of extortion must be removed from office.[41]

Political Coercion

It is unlawful for a public official to coerce or attempt to coerce, directly or indirectly, any other public official or employee to pay, lend, or contribute any sum of money or anything else of value to any person, organization, or party for political purposes. A person engaging in coercion is guilty of a misdemeanor.[42]

Violation of Oath of Office

Any public officer who willfully and intentionally violates the terms of his or her oath of office is to be punished by imprisonment for not less than one nor more than five years.[43]

Conspiracy to Defraud

A public official or other person commits the offense of conspiracy to defraud a political subdivision when he or she conspires or agrees with another to commit theft of any property that belongs to a local government or that is under the control of a public official in his or her official capacity. Conviction calls for imprisonment of not less than one nor more than five years.[44]

Sale of Property to the County

Any public official of a county who for him- or herself, or on behalf of any business, sells real or personal property to the county must, upon conviction, be punished by imprisonment for not less than one nor more than five years. However, civil and criminal liability may be avoided when (1) less than $800 in personal property sales per calendar quarter is involved, (2) sales of personal property are made by way of competitive sealed bid, or (3) for sales of real property, disclosure is made to the grand jury or probate judge at least 15 days before the contract becomes binding, revealing who the public official is, the nature of his or her interest, the purchase price, and the location of the property.[45] A parallel statute addresses the sale of personal property and likewise prohibits sales to a county by a "store" in which a county official has an interest unless the sale is sanctioned by the county governing authority or it is clear that the goods are being sold to the county at least as cheaply as they can be bought elsewhere. Removal from office is the penalty for violating this law.[46]

While these two statutes appear to provide county officials with some flexibility in doing business with their own county, the weight of case law and opinions of the attorney general indicate that neither provision indeed authorizes sales to the county by a public official even when the conditions are met. At best, it would seem to insulate a county official from criminal liability while still exposing an elected official to removal from office. [47] Notwithstanding the foregoing limitations on the sale of property by a public official, a county commissioner may sell real property to a county if the property is adjacent to a landfill owned and operated by the county, will be used in connection with the landfill, the price does not exceed the lowest of three appraisals of the property made by three appraisers appointed by the probate judge, and proper disclosure is made in accordance with O.C.G.A. §16-10-6(c)(3).[48]

The law prohibiting a public official from selling real or personal property to the county for him- or herself or on behalf of any business has been extended to include any employee or appointed officer of an employing local authority. An employing local authority is defined as a local authority or board created by a local act of the General Assembly, by local constitutional amendment, or by general law that requires activation by an ordinance or resolution of the local governing authority. Examples of such entities would include housing authorities and development authorities. Thus, any employee or officer of any such entity is prohibited from selling real or personal property to the county or the local authority that employs him or her, to any agency of the county, or the local board of education. The same exemptions that apply to county officials and employees apply to authority officials and employees.[49]

Offenses Involving Public Records and Documents

A public officer or any other person who steals, alters, forges, defaces, or falsifies any records or documents, including minutes or digital records, shall be guilty of a felony if convicted and be subject to imprisonment for 2 to 10 years. Under this statute, willfully removing public records from the premises of the public office is considered stealing the records.[50]

Malpractice, Partiality, Neglect of Duties, Conduct Unbecoming One's Office, and Demanding Additional Costs

In addition to the infractions previously described, state law also addresses malpractice, partiality, neglect of duties, conduct unbecoming one's office, and demanding more cost than that to which a public official is entitled. Any local elected official charged with the foregoing may be indicted by a grand jury. If a true bill is returned by the grand jury and the public official is found guilty in a criminal proceeding, the official will be subject to fine, imprisonment, or both, at the discretion of the court. In addition, the official will be removed from office.[51]

Illegally Letting Contract

A county official who receives, takes, or contracts to receive or take, either directly or indirectly, any part of the pay or profit arising out of a public works contract is guilty of a misdemeanor.[52]

Federal Law Concerning Criminal Acts of Public Officials

There are several means by which federal law enforcement agencies address criminal acts of public officials. They can be grouped into three categories: criminal action statutes, corrupt act statutes, and honest services statutes.[53]

Criminal Action Statutes

Criminal action statutes refer to general criminal laws that define and prohibit behavior as criminal. They are not designed specifically to address actions by public officials. Any citizen, including public officials and employees, may be charged with their violation. Examples would include embezzlement, drug dealing, tax evasion, and fraud.[54]

Corrupt Act Statutes

Extortion or bribery involving public officials may also be prosecuted under federal law. Two of the core corrupt act statutes employed to address state and local corruption are the Hobbs Act and Program Fraud statute.[55] The Hobbs Act defines extortion as "obtaining of property from another ... under color of official right."[56] It includes as a violation the misuse and potential misuse of a public official's power for personal profit. The bribe need not be initiated or demanded by the public official, and passive acceptance is sufficient for a Hobbs Act violation so long as the public official knows that he or she is being offered the payment in exchange for a requested exercise of official power.[57] For example, accepting cash in exchange for a promise to vote favorably on a rezoning matter would violate the Hobbs Act.[58] Punishment for violation of the Hobbs Act is a fine not exceeding $10,000 or imprisonment for not more than 20 years, or both. Couching a bribe in the form of campaign contributions and reporting the payment as a campaign contribution does not change the nature of the bribe.[59]

The federal Program Fraud statute addresses the actions of those who are responsible for federal funds. At a minimum, jurisdiction is triggered when an organization such as a county or an authority receives federal benefits in excess of $10,000 involving some kind of federal assistance during a 12-month period prior to or following the act in question. The statute prohibits the following: (1) embezzling, stealing, defrauding, or misappropriating property valued at $5,000 or more; (2) soliciting or accepting bribes relating to some matter involving $5,000 or more; and (3) giving, offering, or agreeing to give anything of value to influence or reward action in connection with some transaction valued at $5,000 or more.[60] For example, a chief deputy in a jail that housed federal prisoners in exchange for federal funds well in excess of $10,000 in value was indicted and convicted for accepting a bribe from a prisoner in exchange for special treatment from the deputy.[61]

Honest Services Statutes

Honest services statutes are available when there are no federal program funds involved, when there is no immediately identifiable quid pro quo, or when there is only one actor. Honest services statutes address themselves to fraud including lying, cheating, misrepresenting the truth, self-dealing, nondisclosure of material conflicts of interest, and breach of duty. Using this tool, federal prosecutors must prove the use of either the U.S. mail, an interstate wire communication facility such as a phone or the Internet, or an interstate common carrier such as FedEx or UPS to execute a scheme to defraud someone.[62]

Suspension and Removal of Elected Officials

If a local elected official is indicted by a grand jury, Georgia law provides a procedure whereby elected officials may be suspended from office by the governor upon recommendation of a special commission. The special commission is appointed by the governor and is composed of the attorney general and two other persons holding the same office as the indicted official. The duty of the special commission is to determine if the indictment relates to and adversely affects the administration of the office of the indicted official. If the official is suspended, a temporary replacement official is appointed by the governor unless the applicable enabling act or charter provides for some other means for filling temporary vacancies. If the indicted official is acquitted or a *nolle prosequi* is entered, the official is to be immediately reinstated to his or her position.[63] Upon initial conviction of a public official for any felony, whether or not the official was suspended under the procedure described above, such official is immediately and without further notice suspended from office and a replacement official is named to fill the vacancy created by the suspension according to the local or general law applicable to the position.[64]

LOCAL LOBBYING REGISTRATION AND REPORTING

Current law provides that persons who promote or oppose the passage of legislation by the General Assembly are engaged in the practice of lobbying and must register with the Georgia Transparency and Campaign Finance Commission (formerly the State Ethics Commission).[65] However, as a general rule, elected county officials who advocate for or against legislation and county employees who provide requested information to members of the legislature are not considered lobbyists subject to the registration and reporting requirements.[66]

While the focus of the lobbyist registration and reporting requirement is on lobbying at the state level, the law also requires persons lobbying county officials to register with the commission and file the necessary reports. Even though an individual who expresses personal views on his or her own behalf to the commissioners is not considered a lobbyist, the law defines local lobbyists as those persons who for compensation, promote or oppose the passage of any ordinance or resolution of the county or who spend more than $250 per year promoting or opposing county ordinances or resolutions. However, attorneys appearing before local officials in adversary proceedings on behalf of a client are not considered local lobbyists.[67] State law requires any person meeting the definition of lobbyist to register with the Georgia Transparency and Campaign Finance Commission and file the required disclosure reports with the commission and the county election superintendent by the fifth day of January, May, and September of each year.[68]

EVALUATING ETHICAL DILEMMAS

It may sometimes be difficult for public officials to recognize an ethical dilemma when it presents itself. Perhaps more disconcerting is having to determine what to do after recognizing a potential ethical problem when no clear-cut choice between "right" and "wrong" exists. To help resolve such a dilemma, a public official can apply the following tests:

- *Golden Rule Test.* Would you approve of other public officials doing the same thing?
- *Publicity Test.* How would it look on the front pages of tomorrow's newspaper?
- *Kid-at-Your-Shoulder Test.* Would you be comfortable if your son or daughter was sitting at your shoulder and observing your actions?[69]

In a more direct fashion, former Chief Justice Charles L. Weltner, Georgia Supreme Court, summed up the entire subject of ethics, conflicts of interest, and abuse of office in two lines:

> Public power—not for sale.
>
> Buy or sell it—go to jail.[70]

NOTES

1. Joseph F. Zimmerman, "Ethics in the Public Service," *State and Local Government Review* 14, no. 3 (September 1982): 98.
2. 63A *American Jurisprudence* 2d., Public Officers and Employees, §7.
3. Georgia Department of Human Resources v. Sistrunk et al., 249 Ga. 543, 291 S.E.2d 524 (1982).
4. Malcolm v. Webb, 211 Ga. 449, 459, 86 S.E.2d 489 (1955).
5. Charles D. Gabriel, "The Role of the FBI in State and Local Government Corruption," *City-County Attorneys Institute* (Athens: Institute of Continuing Legal Education, University of Georgia, 2001), 21.
6. Official Code of Georgia Annotated (O.C.G.A.) §45-10-1.

7. 1973 Op. Att'y Gen. No. 73-155.
8. 1976 Op. Att'y Gen., 353; Conflicts of Interest of Public Officers, Employees, and Agents.
9. Louise Kipling McVay and Robert Stubbs II, *Governmental Ethics and Conflicts of Interest in Georgia* (Charlottesville, VA: Michie, 1980), 50.
10. Pope v. Propst, 179 Ga. App. 211, 213, 345 S.E.2d 880 (1986).
11. O.C.G.A. §§45-10-3, 36-62A-1.
12. O.C.G.A. §45-10-4.
13. Dick v. Williams, 215 Ga. App. 629 (1994).
14. Montgomery v. City of Atlanta, 162 Ga. 534, 546, 134 S.E. 152 (1926).
15. 1976 Op. Att'y Gen., 353, 359.
16. Harrison v. McHenry, 9 Ga. 164, 167 (1850).
17. Turner v. City of Atlanta, 160 Ga. 216, 127 S.E. 652 (1925).
18. 1983 Op. Att'y Gen. U83-8.
19. Montgomery v. City of Atlanta, 162 Ga. 534, 546, 134 S.E. 152 (1926); 1982 Op. Att'y Gen. No. 82-82.
20. Mayor and Council of the City of Macon v. Huff, 60 Ga. 221 (1878).
21. 1976 Op. Att'y Gen. U76-55.
22. Department of Transportation v. Brooks et al., 254 Ga. 303, 328 S.E.2d 705 (1985); Dunaway v. City of Marietta, 251 Ga. 729 (1983).
23. Vickers v. Coffee County, 255 Ga. 659, 340 S.E.2d 585 (1986).
24. Bowen v. Griffith, 258 Ga. 162, 366 S.E.2d 293 (1988).
25. O.C.G.A. §45-2-2.
26. Dick v. Williams, 215 Ga. App. 629 (1994).
27. Ibid.
28. O.C.G.A. tit. 36, ch. 67A.
29. O.C.G.A. §45-2-2.
30. Dunn v. Froehlich, 382 A.2d. 686 (N.J. 1978); Gryzik v. State, 380 So.2d. 1102 (Fla.1980).
31. 2004 Op. Att'y Gen. U04-02.
32. Black v. Catoosa County School District, 213 Ga. App. 534 (1994).
33. Bowen v. Griffith, 258 Ga. 162 (1988).
34. 1968 Op. Att'y Gen. No. 68-219; GA. CONST. art. II, §2, ¶5.
35. O.C.G.A. §13-8-2; Dept. of Transportation v. Brooks, 254 Ga. 303 (1985).
36. O.C.G.A. §16-10-2.
37. Ibid.
38. The State v. Agan et al., 259 Ga. 541, 384 S.E.2d 863 (1989).
39. O.C.G.A. §16-10-4.
40. O.C.G.A. §§16-10-4, 16-10-5.
41. O.C.G.A. §45-11-5.
42. O.C.G.A. §45-11-10.
43. O.C.G.A. §16-10-1.
44. O.C.G.A. §16-10-21.
45. O.C.G.A. §16-10-6.

46. O.C.G.A. §36-1-14.
47. 1980 Op. Att'y Gen. No. U80-22; Richardson v. Phillips, 302 Ga. App. 305 (2010).
48. O.C.G.A. §45-10-60.
49. O.C.G.A. §16-10- 6.
50. O.C.G.A. §45-11-1.
51. O.C.G.A. §45-11-4.
52. O.C.G.A. §36-91-21(f).
53. Gabriel, 5.
54. Ibid., 6.
55. Ibid., 9.
56. 18 UNITED STATES CODE ANNOTATED (U.S.C.A.) §1951(b)(2).
57. Evans v. United States, 112 S.Ct. 1881 (1992).
58. Ibid.
59. Gabriel, 12–13.
60. Ibid., 14–15; 18 U.S.C.A. §666.
61. Ibid., 15–16; Salinas v. U.S., 522 U.S. 52, 56–57 (1997).
62. Ibid., 18–19; 18 U.S.C.A §§1341, 1343, 1346.
63. O.C.G.A. §45-5-6.
64. O.C.G.A. §§45-5-6, 45-5-6.1.
65. O.C.G.A. §21-5-70 et seq.
66. O.C.G.A. §21-5-71(i).
67. O.C.G.A. §§21-5-3(22)(F), (G); 21-5-71(i); 21-5-70(D), (E).
68. O.C.G.A. §21-5-73(c).
69. Michael Josephson, "Power, Politics and Ethics," in *Ethics: Easier Said Than Done* 1, no. 2–3 (1988): 52.
70. Charles L. Weltner, "Freeing Government from Corruption," *Georgia County Government* 41, no. 8 (January 1990): 17.

PART 2

Management of County Government

7

Stephen E. Condrey, Benton J. Mathis Jr., William H. Buechner,
Elizabeth Bulat Turner, Sabrina Riles, and Kelly J. L. Pridgen

Personnel Management

This chapter presents ways in which to establish and administer an effective human resource management system. It also discusses the significant issue of constitutional protections afforded to public employees and the large body of case law addressing due process and related rights accorded to public employees. Common legal issues that affect county employers and employees are reviewed such as discrimination laws, drug testing, monitoring of computers and telephones, overtime, compensatory time, and other special laws that apply to county employees.

HUMAN RESOURCE MANAGEMENT

Perhaps the most important, yet least attended to, function of county government is human resource management. Human resource costs can exceed 70 percent of a county's noncapital expenditures but often take a back seat to issues such as taxation, finance, and capital improvements. Human resource management covers a broad range of issues such as recruiting and selecting employees, establishing competitive salary rates for employees, properly training new and veteran employees, motivating employees to achieve desired objectives, and fairly and adequately evaluating employee performance.

This part of the chapter will familiarize elected officials with the basic issues involved in human resource management at the county government level. It also suggests appropriate sources of information for the official seeking further information or direct technical assistance. Subjects covered are employee selection, position classification, salary administration, employee benefits, employee training and development, performance appraisal, and personnel policies and procedures.

Employee Recruitment and Selection

In the past, many county governments recruited their employees by word of mouth. Today, the increasing complexity of the work in which counties are involved, coupled with legal requirements and federal guidelines resulting from legislation such as the Civil Rights Act of 1991 and the Americans with Disabilities Act, calls for increased attention to employee recruitment and selection practices.

Recruitment

A broad-based recruitment program that seeks to incorporate all segments of the community is in the best interest of all concerned. Job announcements should clearly state the duties of the position, minimum and desired qualifications, salary ranges, and special licenses or certificates necessary to adequately perform the major duties of the position. Recruitment activities should be both passive (advertisements on the county's official Web site and in local newspapers) and active (recruitment visits to schools and colleges), depending on the nature of the position to be filled. Position vacancies should be announced for at least 10 working days to allow those interested to learn of the vacancy and to have the opportunity to apply. A longer recruitment period is required for department head or county manager positions that are advertised nationally with organizations such as the International City/County Management Association (www.icma.org) or the American Society for Public Administration (www.publicservicecareers.org).[1] It is advisable to post these positions on the Georgia Local Government Access Marketplace site (www.glga.org). This Web site is sponsored by the Association County Commissioners of Georgia and the Georgia Municipal Association and is perhaps the best site available for local government recruitment in the state.

Selection

The selection of employees has come under increasing scrutiny and legal requirements. Counties should strive to create "selection devices" that help them choose the best-qualified applicants without adversely impacting minority and other protected groups. Selection devices include interviews, training and experience evaluations, written examinations, performance examinations, and assessment centers.

The role of county commissioners in employee selection is usually limited to the positions of appointed county administrators and department heads. Executive search firms are sometimes employed by counties to help them find well-qualified applicants for these high-level positions. Technical assistance is also available through the Carl Vinson Institute of Government.

Hiring in Compliance with the Open Meetings and Open Records Law

There are a few special requirements in the open meetings and open records laws that county commissioners must be aware of when hiring employees. First, if a quorum of the board of commissioners wants to interview applicants for a position, it may do so in executive session, so long as votes are taken in public.[2] Other boards have interviewed applicants in meetings that were properly advertised and open to the public. However, this approach may pose a problem for an applicant for executive head of the county or department who may not want his or her current employer to know that he or she is considering a different job.

Second, the open records law contains requirements that apply when a county is hiring certain employees like county managers, county administrators, or department heads. If the county releases the names of all applicants upon request, the special rules do not apply. However, if the county wants to protect applicants from possible retribution from their current employers, it must observe special rules. The open records law allows the county to keep records that would identify all of the applicants for the position of executive head of an agency (such as county manager, county administrator, or department head) confidential until up to three finalists have been selected. Fourteen days prior to the final decision, the names and application materials of the three finalists must be released, unless an applicant no longer seeks the position. However, the county may be required to provide information regarding the number of applicants and the race and gender of those applicants.[3]

So, when a board of commissioners is hiring an executive head of the county or a department, it has two options:

1. Conduct the entire hiring process in the open, making all of the records available to the public for all of the candidates. Using this method means that the board does not have to wait 14 days before hiring a candidate.

2. Mask the identity of all applicants in order to protect them from retribution from current employers. Once the board has identified up to three best-qualified applicants, it must inform these applicants that their names will be publicly released if they continue to seek the position. Any applicant may decline to have

his or her name publicly released. Using this method means that the board must wait 14 days to hire one of the remaining finalists.

Position Classification

Position classification involves placing similar positions together into groups, or classes. For example, comparable secretarial positions could be grouped under the classification of administrative secretary, or similar equipment operation positions could be grouped under the classification of heavy equipment operator. Positions with the same position classification are assigned the same pay grade and pay range. This practice helps to ensure that a county is providing equitable pay.

Position classification provides the framework for an effective system of human resource management and has an impact on recruitment, selection, and performance appraisal. Job descriptions, which form the basis of a classification plan, should be up to date and specific in their listing of the major duties and responsibilities of positions. If job descriptions are timely and specific, they can be used to create announcements advertising position vacancies and develop performance standards for use in appraising employee performance.

The county commissioner's role in position classification generally involves approving new classification plans or approving modifications to existing ones. For example, a commissioner might approve or disapprove a department's request to reclassify a position from "secretary" to "administrative secretary." In making reclassification decisions, commissioners must be sure that the reclassification request is based on a significant change in duties and not solely on a desire to increase the compensation of the employee.

Salary Administration

The county commission's most visible role in human resource management is salary administration. The commission is called upon to approve new classification plans and annually update the county's pay plan. An effective pay plan is both internally and externally equitable. Being internally equitable means that positions with similar levels of duties and responsibilities are grouped together in the same pay grade. A pay plan is externally equitable when its pay rates are competitive with those of its main competitors.

County commissions will find various publications useful as they administer salaries. The Georgia Department of Community Affairs publishes an annual salary survey of the most common county government positions (www.dca.ga.gov/dcawss/default.asp). The Georgia Department of Labor publishes an annual wage survey for many different types of occupations (www.dol.ga.state.us). The Bureau of Labor Statistics of the U.S. Department of Labor periodically publishes proprietary salary data for the more populous regions of the state (www.bls.gov). Additionally, the International City/County Management Association publishes regional salary data concerning county managers, administrators, and department heads (www.icma.org). When relying on any survey, one should exercise care in interpreting the data contained in published salary surveys. For example, job description titles may have been misinterpreted, resulting in incorrect information being reported. County commissioners should also be sure that they are comparing "apples to apples" and "oranges to oranges." In other words, are the duties and responsibilities of the county positions they are researching sufficiently similar to those reported in the survey? If not, no salary comparison should be made.

An effective pay plan generally has 21 to 29 salary grades. Each of these grades should have a salary range of approximately 50 percent from the minimum to the maximum rate. In order to make salary administration more manageable, steps can be inserted between the minimum and maximum rates. Progression through the steps can be linked to length of service and/or performance. For example, an employee performing at a competent level might be awarded a one-step increase, whereas an employee whose performance was considered outstanding might receive a two-step increase. In the past, many pay plans had steps with values of 4 percent to 5 percent. However, plans with increments of that size should be avoided because they usually require the county to spend a large percentage amount on step raises, resulting in less funds being available for general increases that are applied to the entire salary structure. Over a period of time, the practice of granting large step increases and making small overall adjustments may result in a pay plan that pays tenured employees well but is unable to attract new employees because of low entry rates.

After an equitable classification and pay plan has been implemented in a county, a commission's role in salary administration primarily concerns granting annual and merit increases. Annual (market or cost-of-living) increases should be applied to the entire salary scale and every employee's salary. The Consumer Price Index (CPI) or the Employment Cost Index (ECI), published by the U.S. Bureau of Labor Statistics, should be used as a guide in determining the amount of across-the-board increases. A good rule of thumb is to increase the wage scale by 75 percent of the CPI and then conduct a salary survey every four years or so in order to gauge the county's placement in the labor market. Additionally, 2 percent to 3 percent of the personnel budget should also be set aside for step or merit raises, and merit increases should be separate from cost-of-living raises.

Employee Training and Development

The systematic training and development of county employees can greatly benefit an organization. A number of county positions require certification and continuing education by law.[4] Other training and certification may be optional. Training support can take the form of providing tuition reimbursement for attending college courses; encouraging fire, police, water, and wastewater personnel to seek additional certifications; or sponsoring in-house training courses specifically designed to increase the management and supervisory skills of county employees. The result of an effective training and development program is a more skilled and motivated workforce that is able to provide better service to the county's citizens. The Carl Vinson Institute of Government provides extensive training resources for local governments (www.cviog.uga.edu/services/education/statelocal.php).

Performance Appraisal

There is no foolproof way to appraise employee performance. However, some methods are more legally acceptable and job related than others. For many years, employee performance appraisal consisted of a manager's annual assessment of subordinate employees based on characteristics such as dependability, personality, and appearance. However, trait-based performance appraisal devices are no longer acceptable: the courts have ruled that performance appraisals, such as employment tests, must be job related. In many cases, adhering to these standards may necessitate writing different performance standards for every job classification. The appraisal format itself can be kept simple, but it should require the supervisor and employee to define in writing what the acceptable level of performance is for each major duty that the employee performs. This exercise underscores the necessity for accurate, job-specific position descriptions.[5]

In a job-based performance appraisal system, the employee develops goals and objectives for an evaluation period (usually one year). These goals and objectives are then discussed and weighted in a performance conference involving the employee and supervisor. At the end of the appraisal period, the employee performs the initial self-evaluation, which is then discussed with the supervisor. The advantages to such a system are that it lends itself to employee development and provides an avenue by which to link overall organizational goals to individual and group performance.

Successful employee performance appraisal is a continual process, not just an activity that takes place once a year. Employees who receive constant feedback concerning their work are much more likely to make desired behavior changes than are those who receive periodic or infrequent information about their performance.

Performance appraisal is most successful when it is used primarily as a communication tool between supervisor and employee. However, it is being used increasingly to link employee performance and pay. While, on the surface, a pay-for-performance system seems desirable because of the nature of county jobs, such a system would be virtually impossible for a county government to implement. For example, although it is a fairly common practice in the private sector to base an insurance agent's pay on the number or value of policies he or she sells, basing a deputy sheriff's pay on the number of arrests he or she makes would be inappropriate.[6]

Personnel Policies and Procedures

An up-to-date set of personnel policies and procedures provides the ground rules for county employment. Personnel policies generally contain procedures for employee grievances and appeals, definitions of annual and military leave, and a statement of the county's philosophy regarding human resource administration. Due to the changing nature of personnel-related law, a county should have its personnel policies and procedures reviewed periodically by a labor attorney.

TERMINATION AND DISCIPLINE OF EMPLOYEES

The Terminable At-Will Doctrine and Property Interests

Commissioners who have worked in the private sector are often confused about the process for terminating or disciplining county employees. Because of special constitutional protections, it is not as simple to discipline and terminate a government employee as it is an employee in the private sector. One of the first issues to address when considering disciplinary action is whether an employee has a protected "property interest" in his or her job (i.e., a reasonable expectation of continued employment) or whether the employee is "at-will."[7] In Georgia, unless an employee is given a reasonable expectation of continued employment (i.e., that he or she will not be fired except for cause), then the employee is considered an at-will employee and may be fired for a good reason, a bad reason, or no reason at all as long as he or she is not fired based upon sex, race, national origin, religious belief, disability, or age over 40 years. Employees who have a reasonable expectation of continued employment have a property interest in their county job and may not be fired without receiving their due process rights (e.g., notice of the disciplinary action and a meaningful opportunity to respond at a pretermination hearing and/or post-termination hearing).

Employees Who May Be Terminated without Due Process

An employee does not have a property interest in his or her employment if

1. he or she serves "at the pleasure" of the county or

2. he or she may be terminated if such action is found by a superior to be in the "best interest of the county" and no other applicable laws, provisions, or contracts exist to create a property right.

When a county abolishes positions for budgetary or other reasons, an employee whose position is abolished does not have a property interest in his or her job.[8]

Civil Service Systems

Under Georgia law, a county employee generally has no protected property interest and thus no due process rights unless he or she is employed under a civil service system.[9] The General Assembly may place employees under a county civil service system creating such a property right by passing specific authorizing legislation pursuant to a constitutional amendment.[10]

County governments also have the power to create by ordinance or resolution a civil service system for county employees. Such a civil service system may be extended to any and all county departments that are under the jurisdiction of the board of commissioners. The employees of the county constitutional officers may be added to the civil service system only if

1. the elected county officer applies in writing to the commissioners asking to have the employees covered and

2. the commissioners formally provide by ordinance or resolution that the positions be subject to the civil service system.[11]

If these requirements for placing employees under a civil service system are not met, the employees remain at-will, with no protected property interest.[12] Once positions have been moved under the county's civil service or merit system, they cannot be removed from that system unless a vacancy is created and a county officer fills the vacancy with a new employee who is not subject to the merit system.[13]

Employees Who Are Hired for a Certain Period of Time

In addition to a county's creation of a civil service or merit system providing that employees may only be dismissed for cause, a county employee may have a property interest in his or her employment if the county hired an employee for a definite period of time (i.e., a one-year employment contract) and the employee is discharged before the end of that time.[14] If an employee is hired for an indefinite period of time or an initial trial period, however, there is no property interest in his or her employment.[15] Additionally, if the contract specifically provides for early termination or at-will status, then the employee may not have a property interest in his or her employment.

At-Will Employees with Grievance or Appeal Rights

It is clear that county governments that desire to keep some or all of their employees terminable at-will may do so. A public employer, for example, can establish grievance or appeal procedures for its employees without losing its status as an at-will employer.[16] In addition, a public employer may change its policy with respect to whether its employees are employed at-will so long as affected employees are given notice and an opportunity to be heard regarding such changes.[17]

In order for the at-will employment relationship to be maintained, however, the county must ensure that the grievance or appeal procedure in no way restricts its discretion to terminate or otherwise modify its employees' employment by doing the following:

- Placing a disclaimer in the grievance or appeal procedure clearly stating that the procedure is not intended to restrict or limit the county's discretion in any way and reaffirming that the employment relationship is at-will.

- Avoiding the use of language in the grievance or appeal procedure that mandates the outcome of the grievance or appeal if certain conditions are met (i.e., avoiding statements like, "The employee shall be reinstated if . . ." or "The employer must sustain the grievance if . . .").

- Avoiding language in the procedure that establishes the grounds or reason upon which the employment decision in question (e.g., termination, transfer) must be based.

- Shifting the burden of proof onto the employee.

Changing from Property Interest to At-Will Status

A property interest in continuing employment could be revoked or terminated if the county gives employees reasonable notice and an opportunity to respond and the county demonstrates that such a change is in the public interest and "not taken as a subterfuge merely to single out and discharge particular employees."[18]

Thus, a county employer may eliminate a property interest in continuing employment by

- notifying the affected employees of the proposed conversion to at-will status and the reason therefore;

- permitting the affected employees a reasonable period of time to express their position regarding the proposed conversion (e.g., by written objections or suggestions, meeting with the county manager or personnel director); and

- having the matter considered and decided by the county commission in an open meeting.

Resignations

Resignations are presumed voluntary and thus waive any property interest a county employee might have in employment. If the resignation is found to be involuntary or forced by the county, it is called a constructive discharge and is considered to be a violation of due process if a hearing was not held. An employee's resignation will be deemed involuntary and a deprivation of due process if the county forces the resignation by coercion or duress or if the county obtains the resignation by deceiving or misrepresenting a material fact to the employee.[19]

Elements of Procedural Due Process for Employees with a Property Interest in Their Job

If a county makes an employment decision affecting an employee's property interest, the employee is then entitled to procedural due process, which requires the county to provide the employee with both a pretermination and a post-termination hearing.

The Pretermination Hearing

A county employee with a property interest may not be terminated without a hearing prior to his or her separation from employment.[20] County employees who are terminated because of a reduction in force, however, generally are not entitled to a pretermination hearing, as long as post-termination procedures are available.[21]

A pretermination hearing "need not be elaborate"; it is only "an initial check against mistaken decisions—essentially, a determination of whether there are reasonable grounds to believe that the charges against the employee are true and support the proposed action."[22] When post-termination hearings are provided, the county is not required to provide full "trial-type" rights, such as the right to present or cross-examine witnesses, for a pretermination hearing.[23] The due process requirements for a pretermination hearing are simply (1) notice to the employee and (2) an opportunity for the employee to respond.[24]

An employee must only be given notice and an opportunity to respond to proposed disciplinary action. Any disciplinary action that may affect a property interest (such as a demotion or a transfer from one job position to another that results in less pay, less authority, or less chance for promotion) also may require that the employee be provided with notice and an opportunity to be heard prior to the actual disciplinary action.

The importance of a pretermination hearing cannot be overstated, although its procedural requirements are minimal. The safest course of action for public employers is to provide the employee with notice in writing and provide for a reasonable period within which the employee may respond to the proposed disciplinary action. This eliminates any possibility that the employee may claim that he or she was never given a pretermination hearing. As long as an employee is told why the proposed disciplinary action is being taken and is given the chance to respond to the charges before the action takes effect, pretermination due process requirements have been satisfied.

The Post-Termination Hearing

Where there is a property right to employment (i.e., the employee may be terminated only for cause), procedural due process requires not only a pretermination hearing but also a "post-termination" procedure. The post-termination hearing, as it is commonly called, is a far different procedure than the pretermination hearing. The post-termination hearing must include opportunity to present and cross-examine witnesses. In addition, the post-termination proceeding must be held before an impartial tribunal.

When an employee is entitled to procedural due process, the post-termination hearing is often the event most closely scrutinized by a court. It is critical that the employee be accorded every reasonable procedural right so that the post-termination hearing will be considered proper. In order to eliminate any doubt as to the events that transpired in the post-termination hearing, it is important that the proceedings be recorded by a competent court reporter or the proper minutes be taken. The procedures for the post-termination hearing should be given to the employee in writing at the time the adverse employment decision is made.

The following is a list of recommended procedures that should be followed when conducting post-termination hearings:

1. The employee should be given written notice of the charges against him or her, with sufficient detail to enable the employee to show any errors that may exist.[25]

2. The names of all witnesses who will be called by the county as well as an explanation of their expected testimony should be given to the employee.[26]

3. The hearing must be held within a reasonable time.[27]

4. The employee must be allowed to present evidence on his or her own behalf.[28]

5. The employee must be given an opportunity to be heard at the hearing.[29]

6. The employee must be allowed to cross-examine his or her accusers in the presence of the decision maker.[30]

7. The hearing must be held before a tribunal having apparent impartiality to the charges.[31]

8. The employee must be allowed the right to have a lawyer present to assist him or her.[32]

Name-Clearing Hearings and Liberty Interests

A county employee's right to a "name-clearing hearing" stems from the employee's constitutional "liberty interest," or the protection of an employee's good name and reputation. A county may not deprive a county employee of a protected liberty interest without due process of law.

Damage to an employee's reputation alone is generally not enough to be considered an unlawful deprivation of the employee's liberty interest.[33] However, if other employment opportunities are foreclosed because false information is created and distributed by the governmental employer, then the employee's liberty interest is implicated. A county employee's liberty interest exists regardless of whether the employee is terminable at-will or has a property interest in continued employment.

When a Name-Clearing Hearing Is Required

A violation of a county employee's liberty interests occurs when there has been (1) a false statement that (2) is of a stigmatizing nature, (3) attends to the county employee's discharge, and (4) was made public (5) by the county and (6) the employee has not had a meaningful opportunity to have a name-clearing hearing.[34] These elements are discussed in more detail below.

Procedural Requirements of the Name-Clearing Hearing

A name-clearing hearing is not intended to evaluate the correctness of the termination decision or to reconsider the termination; it is merely a limited procedure provided so that the employee may have an opportunity to clear his or her name or reputation. Because of this, it is not required that a hearing be held before the termination or even before the publication of any stigmatizing material.[35] Thus, the process due for a name-clearing hearing is not as strict as that for a hearing for deprivation of a property interest.[36]

For a name-clearing hearing, the county must give the terminated employee notice of the charges raised and then the opportunity to refute the allegations against him or her through either cross-examination of the accusing witnesses or introduction of independent evidence.[37] The hearing must provide the employee with "an opportunity to support his allegations by argument however brief, and, if need be, by proof, however informal."[38] The hearing must also be held before an impartial tribunal. This requirement has been interpreted rather narrowly. In one case, for example, the court held that the tribunal could be made up of members of the board of commissioners that originally fired her.[39] The hearing must also be given within a reasonable time after the employee's termination. Finally, the county must merely inform the employee of the right to such a hearing. The county does not need to initiate the hearing process unless requested to do so by the employee after being notified of his or her right to the hearing.

Other Aspects of Name-Clearing Hearings

County governments should be especially careful about any information that is put into written reports regarding the termination of employees. Comments about the ethics, honesty, character, or guilt of an employee should be kept to a minimum or avoided entirely. Moreover, any statements—even those concerning the employee's work performance—should be backed up with factual evidence so as to prove the truth of the statements. Truth is a valid defense.

The offer to the employee of a name-clearing hearing should be made in writing so that there is no dispute over whether the offer was made. In light of the fairly flexible procedural requirements held to be sufficient by the courts, there seems little downside for a county to offer a terminated employee the opportunity for a name-clearing hearing. With such minimal requirements, and with such large consequences for failure to meet them, the safest course of action is to offer a name-clearing hearing in each and every case of employee termination.

Personnel Decisions: The Open Meetings Act and the Open Records Act

Personnel files are generally open records, although some of the information contained in them may not be subject to disclosure (see Chapter 25 for more information). For instance, social security numbers, insurance and medical information, confidential evaluations, mother's maiden name, financial data, account numbers, month and day of birth, home address, and telephone number must be redacted from the files before allowing public inspection.[40] Records obtained during investigations related to the suspension, firing, or complaints against county employees do not have to be released until 10 days after the report has been presented to the board of commissioners or department head or until 10 days after the investigation is concluded.[41]

The board of commissioners may deliberate on the appointment, employment, compensation, hiring, disciplinary action, dismissal, or periodic evaluation of a county employee in a closed executive session. However, the board must be in open session when receiving evidence or hearing arguments to determine disciplinary action or the dismissal of a county employee. Any vote on such a personnel matter must be taken in public.[42]

Occasionally, litigation over the termination of an employee may result in a settlement agreement that requires purging certain information about the employee. In such a case, the personnel file must contain a notation that the file has been purged as a condition of a settlement agreement. Furthermore, if another governmental agency contacts the county about the former employee's work history in order to make a hiring decision, the county is required to disclose the fact that the personnel file was purged pursuant to a settlement agreement.[43]

COUNTY EMPLOYEES AND THE FIRST AMENDMENT

Claims for violation of freedom of speech and freedom of association by public employees have been the fastest-growing areas of §1983[44] employment law in recent years. As in the case of a liberty interest claim, it is important to recognize that all county employees have First Amendment rights—regardless of whether they are at-will employees or have a property interest in their jobs. In other words, First Amendment rights do not depend on whether the employee is terminable at-will.[45] A county may be sued for any discharge of an employee "on a basis that infringes his constitutionally-protected speech or associations."[46]

Freedom of Speech Cases

In order for a county employee to prevail on a First Amendment cause of action, the employee must show that

1. he or she engaged in speech on a matter of public concern,
2. his or her interest in the speech outweighs the county employer's countervailing interest in providing efficient and effective services to the public, and
3. speech was a substantial or motivating factor leading to discipline. If the employee is able to make that showing, the county must show that it would have made the same employment decision in the absence of the protected speech.[47]

In order to be protected, a county employee's speech must be related to matters of public concern. The First Amendment does not apply when a public employee speaks on matters that are of a personal interest as an employee.[48] The First Amendment protects speech that relates to political, social, or other matters of concern to the community.[49] In order to determine whether the speech touches a matter of public concern, the courts will look at the content, form, and context of the employee's speech.[50]

If a court determines that an employee's speech is constitutionally protected, the court will then apply what is referred to as the Pickering balance test.[51] The Pickering balance test raises the issue of whether certain types of public employees, because of the duties and requirements for their job, may be limited in speech that otherwise is constitutionally protected. Thus, courts must consider whether the employee's interest in speaking on matters of public concern outweighs the public employer's legitimate interest in promoting efficient public service.

In weighing the competing interests under the Pickering balance test, a court considers

1. whether the nature of the county's public responsibilities are such that a close working relationship is essential;
2. whether the speech at issue impedes the county's ability to perform its duties efficiently;
3. the manner, time, and place of the speech; and
4. the context within which the speech was made.

The more the employee's speech touches on matters of significant public concern, the greater the level of disruption to the government that must be shown.[52] Courts will consider whether the speech at issue "impairs discipline by superiors or harmony among coworkers, has a detrimental impact on close working relationships for which personal loyalty and confidence are necessary, or impedes performance of the speaker's duties or interferes with the regular operation of the [public employer's] enterprise."[53] The First Amendment "does not require a public employer to tolerate an embarrassing, vulgar, vituperative, ad hominem attack," even if such an attack touches on a matter of public concern.[54]

Courts have consistently recognized that quasi-military organizations such as police and fire departments have "special concerns" that tilt the Pickering balance test in their favor. "Order and morale are critical to successful police work: a police department is 'a paramilitary organization, with a need to secure discipline, mutual respect, trust and particular efficiency among the ranks due to its status as a quasi-military entity different from other public employers.'"[55] Courts have found a "need for discipline, esprit de corps, and uniformity" in police departments.[56]

An employee must show that the county took action in retaliation for the employee's use of his or her First Amendment rights. The employee must only show that the employee's speech was a "substantial" or "motivating" factor behind an employment decision. Even if an employee's speech was a substantial factor in the decision to terminate him or her, the county may still win if it can show that the employee would have been discharged in the absence of the speech.[57]

Political Patronage Cases

In general, a county employee may not be discharged because of his or her political affiliation. However, a county employee who holds a position involving policy making or confidentiality may be dismissed, hired, promoted, transferred, and recalled after layoffs for his or her political beliefs.[58] For instance, an assistant public defender fired because he was not affiliated with or sponsored by the Democratic Party violated the First Amendment since his duty was not to the public at large but rather to individual citizens whom he represented in controversies with the state.

The issue of whether an employee is in a confidential and policy-making position has been particularly troublesome in political patronage cases involving deputy sheriffs. The court found in one case that loyalty to a sheriff and the goals and policies he seeks to implement is an appropriate requirement for the effective performance of a deputy sheriff.[59] The court described deputies as the "alter ego" of the sheriff and reasoned that the "closeness and cooperation required between sheriffs and their deputies necessitates the sheriff's absolute authority over their appointment and/or retention." Therefore, it did not violate the First Amendment for a sheriff to decline to reinstate deputies who did not support the sheriff in an election campaign. In another case, a sheriff was found to have the right to promote and demote based on political patronage.[60] Specifically, deputy sheriffs who had supported the incumbent sheriff alleged that it was a violation of the First Amendment for them to be transferred from their probationary lieutenant positions back to their previous positions by a newly elected sheriff. The court found that personal loyalty to a sheriff is an appropriate requirement for effective performance of a deputy sheriff.

Because of the difficulty in determining an employee's policy-making or confidential status, public employers increasingly are confronted with difficult decisions. However, because courts have viewed these types of cases in a particularly fact-specific manner, there is little certainty in the result of any case. Accordingly, terminations based on clearly protected First Amendment implications or patronage factors must be closely examined based on the particular facts associated with the individuals involved. Counties must recognize that courts are giving increasing protection to freedom of speech claims and that terminations that are clearly based on what is arguably protected speech are difficult to sustain, even in situations in which the employee is a policymaker or party affiliation is a legitimate concern.

In addition, counties must be aware of the Hatch Act's prohibitions against active participation in political management or political campaigns. The Hatch Act[61] prohibits political activities among employees whose employment is made possible by use of federal funds or appropriations from the Federal Treasury. The act prohibits a "state or local officer or employee" from

- using official authority or influence for the purpose of interfering with or affecting the result of an election or a nomination for office;

- directly or indirectly coercing, attempting to coerce, commanding, or advising a state or local officer or employee to pay, lend, or contribute anything of value to a party, committee, organization, agency, or person for political purpose; or

- being a candidate for elective office in a partisan election.[62]

However, the act does permit a county officer or employee to be a candidate in nonpartisan elections.[63]

ANTIDISCRIMINATION STATUTES

Race, Sex, Religion, and National Origin: Title VII

Title VII of the Civil Rights Act[64] makes it illegal to make employment decisions like hiring, firing, compensation, and other terms, conditions, or privileges based upon an individual's race, color, religion, sex (including pregnancy), or national origin.[65]

Protection from Intentional Discrimination

Title VII prohibits employers from discriminating against individuals based upon their race, sex, religion, or national origin when hiring, firing, recruiting, testing, compensating, or transferring employees. Title VII also prohibits harassment in the workplace on the basis of race, sex, religion, or national origin. Counties cannot make employment decisions based upon stereotypes about the abilities, traits, or performance of individuals of a certain race, sex, religion, or ethnic group.

Protection from Unintentional Discrimination

Even when a county is not motivated by discriminatory intent, Title VII prohibits the county from having neutral policies that negatively impact a particular race, sex, religion, or ethnic group. For instance, some fire departments have been required to reexamine their physical fitness requirements to ensure that they do not unfairly exclude women.

Protection from Religious Discrimination

County employees are also protected from employment discrimination based on religion.[66] The statute defines "religion" as including all aspects of religious observance and practice as well as belief, unless an employer demonstrates that it is unable to reasonably accommodate an employee's religious observance or practice without undue hardship on the conduct of the employer's business.[67] Title VII requires that employers reasonably accommodate applicants' and employees' sincerely held religious practices, unless doing so would impose an undue hardship on the operation of the employer's business.

Protection for Those Who Oppose Employment Discrimination

A job applicant or current or former employee who internally or informally opposes a discriminatory employment action by the county is protected by Title VII so long as the employee clearly communicates to the county a belief that its activity constitutes a form of employment discrimination protected by Title VII and the manner of the employee's opposition is reasonable.[68] For instance, the county may not retaliate against an employee or job applicant who has "testified, assisted, or participated, in any manner in an investigation, proceeding, or hearing" brought under Title VII.[69] The protections of the participation clause arise out of the filing of a formal charge or complaint of discrimination with the Equal Employment Opportunity Commission or a court, and the protected activity is limited in scope to testimony, assistance, or participation during the course of an investigation, proceeding, or hearing under Title VII.[70]

Age Discrimination in Employment Act

The Age Discrimination in Employment Act protects people who are 40 years old or older from discrimination because of age.[71] The act also makes it illegal to retaliate against a person because the person complained about discrimination, filed a charge of discrimination, or participated in an employment discrimination investigation or lawsuit.

Equal Pay Act

The Equal Pay Act prohibits, with certain exceptions, differentials in pay based on sex in jobs that require equal skill, effort, and responsibility and that are performed under similar working conditions.[72] The Equal Pay Act was recently amended by the Lilly Ledbetter Fair Pay Act (Fair Pay Act) to expand the length of time an employee has to file a claim of discrimination. The Ledbetter Fair Pay Act amends Title VII, the Age Discrimination in Employment Act, the Americans with Disabilities Act, and the Rehabilitation Act to state that an act of discrimination occurs each time wages are paid to an employee following a discriminatory pay decision. As a result, an employee who normally would have been time-barred from asserting a claim of pay discrimination based on a decision made years or perhaps decades in the past can now make a claim as long as it is filed within 180 days of when the employee last received a pay check.

Thus, counties may need to review their record retention policies and consider preserving records of pay decisions for much longer than they have in the past so that they are able to defend themselves in pay discrimination cases that are filed later. These records would include decisions about not only direct pay increases but also promotions, job assignments, layoffs, and other matters that affect compensation. It would also be prudent for counties to document which managers and supervisors make pay decisions or decisions that might affect compensation. Otherwise, if a pay discrimination charge is filed, there may be no way of identifying who made the pay decision at issue.

Americans with Disabilities Act

The Americans with Disabilities Act[73] (ADA) prohibits discrimination by employers against qualified individuals with disabilities in virtually all aspects of employment, including the application process, hiring, advancement, termination, compensation, and training. The ADA contains extensive and sweeping provisions preventing discrimination against persons with disabilities. A disability is a physical or mental impairment that substantially limits one or more major life activities. The definition applies to individuals who have a record of such impairment or who are regarded as having an impairment. Examples of conduct specifically prohibited by the ADA include

1. segregating, limiting, or classifying on the basis of disability a qualified individual with a disability in a way that would adversely affect employment opportunities or status (for instance paying a disabled employee less than is paid a similarly situated nondisabled employee);

2. excluding or denying equal job benefits to a qualified individual because that person has an association or relationship with a disabled person; or

3. using tests or other selection criteria that tend to screen out individuals with disabilities, unless the test is job related and consistent with business necessity.

The ADA prohibits the county from asking an applicant about any disabilities. The only acceptable preemployment questions that the county may ask would pertain to the applicant's ability to perform all of the essential duties of the job.

A county may require a medical examination of an applicant after tendering an offer of employment and before the applicant begins work. The employer may condition the offer on the results of the examination if all entering employees in the same job category are subjected to such an examination.

The ADA requires a county to provide "reasonable accommodation" of an otherwise qualified person with a disability unless the county can show that it would constitute an undue hardship. A reasonable accommodation is any modification or adjustment to a job or the work environment that would allow a qualified employee or job applicant with a disability to perform the essential job functions. Examples of reasonable accommodations include restructuring a job and modifying work schedules or equipment.

The ADA requires the county to determine the essential functions of a job and look at possible modifications and adjustments to the job and/or the work environment that would allow a person with a disability to perform those functions. Counties should make sure that they have written and updated job descriptions that list the essential functions of every job.

Georgia Antidiscrimination Laws

In addition to the federal antidiscrimination statutes, Georgia has enacted the Georgia Fair Employment Practices Act, which specifically prohibits discrimination in public employment on the basis of race, color, religion, national origin, sex, disability, or age.[74] An individual seeking relief under this statute must file a written, sworn complaint with the administrator of the Commission on Equal Employment within 180 days of the alleged adverse employment action. If the administrator finds that there is cause to believe that a violation occurred and efforts at conciliation are not successful, the governor may appoint a special master to conduct a hearing on the complaint.

RIGHT TO PRIVACY: WORKPLACE MONITORING AND SEARCHES

Workplace Searches

Counties are subject to different standards than are private companies with respect to workplace searches. For county employees, searches are governed by the Fourth Amendment. In order to establish a violation of rights under the Fourth Amendment, an employee first must prove that he or she had a legitimate expectation of privacy with regard to the place searched or the item seized. Counties should make it clear from the outset to all employees that all county property, including offices, computers, desks, and file cabinets, are subject to search and that there is no expectation of privacy for employees.

All workplace searches by a county must be reasonable.[75] Typically, a search of an employee's office by a supervisor will be justified if there are reasonable grounds for suspecting that the search will produce evidence of work-related misconduct by the employee or that the search is necessary for some noninvestigatory work-related purpose.

Monitoring of Telephones and E-mail

Rapidly expanding communications technology creates new ways in which an employer can monitor its employees' activities. These methods include telephone surveillance, audio surveillance, and monitoring of employees' electronic and voice mail messages. Many of the same considerations applicable to workplace searches apply to searches of employees' e-mail and phones.

The Electronic Communications Privacy Act of 1986 (ECPA)[76] prohibits an employer from secretly monitoring certain communications of its employees. Both employees and nonemployees who claim to have been monitored as a result of an investigation of an employee may bring a civil action under the ECPA.[77] Furthermore, the ECPA is applicable to the electronic and oral communications of public employees.[78]

There are certain exceptions to the ECPA. A county would not be liable if the "interception" of a communication was by the human ear alone (i.e., overhearing a conversation). Additionally, a county may monitor covered communications when one of the parties has given his or her prior consent.[79]

Finally, pursuant to the "business extension exception" or "telephone extension exception," a county may utilize telephone extension equipment provided by a communications carrier in the normal course of business.[80] For example, a county could monitor employee communications with a special switchboard and other intercom equipment that is a regular component of its business phone system. The federal courts have found that an employer's recording of phone conversations of two of its employees while both were on duty fell within the "telephone extension exception."[81] The court first noted that in order to qualify for the exception, the employer is not required to use a standard telephone extension but rather is permitted to use any telephone instrument, equipment, or facility. The court then held that the employer's interception was in the ordinary course of business and was not the interception of a personal call, reasoning that the conversation occurred during "office hours, between co-employees . . . and concerned scurrilous remarks about supervisory employees in their capacity as supervisors. Certainly the potential contamination of the working environment is a matter in which the employer has a legal interest."

The Stored Communications Act[82] prohibits searching certain stored electronic data without authorization. Although this is a developing area of law, county employers generally have the right to access communications of their employees made on county-owned and -operated devices within the scope of their employment under the ECPA provided that the search is made for a legitimate work-related reason and is not excessive in scope.[83] Counties should consider enacting a clear policy regarding the right to access and monitor the communications of employees on county-owned devices, including obtaining employee consent to search as a general practice, and to follow that policy consistently, emphasizing that employees do not have a reasonable expectation of privacy in communications made on county-provided devices.

Drug Testing

Drug testing of county employees is considered a search. Counties may not require employees to take a drug test without reasonable suspicion that the employee is under the influence of drugs or alcohol unless the county has a compelling special interest. There are two basic types of drug testing:

1. Drug testing when there is a reasonable suspicion of an employee being under the influence of drugs.

2. Random drug testing of employees in "high-risk jobs" (e.g., bus drivers, mechanics who work on buses or Rideshare vehicles), which is considered a compelling interest.

Counties wishing to subject their employees to drug tests must comply with the Fourth Amendment guaranteeing the right against unreasonable searches and seizures.[84] Public employees working in high-risk jobs are subject to random drug testing pursuant to Georgia law.[85]

WHISTLEBLOWER STATUTES

Georgia's Whistleblower Protection Act

Georgia's Whistleblower Protection Act includes protection of county employees.[86] The act prohibits counties from retaliating against employees who "blow the whistle" on waste, fraud, or abuse in government. Specifically, counties are restricted on personnel actions that may be taken against a county employee who refuses to participate in activity that he or she reasonably believes to be in violation of the law. Accordingly, county employees may sue counties for retaliation, thus greatly increasing local governments' exposure to litigation. Commissioners need to be mindful of whether policies and directives comport with the law and can be defended in the face of challenges from alleged whistleblowers.

Federal False Claims Act

The Federal False Claims Act[87] prescribes liability for a person who knowingly presents a false or fraudulent claim for payment or approval to the United States government. The statute includes a whistleblower provision,[88] which prohibits the discharge, demotion, suspension, threat, harassment, or other manner of discrimination in the terms and conditions of employment of an employee because of lawful acts done by the employee in furtherance of an action for a false or fraudulent claim for payment or approval to the United States government.

EMPLOYEE COMPENSATION, LEAVE, AND BENEFITS

Minimum Wage, Overtime, and Compensatory ("Comp") Time: Fair Labor Standards Act

The Fair Labor Standards Act (FLSA) sets standards for minimum wage, maximum hours, overtime pay, record keeping, and child labor for all covered employment, unless a specific exemption applies. The FLSA requires employers to

- maintain payroll records,

- pay men and women equal pay for equal work,

- pay at least the statutory minimum wage,

- pay an overtime premium that must be at least one and one-half times the average hourly straight time pay for the employee or provide compensatory time off at the rate of at least one and one-half times the number of hours worked over 40 in a workweek, and

- maintain established child labor standards.

As employers, counties must be aware that although the FLSA is the primary federal wage law, there are additional federal laws governing the payment of wages to their employees, such as the Equal Pay Act. Like the FLSA, these statutes are designed to ensure the payment of minimum wages, overtime pay, and equal pay for equal work.

For most employees, the FLSA requires the payment of overtime wages in an amount of one and a half times the employee's regular rate for all hours actually worked in excess of 40 in any workweek. If a holiday occurs during the workweek or the employee takes any other time off during the week, these hours do not count toward the 40 hours actually worked. For every hour over 40 actually worked in a workweek, the employee must be paid one and a half times his or her regular rate (i.e., overtime) or receive one and a half hours in paid leave (i.e., compensatory time, or "comp" time).

The FLSA contains a number of exemptions and exceptions. Some county employees, such as elected officials and their staff, policy-making employees, legal advisors, legislative employees, volunteers, and others, simply are not covered by the FLSA. Other types of employees are covered but are exempt. Courts have noted that the FLSA is remedial in nature and should be read liberally in favor of workers.[89] Generally speaking, employees are not considered to be "volunteers" for any work they perform for their employer.

"White-Collar" Exemptions

There are several exemptions to the overtime requirements of the FLSA, the most common of which are for "white-collar" employees. The categories under the FLSA are executive employees, administrative employees, professional employees, and computer-related personnel.

The minimum salary level for all white-collar employees is $455 per week ($23,660 per year). For computer employees, the salary requirement applies, but the regulations also stipulate an hourly rate qualification of at least $27.63 per hour.

For executive employees, the regulations require that

1. the employee's primary duties consist of the management of the enterprise for which he or she is employed or of a customarily recognized department or subdivision,

2. the employee customarily and regularly directs the work of two or more other employees, and

3. the employee has the authority to hire or fire other employees or is able to provide suggestions and recommendations that are given particular weight as to the hiring, firing, advancement, promotion, or any other change of status of other employees.

The duties test for administrative employees requires that

1. the employee's primary duty is performing office or nonmanual work directly related to management policies or general business operations of the employer or the employer's customers and

2. the employee's primary duty includes the exercise of discretion and independent judgment with respect to matters of significance.

The standard test for the professional exemption requires learned professionals to perform work requiring advanced knowledge in a field of science or learning customarily acquired by a prolonged course of specialized intellectual instruction and study. "Work requiring advanced knowledge" is defined as work that is predominantly intellectual in character and that requires consistent exercise of discretion and independent judgment. Creative professional employees are required to perform work requiring invention, imagination, originality, or talent in a recognized field of artistic or creative endeavor. The exemption does not apply to work that can be produced by a person with general manual or intellectual ability and training.

Under the regulations, an exempt computer employee must

1. have a primary duty of performing work requiring theoretical and practical application of highly specialized knowledge in computer systems analysis, programming, and software engineering;

2. be employed as a computer systems analyst, computer programmer, software engineer, or other similarly skilled worker in the computer software field; and

3. consistently exercise discretion and judgment.

Other court decisions indicate that improperly disciplining an employee who is exempt from the FLSA and is paid on a salary basis by suspension without pay may result in that employee and all other similarly situated employees becoming subject to the FLSA and thus entitled to overtime pay or compensatory time off for all hours worked in excess of a 40-hour workweek.[90]

Public Safety Employees

Recognizing that public safety employees often work 12- to 24-hour shifts, the FLSA provides an exception to the general requirement that overtime or compensatory time be computed on a weekly basis and a premium paid for hours in excess of a 40-hour workweek for firefighters and law enforcement personnel.[91] The exemption allows a public employer to have firefighters work up to 212 hours and law enforcement personnel work up to 171 hours in a 28-day work period without incurring overtime pay liability. The work period set out in this provision may be any period of at least 7 consecutive days but not more than 28 consecutive days.

Not included in the exemption are the "civilian" employees of a fire department and law enforcement department dispatchers, radio operators, repair workers, janitors, clerks, or stenographers.[92] Rescue and ambulance service personnel will qualify for the exemption as employees engaged in fire protection activities if they "form an integral part of the public agency's fire protection activities" or as employees engaged in law enforcement activities if they "form an integral part of the public agency's law enforcement activities."[93] Ambulance and rescue service employees may also qualify if they are employees of a public agency other than a fire department or law enforcement agency and their services are substantially related to firefighting or law enforcement activities.[94]

Under the FLSA, courts have held counties liable for overtime pay to law enforcement personnel for off-duty time, including nights, week-ends, and holidays, spent caring for a canine used for law enforcement purposes, either in-house or for outside task force participation with other law enforcement agencies such as those dealing with drug and bomb detection. If an officer is responsible for feeding, training, grooming, and cleaning up after the dog and does this caretaking in addition to his or her regular 40-hour workweek or extended work period, the extra time spent caring for the dog constitutes overtime, and the officer must be compensated.[95]

The FLSA also provides a complete overtime pay exemption for individuals employed by a public agency with fewer than five employees in fire protection or law enforcement activities.[96] In determining whether a public agency qualifies for the exemption, fire protection and law enforcement activities are considered separately. Thus, if a county employs fewer than five employees in fire protection activities but five or more in law enforcement activities, it may claim the exemption for fire protection but not law enforcement.[97]

Compensatory Time Off in Lieu of Overtime Pay

Although public safety employees may accumulate up to 480 hours of compensatory time, other nonexempt employees may accrue only 240 hours. After that maximum is reached, a covered employee must be paid overtime if he or she works more than 40 hours in a workweek. However, the county may require employees to use compensatory time. Employees must be permitted to use their compensatory time within a "reasonable period" of a request unless it would be "unduly disruptive." Employees protected by the FLSA must be paid any unused compensatory time upon separation from employment with the county.[98]

Family and Medical Leave Act

The Family and Medical Leave Act of 1993 (FMLA) requires all public employers to provide unpaid leave to employees in certain situations. Up to 12 weeks of unpaid leave must be provided to an eligible employee during any 12-month period for the birth or adoption of a child or placement of a foster child; in order to care for a spouse, child, or parent with a serious health condition; or due to the employee's own serious health condition. Additionally, eligible employees are allowed 12 weeks of unpaid leave for a qualifying exigency arising out of the fact that the employee's spouse, son, daughter, or parent is a covered military member on active duty (or has been notified of an impending call or order to active duty) in support of a contingency operation.[99] Finally, eligible employees may now take unpaid leave or substitute appropriate paid leave if the employee has earned or accrued it for up to 26 workweeks in a single 12-month period in order to care for a covered service member with a serious injury or illness.[100]

An employee who takes leave under the FMLA must be returned to the same position that he or she held prior to taking such leave or to an equivalent position, and the county must maintain group health insurance coverage for the employee during the period of leave, as if the employee had worked. The leave guaranteed by FMLA is unpaid, although a county may require that an employee use any available vacation, personal, family, or sick leave before the unpaid portion of the 12-week leave period begins. In addition, leave under the FMLA may be taken intermittently or on a reduced schedule when medically necessary.[101]

Military Leave of Absence: Uniformed Services Employment and Reemployment Rights Act and Georgia Law

The Uniformed Services Employment and Reemployment Rights Act (USERRA) is the primary federal law applicable to reemployment rights of employees who are called to active duty.[102] In general, USERRA and Georgia law require employers to reinstate employees who have been absent from work because of active military service, and they prohibit discrimination and/or retaliation against such individuals. All county officers and employees who serve in the Army, Navy, Marine Corps, Air Force, Coast Guard, or National Guard or in any of their reserves are entitled to a military leave of absence while they are engaged in the performance of military duty as well as while traveling to and from such duty.[103] In addition to active duty, both active and inactive duty for training are included.

The employee or the appropriate officer of the military branch in which the employee is serving must provide written or oral notice of the military service unless military necessity prevents the giving of notice or the giving of notice is otherwise impossible or unreasonable.[104] The county may neither refuse to allow an eligible employee or official to take the military leave of absence nor require the employee or official to find a suitable replacement to cover his or her county duties during such absence.

Military leave of absence may not be considered an interruption of employment, regardless of any local legislation or county ordinance to the contrary.[105] Additionally, the county may not discriminate against an employee because of his or her military obligations.[106] This provision includes consideration of military obligations when making decisions to hire, promote, terminate, or provide benefits to individuals.

In general, Georgia law requires counties to pay their officers and employees who are on military leave of absence their regular county salary or other compensation for the first 18 days of ordered military service per federal fiscal year (i.e., October 1 through September 30).[107] In certain circumstances, members of the National Guard may be entitled to their county salary for 30 days per federal fiscal year.[108] Additionally, USERRA provides that these officers and employees may use any vacation leave that accrued prior to their military service. However, the county may not require an employee to use vacation leave.[109]

If the county provides health insurance coverage for employees, it must continue to provide the coverage for the first 30 days of ordered military service. However, after the initial 30 days, if the employee chooses, he or she may elect to continue coverage for up to 18 months or the period of military service, whichever is shorter.[110] The employee may be required to pay up to 102 percent of the cost to provide health insurance coverage after the initial 30 days.

There are specific rules for determining pension and retirement benefits for county employees and officers on military leave of absence.[111] County commissioners are encouraged to consult with their retirement plan administrator as well as the county attorney in order to determine pension or retirement benefits during the military leave of absence.

The time limits for reporting to the county after completion of military leave of absence depend upon the length of military service.[112] When these officers and employees return to the country, they may not lose any benefits or privileges because of their absence. They are entitled to seniority and all seniority rights and benefits that they would have reasonably obtained if they had not taken a military leave of absence.[113] Additionally, they are entitled to non-seniority-based rights and benefits on the same basis as any other employee on any type of leave of absence provided by the county.[114]

The length of service also determines the position into which an employee is reinstated.[115] In general, returning employees and officers are entitled to be reinstated in the job that they would have had if they had remained continuously employed (including any likely promotions) so long as the person is qualified for the job or can become qualified after reasonable efforts are made by the county.

For questions about the USERRA, commissioners should contact the National Committee for Employer Support of the Guard and Reserve or the Veterans' Employment and Training Service division of the U.S. Department of Labor.

Leave for Voting

Each employee must be given up to two hours off of work to vote in any municipal, county, state, or federal election in which he or she is qualified to vote. However, if the county's work hours begin at least two hours after the opening of the polls or end at least two hours prior to the closing of the polls (i.e., if the employee does not have to be at work until 9:00 a.m. or is done with work by 5:00 p.m.), the county does not have to provide additional time off for voting.[116]

Leave for Jury Duty and Court Proceedings

Employees who are summoned to jury duty or served with a subpoena or court order requiring their attendance at a judicial proceeding may not be terminated, disciplined, or otherwise penalized because they are absent from work.[117]

Employee Benefits

The Employment Retirement Income Security Act (ERISA) is the primary statutory scheme governing employee welfare and pension plans. However, ERISA does not apply to government plans such as health and retirement plans established or maintained by local governments.[118] Accordingly, most disputes concerning employee benefits for county employees are governed by state law and the application of general principles of contract and tort law. In this regard, Georgia courts have consistently held that ordinances conferring benefits to government employees create a contractual relationship.[119]

Retirement Benefits

Counties may establish and maintain retirement or pension systems for their employees.[120] Counties are authorized by state law to set up deferred compensation plans for their employees[121] that must not reduce any retirement, pension, or benefit available to them.[122]

Georgia courts have consistently held that plan administrators may correct errors resulting in overpayment of retirement benefits.[123] Local governments may modify or terminate retirement plans—even in the absence of an error—when the plan itself reserves the right to do so.[124] The Court of Appeals has held that an inadvertent clerical error does not modify an existing contract to pay retirement benefits pursuant to a retirement plan.[125] In this case, the court rejected the employee's negligence claim because the employee did not justifiably rely on the oral estimate allegedly given to him, explaining that the plaintiff did not request a written explanation or calculation of his retirement benefits or a written confirmation of the retirement plan's benefits. The court added that if it ruled otherwise, "every retiree would be free to deny having received the written notice of benefits and to contend that [he or she] had been orally advised of a higher benefit."[126]

Social security benefits are also available to county employees.[127]

Medical and Disability Benefits

Counties may provide insurance and hospitalization benefits for their employees.[128] Georgia courts have held that government plans may amend or terminate disability plans if the original legislation reserved the right to do so.[129] Although ERISA does not apply to government plans, counties still must comply with the continuation of medical insurance coverage and notice requirements provided for in the Consolidated Omnibus Budget Reconciliation Act (COBRA). COBRA amended not only ERISA but also the Public Health Services Act (PHSA),[130] which does apply to local governments. Thus, for example, the PHSA provides that local governments must offer to terminated employees continued health plan coverage for a maximum period of 18 months (and in limited circumstances, up to 36 months) after their termination.[131] The PHSA also requires that the plan administrator notify the employee in writing of the employee's right to elect continuing coverage within 14 days of receiving notification of the employee's termination (or other qualifying events).[132] The employee has 60 days after medical coverage otherwise would terminate due to a qualifying event to elect continuation of coverage.[133]

Workers' Compensation Benefits

Georgia's workers' compensation statute applies to county employees.[134] The law specifically encompasses "[a]ll firefighters, law enforcement personnel, and personnel of emergency management . . . agencies, emergency medical services, and rescue organizations whose compensation is paid by . . . any county . . . regardless of the method of appointment, and all full-time county employees and employees of elected salaried county officials." In addition, elected county officers and certain volunteer personnel can be covered if the governing authority adopts the appropriate resolution.[135]

Indemnification and Defense Benefits

Counties have the authority and the discretion to provide legal defense and indemnification to employees.[136] Georgia courts have recognized that a county's enactment of such indemnification and defense ordinances is a form of employee benefit.[137] One court held that by enacting the ordinance, "the county has agreed to indemnify its employees; that is, the county's obligation is like that of a liability insurance company using its attorney to defend the covered employee and cannot renege on that obligation.[138] However, counties are given "considerable latitude in determining what actions will be defended."[139] Absent an abuse of discretion, Georgia courts will not interfere with a county's determination that an employee is not entitled to indemnification based on a provision in the ordinance.[140]

Garnishment

Salaries of county officials and employees are subject to garnishment. However, an employee may not be discharged because his or her earnings have been subjected to garnishment for any one debt obligation, even though more than one summons of garnishment is served.[141]

NOTES

1. For further information on executive recruitment and selection, see David N. Ammons, *Recruiting Local Government Executives* (San Francisco: Jossey-Bass Publishers, 1989).
2. OFFICIAL CODE OF GEORGIA ANNOTATED (O.C.G.A.) §50-14-3(6).
3. O.C.G.A. §50-18-72(a)(7).
4. Boards of assessors O.C.G.A. §§48-5-291, 48-5-294; boards of equalization O.C.G.A. §48-5-311(b)(2), (k); bomb technicians, explosive ordinance disposal technicians, and animal handlers O.C.G.A. §35-8-25; communications officers O.C.G.A. §35-8-23; coroner and deputy coroners O.C.G.A. §45-16-6; county clerks O.C.G.A. §36-1-24; county commissioners O.C.G.A. §36-20-4; elections staff O.C.G.A. §21-2-100; EMA director and deputy directors O.C.G.A. §38-3-27; EMS O.C.G.A. §35-5-3 et seq.; firefighters O.C.G.A. §§25-4-9–25-4-11; jail officers and juvenile correction officers O.C.G.A. §35-8-24; juvenile court clerks O.C.G.A. §15-11-25; magistrate judges O.C.G.A. §§15-10-25, 15-10-137; peace officers O.C.G.A. §§35-8-9, 35-8-12, 35-8-26; police chaplains O.C.G.A. §35-8-13; police chiefs and department heads O.C.G.A. §§35-8-20, 35-8-20.1, 35-8-9; probate judges O.C.G.A. §15-9-1.1; public defenders O.C.G.A. §§17-12-6(3), 17-12-9; sheriffs O.C.G.A. §15-16-3; judges O.C.G.A. §§15-7-26, 15-1-11; superior court clerks O.C.G.A. §15-6-50; tax commissioners O.C.G.A. §48-5-126.1.
5. For a thorough discussion concerning performance appraisal practices, see Dennis Daley, "Designing Effective Performance Appraisal Systems," in *Handbook of Human Resource Management in Government*, 3rd ed., ed. Stephen E. Condrey (San Francisco: Jossey-Bass, 2010).
6. For an excellent discussion on the prospects of pay-for-performance compensation systems, see Christine B. Ledvinka, "The Enduring Importance of Public

Sector Compensation Special Issue Introduction," *Review of Public Personnel Administration* 28 (December 2008): 304–7.

7. See O.C.G.A. §34-7-1.
8. See Newsome v. Richmond County, 246 Ga. 300, 271 S.E.2d 203, 204 (1980).
9. Warren v. Crawford, 927 F.2d 559 (11th Cir. 1991); Dixon v. Metropolitan Atlanta Rapid Transit Authority, 242 Ga. App. 262, 529 S.E.2d 398 (2000).
10. O.C.G.A. §36-1-21(d)(1)(A); Hill v. Watkins, 280 Ga. 278, 627 S.E.2d 3 (2006); Ferdinand v. Board of Commissioners of Fulton County, 281 Ga. 643, 641 S.E.2d 87 (2007).
11. O.C.G.A. §36-1-21(b); Brett v. Jefferson County, 123 F.3d 1429 (11th Cir. 1997).
12. Brett v. Jefferson County, 123 F.3d 1429 (11th Cir. 1997); Hill v. Watkins, 280 Ga. 278, 627 S.E.2d 3 (2006).
13. O.C.G.A. §36-1-21(b).
14. See O.C.G.A. §34-7-1; Mail Advertising Systems, Inc. v. Shroka, 249 Ga. App. 484, 485–86, 548 S.E.2d 461 (2001); Wojcik v. Lewis, 204 Ga. App. 301, 419 S.E.2d 135 (1992).
15. Pickle Logging, Inc. v. Georgia Pacific Corp., 276 Ga. App. 398, 623 S.E.2d 227 (2005); Gunn v. Hawaiian Airlines, Inc., 162 Ga. App. 474, 291 S.E.2d 779 (1982).
16. Wofford v. Glynn Brunswick Memorial Hospital, 864 F.2d 117 (11th Cir. 1989).
17. DeClue v. City of Clayton, 246 Ga. App. 487, 540 S.E.2d 675 (2001), *cert. denied*, (March 19, 2001).
18. See also Peterson v. Atlanta Housing Authority, 998 F.2d 904 (11th Cir. 1993).
19. Hargray v. City of Hallandale, 57 F.3d 1560 (11th Cir. 1995).
20. Cleveland Board of Education v. Loudermill, 470 U.S. 532 (1985).
21. Lalvani v. Cook County, 396 F.3d 911(7th Cir. 2005); Washington Teachers' Union Local No. 6 v. Board of Education, 109 F.3d 774 (D.C. Cir. 1997).
22. Cleveland Board of Education v. Loudermill, 470 U.S. 532 (1985).
23. Kelly v. Smith, 764 F.2d 1412 (11th Cir. 1985) overruled on other grounds; Jones v. City of East Point, 795 F.Supp. 408 (N.D. Ga. 1992).
24. Gilbert v. Homar, 520 U.S. 924 (1997).
25. See Hatcher v. Board of Public Education and Orphanage for Bibb County, 809 F.2d 1546 (11th Cir. 1987) overruled on other grounds.
26. Ibid.
27. Cleveland Board of Education v. Loudermill, 470 U.S. 532 (1985).
28. Adams v. Sewell, 946 F.2d 757 (11th Cir. 1991) overruled on other grounds; McKinney v. Pate, 20 F.3d 1550 (11th Cir. 1994) (en banc); Kelly v. Smith, 764 F.2d 1412 (11th Cir. 1985) overruled on other grounds; Winkler v. County of DeKalb, 648 F.2d 411 (5th Cir. Unit B 1981).
29. Cleveland Board of Education v. Loudermill, 470 U.S. 532 (1985).
30. Hatcher v. Board of Public Education and Orphanage for Bibb County, 809 F.2d 1546 (11th Cir. 1987) overruled on other grounds.
31. See Schweiker v. McClure, 456 U.S. 188 (1982) overruled on other grounds; McKinney v. Pate 20 F.3d 1550 (11th Cir. 1994) (en banc), *cert. denied*, 513

U.S. 1110 (1995); Kelly v. Smith, 764 F.2d 1412 (11th Cir. 1985) overruled on other grounds.

32. See Carter v. Western Reserve Psychiatric Habilitation Center, 767 F.2d 270 (6th Cir. 1985).

33. Paul v. Davis, 424 U.S. 693 (1975).

34. Patterson v. City of Utica, 370 F.3d 322 (2d Cir. 2004); Cox v. Roskelley, 359 F.3d 1105 (9th Cir.), *cert. denied*, 125 S. Ct. 309 (2004); Quinn v. Shirey, 293 F.3d 315 (6th Cir. 2002), *cert. denied*, 537 U.S. 1019 (2002); Wojcik v. Massachusetts State Lottery Commission 300 F.3d 92 (1st Cir. 2002); Cotton v. Jackson, 216 F.3d 1328 (11th Cir. 2000); Hughes v. City of Garland, 204 F.3d 223 (5th Cir. 2000); Strasburger v. Bd. of Ed., Hardin County Community School District No. 1, 143 F.3d 351 (7th Cir. 1998), *cert. denied*, 525 U.S. 1069 (1999).

35. Campbell v. Pierce County, 741 F.2d 1342 (11th Cir. 1984).

36. Harrison v. Wille, 132 F.3d 679 (11th Cir. 1998).

37. Hammer v. City of Osage Beach, 318 F.3d 832 (8th Cir. 2003); Campbell v. Pierce County, 741 F.2d 1342 (11th Cir. 1984).

38. Campbell v. Pierce County, 741 F.2d 1342 (11th Cir. 1984).

39. Ibid.

40. O.C.G.A. §50-18-72(a).

41. O.C.G.A. §50-18-72(a)(5).

42. O.C.G.A. §50-14-3(6).

43. O.C.G.A. §45-1-5.

44. 42 U.S.C.A. §1983 is the federal statute that allows a person to sue the government when he or she has been deprived of a constitutional or statutory right under "color of law."

45. Mt. Healthy City School District Board of Education v. Doyle, 429 U.S. 274 (1977) overruled on other grounds; Sonoda v. Cabrera, 255 F.3d 1035 (9th Cir. 2001); Hennessy v. City of Melrose, 194 F.3d 237 (1st Cir. 1999).

46. Perry v. Sindermann, 408 U.S. 593 (1972).

47. See, e.g., Cook v. Gwinnett County School District, 414 F.3d 1313 (11th Cir. 2005) overruled on other grounds; Jackson v. State of Alabama State Tenure Commission 405 F.3d 1276 (11th Cir. 2005); Brochu v. City of Riviera Beach, 304 F.3d 1144 (11th Cir. 2002) overruled on other grounds.

48. Connick v. Myers, 461 U.S. 138 (1983).

49. Fikes v. City of Daphne, 79 F.3d 1079 (11th Cir. 1996).

50. City of San Diego, California v. Roe, 125 S.Ct. 521 (2004); Connick v. Myers, 461 U.S. 138 (1983).

51. Boyce v. Andrew, 510 F.3d 1333 (11th Cir. 2007); Pickering v. Board of Education, 391 U.S. 563 (1968).

52. Connick v. Myers, 461 U.S. 138 (1983).

53. Rankin v. McPherson, 483 U.S. 378 (1987).

54. Mitchell v. Hillsborough County, 468 F.3d 1276 (11th Cir. 2006).

55. Hansen v. Soldenwagner, 19 F.3d 573 (11th Cir. 1994).

56. Kelly v. Johnson, 425 U.S. 238 (1976); Oladeinde v. City of Birmingham, 230 F.3d 1275 (11th Cir. 2000).

57. Board of County Commissioners v. Umbehr, 518 U.S. 668 (1996).

58. Elrod v. Burns, 427 U.S. 347 (1976); Rutan v. Republican Party, 497 U.S. 62 (1990).

59. Terry v. Cook, 866 F.2d 373 (11th Cir. 1989).
60. Silva v. Bieluch, 351 F.3d 1045 (11th Cir. 2003).
61. 5 UNITED STATES CODE ANNOTATED (U.S.C.A.) §1501 et seq.
62. 5 U.S.C.A. §1502(a).
63. 5 U.S.C.A. §1503.
64. 42 U.S.C.A. §2000 et seq.
65. 42 U.S.C.A. §2000e-2.
66. 42 U.S.C.A. §2000e-2(a).
67. 42 U.S.C.A. §2000e(j).
68. Clark County v. Breeden, 532 U.S. 268 (2001).
69. 42 U.S.C.A. §2000e-3(a).
70. Clover v. Total Sys. Services, Inc., 176 F.3d 1346 (11th Cir. 1999).
71. 29 U.S.C.A. §621 et seq.
72. 29 U.S.C.A. §206(d).
73. 42 U.S.C.A. §12101 et seq.
74. O.C.G.A. §45-19-29.
75. O'Connor v. Ortega, 480 U.S. 709 (1987).
76. 18 U.S.C.A. §§2510–2522.
77. Awbrey v. Great Atlantic & Pacific Tea Co., 505 F. Supp. 604 (N.D. Ga. 1980).
78. 18 U.S.C.A. §2510(6).
79. 18 U.S.C.A. §2511(2)(d).
80. 18 U.S.C.A. §2510(5).
81. Epps v. St. Mary's Hospital of Athens, Inc., 802 F.2d 412 (11th Cir. 1986).
82. 18 U.S.C.A. §§2701–2712.
83. Ontario v. Quon, 130 S. Ct. 2619 (2010).
84. See Everett v. Napper, 833 F.2d 1507 (11th Cir. 1987).
85. O.C.G.A. §45-20-91. See also O.C.G.A. §20-2-1121; Mayo v. Fulton County, 220 Ga. App. 825, 470 S.E.2d 258 (1996).
86. See O.C.G.A. §45-1-4.
87. 31 U.S.C.A. §3729(a).
88. 31 U.S.C.A. §3730(h).
89. See Firefighters Local 349 v. City of Rome, 682 F.Supp. 522 (N.D. Ga. 1988).
90. See Avery v. City of Talladega, 24 F.3d 1337 (11th Cir. 1994).
91. 29 U.S.C.A. §207(k).
92. 29 CODE OF FEDERAL REGULATIONS (C.F.R.) §§553.210(c), 553.211(g).
93. 29 C.F.R. §§553.210(a), 553.211(a), (b).
94. See O'Neal v. Barrow County Board of Commissioners, 743 F.Supp. 859 (N.D. Ga. 1990) overruled on other grounds and vacated and remanded by 980 F.2d 674 (11th Cir. 1993).
95. Reich v. New York Transit Authority, 45 F.3d 646 (2d Cir. 1995); Levering v. District of Columbia, 869 F. Supp. 24 (D.D.C. 1994).
96. 29 U.S.C.A. §213(b)(20).
97. 29 C.F.R. §553.200(b).

98. See Christensen v. Harris County, 529 U.S. 576 (2000); 29 U.S.C.A. §207(o) (5).
99. See 29 C.F.R. §825.126.
100. 29 C.F.R. §825.127.
101. 29 U.S.C.A. §2601 et seq.
102. 38 U.S.C.A. §4301 et seq.
103. See 38 U.S.C.A. §4303; O.C.G.A. §38-2-279 (b).
104. 38 U.S.C.A. §4312(a)(1).
105. O.C.G.A. §38-2-279(d).
106. 38 U.S.C.A. §4311.
107. O.C.G.A. §38-2-279(e).
108. Ibid.
109. 38 U.S.C.A. §4316(d).
110. 38 U.S.C.A. §4317.
111. 38 U.S.C.A. §§4312 (f)(3)(B), 4318; O.C.G.A.§38-2-279(f).
112. 38 U.S.C.A. §4312(e).
113. 38 U.S.C.A. §4316(a).
114. 38 U.S.C.A. §4316(b).
115. 38 U.S.C.A. §4313.
116. O.C.G.A. §21-2-404.
117. O.C.G.A. §34-1-3.
118. 29 U.S.C.A. §§1002(32), 1003(b)(1).
119. See, e.g., Strickland v. City of Albany, 270 Ga. 31, 504 S.E.2d 666 (1998); Pulliam v. Ga. Firemen's Fund, 262 Ga. 411, 419 S.E.2d 918 (1992); DeClue v. City of Clayton, 246 Ga. App. 487, 540 S.E.2d 675 (2000); City of East Point v. Seagraves, 240 Ga. App. 852, 524 S.E.2d 755 (1999).
120. Ga. Const. art. IX, §2, ¶1(f). See O.C.G.A. §36-1-11.1.
121. O.C.G.A. §45-18-31.
122. O.C.G.A. §45-18-34.
123. Withers v. Register, 246 Ga. 158, 269 S.E.2d 431 (1980); O.C.G.A. §47-4-121(b); Tate v. Teachers' Retirement System of Georgia, 257 Ga. 365, 359 S.E.2d 649 (1987).
124. Murray County School District v. Adams, 218 Ga. App. 220, 461 S.E.2d 228 (1995).
125. Dodd v. City of Gainesville, 268 Ga. App. 43, 601 S.E.2d 352 (2004).
126. Ibid.
127. O.C.G.A. tit. 47, ch. 18.
128. Ga. Const. art. IX, §2, ¶1(f). See O.C.G.A. §§36-1-11.1, 36-21-1 et seq.
129. Pulliam v. Georgia Firemen's Pension Fund, 262 Ga. 411, 419 S.E.2d 918 (1992).
130. 42 U.S.C.A. §300bb-1 et seq.
131. 42 U.S.C.A. §§300bb-1–300bb-3.
132. 42 U.S.C.A. §300bb-6.
133. 42 U.S.C.A. §300bb-5(a).
134. O.C.G.A. §34-9-1.

135. Ibid.

136. O.C.G.A. §§45-9-21, 45-9-22.

137. Gwinnett County v. Blaney, 275 Ga. 696, 702–703, 572 S.E.2d 553 (2002); Hendon v. DeKalb County, 203 Ga. App. 750, 755(1), 417 S.E.2d 705 (1992).

138. Chatham County Commissioners v. Clark, 253 Ga. 687, 324 S.E.2d 448 (1985).

139. Haywood v. Hughes, 238 Ga. 668, 669, 235 S.E.2d 2 (1977). See O.C.G.A. §45-9-21(a).

140. See Baker v. Gwinnett County, 267 Ga. App. 839, 600 S.E.2d 819 (2004). See also Cleveland v. Skandalakis, 268 Ga. 133, 133–34, 485 S.E.2d 777 (1997); Prayor v. Fulton County, 2009 WL 981996 (N.D. Ga. April 13, 2009).

141. O.C.G.A. §§18-4-7, 18-4-21.

8

Kelly J. L. Pridgen

Contracting, Purchasing, and Sale of County Property

Since a county governing authority "has the exclusive authority to control the fiscal affairs of the county,"[1] it generally has the authority to enter into a contract on behalf of the county. Despite the fact that the county governing authority is the fiscal authority, other elected county officers may enter into contracts on behalf of a county when authorized by law or when it is necessary for them to perform their duties.[2]

REQUIREMENTS FOR COUNTY CONTRACTS

A county's power to contract is subject to various limitations. In addition to being subject to the principles of general contract law, including immigration law,[3] contracts of the county commissioners must be in writing and entered into the minutes.[4] Also, the contracts are limited in their duration. If the county ignores any one of these limitations in making a contract, the contract may be deemed *ultra vires* (i.e., unlawful, illegal, or unauthorized).[5] Regardless of whether it is called a contract, agreement, lease, memorandum of understanding, memorandum of agreement, or letter of intent signed by both parties, it is considered a contract that is subject to the requirements of this chapter.

Written Contracts Entered into the Minutes

With certain exceptions, any contract entered into by the county commissioners must be in writing, approved by the county governing authority in a meeting, and entered into the official minutes.[6] Any modifications or amendments to an existing contract must also be in writing and entered into the minutes.[7] If a contract is in writing and valid in all respects except that it has not been entered into the minutes, then the other party to the contract can petition the courts to force the commissioners to enter the contract into the minutes.[8] Although the county may not be held liable for an implied contract,[9] it may be liable for the reasonable value of materials furnished and services rendered on an express contract.[10]

Length of Contract

Except as will be explained, most county contracts must be for one year or less. In general, one board of commissioners may not bind itself or future boards to prevent free legislation in matters of local government.[11] However, the courts have recognized that this prohibition must not be too rigidly applied, so each individual contract should be considered individually[12] because certain contracts have been allowed to extend beyond one year.[13]

Multiyear Contracts

Counties may enter into a contract with a private party that automatically renews for one or more years to lease, purchase, or lease-purchase goods, materials, real property, personal property, services, and supplies so long as certain minimum requirements are met.[14] First, the contract must absolutely terminate without any further obligation on the county by December 31 of the year it was executed and by December 31 of each year for which it is renewed.[15] Second, the contract must state the total obligation of the county for the calendar year for which it is executed and the total obligation for each calendar year for which the contract is renewed.[16] Third, the title to the property must either remain in the name of the vendor until it is fully paid for by the county,[17] or it may be in the name of the county so long as the county is authorized to transfer the title back to the vendor if the contract is not fully consummated.[18] Fourth, the amount of the contract plus the total amount of debt incurred by the county may not exceed 10 percent of the assessed value of all taxable property within the county.[19] Fifth, if the contract is for the purchase of property, then it may not have been the subject of a failed referendum (e.g., a referendum to approve a special purpose local option sales tax or bonded indebtedness to fund the purchase of the property) in the four calendar years prior to the contract unless the purchase is required by a court order or it is certified by the governing authority that such a court order is imminent.[20] Sixth, if the multiyear contract is for the purchase of real property, several other conditions must be met:

- *Public hearing.* The county must hold a public hearing that has been advertised for two weeks in a newspaper of general circulation in the county.[21]

- *Maximum amount.* The average annual payments on a contract to purchase real property may not exceed 7.5 percent of the governmental fund revenues of the county for the last calendar year plus any special purpose local option sales tax revenues,[22] and the total amount may not exceed $25 million.[23] These restrictions do not apply to projects that have been approved in a special purpose local option sales tax referendum, to projects that state law allows to be paid from fine revenues, or to projects to build housing for court services.[24]

Finally, multiyear contracts may include a provision that the contract will terminate absolutely if funds for the contract are not appropriated by the county,[25] since the county is only obligated to pay the amount due during the calendar year in which it is executed or renewed.[26]

Other Exceptions

Contracts with private firms may extend beyond one year when specifically provided by law. For instance, counties may enter into contracts to build, maintain, own, or operate a toll road or toll bridge that may exceed one year.[27] Additionally, counties may contract with private parties for up to 20 years to provide for the construction, operation, and maintenance of wastewater treatment systems, storm water systems, water systems, and sewer systems.[28] In evaluating proposals, counties must consider previous performance on projects of comparable magnitude, the environmental compliance record, and the five-year history of relevant civil or criminal penalties incurred by potential firms. If the contracts involve construction of a facility, the contract must comply with Georgia's Local Government Public Works Construction Law[29] discussed later in this chapter.

Intergovernmental Contracts

Counties may contract with the state and other local governments in Georgia for a period not exceeding 50 years.[30] Examples include the following:

- Contracts with the state, a public agency, a public corporation, or a public authority to convey existing facilities to the state and to any public agency, public corporation, or public authority.[31]
- Contracts with the state, a public agency, a public corporation, or a public authority to provide care, maintenance, and hospitalization of its indigent sick.[32]
- Contracts with cities to provide police protection, fire protection, emergency medical services, animal control, hospital, ambulance, garbage and sewage disposal, libraries, building permit

issuance and building code enforcement, street and road maintenance, parks and recreation, and the treatment and distribution of water.[33] In fact, a county may not provide any of those services inside a city's boundaries without such a contract.[34]

- Contracts with cities, other counties, or municipalities to provide industrial wastewater treatment services, in order to comply with applicable state and federal water pollution control standards and to be eligible for grants-in-aid or other allotments.[35]

- Contracts with the State Personnel Board to provide health insurance coverage for county employees.[36]

- Contracts with the Georgia Ports Authority for the leasing, operation, or management of real or personal property in or adjacent to any seaport.[37]

- Contracts with contiguous counties and cities located either in a contiguous or the same county to develop regional facilities. These contracts may provide for allocation of proceeds of ad valorem taxes levied in an assessing county with other counties or municipalities with which it has contracted and for allocation of revenues generated by a regional facility. The allocation of the tax proceeds and the other revenues is to be determined by contract between the affected local governments.[38] Prior to entering into such a contract, a county must hold at least one public hearing, and notice of the public hearing must be published in a newspaper of general circulation within the county. The required public hearing may be held jointly with the other local government to be involved in the contract. If the proposed facility will be located outside a county but will require expenditure of public funds of that county, a financial feasibility study must be conducted prior to the county entering into such contract.[39]

- Contracts with public agencies and private nonprofit entities organized to provide services to persons of low and moderate incomes. Specifically, these are day-care services for children, services for the elderly, health education, literacy and English language instruction, mental health and disability services, legal assistance, and emergency food and medical assistance.[40]

CONSTRUCTION CONTRACTS

When a county undertakes a public works or a road construction project, in addition to the general requirements for county contracts, some special procedures must be observed. The Georgia Local Government Public

Works Construction Law governs construction projects other than roads. Road construction contracts are subject to other requirements.

Public Works Construction Contracts

The Georgia Local Government Public Works Construction Law[41] establishes the basic requirements that counties must follow when hiring private contractors to do construction projects (other than road construction) that cost more than $100,000 to ensure that public works contracts are awarded in a fair and competitive manner.

Construction Projects Subject to the Law

A determination must first be made that a contract is for the construction, alteration, repair, improvement, or demolition of a county building or structure (other than routine operation, repair, or maintenance).[42] The contract must also hold the other party responsible for construction by providing labor and building materials.[43] This means that if the contractor is using his own employees or is responsible for contracting with another firm for labor, the contract is subject to the requirement of the law.

Not all construction contracts are subject to the requirements of the public works law.[44] Road construction contracts are subject to different requirements, explained later in this chapter.[45] Construction contracts that will cost under $100,000 do not have to comply with the requirements of the public works law,[46] but counties may nevertheless choose to observe the requirements to obtain better competition.[47] Counties may use their own employees to construct the building or structure at any amount so long as any subcontracts with private firms costing over $100,000 are competitively awarded in accordance with the public works law.[48] Professional service contracts (e.g., architect or engineering contracts) are not subject to the procurement requirements so long as the professional firm is not "responsible" for construction.[49] Contracts necessitated by an emergency are also exempt, except that the county must ratify the contract in a commission meeting and describe the nature of the emergency in the meeting minutes as soon as practicable.[50] Construction projects using inmate labor are exempt from the law.[51] Additionally, if the construction project is subject to a federal grant with special procurement requirements, the county does not have to comply with any requirements that conflict with federal grant requirements.[52] However, a special notice must be included in the advertisement of the project indicating that the project is subject to federal grant requirements.[53]

Advertising the Proposed Project

Public works construction contract opportunities that are subject to the law must be posted conspicuously in the county governing authority's office and must be advertised.[54] The county may advertise by posting the notice on the Internet for four weeks[55] or may advertise by publishing a notice in the legal organ twice in the four weeks preceding the bid/proposal opening. The first advertisement must be at least four weeks before the bid/proposal opening, and the second advertisement must be at least two weeks after the first advertisement.[56] While these are the minimum requirements, counties may advertise in additional places or more frequently in order to reach a broader audience, creating greater competition and perhaps driving prices down. Defective notice and advertising may make a contract illegal,[57] as does inclusion of a provision that is unauthorized by law.[58] Failure of the advertisement to invite all reasonable competition voids the contract.[59] The price, exact or approximate, at which the contract will be let, need not be stated in the advertisement.[60] Further advertisement is necessary when proposals are rejected and plans are subsequently changed.[61]

Prequalification of Bidders and Offerors

Counties may "weed out" unqualified firms before accepting a bid or proposal, eliminating the need to waste time and resources evaluating bids/proposals from firms that are not candidates for the contract. However, such prequalification procedures must meet certain minimum requirements.[62] For instance, the criteria to prequalify must either be related to the work or the contractor's ability to perform the work (such as related experience on similar projects or financial capability). Additionally, the procedure must include a process for disqualified bidders/offerors to respond to their disqualification. The inclusion of such a process does not mean that the disqualified bidder has the right to appeal his or her disqualification and be reinstated as a bidder; it is merely an opportunity for the disqualified bidder to clear his or her name.[63] The procedure may be as simple as allowing a disqualified bidder to submit a letter responding to the disqualification within a specified number of days to a designated official (i.e., the chairman, manager, clerk, or purchasing agent), or it may be more formalized by providing the opportunity for a hearing before the board.

Competitive Sealed Bids and Proposals

Two methods may be used to procure a public works construction contract: the competitive sealed bid method and the competitive sealed proposal method.[64]

1. *Bid method.* Under the bid method, the county issues an "invitation to bid" that explains the requirements of the project. The contract, if awarded, must be to the lowest responsible bidder who meets all of the requirements of the invitation to bid. Bids are valid for only 60 days unless otherwise agreed by the county and the bidder.[65] Under the bid method, the county may negotiate only with the lowest responsive, responsible bidder if all responsive bids exceed the county's budget.[6]

2. *Proposal method.* The proposal method allows the county to select an offer based upon evaluation factors established in the request for proposal (RFP). In the RFP, the county must list all of the factors that will be used to pick the best proposal. The RFP must also assign a relative weight for each factor. Each responsive proposal is scored according to only those factors listed in the proposals. Once all of the proposals are scored, the relative weight of each factor is applied, and the firm with the best score wins. The scoring sheets must be used to evaluate firms and are subject to open records requirements once the project is awarded. Because price does not have to be an evaluation factor, counties are not restricted to hiring the firm that offers the lowest price. If the contract is awarded, it must be to the firm determined in writing to be most advantageous to the county based upon the factors specified in the RFP.[67] Proposals are valid for as long as specified in the RFP, but offerors not on the short list must be released after 60 days.[68] If specified in the RFP, the county may negotiate with those firms on the short list for purposes of obtaining a best and final offer under the proposal method.

Construction Delivery Systems

Which competitive award method is used depends largely upon the type of construction delivery system the county selects for the project. In order to make an informed selection, county officials should have an understanding of the various construction delivery systems available.

- *Design-bid-build.* Under the traditional design-bid-build method, the county hires either an architect or engineer to design the project. Once the design is complete, the county hires a contractor to build the project. This method may take longer than some of the others, but it can provide the county more control over the design and construction of the project as well as a more accurate price. Additionally, counties receive the benefit of the architect watching for construction errors and the contractor watching for design errors.

- *Design-build.* Using the design-build method, the county hires one firm to be responsible for both design and construction. The firm may provide this service with in-house resources or may contract with another firm to provide the design and/or the construction portion of the contract. This method is faster because construction of the project begins before the design is complete. It may also result in a more efficient project because of the builder's input into the design phase. However, because the design team and the construction team are employed by the same firm, the county does not receive the same "watchdog" benefit that it receives in design-bid-build. Also, the county may not have as much control over either design or construction because of the additional layer between the county and the design and construction teams.

- *Construction manager or program manager.* Under this method, the county hires a firm to coordinate and supervise the project as well as to represent the county under both the construction manager (CM) method and the program/project manager methods. The county has a separate contract or contracts with either a general contractor or the trade contractors for construction. If the county utilizes the CM method, the firm performs the same services as the CM agency but is also responsible for construction of the project.

- *Fast track.* Under the fast-track method, design and construction occur at the same time. In fact, construction begins as soon as the first phase of design is completed, offering the advantage of quick project completion. However, this method requires a great deal of coordination to ensure that contract documents are complete and accurate and that nothing is overlooked.

Method of Competitive Award and Construction Delivery

The bid method works very well with the traditional design-bid-build method. Because the project design is complete when it is time to select a builder, the only remaining factor in the decision is price. The proposal method of competitive award works well with the design-build method and the fast-track method because price is not a required factor. Because design and construction of the project are integrated in the proposal method, the county needs some flexibility in selecting a firm. Innovativeness of proposal, timeliness of projected completion, and quality of past projects and key personnel designated for the project become more important factors in the decision. Also, until there is a final design, it is difficult to have an accurate total price for the project. Similarly, the proposal method works well for both the CM agency and the CM at risk. Because one of the major benefits of using CM is the coordination and supervision of the project, the quality of the firm generally becomes a more important factor in the decision to hire a construction manager than does the price.

Choosing a Construction Delivery System

There is not one "best" construction delivery system because one method may be better suited than another to a particular project. It is very important to understand the various methods as well as their strengths and weaknesses before selecting a construction delivery system. A county governing authority should consider various basic questions when selecting a construction delivery method.

First, does the county governing authority have a clear idea of what the project will look like, or does it want a firm to provide some ideas on what should be included in the project? Design-bid-build works very well when the scope of the project is fairly well established.

Second, will the project need to be completed faster than an average construction schedule will allow? Fast track and design-build are good methods for rapid project completion. Third, does the county have personnel who can supervise and coordinate the project as well as prepare the contract documents? Program/project manager and CM agency work well when the county does not have the in-house resources to manage the project.

Finally, what level of control does the county governing authority want to have over the project? A county will have a greater level of control in the design-bid-build method than in some variations of design-build and CM agency.

Bond Requirements

Bid, payment, and performance bonds protect the county when a contractor fails to meet his or her obligations. These bonds are required on all projects costing over $100,000 that are subject to the public works construction law, although a county may require contractors to submit them on any project.[69] Bid bonds protect the county if the selected bidder/offeror fails to execute the contract. The county will be able to collect the difference between the selected bid/proposal and the next highest bid/proposal, protecting the county financially if the selected bidder/offeror fails to execute a contract. Performance bonds provide the county with reimbursement if the builder/firm fails to complete the project according to the contract. Payment bonds protect the subcontractors and suppliers of the contractor. If the contractor fails to pay the subcontractors and suppliers who assisted in the project, the subcontractors and suppliers seek recovery against the payment bond, not the county.[70] However, if a county fails to obtain a payment bond on a contract that is over $100,000, it may be held liable to pay the subcontractors or suppliers.[71]

Contractor's Oath

Before beginning work on the project, a contractor must make an oath in writing stating that he or she has not directly or indirectly attempted to prevent competition in the procurement of the contract.[72] The local government official responsible for making payments to the contractor must file the oath. If the oath is false, the contract is void, and the local government is entitled to recover any monies paid to the contractor.

Penalties for Failure to Comply with Public Works Law

Compliance with the public works law is mandatory.[73] Any public works contract that is subject to the law and that is entered into without properly using either the bid method or proposal method is invalid.[74] It is considered a misdemeanor for a county commissioner to receive or agree to receive any pay or profit, directly or indirectly, from a public works contract.[75] If the contractor knows that the local government failed to properly advertise the contract opportunity and/or use competitive sealed bids or proposals, the contractor is not entitled to payment for any of the work performed under the contract.[76]

ROAD CONSTRUCTION CONTRACTS

When counties contract with private contractors to build or maintain a county road, the contract is subject to different requirements than those mandated by the Georgia Local Government Public Works Construction Law.

Projects Subject to the Law

Contracts with private firms to build, rebuild, or maintain a road that costs $20,000 or more must be let to the lowest bidder according to the requirements of state law.[77] Contracts with the state, a city, or another county are not subject to the bidding law.[78] If a county performs the road project itself, the purchase of materials, supplies, and equipment is not subject to the state bidding laws.[79] Professional services, such as engineering, are also not subject to the bidding law.[80] Additionally, projects necessitated by an emergency (i.e., bridge repairs, snow and ice removal, flood damage, etc.) are not subject to bidding requirements.[81]

Advertising the Proposed Project

Road construction contract opportunities subject to the bidding law must be advertised in the legal organ or in any other newspaper that will ensure adequate publicity.[82] Unlike public works construction contracts, there is no provision for advertisement on the Internet. While a Web site could be used as a supplemental method of advertising a road construction contract opportunity, a local government must still advertise in the legal organ or other newspaper. The advertisement must run at least two times during the two weeks before the bid opening, with the first advertisement appearing two weeks before the bid opening. The second advertisement must appear one week after the first advertisement.[83] It must include a description of the project; the time allotted for performance; the terms and time of payment; the procedure for and costs of obtaining detailed plans and specifications; the amount of the proposal guaranty; the time and place for the submission and opening of bids; the right to reject any or all bids; and any bonds required other than performance and payment bonds (e.g., public liability and property damage bonds).[84]

Award of Contract

Unlike public works construction projects, only one method—the bid method—can be used to obtain road construction projects. If the contract is awarded, it must be to the lowest reliable bidder.[85] However, the county may choose to reject any and all bids, re-advertise the project, perform the work in-house, or abandon the project.[86] Contracts must be approved by resolution of the board of commissioners, and the resolution must be entered into the minutes.[87] If the successful bidder fails to sign the contract or furnish the bonds, the contract may be re-advertised, performed in-house, or abandoned.[88]

Bond Requirements

Bonds are required on road construction contracts to protect the county. With bids on all road construction contracts, regardless of the dollar amount, the bidders must submit a "proposal guaranty" (certified check or other security) payable to the county in an amount necessary to ensure that the successful bidder will execute the contract (except for contracts for engineering or other professional services only).[89] Similar to bid bonds for public works construction projects, proposal guaranties ensure that the successful bidder honors his or her bid. Failure to sign the contract or furnish the bonds by the successful bidder will result in forfeit of the proposal guaranty.[90] Proposal guaranties must be returned to a bidder if a written withdrawal of his or her bid is received before the scheduled bid opening.[91] When a contract is awarded, proposal guaranties must be returned to all bidders except the lowest reliable bidder.[92] If no contract is awarded within 30 days of the bid opening, then all bids and all proposal guaranties will be returned unless the county and the lowest reliable bidder agree to a longer period of time.[93]

On road construction contracts that are over $5,000, the contractor must provide a performance bond in the amount of the bid for the faithful performance of the contract and to indemnify the county for any damages should the contractor fail to perform the contract on time.[94] On road construction contracts that are over $5,000, the contractor must provide a payment bond in the same manner as for public works construction contracts.[95] If the county fails to obtain a required payment bond, it may be liable to any unpaid subcontractors, laborers, or materialmen.[96] In the case of construction or reconstruction to a bridge or the approach to a bridge, counties may require a contractor to provide a bond to keep the bridge in good condition for at least seven years.[97] The county will be liable for all injuries caused by a defective bridge for seven years if it fails to obtain a bridge-repair bond.[98] Counties may require additional bonds, such as public liability and property damage bonds so long as the project advertisement provided notice of the required additional bonds.[99]

Contractor's Oath

The successful bidder must execute a written oath stating that he or she has not unlawfully restricted competitive bidding on the project.[100]

TOLL ROAD CONTRACTS

Counties may enter into contracts with private companies to finance, construct, maintain, improve, own, or operate private toll roads and bridges.[101]

TRANSIT CONTRACTS

Counties may contract with transit agencies for transit services or transit facilities for up to 50 years.[102] If fares alone will not cover the cost, any tax increase levied to subsidize the transit service must be approved by the voters of the county before the county governing authority enters into such a contract.[103] The county governing authority and the governing authority of any affected city must adopt a transit service plan.[104]

PURCHASING

Local Purchasing Requirements

Very little state regulation exists for county purchasing other than procuring public works and road construction services. The majority of purchasing requirements are found in a county's local legislation and ordinances. Local legislation, sometimes referred to as enabling legislation, is adopted by the General Assembly and dictates what a county governing authority can and cannot do.[105] For instance, local legislation or a county ordinance may require that purchases that exceed a designated monetary amount must be made pursuant to legal advertisement and competitive bidding.[106] Often it is required that a minimum number of bids be obtained, that the bids be formal and sealed, and that they be kept on file.[107] Usually, purchases must be made from the lowest "responsive" and "responsible" bidder.[108] In some counties, purchases in excess of a specified amount must first be approved by the board of commissioners.[109] The law governing one county provides that purchases costing under $15,000 may be made by the purchasing agent on the open market, but a purchase costing over $15,000 may be made only after it has been advertised in the official county newspaper and has received the approval of the board of commissioners.[110] When making purchases, commissioners should examine their local legislation as well as their ordinances to avoid legal complications.

State Law Requirement for Purchases by Counties

There are few requirements for county purchasing under state law. Counties must give preference "as far as may be reasonable and practicable" to items manufactured or produced in Georgia when buying supplies, materials, equipment, and agricultural products, unless giving such a preference will sacrifice quality.[111] For purchases over $100,000, if submitted in writing by a bidder, the county must consider the multiplier effect on the gross state domestic product and the effect on public revenues to purchase a Georgia-manufactured good rather than something produced out of state.[112]

Finally, it a misdemeanor to purchase beef that was not raised and produced in the United States with county funds. Canned meats not available from a source within the United States and not processed in this country may be purchased without penalty.[113]

Purchasing Agreements

Counties are specifically authorized by law to enter into certain purchasing agreements with other governments. For instance, counties may contract with the state and federal government to purchase or lease equipment, supplies, and property.[114] Counties may buy various supplies, materials, and equipment, including motor vehicles "off of the state contract," through the Georgia Department of Administrative Services.[115] Georgia's Correctional Industries Administration may sell items such as washing powders, insecticides, picnic tables, park benches, parking bumpers, and street signs and markers and other products manufactured by state inmates to counties.[116] Finally, counties may increase their buying power by joining other counties, cities, school districts, and other governmental jurisdictions to purchase various items.[117]

Conflicts of Interest

To prevent private gain from public office, the county may not purchase from any county official, from any store in which the county official is an employee or is directly or indirectly interested, or from any person or partnership of which a county official is a member or by which he or she is employed unless such purchases are authorized by the governing authority or it is clearly apparent that the individual, partnership, or owner of the store will sell the goods or property as cheaply or more cheaply than they can be bought elsewhere.[118] A contract made in violation of this prohibition is illegal, and the official who commits the violation may be removed from office.[119] Additionally, it is a felony for any county official or employee to sell any real or personal property, directly or on behalf of a business entity, to the county or the school board unless the sale price is less than $800 per calendar quarter or by competitive sealed bid.[120] However, in the case of real property, such action is not a felony if disclosure is made to the probate judge at least 15 days prior to the execution of the contract.[121] Although criminal charges might be avoided, such sales may be voided. The selling of services to the county is not included in the crime defined in this section of the code.[122] These statutory provisions make it clear that any county official who sells to his or her county could have the contract invalidated and even face criminal charges.

County officials must avoid all situations in which their personal interests affect their public actions or come into conflict with them. When such situations occur, they should disqualify themselves from acting on such matters. It is of no consequence that there is only a potential conflict of interest, that there is no dishonesty or loss of public funds, or that the official is not influenced by the situation. For more information on ethics, see Chapter 6.

SALE OF COUNTY PROPERTY

Georgia law specifies different requirements for selling real property generally than for selling real property used for roads.

Sale of Real Property

Real property (other than roads) sold by the county must be awarded to the highest responsible bidder, either by sealed bids or at auction. The county commissioners cannot contract with an individual to purchase county-owned land—even if it is no longer needed by the county and the proposed buyer is willing to pay fair market value or higher.[123]

Notice of the sale must be published once in the legal organ or in a newspaper of general circulation in the county not less than 15 days or more than 60 days before the date of the auction or the last day for the receipt of proposals.[124] The notice must include a legal description of the property, conditions of the sale, and the date, time, and place of the bid opening or auction.[125] The commissioners may award the sale to the highest bidder or may reject all bidders.

The general requirements for sale of real property (other than roads) do not apply to certain types of sales of county property:

- *Tax deeds.* The sheriff or tax commissioner may sell property held by a county under a tax deed without using this procedure.[126]
- *Exchanges.* A county may exchange a parcel of real property so long as the other property is of equal or greater value than the property held by the county as determined by an appraisal.[127] However, within the six weeks before the closing of the exchange, the county must publish a notice of the proposed exchange in the legal organ once per week for four weeks.[128]

- *Unusable parcels.* Counties may sell small or odd-shaped parcels that cannot reasonably be used under applicable land-use controls to abutting property owners without going to auction or sealed bids, as long as all abutting property owners are given an opportunity to purchase the property.[129]

- *Property to schools.* Counties may sell, lease, or transfer real property to the local board of education or other public education institution for use as a public school or other educational purpose. This transfer may take place without advertisement, bidding, auction, notice, publication, or referendum, provided that the county governing authority holds a public hearing in the area where the affected property is located and at least one subsequent meeting to discuss comments expressed at the public hearing.[130]

- *Recreational set-asides to homeowners' associations.* If the county requires developers to set aside a certain amount of property in each new subdivision for recreational purposes, the county may negotiate a sale of those recreational set-asides to the homeowners' association so long as the recreational set-asides were conveyed to the county at no cost to the county.[131] However, the county must publish a notice of the sale in the legal organ once per week for four weeks.[132]

- *Property to the state.* The county may sell or grant property to the state or any state authority if it determines that the establishment of a state facility would be of benefit to the county by providing activities in an area in need of redevelopment, by enhancing employment activities, or by benefiting the county in other ways.[133]

- *Land to be developed as a lake.* If the county abandoned plans to develop or create a lake on at least 1,000 acres, it may sell the property back to the original owner for at least the price paid by the county or in the case of remnants of the original acquisition, at market value.[134] If the original owner does not purchase the property within 60 days' notice and if the county still desires to dispose of the property, it must do so using the regular requirements for selling real property explained earlier in this chapter.[135]

Personal Property

Other public property (i.e., not real property) such as equipment and vehicles that becomes unserviceable may be disposed of by an order of the governing authority.[136]

Sale of County Roads

A county may, in the public interest, abandon any public road or dispose of or lease property acquired for public road purposes if certain procedures are followed.[137] When property is no longer needed for road purposes,[138] the county must first contact the owner of the property who sold it to the county or his or her successors in title who own the abutting property.[139] The original owner or his or her successors may purchase the property at any price agreed upon so long as it is not less than the amount paid by the county.[140] If only remnants or portions of the property exist, they may be acquired at market value.[141] If the original owner or his or her successors do not exercise their option to purchase the property, it may be sold through one of three methods:

1. *Sealed bid.* The county may sell the former right-of-way property to the highest sealed bidder after advertising for bids.[142] The first advertisement must be at least two weeks before the bid opening, and the second advertisement must be at least one week after the first advertisement.[143] The advertisement must include a description of the property, the time and place to submit and open bids, the right to reject any and all bids, the conditions of the sale, and any other information that the county believes would be advisable in the public interest.[144]

2. *Real estate broker.* The county may list the former road property for sale through a licensed real estate broker who has a business located within the county.[145] If there are no real estate brokers in the county, then the county may use a broker located outside the county.[146] The county must publish the names of the real estate brokers listing property once per week for two weeks in the legal organ.[147] The property must be listed for a minimum of three months and may not be sold for less than fair market value.[148] The county governing authority must approve the sale at a regular meeting after providing opportunity for public comment.[149]

3. *Public auction.* The county may sell the property no longer needed for road purposes at public auction by a licensed auctioneer, provided that it not be sold for less than fair market value.[150] The county must publish in the legal organ once per week for the two weeks immediately preceding the auction a notice that includes a description of the property, the time and place to submit and open bids, a statement of the right to reject any and all bids, the

conditions of the sale, and any other information that the county believes would be advisable in the public interest.[151]

As can be seen from this chapter, it is essential that county officials and staff be aware of the restrictions imposed by state law on the ability of counties to enter into contracts as well as the varying requirements established for different types of county purchases or sales.

NOTES

1. Stephenson v. Board of Commissioners of Cobb County, 261 Ga. 399 (1991).
2. Board of Commissioners of Spalding County v. Stewart, 284 Ga. 573 (2008) (sheriff had authority to enter into contract for inmate medical care); OFFICIAL CODE OF GEORGIA ANNOTATED (O.C.G.A.) §15-16-13(a) (sheriff is authorized to contract with cities to provide law enforcement services subject to the written consent of the board of commissioners); O.C.G.A. §42-4-9 (the "keeper of a county jail" may house federal prisoners in the jail with the consent of the board of commissioners); O.C.G.A. §15-6-96 (clerk of superior court may enter into a contract to distribute, sell, or market records or computer-generated data from the office; a monthly report of any such contracts as well as the revenues received must be submitted to the board of commissioners); O.C.G.A. §15-6-61(a)(18) (clerk of superior court may participate in agreements necessary to file and transmit civil case filing and disposition forms to the Superior Court Clerks' Cooperative Authority); O.C.G.A. §48-5-359.1(a) (county's contract with any city located within the county to prepare the tax digest, assess, and collect taxes for the city must also be approved by tax commissioner); ibid. (tax commissioner may contract to receive additional compensation from the city for collection of city taxes); O.C.G.A. §48-5-147 (in counties where the tax commissioner receives tax payments for both the county and city or receives mailed tax payments for the county, the tax commissioner may enter into a contract for a lock box system with a bank to receive, process, and deposit mailed tax returns and payments); O.C.G.A. §42-8-100(g)(1) (authorizes the probate judge or the chief magistrate judge to enter into a contract with a private probation company to provide probation supervision so long as the contract is approved by the board of commissioners); O.C.G.A. §§15-10-150, 15-10-151 (the board of commissioners and city council of a city located within the county may enter into an agreement, which must be approved by the chief magistrate judge, for the magistrate court to provide municipal court services to the city).
3. See title 13 of O.C.G.A.; O.C.G.A. §36-10-91.
4. O.C.G.A. §36-10-1. See Board of Commissioners of Spalding County v. Stewart, 284 Ga. 573 (2008) (contract by sheriff did not have to be on the minutes); Smith v. Murrath Enterprises, Inc., 243 Ga. App. 856 (2000); Cherokee County v. Hause, 229 Ga. App. 578 (1997); Smith v. Gwinnett County, 182 Ga. App 875 (1987); Commercial Credit Corp. v. Mason, 151 Ga. App. 443 (1979); Lasky v. Fulton County, 145 Ga. App. 120 (1978); DeKalb County v. Scruggs, 147 Ga. App. 711 (1978); Hatcher v. Hancock County Commissioners of Roads and Revenues, 239 Ga. 229 (1977). See also Murray County v. Pickering, 42 Ga. App. 739 (1931); Graham v. Beacham, 189 Ga. 304 (1939); City of Atlanta v. North by Northwest Civic Association, 262 Ga. 531 (1992).

5. Madden v. Bellew, 260 Ga. 530 (1990); compare with Twiggs County v. Oconee Electric Membership Corporation, 245 Ga. App. 231 (2000) (county could not claim that its actions were illegal and *ultra vires* because there was no written contract two years after making payments).

6. O.C.G.A. §36-10-1. See Board of Commissioners of Spalding County v. Stewart, 284 Ga. 573 (2008) (contract by sheriff did not have to be on the minutes); Smith v. Murrath Enterprises, Inc., 243 Ga. App. 856 (2000); Cherokee County v. Hause, 229 Ga. App. 578 (1997); Smith v. Gwinnett County, 182 Ga. App. 875 (1987); Commercial Credit Corp. v. Mason, 151 Ga. App. 443 (1979); Lasky v. Fulton County, 145 Ga. App. 120 (1978); DeKalb County v. Scruggs, 147 Ga. App. 711 (1978); Hatcher v. Hancock County Commissioners of Roads and Revenues, 239 Ga. 229 (1977). See also Murray County v. Pickering, 42 Ga. App. 739 (1931); Graham v. Beacham, 189 Ga. 304 (1939); City of Atlanta v. North by Northwest Civic Association, 262 Ga. 531 (1992).

7. Lester Witte and Company v. Rabun County, 245 Ga. 382 (1980). See John D. Stephens, Inc. v. Gwinnett County, 175 Ga. App. 379 (1985).

8. Hatcher v. Hancock County Commissioners of Roads and Revenues, 239 Ga. 229 (1977); Malcom v. Fulton County, 209 Ga. 392 (1952). There is no time limit as to when a county contract must be entered into the minutes. See also Burke v. Wheeler County, 54 Ga. App. 81 (1936) and Wagener v. Forsyth County, 135 Ga. 162 (1910). In both cases, the contract was entered into the minutes after completion of the work.

9. Harden v. Clarke County Board of Education, 279 Ga. App. 513 (2006); PMS Construction Company, Inc. v. DeKalb County, 243 Ga. 870 (1979); DeKalb County v. Scruggs, 147 Ga. App. 711 (1978); Neely v. Richmond County, 161 Ga. App. 71 (1982); Cherokee County v. Hause, 229 Ga. App. 578 (1997); Barge and Company, Inc. v. City of Atlanta, 161 Ga. App. 675 (1982).

10. PMS Construction Company, Inc. v. DeKalb County, 243 Ga. 870 (1979); DeKalb County v. PMS Construction Company, Inc., 151 Ga. App. 63 (1979); Barge and Company, Inc. v. City of Atlanta, 161 Ga. App. 675 (1982).

11. See O.C.G.A. §36-30-3(a); Madden v. Bellew, 260 Ga. 530 (1990); Ledbetter Bros. v. Floyd County, 237 Ga. 22 (1976); Brennan v. Chatham County Commissioners, 209 Ga. App. 177 (1993); International Brotherhood of Police Officers Local #471 v. Chatham County, 232 Ga. App. 507 (1998).

12. See Jonesboro Area Athletic Association, Inc. v. Dickson, 227 Ga. 513 (1971).

13. See City of Atlanta v. Brinderson Corp., 799 F.2d 1541 (11th Cir. 1986) (prohibition does not apply to construction contracts that typically extend beyond the term of the officer entering into the contract on behalf of the local government).

14. O.C.G.A. §36-60-13(a).

15. O.C.G.A. §36-60-13(a)(1).

16. O.C.G.A. §36-60-13(a)(3).

17. O.C.G.A. §36-60-13(a)(4).

18. O.C.G.A. §36-60-15.

19. GA. CONST. art. IX, §5, ¶1; O.C.G.A. §36-60-13(e).

20. O.C.G.A. §36-60-13(f).

21. O.C.G.A. §36-60-13(g).

22. O.C.G.A. §36-60-13(h)(1)(A).

23. O.C.G.A. §36-60-13(h)(1)(B).

24. O.C.G.A. §36-60-13(h)(2).

25. O.C.G.A. §36-60-13(b)(1).

26. O.C.G.A. §36-60-13(d).

27. O.C.G.A. §36-60-21(c).

28. O.C.G.A. §36-60-15.1.

29. O.C.G.A. §36-91-1 et seq.

30. Ga. Const. art. IX, §3, ¶1.

31. Ibid.

32. Ibid.

33. Ga. Const. art. IX, §2, ¶3; O.C.G.A. §§32-4-60, 36-13-4.

34. Ga. Const. art. IX, §2, ¶3(b)(1).

35. O.C.G.A. §36-60-2.

36. O.C.G.A. §45-18-5.

37. O.C.G.A. §52-2-9(15).

38. Ga. Const. art. IX, §4, ¶4.

39. O.C.G.A. §36-73-1 et seq.

40. O.C.G.A. §36-87-2.

41. O.C.G.A. §36-91-1 et seq.; *A Guidebook to Local Government Construction Projects* (Atlanta: ACCG, 2010).

42. O.C.G.A. §36-91-2(10).

43. See O.C.G.A. §36-91-20(c).

44. O.C.G.A. §36-91-22.

45. See O.C.G.A. §§32-4-60 et seq., 36-91-22(f).

46. O.C.G.A. §36-91-22(a); Griffin Bros., Inc. v. Town of Alto, 280 Ga. App. 176 (2006).

47. O.C.G.A. §36-91-22(a).

48. O.C.G.A. §36-91-22(g).

49. See O.C.G.A. §36-91-20(c).

50. O.C.G.A. §36-91-22(e); Jacks v. City of Atlanta, 284 Ga. App. 200 (2007), *cert. denied*, 2007 Ga. LEXIS 500 (Ga. 2007) (park project not considered an emergency subject to the exception).

51. O.C.G.A. §36-91-22(b).

52. O.C.G.A. §36-91-22(d).

53. O.C.G.A. §36-91-20(b).

54. O.C.G.A. §36-91-20(b)(1).

55. O.C.G.A. §36-91-20(b)(3).

56. O.C.G.A. §36-91-20(b)(2).

57. Dyer v. Erwin, 106 Ga. 845 (1899).

58. Bird v. Franklin, 151 Ga. 4 (1921).

59. Ibid.

60. Pilcher v. English, 133 Ga. 496 (1909).

61. Manley Building Co. v. Newton, 114 Ga. 245 (1901); Glynn County v. Teal, 256 Ga. 174 (1986).

62. O.C.G.A. §36-91-20(f).

63. See also Ruby-Collins, Inc. v. Cobb County, 237 Ga. App. 517 (1999).

64. See O.C.G.A. §§36-91-2(3), 36-91-2(4), 36-91-20(c), 36-91-21(b), 36-91-21(c).

65. O.C.G.A. §36-91-50(b).

66. O.C.G.A. §36-91-21(b)(4).

67. See O.C.G.A. §36-91-21(c)(2).

68. See O.C.G.A. §36-91-50(c).

69. O.C.G.A. §§36-91-50(a), 36-91-70, 36-91-90.

70. McArthur Elec., Inc. v. Cobb County School District, 281 Ga. 773 (2007).

71. O.C.G.A. §36-91-91; see Sims Crane Service, Inc. v. Reliance Insurance Company, 514 F.Supp 1033 (S.D. Ga. 1981), *aff'd*, 667 F.2d 30 (11th Cir. 1982).

72. O.C.G.A. §36-91-21(e).

73. Bird v. Franklin, 151 Ga. 4 (1921).

74. O.C.G.A. §§36-91-21(a), 36-91-21(g).

75. O.C.G.A. §36-91-21(f).

76. O.C.G.A. §36-91-21(a).

77. O.C.G.A. §32-4-63(1).

78. O.C.G.A. §32-4-63(2).

79. O.C.G.A. §32-4-63(3).

80. O.C.G.A. §32-4-63(5).

81. O.C.G.A. §32-4-63(6).

82. O.C.G.A. §32-4-65(a).

83. Ibid.

84. O.C.G.A. §§32-4-65(b), 32-4-69(3).

85. O.C.G.A. §32-4-68.

86. Ibid.

87. O.C.G.A. §32-4-61.

88. O.C.G.A. §32-4-72.

89. O.C.G.A. §32-4-67(a).

90. O.C.G.A. §32-4-72.

91. O.C.G.A. §32-4-67(b).

92. Ibid.

93. Ibid.

94. O.C.G.A. §32-4-69(1).

95. O.C.G.A. §32-4-69(2).

96. O.C.G.A. §32-4-71(a).

97. O.C.G.A. §32-4-70.

98. O.C.G.A. §32-4-71(b).

99. O.C.G.A. §32-4-69(3).

100. O.C.G.A. §§32-4-73, 36-91-21(e).

101. O.C.G.A. §36-60-21.

102. O.C.G.A. §32-9-11(b).

103. Ibid.

104. O.C.G.A. §32-9-11.

105. An index of current local legislation for a particular county may be found in Volume 42 of O.C.G.A. The actual text may be found in Georgia Laws, which is published after each session of the General Assembly.

106. For examples of counties with this requirement, see Ga. Laws 1988, 4877; 1984, 5318; 1983, 4757; 1980, 3809.

107. For examples of counties with this requirement, see Ga. Laws 1988, 4633; 1983, 4757.

108. For examples of counties with these requirements, see Ga. Laws 1992, 7064; 1988, 4877; 1988, 4633.

109. For examples of counties with this requirement, see Ga. Laws 1986, 5668; 1982, 5166.

110. For examples of counties with this requirement, see Ga. Laws 1986, 5668.

111. O.C.G.A. §§36-84-1(b), 50-5-61.

112. O.C.G.A. §36-84-1(c).

113. O.C.G.A. §50-5-81.

114. O.C.G.A. §50-16-81. Counties may enter into certain purchasing agreements with other governments without public advertising for bids, posting notices of expenditures, inviting or receiving competitive bids, or requiring delivery of procedures before payment. This statute does not affect contracting or purchasing requirements set out in general or special laws concerning other types of purchases.

115. O.C.G.A. §§50-5-100–50-5-103, 50-5-143.

116. O.C.G.A. §42-10-4(12).

117. Ga. Const. art. IX, §3, ¶1.

118. O.C.G.A. §36-1-14(a); Dalton Rock Product Company v. Fannin County, 136 Ga. App. 649 (1975).

119. O.C.G.A. §36-1-14(b).

120. O.C.G.A. §16-10-6.

121. Ibid.

122. Ibid.; Defoor v. State, 233 Ga. 190 (1974).

123. O.C.G.A. §36-9-3(a)(1).

124. Ibid.

125. Ibid.

126. O.C.G.A. §36-9-3(a)(2)(A).

127. O.C.G.A. §36-9-3(a)(2)(D).

128. Ibid.

129. O.C.G.A. §36-9-3(h).

130. O.C.G.A. §36-9-3(c).

131. O.C.G.A. §36-9-3(e).
132. Ibid.
133. O.C.G.A. §36-9-3(f).
134. O.C.G.A. §36-9-3(g).
135. O.C.G.A. §36-9-3(g)(5).
136. O.C.G.A. §36-9-2.
137. O.C.G.A tit. 32, ch. 7; McIntosh County v. Fisher, 242 Ga. 66 (1978).
138. O.C.G.A. §32-7-3.
139. O.C.G.A. §32-7-4(a)(1).
140. O.C.G.A. §32-7-4(a)(2).
141. Ibid.
142. O.C.G.A. §32-7-4(b)(1)(A).
143. O.C.G.A. §32-7-4(b)(1)(B).
144. Ibid.
145. O.C.G.A. §32-7-4(b)(2)(A).
146. Ibid.
147. O.C.G.A. §32-7-4(b)(2)(B).
148. O.C.G.A. §32-7-4(b)(2)(A).
149. Ibid.
150. O.C.G.A. §32-7-4(b)(3)(A).
151. O.C.G.A. §32-7-4(b)(3)(B).

9

Annaka Woodruff

Planning and Land Use

As elected officials, county commissioners have the ability to influence the landscape of Georgia in remarkable ways. While the General Assembly is empowered by the state constitution to enact laws restricting land use in order to protect and preserve natural resources and vital areas of the state,[1] most land-use decisions are made at the local level. The constitution in fact vests the power of planning and zoning in local governments. However, it is important to note that the General Assembly is empowered to enact general laws establishing procedures for the exercise of zoning power.[2] Since land-use decisions affect private property, all requests to change designated land uses (usually referred to as zoning changes) must be made by elected officials, never by staff. In short, commissioners are responsible for valuable economic, natural, and community resources within their counties, and their decisions have lasting impacts. How do we, as counties in the largest state east of the Mississippi River, plan for the use of our vast land areas, and how do we build communities that people are glad to call home?

Since 1989, with the passage of the Georgia Planning Act, every local government in Georgia has been required to complete a comprehensive plan in order to maintain its qualified local government status.[3] The act requires that each government update its comprehensive plan at least every 10 years. Throughout the 1990s, as counties and cities completed their plans, the prevailing sentiment in Georgia seemed to be "okay, now that we've completed our plan, we're done." As with any new skill or activity, the first effort was not necessarily the best. The State of Georgia needed some practice in learning how to use the plans its communities had worked so hard to create the first time.

As of 2009, most counties either were beginning the next 10-year planning process or had recently completed it. Moving into the 21st century, counties are seeing the utility of following these plans, not simply completing them. Statewide discussions about water quality and quantity, housing opportunities, transportation, job availability, and land conservation highlight the need for an agreed-upon approach to these difficult topics; county comprehensive plans offer such an approach. Long-range, comprehensive planning presents the best opportunity for creating successful communities for the future.[4]

Plans of any type, whether business, governmental, or personal, ask and answer three basic questions:

1. What do you have? (inventory and assessment)
2. What do you want to have? (needs and goals)
3. What are you willing to do to get it? (implementation strategy)

While Georgia's comprehensive plans provide guidance for a variety of community topics, including economic development and regional cooperation, by and large these plans can be roadmaps for the physical development of a community—how the community uses and shapes the land. "Land use" refers to any decisions made about the land and zoning regulations. Behind the concept of planning and land use is the assumption that decisions regarding a jurisdiction's land are made in accordance with an adopted comprehensive plan. By employing a comprehensive plan, a county commission makes decisions about the shape and form of the land under its jurisdiction and directly affects the design of the county. In short, the commission considers what the county will look like, both now and in the future.

Georgia is changing rapidly—growing in population overall—but some communities and populations in the state are in decline. Leaders who have a clear vision for the future are necessary to guide communities through these tough economic times. Regardless of the population, land mass, and economic makeup of each of Georgia's 159 counties, sound planning (followed by decisions based upon that planning) can make a positive difference in each community and collectively in the entire state.

PLANNING

Purpose and Intent of the Comprehensive Plan

The purpose of the local planning requirements promulgated by the Department of Community Affairs (DCA) is to "provide a framework for preparation of local comprehensive plans that will . . . provide a guide to everyday decision-making for use by local government officials and other community leaders."[5] Decision making is difficult at the best of times, even more so when it is done in the public eye. The plan represents the voice of the citizens of the community—what they want the community to look like, what they cherish, what they would like to change, what they consider to be the prevailing issues and opportunities in the community. As such, the comprehensive plan can and should act as a guide for commissioners when making decisions for the public good.

The physical size of the comprehensive plan for a community can be daunting—in some cases amounting to several hundred pages of material. However, once the plan is explored, it is relatively easy to find the important information that can help a board of commissioners make reasonable, fair, and predictable decisions about the future of a community.

Components of the Comprehensive Plan

The Community Agenda

In order for a comprehensive plan to comply with local planning requirements, it must include three components: (1) a community assessment, (2) a community participation program, and (3) a community agenda. The assessment and community participation program, also commonly referred to as the public participation program, must be submitted to DCA prior to the adoption of the community agenda. The community agenda is what is commonly known as the plan, or the comprehensive plan. The local planning requirements state that the community agenda must include the following three major components:

1. a community vision for the future physical development of the community, expressed in the form of a map indicating unique character areas, each with its own strategy for guiding future development patterns;

2. a list of issues and opportunities identified by the community for further action; and

3. an implementation program for achieving the community's vision for the future and addressing the identified issues and opportunities.[6]

The Future Development Map

The foundation of the agenda is the future development map (often called a character area map). This map should identify the areas of the county that provide character in whatever form the community has deemed important. There are no "right" amounts or types of character areas. Depending on the size, population, developed areas, natural characteristics, and employment centers of a community, a map may show as few as 5 or as many as 20 different character areas.

If the future development map for a county appropriately identifies the unique individual characteristics of the county in a way that makes sense to the board of commissioners and the citizens, then it is a "good" map. When the board of commissioners uses the map to make decisions about land use, community facilities, or capital improvements, the comprehensive plan is being put to its best possible use.[7]

The Defining Narrative

The descriptions of the character areas on a future development map are part of the defining narrative. Local planning requirements state that these descriptions must include the following:[8]

- Written descriptions, pictures, and/or illustrations that make it clear what types, forms, styles, and patterns of development are to be encouraged in the area

- List of specific land uses or (if appropriate for the jurisdiction) zoning categories to be allowed in the area

- List of the quality community objectives that will be pursued in the area

- Identification of implementation measures to achieve desired development patterns for the area

Simply put, the defining narrative should describe clearly what kind of development a county expects—and will approve—in the various character areas. Whitfield County in northwest Georgia provides an excellent example of a defining narrative. The community has defined "rural crossroads" as unique to its rural mountain character:

> The Rural Crossroads character area . . . [is] intended to serve adjacent residential or agricultural areas with limited goods and services concentrated around an intersection rather than spread out in a linear fashion along a roadway. Small scale retail uses, public facilities such as churches, fire stations, post offices and libraries, and agricultural support businesses such as commercial nurseries, farm implement sales and supply stores, farmer's markets and feed and seed stores are appropriate uses in this character area.

Also discussed in the defining narrative are development patterns, primary land uses, and implementation strategies. A development pattern should seek to do the following:

- Protect rural character

- Provide small-scale commercial opportunities for meeting local needs

- Cluster buildings at an area's center

- Maintain open space surrounding the center

- Encourage compatible architectural styles (rather than "franchise" or "corporate" architectural styles) that maintain the regional rural character

- Limit clearing and grading

- Reduce access points along the highway

- Connect to greenways or trail systems wherever possible

Primary land uses include neighborhood or rural commercial uses, civic or institutional uses, and passive or active parks. In terms of implementation strategies, a community may adopt a rural crossroads zoning overlay district that includes minimum standards for commercial building and site design. Another strategy would be to widen roadways only when absolutely necessary.[9]

The description for each character area is followed by implementation measures, which are the means by which a community will achieve its vision (that is, the best-case scenario for the area). In the Whitfield County plan, the community has identified the need to adopt an overlay code to protect its rural crossroads and a policy that it will widen rural roadways only when absolutely necessary. A commitment to those adopted measures will help Whitfield County maintain its mountain beauty in the coming years.

Issues and Opportunities

As a community is developing its plan, elected officials have opportunities to hear from citizens regarding what they think are the biggest challenges facing the community and the biggest opportunities in the future. Along with public opinion, the available data about a community help shape the comprehensive plan. The data will show (among other things)

- whether the community is growing, remaining stable, or losing population;

- the types of jobs that are available in the community;

- the types and levels of education of most citizens in the community; and

- the types of natural resources in the community and their location.

The issues and opportunities in the comprehensive plan are those identified by community members and leaders as being the most important to address over the next 10 years. Accordingly, the local planning requirements state that each of these issues or opportunities must be followed up with corresponding measures in the implementation program.[10]

The Implementation Program

A comprehensive plan is, most of all, a visionary document that helps answer the question, "What do we want our community to be like in 20 years?" In order to achieve that goal, each community will have to take smaller steps over the years that will eventually result in fulfillment of that vision. The short-term work plan should outline those steps in five-year increments. The short-term work plan should consist of actions or activities that will improve or enhance the community. The long-term measures or policies are those items that may be ongoing or are based on the core values of the community. For instance, a community that values transportation options may have a stated policy of providing walking and biking options along with all road improvements. Similarly, a community that values an agricultural lifestyle may choose a policy of maintaining very large land parcels for agricultural use.[11]

Quality Community Objectives

In 1999, the Board of DCA adopted quality community objectives as statements of the development patterns and options that will help Georgia preserve its unique cultural, natural, and historic resources while looking to the future and developing to its fullest potential. The local planning requirements state that each local government should determine which of these objectives are important to pursue in each character area identified on the future development map:

(a) Regional Identity Objective. Regions should promote and preserve an "identity," defined in terms of traditional regional architecture, common economic linkages that bind the region together, or other shared characteristics.

(b) Growth Preparedness Objective. Each community should identify and put in place the prerequisites for the type of growth it seeks to achieve. These may include housing and infrastructure (roads, water, sewer, and telecommunications) to support new growth, appropriate training of the workforce, ordinances to direct growth as desired, or leadership capable of responding to growth opportunities.

(c) Appropriate Businesses Objective. The businesses and industries encouraged to develop or expand in a community should be suitable for the community in terms of job skills required, linkages to other economic activities in the community, impact on the resources of the area, and future prospects for expansion and creation of higher-skill job opportunities.

(d) Educational Opportunities Objective. Educational and training opportunities should be readily available in each community in order to permit community residents to improve their job skills, adapt to technological advances, or pursue entrepreneurial ambitions.

(e) Employment Options Objective. A range of job types should be provided in each community to meet the diverse needs of the local workforce.

(f) Heritage Preservation Objective. The traditional character of the community should be maintained through preserving and revitalizing historic areas of the community, encouraging new development that is compatible with the traditional features of the community, and protecting other scenic or natural features that are important to defining the community's character.

(g) Open Space Preservation Objective. New development should be designed to minimize the amount of land consumed, and open space should be set aside from development for use as public parks or as greenbelts or wildlife corridors.

(h) Environmental Protection Objective. Air quality and environmentally sensitive areas should be protected from negative impacts of development. Environmentally sensitive areas deserve special protection, particularly when they are important for maintaining traditional character or quality of life of the community or region. Whenever possible, the natural terrain, drainage, and vegetation of an area should be preserved.

(i) Regional Cooperation Objective. Regional cooperation should be encouraged in setting priorities, identifying shared needs, and finding collaborative solutions, particularly where it is critical to the success of a venture, such as protection of shared natural resources.

(j) Transportation Alternatives Objective. Alternatives to transportation by automobile, including mass transit, bicycle routes, and pedestrian facilities, should be made available in each community. Greater use of alternative transportation should be encouraged.

(k) Regional Solutions Objective. Regional solutions to needs shared by more than one local jurisdiction are preferable to separate local approaches, particularly where this will result in greater efficiency and less cost to the taxpayer.

(l) Housing Opportunities Objective. Quality housing and a range of housing size, cost, and density should be provided in each community in order to make it possible for all who work in the community to also live in the community.

(m) Traditional Neighborhood Objective. Traditional neighborhood development patterns should be encouraged, including use of more human scale development, mixing of uses within easy walking distance of one another, and facilitating pedestrian activity.

(n) Infill Development Objective. Communities should maximize the use of existing infrastructure and minimize the con-

version of undeveloped land at the urban periphery by encouraging development or redevelopment of sites closer to the
downtown or traditional urban core of the community.

(o) Sense-of-Place Objective. Traditional downtown areas
should be maintained as the focal point of the community, or
for newer areas where this is not possible, the development of
activity centers that serve as community focal points should
be encouraged. These community focal points should be attractive, mixed-use, pedestrian friendly places where people
choose to gather for shopping, dining, socializing, and entertainment.[12]

The Plan Adoption Process and Qualified Local Government Status

The Georgia Planning Act requires that each local government (county
and city) adopt a comprehensive plan in order to maintain its qualified
local government status. Although there is no state-imposed penalty for
not completing and adopting a comprehensive plan according to the
schedule created by DCA, local governments that do not attain qualified
local government status are not eligible for state-administered grants,
loans, and some permits.

Detailed procedures for submitting a plan for review and adoption
by a county board of commissioners are available on the DCA Web
site.[13] The process by which a government may achieve qualified local
government status is as follows:

1. The plan preparer completes a community assessment and community participation plan.

2. After review of the documents, including a public hearing, the
   board of commissioners passes a transmittal resolution to send
   these documents to its regional commission for review.

3. The regional commission and DCA review and comment on the
   assessment and participation program.

4. The board of commissioners publicizes the availability of the assessment and participation program.

5. The plan preparer gathers community input and creates the community agenda.

6. The board of commissioners holds a public hearing prior to passing a transmittal resolution to send the community agenda to the regional commission for review.

7. The regional commission and DCA review and comment on the community agenda.

8. The board of commissioners allows the public 60 days from the public hearing to comment on the plan.

9. Upon receiving comments from the public, the regional commission, and DCA, the board of commissioners authorizes the plan preparer to make any necessary changes.

10. The board of commissioners adopts the comprehensive plan by resolution and notifies the regional commission of the date on which the plan is adopted.

11. Upon receipt of notification of adoption, DCA extends the government's qualified local government status.[14]

Implementing the Plan

Every decision a county commission makes is a step toward implementing the plan—or not. Did the commission consider the description of the character of the area before rezoning a parcel of property? Is its vote consistent with that description? Did the commission look at the future development map? Did it make a decision consistent with the measures outlined there? If the answers to these questions are yes, the commission has helped implement the plan. Conversely, when a commission votes inconsistently with its plan, it becomes increasingly difficult to show that the plan is the guide for community decisions.

The following questions can guide the implementation of a county's comprehensive plan:

- Will this decision further the vision for the character of the area described in the comprehensive plan?

- Is this decision consistent with the future development map?

- Is this decision consistent with a stated policy in the comprehensive plan?

- Does this decision address an issue or opportunity stated in the comprehensive plan?

- Does this decision address an item in the short-term work plan?

LAND USE

The term land use means just that: how a community uses the land within its jurisdiction. Is it used for agricultural or housing purposes? For industry or retail? For conservation? In the mid-20th century, when Georgia had a population of about a million people, land seemed limitless. Now, as Georgia's population approaches 10 million people, discussions about how to use the land have taken on a more urgent tone.

As previously noted, in Georgia most land-use decisions are made by local governments—either county boards of commissioners or city councils. With increasing populations and the same amount of natural resources within the state, these decisions are becoming more and more important each year. Local elected officials have enormous responsibility for the health, vitality, and appearance of Georgia's landscape and natural resources. Making good decisions about available resources may not be simple, but it is possible. Following the agreed-upon comprehensive plan can help take some of the emotion out of land-use decisions and make those decisions more predictable and fair. Decisions by boards of commissioners can be critical in determining the long-term economic and environmental health of not only a community but also the state.

Infrastructure

Infrastructure decisions at the county level concern both the type and location of infrastructure. The most common infrastructure decisions made by boards of commissioners pertain to the following:

- Roads and bridges
- Water
- Sewer
- Storm water facilities
- Parks and recreation facilities
- Police, fire, and emergency medical services facilities
- Libraries
- Schools

Boards of commissioners do not decide the location of schools, but it is important that commissioners make an effort to coordinate school location decisions with local boards of education. Poorly sited schools can create safety, transportation, and other land-use problems that could otherwise be avoided by cooperation.

The placement of public facilities and investments directly affects land use and to a large extent determines the location of future private development in a community. Land adjacent to public infrastructure is more easily developed and likely to be converted from agriculture, conservation, or another "green" use to a more intensive use when public facilities become available. For this reason, boards of commissioners should be careful to avoid environmentally sensitive areas when choosing the location of water, sewer, and road facilities.

Building libraries and public safety facilities (especially fire stations and police precincts) invites nearby residential development. Consulting the comprehensive plan to identify areas that are most receptive to development—and avoiding those areas that cannot support development—helps ensure the long-term viability of the community.

Zoning and Sprawl

Zoning is the primary regulatory method used by local governments to influence, guide, and control development as they carry out their plans for physical and economic growth. Zoning codes are among the "police powers" granted to county boards of commissioners. The administration of these codes is governed by the Georgia Zoning Procedures Act.[15] Failure to observe the procedural requirements in the act may render a zoning ordinance or zoning decision void.[16]

A zoning ordinance consists of (1) a map that divides a jurisdiction into various districts for particular classes of residential, commercial, industrial, and other uses and (2) a written ordinance that establishes the conditions under which land may be developed and used for particular purposes. A zoning ordinance specifies what types of development may take place in each zoning district of the jurisdiction. It stipulates the allowable size and height of structures and sets forth the requirements for lot size, setbacks, street parking, and other related considerations. A zoning ordinance is not a comprehensive plan or a land-use plan, but it can be used to implement such plans by controlling how land is used.

Most elected officials and local government staff recognize and understand what sprawl means in terms of land development, even without a formal definition. Most people would agree that sprawl is, at the very least, unattractive and, at worst, harmful to the natural environment. Zoning codes and sprawl are interconnected. Most local zoning plans are meant to separate different types of property uses. Residential uses may be allowed in one area of a community, while retail and commercial uses are assigned another area. The original intent of zoning codes was to put space between the community and more noxious uses, like heavy industrial uses or landfills. Throughout the 20th century, most states continued to require separation of uses, resulting in communities in which transportation is dominated by the private automobile. Making room for numerous vehicles increased the sprawling landscape, as more parking spaces were required for more vehicles and wider streets were needed in order to accommodate traffic.

Between 1982 and 1997, the amount of urbanized land used for development in the United States increased by 45 percent (from 51 million acres to 76 million acres), and the population grew by 17 percent.[17] Most observers believe that this type of land conversion is unsustainable, which makes the decisions made by boards of commissioners even more pressing in the 21st century. Some zoning code provisions that promote sprawl have to do with the following:

- Parking requirements

- Street connectivity requirements

- Building setbacks (that is, how far away buildings are required to be from each other and the road)

- Building height limitations

- Minimum lot sizes in excess of half an acre in all residential and commercial areas

The DCA Office of Planning and Quality Growth provides a variety of Web-based resources as well as technical assistance for local governments that are interested in changing their zoning codes in order to reduce sprawl.[18]

In addition to the zoning code in a community, decisions concerning rezoning requests have enormous influence on sprawl. When a commission votes to rezone property in order to build houses far away from a town center or a community resource, it is creating sprawl. Such development necessitates roads, public safety coverage, schools, and places for residents to buy goods and services. Over time, these resources creep out toward the housing areas, generally along a single roadway, creating a linear development pattern that devours land formerly used for agriculture, conservation, and other green purposes. This kind of creep tends to weaken the viability of existing town centers, resulting in dead shopping centers, historic downtowns with no businesses, and gaps in productivity throughout the community.

By bearing in mind the stated visions that go along with a community's future development map, commissions can make decisions that may help reduce the spread of sprawl. A comprehensive plan provides commissioners with a foundation on which to consider the best interests of not only the community but also property owners when making decisions about rezoning requests.

The Planning Commission

A planning commission is an advisory board appointed by the board of commissioners. If it is a joint city-county planning commission, some members are appointed by the county governing authority; others, by the mayor and council. The planning commission's mission is to plan for the county's future, looking beyond short-term solutions, the technical views of county staff and department heads, and the particular concerns of local special interest groups. Members of the planning commission should have no actual, or even potential, conflicts of interest. They should be encouraged to attend training programs sponsored by universities, professional associations, and state and regional agencies.

Ordinarily, a planning commission interprets the zoning ordinance and amendments and makes recommendations to the board of commissioners regarding rezoning requests. The planning commission may act as a design review board, meaning that members will review and make recommendations concerning site and building design proposals, particularly for commercial development. The commission may receive technical assistance from a professional staff, department heads, and consultants in performing these functions. If the county does not have a planning commission, the board of commissioners usually assumes planning commission functions.

Transfer of Development Rights

Pursuant to state law, the governing body of any county may establish by ordinance procedures, methods, and standards for the transfer of development rights (TDR) for property within its jurisdiction in order to conserve and promote the public health, safety, and general welfare. Under a TDR program, the development rights from a naturally or historically significant parcel of land, called the sending property, are separated from the land and are sold for higher-density use on a tract more suitable for development, called the receiving property. A permanent conservation easement is placed on the sending property, and the owner of the sending property is compensated for the loss of development rights by the owner of the receiving property. The owner of the receiving property then gains a higher-density usage of the property than is allowable under the zoning ordinance of the county. TDR can help steer development toward areas where growth is more desirable and can help communities preserve green space without having to pay for land. Any proposed transfer of development rights shall be subject to the approval and consent of the property owners of both the sending and receiving property. Prior to the enactment of the ordinance as required in state law, the governing authority shall provide for a public hearing on the proposed ordinance.[19]

Regional Planning and Land Use

Georgia has a great number and variety of natural, historic, cultural, and archaeological resources. Many of these resources do not adhere to formal jurisdictional lines but rather straddle cities, counties, and entire regions. Recognizing the importance of these resources to the state, Georgia has adopted a regional approach to managing, protecting, and enhancing these assets.

Regionally Important Resources

A regionally important resource is a natural or historic resource that is of sufficient size or importance to warrant special consideration by the local governments that have jurisdiction over the resource. The Georgia Planning Act of 1989 (the same law that requires comprehensive planning by local governments) authorizes DCA to establish procedures for identifying regionally important resources statewide. DCA has established rules for use by the regional commissions in preparing a regional resource plan that systematically identifies the regionally important resources in each region and recommends best practices for use in managing these important resources.[20]

As of July 1, 2009, each regional commission is required to prepare a regionally important resources map and an accompanying resource management plan. Georgia's diverse regions range from the Appalachian Mountains to the Coastal Plain. The state's natural resources include floodplains, marshlands, steep slopes, and rivers and streams. Its historic resources include historic properties as well as archaeological and cultural resources.

Each regional commission has a resource nomination process. With regional involvement, a regional commission determines a final list of regionally important resources that form the foundation of the regional resource plan. The state's goal is to create a green infrastructure net-work among these regionally important resources in order to preserve and enhance those elements that Georgians deem important. A green infrastructure network is a strategically planned and managed network of wilderness areas, parks, greenways, conservation easements, and working lands with conservation value that benefits wildlife and people, supports native species, maintains natural ecological processes, sustains air and water resources, links urban settings to rural ones, and contributes to the health and quality of life of the communities and citizens sharing this network. The network should encompass a wide range of elements, including natural areas such as wetlands, woodlands, waterways, and wildlife habitat; public and private conservation lands such as nature preserves, wildlife corridors, greenways, and parks; and public and private working lands of conservation value such as forests, farms, and ranches. It should also incorporate outdoor recreation and trail networks.[21]

Regional Planning

Much like a comprehensive plan for a local government, the regional plan prepared by each regional commission should guide decisions for the region. The regional agenda (the finished product) includes the region's vision for the future as well as the strategy for realizing this vision. Because the regional agenda provides guidance for future decision making about the region, it must be prepared with adequate input from stakeholders and the general public. The regional agenda must include

- a regional vision for the future development of the region,

- a list of regional issues and opportunities for further action, and

- an implementation program for achieving the regional vision and addressing regional issues and opportunities.

The implementation program must include the following:

- Guiding principles to be followed by all actors in making decisions affecting the future of the region

- Performance standards that establish minimum and exceptional levels of performance expected of all actors in implementing the recommendations of the plan

- A list of strategies that may be implemented by any actors in the region to assist with achieving the regional vision or addressing regional issues and opportunities

- A regional work program listing the responsibilities of the regional commission for implementing the plan

- An evaluation and monitoring plan to ensure that the regional plan is accomplishing the desired results[22]

Developments of Regional Impact

Developments of regional impact are large-scale developments that are likely to have regional effects beyond the local government jurisdiction in which they are located. The Georgia Planning Act of 1989 authorized DCA to establish procedures for review of these large-scale projects. These procedures are designed to improve communication between affected governments and provide a means of revealing and assessing potential impacts of large-scale developments before conflicts relating to them arise. At the same time, local government autonomy is preserved since the host government maintains the authority to make the final decision on whether a proposed development will go forward.

Population and Development Thresholds

Thresholds are used to determine whether a proposed development qualifies as a development of regional impact. The thresholds vary by type of development and the population category of the county in which the proposed development will take place. Various categories of development, each with separate thresholds, include office, commercial, hospitals, housing, industrial, hotels, mixed use, airports, recreation, postsecondary schools, waste disposal, quarries and asphalt plants, wastewater treatment, and petroleum storage.

Because communities across the state have a wide range of population and development levels, two tiers, or population categories (metropolitan areas and nonmetropolitan areas), have been established. Thresholds vary for each because a development in a region with low levels of population and development is likely to have a greater relative impact than it would in an area with higher levels of population and development.

Local Government Role

The local government role related to developments of regional impact involves the following:

- Identifying potential developments of regional impact as part of the local development review process (examples of activities triggering the process include rezonings and issuance of development permits or building permits)

- Notifying the regional commission of all potential developments of regional impact for intergovernmental review

- Taking the findings of the regional commission into account when making a decision to approve, approve with conditions, or deny a proposed development of regional impact[23]

SOURCES OF HELP

Most local elected officials play a variety of roles in the community, and most must juggle business and family responsibilities as well. In order to help officials with planning and land-use decisions, the State of Georgia provides a variety of resources, including individual technical assistance and Web-based information. Elected officials should also look to local staff resources. Even if a county does not have a professional planner, other staff members may be able to provide information or insight regarding the matter at hand. Of course, in any situation involving legal matters, the county attorney should be consulted.

Several public agencies and nonprofit organizations are dedicated to assisting local governments in Georgia, including the following:

- Regional commissions provide a wide variety of assistance to local governments in preparing and implementing comprehensive plans and are often the first place to call for planning help.

- Staff at the DCA Office of Planning and Quality Growth—the state agency responsible for implementing the Georgia Planning Act—can help local governments with questions to do with planning, land use, and plan implementation.

- The Association County Commissioners of Georgia serves as the consensus-building, training, and legislative organization for all 159 county governments in the state.

- The University of Georgia's Carl Vinson Institute of Government provides education, assistance, research, policy analysis, and publications to assist public officials in serving citizens in Georgia and throughout the world.

- The Fanning Institute at the University of Georgia works with communities of all types, within and outside of Georgia, and provides customized approaches to developing skilled community leaders, creating vibrant communities, and promoting prosperous economies.

- The Georgia Institute of Technology Center for Quality Growth and Regional Development produces, disseminates, and helps implement new ideas and technologies that improve the theory and practice of quality growth.

- The Georgia Planning Association encourages, promotes, and assists physical, economic, and human resources planning within the state.

- The Georgia Conservancy advocates for the protection of the state's natural environment. Through its focus on clean air and water, land conservation, coastal protection, growth management, and education, the Georgia Conservancy works to develop solutions to protect Georgia's environment and promote the stewardship of the state's vital natural resources.

SUMMARY

The 21st century will be a time of great change for Georgia. Demographics are shifting, and the population continues to increase. In addition, the economy of Georgia—like that of other states—is affected by the national and international economies. It may seem that the decisions made in county commission chambers have little effect on the state, but when taken together, they have great impact.

Counties may have a more difficult job than cities when developing or redeveloping portions of their communities. Usually, there is no "downtown core" from which to start or maintain development. Builders and developers generally deal with one parcel at a time rather than tackling an entire community at once. Commissioners must also consider the effect their decisions concerning the built environment will have on the natural environment. Water quality, air quality, soil quality, and natural terrain are all affected by development decisions. Commissioners have the opportunity to consider the overall look and feel of a community when making land-use decisions. By availing themselves of all the available resources prior to formulating lasting decisions, local elected officials can help shape Georgia in positive ways.

NOTES

1. GA. CONST. art. III, §6, ¶(a)(1).
2. GA. CONST. art. IX, §2, ¶4; OFFICIAL CODE OF GEORGIA ANNOTATED (O.C.G.A) §§36-66-1 et seq., 36-67-1 et seq.

3. O.C.G.A. tit. 36, ch. 70, art. 1; §12-2-8; tit. 50, ch. 8, arts. 1, 2.

4. Herbert H. Smith, *The Citizens' Guide to Planning* (Chicago: Planners Press, 1993).

5. Official Compilation Rules and Regulations of the State of Georgia (Ga. Comp. R. & Regs.) ch. 110-12-1-.01.

6. Ga. Comp. R. & Regs. ch. 110-12-1-.05.

7. Ga. Comp. R. & Regs. ch. 110-12-1-.05(2)(a)(ii).

8. Ga. Comp. R. & Regs. ch. 110-12-1-.05(2)(a)(iii).

9. Whitfield County, Board of Commissioners, *Whitfield County Comprehensive Plan 2008–2018* (Dalton, GA: Whitfield County, Board of Commissioners, 2008), 2–10.

10. Ga. Comp. R. & Regs. ch. 110-12-1-.05(2)(b).

11. Ga. Comp. R. & Regs. ch. 110-12-1-.05(2)(c).

12. Ga. Comp. R. & Regs. ch. 110-12-1-.06(3).

13. Department of Community Affairs, Standards and Procedures for Local Comprehensive Planning, Local Planning Requirements. www.dca.state.ga.us/development/PlanningQualityGrowth/programs/downloads/MinimumStandardsAdopted.pdf. Accessed May 6, 2010.

14. Ga. Comp. R. & Regs. ch. 110-12-1-.08.

15. O.C.G.A. tit. 36, ch. 66.

16. McClure v. Davidson, 258 Ga. 706 (1988); Tilley Properties v. Bartow County, 261 Ga. 153 (1991).

17. Peter Calthorpe and William Fulton, *The Regional City: Planning for the End of Sprawl* (Washington, DC: Island Press, 2001).

18. Department of Community Affairs, Office of Planning and Quality Growth. www.dca.state.ga.us/development/PlanningQualityGrowth/index.asp. Accessed May 6, 2010.

19. O.C.G.A. tit. 36, ch. 66A. See O.C.G.A. §36-66A-1 for definitions.

20. Department of Community Affairs, Regionally Important Resources, Program Description. www.dca.state.ga.us/development/PlanningQualityGrowth/programs/rir.asp. Accessed May 6, 2010.

21. Ga. Comp. R. & Regs. ch. 110-12-4.

22. Ga. Comp. R. & Regs. ch. 110-12-6.

23. Department of Community Affairs, Developments of Regional Impact. www.dca.state.ga.us/development/PlanningQualityGrowth/programs/regionalimpact.asp. Accessed May 6, 2010.

10

Don Christy, Rob McDowell, and Margaret Myszewski

Environmental Management

All levels of government play a vital role in environmental management. The federal government's role generally includes funding research and development activities; establishing minimum national standards; addressing interstate and international issues; providing technical assistance; responding to emergency situations; assuring compliance with federal requirements/enforcement; overseeing implementation of delegated federal programs; and providing funds for program implementation and other purposes. State governments are mostly responsible for day-to-day implementation of federal environmental protection programs, which includes planning; setting standards; issuing permits; monitoring resources (air, water, and other resources); enforcing state laws; providing compliance assistance and training; administering funding (grant and loan) programs; collecting and analyzing data and information; and responding to emergencies.

Local governments often find themselves in a unique situation. As providers of public services, their activities are subject to federal and state environmental requirements. However, in the exercise of their governmental functions, they assume the role of regulator. In many cases, they develop and implement building, fire, health, and safety codes in addition to carrying out delegated state programs, such as erosion and sediment control. Local governments also design, construct, operate, and maintain environmental facilities; finance infrastructure; respond to emergencies; exercise land-use planning and zoning authority; and are required to coordinate service delivery.

Georgia is a state with abundant and diverse natural resources and a temperate climate. Air, land, and water resources support a wide variety of uses, from providing a strong economy to offering recreational opportunities to affording citizens a good quality of life. As a result of these resources and other factors, some areas of Georgia have experienced phenomenal population growth and industrial and commercial development over the past few decades. Georgia agriculture, the backbone of many rural economies, remains strong and continues to prosper. Many local governments look to growth and development in order to provide jobs, tax revenue, and retail business opportunities, thus allowing communities to improve the quality of life for their citizens. However, this growth and prosperity also have affected the state's air, water, and land. In order to address these impacts, state and local leaders must take a thoughtful and comprehensive approach. It is anticipated that Georgia's population growth and economic expansion will continue, further increasing water and energy demands, conversion of land, development of coastal areas, and waste generation. County officials will be called upon to help meet these needs and minimize adverse impacts on their communities.

Local government officials truly are on the front lines of efforts to protect public health and the environment. County commissioners often receive calls from constituents regarding environmental concerns and nuisances, regardless of a commissioner's authority to address a situation. As a result of county operations, counties incur some environmental liabilities. In some cases, those liabilities may remain, even if facility operations or services are contracted out to other parties. For these reasons, county officials should be aware of environmental requirements associated with governmental operations.

This chapter provides an overview of selected federal and state environmental laws and programs, with an emphasis on those aspects establishing responsibilities and/or liabilities or providing opportunities for county governments. It also summarizes basic environmental information so that commissioners will have a better understanding of the basis for environmental requirements associated with county operations. However, it is not intended to serve as a definitive statement on means and approaches for environmental compliance or to provide legal advice. The chapter recognizes that counties are unique entities with differing characteristics, service levels, and capacities to address environmental protection issues.

The chapter addresses four themes: air quality protection, water resources management, land-use management, and other relevant issues. Each section begins with a discussion of relevant federal requirements and roles, followed by information on state-specific matters and other appropriate information. While solid waste management is an essential component of environmental management, that subject is covered in depth in Chapter 12. Readers who would like more information on specific matters may consult the *Environmental Management Handbook for Georgia Local Government Officials*.[1]

Before discussing specific federal and state environmental laws, it is important to set forth a few general principles.[2] Both federal and state governments enact environmental laws and implement environmental programs, usually dealing with activities in a single subject area (such as air pollution control, water pollution control, waste management, endangered species protection, or drinking water quality protection). Rules and regulations set forth detailed requirements that must be followed by regulated parties. Sometimes, particularly on technical matters, rules and regulations may be supplemented by more specific information in the form of guidance, procedures, and policies. Most federal environmental laws discussed in this chapter are implemented by the U.S. Environmental Protection Agency (EPA). The agency has a headquarters office in Washington, D.C., 10 regional offices, and numerous laboratories and support offices and facilities located across the country. Staff at the EPA's Atlanta regional office (Region 4) work with state and local environmental regulatory agencies and programs in eight southeastern states, including Georgia.

In enacting federal environmental laws, Congress usually includes provisions that allow appropriate state agencies to implement day-to-day program responsibilities. In order to obtain the authority to implement federal environmental programs (commonly referred to as program delegation or authorization), states must develop a program at least as strict as and consistent with the federal program. Therefore, most state environmental laws are very similar to the corresponding federal environmental laws. Federal environmental laws typically provide minimum standards that apply nationwide (federal programs provide a "floor"). States may adopt laws regarding matters not addressed by federal law or may adopt requirements that are stricter than federal requirements. For example, the Georgia General Assembly adopted the Erosion and Sedimentation Act in 1975, before the federal Clean Water Act (CWA) had any specific provisions regarding storm water management. However, the erosion and sedimentation program had to subsequently conform to the EPA's storm water management program in the early 2000s.

Although some Georgia environmental laws were enacted before the corresponding federal law, the General Assembly has usually amended those laws over the years in order to minimize the differences. In most instances, the Georgia Environmental Protection Division (EPD) of the

Department of Natural Resources (DNR) is designated as the primary state environmental regulatory agency. The state Board of Natural Resources adopts appropriate rules and regulations for implementation of those laws.

AIR QUALITY PROTECTION   *← Indoor Air Quality Radon Second-hand smoke*

Air pollutants are substances in the air that can cause harm to human health or the environment. These substances can be gases such as carbon monoxide or chemical vapors, liquid droplets, or tiny solid particles such as dust, soot, or smoke. Air pollutants come from numerous sources, including stationary sources (such as smokestacks at factories and power plants), mobile sources (such as tailpipes from on-road vehicles [cars, light-duty trucks, and motorcycles] and nonroad vehicles and equipment [construction equipment, sweepers, and mowers]), and other sources resulting from human activity (open burning or use of solvents) as well as natural sources (dust storms, volcanic activity, and wildfires). Some pollutants, such as ground-level ozone, are not directly emitted but are created by reactions between other pollutants. Since air does not respect political boundaries, wind patterns can move air pollutants locally, across state lines, and even internationally, thereby creating unique regulatory challenges.

Both federal and state laws contain requirements for air pollution control focusing on the establishment and maintenance of healthy air quality in outdoor (also referred to as ambient) air. Federal law sets minimum requirements that must be implemented nationally; however, state agencies, and in some cases local governments, carry out the day-to-day program responsibilities. State and local governments may also adopt broader or stricter requirements or regulations.

Given the broad extent of their operations, county governments may be subject to certain air pollution control requirements and programs. Applicability can vary widely.

Federal Requirements

Nationally, the Clean Air Act (CAA) establishes a framework for the prevention and control of air pollution by federal, state, and local governments.[3] Five major parts of the act are discussed in this section: ambient air quality standards, mobile source control, acid rain control, federal operating permit requirements, and stratospheric ozone protection.

National Ambient Air Quality Standards

PM Standards [handwritten]

The law requires the EPA to establish national standards for the maximum allowable levels of six common pollutants in ambient air.[4] Since 1970, the agency has established and revised national ambient air quality standards for (1) ground-level ozone (the principal component in smog), (2) particulate matter (sometimes referred to as soot), (3) sulfur dioxide, (4) nitrogen dioxide, (5) lead, and (6) carbon monoxide. Because these standards must be reviewed every five years, many standards have either recently changed or may soon change. In order to ensure compliance, a network of air quality monitors across the country checks the concentrations of these pollutants periodically.

When a standard is revised, the EPA, in coordination with state agencies, classifies geographic areas based on the most recent monitoring information as attainment (meeting the standard), unclassifiable, or nonattainment (not meeting the standard). Because local air quality must meet the standards for all pollutants, an area may be classified as attainment for one pollutant and nonattainment for another.

In nonattainment areas, states, and in some cases local governments, must adopt control measures and strategies (rules, regulations, policies, and programs) to attain and maintain a standard. The state air pollution control agency includes these measures and strategies as part of the state's federally enforceable plan for complying with the CAA, commonly referred to as the state implementation plan.[5] Among the programs included in Georgia's plan are a permitting program for major sources of air pollution and a motor vehicle inspection and maintenance program to reduce ozone in the 13-county Atlanta metropolitan nonattainment area *Expanded* [handwritten] (Cherokee, Clayton, Cobb, Coweta, DeKalb, Douglas, Fayette, Forsyth, Fulton, Gwinnett, Henry, Paulding, and Rockdale).

If a county is designated as part of a nonattainment area, it is important that local officials work with state officials to identify, develop, and implement control measures and strategies. In those areas where violations of a standard have been shown (that is, potential future nonattainment areas, since designations are made only after the revision of a standard), county officials should consider adopting reasonable voluntary control measures (such as idling reduction requirements) in order to reduce concentrations of harmful air pollutants. Early implementation of these measures may allow an area to avoid a nonattainment designation. State and federal air pollution control officials can provide assistance in identifying such voluntary control measures.

In order to help meet the ambient air quality standards, the CAA established the New Source Review[6] program to ensure that an area's air quality would not be degraded by the addition of a new or major modification of a stationary source. Stationary sources, including factories, industrial boilers, and power plants, emit air pollution primarily through smokestacks. The New Source Review program requires preconstruction review and permitting for new stationary sources and major modifications focusing on the new or modified source's potential emissions in light of the existing air quality conditions.

County operations may also be subject to CAA requirements for technology-based permit limits under the new source performance standards program. Municipal solid waste or sewage sludge incinerators and landfill gas recovery systems at municipal solid waste landfills may be subject to the new source performance standards nationally uniform emission technology standards.

The CAA also requires the EPA to control emissions of hazardous air pollutants, also referred to as air toxics.[7] The EPA is required to identify categories of industrial sources for 187 air toxics and take steps to reduce emissions from these sources. Particularly relevant to some local governments are the agency's national emission standards for hazardous air pollutants for landfills and wastewater treatment units (also referred to as publicly owned treatment works).

Climate Change and Regulation of Greenhouse Gases

Needs Updating

One area of substantial discussion is climate change and the EPA's efforts to regulate the emission of greenhouse gases. Climate change involves long-term variations in temperature, precipitation patterns, and other aspects of the earth's climate. While scientific consensus exists that climate change is occurring, particularly on a global scale, there is considerable debate regarding the extent to which human activities are contributing to this change. Human activities result in the emission of greenhouse gases, which include carbon dioxide, methane, and nitrous oxide. As the concentration of these gases in the air rises, more heat is trapped in the atmosphere. The buildup of these gases could affect agricultural and forestry production, public health (hotter days or more days with poor air quality), the availability of water resources and thus the economies of local governments.

The U.S. Supreme Court has ruled that greenhouse gases fall within the definition of air pollutant under the CAA and that the EPA may regulate their emissions from new motor vehicles. The EPA is developing regulations to control greenhouse gas emissions from new motor vehicles and other sources. Interested parties have filed lawsuits challenging many of these actions. The regulation of greenhouse gas emissions is likely to be the subject of controversy for the foreseeable future.

Mobile Source Control Program

A second major part of the CAA deals with mobile sources.[8] Efforts to reduce pollution from these sources generally focus on three areas: (1) cleaner engines, (2) cleaner fuels, and (3) education and awareness. A focus on cleaner engines has resulted in tighter emission standards and use of advanced emission control technologies (catalytic converters and particulate filters). A focus on cleaner fuels has led to the introduction and use of low-sulfur diesel fuel and reformulated gasoline as well as progress in the development of electric vehicles, biodiesel, E85 for use in flex-fueled vehicles, and conversion of gasoline-fueled vehicles to operate on compressed natural gas or propane, alcohol fuels, or electricity. *suspect this is dead* In support of these efforts, the EPA has provided significant funding to local governments and others through the National Clean Diesel Campaign (more specifically, the National Clean Diesel Program and State Clean Diesel Grant Program). The focus on education and awareness emphasizes reductions based on activities such as carpooling, teleworking, idling reduction, and other steps that individuals can take. Because of their vehicle and fleet maintenance and fueling operations, counties may participate in mobile source emission reduction programs. County commissioners may become involved in this area while considering policies for growth management, vehicle acquisitions, idling reduction, and commuting alternatives (e.g., teleworking and carpooling/vanpooling subsidies).

Acid Rain Control Program

impact of Power Plant closures & tax base?

The CAA also establishes programs to reduce acid rain by requiring lower emissions of sulfur dioxide and nitrogen oxides.[9] Typically, these programs only affect counties that operate large stationary sources such as waste combustors, sludge incinerators, and large boilers.

Federal Operating Permit Program

Federal and state laws require permits for new or major modifications to stationary sources, particularly larger (major) sources.[10] These permits, which are required before beginning construction and/or operation, include allowable levels of emissions as well as monitoring, recordkeeping, and reporting requirements. The CAA sets forth federal operating permit requirements for major sources and certain smaller sources of air pollution (often referred to as the Title V program). A specific source may require a Title V permit based upon the amount and types of air pollutants emitted. The program, which is designed to streamline regulation of air pollution, allows inclusion of all air pollution control requirements for a source in a single document and contains requirements for public participation in the permitting process. Title V also requires the imposition of a fee on regulated sources to pay for program implementation. Counties that operate incinerators, certain boilers/generation units, or other large sources may be subject to Title V requirements.

Stratospheric Ozone Protection Program

Provisions of the CAA also protect stratospheric ozone by restricting the use of ozone-depleting chemicals.[11] The manufacture of many of these chemicals has already been phased out. These requirements are applicable to local government operations involving repair and maintenance of vehicle or building air conditioning units. Unlike many other CAA programs that are enforced by state or local agencies, the EPA implements this program directly.

Application of Federal Requirements in Georgia

The Georgia Air Quality Act authorizes the adoption of air quality standards and emission limits, requires permits for stationary sources, and mandates enforcement of air quality requirements.[12] The Board of Natural Resources has adopted a range of rules to control pollution from stationary sources, restrict open burning, and implement motor vehicle inspection and maintenance programs.[13] The EPD administers and enforces the law and its associated regulations. The EPA has delegated most of its day-to-day federal air pollution control program implementation and enforcement responsibilities to the EPD and provides some funding to support those activities.

Across Georgia, air quality has historically met or exceeded federal standards for all pollutants; however, controlling ground-level ozone and particulate matter in urban and nearby areas has been challenging. Air pollution in the Atlanta metropolitan area has exceeded federal standards for ozone since the late 1970s. In 1991, the EPA listed the 13-county Atlanta region as a serious nonattainment area for the one-hour ozone standard. Because the area did not come into attainment by 1999, its classification was bumped up to a severe nonattainment area, which required the imposition of more pollution reduction requirements. In order to enhance pollution control efforts, the EPD designated 32 additional counties (Banks, Barrow, Bartow, Butts, Carroll, Chattooga,

Clarke, Dawson, Floyd, Gordon, Hall, Haralson, Heard, Jackson, Jasper, Jones, Lamar, Lumpkin, Madison, Meriwether, Monroe, Morgan, Newton, Oconee, Pickens, Pike, Polk, Putnam, Spalding, Troup, Upson, and Walton) as "contributing counties" and subjected areas in those counties to certain regulations. In 2005, the EPA redesignated Atlanta as an attainment area for the one-hour ozone standard.

Although it has met the one-hour standard, the Atlanta area continues to face challenges in meeting a new eight-hour ozone standard originally adopted in 1997. In 2004, the EPA designated 20 counties (Barrow, Bartow, Carroll, Cherokee, Clayton, Cobb, Coweta, DeKalb, Douglas, Fayette, Forsyth, Fulton, Gwinnett, Hall, Henry, Newton, Paulding, Rockdale, Spalding, and Walton Counties) as the metropolitan Atlanta marginal nonattainment area. Failing to attain this standard by 2007, the Atlanta area was bumped up to the moderate classification in 2008 and was required to attain the standard before June 15, 2010. The area again failed to attain the eight-hour ozone standard, but due to significant improvement, it was granted a one-year extension. The next evaluation in 2011 will rely on air quality–monitoring data from 2008–10.

Metropolitan Atlanta has also faced challenges in meeting the fine particulate matter ($PM_{2.5}$) standard. The EPA designated all or part of 22 counties in the region (Barrow, Bartow, Carroll, Cherokee, Clayton, Cobb, Coweta, DeKalb, Douglas, Fayette, Forsyth, Fulton, Gwinnett, Hall, a portion of Heard, Henry, Newton, Paulding, a portion of Putnam, Rockdale, Spalding, and Walton Counties) as a nonattainment area in 2005. The CAA requires that designated areas achieve the standards in no more than five years but authorizes the EPA to issue a five-year extension. The agency did not designate any additional counties following the 2006 standard revision.

In recent years, other areas of Georgia have begun addressing air quality challenges. Walker and Catoosa Counties are part of the Chattanooga area, which has faced difficulties in meeting the ozone and $PM_{2.5}$ standards. The Macon metropolitan area (Bibb and a portion of Monroe Counties) has also faced challenges with regard to ozone and fine particle pollution. Although the EPA designated a portion of Muscogee County as a nonattainment area for the lead standard in 1992 (redesignated as an attainment area in 1999), more recent concerns have arisen in meeting the ozone and fine particle standards. Other areas in Georgia that have faced and may continue to face air quality issues include a portion of Murray, Richmond, and Houston Counties (eight-hour ozone standard); Floyd, Harris, Dade, Madison, and Oconee Counties ($PM_{2.5}$ standard); and Clarke County (ozone and $PM_{2.5}$ standard). All of these counties were either proposed for a nonattainment designation or were ultimately designated as part of a nonattainment area. Counties in the Chattanooga and Macon areas took aggressive steps to reduce ozone pollution and have been redesignated as attainment areas. The agency has redesignated the portion of Murray County as an attainment area for the ozone standard and Clarke and Muscogee Counties as attainment areas for the fine particle standard.

Moving Forward

Air quality in Georgia has improved as the result of (1) operation of new pollution controls at stationary sources, particularly power plants; (2) use of cleaner fuels; (3) implementation of tighter emission standards; and (4) continued focus on reducing vehicle miles traveled through activities such as carpooling and high-occupancy vehicle lane usage. However, as some areas of Georgia continue to grow, more pollution-reducing actions will be required in order to keep pace with population increases, additional energy demands, and tightening federal standards.

The time frames for implementation of effective air pollution control programs are often lengthy. The EPA has been criticized for adopting tighter standards when programs to obtain reductions under previous standards have often just begun. The five-year standards review cycle under federal law may be too ambitious; however, the EPA will continue its best efforts to comply with the legal time frames in reviewing and revising standards if necessary.

Georgia will continue to face deadlines for meeting federal air quality requirements. As standards are revised, it is incumbent upon local governments to implement policies and programs (some at little or no cost) in order to reduce the odds of being designated a nonattainment area. While such a designation often does not produce the perceived disastrous economic consequences, as evidenced by the continued growth in the Atlanta metropolitan area, it is designed to force actions to reduce air pollution that may be better achieved voluntarily.

WATER RESOURCES MANAGEMENT

Like air, water is a life-sustaining resource that is essential to the survival of humans and all other life on earth. Water also has significant economic value to businesses and industries that use it as part of their processes. It can be used directly to generate power or as coolant, thereby allowing other technologies to produce power. Water is vital in agricultural and forestry operations, producing the food and fiber that is used daily.

Water and waterways continue to play important roles in commerce and recreational uses and in supporting ecological needs, including providing an aquatic habitat for plants and animals.

Given the extensive need for water and its limited availability, competition among uses (and users) of water has increased. This competition exists not only within the state but also on an interstate basis, resulting in environmental conflicts. Intrastate competition has historically been manifested in numerous attempts to limit interbasin transfers. Current state surface water allocation laws contain a provision limiting interbasin transfers.[14] In addition, the law creating the Metropolitan North Georgia Water Planning District specifically prohibits the district from including in its studies or planning any interbasin transfers of water into the district.[15]

Interstate conflicts have been most pronounced in the Apalachicola-Chattahoochee-Flint and Alabama-Coosa-Tallapoosa river basins. Concerns have also been expressed about potential withdrawals from the Savannah River and the Tennessee River. Most interstate concerns/conflicts have focused on water use in the metropolitan Atlanta area. In addressing these concerns, Georgia officials have held conversations and negotiations with leaders from Alabama, Florida, and South Carolina. Potential disputes remain largely unresolved. However, a federal district court ruled that water supply withdrawals for metropolitan Atlanta are not among the authorized purposes for Lake Lanier. The U.S. Army Corps of Engineers must end most water supply withdrawals from the lake by July 2012 unless specific authorization for these withdrawals is given by Congress. Georgia leaders are currently working to address this situation.

Laws regarding water resource management are fragmented. Although general agreement exists among policymakers regarding the interrelatedness of water quality and quantity (supply and use) as well as the interconnection between surface water and groundwater in many areas, laws and policies have typically focused on major issues occurring at the time of their adoption and legal constraints on federal, state, and local governmental authority in water resources-related matters. Given that water resources are vital for so many reasons, it is important for county officials to be aware of local water resource conditions and be informed about opportunities and responsibilities relating to water resource management issues.

This section reviews federal and state laws related to surface water quality protection, drinking water quality protection (including policies protecting groundwater resources), and water supply and allocation.

Federal requirements provide the overall framework. As with most major environmental protection programs, Georgia has enacted corresponding state statutes, thus allowing the EPD to implement the federal programs in Georgia. As is the case in many environmental management programs, county governments may find themselves to be regulated entities as well as regulators or managers. For example, counties' drinking water and wastewater management services are regulated, but counties may be regulators of industrial wastewater pretreatment programs.

Water Quality Protection

Federal water pollution control efforts began in the 19th century with the enactment of the Rivers and Harbors Act, prohibiting obstruction of navigable waterways without a permit from the Secretary of the Army. It also prohibited the placement of materials such as solid waste or sewage sludge on the banks of those waterways if the material was likely to be washed into a river or stream. The implementation of provisions that are still applicable has been consolidated with the Army Corps of Engineers' responsibilities under the dredge and fill permitting program of the CWA.

The CWA (formerly known as the Federal Water Pollution Control Act) sets forth the framework for protecting and restoring surface water quality.[16] Programs implemented under the act seek to restore and maintain the chemical, physical, and biological integrity of the nation's waters. These programs involve water pollution control permitting, water quality standards development and implementation, wetlands permitting, sewage sludge management, spill prevention and reporting, nonpoint source pollution management, and provision of financial assistance for construction of wastewater treatment systems. The EPA primarily oversees implementation of these programs, while the EPD implements the federal requirements as well as other state-specific water pollution control programs under the Georgia Water Quality Control Act.[17]

Water Pollution Control Permitting Programs

Before discussing the specific regulatory requirements, it is important to clarify that the CWA's regulatory provisions apply to navigable waters, which include all waters of the United States. Federal regulations define waters of the United States as intrastate lakes, rivers, streams (including intermittent streams), mudflats, sandflats, "wetlands," sloughs, prairie potholes, wet meadows, playa lakes, natural ponds, and interstate waterways; intrastate waterways that could be used in interstate or foreign commerce; tributaries of these waterways; certain coastal waters; and wetlands adjacent to any of these waters.[18]

The CWA prohibits the discharge of a pollutant by any person into navigable waters, unless that discharge is permitted under the act through the National Pollutant Discharge Elimination System (NPDES) program. In general, permits must be obtained by point sources, which include industrial, municipal (which includes county governments), commercial, and agricultural activities discharging through pipes or ditches. Those permits, which are issued by the EPD, contain specific conditions regarding the quality and amount of the discharge as well as monitoring, recordkeeping, and reporting requirements. Effluent limits, which limit the concentration of pollutants in a discharge, are based on industry-specific technology standards for reducing pollutants and/or water quality–based limits that are imposed in order to address location-specific concerns. Permits must be renewed at least once every five years. County governments that operate publicly owned treatment works with a direct discharge into waters of the United States must have an NPDES permit.

Dealing with pollution from storm water discharges (runoff from rainfall events) such as combined sewer overflows, sanitary sewer overflows, and runoff from industrial and construction sites has posed unique challenges. Combined sewers (which exist mainly in older urban areas) carry both domestic sewage and runoff from storm events. In order to address pollution problems, combined sewer overflows must now be permitted under the NPDES program, and permitted local governments must take steps to minimize those overflows in the short term and eliminate them in the long term. Sanitary sewers are constructed to carry only domestic sewage. Overflows of raw sewage generally occur as a result of poor maintenance, improper operation, or inadequate capacity. These overflows constitute a violation of the CWA.

The NPDES program also requires permits for storm water discharges from industrial activities, construction sites, and municipal separate storm sewer systems.[19] The EPD may authorize or permit storm water discharges through individual NPDES permits or coverage under a general permit (an NPDES permit that allows discharges from a category of sources within an area). During the first phase of the storm water management program, operators of large and medium-sized municipal separate storm sewer systems located in urbanized areas and construction site operators who engage in activities disturbing five acres or more of land were required to obtain permits. The programs also required permits for storm water discharges from 10 categories of industrial activities. The *define who*

second phase addressed discharges from regulated small municipal separate storm sewer systems and construction sites that disturb one acre or more of land. Today, numerous local governments across the state must meet storm water management requirements. These governments, which generally engage in land-disturbing activities, must implement storm water management controls in order to meet permit conditions.

Another CWA permit program regulates indirect discharges—those made by industrial users into publicly owned treatment works—through the national pretreatment program.[20] This program allows the establishment of effluent limits (in accordance with industry-specific, technology-based limitations or local limits) in order to protect publicly owned treatment works operations and reduce undesirable chemicals in the sludge. In Georgia, the EPD issues pretreatment permits to any industrial users who release pollutants into a treatment works. Operators of publicly owned treatment works typically become regulators by enforcing permits and limitations on users of their systems.

Establishing and Protecting Water Quality Standards

The CWA requires states to establish water quality standards based upon a water body's particular characteristics and use. The EPD's standards may be numeric (e.g., a limit of 0.000064 micrograms per liter of polychlorinated biphenyls [PCBs]) or narrative (e.g., waters shall be free from oil, scum, and floating debris).[21] States must periodically determine if the water bodies are meeting those standards. If a portion (segment) of a water body is impaired (not meeting a standard for a particular pollutant), that portion is listed, and the process of developing a total maximum daily load is begun. During the total maximum daily load process, the EPD examines all sources for that pollutant and determines how much reduction is needed in order to allow the segment to meet the standard. The reductions may be obtained through tighter requirements on NPDES permits or increased use of best management practices for runoff. While the EPA does not set water quality standards, most states follow the agency's guidelines for those standards.

Permitting the Discharge of Dredged or Fill Materials (Wetlands Program)

Operations that dispose of dredged or fill materials in waters of the United States require a permit from the Army Corps of Engineers, subject to guidance issued by the EPA.[22] In order to facilitate implementation of this program, commonly referred to as the wetlands program, the corps and the EPA have entered into an interagency agreement. As part of its evaluation of a permit application, the corps conducts a public interest review, assesses probable adverse impacts, and ensures that the applicant has taken appropriate steps to avoid, minimize, and/or mitigate those impacts. Federal regulations provide that the corps issue a permit if no practicable alternative exists to the proposed project, no significant adverse impacts on aquatic resources will result, all reasonable mitigation measures are employed, and the proposed project will not violate any other statute.[23] However, before the corps can issue any dredge-and-fill permit in Georgia, the EPD must certify that discharges from the requested activity will not cause a violation of state water quality standards.

Managing Sewage Sludge

The CWA also requires the development of regulations for the use and disposal of sewage sludge (also referred to as biosolids).[24] The Biosolids Rule (Section 503 Program) regulates sludge management practices. Federal requirements contain limits on toxic chemicals in the sludge based on the proposed disposal practice such as land application, surface disposal, or incineration. The requirements also require controls for pathogens (e.g., bacteria, viruses, and certain fungi) in the sludge and practices to reduce the attractiveness of the sludge to disease-carrying vectors such as flies. Publicly owned treatment works in Georgia that generate biosolids must obtain an NPDES permit, a land application system permit, or a pretreatment permit from the EPD and may have to submit a sludge management plan. Depending on the selected management method, a local government may also be required to obtain additional approvals or permits.

Spill Management

The CWA requires certain facilities that store and use oil to develop a plan for the control and prevention of spills. Spills must be reported, and the facility owner/operator must pay the cleanup costs.[25] If local governments operate fueling facilities, they may be subject to the spill prevention, control, and countermeasures program.

Nonpoint Source Pollution Management

In addition to its regulatory provisions, the CWA contains assistance provisions. Dealing with nonpoint sources pollution (i.e., runoff from agricultural and forestry operations and mining, urban areas, or construction activities) has been and continues to be a challenge in certain areas, despite the best efforts of some operators engaged in those activities to reduce the pollution. Under the CWA's nonpoint source pollution management program (Section 319 program), states must identify water bodies that cannot meet water quality standards due to nonpoint sources pollution, identify the activities responsible for the problem, and prepare management plans specifying controls and programs to reduce pollution from those sources.[26] The EPA also provides states with funding to implement programs and projects in order to prevent or reduce nonpoint sources pollution. County governments that have eligible projects may receive 319 funding.

Clean Water State Revolving Fund Loan Program

The most notable CWA assistance program involves the distribution of funds to local governments for the construction of wastewater treatment facilities and associated sewage collection systems. The federal government has historically provided funds for the design and construction of these facilities. The CWA originally provided for a construction grants program.

As a result of continuing federal budgetary challenges, a Clean Water State Revolving Fund loan program was created in 1987.[27] The EPA provides states with annual capitalization grants for use in their programs, and the states in turn make low-interest loans to local governments for eligible projects. The program, administered by the Georgia Environmental Finance Authority (GEFA), makes loans for a broad range of projects, including construction of new wastewater treatment plants, expansion or upgrade of existing plants, installation of new sewage collection lines, system rehabilitation, efforts to maintain compliance, and other water security measures.

Erosion and Sediment Control Program

Many provisions of the Georgia Water Quality Control Act correspond to CWA provisions. The authority of the state to regulate water quality is similar to that of the federal government. State law and the associated rules authorize the EPD to implement a variety of water pollution control programs in Georgia.[28] The remainder of this section briefly describes some state-specific laws.

Georgia's Erosion and Sedimentation Act protects the state's land and water resources from adverse impacts associated with land-disturbing activities.[29] Under this law, areas within local jurisdictions are either covered under state requirements enforced by the EPD or local ordinances enforced by local issuing authorities. In order to be certified as a local issuing authority, a county must adopt an erosion and sediment control ordinance at least as stringent as state requirements and hire qualified inspectors.[30] Local issuing authorities must respond to requests for permits for land-disturbing activities and enforce their ordinances. Those who want to engage in land-disturbing activities (i.e., clearing and grading a site) must prepare and submit an erosion and sediment control plan with the permit application. If permitted, those operators must use best management practices consistent with the Georgia Soil and Water Conservation Commission's *Manual for Erosion and Sedimentation Control in Georgia* to reduce erosion as well as other requirements contained in the permit. The act prohibits land-disturbing activities in certain areas (e.g., stream buffers and floodplains) and specifies activities that are exempt from its requirements. The Erosion and Sedimentation Act also has education and training certification requirements for certain individuals engaged in erosion and sediment control activities.

Georgia law authorizes the EPD to regulate the disposal of treated wastewater onto land instead of discharging it into waters of the United States (which requires an NPDES permit). Any person discharging domestic, municipal, commercial, or industrial wastewaters into a land disposal system must obtain a land disposal permit.[31]

Septic System Regulation

Publicly owned treatment works and associated sewer systems and other types of on-site sewage management systems are used primarily in more heavily populated areas. In rural areas, septic tanks are predominantly used. If these systems are not properly operated and maintained, they can be sources of surface water or groundwater pollution. State law designates the Department of Community Health as the agency responsible for regulating on-site sewage management.[32] The department's requirements govern the location, design, permitting, construction, inspection, maintenance, and operation of septic systems. Local governments may adopt additional requirements for septic systems. County health department personnel conduct permitting and inspection activities.[33] Any person wanting to build a structure in which a septic system will be used or install a septic system must have a permit from the appropriate county health department. State rules require the property owner to maintain and operate the septic system in a safe and sanitary manner.[34] County health department personnel may be called upon to investigate and cite property owners for failure of a septic system (i.e., when seepage or discharge of sewage to the surface occurs).

State Financial Assistance

In addition to funds available through the Clean Water State Revolving Fund, GEFA offers qualified local governments low-interest loans through the Georgia Fund Program for water and wastewater infrastructure projects. The Environmental Emergency Loan Program provides funding to address public health hazards or environmental violations resulting from an unanticipated event. In addition, GEFA offers certain small cities, counties, and water and sewer authorities the opportunity to receive a one-time grant up to $100,000 to build or expand a public sewer system.[35]

Drinking Water Quality Protection

The federal Safe Drinking Water Act has four main purposes:

1. To establish standards and treatment requirements for public water systems
2. To control injection into underground sources of drinking water
3. To protect sources of drinking water
4. To provide financing for drinking water infrastructure[36]

This law specifically recognizes the state's lead role in implementation and enforcement.

Drinking Water Quality Standards

The Safe Drinking Water Act requires the EPA to adopt national health-based standards setting enforceable maximum contaminant levels (primary drinking water standards) for public water systems (defined as a system providing water to the public for human consumption through pipes, if that system serves at least 15 connections or a minimum of 25 people for at least 60 days annually).[37] Certain public water systems in Georgia are exempt from compliance with the primary standards. Secondary standards provide nonenforceable guidelines to address substances affecting the odor, color, or aesthetics of drinking water. The Safe Drinking Water Act does not regulate the quality of water from private wells or bottled water.

Regulation of Public Water Systems

Owners and operators of public water systems in Georgia must obtain a permit from the EPD. Public water systems must monitor water quality, conduct periodic laboratory analyses, maintain records, and notify customers if there have been any violations of standards that could result in serious health effects. Most systems must also annually provide customers with a report disclosing information on water sources, contaminant testing, and any health concerns (Consumer Confidence Report). Drinking water treatment plants must be operated by certified operators. The Georgia State Board of Examiners for the Certification of Water and Wastewater Treatment Plant Operators and Laboratory Analysis certifies 13 classes of licenses. The Safe Drinking Water Act gives small water systems special consideration regarding use of treatment technologies and other resources and calls for implementation of programs to ensure these systems have the technical, financial, and managerial capacity to comply with drinking water standards. The act also requires certain public water systems to conduct assessments of their vulnerability to terrorist acts and other intentional acts of contamination. Systems are required to have emergency response plans specifying response measures that will be taken in the event of an incident.

Protecting Underground Sources of Water

The act also requires the EPA to develop and implement an underground injection control program to protect underground sources of drinking water.[38] This permitting program regulates the construction, operation, and closure of injection wells that are used for the storage or disposal of fluids. Wells are classified into one of five categories. Local governments that operate Class V (i.e., shallow wells injecting nonhazardous fluids) are subject to these regulations. The EPD implements the underground injection control program in Georgia.

Provisions of the Safe Drinking Water Act also seek to protect sources of drinking water. Through the wellhead protection program, activities on land around public water supply wells or well fields can be controlled in order to prevent uses that may result in contamination. States are required to submit a source water assessment plan (for both surface water and groundwater). The EPD has completed source water assessment plans for existing surface water–supplied drinking systems that use groundwater. The EPD continues to develop wellhead protection plans for proposed new drinking water systems.

The Resource Conservation and Recovery Act addresses concerns regarding water pollution, particularly groundwater pollution, resulting from leaking underground storage tanks (USTs).[39] A UST system includes the tank and any underground piping to the tank that has at least 10 percent of its combined volume underground. Most USTs contain petroleum products such as gasoline. Tank owners and operators, including county governments, must comply with program requirements for the following:

- Tank system installation
- Leak detection
- Spill/overfill protection
- Corrosion protection
- Tank closure
- Reporting and record keeping

The UST provisions in the Resource Conservation and Recovery Act also require that owners and operators demonstrate their financial ability to take corrective action and compensate third parties for bodily injury and property damage. In order to meet these requirements, Georgia established the Underground Storage Tank Trust Fund.[40] This fund receives the proceeds from a state environmental assurance fee of $0.005 on each gallon of gasoline sold in the state.[41] If local government tank owners and operators meet certain requirements set out by the EPD, they may be partially reimbursed for costs associated with release response and corrective action as well as for compensation of third parties for bodily injury and property damage caused by an accidental release. However, the local government is liable for the first $10,000 in costs and must provide financial assurance for that amount. If a local government is not in compliance with the EPD requirements, it is liable for all costs associated with an accidental release.

Drinking Water State Revolving Fund Loan Program

The Drinking Water State Revolving Fund loan program helps eligible owners and operators of drinking water systems fund infrastructure and improvements.[42] The EPA provides states with annual capitalization grants for use in their programs, and the states in turn make low-interest loans to local governments for eligible projects. Like the Clean Water State Revolving Fund loan program, the Drinking Water State Revolving Fund loan program is administered by GEFA and provides funds for a broad range of projects, including construction of new drinking water systems, expansion or upgrade of existing systems, installation of new water distribution lines, system rehabilitation, efforts to maintain compliance, and other water security measures. Georgia may also set aside and use funds for small system assistance, funding for economically disadvantaged systems, technical assistance and capacity development programs, and source water protection efforts.

Georgia Safe Drinking Water Act

The Georgia Safe Drinking Water Act of 1977 is the state's counterpart to the federal Safe Drinking Water Act and provides the legal basis for the regulation of drinking water systems in Georgia.[43]

Georgia Underground Storage Tank Act

The requirements under Georgia's Underground Storage Tank Act[44] are similar to those of the federal government. State law exempts the following:

- Tanks storing heating oil to be used on the premises
- Tanks on or above the floor of underground areas
- Septic tanks and systems used for collecting storm water and wastewater
- Tanks holding 100 gallons or less
- Emergency spill and overfill tanks from UST requirements[45]

Water Well Standards Act

The EPD also administers the Water Well Standards Act,[46] which creates a program for licensing water well contractors (i.e., well drillers and drilling contractors) in accordance with standards set by the Water Well Standards Advisory Council. The law prohibits any person from drilling a water well without a water well contractor's license.[47] In addition, the law sets forth standards for the siting, construction, and abandonment of individual wells (single-family residence/domestic use); nonpublic water wells (wells that provide drinking water to the public but are below the size threshold for a public water system), irrigation wells, industrial wells, and dewatering wells.[48]

Water Supply/Allocation

Federal regulatory requirements regarding water supply and allocation are very limited. The Army Corps of Engineers has undertaken numerous water infrastructure projects and remains responsible for operating reservoirs around Georgia. The corps can also provide assistance through its continuing authorities program, which focuses on water resource–related projects that are smaller in scope and cost. Among the potentially eligible projects are those that address flood damage reduction, aquatic system restoration, and snagging and clearing of waterways for flood control.[49]

Another federal program that arguably falls into this category is the National Flood Insurance Program. This program provides flood insurance for structures and contents in communities that adopt and enforce an ordinance outlining minimal floodplain management standards. The three components of the National Flood Insurance Program are flood insurance, floodplain management, and flood hazard mapping.[50] The Federal Emergency Management Agency implements this program federally, and the EPD assists local governments by providing flood maps, flood hazard data, and guidance in understanding, implementing, and maintaining program compliance.

With regard to water allocation, the CWA gives each state the authority to allocate quantities of water within the state. Nothing in the CWA may supersede the state's authority to allocate its water resources. Further, federal agencies must to cooperate with the state and local governments to develop comprehensive solutions to prevent, reduce, and eliminate pollution while managing water resources. [51]

Any federal role in water allocation has resulted primarily from the federal operation of reservoirs, the participation of federal representatives in interstate water compacts, and water allocation decisions issued by the U.S. Supreme Court.

Several key aspects of Georgia law relating to water withdrawal permitting, reservoirs, water conservation, flood protection, and drought management are discussed in the following sections. However, today, the most notable water resource management program involves the ongoing statewide water resources planning effort.

Comprehensive Statewide Water Management Plan

The Comprehensive Statewide Water Management Planning Act created a framework and process for the development of a state water management plan, with the EPD designated as the lead agency.[52]

Under the plan approved by the General Assembly and the governor, the EPD will facilitate an ongoing, substate/regional planning process consisting of four major steps:

1. Provision of water resource assessments that describe water supply and wastewater treatment capacities of regional water resources to regional water planning councils

2. Forecasting of needs for water supply and wastewater treatment capacities by regional councils based upon population and employment projections

3. Preparation of a regional water development and conservation plan that identifies management practices for meeting forecasted water supply and wastewater management needs

4. Review and adoption of the regional plan, if it is consistent with the criteria established in the statewide plan

Once the EPD adopts a plan, the water users in the region must implement the plan. The plan will also serve as the basis for the division's water permitting decisions.[53]

Water Withdrawal Permitting

In the area of water rights, Georgia has adopted a regulated riparian approach in order to allocate surface water and a regulated reasonable use approach for use of groundwater. Under both approaches, the state regulates water withdrawals and transfers to ensure that uses of large amounts of water are reasonable. The Georgia Ground-Water Use Act and water withdrawal provisions of the Georgia Water Quality Control Act both require a permit from the EPD for any water withdrawal exceeding 100,000 gallons per day.[54] Applicants requesting new or additional surface water or groundwater withdrawals must submit a water conservation plan to the EPD for approval. Before granting a permit, the agency must consider the reasonableness of the withdrawal and the effect on other water resource users. Municipal (i.e., local government) and industrial water withdrawal permits contain limits on the amount of water that may be withdrawn as well as requirements pertaining to monitoring and reporting. Permit terms are usually 10 to 20 years but may extend up to 50 years.

Reservoirs

Georgia law contains several provisions that address reservoirs. Many local governments in Georgia, particularly in North Georgia, use reservoirs to store water for public water supply needs. Local governments that seek to construct a new reservoir must obtain federal authorization, including a permit for the disposal of dredged-and-fill material from the Army Corps of Engineers (for more on these requirements, see the earlier discussion on surface water quality protection), and meet applicable state requirements. In addition, local governments must obtain a water withdrawal permit[55] and may be required to obtain a dam safety permit[56] and special approval, if the reservoir is to be built on a designated trout stream. Local governments that own a water supply reservoir must develop and implement a reservoir management plan.

In accordance with the Georgia Water Supply Act of 2008, GEFA conducted an inventory of potential sites for multi-jurisdictional water supply reservoirs. The final report identified 161 existing water supply reservoirs and 114 sites from previous studies. Sixteen reservoirs were deemed to have the "potential for increased water supply yield." In addition, eight reservoirs are under development or currently in the permitting process.[57]

If a local government wants to construct a reservoir for which more than 50 percent of the total cost is funded by a grant from a state agency or a grant of more than $250,000 from a state agency is used, that local government must prepare an environmental effects report if the construction of the reservoir might have a significant adverse effect on the natural environment.[58] GEFA is authorized to provide loans or grants to local governments to expand or increase the capacity of existing reservoirs.[59]

Water Conservation

Water conservation efforts are also very important. In order to promote greater efficiency in residential and commercial water use, Georgia law requires all residential and commercial buildings constructed after 1992 to have low-flow toilets, showerheads, and faucets installed in them.[60] Other than for plans associated with water withdrawal permits, drought mitigation measures, and plumbing code requirements, Georgia law contains few requirements pertaining to water conservation. However, local governments have numerous opportunities to implement policies requiring water conservation measures, including the following:

- Use of conservation pricing for locally owned water utilities

- Installation of low-flush urinals for new industrial, commercial, and institutional buildings

- Use of rain sensor shutoff switches on new irrigation systems

- Requirements for subunit meters in new multifamily buildings

- Assessment and reduction of water system leakage

- Implementation of residential and commercial water audits

- Provision of low-flow retrofit kits for residential toilets

- Adoption of an e-education and public awareness plan

- Review and oversight of water conservation implementation and performance[61]

In response to the 2009 federal district court ruling regarding continued water withdrawals from Lake Lanier, the Georgia Water Stewardship Act of 2010 was passed.[62] Key provisions of the act include

1. requirements for certain state agencies to review policies and programs to encourage water conservation and enhance water supply;

2. mandates for some public water systems to detect water losses;

3. revisions to state minimum construction standards for new buildings, including use of high-efficiency plumbing fixtures and sub-metering for water use;

4. modification of state and local government authority to impose outdoor watering restrictions;

5. amendments to the permitting system for agricultural water withdrawals; and

6. creation of a joint legislative committee on water supply to examine opportunities for enhancing the state's water supply.

Drought Management Planning

Provisions of Georgia law also provide for drought management planning. The Georgia Drought Management Plan adopted by the Board of Natural Resources includes pre-drought mitigation strategies (water conservation measures) and drought response strategies used in the phased response approach based on drought severity.[63] Local governments may adopt mitigation or response strategies beyond those required by the state.

Moving Forward

Counties in many parts of Georgia will continue to face water resource management challenges in the foreseeable future. Demands from population increases and economic expansion coupled with periods of water scarcity and water quality concerns may create difficulties in meeting water supply needs. These difficulties may be intensified by continued interstate water conflicts. Through its current water management planning process, the state is making great strides toward addressing many of these issues, and its regional approach to water resource management shows great promise in reducing intrastate water-use conflicts.

As service providers, county governments will also likely continue to struggle with drinking water and wastewater management costs. Notwithstanding the need for new service, rehabilitation and replacement of aging infrastructure remain issues. In order to address these needs, local governments may be forced to focus more attention on water and wastewater rate structures, which are generally controversial issues. In addition, as regulatory programs continue to tighten standards on contaminants and pollutants, management costs may increase in order to meet those new requirements.

LAND-USE MANAGEMENT

Through the establishment of sound land management policies, local government officials can protect public health and welfare, enhance the quality of life for local citizens, and preserve the community character. The Georgia Constitution places the authority for land-use management decisions primarily at the local level.[64] Using this authority, officials can direct growth and development, including the density and location of houses, industries, business and commercial establishments, farming operations, and other land uses, thereby separating incompatible land uses. Although the imposition of land-use controls is often controversial, many counties have discovered too late that without these measures in place, local control may not be available to prevent undesirable land uses that could create nuisance conditions associated with noise, odors, or aesthetics.

Moreover, land-use decisions can influence the amount and types of pollutants generated within a county. For example, poor land-use planning often results in sprawl, which likely increases air pollution. In addition to reducing air pollution, proper land-use planning can mitigate adverse impacts to water quality from storm water runoff, which carries oil, litter, sediment, and chemicals into local waterways.

Land-use decisions also determine the need for a county to provide public infrastructure and services as well as its revenue capacity to finance those services. This aspect of land-use management is particularly important in areas of higher population density. Residents moving from urban areas to rural areas often expect the same availability of services. In terms of the revenue capacity to provide county services, certain land uses do not require a high level of local government or school system services. Thus, land used for commercial, agricultural, or forestry purposes actually generates more tax revenue than the county spends on services. The opposite is true of land developed for residential purposes, as levels of service exceeding the tax revenues generated are required.[65] If overall revenues become insufficient to pay the service costs, county officials may be forced to either raise revenue (by imposing fees or taxes) or cut services.

Land-use management decisions also play a key role in preserving vital areas and community character. In many cases, development results in a change in land use—conversion of farms, forests, or other rural lands to a residential, commercial, or industrial use. Moreover, additional property may be converted, taking the form of roads, parking lots, homes, stores, and other developments in order to support the new use.[66]

This section provides an overview of the roles of federal, state, and local governments with regard to land-use management, including regulatory provisions and nonregulatory programs.

Federal Governmental Role

The primary interest of the federal government in land-use management arises from its property ownership and management responsibilities and efforts to restrict discriminatory land-use practices. The U.S. Constitution authorizes Congress to regulate federal property[67] and gives Congress preemptive power over state and local control of federal lands.[68] Although that preemption is absolute in many cases, activities regarding certain federal property may be subject to local constraints.

Various federal agencies own and/or protect more than two million acres of property across Georgia. These agencies include the U.S. Forest Service, the U.S. Fish and Wildlife Service, the National Park Service, and the U.S. Department of Defense, including the Army Corps of Engineers.[69] Georgia also contains nearly 57 miles of federally protected wild (40 miles), scenic (2.5 miles), and recreational (15 miles) rivers.[70]

Since land-use management authority lies primarily at the state and local level, there is no comprehensive federal land-use planning or federal land-use plan. Thus, federal authority over private land-use decisions is limited. Congress has continued to limit any federal land-use authority.[71]

Federal Statutes That May Affect Land Use

Despite the lack of direct land-use control authority, the federal government may indirectly control land use through several statutes. Section 404 of the CWA requires localities to obtain a permit from the Army Corps of Engineers in order to discharge dredged or fill materials into waters of the United States. In most cases, these permits are being sought in order to fill wetland areas. Federal law exempts certain activities from the permitting requirements. Permits issued by the Army Corps of Engineers often contain conditions, restrictions, and requirements for mitigating adverse impacts.

The Endangered Species Act seeks to prevent extinction of threatened and endangered species as well as provide protection for critical habitat areas on which those species rely.[72] Administered by the U.S. Fish and Wildlife Service and the National Marine Fisheries Service, the Endangered Species Act provides a process for species listing and critical habitat designation and limits certain activities on land designated as critical habitat. Because critical habitat may include nonfederally owned lands, the Endangered Species Act provides for the issuance of incidental taking permits, which allow limited destruction or harm to a species, and the development of habitat conservation plans, which allow land uses not jeopardizing the listed species or its recovery. Upon approval of a plan by the U.S. Fish and Wildlife Service, the agency will issue an incidental take permit. The agency has taken other actions to reduce adverse impacts on nonfederal landowners (e.g., "no surprises" rule, safe harbor agreements, and candidate conservation agreements).

The National Environmental Policy Act establishes procedural requirements for federal agencies to follow when taking any action that significantly affects the quality of the human environment.[73] Defined broadly, major federal actions include situations in which federal agencies provide assistance, financing, or approval of projects as well as those in which an agency conducts the action. The act's guidelines contain exemptions and exclusions for certain projects and programs. For actions that are subject to the requirements of the National Environmental Policy Act, agencies must conduct environmental assessments. If the assessment finds no substantial effects on the environment, the agency may produce a Finding of No Significant Impact. If the assessment finds significant impacts, the agency must conduct a more detailed evaluation of those impacts and produce an Environmental Impact Statement. The act does not require an agency decision maker to select the environmentally preferred alternative or prohibit adverse environmental effects. Given the breadth of National Environmental Policy Act requirements, many local government activities may be affected, particularly those funded in part with federal assistance.

Congress enacted the federal Coastal Zone Management Act to preserve, protect, and where possible, restore or enhance the many natural and unique resources of coastal areas.[74] Recognizing the primacy of state decision making, the law encourages coastal states to develop and implement coastal zone management plans. Once the National Oceanographic and Atmospheric Administration approves a state plan for program development, it provides funds for program implementation. State plans define the boundaries of the coastal zone, identify uses subject to state regulation, specify the mechanism(s) used in regulation, and provide guidelines on use priorities. A significant provision in the law requires that activities needing a federal license or permit or receiving federal financial assistance that have reasonably foreseeable adverse coastal effects be fully consistent with the state coastal management programs.

Federal Assistance Programs

Federal programs also provide nonregulatory means by which to assist local governments in land-use management, mostly through financial assistance programs. Some of these programs are as follows: [75]

- *Habitat Conservation Plan Land Acquisition Grants*. Pertains to acquisition of lands associated with existing habitat conservation plans.

- *Land and Water Conservation Fund*. Pertains to the purchase of lands for new or existing parks and recreation lands.

- *Wildlife Habitat Incentives Program*. Pertains to incentives for the creation, maintenance, and protection of certain wildlife habitats, with emphasis on those for rare species.

- *The Farm and Ranch Lands Protection Program*. Pertains to support for state and local farmland protection efforts.

- *The Coastal and Estuarine Land Conservation Program*. Pertains to the purchase of land or easements to protect important coastal and estuarine lands.

Cleaning Up Contaminated Properties

Recognizing that there are many areas with abandoned or underutilized properties, particularly urban areas, that face challenges in terms of revitalization and redevelopment, Congress passed the Small Business Liability Relief and Brownfields Revitalization Act of 2002.[76] The EPA defines brownfields as property, the expansion, redevelopment, or reuse of which may be complicated by the presence or potential presence of a hazardous substance, pollutant, or contaminant. Because these properties are often found in commercial areas that have appropriate transportation, electrical, and water management infrastructure, they have an increased potential for reuse or redevelopment. Brownfields redevelopment is generally considered to be an urban issue. However, rural areas also have brownfields in the form of old gas stations or closed factories.

Developers are usually reluctant to redevelop brownfields out of concern for cost and liability issues. Costs associated with the actual development of brownfields are 20 percent to 60 percent higher than comparable projects at the urban fringe.[77] Federal and state laws also impose financial liability on previous and current owners of contaminated property, regardless of fault. Moreover, brownfields owners may be hesitant to sell out of fear that they may be liable for as yet unidentified contamination or undetermined cleanup costs.[78]

The EPA has implemented a brownfields revitalization program that provides technical and financial assistance to states, communities, and stakeholders. The brownfields grants program provides funds to eligible participants, including local governments, for site assessments, cleanup activities, capitalization of revolving loan funds for site cleanups, and job training. Grantees have leveraged an average of $18.68 for each federal dollar spent and an average of 7.75 jobs per $100,000 of federal funding. Other benefits include decreases in air and water pollution, increases in property values, and reduction in crime.[79] Although all local governments are eligible for brownfields program funding and several Georgia municipalities have received such funding, historically it has been more difficult for counties to obtain this funding.

State Governmental Role

In order to better address planning and growth-related concerns, the Georgia General Assembly passed the Georgia Planning Act in 1989 (see Chapter 9 for a comprehensive discussion of planning requirements). The law recognizes that there is an essential public interest in establishing minimum standards for land use in order to protect and preserve the state's natural resources, environment, and vital areas.[80] The law authorizes the DNR to develop minimum standards and procedures for the protection of these assets.

Georgia law addresses vital areas of the state—those natural resources deemed to be in the interest of the public to protect and preserve, such as wetlands, water supply watersheds, significant groundwater recharge areas, higher elevations in the mountains, and river corridors. The Board of Natural Resources has developed minimum standards and procedures for protecting vital areas, known as environmental planning criteria, which may include requirements for resource assessments, management plans, and protection ordinances.

In order to fulfill the mandate of protecting vital areas, local officials must identify such areas within their jurisdiction in the local comprehensive plan. If vital areas are present, county officials must determine whether all or a portion of the environmental planning criteria will be implemented through local protection measures. The Department of Community Affairs reviews local comprehensive plans and protection measures to determine consistency with the requirements of the Georgia Planning Act and environmental planning criteria. Satisfying these requirements allows counties to maintain qualified local government status, which establishes eligibility for financial assistance programs.

Protecting Coastal Areas

Three state laws control development in coastal areas: the Coastal Marshlands Protection Act, the Shore Protection Act, and the Georgia Coastal Management Act. The Coastal Marshlands Protection Act authorizes the Coastal Resources Division of the DNR to require permits for erecting structures such as docks, walkways, and buildings and for dredging or filling in estuarine areas.[81] The Shore Protection Act prohibits use of motor vehicles on dunes and beaches while authorizing the Coastal Resources Division to issue permits for limited construction activity in the sand dune areas.[82]

The Georgia Coastal Management Act enables Georgia to reenter the federal Coastal Zone Management Program.[83] The Coastal Resources Division must prepare a coastal zone management plan that includes locally developed policies to guide public and private uses of land and waters in the coastal area. The Georgia Coastal Management Program balances the economic development concerns and natural resource preservation issues identified by the public. This program works with local governments in the 11-county coastal zone service area to monitor water quality, implement the coastal nonpoint source pollution and shellfish sanitation programs, provide education and outreach, and review federal actions (licenses, permits, and projects as well as federally funded activities) in order to ensure consistency with the program.[84]

The Coastal Management Program offers technical assistance to local governments on a variety of coastal issues and provides funding to eligible parties (including county governments) through the Coastal Incentives Grant Program. Under this competitive grant program, a request for proposal is issued outlining the aspects of the project that should receive priority funding. The program has also developed and submitted a Coastal and Estuarine Land Conservation Program plan to the National Oceanic and Atmospheric Administration, thus allowing potential federal funding for acquisition of lands for preservation.

Georgia Environmental Policy Act

The Georgia Environmental Policy Act requires state agency heads to consider potentially adverse environmental impacts resulting from the actions of their agencies.[85] The law also applies to any action by a county that receives more than 50 percent of the total project cost from the state or a grant of more than $250,000 from the state. If the proposed action may result in a significant adverse environmental impact, the responsible agency must prepare an environmental effects report that examines the nature of the impact, alternative actions, measures to avoid or minimize the impact, and other specified factors. The responsible official must publish the report, send it to the EPD, provide legal notice and an opportunity for public comment, and consider all received comments before deciding on a course of action. A public hearing may also be required. Finally, the official must provide notice of his or her final decision.

Nonregulatory Land Conservation Initiatives

The State of Georgia implements several nonregulatory programs to provide funding for land conservation and preservation at the local level. The Georgia Land Conservation Act created a framework for local governments, state and federal agencies, and private partners to protect the state's natural resources.[86] The Georgia Land Conservation Council, composed of state agency heads and gubernatorial appointees, considers and approves eligible land conservation project proposals. The DNR serves as the lead programmatic agency; however, GEFA reviews the financial aspects of project proposals and makes recommendations to the council. The Georgia Land Conservation Trust Fund provides grant funds annually to local governments that implement approved land conservation projects. In addition, the Georgia Land Conservation Revolving Loan Fund provides loans annually to local governments and state authorities for approved projects. Funds must be used for the acquisition of conservation land or conservation easements supporting the goals of the act.

Georgia has also encouraged land conservation through tax policy. The Land Conservation Tax Credit Program provides income tax credits for donations of real property for conservation purposes.[87] Because real property tax assessments are based on property value, land committed to conservation purposes (e.g., through conservation easements) may be subject to a reduction in ad valorem taxes under the program.[88] In addition to its other duties, the Georgia Land Conservation Program provides assistance with implementation of the Land Conservation Tax Credit Program. Since the program was created in 2005, 210 grant, loan, and tax credit applications have been approved to help preserve over 150,000 acres in Georgia.[89]

Local Governmental Role

Because authority for land-use decisions rests primarily with local governments, county officials can exercise significant influence over land-use management. Local governments have several regulatory mechanisms by which to direct and/or control local land uses.

Over the years, land-use planners have become more innovative with zoning schemes, thereby allowing public officials some flexibility. Available options include the following:

- Conventional zoning

- Incentive zoning

- Nonexclusive agricultural zoning

- Floodplain zoning

- Cluster zoning

- Performance zoning

- Overlay zoning[90]

County governments can adopt subdivision regulations in order to establish minimum standards for subdivision development. These regulations can set requirements for storm water drainage and retention, streamside buffers, wastewater management, drinking water systems, and recreational areas. In many cases, subdivision regulations protect communities by ensuring a properly built environment. They also typically make developers responsible for the installation of basic public infrastructure before the sale of parcels.

Nonregulatory Land Conservation Initiatives

County governments can also play nonregulatory roles in land-use management through land-use planning, acquisition of property or an interest in property, and the creation of tradable development rights programs.[91] Land-use planning identifies unique areas (such as environmentally sensitive areas, historical sites, and parks) that may be targeted for acquisition or preservation. While effective land-use planning can certainly serve as a strong basis for zoning ordinances or subdivision regulations, the practice itself is not regulatory.

Another land-use management tool available to local governments is conservation easements. Georgia law defines a conservation easement as a "non-possessory interest of a holder in real property imposing limitations or affirmative obligations, the purposes of which include retaining or protecting natural, scenic, or open-space values of real property; assuring its availability for agricultural, forest, recreational, or open-space use; protecting natural resources; maintaining or enhancing air or water quality; or preserving the historical, architectural, archeological, or cultural aspects of real property."[92]

Local governments may also purchase development rights. In these situations, a landowner typically sells the rights to develop a parcel to a government entity. The landowner retains all remaining property rights. Georgia law allows local governments to create Transfer of Development Rights programs.[93] This concept allows landowners in restricted areas (sending areas) to transfer certain development rights to landowners in areas where higher-density development may be appropriate and/or supported (receiving areas). In order to create a Transfer of Development Rights program, a local government must pass an ordinance outlining the specifics of the program and may also be required to amend zoning and planning documents.[94] (For more information on Transfer of Development Rights programs, see Chapter 9).

Tree Ordinances

A number of counties and cities in Georgia have enacted tree ordinances in their communities. Tree ordinances are developed for a variety of reasons, most often in response to rapid land development or in order to improve water quality, protect quality of life, and address natural resource issues. Tree ordinances can range in complexity from simple tree replacement standards to more comprehensive ordinances that address a vast number of natural resources and tree replacement and banking policies.

Moving Forward

Local government land-use controls and land-use management initiatives will remain important to protecting Georgia's environment and natural resources. As populations increase in parts of the state, land-use controls will be needed in order to direct growth and development, thus inhibiting sprawl. In more rural parts of the state, land-use controls should be considered in order to prevent locally unwanted land uses. Throughout the state, it is essential that county governments consider implementing land conservation initiatives in order to preserve sensitive areas that contribute to the character of the state.

ENVIRONMENTAL ENFORCEMENT

Federal and state environmental protection agencies have several approaches to enforcement: administrative enforcement, civil enforcement, and criminal enforcement. Citizen lawsuits are another means by which violators may be brought into compliance.

Administrative Enforcement

Administrative enforcement typically provides the most flexibility in resolving an enforcement issue. Within this process, agency staff may conduct facility inspections, investigate activities, request records and information, and issue administrative orders or consent orders. These orders may require alleged violators to take certain actions and may include monetary penalties. Within the EPA, administrative enforcement is considered part of the civil enforcement program.

Civil Enforcement

In the civil enforcement process, the agency files a lawsuit, usually seeking injunctive relief and a civil penalty. An injunction is a court order that either compels a party to take or prohibits a party from taking an action. Policies adopted under some federal environmental laws require that actions seeking a penalty amount above a certain threshold be referred to the U.S. Department of Justice for civil enforcement. The goal of civil enforcement in environmental protection laws is to return an alleged violator to compliance.

Civil and administrative penalties associated with each violation of federal and state environmental laws can be substantial. Under the CAA and the CWA, civil penalties for some violations could bring a maximum fine of $25,000 per day per violation. Since 1996, the EPA has been required by federal law to adjust federal environmental civil penalties for inflation every four years. As a result, the agency revised the $25,000 daily maximum penalty to $37,500 per day effective January 2009. It should also be noted that in this area, Georgia law is stricter than federal law.

Georgia law provides a maximum civil penalty of $50,000 per day for the first violation of the Georgia Water Quality Control Act and $100,000 per day for subsequent violations within a 12-month period.[95]

In considering penalty amounts, environmental regulatory agencies usually take into account several factors such as whether the violation was deliberate, damages to the environment and natural resources, past performance history of the alleged violator, and any economic benefits that accrued as a result of noncompliance. Incentives (reduction in penalties) may exist if regulated organizations self-report violations they discover through environmental self-audit programs or evaluations.

Another aspect of the civil enforcement process involves the use of supplemental environmental projects to reduce the penalty amount that may be paid. As part of a settlement agreement, an alleged violator may agree to perform an environmentally beneficial project (a supplemental environmental project) that is somewhat related to the alleged violation. That project cannot be legally required in order to bring the violator back into compliance. For example, a company alleged to have violated sections of the CAA may propose funding for technical assistance to local governments on air quality issues or for retrofits of diesel-powered public equipment in order to reduce emissions. The EPA has a supplemental environmental projects policy that provides further details.

Criminal Enforcement

Criminal enforcement is usually reserved for the most serious environmental violations. Violations for which criminal sanctions are sought involve serious negligence, intentional acts, and "knowing" disregard for the law. Particular attention is paid to situations in which the violator knowingly places another person in imminent danger of death or serious bodily injury. Convictions for criminal violations of environmental laws can carry very significant fines and prison sentences. For example, criminal penalties for tampering with a public water system carry a fine and prison sentences (10 to 20 years).[96] As expected, the goals of criminal enforcement are punishment and prevention of future crimes.

Citizen Lawsuits

Another approach to environmental enforcement involves citizen lawsuits. Many major federal environmental laws contain sections that allow "citizens" (defined in the broadest sense and including public interest environmental groups, such as the Southern Environmental Law Center or Greenlaw) to file lawsuits in federal court against regulated parties for alleged violations of environmental laws. Before filing the lawsuit, the citizen (or his or her legal counsel) must provide a 60-day notification (referred to as an intent to sue) to the alleged violator and the EPA. In addition, a continuing violation must exist at the time the lawsuit is filed. Citizen lawsuits are not allowed if a federal or state regulatory agency is diligently prosecuting the alleged violation. While citizens may recover attorney fees in successful actions, they cannot recover any monetary amounts for damages.[97] Citizens may also sue the administrator of the EPA for failing to perform a duty mandated by federal law. The lawsuit would seek a court order requiring the administrator to perform that duty within a given time. Georgia environmental protection laws do not contain citizen lawsuit provisions.

FEDERAL ENVIRONMENTAL GRANTS AND CONTRACTS

One area that receives little mention in discussions regarding environmental management involves the use of federal grant funds. The EPA provides numerous financial assistance opportunities in many different programs, and county governments are among the eligible participants. Federal environmental grants come with many conditions involving recordkeeping and reporting, procurement of goods and services (typically requiring competition in procurement of services), avoidance of conflicts of interest, and requirements for closeouts. Problems may also arise regarding contracts that use federal environmental funding.

Most local government officials are aware that violations can result in withholding of funds or demands to repay improperly spent funds. However, many officials are not aware that very serious violations may result in suspension or debarment. Suspension usually results in individuals or organizations (including local governments) being denied access to all federal grants and contracts on a temporary basis. Debarment actions usually cover a longer term and may be permanent. In order to avoid these outcomes, county personnel should remain well trained and up-to-date on federal grant/contracting requirements as well as the list of persons who are currently suspended or debarred. Staff at the EPA regional office can provide assistance.

CONCLUSION

Environmental protection efforts have resulted in progress toward better quality of life over the past few decades. Air and water quality have improved. Contaminated property has been identified and cleaned up. As highlighted in Chapter 12, waste generation has been reduced in some areas. People have generally become more aware of environmental issues. Much of this improvement has occurred while the population has increased, the economy has prospered, energy consumption has risen, and vehicle miles traveled have increased. Improvements in environmental quality have occurred as a result of not only regulatory programs but also voluntary and collaborative efforts.

County governments have assumed more responsibilities in response to public expectations for services and actions. They have been delegated greater responsibility for environmental programs from federal and state governments and have made commitments to improve the quality of life for local citizens. As a result, local governments generally provide more services and implement more programs than at any time in the past.

Attention continues to be given to conservation of water, energy, and other resources. County governments can practice conservation in their operations, thereby reducing costs and providing other benefits. As respected members of the community, county officials can encourage business owners, industry leaders, and constituents to incorporate conservation measures into their daily practices. In some cases, these measures can be taken at little or no cost. With a renewed focus on sustainability, county governments across the country are undertaking "green" building projects and implementing other green practices in their operations. Successful implementation of conservation measures and sustainable projects reduces not only current use but also the vulnerability to increased future costs.

It is vital that individuals conducting and supervising county environmental management responsibilities maintain a working knowledge of current requirements. Environmental regulatory requirements are numerous, complex, and ever changing. Given tighter budgets and scores of other priorities, environmental regulatory issues may not always be at the top of the list. However, attention to these details can help local governments avoid future problems.

NOTES

1. Margaret Myszewski, James Kundell, Terry DeMeo, and Don Christy, *Environmental Management Handbook for Georgia Local Government Officials* (Athens: Carl Vinson Institute of Government, University of Georgia, 2006).
2. Adapted from "Basics of Environmental Law," www.wildlaw.org/Eco-Laws/basics.htm. Accessed March 19, 2010.
3. 42 UNITED STATES CODE ANNOTATED (U.S.C.A.) §7401 et seq.
4. 42 U.S.C.A. §§7408–7409.
5. 42 U.S.C.A. §7410.
6. U.S. Environmental Protection Agency, *Profile of Local Government Operations* (Washington, DC: USEPA Office of Enforcement and Compliance Assurance, 1999).
7. 42 U.S.C.A. §7412.
8. 42 U.S.C.A. §§7521–7590.
9. 42 U.S.C.A. §§7651–7651o.
10. 42 U.S.C.A. §§7661–7661f.
11. 42 U.S.C.A. §§7671–7671q.
12. OFFICIAL CODE OF GEORGIA ANNOTATED (O.C.G.A.) §12-9-1 et seq.
13. OFFICIAL COMPILATION RULES AND REGULATIONS OF THE STATE OF GEORGIA (GA. COMP. R. & REGS.) ch. 391-3-1.
14. O.C.G.A. §12-5-31(n).
15. O.C.G.A. §12-5-584(f).
16. 33 U.S.C.A. §§1251–1387.
17. O.C.G.A. §12-5-20 et seq.
18. 40 CODE OF FEDERAL REGULATIONS (C.F.R.) §122.2.
19. 33 U.S.C.A. §1342.
20. 33 U.S.C.A. §1317.
21. GA. COMP. R. & REGS. ch. 391-3-6-.03.
22. 33 U.S.C.A. §1344.
23. 40 C.F.R. §230.10(a)–(d).
24. 33 U.S.C.A. §1345.
25. 33 U.S.C.A. §1321.
26. 33 U.S.C.A. §1329.
27. 33 U.S.C.A. §§1381–1387.
28. GA. COMP. R. & REGS. ch. 391-3-6.
29. O.C.G.A. §12-7-1 et seq.
30. O.C.G.A. §12-7-8(a)(1).
31. O.C.G.A. §12-5-23.
32. O.C.G.A. §31-2-12.
33. O.C.G.A. §31-3-5.
34. GA. COMP. R. & REGS. ch. 290-5-59-.03(1).
35. Georgia Environmental Finance Authority, The Georgia Fund Loan Program, gefa.org/Index.aspx?page=78. Accessed March 3, 2010.
36. 42 U.S.C.A. §300f et seq.

37. 42 U.S.C.A. §300g-1.
38. 42 U.S.C.A. §300h.
39. 42 U.S.C.A. §6991–1i.
40. O.C.G.A. §12-13-9.
41. O.C.G.A. §12-13-10.
42. 42 U.S.C.A. §300j-12.
43. O.C.G.A. §12-5-170 et seq.; GA. COMP. R. & REGS. ch. 391-3-5.
44. O.C.G.A. §12-13-1 et seq.
45. O.C.G.A. §12-13-4.
46. O.C.G.A. §12-5-120 et seq.
47. O.C.G.A. §12-5-125.
48. O.C.G.A. §12-5-134.
49. U.S. Army Corps of Engineers, The Continuing Authorities Program, Charleston District, www.sac.usace.army.mil/?action=programs.continuing_authorities_program. Accessed March 3, 2010.
50. U.S. Federal Emergency Management Agency, National Flood Insurance Program, www.fema.gov/about/programs/nfip/index.shtm. Accessed March 3, 2010.
51. 33 U.S.C.A. §1251(g).
52. O.C.G.A. §12-5-520 et seq.
53. *Water Quality in Georgia 2006–2007* (Atlanta: Georgia Department of Natural Resources, Environmental Protection Division, 2008).
54. O.C.G.A. §§12-5-90 et seq., 12-5-31.
55. O.C.G.A. §12-5-31.1.
56. O.C.G.A. §12-5-370 et seq.
57. *Georgia Inventory and Survey of Feasible Sites for Water Supply Reservoirs* (Atlanta: Georgia Environmental Facilities Authority, October 31, 2008).
58. O.C.G.A. §§12-16-3, 12-16-4.
59. O.C.G.A. §50-23-28.1.
60. O.C.G.A. §8-2-3(b).
61. Metropolitan North Georgia Water Planning District, "Water Supply and Water Conservation Management Plan," www.northgeorgiawater.com/files/Water_Supply_Water_Conservation_Plan_May2009.pdf. Accessed March 3, 2010.
62. Senate Bill 370, 2010 Georgia General Assembly (O.C.G.A. §§12-5-4, 12-5-4.1, 12-5-7, 12-5-31, 12-5-1-5, 12-5-180.1, 8-2-3, 8-2-23).
63. O.C.G.A. §12-5-8; Georgia Environmental Protection Division, "Georgia Drought Management Plan," www.gaepd.org/Files_PDF/gaenviron/drought/drought_mgmtplan_2003.pdf. Accessed August 19, 2010.
64. GA. CONST. art. IX, §2 ¶4.
65. Jeffrey Dorfman, Dawn Black, David Newman, Coleman Dangerfield, and Warren Flick, *The Economic Costs of Development for Local Governments* (Athens: Department of Agricultural and Applied Economics, University of Georgia, 2002).
66. Robert Healy, *Competition for Land in the American South: Agriculture, Human Settlement and the Environment* (Washington, DC: The Conservation Foundation, 1985).

67. U.S. Const. art. IV, §3, cl. 2.

68. U.S. Const. art. VI, cl. 2.

69. Georgia Department of Natural Resources, "Federally Protected Lands," www.dnr.state.ga.us/greenspace/pdfs/gspce_fedac.pdf. Accessed February 8, 2010.

70. National Wild and Scenic Rivers, "River Mileage Classifications of the National Wild and Scenic River System," www.rivers.gov/publications/rivers-table.pdf. Accessed February 8, 2010.

71. 2 U.S.C.A. §7431.

72. 16 U.S.C.A. §1531 et seq.

73. 42 U.S.C.A. §4321 et seq.

74. 16 U.S.C.A. §1451 et seq.

75. *Environmental Management Handbook for Georgia Local Government Officials.*

76. Pub. L. 107-118 (2002); 42 U.S.C.A. §9601 et seq.

77. *Environmental Management Handbook for Georgia Local Government Officials.*

78. Hope Whitney, "Cities and Superfund: Encouraging Brownfield Redevelopment," *Ecology Law Quarterly* 30 (2003): 59.

79. U.S. Environmental Protection Agency, "EPA Brownfields Program Produces Widespread Environmental and Economic Benefits," www.epa.gov/brownfields/overview/brownfields_benefits_postcard.pdf. Accessed February 8, 2010.

80. O.C.G.A. §12-2-8.

81. O.C.G.A. §12-5-280 et seq.

82. O.C.G.A. §12-5-230 et seq.

83. O.C.G.A. §12-5-320 et seq.

84. Georgia Department of Natural Resources, Coastal Resources Division, "Overview of the Coastal Management Program," crd.dnr.state.ga.us/content/displaycontent.asp?txtDocument=54. Accessed February 8, 2010.

85. O.C.G.A. §12-16-1 et seq.

86. O.C.G.A. §12-6A-1 et seq.

87. O.C.G.A. §48-7-29.12.

88. O.C.G.A. §48-5-7.4.

89. Georgia Land Conservation Program, *Annual Report: July 2008 to December 2009* (Atlanta: Georgia Department of Natural Resources, 2010).

90. James McElfish, *Nature-Friendly Ordinances: Local Measures to Conserve Biodiversity* (Washington, DC: Environmental Law Institute, 2004).

91. *Environmental Management Handbook for Georgia Local Government Officials.*

92. O.C.G.A. §44-10-2(1).

93. O.C.G.A. §36-66A-1 et seq.

94. O.C.G.A. §36-66A-2(c) et seq.

95. O.C.G.A. §12-5-52.

96. 42 U.S.C.A. §300i–1(a).

97. Jeffrey Sanders, "Citizen Suits: The Statutory Power to Abate Environmental Pollution and to Enforce Federal Environmental Statutes as a Private Attorneys General," jeffreymsanders.files.wordpress.com/2009/06/citizen-suit-provisions-in-major-environmental-statutes.pdf. Accessed June 14, 2010.

PART *3*

County Services

11

Matthew Hicks and Saralyn Stafford

Economic Development

Ask 10 people to define economic development and you are likely to hear 10 different answers. In general, economic development refers to the creation and retention of wealth in a community and the improvement of living standards. The public policy benefits of economic development include expanding and diversifying the tax base, reducing unemployment, improving overall quality of life, and enhancing a community's image. In the past, economic development meant landing the next large manufacturing or distribution facility in one's county. Today a number of strategies may be used such as supporting entrepreneurs, promoting tourism, assisting existing businesses, recruiting big box retailers, building industrial parks, encouraging mixed-use developments, incubating technology start-ups, and locating manufacturing and distribution centers. In order to implement these strategies, counties generally focus on putting in place needed infrastructure. They offer tax incentives and foster an educated workforce in addition to forming economic development leadership teams and funding development authorities.

Despite the myriad definitions of economic development and the activities that support it, county commissioners must understand the problems their particular communities face and help them identify priorities. Should the county focus on recruiting a particular sector such as the biotechnology, energy, or health-care industry? Is the county better suited for call centers, agribusiness, or some other specialty? Are there cultural and historical assets that make the county ideal as a tourist destination? A county may be so diverse that multiple goals should be established. It is up to elected, business, and civic leaders to realistically answer these questions, define what economic development means in their respective counties, and direct resources in order to achieve specific economic goals.

STATE AND LOCAL ROLES IN ECONOMIC DEVELOPMENT

Several state and regional organizations are engaged in economic development and are available to assist counties. These include the Department of Economic Development, the Department of Community Affairs, the Small Business Development Center, Georgia Power, and local electric membership corporations. The Georgia Department of Economic Development is the official marketing arm of the state, responsible for promoting Georgia to prospective businesses, tourists, and new residents, among others. Project managers employed by the department are responsible for working with companies that have expressed an interest in Georgia. Their job is to "sell Georgia"—in other words, to recruit business—by providing specific information on communities that meet the needs outlined by prospective companies. Like the department, several major utilities (Georgia Power Company, Georgia Electric Membership Corporation, and Electric Cities of Georgia) have statewide project managers who work with businesses and consultants to provide information and services in order to encourage their location or expansion within the state.

The role of the local economic development team is to provide the product—the buildings, sites, infrastructure, workforce, and quality of life—that the statewide partners are selling. In addition, the local economic development team must actively market the local community, in part by developing and maintaining a community Web site with current and in-depth information important to businesses, tourists, consultants, and other groups who are researching locations. Most searches by economic development prospects begin with a Web site review. If a county does not have an informative Web site, it will not make it through this first review. Community marketing also includes conducting outreach to targeted prospects and developing and maintaining good relationships with statewide partners. It is important to keep them informed of available properties and events in the community. Trust is also crucial between local and statewide partners because both entities' reputations are at stake when sharing prospective locations for a company or consultant review.

Statewide partners are responsible to the prospect first; their job is to suggest locations in Georgia that meet the needs of the business or consultant. The job of the local economic development team is to have, maintain, and present the local community's product to the world. A community may be invited to work with the statewide project managers or to interact directly with a business or consultant. Information requests must be answered promptly and accurately. If a prospect does visit a community, the local team should follow the agenda in order to meet the prospect's needs.

Quite often, a company or consultant will request complete confidentiality regarding its identity and interest and will limit the number of contacts on a first visit to just one local representative. Should that confidentiality be breached, the consequences would negatively affect not just that particular opportunity but also the community's reputation among future prospects and statewide economic development partners. Because of the open records act, companies and consultants desiring confidentiality should limit documents, letters, e-mails, or other records that reveal the company's identity. Counties are required to comply with the open records act.[1] If the county has documents, letters, e-mails, or other records identifying an interested company, those records must be released, if requested, unless those records fall into a specific exemption.[2]

ROLE OF THE COUNTY COMMISSIONER

Companies that are considering investing in a community look for stability, predictability, and a united approach by county leaders. It can shake the confidence of an economic development prospect to discover that local elected officials are divided or not "on the same page" as other county leaders. A team approach involving a number of private and public stakeholders (one being the county commission) is generally the most effective way for a county to address economic development. A county's "economic development team" or "community sales team" may consist of chamber of commerce and other business leadership, development authority staff, regional commission staff, county and municipal officials, local college and technical education officials, or other parties. This team will usually lead, formally or informally, efforts related to the establishment of goals and implementation of necessary activities.

The county commissioner plays a critical role as a member of a county's economic development team by both serving as an ambassador for the county and making critical funding and resource decisions. The level of hands-on involvement by a county commissioner largely depends on whether the county has a professional economic development staff. The staff can be employed directly by the county or by a development authority, chamber of commerce, or some related entity. It is best to have a single point of contact, often referred to as the economic developer, who is able to address economic development–related matters that arise within the community. This contact person should be authorized to speak and act on behalf of the local community in dealings with both statewide partners and businesses. A commission that displays a united effort, with a single point of contact, presents the most professional image and simplifies efforts, especially when statewide project managers are involved.

Every county commissioner should know his or her county's strengths and assets and economic development goals. A commissioner should also know the members of the county's economic development team. Becoming familiar with existing industries and workforce statistics can also be very helpful.

The county commission plays a crucial role in economic development through its budget process and funding decisions. Types of budget decisions that can assist in economic development include funding utility and public works infrastructure and economic development organizations, such as development authorities. A county is authorized by law to dedicate up to one mill of property taxes to fund a development authority for the purpose of developing trade, commerce, and industry.[3] A city may levy up to three mills.[4] In addition, a county or city may levy a hotel-motel tax, which can be used to promote tourism, conventions, and trade shows and fund facilities such as convention and conference centers.[5]

The county commission is also responsible for making land-use decisions[6] such as zoning[7] and comprehensive planning[8] and setting permitting policies that affect the location of industries and the use of public infrastructure investments.[9] Further, county leaders must be involved in deciding upon an incentives policy that makes sense in meeting local economic development goals. Promoting economic development is not a single event but rather a process that requires a long-term commitment of time and resources by the county commission.

BUSINESS RETENTION AND JOB CREATION

The local economic development team also plays an extremely important role with regard to existing businesses and industries in a community. In fact, business retention may be the most important role a local team can assume since existing businesses and industries in a county already contribute to the local economy and any necessary infrastructure investment has already been made. The team's relationship with existing businesses and industries will also help determine whether a company should expand in a county or go to a more hospitable location when economic times are difficult. New business prospects will look at the relationships that existing businesses have with local officials when they visit. Often, they will have private discussions with existing industries to see what kind of support the local government gives after a location decision has been made.

Traditionally, expansion of existing businesses creates more new jobs in a community than does recruitment of new businesses. These additions to the workforce are often few, resulting in perhaps only a couple of new jobs, and receive little attention, but they do add up over time. Many industries have multiple locations, and when decisions must be made regarding cutting or adding a product line, they will look to the communities with the best business environment and local support in their decision-making process. Regular communication between the local government and established companies can reveal problems, such as public infrastructure or regulatory issues, before they become insurmountable.

Local industry councils are one type of forum in which industry managers can share the challenges they are facing and collaborate with other business owners and local leaders to overcome competitive hurdles. Ultimately, this type of effort ensures that good relationships are developed and maintained between existing industries and local leaders. It is important for county commissioners to support existing local industry council efforts or encourage the establishment of such a council if the county does not have one.

Job creation is accomplished through not only recruitment and retention of industry but also the support of small businesses and entrepreneurs. Most businesses in the United States are categorized as small businesses (fewer than 20 employees), and many have no employees, as they are solely owned and operated by entrepreneurs. These businesses generally are the largest sources of new job creation annually across the country. A supportive environment for their growth can be an effective means of job creation and retention in many communities. The Georgia Department of Economic Development has coordinated resources and assistance available for small businesses and entrepreneurs and can assist local communities in developing support programs.[10] Further, the state-sponsored Small Business Development Center offices provide technical assistance for existing small businesses and individuals who are interested in starting a business.[11]

DEVELOPMENT AUTHORITIES

Authorities are creations of government.[12] They are, therefore, public bodies whose boards comprise appointed public officials who are subject to many of the same responsibilities as elected officials. These officials are appointed in order to accomplish specific duties on behalf of local or state governments.[13]

Development authorities bridge the gap between the public and private sectors to facilitate job creation projects that are desirable to both. Most communities have some form of development authority (also called an industrial authority or payroll authority) that works for the county and/or city in economic development efforts.

A development authority may have been created by one of three methods: local constitutional amendment, general law, or local act. New development authorities may not be created by constitutional amendment. However, development authorities created by local constitutional amendment before the 1983 Constitution may continue to exist. The General Assembly has authorized a development authority for each county and city.[14] However, the development authority is not fully created until the county commission (or city council, in the case of a city) adopts a resolution declaring a need for the development authority.[15] A copy of the resolution must be submitted to the secretary of state.[16]

The method of creation determines the specific powers of the authority. In general, a development authority is charged with the "development of trade, commerce, industry, and employment opportunities," which is a "public purpose vital to the welfare of the people of the state."[17] The Georgia Department of Community Affairs maintains records on development authorities and requires a yearly registration for active development authorities. The department also maintains a database that lists all authorities within a community, which method was used to form the body, who serves on the authority, and contact information.[18]

The county commission appoints members to the development authority.[19] Commissioners should be familiar with current members and when new appointments or reappointments are due.

As previously noted, the county commission may also fund the work of the development authority through general fund appropriations or millage allocations. Local governments may also include capital projects, such as the purchase and development of land for industrial parks, in special purpose local option sales tax projects.[20] An assured funding source for a development authority will facilitate its long-range planning on behalf of the community.

Joint development authorities may be formed between multiple cities and counties in order to accomplish regional goals for economic development.[21] This type of authority is created through resolutions being adopted by the governing authorities of each participating government.[22] Typically, a joint development authority is formed for the purpose of sharing resources for developing product and marketing an area, with revenue generation shared between the jurisdictions that are represented on the authority. In addition to allowing for the pooling of resources by multiple communities, the use of joint development authorities offers an increased state job tax credit of $500 for job creation as an incentive for new or existing industry expansion within the areas served by the authority.[23]

INDUSTRIAL REVENUE BONDS AND OTHER INCENTIVES

One of the ways in which development authorities can attract new business is to issue revenue bonds for industrial purposes.[24] This type of bond is issued on behalf of a private company, and repayment is guaranteed by that company. It does not obligate county funds. The bonds may be income tax free, which can allow for a lower rate of interest. The authority serves as a conduit, enabling a project to be financed at rates well below those that would be available through commercial lenders. Bond proceeds typically are used by the company to purchase land, buildings, and equipment through a lease-purchase arrangement with the authority. The property is actually owned by the development authority, which makes the property tax exempt, and then leased to the company. The lease payments made by the company provide the revenue for the authority to make the interest and principal payments due on the bonds.

Since the development authority is the legal owner of assets purchased through the bond issue, and because it is a governmental entity, its property is not subject to ad valorem taxes.[25] If the board of tax assessors and the tax commissioner recognize that the company's interest in the lease is tax exempt, too, then the company receives a tax abatement. In the state of Georgia, this is one of the only ways in which a county can provide a property tax abatement to a private company. It can be an incentive for a company to locate a project in a community.

Typically, the contract between the development authority and the private company provides that the company pay charges based on its ownership in the project, which would increase each year for the duration of the contract. This type of agreement is referred to as payment in lieu of taxes, or PILOT. Most counties do not include school taxes in this agreement, so the private company would pay school taxes each year at the full rate.

A community might consider other incentives to attract business. These incentives should be agreed upon in advance of any marketing activities. The local economic development team (that is, the community sales team) should determine what is reasonable and what the person who is designated as the single point of contact or the economic developer may offer in negotiations with a prospect.

Several tools exist that can assist a county in developing a reasonable incentives policy that ensures a return on investment. Many counties, through their development authorities, offer incentives that are based on a combination of the number of jobs anticipated and the private investment made in the community. Such incentives might include the following:

- Fee waivers (permits, impact fees, etc.)

- Infrastructure improvements

- Free or reduced-cost land from the development authority

- Free or reduced-cost services from local businesses

- Lowered or eliminated building lease costs

- Other creative ways to save a company initial start-up costs

An incentive or package of incentives, will not "win" a new business location for a community if the business needs of the company cannot be met as well. Typically, incentives come into play when a company has narrowed down its options to just two or three communities that meet all its business requirements. A community should never invest more in incentives than it expects to receive in benefits. A structured memorandum of understanding should be signed by representatives of both the community and the company specifying exactly what is expected and agreed upon by both sides and outlining the penalties for failure to fulfill the agreement. Ultimately, if anything is being offered by the county in the memorandum of understanding or any other form of agreement, it must be approved by the county commission in a meeting.[26]

The State of Georgia also offers incentives to attract and retain business and industry, including the Job Tax Credit Program, and financing assistance programs through the Georgia Department of Community Affairs and the OneGeorgia Authority.[27] One of Georgia's most valuable incentives is the QuickStart training program, which is facilitated by the Technical College System of Georgia and local technical colleges and which offers free customized training to companies that provide new jobs in Georgia.[28]

The state's incentives are available to both new and existing industries that are creating new jobs in Georgia or making new capital investments. County commissioners should ensure that existing companies are treated in the same manner as new companies. In other words, it is not wise to offer an incentive to a new company that would not also be offered to an existing company under the same job creation or capital investment circumstances.

CREATING A SUCCESSFUL ECONOMIC DEVELOPMENT STRATEGY

Every community has distinctive attributes and assets that should be considered in creating a successful strategy for economic development. The realities of funding availability and partnerships to support development efforts are also important considerations. As mentioned earlier, many primary responsibilities of a county commission—such as comprehensive planning,[29] land-use regulation,[30] and provision of adequate public services[31]—set the stage for successful economic development efforts.

Industrial recruitment is just one aspect of economic development, and it may not be the best focus for some communities. Those that do not have the necessary flat land for industrial parks or sufficient water and sewer infrastructure to support industries should explore other strategies in their economic development efforts. Additional economic development strategies that a county may consider include tourism development, small business development, and downtown development, all of which can benefit a county's tax base.

Successful economic development involves having the following:

- a cohesive, well-prepared local sales team with a professional economic developer who represents the community

- a product—whether it is an attractive, well-maintained downtown business district or a new industrial park

- a qualified workforce

- a plan that includes multiple strategies to create jobs and investment and to capitalize on a community's assets

- a marketing effort that includes an excellent Web site

- a long-term commitment to the process, recognizing that economic development is an effort that brings benefits over time

Many public and private entities offer assistance to communities in developing a strategic plan for economic development. Among them are the Georgia Electric Membership Corporation, Georgia Power Company, Electric Cities of Georgia, the Georgia Department of Community Affairs, the Georgia Department of Economic Development, the Georgia Institute of Technology, the University of Georgia, and regional commissions. With the help of these agencies, communities can engage in a collaborative effort to determine their strengths and weaknesses as well as opportunities and threats to success. These organizations show communities how to use this information in order to achieve their aspirations and thereby develop a workable economic development plan that will bring long-term benefits and improve residents' quality of life.

NOTES

1. OFFICIAL CODE OF GEORGIA ANNOTATED (O.C.G.A.) §50-18-70 et seq.
2. O.C.G.A. §50-18-72.
3. O.C.G.A. §48-5-220(20).
4. O.C.G.A. §48-5-330.
5. O.C.G.A. §48-13-51.
6. GA. CONST. art. IX, §2, ¶4.
7. O.C.G.A. §36-66-1 et seq.
8. O.C.G.A. §36-70-1 et seq.
9. GA. CONST. art. IX, §2, ¶1.
10. Georgia Department of Economic Development (www.georgia.org).
11. Small Business Development Center (www.sbdc.uga.edu).
12. GA. CONST. art. IX, §6, ¶3.
13. O.C.G.A. §36-62-4.
14. O.C.G.A. §36-62-4(a).
15. O.C.G.A. §36-62-4(c).
16. Ibid.
17. GA. CONST. art. IX, §6, ¶3.
18. Georgia Department of Community Affairs Directory of Registered Local Government Authorities (www.dca.ga.gov/development/research/programs/RASearch.asp).
19. O.C.G.A. §36-62-4.
20. O.C.G.A. §§48-8-111(a)(1)(C), (D).
21. O.C.G.A. §36-62-5.1.
22. Ibid.
23. O.C.G.A. §36-62-5.1(e)(2).
24. O.C.G.A. §36-62-9.
25. O.C.G.A. §48-5-1.
26. O.C.G.A. §36-10-1.

27. O.C.G.A. §48-7-2; www.dca.ga.gov/economic/TaxCredits/index.asp; Georgia Department of Community Affairs Financing programs (www.dca.ga.gov/economic/Financing/index.asp); One Georgia Authority (www.onegeorgia.org).

28. Quick Start program (www.georgia.org/WhyGeorgia/FirstClassWorkforce/Pages/QuickStart.aspx).

29. O.C.G.A. §36-70-1.

30. O.C.G.A. §36-66-1; GA. CONST. art. IX, §2, ¶3.

31. GA. CONST. art. IX, §2, ¶3.

12

Randy Hartmann and Kelly J. L. Pridgen

Public Works and Public Utilities

Counties in the state of Georgia appropriate considerable funds for public works projects. Those individuals responsible for public works projects are guided by policy decisions regarding these expenditures, and the implementation of these projects requires considerable time and a basic understanding of the public works, civil engineering, and associated activities.

This chapter describes typical public works facilities, activities, and associated services that are financed and owned by Georgia counties. Each of these public works programs fulfills a community need by promoting health, protecting life and property, aiding economic development, and protecting the environment. This list is not considered to be all-inclusive but instead represents a significant number of responsibilities typically observed in the public works setting in counties throughout the state of Georgia, including the following:

- Project oversight and delivery
- Road construction and maintenance
- Transportation and traffic engineering
- Road lighting
- Transit
- Airports
- Transportation and environmental regulation
- Water
- Environmental protection

- Sanitary sewer

- Sanitation/solid waste

- Cable TV

- Building codes

- Vehicle/equipment purchase and maintenance

The discussion in this chapter is applicable to Georgia and federal laws, standard construction and maintenance practices, and other practical management concerns for each public works item listed.

PROJECT DELIVERY

The oversight and method of delivering construction and public works services are key priorities of county officials. Additional contracting and construction delivery methods are covered in Chapter 8.

Engineering

For the supervision of any public works project, qualified engineering services are a primary concern. A professional engineer can protect the public from excessive costs and from unsafe construction and maintenance practices that fail to meet minimum standards. Georgia law defines a professional engineer as one who is qualified and who is properly certified.[1]

Georgia law further defines professional engineering practice as it applies to public works construction and maintenance to include

> any professional service, such as consultation, investigation, evaluation, planning, designing, or responsible supervision of construction or operation, in connection with any public or private utilities, structures, buildings, machines, equipment, processes, works, or projects, wherein the public welfare or the safeguarding of life, health, or property is concerned or involved, when such professional service requires the application of engineering principles and data and training in the application of mathematical and physical sciences.[2]

Except for construction (including alterations) that costs less than $100,000, Georgia law prohibits counties from engaging in public works design, construction, or supervision unless such activity is under the direct authority of a registered professional engineer or architect.[3]

Engineering activities are often separated into two types: one requiring the services of consulting engineers, the other using in-house staff engineers.

Specialized Projects Designed by Consulting Engineers

These projects include water treatment plants, sewage treatment plants, and major road and drainage construction. They are usually built by private contractors whose work can be supervised by either the consulting engineers who designed the project or program management consultants working on behalf of and as staff extension for public works operations. Typically, program management consultants can provide a greater measure of protection of the local government's resources because they are not involved with the actual design of the public works project.

Selecting a consulting engineer should be done carefully. With larger public works projects, a request for qualifications occurs prior to submitting costs proposals. A request for qualifications usually includes past experience on similar projects, qualifications of personnel assigned to the project, ability to meet deadlines, and other related issues. Once the qualified firms are selected, local authorities can either request a cost proposal that contains both the cost and the technical approach to solving the problem for the local authority or a separate technical and cost proposal. This latter approach of separate and distinct proposals is authorized in the federal Brooks Architect–Engineers Act, commonly referred to as the Brooks law.[4] This law establishes the procedures for the procurement of engineering services by federal agencies and certain federally funded projects. Generally speaking, selecting engineering consultants based on their technical merit and expertise followed by separate negotiations for cost based on the highest ranked technical firm is the preferred approach for procuring engineering services. This is known as Qualifications-Based Selection.

Compensating a consultant for engineering services may take the form of lump sum, cost plus fixed fee, percentage of construction costs, or multiple of payroll costs. Regardless of the type of payment chosen, careful attention should be given to any additional services that may involve further costs, such as design changes, soil tests, resident inspection, planning survey, and duplicate copies of drawings.[5]

Activities and General Projects Administered by In-House Engineers

These activities include contract administration associated with consulting engineers; public works supervision; compliance with mandated federal, state, and local regulations associated with public works; and engineering feasibility studies and design for minor public works projects.

Coordinating and controlling the numerous construction and maintenance activities associated with public works entails keeping three categories of maps and records. These records can be maintained in a geographic information system as a managerial control function.[6] The categories are as follows:

1. An official map depicting public rights-of-way and property lines.

2. Detail-supporting maps and records that tie into the official map. Data in these detailed maps include bridges and bridge pier details, subsurface utilities, utility poles, streetlights, pavement surfaces, curbs and gutters, storm drains, topographic elevations, traffic control devices, parking restrictions, pedestrian crosswalks, bridges, and railroad crossings, among others.

3. "As-built" drawings that reflect changes in public works construction and maintenance, such as relocation of water and sewer lines, alterations to water treatment plants and sewage lift stations and treatment plants, and modifications to buildings owned by the county.

PRIVATIZATION AND FINANCING

Privatization of water and sewer operations, government facilities maintenance, and public works operations such as vehicle maintenance and mowing of right-of-ways may be the best choice when localities must address issues related to costs, efficiency, and public perception of government services. Contract services, unit price contracts, and on-demand contract services are among the options for privatization.

Public-private partnerships will become increasingly more important as both large and small governments throughout the state continue to balance operation costs with meeting ever-changing state and federal regulations.

TRANSPORTATION: ROAD CONSTRUCTION AND MAINTENANCE

The Georgia Code of Public Transportation governs county roads.[7] This code forbids construction or maintenance of private roads by a county,[8] specifies property acquisition procedures for public road purposes,[9] and requires notification to the Georgia Department of Transportation (DOT or GDOT) within three months after a county road is added or abandoned.[10] This code empowers counties to contract with other governments; use authorized federal and state funds; and acquire, manage, receive, and make payment for all personal property (e.g., equipment, machinery, and vehicles) used in operating the county road system.[11] Counties may employ personnel and contract with additional persons whose services may be required for construction and maintenance of public roads.[12] Counties are also permitted to enter into contracts with private companies to finance, construct, maintain, improve, own, or operate private toll roads or bridges.[13]

A county may regulate the use of those public roads on its county road system that are located outside the corporate limits of a municipality.[14] In regulating these roads, counties may require that proposed installation and maintenance of utilities be accompanied by written request.[15] Also, with GDOT permission, counties may set vehicle parking requirements and place parking meters on any public road on the state highway system that is outside the corporate limits of any municipality.[16]

With further respect to county road systems, counties can purchase supplies through the state and require contractors who work on county roads to post indemnity bonds or other security for any damages resulting from a contractor's failure to complete the work on time.[17] Counties may provide for surveys, maps, and specifications as are necessary in supervising and maintaining county roads that are in both the unincorporated and incorporated areas of the county.[18] Counties are empowered to contract for public road maintenance or construction.[19] All contracts are required to be let by public bids, except when a county is specifically permitted by law to negotiate contracts. For example, counties may negotiate contracts involving expenditures of $20,000 or less.[20] (For details, see Chapter 8.)

This code further regulates counties with regard to

- control of advertising, erection of informational and directional signals, regulation of limited access roads, and regulation of roads under a county's exclusive jurisdiction;[21]

- relocation of public utilities and railroad grade crossings and payment for these costs;[22]

- junkyards that are within 1,000 feet of the rights-of-way of interstate or federal aid primary highways;[23] and

- acquisition of property, scenic easements, air space, and rights of access for present or future public road or transportation purposes.[24]

Potential for Financial Benefits

Compliance with this code and taking other prudent steps can result in some noteworthy economic benefits for counties. For example, costly damage to county roads can be curtailed by reporting suspected over-weight vehicle violations on county roads to the Georgia Department of Public Safety (DPS). The DPS is authorized to enforce load limitations on all public roads in Georgia.[25] Revenues from ensuing fines and forfeitures are distributed between the state and the county where the violation occurred.[26]

As a means of regulating the maintenance and use of public roads, a county can control vehicle parking and place parking meters (a source of revenue) on its county road system, except on extensions of the county road system into municipalities. It also may place parking meters on state highway system roads outside municipal corporate limits when authorized by DOT.[27]

Counties may limit liability concerns and expenses by building roads to nationally recognized standards such as those published by the American Association State Highway Transportation Officials and the "Greenbook" Committee of Public Works Standards, Inc.

Funding, Regulating, and Maintaining Roads

In constructing roads, the governing authority's policy should consider financial alternatives. Because road construction and right-of-way costs may command a large portion of the county budget, the board may need to spread out these proposed expenditures over several years. This process requires the use of a long-range capital improvements program that permits funding from the following sources:

- Current revenues
- State grants to counties
- State contracts from DOT
- Local option sales tax (LOST)
- Regional local option sales tax
- Special purpose local option sales tax (SPLOST)
- General obligation bonds

- Assessments on adjoining property owners

- Homestead option sales tax (HOST)

- Impact fees

- Public/private partnerships

- Georgia Transportation Infrastructure Bank loans

Two activities in particular are necessary in protecting a county's investment in its paved roads:

- *Regulatory enforcement.* To prevent damage to road surfaces by overweight vehicles, counties should adopt an ordinance that specifies maximum gross vehicular weights on designated streets.

- *Preventive maintenance.* To protect road surfaces and subsurfaces from deterioration due to excessive moisture, a county must promptly patch potholes and effectively seal "alligator cracks."

In order to prevent excessive moisture, all gutters, inlets, catch basins, and storm drainpipes should be kept clear of debris. In urban sections, a regular schedule for street sweeping, leaf collection, and catch basin or outlet cleaning will require expenditures in personnel and equipment; however, this can prevent far heavier outlays in costly resurfacing projects.

Surveys should be performed on a periodic basis in order to adequately define the condition of a county's roadways. A variety of condition survey techniques exist to assist local governments with the maintenance and rehabilitation necessary to maintain their roadway infrastructure and with adequately addressing funding necessary to perform this work. Typically, the Georgia DOT requires that local governments provide a condition survey of local asphalt resurfacing needs for eligibility of state funding for the local road assistance program.

An inventory of roadway striping is also critical to providing a safe roadway for the motoring public. A periodic inventory of existing striping conditions will also help protect the local government from potential litigation.

Right-of-Way Maintenance

It is generally the responsibility of the county public works department to maintain the public right-of-way on the county roads in both the unincorporated and the incorporated areas of the county. The responsibility for maintenance of state rights-of-way is generally the responsibility of the DOT unless a contractual relationship exists between the local government and the DOT. Right-of-way maintenance usually consists of, but is not limited to, (1) removal of shrubbery, trees, and other obstructions for safe operation of the public use of the road; (2) removal of brush and trees that could cause restrictions to sight distance, particularly horizontal and vertical sight distance at intersections; (3) mowing of grass within the right-of-way; and (4) maintenance of a roadway shoulder to ensure that the shoulder elevation matches the roadway elevation in order to avoid drop-offs on the edge of pavement and other irregularities in the shoulder that may result in vehicular accidents.

Proper traffic control during maintenance of the right-of-way is critical during these operations. The Manual for Uniform Traffic Control Devices must be utilized during right-of-way maintenance operations.

Roadway Rehabilitation Techniques

Patch-and-Repair

A number of construction techniques exist for the rehabilitation and repair of public roads. The normally accepted practice by most local governments is to remove those areas that are in need of repair and replace the deteriorated areas with full depth asphalt or a combination of asphalt and underlying graded aggregate base. If a county's public works crews can accomplish this work, the cost usually is minimal except for the time and the cost of materials. The need to contract out patch-and-repair operations can result in significant costs to the local government.

Resurfacing

In those cases where the patch-and-repair operation is extensive or where the cost of patch-and-repair exceeds the cost of resurfacing, the county should assess whether removal of the existing road, through methods defined as reclaiming, is appropriate. Additionally, depending on the condition survey of the roadway, several interim repair measures such as crack sealing (normally done as a preventive measure several years prior to resurfacing) or a single or double surface treatment on the existing roadway surface prior to asphalt resurfacing are available as alternatives to resurfacing.

Reclaiming

Reclaiming is a method by which the existing underlying stone base (if one exists) is removed with the asphalt pavement and the combined material is reclaimed in place and recompacted and utilized as a base course for a new asphaltic concrete pavement surface. This reclaiming operation, although three to four times the cost of a typical asphalt overlay project, will result in a roadway with a lifespan substantially greater than a patch-and-repair or a resurfacing project. Depending on weather, traffic loading conditions, and construction methods and materials, a reclaimed roadway typically has a lifespan of two to three times that of a typical resurfacing project. Moreover, the time, monetary costs, and, in highly urbanized areas, effects of traffic control associated with resurfacing every five to seven years may justify a local government's decision to use the reclamation approach.

TRANSPORTATION AND TRAFFIC ENGINEERING

Vehicular and pedestrian flow on streets is regulated under the Georgia Uniform Rules of the Road.[28] These regulations are also enforceable on privately owned shopping center parking lots or similar areas used by the public as through streets or connector streets.[29]

In their broad scope, the Uniform Rules of the Road regulate the use of traffic signs, signals, and markings;[30] driving on the right side of the roadway, overtaking, and passing;[31] the right of way of approaching vehicles;[32] the rights and duties of pedestrians;[33] turning starting, and signaling;[34] stopping at railroad crossings and entering highways from private drives, alleys, and buildings;[35] school buses;[36] speed restrictions;[37] stopping, standing, and parking;[38] backing, driving on sidewalk, driving on mountain highway, crossing a fire hose, littering, "laying drags";[39] duties in an accident;[40] and the use of bicycles, play vehicles, motorcycles, motorized carts, and mopeds.[41] They also define and specify penalties for serious traffic offenses.[42]

These rules apply throughout Georgia.[43] Counties are given powers to adopt regulations that are supplemental to the Uniform Rules of the Road.[44] They also may adopt by ordinance any or all of these rules by reference; publishing or posting the provisions in full is not required.[45] The adopting ordinance must use the same or similar wording as that appearing in Figure 12-1.[46]

In managing traffic control, a comprehensive transportation and roadway thoroughfare plan is needed that includes the following elements:

1. Road plan. Evaluates roads in meeting objectives. Assigns roads to categories (i.e., arterials, collectors, or local roads).

2. Land-use plan and zoning maps. Determines traffic needs in accommodating land-use patterns. Maps roads to meet traffic flow according to uses (e.g., residential, business, industrial, schools, playgrounds, and hospitals).

Figure 12-1. *Model Ordinance: Georgia Rules of the Road*

County of _____

Ordinance number _____

An ordinance adopting the Georgia Uniform Rules of the Road, Code Sections [_____ to _____ (except for Code Sections _____)] of Chapter 6 of Title 40 of the Official Code of Georgia Annotated, to regulate traffic upon the public streets of the County of _____ and repealing ordinance number _____ and all other ordinances and sections of ordinances in conflict herewith.

It is ordained by _____ as follows:

Section 1. Adoption by reference. Pursuant to Chapter 6 of Title 40 of the Official Code of Georgia Annotated, Code Sections 40-6-372 through 40-6-376, Code Sections [_____ to _____ (except for Code Sections _____)] of that chapter known as the Uniform Rules of the Road and the definitions contained in Code Section 40-1-1 are hereby adopted as and for the traffic regulations of this County with the effect as if recited herein.

Section 2. Penalties. Unless another penalty is expressly provided by law, every person convicted of a violation of any provision of this ordinance shall be punished by a fine of not more than _____ dollars or by imprisonment for not more than _____ days or by both such fine and imprisonment.

Section 3. Repeal. The (existing ordinances covering the same matters as embraced in this ordinance) are hereby repealed and all ordinances or parts of ordinances inconsistent with the provisions of this ordinance are hereby repealed.

Section 4. Effective date. This ordinance shall take effect from and after the _____ day of _____, 20 _____ .

O.C.G.A. §40-6-374

3. Subdivision street plans. Examines subdivision proposals for potential impact from through traffic and other safety hazards. Assigns street speed limits. Reviews curvatures, cul-de-sacs, T intersections, distances between intersections. Encourages minimum number of intersections at one location.

4. Origin-destination study. Collects information for forecasting increases in traffic volume.

5. Sight distance analysis.[47] Evaluates obstruction removal necessary to aid motorist vision at designated intersections under varying approach speeds (e.g., at an intersection on a hill).

6. Traffic warrant analysis.[48] Investigates traffic conditions at a location to determine if a signal installation is warranted. Data collection includes the number, type, and speed of vehicles from each approach; pedestrian volume; accident experience; and geometric conditions.

Comprehensive Transportation Studies

Most urbanized areas in Georgia are faced with the need to make transportation improvements. Transportation improvements facilitate economic vitality, quality of life, and transportation safety by identifying needs in the short, intermediate, and long term. The Comprehensive Transportation Plan typically provides recommendations for transportation improvements that address countywide, intercounty, and regional travel needs. Various modes of transportation are also typically addressed, including roadway, transit, bicycle, and pedestrian facilities. The transportation plan is submitted when urbanized counties seek to obtain state and federal funding, and it provides technical documentation for addressing air quality concerns as required under the Clean Air Act.[49] Factors typically considered in the development of Comprehensive Transportation Plans include coordination of all transportation improvement plans with the local government's current and future land-use and zoning plans; travel demand forecasting models for the development of analyzing transportation alternatives; coordination with studies of transportation plans of adjoining jurisdictions; development of a countywide thoroughfare plan with roadway functional classifications; identification of current and future transportation deficiencies, trends in patterns of development, and the effects on the transportation network; and the development of conceptual cost estimates for construction of transportation projects.

Roadway Modeling

Transportation modeling is a necessary element in the development of transportation thoroughfare plans. The assessment of future travel demands and patterns can be done through computer modeling. Modeling programs typically reflect current travel patterns and anticipate future population, employment, and travel growth.

Traffic-Calming Devices

The technique known as traffic calming is quickly becoming an accepted traffic control measure for addressing a wide range of citizen concerns within residential neighborhoods. Traffic calming includes slowing traffic speeds; reducing cut-through traffic and traffic-related noise; improving the aesthetics of the street; and increasing safety for pedestrians, bicyclists, and vehicles, with the ultimate goal of improving the overall quality of life within a neighborhood. Traffic circles, chicanes, chokers, narrowing roads, changes in road texture, direction changes, and a variety of other mid-block design changes can alter the movement of vehicles on residential streets. It is critical that the use of traffic-calming measures be coordinated with the DOT because it has had policies that prohibited state funding on roads that incorporated certain types of traffic-calming devices.

A number of professional organizations, such as the Institute of Transportation Engineers, have developed technical specifications and guidelines for traffic-calming devices. Governments that have instituted such traffic control measures are another source of information.

Asset Management and Traffic Signs, Striping, and Other Roadway Inventory Attributes

The development of a database for a county's public works infrastructure, such as signs, striping, and work orders initiated and completed within the road right-of-way, is critical for budgeting, scheduling, and protecting the local government in the event of litigation. Numerous types of software exist for the creation of this database. Integration of this inventory of public works infrastructure can be accomplished with minimal training of public works staff. In addition, maintaining an accurate and up-to-date inventory of public works infrastructure is an important step toward properly managing county assets.

Road Lighting

County road-lighting policies should consider crime control, highway safety, business convenience, and beautification. Policies should establish priorities, particularly when funding for road lighting is limited. Essential roadway-lighting standards can be adopted regarding minimum levels of illumination, maximum permissible ratios of average to minimum illumination, and minimum mounting heights. Roadways are classified by traffic use and access. Areas may be commercial, residential, or some combination of these.[50]

Policymakers may also need to consider the efficiency of lighting units and the amount of vertical and lateral light they will emit. Assistance may be found in *American National Standard Practice for Roadway Lighting*, as developed by the Illuminating Engineering Society, and in *Lighting Handbook*.[51] In selecting lighting, the costs must be weighed against the benefits of alternative electrical light sources. Maintenance of a road-lighting program is also important. Reflectors need to be washed regularly, trees trimmed, lamps replaced, and damaged, rotted, or rusting poles replaced.[52]

Transit

Counties may contract with transit agencies for transit services or facilities within the county or between that county and any area in which the transit agency already provides such services or facilities. However, if transit services are to be subsidized by fees, taxes, or assessments levied in a special service district, the voters of the county must approve the contract. The governing authority of an affected county must adopt a transit service plan.[53]

Airports

Among the more than 100 airports in Georgia, some are the responsibility either jointly or fully of one or more counties. Usually managed by a fixed-base operator (FBO), most small airports are only marginally profitable at best. For this reason, the governing authority may not expect to operate an airport solely from airport revenues.

Liability prevention and the development of standard management practices have been cited by Georgia FBOs/airport managers as critical areas for improving profits and achieving greater stability.[54] In deciding on lease arrangements with FBOs/airport managers, governing authorities should be prepared to deal with the various concerns. In terms of liability prevention, these include noise, selling of new and used parts, bailor-bailee relationships, renting of airplanes to incompetent pilots, negligent instruction, and defective rental aircraft. In terms of management practices, such concerns include safety procedures, accident notification, fire regulations, emergency weather procedures, fuel facilities inspection and maintenance, and testing of fuel storage for water and foreign matter.

Airport mowing, public works projects, passenger and visitor services, and revenue charges are other issues that FBOs must address when they serve as airport operators. Information on these concerns is available in the *Small Airport Management Handbook*.[55]

TRANSPORTATION AND ENVIRONMENTAL REGULATIONS

The construction and maintenance of county roads and bridges will likely involve activities, equipment, and materials that can significantly impact air and water quality as well as produce significant noise levels. As a result, county construction and maintenance activities are likely to be subject to state and federal environmental laws and regulations, including the Clean Water Act,[56] the Clean Air Act,[57] the National Environmental Policy Act,[58] the Resource Conservation and Recovery Act (RCRA),[59] the Endangered Species Act,[60] the Rivers and Harbors Act,[61] the Toxic Substances Control Act,[62] and noise abatement regulations. For more information on environmental laws and regulations that affect counties, see Chapter 10.

New construction often involves clearing land prior to the beginning of the actual construction activity. Land-clearing activities such as the removal of vegetation and existing structures can affect the structural makeup of the soil, increase soil erosion and sedimentation, and cause flooding, which may affect downstream property owners and aquatic resources, particularly wetlands and floodplains. Sensitivity to downstream impacts is vitally important in road construction activities, and great care must be taken to ensure that such impacts are eliminated or minimized. These land-disturbing activities must observe the best management practices established in the Erosion and Sedimentation Act of 1975.[63] Other potential impacts as a result of construction activities include air emissions, noise, vibrations from construction equipment, and dust and/or odors from construction traffic.

The 1970 Clean Air Act established a regulatory structure that required states to meet air quality standards and transportation plans in order to conform to state strategies to meet those air quality standards. Air pollution must then be reduced by certain attainment dates or deadlines. The act defines two types of stationary air pollution sources: existing and new. New sources are subject to one set of technology-based requirements; existing sources are subject to a more lenient approach to resolving an air quality violation.

Additional amendments to the Federal Highway Funding Program resulted in complementary environmental requirements identified as the

Intermodal Surface Transportation Efficiency Act (ISTEA). Within the ISTEA program, metropolitan planning organizations (with populations greater than 200,000) must adopt 20-year transportation plans and Transportation Improvement Programs (TIP) consisting of projects funded or approved by the Federal Highway Administration or the Federal Transit Administration. The transportation improvement plan must result in emissions that conform to the State Implementation Plan for Air Quality (SIP) budget for mobile source emissions. ISTEA's metropolitan planning requirements prohibit federal approval, funding, or implementation of transportation projects that do not conform to the SIP.

The ISTEA program not only strengthened metropolitan planning organizations' authority to conduct transportation planning and allocate federal funds but also created separate categories of projects and programs eligible for federal funding under the Congestion Mitigation and Air Quality program for the express purpose of supporting improvements in air quality. ISTEA also encouraged multimodal planning, requiring a set of management systems for intermodal facilities, bridges, pavement, public transportation, safety, and congestion.[64] The influence of the Clean Air Act and ISTEA amendments shifted the emphasis in metropolitan transportation planning toward projects that improve air quality and away from those that impair it.

WATER

In a county that distributes water, supply must be adequate to satisfy needed peak hourly flows for both domestic purposes and required fire flows. For domestic uses, the water supply must meet state health standards regarding clarity, softness, palatability, and purity. In order to meet required fire flows, additional water must be provided in amounts above the quantities needed for peak domestic demand. This required fire flow amount must be in elevated storage in case of electrical malfunctioning.

The policy of the county governing authority should assure that these two separate purposes—domestic needs and fire flows—are satisfied in evaluating the water supply in terms of its source, pumping capacity, and elevated storage reservoirs. The water supply may come from a surface supply (a river or lake) or from an underground supply (wells). Calculations for determining the total water supply are usually prepared by consulting engineers. Regardless of the source of the water supply, policy should be dedicated to meeting long-range capital needs and assuring an adequate supply of water to satisfy both domestic needs and required fire flows. One consequence of poor planning for the water needs of the county may be higher insurance premiums in a community as a result of a low fire defense rating by the Insurance Services Office because of inadequate water supply.

A good water distribution system provides adequate quantity and pressure. Adequate quantity refers not only to the amount of water available, but also to the need to have a supply from two different directions using a series of "loops" to all points in the system. Adequate pressure requires the use of elevated storage tanks or standpipes to equalize pressure in the system and to provide for maintaining pressure in case of pump failure. In counties that have dispersed clusters of urban subdivisions, it may be necessary to operate more than one water system.

Charging for Water

The general practice in most counties is to charge consumers regardless of type—residential, commercial, or industrial—for the actual amount of water used during a specific period.[65] Meter reading and billing are ordinarily done under a cycle plan whereby meters are read either monthly or bimonthly. Meters are divided into divisions or zones, and all meters in a single zone are read and billed according to that zone. In this way, the billing clerk avoids a peak load of preparing bills in a short time span. Unit prices are specified per 100 or 1,000 cubic feet or gallons of metered water used. If the cost per unit of water delivered is lower as quantities increase, the unit price for the water decreases. Prices change according to several "blocks" or steps in the rate schedule.

If customers use unusually large volumes of water, requiring larger treatment systems or larger distribution systems, the unit price may rise to offset increased costs. Two examples of demand-charge customers are (1) industries that process large volumes of water and (2) customers in sparsely developed areas that are distant from previously planned main extensions and elevated storage tanks. Conservation billing—consumers paying more based upon consumption—is a growing practice.

Management Policy

The following suggestions provide policy guidance in managing the county water system:

- Water pricing should be adjusted at least annually in order to keep pace with inflation as well as to offset any expected increased costs in capital improvements in the water system. Because sanitary sewer rates are usually a percentage of the water bill, the water pricing ultimately determines the funds available for sewer operation and capital plans. Incremental annual or semiannual increases in water and sewer rates are usually more acceptable to the public than large increases every two or three years.

- Persons supervising the operation of public water supply systems and wastewater treatment plants must be certified by the State Board of Examiners for Certification of Water and Wastewater Treatment Plant Operators and Laboratory Analysts.[66] There are several classifications of water supply systems and several certification classes established by the Environmental Protection Division (EPD) of the Georgia Department of Natural Resources.[67]

- Water quality test results should be summarized quarterly and explained to the governing authority. Plant operators are required to perform laboratory tests on water from their system at specified intervals and to send water samples to the EPD for analysis.[68] Water quality should be protected by periodic inspections at customer locations, especially commercial establishments. Particular attention should be given to ensure that improper cross-connections and backflows are prevented from contaminating the entire distribution system.

- Unaccounted water losses should be identified and reduced.

- Policies should be reviewed if they result in water subsidies to any group at the expense of paying customers. The county should have a policy governing the extension of water mains, particularly with respect to who will pay for them.[69] The county should extend service to developers and industry only when they are willing to pay for the extension. Provisions can be made for rebating some or all of the extension cost to developers and industry as customers are added to new lines. The extension policy should also cover the size of the line. In this case, the county would want to consider requirements for customer usage and fire protection. Water mains should be sized to meet domestic needs and to support required fire flows. Although it is less expensive to install smaller domestic lines, eventually they will probably need to be replaced to provide adequate hydrant service and improve the fire insurance rating.

- Each water system customer should be individually metered so that payment will be on the basis of amount actually used.

There should be no "flat-rate" or "nonmetered" customers. The amount of water used by flat-rate customers and the consequent revenue lost is almost always significantly higher than expected and usually warrants the expense of installing and reading meters.

- Water meters should be tested or meter heads replaced regularly to ensure proper operation. Counties should adopt a rotation schedule to periodically test and identify malfunctioning meters. Obviously, the continued existence of many defective meters can cause considerable revenue loss to the county.

- Meters should be read frequently. While many water systems read meters every 30 days, reading and billing might be performed every 60 days. A 60-day billing period would provide more time for meter reading and would reduce by half the number of water bills to be mailed each year.

SANITARY SEWER

In a modern county sanitary sewer system, liquid wastes are collected in a network of drains from two basic types of sewers: sanitary and storm sewers. Sanitary sewers collect contaminated, putrescible liquid from the plumbing systems of buildings and carry it to a sewage treatment plant or other suitable place for disposal. Storm sewers collect rainwater and carry it to natural water courses or bodies of water in such a way as to prevent flooding.[70] Because of space limitations and the extreme importance of sanitary sewers (and because, in many cases, storm sewers and sanitary sewers are combined), this section does not discuss enclosed storm sewer systems.

Where physically possible, sanitary sewer systems depend upon gravity to move the sewage through the lines. For this reason, the location of sewer lines must be carefully planned to follow the topography of the land and to ensure that sewage flows downhill toward the treatment plant. If this is not possible, pumping stations must be installed, where necessary, to lift the sewage and force it up and over a grade for additional gravity flowage.

Sanitary Sewer Treatment Methods

Once sewage has been collected and piped to a place of disposal, it must be given primary, secondary, and sometimes tertiary, treatment.[71] With primary treatment, raw sewage undergoes digestion by bacterial action and is pumped through a series of screens that remove successively smaller particles of insoluble solid matter. When the screening process is completed, the remaining sewage is pumped into a sedimentation tank, where additional solid waste is allowed to settle to the bottom of the tank. This solid matter, called sludge, is periodically removed from the tank and used for fertilizer, burned, dumped in a landfill, or disposed of in some other manner. As a final step in primary treatment, the liquid waste is treated with chlorine gas for a minimum period of time to destroy disease-causing bacteria and to make it less offensive. The chlorinated liquid is then discharged into a stream or river.

Secondary treatment adds a step in which bacteria in the sewage are further utilized to decompose organic matter. After passing through a sedimentation tank, as in primary treatment, the liquid waste is pumped into another facility. There, it is either trickled slowly through a bed of stones or exposed to "activated sludge." In the trickling-filter process, liquid waste passes slowly over layers of stone that become covered with bacteria that decompose organic matter remaining in the sewage. In the activated sludge process, sewage is pumped into an aeration tank, where—through exposure to oxygen and sludge containing a high bacteria count—it is further decomposed. As in primary treatment, the last stage in secondary treatment is to chlorinate the remaining liquid waste before pumping it into a stream or river.

In addition to primary and secondary treatment, more advanced techniques have been suggested and/or tried, including the following:

- Coagulation-sedimentation—to increase the removal of solids and to remove phosphate

- Absorption—to remove more organic matter than can be eliminated in secondary treatment

- Electrodialysis—to remove salts and then restore, or even improve, the salt content of the water

These techniques, when used in succession, return the county's water to a quality appropriate for any reuse by keeping rivers clean. State and federal regulations mandate minimum wastewater treatment practices for county sewage treatment systems. These regulations are administered by the EPD.[72]

In managing the county sanitary sewer system, several alternative customer billing approaches are available, including

- flat rate,

- number of fixtures,

- flat rate according to water bill,
- percentage of water bill,
- flat minimum rate plus percentage of water bill,
- percentage of average winter water bill, and
- proration based on water consumption.[73]

It has been noted that a "good argument can be made in favor of basing the sewer service charge on the quantity of water used or some variable indicating water or consumption, such as size of water meter. This approach at least recognizes the fact that a large proportion of the water delivered to the customer is later returned to the sewer."[74]

Suggestions for overseeing sanitary sewer activities include the following:

1. Periodically evaluate the nature and condition of the present sewer system regarding treatment plant capacity and major repairs to the plant or to the collection system that may be needed.
2. Consider all planning for residential, commercial, and industrial expansion or redevelopment that may reveal future needs for additional sewer capacity.
3. Explore financial implications of sewerage plans.
4. Phase any untreated sewage into an expansion program as feasible. Consult EPD officials before proceeding with major expansions.
5. Monitor industrial wastes to the sewerage system to assure adequate pretreatment processes.
6. Reconcile the sewerage system with plumbing regulations of the county.
7. Clarify county policy on sewer connections as to who can do the work and under what conditions.
8. Make provisions for disposing of roof drain, septic tank outlet, car wash, laundry, and air-conditioning water.

Combined Sewer and Sanitary Sewer Overflows

The Federal Clean Water Act requires local governments to rehabilitate combined sewer overflows (CSOs) and sanitary sewer overflows (SSOs), which will require an enormous investment, particularly in urban areas within the state of Georgia that have an aging sewer infrastructure. Both types of sewage collection and treatment systems in older communities can release raw sewage into our streams and rivers.

Combined sewer overflows result from a design technique used for the construction of municipal sewers many years ago. Sewer collection lines were frequently designed to handle both sanitary sewer and storm water runoff from streets, roofs, and buildings. These combined systems were usually built prior to municipal, state, or federal requirements for sanitary sewer treatment. When wastewater treatment plants were constructed, the plants and their collector sewers were provided with bypasses to prevent them from being overwhelmed with large volumes of mixed sanitary sewer and storm water during periods of rainfall. Combined sewer overflows are the discharge of mixtures of storm water and untreated sewage from these combined systems.

In order to gain further control over CSO discharges and to eliminate and reduce them, the federal EPA, working through the state EPD, requires systems with CSOs to implement the following nine minimum controls:[75]

1. Implement proper operation and maintenance programs for the sewer system and the combined sewer overflows.

2. Maximize use of the collection system for storage of combined storm water and sewage before later treatment.

3. Review and modify industrial wastewater pretreatment requirements to ensure that adverse CSO impacts are minimized.

4. Maximize flow to the wastewater treatment plant for treatment.

5. Prohibit CSO discharges during dry weather.

6. Control solid and floatable materials in CSOs.

7. Implement pollution prevention measures.

8. Provide adequate notification to the public about CSO occurrences and impacts.

9. Monitor and characterize CSO impacts and the effectiveness of CSO controls.

Sanitary Sewer Overflows

Sanitary sewer overflows occur when sewer collection lines that are designed to handle only sanitary sewage become overcharged with storm water entering the system from a variety of external sources. These sewer lines then either back up and discharge from manholes or other outlets into homeowners' basements or through designed diversion structures that are intended to limit the amount of flow into large interceptor sewers. These discharges are SSOs.

Sources of the storm water entering the sanitary sewer systems include inflow and infiltration. Inflow comes from such design defects as low manholes and other features below grade so that they serve as a conduit for storm water into the sanitary sewer system. Other sources of inflow include breaks or gaps in collectors that admit stream flows and hookups of residential roof drains and foundation drains into the sanitary sewer system. Infiltration comes from the deterioration of collectors and house sewer laterals (the homeowner portion of the system that conveys wastewater to the municipal collector), allowing storm water to enter the lines.

Technical solutions to CSOs and SSOs and alternatives could include

- reducing the amount of inflow and infiltration from house laterals and other private sources such as roof and foundation drains;

- reducing the amount of storm water in separate sanitary sewers through substantial repair, replacement of municipal collectors, and better municipal maintenance programs that schedule inspections and replacement of deteriorated lines and cleanouts of obstructions;

- conveying more or all of the mixed storm water and wastewater to the wastewater treatment plant and providing additional treatment capacity for this volume; and

- constructing storage tanks and retention basins in individual local governments to contain wet water volumes that can be treated later during lower flow periods.[76]

Alternative Wastewater Systems

A number of alternatives exist to on-site, individual septic tank systems or centralized wastewater systems. Such systems are described as community-based septic tank systems. These decentralized systems essentially redirect effluent to a centralized large-scale holding tank and leach field. Advanced on-site systems must be designed for a particular set of environmental parameters. Where restrictive soils exist, recirculating sand filters can be used in combination with absorption systems to enhance pathogen reduction and lower absorption area requirements, for example. Discharge of any wastewater system greater than 10,000 gallons per day requires an EPD permit. Such decentralized systems must consider the following factors:

- Management and maintenance of community-based systems should be accomplished through a homeowners association or by annual fees. The association fees are then used to perform annual or more frequent cleanout of the systems and inspection of such systems.

- The removal of effluent must be sufficiently removed through a biological system to ensure that communal drain fields function properly.

- A proper design, with particular attention given to installation, is critical to the success of community-based systems.

The benefits of such systems are as follows:

- A community-based septic tank system will generally increase the value of the lots similar to that of a subdivision development with sanitary sewers.

- Removal of on-site septic tank systems will allow for saving of more trees on each individual lot.

- Long-term cost for sewer will be reduced as a result of connections to a community-based septic tank system. (Extension of sewer lines throughout a subdivision would not be necessary. Direct connection to a community-based system would reduce costs to a local government.)

- Environmentally, a community-based system can be more easily maintained and managed as opposed to individual septic tank systems, which may not be properly inspected or maintained by homeowners.

PRIVATIZATION OF WATER, WASTEWATER, AND STORM WATER SYSTEMS

Public-private partnerships in the areas of water, wastewater, and storm water may take the form of privatization; contract operation, maintenance, and management; or contract management.

Privatization

Privatization can take the form of (1) purchase of an existing facility, (2) creation of a new facility (from the initial planning to the design of the infrastructure) and long-term operation, (3) expansion or enhancement of an existing facility, or (4) long-term lease of treatment works.

Contract Operations, Maintenance, and Management

A contractor generally performs contract operations, maintenance, and management services under a negotiated agreement to provide necessary government services. The contractor is responsible for the routine operation, maintenance, and management of the treatment facilities while the ownership remains with the government. The contractor normally guarantees performance of the facilities while complying with all regulations. The contractor is generally responsible for all routine costs associated with the operations of the facilities. Large capital expenditures for expansion and upgrade remain the responsibility of the local government.

Within a contract management partnership, the government retains ownership of the facility and is responsible for purchasing supplies and equipment and regulatory compliance. The private sector is a partner with the local government and assumes all personnel and management responsibility. Public-private partnerships for storm water projects are just beginning to be examined in Georgia, but the need for such partnerships will become increasingly more important over the next decade.

Funding Storm Water Systems

The financing of storm water projects is generally relegated as a line item within the general fund of local governments, often competing with other funding needs (e.g., fire, sheriff) within a community. With the increased emphasis on environmental issues (and associated mandates) in the United States, storm water and related water quality issues will require dedicated funding sources.

A storm water utility is an example of dedicated funding that more than 40 city and county governments in Georgia have initiated, and more are coming on line each year. A fee is assessed to the property owners of land within a county setting based on their amount of impervious surface (or their storm water contribution), and this fee is used exclusively to address storm water and associated water quality concerns. Other funding opportunities include impact fees, EPA Clean Water Act Section 319 and community development block grant funds, and increasing millage rates and other fees.

SANITATION

Managing Solid Waste

Management of the county's solid waste is a significant responsibility of county government. Under the Georgia Comprehensive Solid Waste Management Act, counties are required to adopt solid waste management plans and to update these plans every 10 years.[77] The adopted solid waste management plan must demonstrate 10 years of solid waste collection capability and disposal capacity. It must also include a strategy to reduce the per capita disposal rate within the county. ~~The plan must also~~ include *and* a "land limitation" element that governs the siting of new solid waste–handling facilities within the county. This land limitation element, if written and implemented properly, is a powerful tool in managing where and how both public and private solid waste–handling facilities are sited and operated. The Department of Community Affairs (DCA) ~~reviews and approves solid waste management plans and~~ collect*s* *other* solid waste management information from local governments annually. ~~The EPD implements the regulatory provisions of local plans.~~

Collection of Solid Waste (Refuse), Recyclables, and/or Yard Trimmings

While landfilling remains the most widely used solid waste disposal method, many county sanitation systems throughout the state have made or are making the transition from "waste" management to "resource" management. Citizens are increasingly demanding separate collection services for solid waste, recyclables, and yard trimmings so that these materials may be put to beneficial use. A growing trend, primarily in the commercial sector, is to separate organics collection for composting and/or biofuel production.

A county may choose from among six basic arrangements for the collection of refuse, recyclables, and/or yard trimmings:

1. Provide the service using county employees and equipment
2. Contract, with private haulers or another local government, for collection services for the entire unincorporated county or parts of the county
3. Establish a franchise for collection services for the entire unincorporated county or parts of the county
4. License private collectors who provide collection services directly with homeowners and/or commercial property owners

Promote

5. Adopt an ordinance governing refuse, recycling, and/or yard trimmings collection services within the county

6. Open competition enabling private haulers to provide collection services directly to homeowners and/or commercial property owners without any oversight.

Counties may use a combination of these methods. For example, county crews may collect from bins that are set out along the road in rural areas and license private haulers to collect from densely populated subdivision residents, businesses, and industrial firms. Alternatively, they may elect to use their own crews to collect yard trimmings and recyclables and contract out the collection of refuse.

In order to capture the economic benefit of the collected materials, refuse, recyclables, and yard trimmings need to be kept separate. In most cases, keeping materials segregated from refuse results in a higher economic value of the individual materials collected. If recyclables are "source separated" during collection (e.g., each material is separated from the other), they can be processed and sold directly to end-market users of those materials. However, a source-separated recycling collection system typically costs more, has less participation, and has lower recycling recovery rates than does a single-stream/comingled recycling collection system. Trying to capture recyclables or energy from recyclables mixed together with refuse typically has the highest cost and results in the lowest recovery rate of any collection program.

There are five commonly used methods for the collection of solid waste, recyclables, and/or yard trimmings:

a system where all the recyclables are collected from one container

1. <u>Roadside or curbside service</u>. On a regular schedule (typically either weekly or twice a week for refuse, sometimes less frequently for recyclables and yard trimmings), residents carry and set out at the "curb" their refuse, recyclables, and/or yard trimmings contained in separate containers, where they are picked up by a county crew or private collection hauler. Residents return the containers to their original location stored on their property. This service can be provided using either an automated collection vehicle with one driver and an automated "sidearm" to collect and empty the containers or a rear load packer truck typically with a two- to three-person collection crew. Yard trimmings, especially storm debris, are often collected using a grapple or claw bucket and dump trucks.

2. Backdoor service. Collection crews collect refuse, recyclables, and/or yard trimmings in large containers, baskets, or disposable paper or plastic sacks from the "backdoor" of a residence and carry them to a collection vehicle and return the container to the location where they found it. Many counties either provide or require a private hauler to provide this service to elderly or disabled residents.

3. Convenience centers. Refuse, recyclables, and/or yard trimmings are delivered to either a staffed or unstaffed location or locations in the county by residents or businesses. Unstaffed locations typically consist of a series of "green" container boxes that are serviced by county crews, but more typically private waste haulers take the refuse to a solid waste transfer station or landfill. Most unstaffed locations do not collect recyclables or yard trimmings in separate containers. Staffed convenience centers have set hours of operation, typically accept both refuse and recyclables, and are secured during nonoperating hours in order to prevent illegal dumping and use by nonresidents. Residents and businesses typically are required to separate their recyclables into separate roll-off containers for each recyclable accepted; however, many counties are starting to take advantage of single-stream recycling collection whereby all the recyclables are mixed together into one collection container and collected either by a county crew or private hauler and delivered to a material recovery facility for processing and delivery to an end market or an industrial user of the recyclable materials. Collected yard trimmings are either ground and managed on site and delivered to a composting facility and/or an inert or construction and demolition landfill.

4. Vacuum collection. Used for yard trimmings collection only. Leaves are raked to the curb and collected by a county collection crew using a vacuum collection vehicle. The collected materials are delivered to a composting facility, inert landfill, or construction and demolition landfill. This service typically is only provided in densely populated areas of a county.

5. Special events. On a periodic basis, counties may host a special event to collect hard-to-dispose-of items, including tires; bulky items like couches, mattresses, and other furniture sometimes referred to as "brown goods"; electronic items; computers and

televisions; appliances or "white goods"; or household hazardous waste. These events either are held at county facilities or involve hiring a private contractor to provide the collection containers (e.g., roll-off box, tractor trailer, or van truck, depending upon the materials being collected).

Management of Collected Solid Waste (Refuse), Recyclables, and/or Yard Trimmings

Most areas in the state use a combination of sanitary landfill, ~~incinera-tor, and/or~~ recycling, composting, and/or bioconversion facility to manage the discarded resources collected within their county. Open dumps, which attract insects and rodents, are highly undesirable and illegal. ~~Many public agencies have abandoned the incineration process because of air pollution and the high cost of approved incineration methods.~~ The majority of counties in the state now use a sanitary landfill, where refuse is compacted and covered with a layer of dirt on a daily basis. Due to the increased environmental regulatory costs of constructing and operating a lined sanitary landfill, such landfills have become larger and more regional in nature. Approximately two-thirds of the disposable waste in Georgia is disposed of in one-third of the landfills in the state, which are privately owned and operated.

Minimizing transportation costs to these regional landfills has given rise to the siting and operation of solid waste transfer stations. Solid waste transfer stations typically are roofed structures, often three-sided buildings, where solid waste haulers, individuals, and businesses deliver collected waste. The waste is then loaded onto semi-trailers or placed into trash compactors for delivery to a sanitary landfill. Solid waste transfer stations do not require a solid waste–handling permit from the EPD; the siting and operational management are governed primarily by local zoning regulations and provisions included in a county solid waste management plan.

Recycling

Community recycling initiatives can support Georgia-based manufacturers and extend landfill life by reducing the amount of the waste stream.[78] Recycling stations or centers are alternatives to landfill disposal. These centers typically accept recyclables such as newspaper, magazines, cardboard, plastic, scrap metal, and glass that are kept separate from each other. The centers typically have a baler to process the collected materials so they can be cost effectively shipped to markets/manufacturers that use the materials by recycling them into new products. These centers are typically operated by local governments or nonprofits that also have the responsibility for finding a market for these materials.

A Material Recovery Facility (MRF) is another type of recycling center. At a MRF, recyclables that are collected "single stream" (i.e., collected comingled in one container or vehicle) are accepted and [and delivered for] processing. At a MRF, materials are separated by type, processed, and delivered to end users or markets. Depending upon recyclable commodity market conditions, counties and private haulers can expect to get paid a nominal amount for the materials delivered to a MRF or be able to deliver the materials and drop them off free of charge.

Recycling has a major impact upon the environment and Georgia's economy. Recycling conserves the state's natural resources, reduces the volume of waste disposed of in landfills, and results in less energy and water consumption when the materials are used to make new products. [Fact] Recycling also supports the markets [Georgia jobs] the industries in Georgia that need these materials for their operations. Georgia has strong markets for all the recyclables collected in a curbside recycling program. For example, the state has 16 paper mills, 9 of which rely exclusively on recycled fiber [?] for their operations; one-third of all plastic beverage containers recycled in North America are recycled into carpet in north Georgia; aluminum cans are being recycled and readied for use in less than 30 days in Greensboro; and three Georgia manufacturers use recycled glass in their operations. Recycling these materials in Georgia means these materials are available locally, reducing the cost and environmental emissions associated with transporting these materials to markets in the state.

Composting/Bioconversion

Counties are required to [may] impose restrictions on the disposal of yard trimmings.[79] Under current law, counties are required to have [may require] yard trimmings [to be] collected separately from refuse and to keep the collected yard trimmings from being disposed of at lined landfills and preferably be put to beneficial use. Another method of reducing the solid waste stream is composting, a process of aerobic biological decomposition of organic materials to produce a stable and usable organic topsoil that does not require disposal. Resources used to create the final compost product originate from the roughly 60 percent of the municipal solid waste stream that is organic material (e.g., food waste, scrap paper, yard and lawn clippings). The primary activities associated with composting are (1) collections/receiving wastes for composting, (2) processing of waste, and (3) marketing. A local government can collect or receive waste for composting from a variety *curbside*

of sources, such as active yard waste collection programs, vacuuming of leaves, and organics-only collection.

Another source of compostable materials is biosolids—sewage sludge, the solid, semisolid, or liquid residue generated during the treatment of domestic sewage in a wastewater treatment plant. Given the federal guidelines and restrictions on the land application of biosolids, composting may be a viable option for managing this resource.[80]

Composting of household organic materials is not regulated by any major federal statute, although Georgia does have composting standards and regulations if the composting operation involves processing any organic materials beyond yard trimmings.

The processing or decomposition stage of composting involves both a physical and biological process. In order to accelerate the decomposition process and minimize odors, composters typically shred or grind the organic materials they accept into smaller particle sizes and frequently rotate or "turn" the composting materials. Composters must also carefully balance the carbon-nitrogen mix of the materials they accept in order to successfully stimulate the biological process of decomposing organic materials into a stable, usable soil amendment.

Bioconversion is another growing trend for managing organics in the waste stream. Bioconversion is the conversion of the organic waste stream to energy through a biological process or agents such as certain microorganisms or enzymes.

Charges for Solid Waste Disposal

Solid waste management services may be financed through the county general fund, an enterprise fund (supported by a special assessment, a user fee collected by the county or private contractor) or the creation of a special service district. A special assessment and user fee are typically preferred over using the general fund, given that there is not necessarily a correlation between the value of someone's property and the amount of trash they generate. A special assessment may be assessed using a number of factors and collected as a line item on property tax bills, or a user-fee bill may be sent monthly or quarterly by either the county or a private contractor to individual residents or commercial waste generators. If a particular service such as residential collection is provided only to a particularly densely populated area, the county may create a special service district to finance this effort.[81] The special service district can give relief to urbanized residents in unincorporated parts of the county while avoiding the imposition of charges to rural landowners of large tracts of land who may not need this service. Similarly, a service district can consist of the entire unincorporated area of the county, ~~with municipalities providing disposal services using municipal revenues.~~ -is

A ~~The~~ flat minimum rate ~~was previously~~ the most popular fee plan in *and promote recycling* most counties. In an effort to reduce the waste stream, ~~however,~~ some counties have instituted a "pay-as-you-throw" system, with fees based on the amount or volume of solid waste collected. Under this program, households are charged a higher rate for larger trash containers (e.g., a 95 gallon cart versus a 35 gallon cart). Because recycling containers and services are typically provided without an itemized fee, a pay-as-you-throw program supports recycling efforts by charging a higher rate for the collection of larger trash containers. This practice is consistent with commercial accounts, which usually ~~are~~ charged on the basis of quantity and frequency of collection services.

CABLE TELEVISION

Many counties have franchise agreements with cable television providers. A franchise agreement is a contract between the county and the cable provider in which the county allows the cable provider to locate its cables and equipment in the public rights-of-way of the unincorporated area of the county in exchange for a franchise fee.[82] A county may charge up to 5 percent of the cable company's gross revenues[83] as a franchise fee.[84] Unlike cities, the only service for which counties may collect a franchise fee is cable service.[85]

Cable franchise agreements may no longer contain build-out requirements for any cable providers.[86] Cable providers can expand or shrink their service area as long as they do not discriminate based on the income of the subscribers in an area.[87] Any discrimination claims will be brought to the local government and addressed through nonbinding mediation or the courts.[88]

Cable providers are required to follow any county ordinances and regulations regarding excavation, permitting, bonding, indemnification, and placement and maintenance of facilities in the public right-of-way that are applicable to all users of the right-of-way, regardless of the type of franchise agreement held by the cable provider.[89]

Since 2008, cable providers have had the option of obtaining a franchise agreement from the county or the state.[90]

Local Franchise Agreements

If the cable provider chooses to have a local franchise, it can negotiate a franchise agreement with the county or adopt the terms of any other franchise agreement that the county may have with another provider.[91] If the cable provider chooses to negotiate a franchise agreement, the rate of the franchise fee and the frequency with which it may be changed is subject to the terms of the franchise agreement.

In negotiating a franchise agreement, the county may require public, educational, and governmental (PEG) channels.[92] However, cable providers have the option of terminating their existing local franchise agreements in order to obtain a state franchise.[93] In doing so, the cable provider must continue to provide PEG access support according to the terms of the local franchise as if the local franchise had not been terminated early.[94]

Federal law and the Federal Communications Commission (FCC) establish regulation of cable providers. Counties "regulate" subscriber rates for "basic services tier" cable channels (e.g., local broadcast stations and PEG channels) and customer service of cable service by ensuring that the rates and the customer service meet the requirements of federal law.[95]

State Franchise Agreements

If a cable provider decides to obtain a franchise through the state, the county may object to the franchise if the board of commissioners reasonably believes that the cable provider does not have financial and technical capability to provide cable or video service or is not authorized to do business in Georgia.[96] If the state franchise is granted, the county must also set the franchise fee rate (up to 5 percent) and notify the secretary of state and the cable provider.[97] The county may change the franchise fee on a state franchise once every two years.[98] Even with a state franchise agreement, counties may audit a cable provider once per year.[99]

Under the state franchise, counties are limited to a maximum of two or three public access or PEG channels, depending on their unincorporated population.[100] If a county cannot meet the utilization requirements, it can place its PEG content on a shared channel controlled by the cable provider.

The governor's Office of Consumer Affairs is responsible for establishing a uniform set of rules for counties and cable service providers to resolve subscriber complaints.[101] Under the state franchise, counties may enforce federal customer service standards until 50 percent of the potential subscribers within the unincorporated county are offered cable service by two or more service providers holding a state or local franchise. After this threshold is met, the county may adopt a resolution to discontinue receiving complaints regarding billing and customer service from citizens.[102]

BUILDING CONSTRUCTION AND BUILDING CODES

County public works departments may also be associated with the construction or renovation of county buildings such as courthouses, administrative buildings, and fire stations as well as older buildings and the demolition of other structures. When contractors are hired, such projects may be subject to the Georgia Public Works Construction Law.[103] Whether performed with county labor or by a private contractor, as with the construction and maintenance of roads, these activities may be subject to numerous state and federal environmental regulations. If the building is within the city limits, the project will be subject to city building codes and inspections.[104] Land-disturbing activities may require permits from state and federal agencies, for example. The waste generated through building construction activities can be hazardous or nonhazardous, and disposal of such waste is generally regulated under a variety of federal, state, and local laws. If hazardous construction wastes are generated, federal RCRA Hazardous Waste Regulations[105] are applied.

Of particular concern is the presence of asbestos in county-owned buildings. Decades ago, asbestos was often used for insulation and as a fire retardant. All renovation or demolition activities involving asbestos materials are regulated under the Clean Air Act, and local governments are required to contact the federal EPA prior to any renovation or demolition. Removal and disposal of asbestos must be performed by accredited, trained personnel utilizing appropriate equipment. It is also important to note that lead-based paint is typically found in the interiors and on the exteriors of buildings constructed prior to 1978. During demolition and renovation activities, federal guidelines must be followed with regard to the removal and disposal of such paint.

Building codes are a set of rules adopted by the state that specify the minimum acceptable level of safety for constructing buildings and other structures. They are designed to protect health, safety, and property during construction and occupancy of a building or structure.

The State of Georgia has adopted eight "mandatory" building codes:

1. Georgia State Minimum Standard Building Code (International Building Code with Georgia State Amendments)

2. Georgia State Minimum Standard One and Two Family Dwelling Code (International Residential Code for One- and Two-Family Dwellings with Georgia State Amendments)

3. Georgia State Minimum Standard Fire Code (International Fire Code with Georgia State Amendments)

4. Georgia State Minimum Standard Plumbing Code (International Plumbing Code with Georgia State Amendments)

5. Georgia State Minimum Standard Mechanical Code (International Mechanical Code with Georgia State Amendments)

6. Georgia State Minimum Standard Gas Code (International Fuel Gas Code with Georgia State Amendments)

7. Georgia State Minimum Standard Electrical Code (National Electrical Code with Georgia State Amendments)

8. Georgia State Minimum Standard Energy Code (International Energy Conservation Code with Georgia State Supplements and Amendments).[106]

While counties have the option of enforcing some or all of these codes in the unincorporated areas, builders are required to comply with them.

The state has also adopted two "permissive" codes: the International Property Maintenance Code and the International Existing Building Code.[107] Counties have the option of adopting and enforcing these two codes. Counties desiring to enforce these codes may do so by adopting a resolution or ordinance providing procedures necessary to administer the codes.

DCA is charged with developing and updating building codes. A copy of the adopting ordinance or resolution must be forwarded to DCA.[108]

A county may amend any of these codes to meet local conditions, provided that the requirements are not made less stringent and they are based on local climatic, geologic, topographic, or public safety factors.[109] The amended codes must be submitted to DCA for review. The final decision remains with the county.[110]

In addition to these codes, the Georgia State Fire Code, as adopted by the Georgia Safety Fire Commissioner, remains mandatory throughout the state.[111] That office determines the construction standards for manufactured homes (i.e., mobile homes).[112] Although state minimum standards do not exist for historic preservation, high-rise construction, or architectural design standards, counties may adopt related building codes or ordinances for enforcement purposes. Review by DCA is required to ensure that the restrictive nature of state-mandated codes is not diluted.[113]

Once codes are adopted, they are enforced through a system of permits and inspection. Anyone planning construction or alterations covered by county codes must first submit a set of plans and specifications to the building inspector. If these plans meet county code standards and zoning requirements (if any), a building permit is issued. The permit allows construction to proceed on the condition that the approved plans are followed. Periodic inspections are made by the building inspector. If the county is unable to review the plans within 30 business days of receiving a written application for permitting or if the county is unable to provide an inspection within 2 business days of receiving a request for inspection, the builder may hire a private professional provider (i.e., an engineer or architect) to review the plans or perform the inspection.[114]

If a city constructs a building or structure in the unincorporated area of a county that has adopted building codes, the city is subject to the same permit and inspection process as any other builder. Conversely, if a county constructs a building or structure in a city that has adopted building codes, the county is subject to the city's permit and inspection process.[115]

Personnel requirements for code enforcement vary with the size of the county, the volume of building activity, and the kinds of codes being enforced. In larger counties, code enforcement may require a department with several full-time staff members.

Counties are required to post a notice stating whether their building inspectors are qualified through certification by the International Code Council.[116] If the county does not have certified inspectors, a builder has the option of retaining, at his or her own expense, a person who is certified by the council.[117]

Counties may choose to contract with a municipality or adjoining county that has a code enforcement department or enter into an intergovernmental agreement establishing a joint code enforcement system.

Code enforcement should be organized so that the inspector's performance is reviewed only by an official directly concerned with enforcing county codes.[118] Criteria for successful code enforcement have been defined as follows:[119]

- All code enforcement should be in one agency.

- Code enforcement should be the sole function of that agency.

- The code enforcement agency should have department status.

- The code enforcement administrator should be responsible directly and exclusively to the person serving as chief administrative officer of the county.

Counties are allowed to charge inspection fees; permit fees are regulatory fees designed to help defray code enforcement costs.[120] The Southern Building Code Congress International and the International Code Council publish building valuation data on which some local governments base their permit fees. However, counties must take care to ensure that the cost of the regulatory fees does not exceed the cost of inspection.[121]

VEHICLE/EQUIPMENT PURCHASE AND MAINTENANCE

County vehicles may be purchased within either the fleet maintenance division of the public works operation and/or the finance department of a local government setting. Purchasing normally includes the acquisition of vehicles, equipment, and materials. Purchasing activity is directly regulated by environmental laws only with regard to the purchasing of clean fuel vehicles for local governments that have large vehicle fleets. Under the Clean Air Act, local governments that purchase new vehicles for fleets of a certain size are required to purchase a specified percentage of clean fuel vehicles during each year in order to satisfy pollutant emissions reduction goals in a nonattainment area.

Public works departments within local governments are generally responsible for operating, maintaining, and purchasing motor vehicles and equipment to perform government services. The types of vehicles can range from fire trucks, heavy construction equipment, administrative staff vehicles, and vehicles and equipment used by the sheriff/police department and other officials within a variety of departments within the local government. Equipment needed in order to maintain these vehicles can cover a broad spectrum, from generators to normal mechanics' tools to pumps and boilers. Public works fleet operations generally include vehicle repair shops, fueling stations, purchasing operations, and paint and body shops.

Within vehicle repair shops, several activities have the potential to impact the environment and are regulated under U.S. environmental laws and regulations. Changing fluids (e.g., oil, antifreeze), cleaning parts, maintaining batteries, repairing air conditioners, washing vehicles and shop floors, repairing and replacing exhaust systems, painting vehicle bodies, and storing materials are all subject to regulation under federal environmental laws such as the RCRA, the National Pollutant Discharge Elimination System, and others. For a fuller explanation of state and federal environmental laws, see Chapter 10.

Vehicle fueling stations are also often associated with public works operations and, generally speaking, are located within a vehicle fleet maintenance operation within the public works department. Vehicle fueling stations provide fuel to government vehicles and include activities such as fuel storage, fuel dispensing, and disposal of unusable fuel. Moreover, they provide alternative fuel options such as compressed natural gas and methanol. Fuels can be stored in underground or above-ground storage tanks and are connected by piping to the fuel-dispensing unit. Operation and maintenance of these tanks are generally regulated under either the federal Clean Water Act, which requires development and implementation of spill prevention plans and secondary containment for aboveground tanks, and/or the provisions of the underground storage tank section of the RCRA.[122] Fuel-dispensing units used in public works vehicle fueling stations are similar or identical to those used at retail service stations. Because these dispensing units may potentially emit organic vapors into the atmosphere, they may be subject to regulation under the Clean Air Act. These laws also contain requirements for handling, storage, and disposal of unusable fuel. In the event of spills, the repair shop is required to report such spills to the local hazardous waste–reporting agencies within the local government setting or state agency.

NOTES

1. OFFICIAL CODE OF GEORGIA ANNOTATED (O.C.G.A.) §43-15-2(10).
2. O.C.G.A. §43-15-2(11).
3. O.C.G.A. §43-15-24.
4. 40 UNITED STATES CODE ANNOTATED (U.S.C.A.) §1101 et seq.
5. Charles K. Coe, *Getting the Most from Professional Services: Consulting Engineer* (Athens: Institute of Government, University of Georgia, 1978).
6. A geographic information system enables the collection of technical data from maps, surveys, aerial photography, and text that can be inserted into a computer program for planning and monitoring proposed construction throughout the area.
7. O.C.G.A. tit. 32.

8. O.C.G.A. §32-1-8.
9. O.C.G.A. tit. 32, ch. 3.
10. O.C.G.A. §32-4-41(4).
11. O.C.G.A. §32-4-42.
12. Ibid.
13. O.C.G.A. §36-60-21.
14. O.C.G.A. §§32-4-42, 32-6-2(2).
15. O.C.G.A. §32-4-42(6).
16. O.C.G.A. §32-6-2.
17. O.C.G.A. §§32-4-42(6), 32-4-69.
18. O.C.G.A. §32-4-42(4).
19. O.C.G.A. §32-4-42(1).
20. O.C.G.A. §§32-4-63, 32-4-64.
21. O.C.G.A. tit. 32, ch. 6, arts. 1, 3, 4, 5.
22. O.C.G.A. tit. 32, ch. 6, art. 6.
23. O.C.G.A. tit. 32, ch. 6, art. 8.
24. O.C.G.A §32-3-1 et seq.
25. O.C.G.A. tit. 32, ch. 6, art. 2.
26. O.C.G.A. §32-6-27(d).
27. O.C.G.A. §32-6-2.
28. O.C.G.A. tit. 40, ch. 6.
29. O.C.G.A. §40-6-3.
30. O.C.G.A. tit. 40, ch. 6, art. 2.
31. O.C.G.A. tit. 40, ch. 6. art. 3.
32. O.C.G.A. tit. 40, ch. 6. art. 4.
33. O.C.G.A. tit. 40, ch. 6. art. 5.
34. O.C.G.A. tit. 40, ch. 6. art. 6.
35. O.C.G.A. tit. 40, ch. 6. art. 7.
36. O.C.G.A. tit. 40, ch. 6. art. 8.
37. O.C.G.A. tit. 40, ch. 6. art. 9.
38. O.C.G.A. tit. 40, ch. 6. art. 10.
39. O.C.G.A. tit. 40, ch. 6. arts. 7, 11.
40. O.C.G.A. tit. 40, ch. 6. art. 12.
41. O.C.G.A. tit. 40, ch. 6. art. 13.
42. O.C.G.A. tit. 40, ch. 6. art. 15.
43. O.C.G.A. §40-6-370.
44. O.C.G.A. §40-6-371.
45. O.C.G.A. §40-6-372.
46. O.C.G.A. §40-6-374.
47. American Association of State Highway and Transportation Officials, *A Policy on Geometric Design of Highways and Streets, 1990* (Washington, DC: AASHTO, 1990). For a general overview of this topic, see chapter 3, "Elements of Design." A more detailed, technical application to assist in making decisions on sight distance problems is found in chapter 9, "At-Grade Intersections."

48. Federal Highway Administration, *Manual on Uniform Traffic Control Devices for Streets and Highways* (Washington, DC: U.S. Government Printing Office, 1988), 4C-14C-12.

49. 42 U.S.C.A. §7401 et seq.

50. American Standards Association, *American National Standard Practice for Roadway Lighting* (New York: Illuminating Engineering Society, 1983).

51. Ibid.

52. International City Management Association, *Urban Public Works Administration* (Washington, DC: ICMA, 1976), 366–83.

53. O.C.G.A. §32-9-11.

54. Jerry A. Singer, "Survival Techniques for FBO/Airport Managers," in *Small Airport Management Handbook* (Athens: Carl Vinson Institute of Government, University of Georgia, 1985).

55. Ibid.

56. 33 U.S.C.A. §1251 et seq.

57. 42 U.S.C.A. §7401 et seq.

58. 42 U.S.C.A. §4321.

59. 42 U.S.C.A. §6901.

60. 16 U.S.C.A. §1531.

61. See 33 U.S.C.A. §407 et seq.

62. 15 U.S.C.A. §2601 et seq.

63. O.C.G.A. §12-7-6.

64. Intermodal Surface Transportation Efficiency Act of 1991, Pub. L. 102-240.

65. Georgia Municipal Association, *A Study of Municipal Water and Sewer Utility Rates in Georgia* (Atlanta: GMA, 1971).

66. O.C.G.A. §§43-51-1, 43-51-6; OFFICIAL COMPILATION RULES AND REGULATIONS OF THE STATE OF GEORGIA (GA. COMP. R. & REGS.), ch. 750.

67. O.C.G.A. §43-51-10.

68. GA. COMP. R. & REGS. , ch. 391-3-5.

69. O.C.G.A. tit. 36, ch. 71.

70. International City Managers' Association, *Municipal Public Works Administration*, 5th ed. (Chicago: ICMA, 1957), 289.

71. This discussion of treatment processes is drawn from Arnold W. Reitze Jr., *Environmental Law*, 2nd ed., vol. 1 (Washington, DC: North American International, 1972), 4–17.

72. O.C.G.A. tit. 12, ch. 5, art. 2; GA. COMP. R. & REGS., ch. 391-3-6.

73. Georgia Municipal Association, *A Study of Municipal Water and Sewer Utility Rates in Georgia* (Atlanta: GMA, 1971), 20. Pursuant to the FTC's Red Flag Rules, counties must also protect customers from identity theft. See *ACCG Identity Theft Prevention Program* (June 2010). www.accg.org/library/ACCG_Sample_Identity_Theft_Prevention_Program.pdf.

74. Ibid.

75. Combined Sewer Overflow Control Policy, 59 Federal Register 18688 (April 19, 1994).

76. U.S. Environmental Protection Agency, Seminar Publication: National Conference on Sanitary Sewer Overflows (SSOs), April 24–26, 1995, EPA/25/R-96/0007 (Washington, DC: EPA, September 1996).

77. O.C.G.A. tit. 12, ch 8.

78. Examples of programs directed at landfill waste stream reduction include residential participation in separation of recycling products from household waste collection; recycling of recoverable materials such as used motor oil, batteries, and tires; roadside litter prevention and patrols; composting; and Christmas tree chipping. Information on these and other programs aimed at landfill waste reduction can be obtained from the Georgia Department of Community Affairs, Office of Environmental Management (www.dca.state.ga.us/development/ EnvironmentalManagement/index.asp) and from Keep Georgia Beautiful (www. KeepGeorgiaBeautiful.org).

79. O.C.G.A. §§12-8-21(g), 12-8-40.2.

80. 40 CODE OF FEDERAL REGULATIONS (C.F.R.) part 503.

81. O.C.G.A. §36-70-24.

82. O.C.G.A. §36-76-2(6).

83. O.C.G.A. §36-76-2(8).

84. 47 U.S.C.A. §542(b); O.C.G.A. §§36-18-2, 36-76-6.

85. See O.C.G.A. §§36-18-1 et seq., 36-76-1 et seq.; DeKalb County v. Georgia Power Company, 249 Ga. 704 (1982); DeKalb County v. Atlanta Gas Light Company, 230 Ga. 65 (1973); DeKalb County v. Atlanta Gas Light Company, 228 Ga. 512 (1972).

86. O.C.G.A. §36-76-10.

87. O.C.G.A. §36-76-11(a).

88. O.C.G.A. §36-76-11(c).

89. O.C.G.A. §36-76-10(4).

90. O.C.G.A. §36-76-3(a).

91. Ibid.

92. 47 U.S.C.A. §531

93. O.C.G.A. §36-76-4(g)(2).

94. O.C.G.A. §36-76-4(g)(4).

95. 47 U.S.C.A. §541 et seq.; 47 C.F.R. 76.309(c), 76.922.

96. O.C.G.A. §36-76-4(f).

97. O.C.G.A. §36-76-6(a)(2).

98. O.C.G.A. §36-76-6(a)(3).

99. O.C.G.A. §36-76-6(c).

100. O.C.G.A. §36-76-8.

101. O.C.G.A. §36-76-7(c)(1).

102. O.C.G.A. §36-76-7(c)(2).

103. O.C.G.A. §36-10-1 et seq.

104. City of Decatur v. DeKalb County, 256 Ga. App. 46 (2002).

105. 40 C.F.R. Part 260.

106. O.C.G.A. §§8-2-20(9)(B)(i)(I)–(VIII), 8-2-25(a).

107. O.C.G.A. §§8-2-20(9)(B)(i)(IX)–(XI), 8-2-25(b).

108. O.C.G.A. §8-2-25. Once the state receives a copy of the county adopting ordinance or resolution of any of these six optional codes, subsequent amendments can be forwarded for the purpose of keeping the county informed about the code changes.

109. O.C.G.A. §8-2-25(c)(1).

110. O.C.G.A. §8-2-25.

111. O.C.G.A. §§8-2-20(9)(D), 25-2-13.

112. O.C.G.A. tit. 8, ch. 2, art. 2, pt. 2.

113. O.C.G.A. §8-2-25.

114. O.C.G.A. §8-2-26(g)(1).

115. City of Decatur v. DeKalb County, 256 Ga. App. 46 (2002).

116. O.C.G.A. §8-2-26.1(b).

117. O.C.G.A. §8-2-26.1(c).

118. Richard L. Sanderson, *Code and Code Administration* (Chicago: Building Officials Conference of America Inc., 1969).

119. Ibid., 110.

120. O.C.G.A. §8-2-26(a)(4).

121. O.C.G.A. §48-13-9; Greater Atlanta Homebuilders Association v. DeKalb County, Georgia, case no. 1:00-CV-1290-GET, U.S. District Court, Northern District of Georgia, *aff'd without opinion*, 37 Fed. Appx. (May 30, 2002); Homebuilders Association of Savannah Inc. v. Chatham County, 276 Ga. 243 (2003).

122. 42 U.S.C.A. §6901 et seq.

13

Michele NeSmith and Daniel Hope

Recreation and Parks

The role of government in providing public parks for Georgia's citizens is as old as the state itself. The precedent was set by General James Edward Oglethorpe when he designed and developed the city of Savannah in 1733. The local government role became more formal in 1911, when Atlanta started the first city parks department to provide park and recreation services. Today, there are 2,340 sites managed by local governments in Georgia totaling 63,110 acres.[1]

As used in this chapter, "recreation and parks" refers to youth and adult sports, festivals and special events, senior centers, recreational classes, the visual and performing arts, community centers, gymnasiums, public parks and open space, golf courses, swimming pools, greenways, trails, and other such programs and facilities.

BENEFITS OF PROVIDING RECREATION AND PARK SERVICES

Parks, open spaces, tree lined streets, museums, festivals, recreation programs, and special events all help to shape the identity of a community. These factors combined with a wide range of elements such as health, safety, education, housing, and transportation define "quality of life" and determine whether a community is a desirable place to live and work.[2]

According to Partners for Livable Communities,[3] capital investments intended to provide recreation, entertainment, and cultural enrichment to community residents often have a low priority, particularly in times when budgets are tight. When parks, museums, libraries, performing arts facilities, and other amenities that require land and structures are allowed to deteriorate or do not keep pace with population or changing demands, a community may lose the features that make it attractive. As amenities grow more important with urban development, their loss may be counted in dollars lost to the local economy as well as a declining quality of life.[4]

There is a common belief that recreation and park services are not necessary. Another assumption is that the benefits of such activities affect only certain individuals and not the community at large. This train of thought often leads elected officials to underfund recreation and park services. In reality, however, the public assigns a very high level of importance to the benefits garnered from the use of these services.[5]

The Georgia General Assembly mandates the development of state policies on outdoor recreation.[6] Accordingly, Georgia's Department of Natural Resources produced the Statewide Comprehensive Outdoor Recreation Plan (SCORP), which identifies trends, priorities, and goals regarding outdoor recreation in Georgia. This plan is updated every five years in order for Georgia to be eligible for recreation dollars through the federal Land and Water Conservation Fund.

According to the results of the 2008 SCORP Survey, 88 percent of Georgians support public funding of outdoor recreation, and 74 percent of those respondents support additional public funding. The survey further revealed that 68 percent of Georgians had participated in outdoor recreational activities within the past year and that nearly three out of every four Georgians had visited a recreation park within that time frame.[7]

The popularity of parks is why county governments have become increasingly involved in funding outdoor recreation. But why should a county put time and money into these services when many civic organizations, nonprofit agencies, or the private sector already provide recreational activities? Providing recreation services has become an accepted governmental role for several reasons:[8]

- Only when recreation and park services are provided by governmental agencies and therefore offered at little or no cost can the largest segment of the population take advantage of them.

- With the growing value of land, the county is often the only organization with resources for acquiring, developing, and maintaining land for public recreation, park, and open space purposes.

- Only local government can ensure the provision of recreation and park services on a permanent basis. Private or volunteer agencies may be abolished, may remove facilities from public use, or may divert their use from recreational purposes. Public agencies, however, have greater permanency and are subject to public control and accountability.

- The potential rewards to the county for providing adequate recreational opportunities often make them profitable investments.

- Citizens have demanded it.

Recreation and park departments provide numerous benefits to the county. These include increased self-esteem for kids through participation in youth recreation programs and sports, better physical and mental health and decreased stress for individuals, increased economic activity due to the community's attractiveness to business and industry, and an increased quality of life for the community as a whole. Further, providing recreation and park services fosters the development of a stronger environmental ethic and a better understanding of the need for stewardship.[9]

LEGAL AUTHORITY FOR CREATING A RECREATION AND PARK SYSTEM

Title 36, Chapter 64, of the Official Code of Georgia Annotated authorizes local governments to establish and expend funds on recreation and park services. Often referred to as the Recreation Enabling Law, it empowers the governing body of any county or municipality, or combination thereof, to provide, establish, maintain, and conduct a recreation system and to acquire the property necessary to establish and maintain playgrounds, recreation centers, parks, and other recreational facilities and activities. It also enables municipalities and counties to create recreation boards or commissions and outlines their powers and duties.

In order to carry out the provisions of this law, local governments, or any board they designate, may employ playleaders, playground or community center directors, supervisors, recreation superintendents, or other officers or employees needed to carry out the services. The basic provisions of the law are as follows:

1. The governing body of any county or municipality may establish a system of supervised recreation. It may, by resolution or ordinance, vest the power to provide, maintain, and conduct

parks, playgrounds, recreation centers, and other recreational activities and facilities in the board of education, park board, or other existing body or in a recreation board, as the governing body may determine.

2. The governing authority may appropriate general funds to conduct, equip, and maintain recreational lands and buildings. Staff may also be employed to manage the recreation and parks system. In addition, grants, gifts, money, or property for recreational purposes may be accepted by the agency responsible for recreation programs, with governing authority approval required when acceptance of real estate will subject the county to additional expense.[10]

3. Ten percent of the qualified and registered voters of a county may sign a petition requesting the governing authority to provide a supervised recreation system and to levy a recreation tax for that purpose, subject to approval by referendum. Once the levy has been approved, in order to remove the recreation tax, the county must adopt a resolution to that effect, subject to approval by referendum. After the tax is removed, the funding for the county recreation system can be determined at the discretion of the county governing body.[11]

4. The governing authority may propose that bonds be issued for the purpose of acquiring lands, buildings, or equipment for recreation purposes. Special purpose local option sales tax (SPLOST) funds may also be used for recreation and parks capital projects if approved in a voter referendum.[12]

5. Counties and cities, as well as school boards, may jointly establish and maintain a recreation system.

COMPONENTS OF A RECREATION AND PARK SYSTEM

A recreation and park system is a major contributor to the overall quality of life in the county. In order to help ensure the professional competence and effectiveness of park and recreation agencies, the Commission for Accreditation of Park and Recreation Agencies (CAPRA) developed best practices standards organized into 10 major categories: agency authority, role, and responsibility; planning; organization and administration; human resources; finance management; program and services management; facility and land-use management; public safety, law enforcement, and security; risk management; and evaluation and research.[13]

Structure and Organization

The most commonly found structure for public recreation, park, and leisure service departments includes the following elements:

- *Organization and Administration.* Organization is the structure that clarifies the lines of authority and areas of responsibility for the agency to accomplish its mission. Administration is the process that ensures that an agency's resources are used to attain its predetermined goals. It must also provide maintenance for the care and upkeep of the areas, facilities, and structures; ensure that they are accessible; and protect the health and safety of the users.

- *Parks and Facilities.* Parks are areas of land and water not intensively developed for residential or economic purposes. They are set aside for their aesthetic, environmental, recreational, educational, or cultural value and may also serve transportation and historic preservation purposes. Facilities are the buildings and structures in parks needed to deliver recreation services (e.g., swimming pools, ball fields, community centers, and performing arts centers).

- *Programs and Services.* The activities or experiences offered are designed to enable the individual to maximize the use of his/her leisure time. These may be active or passive in nature and range from sports to the performing arts to environmental education.

Open Space

Closely related to recreation is the provision of open space by the county, especially in urban counties. In its broadest definition, open space is considered to be space that is not used for buildings or structures. Without open spaces, our communities would be unrecognizable and unmemorable.[14] People in urban areas need open space for many different purposes: to conserve water and other natural resources, as a reserve for often unpredictable future needs, to prevent building in undesirable locations in order to avoid flood hazard or a wasteful extension of services, for pleasant views from urban areas, for a sense of urban identity, for buffers against noise and other nuisances, and above all, for recreation, which can be combined with many other uses.[15]

Counties can utilize state conservation funds, if available, to finance land acquisition for passive recreation such as boating, hiking, camping, fishing, hunting, jogging, biking, or similar outdoor activities.[16] Grants and low interest loans are available to counties to implement approved projects through the Georgia Land Conservation Program, which is administered by the Georgia Environmental Finance Authority (GEFA). For more information on land protection and conservation tools, see Chapters 9 and 10 on planning and environmental management.

RECREATION AND PARK SYSTEM MANAGEMENT

Once the decision to establish a recreation and park department has been made, the county governing authority must decide how it will be structured and who will be responsible for its operation. As previously noted, the county commission may, by resolution or ordinance, vest the power to provide, maintain, and conduct parks, playgrounds, recreation centers, and other recreational activities and facilities in the board of education, park board, or other existing body or in a recreation board. Though not mentioned in the enabling legislation, the county commission may establish an advisory board in lieu of a policy board. In either case, the ordinance or resolution must clearly define the specific functions, organization, and responsibilities of the recreation and parks department. The department can operate as a line department reporting directly to the county administrator, to the chair of the board of commissioners, to the entire board of commissioners, or to a recreation and parks policy board. If a policy board or an advisory board is created, bylaws should be developed for operation of the board.

Regardless of how the chain of command is set up, counties can utilize an advisory committee as a way of involving citizens with the department. When a county and city operate a recreation and park department jointly, a policy board, with members appointed by each government, is recommended.

Functions of a Recreation and Park Policy Board

The Recreation Enabling Act provides for the establishment of a policy board (also known as a legal board) and defines the powers and duties of the board, the number of board members and how they are appointed, the selection and replacement of individual members, and the length of a member's term.[17] A county that decides to have an advisory board or committee rather than a policy board should also address these four points in the local ordinance or resolution creating it.

Recreation and park policy boards have five major functions:

1. Policymaking. The board sets policies to govern all phases of the department's operations. These policies should specify how the board wants to use its resources (human and fiscal). Equally important, the policies should be designed to assure the health, safety, and well-being of participants.

2. Program planning, review, and evaluation. The board establishes long-range goals, approves yearly operating objectives, and annually reviews and evaluates the progress made toward achieving its goals and objectives.

3. Financial management. The board is responsible for assuring that sufficient income is generated from various sources to carry out the programs and operate the facilities that are approved by the board. Normally, the department's director develops the budget, and the board, after reviewing and modifying it as needed, recommends it to the county commission, which has final approval.

4. Evaluation of the performance of the director. The policy board provides an objective evaluation of the department's director. The county commission, the policy board, and the director must have a clear understanding of the director's responsibilities, authority, and duties.

5. Community relations. The board is obligated to make recreation programs and facilities available to all citizens within its jurisdiction who want to participate. It should maintain high standards for the programs conducted and facilities operated and ensure the accessibility, safety, and welfare of participants. The board should make itself known to the community through reports, earn respect through the integrity of its management, and achieve acceptance by striving to serve everyone in the community and by involving the community constructively in planning and evaluating its programs and facilities.

Recreation and Park Authorities

The Constitution of Georgia provides for the creation of development authorities and community improvement districts.[18] Community improvement districts are managed by a governing authority and are created to provide several types of governmental services and facilities, including parks and recreation. The General Assembly may authorize the administrative body that oversees a district to incur debt and to levy taxes, fees, and assessments within its jurisdiction only on real property used nonresidentially.[19]

DETERMINING WHICH RECREATION AND PARK SERVICES TO OFFER

There are a variety of methods for gathering information about recreation and park services. Depending on the resources of the county staff, these methods can be used in-house or they can be contracted.

The most common way to determine people's attitudes about the provision of recreation and park services is to collect information through a survey. Surveys can vary in length and be administered in several ways: by telephone, through a Web-based survey tool, by e-mail, or by mail. Each method has good and bad points, and there are costs that should be considered when determining which method is best for your county.

In addition to obtaining specific information about recreation and park issues, it is important to understand the demographic makeup of the county. Demographic information is usually available through the county's planning office, regional commissions, local libraries, colleges and universities, or on Web sites (through ACCG, the Department of Community Affairs, and the U.S. Bureau of the Census, for example).

A community's residents are the best source of information about what kinds of recreation and park services are needed. Therefore, a community-based decision-making process is often the most effective means for determining the kind of services citizens desire.[20] It places the people who live in the county on the planning committee and invites them to open forums to discuss the issues. It is a strategic process for determining where the county is now, its preferred future, and how to get there.

The strategic plan develops the vision and mission for recreation, parks, and leisure services along with goals, objectives, and an action plan. It is broader in scope than the site plan, which is the design for an individual park or facility. From this, a comprehensive plan that looks at the specific long-term and short-term dimensions of the recreation programs and the physical resources of the delivery system is developed.[21] Both of these plans should be included in the county's comprehensive plan.

SUMMARY

The role of county government is to ensure the quality of its citizens' lives through the organization and delivery of services. Important among these services is the recreation, parks, and leisure delivery system, which contributes to the overall quality of life for the community and provides a significant contribution to the county's economy. A community's open spaces, parks, streetscapes, cultural facilities, and recreation programs are all part of its leisure services delivery system. These amenities help create a sense of place, making a community one in which people want to live, work, and raise their families.

NOTES

1. *Georgia Statewide Comprehensive Outdoor Recreation Plan 2008–2013* (Atlanta: Georgia Department of Natural Resources, 2008), 22.

2. R. H. McNulty, D. R. Jaconson, and R. L. Penne, *The Economics of Amenity: Community Features and Quality of Life* (Washington, DC: Partners for Livable Places, 1985).

3. See www.liveable.com.

4. McNulty, Jaconson, and Penne, *Economics of Amenity*.

5. J. Harper, G. Godbey, and S. Foreman, "Just the Facts: Answering the Critics of Local Government Park and Recreation Services," *Parks & Recreation* (August 1998): 78–81.

6. OFFICIAL CODE OF GEORGIA ANNOTATED (O.C.G.A.) §12-3-1.

7. *Georgia Statewide Comprehensive Outdoor Recreation Plan 2008–2013*, 26.

8. G. Lutzin Sidney, ed., *Managing Municipal Leisure Services* (Washington, DC: International City Management Association, 1980), 1–12.

9. L. Allen, B. Stevens, K. Hurtes, and R. Harwell, *Benefits-Based Programming of Recreation Services: Training Manual* (Ashburn, VA: National Recreation and Park Association, 1998).

10. See also O.C.G.A. tit. 36, ch. 71, on development impact fees.

11. O.C.G.A. §36-64-15.

12. O.C.G.A. §48-8-111(a)(1)(E).

13. *National Accreditation Standards*, 4th ed. (Ashburn, VA: Commission for Accreditation of Park and Recreation Agencies, National Recreation and Park Association, April 2009).

14. P. Harnik, *Inside City Parks: Report from the Trust for Public Land and the Urban Land Institute* (Washington DC: Urban Land Institute, 2000).

15. President's Commission on National Goals, *Goals for Americans* (Englewood Cliffs, NJ: Prentice-Hall, 1960), 239.

16. O.C.G.A. §12-6A-1 et seq.

17. O.C.G.A. §36-64-5.

18. GA. CONST. art. IX, §7.

19. GA. CONST. art. IX, §7, ¶3(c).

20. Daniel Hope and Steven L. Dempsey, "Achieving Consensus in Planning Recreation and Park Services," *World Leisure Journal* 42, no. 4 (2000): 56–64.

21. B. Van der Smissen, M. Moiseichik, V. Hartenburg, and L. Twardzik, eds., *Management of Park and Recreation Agencies* (Ashburn, VA: National Recreation and Park Association, 1999), 100.

14

Kelly J. L. Pridgen, Clint Mueller, Charles R. Swanson Jr., Jerry
A. Singer, Mike Sherberger, and J. Devereux Weeks

Public Safety

County commissioners provide more county services than ever before, but protecting life and property will always take precedence over other county functions. In fulfilling their public safety responsibilities, counties provide services such as law enforcement, corrections, fire, 9-1-1, emergency management, emergency medical services, and animal control. Although multiple departments may provide these services, a coordinated effort must exist among the various service providers in order to keep the public safety system functioning properly so as to ensure the safety and welfare of the public.

LAW ENFORCEMENT

Sheriff's Office

Law enforcement for counties is primarily provided by the sheriff. Every Georgia county has an elected sheriff. The constitutional and statutory authority of the office of sheriff is statewide. In all but a few counties, the sheriff's office is the sole law enforcement agency serving the unincorporated area and shares law enforcement authority within the cities.[1] Because the sheriff is a "county officer," the commissioners' role with respect to law enforcement is limited to providing reasonable funds in the budget for the sheriff to provide law enforcement for the county.

Police Departments

There are only 13 county police departments in Georgia.[2] These departments are subject to the direction and control of the county governing authority through a police chief appointed by the county commissioners.

Counties that would like to start a county police department must obtain voter approval through a public referendum before creating a new county police department.[3] All existing county police departments were created prior to imposition of this referendum requirement.

Counties served by both a sheriff's office and a county police department usually transfer peacekeeping and law enforcement functions to the county police, while the sheriff continues to carry out his or her other duties, such as maintaining the county jail and serving the courts. The sheriff's authority to fulfill his or her responsibilities is not lessened or diminished by the existence of the county police departments that have been established by county governing authorities to perform additional services within the unincorporated areas of the county.[4]

Accreditation of Law Enforcement Agencies

The Commission on Accreditation for Law Enforcement Agencies (CALEA) is a private, nonprofit organization that was formed by the International Association of Chiefs of Police, National Organization of Black Law Enforcement Executives, National Sheriffs' Association, and Police Executive Research Forum (www.calea.org). CALEA has developed a national set of law enforcement standards for all types and sizes of county police departments and sheriffs' offices.

Although CALEA accreditation is voluntary, many sheriffs, commissioners, and police chiefs seek accreditation because most of the standards identify topics and issues that must be covered by written policies and procedures. Successful accreditation may provide counties a defense or "liability shield" against civil litigation.[5] Also, CALEA provides a nationally recognized system for improvement.[6]

Not all law enforcement agencies that wish to undergo self-evaluation and improvement are financially willing or able to make the commitment to the CALEA process. The State of Georgia Law Enforcement Certification Program offers a professionally recognized methodology to make systematic improvements to such agencies. Satisfying these standards may also serve as a "stepping stone" toward CALEA accreditation.

The State of Georgia Law Enforcement Certification Program was developed through the collaborative efforts of the Georgia Association of Chiefs of Police, the Georgia Sheriffs' Association, the Georgia Peace Officer Standards and Training Council, the Association County Commissioners of Georgia, the Georgia Municipal Association, and the Georgia Police Accreditation Coalition (www.gachiefs.com/statecertification/index.htm). Although voluntary, the certification provides a comprehensive blueprint for effective, professional law enforcement.

Employment and Training Standards

State law requires county law enforcement officers to become certified by the Peace Officers Standard and Training Council (i.e., "POST certified"), in accordance with the minimum standards of the Georgia Peace Officer Standards and Training Act.[7] In order to be employed by a county as a peace officer, individuals must complete a basic law enforcement training course and meet other minimal requirements pertaining to age, citizenship, education, criminal background, etc. [8]

Sheriffs must meet certain requirements to be eligible to hold the office. Every newly elected sheriff is required to complete a four-week training session. A sheriff must become certified within six months of assuming office, unless the requirement has been previously met.[9] As do all Georgia peace officers, sheriffs are required to have additional training every year. A sheriff who fails to complete such training may lose his or her power of arrest and may be suspended from office without pay unless the sheriff qualifies for and obtains a waiver of this training requirement.[10]

With limited exception, a police chief must receive executive law enforcement training in addition to the basic required training.[11]

CORRECTIONS

County Jail

Most counties operate a jail that is run by the sheriff. A county jail may contain the following:

- Persons arrested and waiting for their trail. The county receives no reimbursement from the state for these inmates who are awaiting trial.

- Inmates who have been convicted of a misdemeanor and sentenced to 12 months or less. The county is responsible for the cost of the upkeep of these county inmates.

- Prisoners who have been convicted of a felony, sentenced to serve their time in the state prison system, and are waiting for the Department of Corrections to take them. These prisoners are state inmates awaiting pickup. The state will provide a per diem to cover a portion of the cost to house these inmates if they are not picked up by the state within the first 15 days after the Department of Corrections receives the "sentencing package" from the clerk of court.[12]

- Probationers and parolees who have made a "technical violation" of their probation or parole. Although many of these individuals are felons who would ordinarily be considered state inmates, counties do not receive a per diem from the Department of Corrections for these technical violators.[13]

- Prisoners awaiting an appeal of their conviction.

- Inmates from neighboring counties being temporarily housed because of overcrowding in their "home" facility.

- If an agreement exists, federal prisoners housed on a short-term basis.

- If an agreement with the city exists, city inmates who are serving sentences for violations of city ordinances and other misdemeanors.

Care of Inmates

The sheriff, as the chief jailer, is responsible for the health, safety, and welfare of all prisoners. County governing authorities and sheriffs have been successfully sued for jail conditions that adversely affect the health, welfare, and/or rights of inmates. Because jail conditions or procedures have been the basis of a number of catastrophic awards to those suing the county, no effort should be spared to ensure proper functioning of the county jail.

Georgia law requires the sheriff to provide prisoners with medical aid, heat, blankets, and other essentials.[14] County commissioners must provide the sheriff with adequate funds for food for prisoners so that their strength and health are not impaired as a result of an insufficient diet. If the budget does not provide adequate funds to handle such expenses, the sheriff may personally make the necessary purchases. In this instance, the county is required by law to reimburse the sheriff for such expenditures.[15]

The sheriff must also protect the rights of all prisoners held in the county jail. In addition to the basic right to receive food, shelter, and medical aid, the courts have ruled that confined persons enjoy all the rights guaranteed under the U.S. Constitution. Those rights are not limited by a facility's interest in operating a safe, secure, and orderly facility. Public officials may be liable for any unlawful taking of or failure to protect those rights.

Medical Treatment for Inmates

Medical care for inmates is expensive for a county. If an inmate has medical insurance, a claim may be made against the inmate's insurance for his or her care.[16] Unfortunately, many inmates have no medical insurance. The sheriff is responsible for providing any necessary medical treatment for the inmates. The Georgia Supreme Court has held that the sheriff is authorized to enter into agreements with medical care providers without going through the board of commissioners.[17]

Sheriffs and judges cannot release an arrestee on his or her own recognizance while the arrestee is receiving medical treatment in order to avoid the responsibility of the medical bills. The courts have found counties liable for the medical bills of arrestees who were released after being admitted to the hospital.[18] However, the sheriff is entitled to refuse to accept into the jail any person from another agency who has not received medical treatment for obvious physical injuries or conditions of an emergency nature until the arresting agency has obtained a medical release for the individual from a health care facility or provider. However, if there is no health care facility in the county, the sheriff or keeper of the jail must accept the individual, in which case the county governing authority must pay all costs related to the medical release.[19]

Inmates of county jails who do not have health insurance or are not eligible for health care benefits are liable for the costs of medical care provided to them, and the assets and property of an inmate may be subject to levy and execution for such costs.[20] Alternatively, the sheriff or other keeper of the jail may establish rules for deduction from money credited to an inmate's account to defray the costs of medical treatment requested by an inmate, within certain limits. Amounts collected from an inmate's account are to be reimbursed if the inmate is subsequently acquitted or exonerated of the charges on which he or she was being held.[21]

Jail Standards

The sheriff is responsible not only for the health of the inmates but also for maintaining and protecting the physical facilities of the jail itself. Georgia state statutes provide some guidance or standards for jail operations pertaining to such matters as inmate care, safety and security, and sanitation and health.[22] The Georgia Jail Standards Study Commission prepared the *Standards for Georgia Jail Facilities*,[23] which provides voluntary standards, often based on case law, for all areas of jail operation, including administration and management, facility planning, programs and activities, classification, screening, facility safety, inmate communications, and visitation procedures. Although these standards remain voluntary, the courts have mandated their adoption in several cases.

Much improvement in the planning, design, construction, and operation of county jails has been achieved recently through specialized jail assistance services offered at no cost to counties through the Georgia Sheriffs' Association. These services are acquired upon the request of a county's sheriff.

Jail Construction and Staffing Fee

To assist in funding the jail, counties may adopt a resolution imposing an additional penalty of 10 percent on all criminal and traffic fines in superior court, state court, probate court, or magistrate court.[24] The 10 percent penalty is also imposed on the original amount of any bail or bond posted.[25] This money paid by criminal defendants may be used only for jail construction and staffing.

Any city may likewise impose this 10 percent penalty through municipal court if it enters into an intergovernmental agreement with the county for providing the use of the county jail, correctional institution, or other detention facility by city prisoners.[26] If the county houses city prisoners, this money may be used to help cover the cost of the city to house its prisoners in the county jail. However, the intergovernmental contract with the city should include the entire cost of housing the city inmates (i.e., the true per diem cost, the cost of medical services, etc.).

The funds generated from this 10 percent penalty must be paid over to the county commissioners from the various courts, including municipal courts, by the tenth day of the month, and the funds must be deposited in a special account called the county jail fund.[27] The money may only be used by the county to build, operate, or staff the county jail, county correctional institution, or other county detention facility or to contract for the use of such facilities with other counties, the state, cities, or regional jail authorities.[28]

County Correctional Institutions

County correctional institutions, sometimes referred to as work camps, are operated in 24 Georgia counties.[29] These counties have contracted with the Georgia Department of Corrections to house low-security, long-term inmates sentenced to the state prison (i.e., state prisoners). The state pays the county a per diem to house the inmates, and the county gets the benefit of the labor of these inmates. Correctional institutions are under the control of a warden, who is appointed by the county governing authority. Although the counties operate, maintain, and staff the institutions, correctional institutions must comply with regulations of the Georgia Department of Corrections. Inmates housed in correctional institutions are required to work on maintenance of roads and parks, work at landfills, serve on local fire crews, and assist in county construction projects.

Jail Training

Any person employed as a jail officer or juvenile correctional officer must successfully complete the required training course within six months after the date of initial employment. Persons employed as jail officers or juvenile correctional officers prior to October 12, 1999, are exempted from this certification requirement.[30]

FIRE PROTECTION

In Georgia, there are two basic types of fire departments. There are "career departments" that employ full-time paid employees, and there are volunteer departments that rely primarily on volunteers. The majority of career departments can be found in the major urban and suburban areas, while volunteer departments primarily function in less densely populated rural areas.

The basic mission of fire departments is to save lives and protect property. Today's fire department reflects an all-hazards response organization for multiple emergency events that may include emergency responses to medical calls such as heart attacks and other illnesses, extrication of victims from automobile accidents, rescues and responses to hazardous incidents such as cave-ins and downed power lines, emergency management activities, and disaster response. By law, fire departments have primary responsibility for first-response to chemical incidents with toxic potentials.[31] Law enforcement–related activities often require the intervention of firefighters, including responses to bombings and other terrorism incidents.

In order to be legally organized, a county fire department (whether comprising full-time, paid staff or volunteers) must

- be established in accordance with the provisions of National Fire Protection Association Standard 1201-1984;

- be capable of providing fire protection 24 hours a day, seven days a week;

- be responsible for a defined area of operations depicted on a map located at the fire station;

- be staffed with a sufficient number of qualified firefighters who are full-time or part-time workers or volunteers who have successfully completed an approved basic fire-fighting course conducted by or through the Georgia Fire Academy;

- possess certain minimum equipment and protective clothing; and

- maintain sufficient insurance coverage on all members to cover injuries sustained when answering fire calls or other emergencies and when participating in scheduled training sessions.[32]

In addition, the county fire department must comply with the minimum standards established by the Georgia Firefighter Standards and Training Council. Failure to meet and maintain these requirements may result in the loss of a fire department's certification.[33]

Each department should have the following:

- Master planning

- Adequate equipment and facilities

- Effective communications

- Employment and training standards

- Ongoing training

- A fire prevention program

- Knowledge of the fire-rating process

- Sufficient water supply

Fire departments need various types of equipment, including the following:

- Vehicles to transport firefighters to fires

- Vehicles to transport and pump water to fires

- Fire-fighting equipment on the vehicles, such as pumps, ladders, hose, self-contained breathing apparatus, and fire extinguishers

- Protective clothing, such as coats, helmets, and boots

Fire departments depend upon an adequate supply of water for extinguishing fires. Flow and pressure required in order to combat industrial and commercial fires are typically greater than that required for residential fires. In the absence of pressurized systems, counties can establish alternative water-delivery capabilities, including the ability to shuttle or haul water from static water sources such as ponds, streams, lakes, or cisterns. Dry or draft hydrants can facilitate and improve the time required for conducting these activities.

Fire stations should be strategically deployed throughout the community to provide for effective response times to emergencies. The primary purpose of strategic station distribution is to minimize response times and enable firefighters to suppress reported fires in a time-critical manner prior to flashover (i.e., when all flammable contents within a structure spontaneously ignite). From a medical perspective, response time should be structured to allow personnel to intervene and provide life-saving procedures such as CPR during the first four to six minutes of an emergency event.

Fire stations can also be constructed to provide a safe haven for community residents during periods of inclement weather or other natural or man-made disasters. Sufficient space should be provided to allow business to be conducted normally, as well as allow personnel to be able to function on around-the-clock schedules.

The Fire-Rating Process

Fire departments are evaluated for insurance purposes by the Insurance Services Office (ISO). Fire personnel should understand the basis for the department's existing rating and what is required to improve it.

For the purpose of establishing homeowners and fire insurance rates, each fire department is rated or classified by ISO. In making an evaluation, ISO uses the *Fire Suppression Rating Schedule* as a guide for evaluating fire suppression capabilities. The better the ISO rating, the less property owners pay for their property insurance. ISO places departments in one of 10 classes, with Class 1 rating being the highest and Class 10 being the lowest. To meet the minimum level of protection recognized by ISO, a fire department must have at least a Class 9 rating. In evaluating fire departments, the three principal features that ISO representatives measure are fire alarms, fire department, and water supply.

Employment and Training Standards

Fire departments are required to adhere to the training requirements identified by the Georgia Firefighters Standards and Training Council.[34]

The standards set forth by this agency are not limited to career employees (i.e., full-time rather than volunteer) and include initial training for new firefighters and annual refresher or in-service training. Failure to comply with these mandates will result in a firefighter losing his or her certification and ability to be gainfully employed. As legally organized agencies, fire departments are responsible for providing the required training to maintain individual certification.[35]

Training requirements for volunteer firefighters differ from those for career personnel. The Georgia Fire Academy provides the training for volunteer departments.

EMERGENCY 9-1-1 SERVICES

Communication is the backbone of an emergency services program. A 9-1-1 emergency telephone system provides a simple single telephone number that citizens can use to access fire, law enforcement, emergency medical, and other services when there is an emergency. A county is not mandated by law to provide 9-1-1 services. However, once a county decides to provide this service, it must follow a number of state and federal laws, rules, and regulations governing provision of 9-1-1 service.[36] The 9-1-1 service may be provided by a single county or city or by multiple local governments.

Many counties combine their 9-1-1 system with the dispatching of their local public safety agencies (e.g., fire, law enforcement, ambulance, and emergency management). Combining 9-1-1 call answering and dispatching functions achieves time and cost savings. However, some counties separate the service of answering a 9-1-1 call from the service of sending out or dispatching the requested public safety service. In these cases, the 9-1-1 call is transferred to the appropriate dispatching agency (i.e., the sheriff's office, the city police department, the fire department, etc.). This is particularly true when an independent officer or entity is part of the 9-1-1 system. For instance, some sheriffs may prefer to dispatch their calls. Similarly, many cities may contract with their county to receive 9-1-1 calls, but the 9-1-1 calls are transferred to the city for dispatch.

Counties are encouraged to provide enhanced 9-1-1 services, rather than just basic 9-1-1 service. Enhanced 9-1-1 provides the caller's telephone number and location; basic 9-1-1 does not. Enhanced 9-1-1 also allows easier transfer of calls to another agency.

Funding for 9-1-1 Services

As an alternative to funding 9-1-1 service solely through property tax, counties are authorized to impose a 9-1-1 user fee on telephone and wireless telephone customers in the county. The 9-1-1 user fee is imposed by the county but is collected by landline and wireless telephone companies on behalf of the county.

The maximum 9-1-1 user fee for a landline telephone is $1.50 per month[37] unless two counties create a new joint system, in which case the 9-1-1 user fee is $2.50.[38] The maximum 9-1-1 user fee for a wireless phone is $1.00 per month if the 9-1-1 system can identify the telephone number of the caller and the base station or cell site.[39] The maximum 9-1-1 user fee for a wireless phone is the same as that for a landline phone (i.e., $1.50 or $2.50, depending upon whether it is a single-county or multicounty system) if the 9-1-1 system can identify the wireless phone number and location of the cell phone caller (i.e., automatic location identification, or ALI).[40] The county must reduce the 9-1-1 user fee if the projected 9-1-1 user fee revenues will cause the unexpended revenues in the Emergency Telephone System Fund at the end of the fiscal year to exceed by 1.5 times the unexpended revenues in the fund in the previous fiscal year.[41]

Before any fee can be collected by the telephone company, the local government must hold either a referendum or a public hearing.[42] Once collection of the fee begins, local governments have up to 18 months to implement the service.[43] All user fees collected must be maintained in a separate account known as the Emergency Telephone System Fund. Any income earned on the money in the fund must be kept in the fund.[44] The 9-1-1 user fees may only be used for the following purposes:

- *9-1-1 building.* Leasing or purchasing a building to be used for the 9-1-1 center once the county has completed its street address plan.[45]

- *Computer hardware and software.* Lease, purchase, or maintenance of computer hardware and software used at the 9-1-1 center, including computer-assisted dispatch systems.[46]

- *Logging recorders.* Lease, purchase, or maintenance of logging recorders used to record telephone and radio traffic.[47]

- *Emergency telephone equipment.* The lease, purchase, or maintenance of emergency telephone equipment (including necessary computer hardware, software, and database provisioning; addressing; and nonrecurring costs of establishing a 9-1-1 system).[48]

- *Supplies.* Office supplies and other supplies used directly in providing 9-1-1 services, including the printing of 9-1-1 public education materials.[49]

- *Service supplier fees.* 9-1-1 service suppliers' rates and other service suppliers' recurring charges.[50]

- *Wireless companies' cost recovery.* Cost recovery for the wireless companies of up to 30¢ to 45¢ of every dollar collected.[51]

- *Salaries.* Actual cost of salaries (including benefits) of county employees hired solely for the operation and maintenance of the 9-1-1 system.[52]

- *Training.* Actual cost of training county employees who work as dispatchers or directors (i.e., the person who has direct operational or management control of a public safety answering point or who supervises one or more communication officers or employees who answer 9-1-1 calls).[53]

The 9-1-1 user fee money (and any interest earned on this money) may be used only for the above purposes.[54] Every year, the county must file a report of its 9-1-1 fee collections and expenditures with the annual audit. This report requires that the county and its auditor certify that the 9-1-1 user fees were expended only for these purposes.[55] Any county that uses 9-1-1 user fee money for any other purpose may be liable to pay back the amounts that were illegally used to the telephone and wireless phone customers.[56]

State Responsibilities

The Georgia Emergency Management Agency (GEMA) is responsible for helping local governments develop plans for their 9-1-1 systems and secure funding. In addition to developing guidelines for implementing 9-1-1 service, the director of GEMA, with the approval of the governor, can establish minimum standards for training and equipment. GEMA is also the coordinating agency among the local 9-1-1 systems, state agencies, and telecommunication companies.

Training Requirements

Communications officers who respond to 9-1-1 calls and receive, process, or transmit public safety information and dispatch law enforcement officers, firefighters, medical personnel, or emergency management personnel are required to complete a basic training course approved by the Peace Officer Standards and Training Council. Every dispatch center operated by a county to dispatch law enforcement officers, firefighters, emergency medical personnel or emergency management personnel must have on duty at all times at least one communications officer certified in the use of telecommunications devices for the deaf (TDDs). If a county fails to comply with this requirement, it will not be permitted to impose a monthly 9-1-1 charge.[57]

EMERGENCY MANAGEMENT

County commissioners are on the front line when an emergency or disaster strikes. As the level of government closest to the people, the county is the first and primary agency to provide aid and relief to the citizens impacted by the disaster. Emergency management is a critical government function that coordinates available resources to be used in planning for, lessening the impact of, responding to, and recovering from a wide variety of natural or man-made events that can kill or injure significant numbers of people, do extensive damage to property, and generally disrupt community life.

The function of emergency management has radically evolved and drastically expanded from a civil defense function into an all-hazards approach. The current approach addresses a wide range of disasters and emergencies, including severe weather events, hazardous materials and radiological incidents, school violence and terrorism, pandemics, and other possible occurrences that may be unique to individual communities. County elected officials have the primary responsibility for providing emergency management services to their communities as an essential part of their duty to maintain law and order and protect lives and property. The general legal authority for emergency management is found in federal and state law[58] as well as in presidential decision directives.

County Emergency Management Agency

Each county is required by state law to establish an emergency management agency in order to receive state or federal funding for disaster relief.[59] The agency structure, the number of staff, and the complexity of operations vary widely depending on a county's needs and resources. Although some federal funds are available to support county programs, most activities are funded through local revenues.

Assistance from the State and Federal Governments

At the state level, emergency management is the responsibility of GEMA, which carries out its duties in collaboration with local emergency management agencies, the Federal Emergency Management Agency (FEMA), other state agencies, the private sector, and the volunteer community. When an emergency strikes, it is the governor who declares a state of emergency, which puts into play all of the emergency powers that the state and counties may exercise.[60]

When appropriate, the president may also make a federal disaster area declaration. In such a case, the citizens of any county included in the declaration may have access to federal grants and low-interest loans to help them repair and restore their property. Also, any county included in the declaration may be reimbursed some of the costs of recovering from the disaster through FEMA. In order to be eligible for FEMA reimbursement, counties must comply with several requirements, some of which are discussed later in this chapter.

Prepare, Review, and Update Emergency Operations Plan

A county's emergency management agency is required to prepare an Emergency Operations Plan (EOP).[61] The EOP is crucial to the ability of a county to be prepared for and adequately respond to natural and man-made disasters and emergencies. In order to properly prepare a plan, county officials should first conduct a hazard and risk analysis of the county, assess current capabilities, and take the necessary action to ensure that additional resources are available when needed through the use of such measures as mutual aid agreements, which must be in place prior to a disaster in order to qualify for any reimbursement from FEMA. In addition, the plan should be routinely exercised and updated so that it is effective and current. Finally, key emergency management staff from all affected agencies and social service groups such as the Red Cross should receive appropriate training in response and recovery activities.[62]

Commissioners Participation

County commissioners should be aware of the basics of their EOP. They also need to think about how they would conduct business and plan for how they would continue providing services in the event of an emergency. There are so many urgent and pressing needs during an emergency that it is often difficult to properly draft and follow appropriate procedures, policies, and agreements in the midst of a crisis. However, having these documents drafted and adopted prior to an emergency may save the county millions of dollars in the event of an emergency.

Emergency Ordinances

One way for commissioners to prepare for an emergency is to adopt ordinances that would govern if the governor were to declare a state of emergency in the county.[63] It is much easier to draft these ordinances before an emergency strikes than to wait and try to figure it out in the middle of the emergency.

One of the many requirements for FEMA reimbursement is that the county follow its established procedures in responding to the emergency. In the midst of a disaster, there may not be time to bid out emergency supplies or services according to the county's regular purchasing ordinance or policy. If the county has an established exception in its ordinances for emergency purchases and follows it when buying emergency supplies, the county may be entitled to FEMA reimbursement. If the county does not have an exception and does not follow its regular procedures, then it will be very difficult for it to receive FEMA reimbursement. It is important that commissioners review their purchasing ordinance or policy to make sure that purchases made during an emergency are addressed.

Counties may adopt an ordinance requiring emergency registration of all or certain designated classes of business during the state of emergency and for a recovery period of up to three months.[64] No business may do business within the county without first registering in conformance with the ordinance. This policy is a good way for county commissioners to protect their citizens from unscrupulous building contractors who go from community to community in the wake of a disaster to take advantage of unsuspecting property owners.

Agreements

Another way for a county to prepare is to have mutual aid agreements in place with neighboring jurisdictions in order to assist one another in the event of an emergency.[65] Properly executed mutual aid or other intergovernmental agreements are useful when seeking reimbursement from FEMA. It is often much easier to draft these agreements and have them in place before an emergency.

Oftentimes, in a state of emergency, the county needs to use private property as a staging area, distribution area, or shelter. A sample agreement prepared ahead of time that allows the county to use such property may be a useful tool. If the property owner allows the county to use the property free of charge, then the property owner is granted sovereign immunity (i.e., the property owner cannot be sued successfully for any damages occurring on the property during the emergency).[66]

Governance

Another issue that county commissioners should consider is how the business of running the county will happen during an emergency. Commissioners are supposed to provide for emergency interim successors for county officials (other than constitutional officers, who appoint their own deputies) in the event of a declaration of emergency.[67]

There are special rules that apply only if the governor declares a state of emergency. For instance, if it is imprudent, inexpedient, or impossible to conduct the county's business at the courthouse (or usual place of business), commissioners may meet at any place within the county or outside the county on the call of the chairperson or any two members of the board.[68] The board should adopt an ordinance or resolution designating the alternative or substitute sites as an emergency temporary location of the county government where public business may be transacted during the state of emergency called by the governor. The emergency temporary location may be in another county or even another state. The commissioners and other county officers have the same powers and functions at the emergency temporary location during the state of emergency as they would under normal circumstances. They may conduct business without following time-consuming procedures and formalities otherwise prescribed by law during the state of emergency.[69]

EMA Directors

A county's emergency management agency is headed by a director appointed by the director of GEMA but nominated by the county commissioners.[70] The emergency management agency director serves at the pleasure of the county commissioners. State law establishes certain minimum requirements.[71] Some county emergency management agencies are headed by paid, full-time directors, while others are directed by part-time employees or volunteers. It is permissible for a director to also hold other positions, such as fire chief or 9-1-1 director so long as certain minimum state requirements are met.[72]

ANIMAL CONTROL

County officials often receive complaints about animals. Although taxpayers may complain about the cost of an animal control program, citizens generally expect the local government to not only control rabies but also solve nuisance animal problems. The county's authority to provide animal control services is provided by the Georgia Constitution[73] as well as several state statutes.

Rabies

State law requires counties to regulate or license animals in order to control rabies.[74] The county board of health has primary responsibility for prevention and control of rabies and must appoint a county rabies control officer.[75] County commissioners are authorized to impose a fee of up to 50¢ per dog receiving a rabies vaccine to be collected by veterinarians in the county and to be used to help pay the salary of the county rabies control officer.[76]

Animal Protection

Many counties have ordinances protecting the welfare of animals. These ordinances require outside animals to have amenities such as adequate shelter and access to food and water. Counties are authorized to enforce provisions of the Georgia Animal Protection Act.[77] For instance, the county animal control officer may impound an animal that has been subjected to cruelty or inhumane treatment.[78] When directed by the county commissioners, the county attorney is authorized to obtain an injunction or restraining order.[79]

"Dangerous" and "Vicious" Dogs

Georgia law establishes two categories of dogs that must be confined in special enclosures: "dangerous dogs" and "vicious dogs." These dogs have bitten or have caused severe injury or death to a person without provocation.[80] Commissioners may adopt an ordinance or resolution to create an animal control board to hold hearings in order to classify dogs as dangerous or potentially dangerous.[81] Counties are also responsible for local enforcement of the Dangerous Dog Control Law within their unincorporated areas[82] as well as Georgia's law on vicious dogs ("Mercedes' Law").[83]

A county may contract with a municipality and/or with other counties for joint dog control services.[84] Counties are required to appoint a dog control officer.[85] This responsibility may be assigned to a deputy sheriff or the rabies control officer, with the approval of the sheriff or the county board of health, respectively. The dog control officer is required to investigate reports of dangerous or potentially dangerous dogs, classify dogs as dangerous or potentially dangerous, register dangerous and potentially dangerous dogs within the jurisdiction, verify that the owner is complying with the requirements for confining a dangerous dog, and confiscate and, if necessary, destroy any dangerous dog whose owner fails to comply with the requirements of the law. Counties may charge annual fees in addition to dog-licensing fees for the registration of dangerous and potentially dangerous dogs.[86]

Mandatory Sterilization in Shelters

In recognition of the public health problem created by the uncontrolled breeding of stray cats and dogs, county animal shelters must provide for the sterilization of all dogs or cats adopted from their organizations.[87] The sterilization may be done by the animal shelter or control agency before adoption, or the person adopting the animal must agree to have it sterilized prior to its sexual maturity. If the county animal shelter or animal control agency performs the sterilization, it may add the cost of the sterilization to the fee charged for the animal. Counties are permitted to adopt more stringent requirements than those required by general law.[88]

Nuisance

Many of the complaints county commissioners receive about animals are related to behavior that interferes with the quality of life of neighbors. Some counties have therefore adopted ordinances aimed at reducing nuisance behaviors.

One problem is animals running at large. Many counties have enacted leash laws requiring any animal that is off its property be under its owner's control (i.e., on a leash). Another tactic employed by animal shelters is to require that anyone wishing to adopt an animal have a properly fenced yard.

Barking dogs are another problem. Some counties have tried to use noise ordinances to combat the aggravation created by barking dogs. Some counties have adopted "anti-tethering" ordinances that prohibit or restrict the amount of time a dog can be chained outdoors.

Livestock

The sheriff is required to impound livestock found to be running at large or straying.[89] County commissioners are required to establish and maintain a suitable place to keep impounded livestock until they are sold, redeemed, or otherwise disposed of.[90] Commissioners are also responsible for providing truck transportation of the impounded livestock.

NOTES

1. OFFICIAL CODE OF GEORGIA ANNOTATED (O.C.G.A.) §15-16-10(a)(9).

2. The following 13 counties have county police departments: Athens-Clarke, Clayton, Cobb, Columbus-Muscogee, DeKalb, Dougherty, Floyd, Fulton, Glynn, Gwinnett, Henry, Polk, and Ware.

3. O.C.G.A. §36-8-1(b).

4. Part of this section is drawn from Charles R. Swanson Jr., Leonard Territo, and Robert Taylor, *Police Administration: Structures, Processes, and Behavior*, 5th ed. (New York: MacMillan, 2001).

5. Gary W. Cordner, "Written Rules and Regulations: Are They Necessary?" *FBI Law Enforcement Bulletin* 58, no. 7 (July 1989): 18.

6. Russell Mass, "Written Rules and Regulations: Is the Fear Real?" *Law and Order* 38, no. 5 (May 1990): 36.

7. O.C.G.A. tit. 35, ch. 8.

8. O.C.G.A. §§35-8-9(a), 35-8-8. See also O.C.G.A. §§35-8-20, 35-8-20.1 regarding police chiefs and department heads.

9. O.C.G.A. §15-16-1.

10. O.C.G.A. §15-16-3(e).

11. O.C.G.A. §35-8-20.1.

12. O.C.G.A. §42-5-51(c).

13. O.C.G.A. §17-10-1.

14. O.C.G.A. §42-4-4(a)(2).

15. O.C.G.A. §§42-4-4(a)(2), 42-4-32. See Lumpkin County v. Davis, 185 Ga. 393, 195 S.E. 169 (1938).

16. See O.C.G.A. §42-4-51.

17. Board of Commissioners of Spalding County v. Stewart, 284 Ga. 573, 668 S.E.2d 644 (2008).

18. Macon–Bibb County Hospital Authority v. Houston County, 207 Ga. App. 530, 428 S.E.2d 374 (1993).

19. O.C.G.A. §42-4-12.

20. O.C.G.A. §42-4-51(d).

21. O.C.G.A. §42-4-71.

22. O.C.G.A. §§42-4-4, 42-4-31, 42-4-32.

23. Georgia Jail Standards Study Commission, *Standards for Georgia Jail Facilities* (Atlanta: Department of Community Affairs and Georgia State Crime Commission, 1986).

24. O.C.G.A. §§15-21-92, 15-21-93(a)(1).

25. O.C.G.A. §15-21-93(a)(2).

26. O.C.G.A. §15-21-92.

27. O.C.G.A. §15-21-94(a).

28. O.C.G.A. §15-21-95.

29. Georgia Department of Corrections (www.dcor.state.ga.us/Divisions/Corrections/CountyPrisons.html).

30. O.C.G.A. §35-8-24.

31. Emergency Planning and Community Right-to-Know Act of 1986, 42 UNITED STATES CODE ANNOTATED (U.S.C.A.) §§11001–11050.

32. O.C.G.A. §§25-3-22, 25-3-23.
33. O.C.G.A. §25-3-25.
34. O.C.G.A. tit. 25, ch. 4, art. 1.
35. Ibid.
36. O.C.G.A. tit. 46, ch. 5, art. 2, part 4.
37. O.C.G.A. §46-5-134(a)(1)(A).
38. O.C.G.A. §46-5-138.1.
39. O.C.G.A. §46-5-134(a)(2)(A).
40. O.C.G.A. §46-5-134(a)(2)(B).
41. O.C.G.A. §46-5-134(d)(5).
42. O.C.G.A. §46-5-133(b)(1).
43. O.C.G.A. §46-5-134(k).
44. O.C.G.A. §46-5-134(d)(2).
45. O.C.G.A. §46-5-134(f)(5).
46. O.C.G.A. §46-5-134(f)(6).
47. O.C.G.A. §46-5-134(f)(8).
48. O.C.G.A. §46-5-134(f)(1).
49. O.C.G.A. §46-5-134(f)(4), (7).
50. O.C.G.A. §46-5-134(f)(2).
51. O.C.G.A. §46-5-134(e), (f).
52. O.C.G.A. §46-5-134(f)(3).
53. O.C.G.A. §§46-5-134(f)(3), 46-5-138.2(a).
54. O.C.G.A. §46-5-134(d)(2), (m)(2).
55. O.C.G.A. §46-5-134(m)(1).
56. O.C.G.A. §46-5-134(m)(2).
57. O.C.G.A. §§35-8-23, 36-60-19. No funds have been appropriated to the Georgia Peace Officer Standards and Training Council for this training. Counties must fund this training for their employees.
58. 42 U.S.C.A. §5121 et. seq.; O.C.G.A. tit. 38, ch. 3, art. 1.
59. O.C.G.A. §38-3-27(e)(1).
60. O.C.G.A. §38-3-51(b).
61. O.C.G.A. §38-3-27.
62. GEMA provides emergency management planning and other types of assistance to local governments. For information, contact the Director of GEMA, 935 E. Confederate Avenue, S.E., P.O. Box 18055, Atlanta, GA 30316-0055; www.gema.state.ga.us.
63. O.C.G.A. §38-3-27; 1989 Op. Att'y Gen. No. 89-56.
64. O.C.G.A. §38-3-56.
65. O.C.G.A. §38-3-29.
66. O.C.G.A. §38-3-32. See O.C.G.A. §38-3-33 regarding use of equipment.
67. O.C.G.A. §38-3-50.
68. O.C.G.A. §38-3-54.
69. O.C.G.A. §§38-3-54, 38-3-55.
70. O.C.G.A. §38-3-27(a)(1).

71. O.C.G.A. §38-3-27(a)(2).
72. See O.C.G.A. §38-3-27(a)(3).
73. GA. CONST. art. IX, §2, ¶3(a)(3).
74. O.C.G.A. §31-19-3.
75. O.C.G.A. §§31-19-1, 31-19-7(a).
76. O.C.G.A. §31-19-7.
77. O.C.G.A. tit. 4, ch. 11, art. 1.
78. O.C.G.A. §4-11-9.2(c).
79. O.C.G.A. §4-11-15.
80. See O.C.G.A. §§4-8-21(1), 4-8-41(6).
81. O.C.G.A. §§4-8-22(d), 4-8-24.
82. O.C.G.A. tit. 4, ch. 8, art. 2.
83. O.C.G.A. tit. 4, ch. 8, art. 3.
84. O.C.G.A. §4-8-22(b).
85. O.C.G.A. §4-8-22(c).
86. O.C.G.A. tit. 4, ch. 8, art. 2.
87. O.C.G.A. §4-14-3.
88. O.C.G.A. §4-14-5.
89. O.C.G.A. §4-3-4(a).
90. O.C.G.A. §4-3-11.

15

John A. O'Looney, Charlie Walters, and Kelly Joiner

Health and Human Services

A growing cost to counties is the provision of health and human services. In Georgia, the largest expenditures are for uncompensated and indigent health care costs, emergency medical services, hospitals, public health, and public welfare and social services—generally in that order. Other large outlays of county funds are also made for community action agencies, centers for older persons, and behavioral health services, including substance abuse, mental health, and mental retardation.[1] An area of increasing concern and cost for counties is the provision of medical, mental health, and addictive disease services to inmates of county jails.[2]

EMERGENCY MEDICAL SERVICES

Although counties are not required to provide emergency medical services (EMS), many elect to do so for the benefit of their citizens. In most counties, particularly those in rural Georgia, the population density and/or insurance payer mix do not allow for an EMS service to operate at a profit. In these counties, the government often pays a subsidy to the provider of the service. Counties can choose to furnish EMS directly or contract with private providers or neighboring governments; some provide EMS through local public or private hospitals. Because most urban counties in Georgia have a number of private EMS providers located in their jurisdictions, they often leave EMS to the private sector.[3]

Regardless as to the method by which EMS is furnished, all counties that elect to participate must meet or exceed the applicable state statutory and regulatory requirements. Rules and regulations for the EMS program are promulgated and enforced by the State Office of

EMS and Trauma, an agency of the Department of Community Health (DCH). Emergency ambulance services are coordinated by a Regional EMS Council (also referred to as the local coordinating entity), which assigns 9-1-1 zones to ambulance services. In order for an ambulance service to provide emergency EMS care, it must be approved by the regional council.[4]

In order to receive a license, a service provider must meet standards for medical and communications equipment, insurance, and staffing. Each service provider is also required to have a physician medical advisor/director to ensure a high quality of patient care. This requirement can be waived if the county has fewer than 12,000 population, but most counties have made provisions to offer this valuable service.[5]

When providing EMS, a county can choose to provide a basic life support service, advanced life support service, or a combination of both. As the name implies, the advanced life support is the higher level of service and requires paramedics to be aboard the ambulance. At a minimum, each ambulance must be staffed with at least a basic EMT and an intermediate EMT.[6] EMS personnel are also allowed to carry controlled substances (IV fluids and medications). In order to do so, the service provider must have a contract with both a pharmacist and a physician to ensure the appropriate use and storage of such substances.[7]

Counties providing EMS or ambulance services may be considered health care providers who are subject to Health Insurance Portability and Accountability Act of 1996 (HIPAA) regulations. HIPAA requires EMS to limit the disclosure of a patient's medical and other protected health information. A county that operates an ambulance service is required to pay an annual license fee to the DCH, the amount of which is set by the Board of Community Health and is dedicated to the Indigent Care Trust Fund.[8] DCH is also authorized to enforce laws regarding EMS programs by imposing fines[9] and requiring continuing education of technicians.[10]

Emergency medical services are costly to provide for two reasons. First, fully equipped EMS vehicles are expensive and often require high levels of maintenance. Second, staffing these vehicles with qualified personnel on a 24-hour basis can result in substantial personnel costs, depending on the level of service and prevailing wages. Cost-management measures for ambulance services could include any of the following:

- Limiting subsidies for private providers of services to low-income patients

- Providing vehicle maintenance through county maintenance shops in return for discounts on service subsidies required by private providers

- Combining with other local governments to provide joint overhead for services

Funding for EMS comes from both private payers (i.e., patients and insurance companies) and public payers such as Medicaid and Medicare. Rates for Medicaid reimbursement are set by DCH.

HOSPITALS

As with EMS, counties are not required to provide for local hospital care. However, many counties have public hospitals (see Chapter 4, which describes hospital authorities). Both public and private hospitals are regulated under the Georgia Health Planning and Development Act. This law provides for a health strategies council that recommends state health policy to the governor; health planning and coordination through a state health planning agency that sets guidelines for services, collects data, and administers health services certificates of need; and a health planning review board to hear certificates of need appeals from the planning agency. In order for a hospital to expand its mix of services, it must first secure a certificate of need from the Division of Health Planning of DCH. During this process, a copy of the application for the certificate of need must be provided to the county board of commissioners.

While most public hospitals were built to serve the residents of a particular county and are governed by one county's hospital authority, a number of hospitals have become regional providers of hospital care. The trend toward regional hospitals is due to the impracticality of locating sophisticated and costly medical technology in every local hospital, the inability of small counties to attract physicians, and state and federal incentives for preventing unnecessary duplication of health resources. When combined with static or declining rural populations and the changing climate of health care financing, this trend toward regional hospitals has made small public hospitals less economically viable. Counties that have regional hospitals receive benefits in terms of economic development but incur above-average costs due to increased numbers of uninsured patients coming from outside the county. Counties can contract with hospitals for uninsured patient and other medical care, but they are not required to do so. An as yet unfunded state law authorizes the state to assist counties in paying for the care of nonresident indigent patients. If implemented, the law would require each county to appoint a health care advisory officer to maintain a file of indigent county residents. Upon receipt of a request from a hospital in another county for a determination of a patient's indigency, the advisory officer would determine whether the patient is indigent under state standards and so notify the hospital. For patients found to be indigent, the state pays all or part of the patient's health care costs. If the advisory officer were to fail to respond within 30 days, the county of residence would be liable for these expenses. Since the law is not funded, payment of nonresident indigent health care costs to hospitals is currently voluntary on the part of counties.[11]

Another state law requires a hospital operating an emergency service to provide appropriate and necessary emergency services to any pregnant woman who "presents herself in active labor."[12] If the patient receives health care and claims to be indigent, the hospital must determine if any portion of the cost can be paid by insurance or any federal, state, or local program. It then must communicate its findings, revealing any portion that may be payable from other programs, to the health care advisory officer of the patient's county of residence and request a determination as to whether the patient is indigent under state standards. If the advisory officer concludes that the patient is indigent or fails to respond within 60 days, the county of residence is liable for the patient's costs.[13] Since this law was enacted, a change in Medicaid guidelines has essentially provided for the payment of most of these costs. While state law applies only to pregnant women in active labor, federal "antidumping" regulations prohibit hospitals accepting Medicaid or Medicare from refusing to treat patients who present themselves in emergency condition.[14]

An additional law establishes a state Indigent Care Trust Fund. One of the purposes of this fund is to help defray the cost of uncompensated care at disproportionate share hospitals.[15] DCH[16] is authorized to provide special assistance to hospitals that serve rural communities, with the condition that these hospitals continue to furnish essential health care services to residents in their service areas and engage in long-range planning for cost-effective service delivery.[17] More generally, counties are authorized to levy up to 7 mills on behalf of a hospital authority and are authorized to cover the cost of indigent care. Public hospital authorities have no more legal responsibility to deliver indigent care than do other hospitals. Federal regulations require all hospitals to treat any person, insured or not, who presents him- or herself for emergency care.[18]

The Rural Hospital Authorities Assistance Act provides for the certification of certain rural hospitals (e.g., hospitals operated by a hospital authority, serving indigent patients, maintaining a 24-hour-a-day emergency room, in counties with fewer than 35,000 population) for grant eligibility. However, funding for these grants may not be available due to budget restrictions.[19]

Hospital authorities and nonprofit facilities are, with some exceptions, exempt from ad valorem taxes. Counties with populations of 50,000 or more may tax hospital authorities that have at least 100 beds on real property in which 50 percent of the property is leased to for-profit business or professions. In the case of nonprofit facilities, exceptions include property held for investment purposes that are unrelated to providing health care services, patient care, or training of health professionals.[20]

PUBLIC HEALTH, MENTAL HEALTH, DEVELOPMENTAL DISABILITIES, AND ADDICTIVE DISEASES

The division of responsibility for administering public health, mental health, developmental disabilities, and addictive diseases services among public organizations involves some overlap. Based on state matching fund formulas, county boards of health (see Chapter 4) are authorized to provide services in four general areas: physical health and disease control, environmental health, mental health and addictive disease, and developmental disabilities.[21] In reality, although county boards of health conduct local assessment of health needs and health planning in all of the four primary and preventive health areas, the actual administration and delivery of mental health, developmental disabilities, and addictive diseases services is provided through the state Department of Behavioral Health and Developmental Disabilities.[22]

County boards of health oversee the delivery of physical and environmental health services and gather valuable information about specific local health risks. Typically, they collect data on key indicators such as infant mortality and low birth weight, teenage pregnancy, health risk behaviors of adults and teens, accident patterns, the West Nile virus, rabies, sexually transmitted diseases, alcohol and substance abuse, and suicides.

The Department of Behavioral Health and Developmental Disabilities operates regional offices that establish, monitor, and evaluate mental health, developmental disabilities, and addictive diseases services in local communities. The regional offices also work with regional planning boards to provide and facilitate coordinated and comprehensive planning for their regions. Regional planning board members, in partnership with the Department of Behavioral Health and Developmental Disabilities, are charged with planning service delivery systems that focus on a core set of consumer-oriented, community-based values and principles. These principles provide effective and efficient delivery of services to individuals, families, and communities.

The governing authorities of the counties within each of the regions appoint members to the multicounty boards. The county commission, as the governing authority responsible for the appointment of representatives, in collaboration with the regional office and the regional planning board as well as other advocacy organizations, has the duty of ensuring that the most vulnerable citizens of the county are afforded optimal representation. The county governing authorities must ensure that appointments reflect the cultural and social characteristics of the regional and county population. For balance, each disability should be represented on the regional planning board. The regional planning boards meet at least once every two months.[23]

Community service boards, whose members are also appointed by the county governing authorities, have traditionally been the providers of public mental health, developmental disabilities, and addictive diseases services. Reform of the system grants additional authorities to the community service boards and establishes options for them to reorganize. The intent is to provide for an expansion of provider choices. The boards are not required to provide a comprehensive range of services. Along with other providers, they negotiate a contract annually with the Department of Behavioral Health and Developmental Disabilities for the services to be provided.[24]

In addition to these community-based services, the Department of Behavioral Health and Developmental Disabilities operates seven psychiatric hospitals across the state. These psychiatric hospitals serve people who cannot be served in the community. The catchment areas for these hospitals ensures that the people of Georgia have access to such services when they are determined to be a danger to themselves or others because of a disorder of mood or thought.

The Department of Behavioral Health and Developmental Disabilities also provides mental health treatment to defendants who are found to be incompetent to stand trial or not guilty by reason of insanity by a state or superior court. These forensic services have largely been inpatient but are beginning to be offered to nonviolent offenders on an outpatient basis.

In FY 2010, psychiatric hospitals expect to admit more than 9,000 people. The hospitals are located in the following counties:

- Floyd (North West Georgia Regional Hospital in Rome)

- Richmond (East Central Regional Hospital in Augusta, including the Gracewood campus)

- DeKalb (Georgia Regional Hospital Atlanta)

- Baldwin (Central State Hospital in Milledgeville)

- Muscogee (West Central Georgia Regional Hospital in Columbus)

- Thomas (Southwestern State Hospital in Thomasville)

- Chatham (Georgia Regional Hospital Savannah)

Over time, the use of hospitals for treatment of mentally ill, developmentally disabled, and addicted persons will decrease as community options are improved and expanded.

Physical Health and Disease Control

Services offered by the county board of health include family planning, maternal and infant health, immunization, vision, and dental clinics and programs for sexually transmitted disease, AIDS testing and education, and coronary, cardiac, and communicable disease. Generally, about 10 percent of these programs are paid for through patient fees, 50 percent through state and federal grants, and 30 to 40 percent through county funds. These programs serve patients on an occasional basis, but the largest proportion of those being served by all public health programs fall into this category.

Environmental Health

Services provided by the county board of health include inspection of food establishments, water supplies, sewage disposal, swimming pools, and public premises. Most of these services are provided through county funds supplemented by state grant-in-aid funds. The county boards of health in counties with populations of 400,000 or more are also authorized to develop and implement activities for the prevention of injuries and incorporate injury prevention measures in rules and regulations that are within the purview of the county board.[25] Because the county board of health is limited in its enforcement powers, some counties have adopted the board of health's regulations as ordinances and have designated a board of health code enforcement officer. This arrangement allows the regulations to be enforced as ordinance violations in magistrate court. The magistrate judge may impose penalties and even jail time for code violations.[26]

Mental Health and Addictive Diseases

These services include child, adolescent, and adult counseling and addictive diseases programs and treatment. Most of the funding for these programs is derived from state and federal sources. The counties furnish a small amount, and a very small amount is supplied through fees. These programs serve about 10 percent of those receiving public health services, but they provide more intensive and long-term services than is generally the case with public health.

Developmental Disabilities

These services include early intervention, habilitation, community living, and supported employment programs. The program activities are mostly supported through Medicaid waiver dollars, with some state dollars. Persons with developmental disabilities receive the most intensive services within the service array, usually on a lifetime basis.[27]

Key public health, mental health, developmental disabilities, and addictive diseases issues for county commissioners include the following:

- Developing, in coordination with state and district health systems, preventive and wellness services designed to reduce public health costs in the long run

- Increasing the capacity of the health and mental health systems to use Medicaid programs for revenue maximization. Although state Medicaid plans can change significantly, they have tended to become more supportive of preventive services such as early periodic screening and diagnostic testing for infants and children.

- Increasing participation in PeachCare for Kids, the child health insurance program for low- and middle-income families[28]

- Increasing the capacity to address addictive diseases and mental health problems of county jail and probation populations

- Increasing successful transition from school to adult life for individuals with developmental disabilities through outreach and education to families

- Addressing the waiting list for developmental disabilities services by identifying specific needs by county

- Promoting the use of community-based services to ensure that people with mental illnesses can be served in their home communities as much as possible and defray the costs associated with transporting county residents to psychiatric hospitals

- Ensuring that every county in the state has representation on both the regional planning boards and community service boards

- Providing for the transport of citizens through the sheriff's office from their communities to psychiatric hospitals when involuntary admission has been ordered by a physician or appropriate judge

FAMILY AND CHILDREN SERVICES

Family and children services are the responsibility of the DHS Division of Family and Children Services. At the local level, the board of the county department of family and children services (DFCS) makes recommendations to DHS regarding county policy and appointment of the county director (discussed in Chapter 4).

DFCS has two major areas of responsibility. One area is employability and related assistance programs, which includes the following:

- *Food stamps.* Provides food vouchers for impoverished individuals.

- *Temporary Assistance to Needy Families (TANF).* Provides up to 48 months of cash assistance to families with dependent children, minimal resources (e.g., less than $1,000 for a mother and two children), and incomes not exceeding approximately 45 percent of federal poverty guidelines. Work activities and a Personal Responsibility and Work Plan are required.

- *Medicaid.* Eligibility varies with programs but generally only covers pregnant women, elderly and disabled adults, and children.

- *Other.* Includes general assistance, transportation vouchers, energy assistance, and child care.

The second area of DFCS responsibility is social services, which includes activities to protect family members from abuse and neglect and to keep families together and children in safe and caring environments. Because these goals are sometimes contradictory, services are usually divided into protective services (child and adult protective services) and services such as adoption, homemaking, respite, and foster care that promote family functioning.[29]

The department can request the juvenile court to award it the temporary custody of a child who is in danger of abuse or neglect and in more extreme cases, can ask that the court terminate parental rights. Because of the complex nature of abuse and foster care cases, the state has required that counties

1. establish in writing a child abuse protocol, an interagency agreement for clarifying the roles and responsibilities of law enforcement, DFCS, school officials, hospitals, district attorneys, boards of health, and mental health centers in the investigation and processing of child abuse cases;

2. provide for a review of the current status and plans for permanent care of children placed in foster homes.[30] Many juvenile court judges have appointed a foster care review board of citizen volunteers in order to meet the placement review requirement;[31] and

3. establish a Child Fatality Review Committee (as a subcommittee of the child abuse protocol committee) to oversee the local child fatality review process and report to the Child Fatality Review Panel on the incidence of child deaths, with recommendations for prevention.[32]

OTHER SERVICE PROVIDERS

Housing assistance for county residents is provided through a variety of public organizations, which include the following:

- *Public housing authorities.* Although public housing authorities typically have local boards, these authorities are chiefly funded through the federal government and guided by federal regulations related to eligibility and allowable rental rates. Some housing authorities have begun to work with communities to develop affordable homeownership opportunities, and counties will sometimes supplement housing authority funds for special projects.

- *Georgia Housing and Finance Authority.* This state agency operates a program known as Section 8 housing through which an eligible person's rent is partially or fully paid to qualified landlords operating low-income housing.[33]

- *Housing Trust Fund for the Homeless.* Counties can draw from this state trust fund to help remedy local housing problems.[34]

- *Department of Community Affairs.* This state agency operates a First-Time Home Buyers program and provides funding to local governments for projects that assist low-income residents.

Community action agencies are nonprofit organizations that help families that live below poverty level to move toward independence. While these agencies are not tied to local governments, they are the chief recipients of federal Community Services Block Grant funds that are used to provide services such as transportation, housing, nutrition, and promotion of employability. Funds for community action agencies and for initiatives such as homeless programs, welfare reform support, emergency management, and specialized projects are channeled through DHS. Although these funds have traditionally been appropriated to community action agencies, some local governments have developed their own programs in these areas.

Regional commissions (RCs) and Workforce Investment Act boards play a role in regional planning for and technical assistance to (but not provision of) employment and other human services.[35] RCs typically play an administrative role with respect to programs for the elderly and workforce development (e.g., providing staff support to the Workforce Investment Act boards and programs). While RCs are often the lead or area agencies on aging, DHS can designate any appropriate organization as the area agency on aging.[36] Similarly, while RCs often support the work of the Workforce Investment Act boards, these boards are independently established by federal and state legislation.

Although juvenile courts are not social service agencies, they tend to act as brokers and monitors of services supplied by other agencies, such as DFCS and the Department of Juvenile Justice (DJJ), as well as providers of services designed to divert children away from formal court proceedings or prevent them from becoming career offenders. In a majority of counties, basic juvenile court services such as diversion, intake, and probation are provided by the state DJJ. A few counties provide funding or staff in order to augment these state-supplied services. Although the function of the DJJ in all counties is to rehabilitate youth whose behavior warrants commitment to state custody, some urban counties fund basic juvenile court services such as intake and probation on their own. Prior to committing persons to the state DJJ, counties are responsible for covering the cost of any necessary medical examinations and/or treatment for juveniles upon certification of the expenses by the judge of the court of adjudication, even when the juvenile is housed in another county.[37]

MAJOR ISSUES IN HEALTH AND HUMAN SERVICES

As the cost of providing health and human services continues to grow, counties may have to examine new approaches to effect cost management as well as early intervention activities in order to minimize or even prevent long-term or down-the-line treatment and its associated costs. A number of issues will have to be addressed.

Providing Health Care

Generally, uncompensated health care costs are increasing due to the lack of primary care facilities and an appropriate mechanism for steering patients who need only basic or low-level services away from expensive emergency room care. As a result, there is increased pressure on county governments to subsidize hospitals and other providers. Cost management activities in this area might include the following:

- More use of case management and improved access to and availability of prevention, wellness, and primary care
- Provision of health promotion programs, with increased support for health education, exercise, and nutrition
- Increased education and training of health care practitioners on disability competency issues
- Increased use of Medicaid outreach, clinic, and case management services
- Provision of prenatal care and clinics
- Implementation of programs to manage chronic disease through increased knowledge of how lifestyles affect conditions
- Provision of supplements to physicians for indigent care of patients who would otherwise go to hospitals
- Improved prevention, wellness, and primary care for inmates and persons living with mental illnesses
- Provision of preventive/early detection services not paid for by Medicaid

County commissioners also should be aware of the health needs of children, particularly related to dental care and behavioral health, and of the potential for strategies such as school-based health services to address these needs.[38]

Welfare Reform

While welfare reform has been very successful in reducing the provision of cash public assistance and redirecting the blocked funds to employment support programs such as childcare, economic downturns place the system under severe stress. County governments must be prepared to address a possible gap in funding at least on an emergency basis.

Because the area of family services involves law enforcement and custodial functions, DFCS can become liable for not meeting constitutional and statutory mandates or for not delivering services in accordance with reasonable professional standards. Recent lawsuits, such as *Kenny A. v. Perdue*, have forced several states to address problems relating to excessive worker caseloads, the lack of case responsiveness, the use of emergency care for long-term care, the lack of appropriate placements for foster children, and the absence of specialized placement for troubled children.[39] The root cause of litigation in this area has been the dramatic increase in the demands placed on the family service system without a comparable increase in resources to meet those demands. Due to the downturn in the economy, increased state funding for this system has been reduced, and DFCS has suffered budget reductions of $18 million in FY 10 and FY 11. Many child and family experts and advocates feel that addressing family and child development problems in the state will demand substantially more resources in order to overcome multigenerational problems. Therefore, many counties are recognizing the need for comprehensive early intervention when family and youth crises develop. The Governor's Office for Children and Families[40] provides support to local human services providers for a variety of prevention programs and community-based services.

GEORGIA'S INITIATIVE TO IMPROVE RESULTS FOR CHILDREN AND FAMILIES

Beyond providing the basic level of resources needed to meet legal, professional, and program standards for human services delivery, the key health and human services challenge for the coming decade is two-fold: (1) to address the results accountability issue and (2) to create a solid and efficient system of care—one without service gaps or excess duplication.

With respect to results accountability, some counties are beginning to follow a more proactive strategy for health and human services programming that focuses on return on investment. Such counties appear increasingly willing to provide support for preventive services related to health, housing, behavioral health, and delinquency problems— if these services can demonstrate high net benefits. In order to achieve these net benefits, however, counties must be willing to redirect some resources to areas where the desired impacts are most likely to be realized.

Resources and redirection alone, however, cannot produce the desired benefits. What is needed is a system of care that can exist only when human services organizations and schools work together to provide early identification of problems and family-focused treatments and to share facilities, staff, information, transportation, training experiences, and other resources. Similarly, more systematic and strategic use of Medicaid and other federal funding opportunities is likely to occur only when members of the local human services community work together.

The Family Connection Initiative, a collaborative effort of state agencies (e.g., DHS, the Department of Education, the Department of Juvenile Justice) and local service agencies, provides a model for addressing results accountability[41] and service delivery issues. Most counties in Georgia now have their own Family Connection partnership. In some counties, this partnership has been designated by the county government as the single point of planning and accountability for the human services system in the community. Because many of the partners in The Family Connection are county-operated or county-related organizations, county commissioners should consider assuming significant supporting, coordinating, and leadership roles in such partnerships.

NOTES

1. Interview with ACCG staff, October 1991.
2. Conversation with Suzanne Nieman, ACCG staff member for Health and Human Services, June 2001.
3. Interview with DHR staff member in Emergency Health, October 1991.
4. OFFICIAL CODE OF GEORGIA ANNOTATED (O.C.G.A.) §31-11-3.
5. DCH Regulation 290-5-30-.07; O.C.G.A. §31-11-50.
6. DCH Regulation 290-5-30-.07(c).
7. O.C.G.A. §31-11-60.
8. O.C.G.A. §31-11-31.1.
9. O.C.G.A. §31-11-9.

10. O.C.G.A. §31-11-58.
11. O.C.G.A. tit. 31, ch. 8, art. 2.
12. O.C.G.A. §31-8-42.
13. O.C.G.A. §31-8-43.
14. 42 C.F.R. §482.1(a)(3).
15. O.C.G.A. tit. 31, ch. 8, art. 6.
16. See the Department of Community Health Web site at dch.georgia.gov.
17. O.C.G.A, §31-7-94.1.
18. Excerpted from Ann Marchetti, *Quick Facts* (Atlanta: ACCG, August 1996); O.C.G.A, §31-7-84(b).
19. O.C.G.A. §31-7-94.1.
20. Marchhetti, *Quick Facts*; O.C.G.A, §31-7-72(e).
21. Plan for Financial Assistance to County Boards of Health, based on O.C.G.A. §§31-2-1, 31-2-2; O.C.G.A. tit. 31, ch. 3.
22. Ga. Laws 2002, 1324.
23. O.C.G.A. §§37-2-1–37-2-5.2.
24. O.C.G.A. §37-2-6.
25. O.C.G.A. §31-3-4(8).
26. See O.C.G.A. §§31-3-5.1, 31-3-5.2, 31-3-16.
27. Interviews with ACCG and DHR staff, October 1991.
28. PeachCare for Kids is administered by the Department of Community Health (www.peachcare.org). See also the Covering Kids and Family Initiative in Georgia (www.coveringkidsandfamilies.org/projects/index_StateID=GA.php), which is part of a national health access initiative funded by the Robert Wood Johnson Foundation designed to help local communities identify potentially eligible children and enroll them in available state health insurance programs.
29. Interviews with Clarke County Department of Family and Children Services staff, October 1991.
30. Child Abuse Protocol, O.C.G.A. tit. 19, ch. 15.
31. Foster Care Review, addressed in various sections of O.C.G.A. §15-11-58.
32. See O.C.G.A. §19-15-3 for committee duties and composition; O.C.G.A. §19-15-2, which outlines the requirements for a child abuse protocol committee and a written child abuse protocol; O.C.G.A. §19-15-4, which describes the relationship between the child abuse protocol committee, the county child fatality review subcommittee, and the state child fatality review board.
33. Interview with the director of the Athens Housing Authority, October 1991; O.C.G.A. tit. 50, ch. 26.
34. O.C.G.A. tit. 8, ch. 3, art. 5.
35. O.C.G.A. §§50-8-35, 50-8-36.
36. O.C.G.A. §49-6-63.
37. O.C.G.A. §§15-11-4–15-11-8. For more information on juvenile courts, contact the Council of Juvenile Court Judges.
38. *Child Policy Reports* (Atlanta: Georgia Health Policy Center, School of Policy Studies, Georgia State University, 2001).
39. See Kenny A. v. Perdue, 365 F.Supp. 2d 1353 (N.D. Ga. 2005), in which Children's Rights Inc. sued state and county officials responsible for the foster care system in order to require improvements in systemic deficiencies, including

excessive stays in dangerous emergency shelters, high levels of maltreatment in foster care, and inadequate health care, educational services, and legal represen-tation. A settlement agreement was reached in July 2005 requiring infrastructure changes, service guarantees, and improved oversight of child safety. The state is being monitored in its efforts to meet 31 specific benchmarks in reforming the child welfare system. Two additional settlements were reached with Fulton and DeKalb Counties regarding the right to effective legal representation for children involved in abuse and neglect proceedings.

40. O.C.G.A. §49-5-131 et seq. As of 2008, the former Children and Youth Coor-dinating Council and the Children's Trust Fund Commission were merged to form the Governor's Office for Children and Families. See O.C.G.A. §§19-14-1, 49-5-155.

41. The Family Connection has a Web-based data repository to help citizens measure community and state progress (www.gafcp.org/index.php).

Financing and Revenue

16

Paul E. Glick and Sabrina Wiley Cape

Understanding County Finance

During each year, usually monthly, county finance staff prepare financial statements for the county commissioners. At the end of the fiscal year, the auditors spend one to three months preparing their report and audited financial statements, which they ultimately present to the commissioners. What do the numbers in these financial statements mean? Are they important? How can county commissioners better understand them? This chapter answers these questions and addresses other county financial reporting issues.

In the past decade, Georgia counties have seen major changes in accounting and financial reporting. The Department of Community Affairs (DCA) developed a local government uniform chart of accounts that county governments began using in 2000. After a decade of using the chart of accounts, DCA is considering making changes and additions to it in order to increase the level of uniformity across local governments in Georgia.

In addition, the Governmental Accounting Standards Board (GASB), which sets the accounting and financial reporting rules, has made two major changes to the financial reporting standards that county governments follow. This chapter discusses financial reporting requirements, including these new standards.

FINANCIAL REPORTING

Financial reports are classified according to their content and the purposes for which they are issued. Different types of financial reports may be issued for different user groups according to how the reports will be used (internal or external) and when they are completed (interim or annual).

Interim financial reports are prepared on a monthly basis by management, normally for internal use, including that of the county commissioners. Most counties issue some type of interim report to assist with their day-to-day management. Annual financial reports, which include data regarding operations in the previous year, are designed for external readers, such as citizens or bond rating services. Annual reports are less useful to county commissioners because of the timing of their preparation. Because these reports usually are independently audited by a certified public accounting firm, it may take up to six months after the close of the fiscal year to entirely complete this annual report. In addition to the regular annual report, some counties prepare a comprehensive annual financial report, which includes introductory, financial, and statistical information.

TYPES OF STATEMENTS

Generally, governments prepare two types of financial statements: balance sheets (sometimes called statements of net assets) and operating statements (sometimes called statements of activities). Balance sheets are financial statements that present what the county owns, what it owes, and its worth (i.e., fund balance or net assets).

Operating statements are directed toward control over revenues and expenditures in the primary operating funds. The budgetary operating statement, which includes revenues and expenditures that are compared with the final revised budget and changes in fund balance, is most commonly used. A budgetary operating statement should be most useful to county commissioners, particularly during the year, because it compares budgeted revenues with actual revenues and budgeted expenditures with actual expenditures. This kind of statement allows county commissioners to monitor overspending and to determine if revenues are being received as projected.

COUNTY VERSUS BUSINESS FINANCES

Before one can understand county financial statements, it is important to note the differences between the financial operations of a county and those of the business world. Counties have objectives that are different from those of commercial enterprises; they operate in a different economic, legal, political, and social environment. Counties use capital assets to provide services, whereas businesses use capital assets to generate revenues. These differences often require accounting and financial reporting techniques unique to local governments.

Business enterprises exist to maximize economic profits. The "bottom line," or profits and losses presented on an operating statement, is a reasonable indicator of the success of a business. For a county, however, the bottom line usually is not an accurate indicator of its success. If a county reports more revenues than expenditures in a fiscal year, is that good? If a county spends more than it receives in a fiscal year, is that bad? Whether a county reports more revenues than expenditures or spends more than it receives in a fiscal year is not all-important. The primary objective of a county is to provide services to its constituents within budgetary constraints. There is little regard for the bottom-line concept. The GASB's new financial reporting standards (discussed later in this chapter) tend to move county financial reporting toward business-type accounting.

Legal Requirements

In business, substantial discretion is allowed in obtaining and using resources. By contrast, Georgia county government financing and spending activities are subject to very specific legal and contractual provisions. To adequately review county financial reports, commission members should be familiar with county legal requirements. For instance, Georgia law dictates how a budget is adopted and amended as well as how often audits are conducted.

Annual Operating Budget

Each year, Georgia counties adopt a budget showing where the money to operate the county comes from and how it will be spent (see Chapter 19). The annual operating budget plays a more expanded role in county government than it does in business. Budgets are an important internal planning tool for both business and government, but in county government they also play an important external role. Because a county is a public entity, parties inside (e.g., department directors) and outside (e.g., citizens) the county government may participate in the development of the annual operating budget. The law requires Georgia counties to conduct public budget hearings in which interested parties have an opportunity to ask questions and offer suggestions about the proposed budget.[1] Very few people participate in budget hearings in most counties, but occasionally interested constituents attend budget hearings to express their opinions. For example, because the size of the budget usually affects property taxes, it is not uncommon for property owners to attend budget hearings.

Once the board of county commissioners adopts the budget, it establishes spending limits that departments normally cannot exceed unless the board of commissioners legally changes (i.e., amends) the budget through a commission meeting. State law establishes the legal level of budget control, referred to as the legal level of control, at the department level (i.e., money cannot be moved between departments without a budget amendment approved by the commissioners in a meeting), but commissioners have the authority to establish a more detailed legal level of control.[2] These limits create spending constraints for county administrators that usually do not exist in the commercial sector.

Accounting and Financial Reporting Rules

Generally accepted accounting principles (GAAP) are the accounting rules followed by most accountants in business and government alike. GAAP provide a set of uniform minimum standards and guidelines for financial accounting and reporting. Therefore, all financial statements prepared on a GAAP basis are comparable, regardless of the legal jurisdiction or geographic location of the government. Georgia law requires counties to prepare their audited financial statements in conformity with GAAP.[3]

GAAP is used differently in business and government. GASB establishes GAAP for governments, and the Financial Accounting Standards Board sets standards for business. GASB, a nonprofit entity located in Norwalk, Connecticut, is made up of a full-time chairperson and six part-time board members and has a research director and a permanent staff of accountants working under the direction of the chairperson. When applied to business financial statements, GAAP provide information (i.e., the profit or loss) that investors and creditors need to decide whether (and how much) to invest in stock or to loan money to a particular business. By contrast, individuals do not invest capital in government; therefore, governmental GAAP financial statements emphasize legal compliance (e.g., budget information).

Because county commissioners have oversight responsibility for county financial operations, the rules that GAAP provide for preparing financial information to demonstrate accountability are very useful. County commissioners are responsible for setting financial policies, which includes determining how much money the county may spend through the adoption of the annual operating budget and monitoring progress toward meeting those budgetary goals.

INDEPENDENT AUDITS

Most counties have independent audits conducted in conformity with GAAP and generally accepted governmental auditing standards (GA-GAS). GAGAS consist of the auditing rules that independent certified public accountants (CPAs) must follow when auditing county financial statements. In an independent audit, the CPA expresses an opinion as to the fairness of a county's basic financial statements in conformity with GAAP. In other words, the auditor verifies that the financial statements present the actual financial position and results of operations for the year ended.

The GASB and the Government Finance Officers Association (GFOA) have long recommended that the financial statements of all local governments be audited independently in accordance with GAGAS. In addition, Georgia law requires counties that spend at least $300,000 annually or have a population in excess of 1,500 to be audited annually[4]; most other counties are required to be audited at least every two years (see Chapter 19).[5] Local governments that do not meet the minimum levels for spending or population must, at a minimum, provide evidence of reconciliation of cash, confirmation of cash balances, a listing of bank balances by bank, a statement of cash receipts and cash disbursements, a review of compliance with state law, and a report of agreed-upon procedures.[6] Because counties operate largely on involuntary resources in the form of taxes, which are entrusted to elected and appointed officials for the provision of public services, an audit by an independent certified public accounting firm is essential to ensure that public funds have been expended as legally required. There is another significant reason for an independent audit: because some of the country's larger counties have experienced financial difficulties, buyers of local government debt securities often rely on financial statements as a basis for investment.

County officials can realize many benefits from obtaining independent audits:

1. The results of financial and compliance audits can help elected and appointed officials in their decision-making roles.

2. The additional assurances provided by audited financial statements and the audit testing of legal compliance allow officials to make more confident decisions concerning the future of county operations.

3. Audit results also may point the way to constructive changes that benefit the county and its officials.

4. Audits include a review of a county's internal accounting controls that helps curtail circumstances permitting inefficiencies or fraud.

TYPES OF AUDITS

Most independent audits conducted on behalf of counties are classified as both financial and compliance audits, whereas audits in the private sector are almost always financial audits. A financial and compliance audit expands the scope of the audit beyond validating financial records to include the county's compliance with the various finance-related legal and contractual provisions. This aspect of auditing is very important because, as mentioned earlier, counties must operate within a legally regulated environment.

Most counties in Georgia have an annual audit conducted by a CPA, in accordance with GAGAS. One type of financial audit is the single audit mandated by the provisions of the 1996 amendments to the U.S. Single Audit Act of 1984.[7] The purpose of the single audit is to have one countywide audit that will encompass not only local resources, but also all state and federal grants.[8]

THE UNIFORM CHART OF ACCOUNTS

In 1997, the Georgia General Assembly passed legislation with significant implications for county financial reporting. It required that DCA develop a local government uniform chart of accounts and a set of community indicators that will allow state and local policymakers to monitor the social and economic conditions of Georgia communities.[9]

The uniform chart of accounts was approved by the state auditor and adopted by DCA in 1998. In developing the uniform chart, DCA solicited input and advice from local government officials around the state. Adapted from the GFOA's "Illustrative Chart of Accounts" contained in Appendix C of the "Blue Book," the Georgia chart's primary purpose is to provide a uniform format for local government financial reporting and accounting, allowing state agencies to collect more reliable and meaningful financial data and information from local governments.

Counties are required to use this uniform chart of accounts in reports to state agencies. Counties must also classify their transactions in conformity with the fund, balance sheet, revenue, and expenditure classification descriptions in the chart, and their accounting records should reflect these account classifications. Although local governments are not required to use the chart's numbering system in their own accounting systems, they may find that using the uniform chart of accounts for accounting purposes facilitates their financial reporting to DCA and other state agencies.[10]

DCA requires local governments to submit reports on their services and operations as a condition of receiving state-appropriated funds from the department.[11] These reports are produced using data from the local government finance and operations surveys administered by the department. The community indicators report is developed using data from these surveys and other sources for all local governments in the state with annual expenditures of $250,000 or more.[12] A community's report focuses on demographic patterns, economy, finance, education, health, social environment, civic participation, and selected county government services. Any county that receives state funds from the governor's emergency fund or from a special project appropriation must submit a grant certification form to the state auditor in conjunction with its annual audit. This form requires the governing authority and the auditor of the county to certify that the grant funds were used solely for the purpose or purposes for which the grant was made. Failure to submit this certification results in forfeiture of the grant and the return of any grant funds already received by the local government.[13]

FUND ACCOUNTING

Fund accounting requires counties to keep separate records for each individual fund. GAAP define a fund as an entity with separate accounting records for a specific activity. For example, a county might account for a state grant in one fund and record the proceeds from a building bond sale in another fund. Fund accounting can complicate manual bookkeeping. The use of a computer and computerized government accounting systems for fund accounting greatly simplify the process. Also, GAAP encourages counties to maintain a minimum number of funds.

For county commissioners to be able to read and understand county financial statements, they need to know the nature and purpose of eight fund types (defined by GAAP as generic fund types), which are grouped into three categories. These categories are important because the accounting rules that counties must follow may be applied differently to each of the fund categories.

Figure 16-1 presents a fund organizational chart illustrating the four categories and the relationship of categories A, B, and C to the eight generic fund types. The categories are briefly described here:

A.   Governmental fund types. Used to account for general county operations (e.g., sheriff's department, public works, parks and recreation).

B.   Proprietary fund types. Used to account for county activities that are similar to the commercial sector (e.g., a water and sewer utility).

Figure 16-1. *Governmental Accounting and Financial Reporting*

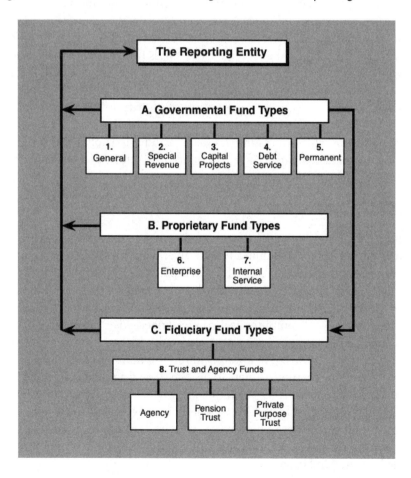

C. Fiduciary fund types. Used to account for assets held by a county in a trustee or agent capacity (e.g., property taxes collected by the county for the county school system).

Five generic fund types are categorized within governmental funds:

1. General fund. Used to account for all resources that GAAP do not require to be accounted for in another fund. Counties report most of their financial transactions in this fund, including some of the activities of the constitutional officers. Expenditures in this fund might include road maintenance, the court system, police and fire, the county clerk's office, and parks and recreation.

2. Special revenue funds. Used to account for resources that are legally or administratively restricted for specific purposes. A federal grant fund might be classified here.

3. Capital projects funds. Used to account for resources restricted for major capital outlays. The proceeds from building bond issues to build new jails that will be repaid from property taxes would be accounted for here.

4. Debt service funds. Used to repay the principal and interest on general long-term debt, such as a building bond issue.

5. Permanent funds. Used to report resources that are legally restricted to the extent that only earnings, and not principal, may be used for purposes that support the county's programs (that is, for the benefit of the county or its citizenry). For example, the perpetual care of a cemetery that the county operates would be classified as a permanent fund.

The two following generic fund types are classified as proprietary fund types:

6. Enterprise funds. Used to account for operations that are financed and operated in a manner similar to business enterprises. Public utilities are the most common county activity reported in this way.

7. Internal service funds. Used to account for operations similar to those under enterprise funds that provide goods or services primarily to other departments within the same county on a cost-reim-

bursement basis. Counties often report as internal service funds activities such as data processing, motor pools, and print shops. Normally, the larger counties use internal service funds.

Included in fiduciary fund types is the eighth generic fund type, which is subdivided into three funds:

8a. Agency funds. Used as holding accounts for assets belonging to some entity other than the county. For example, a tax fund holding a county's collected property taxes for the school system is classified as an agency fund.

8b. Pension trust funds. Used by counties to account for their own (single employer) pension plans. In other words, the retirement assets held for the county's employees who have retired or will retire are reported here. Only a few Georgia counties maintain their own single employer pension plans.

8c. Private purpose trust funds. Used to report trust arrangements under which principal and income benefit individuals, private organizations, or other governments. These funds do not benefit the reporting county.

FINANCIAL REPORTING FOLLOWING GASB STATEMENT 34

County commissioners can expect to see the results of GASB Statement 34 in their annual audited financial statements. GASB Statement 34 includes two levels of reporting in the annual financial report: fund-level reporting and government-wide reporting.[14]

Fund-Level Financial Reporting

GASB Statement 34 requires counties to continue to do what annual reports already do: provide information about funds. The focus of financial statements has been sharpened, however. Pre–GASB Statement 34, fund information was reported in the aggregate by fund type, which often made it difficult for users to assess accountability. Now, counties are required to report information about their most important (or "major") funds, including the county's general fund.

Fund statements continue to assess the "operating results" of many funds by reporting the amount of cash on hand and other assets that can easily be converted to cash. These statements show the performance—in the short term—of individual funds using the same indicators that many counties use when financing their current operations.

Fund-level reporting basically requires counties to present balance sheets and operating statements for each fund category (i.e., governmental, proprietary, and fiduciary). In addition, counties are required to continue to provide budgetary comparison information in their annual reports. An important change, however, is the requirement to add the government's original budget to that comparison. Many counties revise their original budgets over the course of the year for a variety of reasons. Requiring counties to report their original budget in addition to their revised budget increases the usefulness of the budgetary comparison.

Government-wide Financial Reporting

GASB Statement 34 also implemented a requirement to provide government-wide financial reporting in order to give users of the financial statements a complete picture of the government's fiscal operations using accrual accounting methods. The requirements also called for county financial managers to share their insights in a required management's discussion and analysis, giving readers an objective and easily readable analysis of the government's financial performance for the year. Most governmental utilities and private-sector companies use accrual accounting, which measures not only current assets and liabilities, but also long-term assets and liabilities, such as capital assets (including infrastructure) and general obligation debt. It also reports all revenues and all costs of providing services each year—not just those received or paid in the current year or soon after year-end (like the modified accrual basis). Counties prepare both a government-wide balance sheet (known as the statement of net assets) and a government-wide operating statement (known as the statement of activities), with governmental activities aggregated together and business-type activities aggregated together.

These government-wide financial statements help users

- assess the finances of the county in total, including the current year's operating results;

- determine whether the county's overall financial position improved or deteriorated;

- evaluate whether the county's current-year revenues were sufficient to pay for current-year services;

- understand the cost of providing services to its citizenry;

- see how the county finances its programs—through user fees and other program revenues versus general tax revenues; and

- understand the extent to which the county has invested in capital assets, including roads, bridges, and other infrastructure assets.

GASB STATEMENT 45

GASB Statement 45 requires local governments to report on certain obligations that it has to employees in the form of post-employment benefits. Previously, most local governments had reported obligations for pension liabilities. The new standard requires disclosure of so-called other post-employment benefits (OPEB). The largest of these is typically health insurance, but they may include life insurance or other types of benefits that constitute a financial obligation.

While most local governments fund their pension obligations as they are incurred, prior to GASB Statement 45, OPEB obligations were typically charged in the accounting period when they were provided. For instance, health insurance benefits for retirees may be funded this year along with those of current employees. This practice understated the financial obligations made during retirees' working years. In some local governments in which baby boom generation workers are nearing retirement, the understatement of these obligations may be significant.

GASB Statement 45 requires local governments to provide a report on the liability incurred as a result of OPEB obligations and the amount that is funded. The report must also include a description of each OPEB plan, the funding policy followed, and a projection of future cash outlays for benefits discounted to present value. In order to show the present value of benefits to those future periods, the report must use an actuarial cost method.[15]

If the local government is the sole plan participant with fewer than 100 benefits-eligible participants, an alternative simplified evaluation method can be used. However, that method includes most of the same steps and calculations as an actuarial evaluation.

BASIS OF ACCOUNTING

When does a county record the sale of water? When the customer uses the water, when the county reads the meter, or when the customer pays the bill? The basis of accounting answers this type of question. Basis of accounting refers to when revenues, expenses (on the accrual basis of accounting) or expenditures (on the modified accrual basis of accounting), and related assets and liabilities are formally recognized in the accounting process and reported in the financial statements.

Like basis of accounting, the "measurement focus"—an interrelated concept—is reflected in a county's financial statements. Measurement focus indicates what the financial statements are trying to communicate; that is, what is being measured by the statements. Most counties use two types of measurement focus:

- *Current financial resources measurement focus.* Financial statements using this focus, commonly known as "flow of funds," report only current assets (i.e., those that the county can convert to cash quickly) and current liabilities (i.e., those due in the short term) on their balance sheets. The difference between these assets and liabilities, or the fund balance, is considered to be the amount available for spending. On these statements, the emphasis is on accountability. The financial data and information assist county commissioners in their oversight function.

- *Economic resources measurement focus.* Financial statements using this focus report all assets and liabilities on their balance sheets. The difference between all assets and all liabilities is the capital, or equity of the fund. On these statements, the emphasis is on "profit" or "loss." County commissioners can thereby monitor financial projections.

Measurement focus determines *what* is measured in the financial statements; the basis of accounting determines *when* transactions are formally recognized in the financial statements. When measurement focus is determined, the basis of accounting to be used is determined. Basis of accounting is a difficult concept. However, in order to understand county financial statements, county commissioners need to understand the different bases of accounting and which funds in their county use which basis at which financial reporting level.

As alluded to previously, there is more than one basis of accounting. GAAP find two bases of accounting acceptable for counties: accrual and modified accrual. Others exist that are unacceptable. The most common unacceptable basis of accounting is the cash basis. On the cash basis, when the money comes in, the county records the revenue; when the county writes the check, it reports the cost. While using this type of basis may be simple, ultimately it is not truly informative. The cash basis of accounting fails to recognize receivables and payables (i.e., amounts still due to or owed by the county). Therefore, under the cash basis of accounting, the financial statements do not accurately represent the financial position or results of county operations.

The Accrual Basis of Accounting

Counties use the accrual basis, which is used by most major corporations, on all government-wide statements and for their proprietary and fiduciary fund types. When counties use the accrual basis, they report revenues in the financial statements when they earn revenue: a county earns the revenue when it provides the service. For example, when a resident waters his or her yard, the county has provided for the use of water and earned that revenue, even though the county does not record the revenue until the water meter is read and the number of gallons the customer used is calculated. A county reports expenses when they are incurred; that is, when the county owes a supplier for an item purchased or owes an employee for a service performed. For example, once an employee works one day, an expense is incurred because the county owes the employee a day's pay. GAAP has special rules regarding when counties must formally recognize taxes and grants.

Using the accrual basis of accounting, a county can purchase fixed assets (equipment, vehicles) and report them on the balance sheet as assets and not as costs in the operating statement. However, each year the county must include in the operating statement a charge for the use of each fixed asset, based on its estimated useful life. This charge is called depreciation.

On the accrual basis of accounting, all liabilities (both short- and long-term) are included on the balance sheet. For example, when a county issues long-term bonds for an enterprise fund (e.g., the water fund), the bonds payable are reported as a liability on the balance sheet of the enterprise fund, but this transaction is not reported on the operating statement. When a portion of the principal is paid, the liability is reduced but the operating statement is not affected. However, any interest costs are reported as an expense.

The Modified Accrual Basis of Accounting

The other acceptable basis of accounting, the modified accrual, is used by counties to report their governmental fund types at the fund reporting level. Under modified accrual accounting, revenues are reported when they are considered to be available—not when they are earned, as in the accrual basis of accounting. Availability of revenue (i.e., when it is formally recognized as revenue) is primarily what differentiates these two bases of accounting.

"Available" means the county will collect the revenue in the current year or shortly after the end of the year to pay liabilities from the current year. For example, if the fiscal year ends on June 30 and the county will receive revenue for that fiscal year in July, it will probably be reported as revenue as of June 30, as long as it relates to the year just ended. However, if the available revenue is not received until December, it will probably not be reported as revenue for the year ending June 30 because it cannot be used to pay outstanding liabilities at June 30.

On both the accrual and modified accrual bases of accounting, an expense or expenditure, respectively, is recognized when the liability is incurred, but the due date for payment of a liability affects how it is reported. If payment for the liability is not due at year-end, on the modified accrual basis, the liability is not reported as an expenditure at the time incurred. On the accrual basis, the due date of the payment, or when the county pays the liability, does not affect when the county reports the expense.

On the modified accrual basis, counties report capital assets, such as equipment and vehicles, as expenditures on the operating statement; they are reported as assets on the balance sheet on the accrual basis. However, because the county has acquired assets, these purchases also are reported separately in the county's capital asset system but not on its governmental fund type balance sheet. Using the modified accrual basis of accounting, depreciation is not reported in the operating statement because the county already has reported the total cost of the capital asset as an expenditure when purchased.

Long-term debt generally cannot be reported on the balance sheet of a fund that uses the modified accrual basis of accounting. When a county sells bonds and cash is received, the proceeds from the sale of bonds are reported on the operating statement in a special section called "other financing sources/uses." Although the county must pay back the principal on the bonds, the liability is not reported in the governmental fund type. Therefore, a balance sheet reporting governmental funds usually will not include any long-term liabilities. However, counties do report both their capital assets and their long-term debt at the government-wide reporting level.

The repayment of governmental fund debt usually is paid from a debt service fund and is reported as an expenditure on the modified accrual basis of accounting. On the accrual basis, the repayment of debt principal is reported as a reduction of a liability and not as an expense.

NOTES

1. OFFICIAL CODE OF GEORGIA ANNOTATED (O.C.G.A.) §36-81-5(e), (f), (g).
2. O.C.G.A. §36-81-3(d).
3. O.C.G.A. §36-81-7(b), (c)(1).
4. O.C.G.A. §36-81-7(a)(1).
5. O.C.G.A. §36-81-7(a)(2).
6. O.C.G.A. §36-81-7(a)(3).
7. 31 UNITED STATES CODE ANNOTATED (U.S.C.A.) §§7501–7507.
8. For a more in-depth discussion on compliance auditing, see Paul T. Hardy, Betty J. Hudson, Myra Byrd, Richard W. Campbell, and Paul E. Glick, *Compliance Auditing in Georgia Counties and Municipalities: A Practical Guide to State Laws for Auditors and Local Government Officials* 2010 (Athens: Carl Vinson Institute of Government, University of Georgia, 2010).
9. O.C.G.A. §36-81-3(e).
10. Ibid.; *Uniform Chart of Accounts for Local Governments in Georgia*, 2nd ed. (Atlanta: Georgia Department of Community Affairs, 2001); www.dca.ga.gov/development/research/programs/downloads/UCA2ndEdition.pdf. Accessed September 22, 2010.
11. O.C.G.A. §36-81-8(c).
12. O.C.G.A. §36-81-8(h).
13. O.C.G.A. §36-81-8.1.
14. *GASB Statement No. 34, Basic Financial Statements—and Management's Discussion and Analysis—for State and Local Governments* (Washington, DC: Governmental Accounting Standards Board, 1999).
15. *GASB Summary of Statement No. 45, Accounting and Financial Reporting by Employers for Postemployment Benefits Other Than Pensions* (Norwalk, CT: Governmental Accounting Standards Board, 2004).

17

Myra L. Byrd and Virgil Moon

Financial Policies

County commissioners make decisions relating to financial matters on a regular basis. County finance staff members rely on these decisions to successfully perform their assigned responsibilities. However, only a limited number of counties have adopted financial policies to assist in making these decisions. What are financial policies? Why should county commissioners adopt them? What obstacles will need to be overcome in developing financial policies? How are financial policies developed? This chapter reviews each of these questions.

WHAT ARE FINANCIAL POLICIES?

Financial policies are the rules that govern financial decisions in a county. County commissioners adopt and, along with their staff, follow these policies when making financial decisions about the future of their counties. Once county commissioners adopt financial policies, most subsequent financial decisions are simplified because the issues have been deliberated during the policy adoption stage.

Counties might adopt financial policies covering the following topics:

- Operating budget and equity (fund balance) reserves
- Capital improvements plan or program (CIP)
- Debt
- Revenue
- Accounting, auditing, and financial reporting
- Purchasing
- Cash and investments
- Pension/other post-employment benefits (OPEB)

Questions that county commissioners need to ask with regard to each of these policy issues are presented in Table 17-1.

Many counties have informal financial policies. Often resulting from precedent, these informal policies become standing practices within a county. For example, a county's property tax rate might not have been changed for a number of years. The county has no written policy that

Table 17-1. *Questions to Ask and Issues to Resolve When Establishing Financial Policies*

Operating budget and equity (fund balance) reserves	Which funds should be budgeted?
	Is the budget balanced?
	Is a contingency budgeted?
	What types of review and comment are the public provided?
	How much fund balance is maintained?
	Is the fund balance used in balancing the budget?
	When and how is fund balance replenished if used in balancing the budget?
	What is the legal level of budgetary control?
	Should a more detailed level of budgetary control be established?
	Is the budget process centralized or decentralized?
	Is the budget prepared on an annual basis or for another period of time (i.e., two years)?
	What happens to appropriations at the end of the year?
	What budgetary basis of accounting is used?
	Is a budgetary reporting system maintained?
	Who will perform and/or approve budget adjustments during the year?
	Does the county participate in the GFOA Certificate of Achievement Program for the annual budget?
Capital improvements program (CIP)	How are capital projects defined?
	What period of time does the CIP cover (i.e., is the CIP plan for 3, 5, 10, or 20 years)?
	What evaluation criteria are used to prioritize capital projects?
	How much of the CIP is funded each year from the annual operating budget?
	Are funding sources identified and prioritized?
	Is the impact of the CIP on future years' operating budgets included?
	Should the program include a replacement schedule for buildings and equipment?

Table 17-1. *Questions to Ask and Issues to Resolve When Establishing Financial Policies*

Debt	When is debt issued?
	What type of debt is issued?
	How much debt is issued?
	What type of sale is permitted (i.e., negotiated or competitively bid)?
	What are the maturity dates of debt issuances?
	What actions are undertaken to maintain positive relations with bond rating agencies?
	When will outside professional assistance be utilized?
	When is debt refunded?
Revenue	Should the county develop a revenue manual?
	What is the goal for establishing and maintaining a diversified revenue source?
	Are state laws followed in regard to the types of revenues collected?
	How are property taxes calculated?
	How are user fees and charges set, and how often are they updated?
	How are revenue projections developed, how often, and what periods of time are covered?
	How often are revenue projections reviewed, monitored, and reported to the county commissioners?
	What are the collection policies?
	What collection methods (such as tax sales, liens, collection agencies, etc.) are used?
Accounting, auditing, and financial reporting	How is the independent auditor selected?
	What is the level of audit coverage?
	Are generally accepted accounting principles (GAAAP) being followed?
	Who prepares financial reports for internal use, what type of reports will be prepared, and how often are the internal reports communicated to elected officials?
	Does the county participate in the GFOA Certificate of Achievement Program in the preparation of popular reports?
	Does the county use audit or finance committees?
	Does the county have an internal audit staff?
	Does the county participate in the GFOA certificate of achievement program with the production of a comprehensive annual financial report (CAFR)?

limits increasing the tax rate, yet everyone "just knows" that the position of the county commissioners is not to raise property taxes. Obviously, an informal policy is at work in this instance.

ADOPTING FINANCIAL POLICIES

Considerations

There are a variety of reasons why county commissioners should adopt financial policies:

Financial policies can provide county commissioners with the opportunity to review their present approach to financial management with an overall, long-range perspective.

Generally, during budget preparation, county commissioners spend most of their meeting time reviewing the annual operating budget. Therefore, because of the annual budget process, county commissioners are generally "annually oriented" in their financial planning. Fortunately, financial policies require county commissioners to conduct financial planning on a long-range basis, which can only improve a county's financial management.

Financial policies can improve county commissioners' credibility and the public's confidence in them.

When citizens are aware that the county commission has adopted meaningful financial policies, they feel confident that the commissioners are providing sound financial management for the county. As the adopted policies are consistently applied to financial decisions, the credibility and integrity of county commissioners are oftentimes improved. In addition, financial policies can provide the support needed to either improve or maintain a county's credit rating.

Financial policies can save time and energy for both the county commissioners and the county's administrative staff.

It has been said that 80 percent of the decisions that county commissioners make relate in some way to finance (e.g., hiring additional personnel, purchasing new vehicles, evaluating where to locate a new fire station). Therefore, if financial policies are in place, the amount of time at commissioners' meetings spent on financial issues can be minimized. Such policies also allow the county's administration to move ahead with financial matters as it follows the adopted financial policies, rather than wait for decisions from the county commission.

Formulating financial policies can be educational for county commissioners.

Because most county commissioners have a heavy workload, discussions of financial issues are sporadic. The process of developing financial policies provides county commissioners the opportunity to become educated on all facets of county financial management.

Financial policies can provide continuity for the county and its county commission.

If financial policies already exist, newly elected officials should not have to make major changes in the financial management of the county. Of course, the fact that financial policies are in place does not mean that newly elected officials cannot or should not change the policies. It simply means that existing financial policies promote necessary continuity for county operations.

Financial policies can provide a basis for coping with fiscal emergencies.

Financial policies are critical in order for a county to maintain financial solvency. Revenue shortfalls and emergencies requiring unanticipated expenditures can have a severe fiscal impact on a county unless financial plans and policies have been established to handle them.

Obstacles

When considering the development of financial policies, county commissioners may face many obstacles. Certain perceptions and oftentimes very real situations inhibit progress in creating long-term financial policies.

County commissioners themselves may resist developing long-range financial plans. As stated earlier, because of the annual budget cycle, commissioners tend to think of financial planning as an annual process. Also, the commissioners may believe that developing a long-range financial plan is not worthwhile because so many things can change over time.

Consideration must also be given to the county's political environment. In the process of developing financial policies, many important issues will be discussed at public meetings and each elected official's position on specific financial subjects becomes public knowledge. Some county commissioners may be reluctant to reveal too much about how they feel about a particular issue (e.g., increasing property taxes).

Furthermore, the task of developing financial policies is very time consuming and is therefore perceived as a drawback. It usually takes a number of special meetings or work sessions for the county commissioners to deliberate the proposed policies. Weighing these very real concerns against the benefits of adopting financial policies should make overcoming hesitations more acceptable and certainly possible. The time and effort necessary will be well rewarded.

HOW TO DEVELOP FINANCIAL POLICIES

County commissioners must complete various steps before they can adopt financial policies. One of the first steps is to have the county administration begin developing and drafting financial policies. The county administration might present the county commission with a work plan for developing financial policies, which would include most of the topics covered in this chapter. For example, the work plan might include

- defining financial policies;
- the purpose and benefits of financial policies;
- a review of the obstacles to developing financial policies;
- types of financial policies to be considered, with samples for each topical area;
- methods of developing financial policies; and
- strategies for using financial policies.

Once the county commission concurs and chooses the areas for policies, the county administration should begin drafting policies consistent with other adopted policies, as necessary. A good way to begin is to review policies adopted by other counties in the state and nation. Sample policies are available from the Carl Vinson Institute of Government. Another source of sample policy information is the Government Finance Officers Association, which publishes on its Web site (www.gfoa.org) policy statements, recommended practices, and best practices on a variety of finance-related subjects.

After the county administration drafts the policies, the county commission should devote as many work sessions as necessary to reviewing these policies. This process will be educational for the county commissioners but time consuming.

The county commission might decide to hold a public hearing on the financial policies to allow for citizen input. Finally, the policies should be adopted formally through a resolution or ordinance. All policies should be maintained in a policy book and be reviewed periodically (possibly annually and/or after newly elected county commissioners take office). Often, policies are incorporated into the county finance ordinance or resolution. See Table 17-2 for a selection of financial policy areas, issues, and sample policies.

Table 17-2. *Sample Financial Policies*

Area	Issue	Sample Policy
Operating budget and equity reserves	Fund balance amounts to maintain	The county will attempt to establish a fund balance reserve for the general fund to pay expenditures caused by unforeseen emergencies, to cover shortfalls caused by revenue declines, and to eliminate any short-term borrowing for cash flow purposes. This reserve will be maintained at an amount that represents approximately $300,000 or two months of regular general fund operating expenditures, whichever is greater.
Capital improvements program	Capital assets thresholds	For the capital improvements program, all land improvements, and buildings projects costing $25,000 or more are classified as capital assets. Equipment costing $5,000 or more with an estimated useful life of two or more years is considered a capital asset.
Debt	When to use capital leases rather than outright purchases	Capital leases are used to finance equipment purchases when the cost of the equipment purchases exceeds 12 percent of the general fund budget.
Revenue	Review of fees and charges	The government will review all fees and charges annually in order to keep pace with the cost of providing that service.
Accounting, auditing, and financial reporting	Auditor selection	Every five years the county will issue a request for proposal to independent auditors to provide an audit for the county's operation. The current auditing firm is eligible to propose on this audit.
Purchasing	Centralized purchasing	The county will maintain a centralized purchasing system through which all county purchases for both goods and services will be coordinated by the purchasing department

SUMMARY

The importance of financial policies cannot be overemphasized. Laws provide specific guidance regarding some of the issues that financial policies address. However, county commissioners are given much latitude regarding the context of the financial policies. The county and its elected officials should make every effort to adopt meaningful financial policies. Subsequently, both the county administration and county commission must follow these policies.

18

Betty J. Hudson, Richard W. Campbell, Clint Mueller, and Wes Clarke

County Revenues

Counties operate and finance their activities within a federal system. Like municipalities, they are not stand-alone units of government. They are "offspring" of the state and must function within constraints imposed by the state and, to a lesser degree, the federal government. As creations of the state constitution, counties must adhere to state laws, rules, and regulations, and their capacity to generate revenue is determined by the explicit revenue-raising authority granted to them under state law. As noted in Chapter 19, Georgia, like most states, requires that county budgets be balanced. This means that local budgeting processes are to a large extent revenue driven because "available revenues determine the level of spending for any given year."[1]

This chapter describes the revenue sources currently available to Georgia counties, discusses several criteria used in evaluating alternative revenue sources,[2] and examines revenue patterns based on the yield from specific revenue sources. (For a discussion of county financial policies to guide revenue decisions, see Chapter 17.)

TAX REVENUE

Tangible Property Tax

Over the last three decades, the property tax has declined in importance as a revenue source for local governments in the United States.[3] Despite the decline, nationally the property tax remains the major source of revenue for counties. In Georgia, property taxes accounted for 39.5 percent of total county revenues in 2008.[4]

While the property tax has been the object of criticism (e.g., inequitable appraisals and anxiety about reappraisal, cumbersome and expensive to administer), it is likely to remain a permanent fixture of county revenue systems. Its attributes include the following:

1. It provides a stable source of revenue since property values typically do not fluctuate widely from year to year.

2. It taxes nonresident property owners who benefit from local services.

3. It is used by counties to finance property-related services that add value to property such as law enforcement, fire protection, parks, comprehensive land-use planning, and the construction of publicly owned infrastructures such as roads, bridges, curbs and sidewalks, and storm drainage systems.

4. The tax on real property is difficult to evade, thus making collection and enforcement easier for county governments.

5. The tax has enabled local governments in the United States to achieve their unique form of autonomy from state and federal control, thereby forestalling centralization of power at higher levels of government.

In Georgia, the ad valorem (according to value) property tax remains the major revenue source for counties, generating $3.27 billion in FY 2008.[5] Ad valorem taxes are levied on the following types of property:

1. Real property—land, buildings, permanent fixtures, and improvements

2. Personal property—property that can be moved with relative ease, such as motor vehicles, boats, machinery, and inventoried goods

3. Intangible property—long-term notes secured by real estate and the transfer of real property

General law dictates that tangible real and personal property for counties be assessed at 40 percent of its fair market value.[6] The state reviews the correctness of county assessments once every three years and will impose sanctions, including fines, if the average level of assessment for each class of property is not between 36 percent and 44 percent of fair market value.[7] The state constitution authorizes special favorable assessment values for certain kinds of property. Examples are rehabilitated historic property, landmark historic property, bona fide residential transitional property, bona fide conservation-use property not exceeding 2,000 acres, and forest land conservation-use property exceeding 200 acres.[8] Also, real property of no more than 2,000 acres owned by a single property owner and devoted to bona fide agricultural purposes must, if certain conditions are met, be assessed at 30 percent of market values (i.e., at 75 percent of 40 percent of fair market value).[9] Standing timber is to be assessed one time, rather than annually, at 100 percent of fair market value at the time it is cut.[10] Timber land is assessed annually as other property and may qualify as bona fide conservation-use property, agricultural-use property, or forestland conservation–use property and qualify for those favorable assessment classifications.[11] General law provides for the assessment of combined real and personal property of public utilities, airlines, and railroads by the state revenue commissioner and for apportionment of valuation among the applicable local tax jurisdictions.[12]

After real property has been assessed, all applicable exemptions must be deducted from the assessed value of the property before the millage rate is applied. The most common of these exemptions are the state general homestead exemption, exemptions for persons over age 62 and for disabled veterans, and various local homestead exemptions.[13]

The tax rate is stated in terms of mills, with 10 mills equal to 1 percent of a property's assessed valuation. County ad valorem tax (millage) rates are set by the county governing authority before the county tax digest is approved by the Georgia Department of Revenue.[14] The tax rate is set by dividing the amount of money the county needs from property taxation by the amount of the tax digest: tax (millage) rate = amount needed from property taxation / tax digest. The amount of taxes due from an individual property owner is the tax rate times the assessed value of the individual's property: tax (millage) rate x assessed value = taxes due.

Taxpayer Bill of Rights

There is an additional issue that a county governing authority must consider when setting the millage rate. Local governments must acknowledge to the public that property taxes may be increased even when the millage rate does not increase. In order to determine if there is an increase in property taxes, the previous year's millage rate minus the millage equivalent of the assessed value added by reassessment is known as the "rollback rate." If the county proposes a millage rate greater than the rollback rate (i.e., one that would result in a tax increase from the previous year), the county must advertise its intent and conduct at least three public hearings prior to adoption of the millage rate.[15]

Intangible Tax

The intangible personal property tax was repealed in 1996; however, the intangible tax on long-term real estate notes and the real estate transfer tax were preserved. Long-term real estate notes, which are notes that fall due more than three years from the date of execution and are secured by real estate, are subject to an intangible recording tax of $1.50 for each $500 of the face amount to be paid before such notes can be recorded in the superior court clerk's office. The maximum intangible recording tax on a note is $25,000. Examples are mortgages, deeds to secure debt, bonds for title, or any other real estate security instrument that gives the lender a resource to be used if the principal obligation is not paid. In counties with a population of 50,000 or more, this tax is collected by the superior court clerk, and in counties with a population of less than 50,000, this tax is collected by the county tax commissioner. Revenue from the intangible tax on long-term real estate notes is distributed to the state, the county, municipalities, the school district(s), and to other local taxing districts, in proportion to relative millage rates levied by the state and each local taxing district. If property is located in more than one county, this tax is prorated among those counties.[16]

Real Estate Transfer Tax

With certain exceptions, a real estate transfer tax is imposed at the rate of $1 on the first $1,000 and 10 cents on each additional $10 on any conveyance of real property when the value of the interest transferred exceeds $100. The clerk of superior court collects and distributes the tax to the state, county, municipalities, school districts, and other local taxing jurisdictions in proportion to the millage rate levied by each taxing jurisdiction or district.[17]

Local Option Sales and Use Tax

A second major source of revenue for most counties is the joint county and municipal local option sales tax.[18] Subject to voter approval, a sales and use tax of 1 percent may be imposed on the purchase, sale, rental, storage, use, or consumption of tangible personal property and related services.

Proceeds from this tax are collected by the Georgia Department of Revenue and disbursed to the county and its qualified municipalities based on the percentages negotiated by the county governments and the cities within each county. However, in eight counties, a local constitutional amendment dedicates the local option sales tax (LOST) to the school system instead of the county and cities.[19] One percent of the amount collected is paid into the general fund of the state treasury to defray the costs of administration, and a percentage is paid to the dealer for collecting and reporting the tax.[20] This tax is subject to the same exemptions that are in the state sales tax, except for the sales tax exemption for eligible food and beverages and a few other minor exemptions.[21]

The tax bill of each property taxpayer must show the reduced county and city millage rate resulting from the receipt of sales tax revenue from the previous year, as well as the reduced dollar amount of the person's property tax resulting from the receipt of such revenue.

All counties and municipalities that impose a joint sales and use tax are required to renegotiate the distribution certificate for the proceeds of the local option sales tax following each decennial census. The criteria to be used in the distribution of such proceeds and for the resolution of conflicts between the county and qualified municipalities are set by state law. In the event that the county and cities fail to reach an agreement, a judge will be appointed to serve as arbitrator and will issue an order containing the new distribution certificate, which is binding on all parties.[22]

Special Purpose Local Option Sales and Use Tax

The special purpose local option sales tax (SPLOST) is another significant source of county revenue.[23] The revenues from this tax must be used for capital outlays, and the tax is subject to voter approval. This additional 1 percent sales and use tax may be imposed on the purchase, sale, rental, storage, use, or consumption of tangible personal property and related services. The tax is collected by the Georgia Department of Revenue and disbursed to the county. Qualified cities receive their share of the tax collections from the county. A distinguishing feature of this tax is that it is a county tax rather than a joint county-city tax and can only be initiated by the board of commissioners. Counties must negotiate an intergovernmental agreement with their qualified cities or share the funds with the cities based upon the distribution requirements in the law unless only level one countywide capital projects (courthouse, administrative building for elected officials or constitutional officers, county or regional jail or correction facility, and county health department facility) are to be financed with the SPLOST.[24] As a condition to levying a SPLOST, the county must meet and confer with their qualified city officials at least 30 days before the board of commissioners issues the call for the referendum in order to consider any capital projects for presentation to the public in the referendum.[25] One percent of the amount collected is paid into the general fund of the state treasury to defray the costs of administration. This tax is subject to the same exemptions that are in the state sales tax, except for the sales tax exemption for eligible food and beverages and a few other minor exemptions.

The proceeds are to be used for projects anywhere in the county, including the incorporated area, or outside the county for regional facilities and may include the following:

1. Roads, streets, and bridges, which may include sidewalks and bicycle paths

2. A capital outlay project consisting of a county courthouse or administrative buildings; a civic center; a hospital; a county or regional jail, correctional institution, or other detention facility; a county library; a coliseum; local or regional solid waste–handling facilities; local or regional recovered materials processing facilities; or any combination of such projects

3. A capital outlay project to be operated by a joint authority of the county and one or more municipalities within the county for the use or benefit of county citizens and the citizens of one or more municipalities

4. A capital outlay project to be owned or operated by the county, one or more municipalities in the county, one or more local authorities within the special district, or any combination thereof

5. A capital outlay project consisting of a cultural, recreational, or historic facility or a facility for some combination of these purposes

6. A water or sewer capital outlay project or combination thereof to be owned or operated or both by a county water and sewer district and one or more qualified municipalities in the county

7. The retirement of existing general obligation debt of the county, one or more qualified municipalities, or any combination thereof

8. A capital outlay project consisting of public safety or airport facilities or both or related capital equipment used to operate such facilities or any combination of such purposes

9. A capital outlay project consisting of capital equipment for use in voting in official elections or referendums

10. A capital outlay project or projects consisting of any transportation facility designed for the transportation of people or goods,

including but not limited to railroads, port and harbor facilities, mass transportation facilities, or any combination thereof

11. A capital outlay project consisting of a hospital or hospital facility owned by the county, a qualified municipality, or the hospital authority and operated by the county, municipality, or hospital authority or an organization that is tax exempt under Section 501(c)(3) of the Internal Revenue Code, which operates the hospital through a contract or lease with such county, municipality, or hospital authority

12. Any combination of two or more of these projects

This special tax cannot be levied for more than five years, stated in either calendar years or quarters, nor can it be levied in order to raise more than the maximum cost of the project or projects to be funded from the proceeds of the tax, unless there is an intergovernmental agreement or level one projects are included in the referendum. If there is an intergovernmental agreement, the tax may be levied for a full six years regardless of when the projected revenue estimate is reached. If there is not an intergovernmental agreement and level one projects are included that consume less than 24 months of estimated revenues, the tax shall be collected for a five-year period. If the level one projects exceed 24 months of estimated revenue collections, the tax shall be collected for a six-year period.[26] With voter approval, a SPLOST may be reimposed following the expiration of the existing tax. If the call for the referendum is properly timed, the levy can continue without interruption. A referendum to impose a SPLOST, however, can only take place on the third Tuesday in March or the Tuesday after the first Monday in November in odd-numbered years and on the date of the presidential preference primary, general primary, or the Tuesday after the first Monday in November in even-numbered years.[27]

General obligation debt may be incurred for all purposes, including roads, streets, and bridges, but if it is not repaid by the tax, the remaining debt must be satisfied from county general funds. Only one SPLOST may be levied at any time. Moreover, the aggregate of all local sales and use taxes imposed in any period cannot exceed 2 percent.[28] However, there are three exceptions to this cap. First, a sales tax for education purposes does not count toward this limit. Second, the sales tax created to support improvements to Atlanta's water and sewer system is not subject to the cap. Third, the regional transportation sales tax, if enacted, is not subject to this restriction.

Regional Transportation Sales Tax

In 2010, the General Assembly enabled voters in regions, defined by regional commission boundaries, to approve the levy for 10 years of a 1 percent sales tax for transportation. A regional roundtable, made up of the chairman and one mayor from each county, chooses projects for approval by the voters and calls for the election. Failure to call for the election or failure by voters to approve the tax increases the amount of local match required for future state transportation funds. A portion of the revenues raised in each region are distributed back to each county and city based on a formula defined by law for their own discretionary transportation purposes.[29]

Sales Tax for Education Purposes

Subject to voter approval, the board of education of a county school district (if there is no independent school district in the county) or the board of education of a county school district together with the boards of education of each independent school district located in the county may levy a 1 percent sales and use tax. The revenue from this tax is not distributed to county government.

Imposition of this tax does not affect the authority of a county or city to impose other local option sales and use taxes. This tax is not subject to the 2 percent cap on local sales taxes.[30] The school board or boards calling for the referendum, not the county commissioners, are responsible for the cost of holding the referendum.[31]

Homestead Option Sales and Use Tax

Subject to enactment of local legislation by the General Assembly and voter approval in a local referendum, those counties that do not levy a joint county-municipal local option sales and use tax are authorized to impose a 1 percent sales and use tax on the purchase, sale, rental, storage, use, or consumption of tangible personal property and related services, in conjunction with an additional homestead exemption. Voters must approve both the homestead exemption and the sales tax, and once imposed, this tax may only be discontinued with voter approval to end both the tax and the homestead exemption.

Proceeds of this tax are collected by the Georgia Department of Revenue and disbursed to the county. One percent of the amount collected is paid into the general fund of the state treasury to defray costs of administration. This tax is subject to the same exemptions as the state sales tax, except for a few other minor exemptions.

At least 80 percent of the revenue from the homestead option sales tax must be used to provide for the homestead exemption; however, a county can apply up to 100 percent of the homestead option sales tax revenues to fund the exemption. Whatever is not used for the exemption (i.e., up to 20 percent of the revenue from the homestead option sales tax) may be used to fund capital projects. Any surplus funds remaining, after the county provides a 100 percent homestead exemption, must be used to rollback the county millage rate on non-homesteaded property on the digest. If a surplus remains after this rollback, such surplus funds may then be used to fund other services in the county. The homestead exemption imposed in conjunction with this tax is in addition to any other homestead exemption granted in a county. The homestead exemption begins only after the tax has been levied for a complete calendar year. Proceeds of this tax received during the first year may be used by the county to fund general county services or capital outlays.[32]

Alcoholic Beverage Excise Taxes

Counties may levy an excise tax of no more than 22 cents per liter of wine and no more than 22 cents per liter of distilled spirits, but not within cities imposing an excise tax.[33] General law requires counties to impose an excise tax of 5 cents per 12 ounces on all bottles, cans, and like containers of beer sold in the county. Containers of draft beer are taxable at the rate of $6 for every $15^1/_2$ gallons. This tax can be levied only in the unincorporated portions of the county.[34]

Local Option Mixed Drink Tax

Where distilled spirits that are sold by the drink, an excise tax not exceeding 3 percent may be imposed by the county on such sales, but not within cities imposing an excise tax. This tax may not be imposed on sales of fermented beverages made wholly or in part from malt (i.e., beer) or any similar fermented beverage.[35]

Franchise Tax

Counties do not have the authority to levy franchise charges on electric, gas, or telephone companies. They can, however, impose charges on private cable and video television systems in the unincorporated areas but not within a municipality, except by agreement. Cable and video service providers can apply for a predefined state franchise or a custom local franchise. Counties can require the service provider operating under a state or local franchise to pay the county a fee not to exceed 5 percent of the company's gross revenues.[36]

Insurance Premium Taxes

A tax of 1 percent is levied on life insurance companies based on gross direct premiums on policies of persons residing within the unincorporated area of a county. The tax is collected by the Georgia Commissioner of Insurance and distributed on a population ratio basis. No administrative fee is authorized for the collection of this tax. On all other types of insurance companies, counties may levy a gross premium tax of no more than 2.5 percent. High-deductible health plans sold or maintained in connection with a health savings account are exempt from the local insurance premium taxes until January 1, 2015. This tax is collected by the Georgia Commissioner of Insurance and distributed to the counties levying the tax, based on premiums allocated on a population ratio formula to the unincorporated area.[37] No administrative fee is authorized for the collection of this tax.

County revenue from the life insurance premium tax must be utilized in a certain way. Proceeds are to be spent for police (excluding the sheriff) and fire protection, solid waste collection, and curbs, sidewalks, streetlights, and any other services provided primarily to the inhabitants of the unincorporated area. Any revenues remaining after incorporated services are paid must be used to roll back property taxes of unincorporated property owners.[38] In essence, state law requires that counties use insurance premium taxes to benefit unincorporated residents and property owners. Municipalities also receive a pro rata share of insurance premium tax revenues, and city residents get that portion of the tax through their city.

Business and Occupation Tax

The Georgia Constitution provides that counties may levy and collect business and occupational taxes in the unincorporated areas of the county.[39]

With certain limited exceptions, applicable primarily to out-of-state businesses, a county may tax a business or the practitioner of an occupation or profession only if the business or practitioner maintains a location or office within the unincorporated county. Counties may use one or a combination of the four acceptable methods of taxation: the flat tax, profitability ratios, gross receipts, and number of employees.[40]

The law distinguishes between the imposition of a tax, a regulatory fee, and an administrative fee. A county may impose a tax on a business or practitioner solely for the purpose of raising revenues. However, it may only impose a regulatory fee if the county actually regulates the particular type of business or practitioner, and any regulatory fee must approximate the reasonable cost of the actual regulatory activity performed by the county.[41] Counties may impose an administrative fee as a part of an occupation tax to cover the reasonable cost of handling and processing the occupation tax.[42]

There are 18 professions that are permitted by law to choose between payment of an occupation tax imposed under the county's normal business taxation ordinance or a flat fee, not to exceed $400, set by the county.[43] Examples include lawyers, doctors, dentists, veterinarians, and accountants.

Counties are not required to impose an occupation tax, but if they choose to do so they must adopt an ordinance or resolution imposing the business and occupation taxes and regulatory fees according to the requirements of general law.[44] The authority granted to counties to levy occupation taxes on other types of business (e.g., banks, utility companies regulated by the Public Service Commission, and insurance companies) by other general laws remains unchanged.[45] In addition, counties may levy a local occupational license tax on banks.[46]

Financial Institutions Business License Tax

Counties and municipalities may each levy a business license tax on depository financial institutions (i.e., banks and savings and loans) that have an office located within their jurisdictions. The rate of such tax is 0.25 percent of the financial institution's Georgia gross receipts, with the minimum tax being $1,000. Each county is assigned the gross receipts of a financial institution as allocated by the home office to its branches.[47] Unlike other occupation and business taxes, the county collects this tax on offices located in the unincorporated areas of the county as well as locations within municipalities.

Hotel-Motel Tax

Counties may impose an excise tax on charges made for rooms, lodging, or accommodations furnished by hotels, motels, inns, lodges, and tourist camps, campgrounds, or any other place in which rooms, lodgings, or accommodations are regularly furnished for value. Counties may impose a levy of 3 percent or 5 percent. Different conditions apply, depending on which alternative is chosen. The hotel-motel tax cannot be levied within cities imposing a hotel-motel tax or on rooms, lodgings, or accommodations after the first 30 consecutive days of continuous occupancy; charges for the use of meeting rooms and other facilities or to any rooms, lodgings, or accommodations provided without charge; or rooms, lodgings, or accommodations furnished for one or more days to Georgia state or local government officials and employees traveling on official business.[48]

If a county's levy is at a rate of up to 3 percent, from these tax revenues, the county must spend for promoting tourism, conventions, and trade shows a percentage of the revenue that is not less than the percentage spent in the previous year for these purposes. If, during the previous year, any portion of the receipts from the tax was spent for these purposes through a grant to or contract with the state, a state department or authority, or a private-sector, nonprofit organization, at least the same percentage must be spent each year thereafter for those purposes through a contract with one or more of those entities.[49] Any balance may be placed in the general fund for any governmental purpose.[50] If a county levies the tax at the rate of 5 percent, the additional 2 percent levy must be used to support tourism, convention, or trade activities by supporting state, county, or nonprofit facilities or programs that promote these activities.[51]

The law allows counties to levy this tax at 6, 7, or 8 percent for certain purposes.[52] Typically, the higher tax rate is authorized as a means of financing a specific facility such as a conference or convention center in a given county or city. Counties that levy a hotel-motel tax at these rates must meet specific conditions set forth in general statute or must be authorized to levy the tax through the adoption of a resolution and local act.[53] The distribution of the tax above the rate of 5 percent is set by statute or, if passed by a local act, is divided between tourism promotion and tourism product development, with at least 50 percent of the taxes collected dedicated to tourism promotion.[54]

Each county that levies a hotel-motel tax must file an annual report with the Department of Community Affairs specifying the rate of the tax and the amount collected and expended.[55] Complaints regarding the misuse of the funds may be filed with the Hotel Motel Tax Performance Review Board.[56]

Excise Taxes on Rental Motor Vehicles

Counties may impose an excise tax of 3 percent on the rental charge for the rent or lease of a motor vehicle for 31 or fewer consecutive days. A county may not levy this tax within any city that imposes the tax or if the vehicle is either picked up or returned outside the state of Georgia. A county must expend the proceeds of this excise tax on promoting industry, trade, commerce, and tourism; capital outlay projects for the construction and equipping of convention, trade, sports, and recreation facilities or public safety facilities; and for maintenance and operation expenses or security and public safety expenses associated with those capital outlay projects. Proceeds may also be expended pursuant to intergovernmental contracts for those types of capital outlay projects. This excise tax is scheduled to terminate no later than December 31, 2038.[57]

NONTAX REVENUE

Nontax revenues are an important source of general fund revenues for counties. Primary among nontax revenues are fines, forfeitures, civil filings, court fees, and interest earned on invested funds. Service charges, building permit and license fees, and intergovernmental and miscellaneous revenues make up the remainder of other general funds received.

Fines, Forfeitures, and Court Fees

Revenue from these sources includes traffic and parking fines, fines from violations of the wildlife laws, forfeitures of money posted to guarantee appearance in court, civil filings, and court fees. Counties may adopt any or all provisions of the Georgia Uniform Rules of the Road law and prescribe fines for violations, except where otherwise expressly provided by law.[58] Certain funds, such as those for the Drug Abuse Treatment and Education program, are restricted to specific uses. These funds may be used only for drug treatment and education programs related to controlled substances and marijuana.

Investments

Counties can earn interest from investment of idle funds. Monies can be invested in bank savings accounts, certificates of deposit, a variety of U.S. government securities, and the state-managed Local Government Investment Pool, which permits counties to pool their idle funds with those of the state and other local governments to earn higher interest rates.[59]

User Charges

Counties can charge citizens or other governments for services. The amount of such charge may partially or totally offset the cost of providing the service. Services for which user fees can be charged include water, sewage disposal, garbage collection, and recreation. General law provides that fees charged for water or sewer services outside the geographical boundary of the provider must not be unreasonable or arbitrarily higher for customers located outside its boundaries than for those located within its boundaries.[60]

Counties are also authorized to impose a user fee on telephone and cellular telephone customers to support 9-1-1 service.[61] For a discussion of this fee, see Chapter 14.

Building Permit Fees

Counties may charge building permit and inspection fees to help defray the actual cost of enforcing their building codes.[62] However, the fees charged cannot generate more in revenue than would cover the approximate cost to the county of providing the service.

Alcoholic Beverage Licenses

The state constitution provides that, in the absence of a general law, counties may be authorized by local law to levy and collect license fees in the unincorporated area of the county.[63] Counties are authorized to license and regulate the manufacture, distribution, and sale of distilled spirits, malt beverages, and wine within their unincorporated areas. In addition to the excise tax on alcoholic beverages, discussed earlier in this chapter, county governing authorities are authorized to establish the amount of such an annual license fee, with the limitation that they may not charge dealers in distilled spirits more than $5,000 annually for each license.[64]

Development Impact Fees

Development impact fees may be imposed by counties to finance the following public facilities needed to serve new growth and development:[65]

1. Water supply production, treatment, and distribution
2. Wastewater collection, treatment, and disposal
3. Roads, streets, and bridges, including rights-of-way, traffic signals, landscaping, and local components of state or federal highways
4. Storm water collection, retention, detention, treatment, and disposal, flood control, and bank and shore protection and enhancement
5. Parks, open space, and recreation areas and related facilities
6. Public safety, including police, fire, emergency medical, and rescue facilities
7. Libraries and related facilities

Storm Water Fees

The federal government mandates that local governments manage storm water runoff and preserve surface water quality through the Clean Water Act. In order to secure adequate funding to address these mandates, more than 40 Georgia counties and cities have created storm water utilities. These utilities are funded by user fees, with a rate structure designed so that all property owners, including those that are tax exempt, pay a fee based on the relative amount of storm water runoff they put into a public storm drainage system. The amount is based on a calculation of the amount of impervious area on the property.

Motor Vehicle Tag Collection Fees

The county tax commissioner can charge a $1 fee for each motor vehicle tag or revalidation decal issued; all or part of this fee is available to counties.[66]

Sale of Contraband Property

Counties are usually entitled to the proceeds from the sale of confiscated contraband property, but all or part of the proceeds must be used for law enforcement purposes, depending on whether the property is seized under state or federal law. Also, under some circumstances, proceeds may have to be shared with the state. The sale procedures also vary.

Alcoholic Beverages

Except for beer, contraband alcoholic beverages on which taxes have been paid can be sold at public auction by the Georgia Department of Revenue, with the proceeds to be paid to the state. Vehicles, conveyances, and vessels used to transport or conceal distilled spirits in violation of law are to be condemned through court action and sold, with the proceeds to be paid to the county.[67]

Controlled Substances ("Drug Fund Money")

All property (e.g., real property and personal property, including weapons, currency, securities, or any kind of privilege, interest, claim, or right) used or intended for use in violation of state or federal drug laws (i.e., controlled substances acts) can be forfeited by court action and sold. Proceeds from forfeited property, plus confiscated money, are distributed pro rata to the state and local government law enforcement agencies according to the role their law enforcement agencies played in seizing the property and money, with the limitation that the state cannot receive more than 25 percent of the distribution.[68]

Funds must be utilized by the law enforcement agency to which they are transferred for law enforcement purposes except that they may not be used to pay salaries or rewards to law enforcement personnel. Money given to the sheriff's office is within the discretion of the sheriff to use. The sheriff does not have to include federal drug fund money in the budget, but he or she must provide to the commissioners an annual report of state drug money and its use from the preceding year with the budget request.[69] Drug fund money may not be used to supplant the county's funding of the sheriff's office (i.e., the sheriff's budget funded by the county may not be reduced to reflect the amount of drug fund money). If there is any money left over, the county may apply it to uses such as law enforcement purposes, indigent defense, drug treatment, and victim-witness assistance programs.

Gambling

Vehicles, airplanes, and vessels used in or derived from gambling activities are subject to forfeiture and, if ordered by the court, may be sold, with the proceeds to be paid to the county.[70]

Racketeering

Property used in, derived from, or realized through racketeering activities is subject to forfeiture proceedings.[71]

Unauthorized Dumping of Sewage

Vehicles, trailers, and equipment used in the unauthorized dumping of sanitary sewage or commercial or industrial waste into public sanitary or storm sewers are to be condemned through court action and can be sold, with the proceeds to be paid to the local government or district owning the sewer system.[72]

Weapons

Weapons used in the commission of a crime and owned by the person convicted can be sold at public auction by the sheriff, with the proceeds to be paid to the county or, if the crime was committed within a city, to be paid to that city.[73]

Intergovernmental Revenues

Counties receive funds from the federal and state governments and often from other local jurisdictions as described under "User Charges."

Historically, federal funds have generally come to counties through general revenue sharing and block and categorical grant programs. General revenue-sharing funds are no longer available to local governments. Unlike revenue-sharing funds, which could be spent with wide discretion and did not require recipients to provide a matching contribution, block and categorical grants must be spent for specific purposes and usually require a matching contribution. For example, block grants are available to smaller counties under federal community development block grant programs. Their primary objective is to expand economic opportunities, principally for persons of low or moderate income. Also, federal funds are available on a competitive basis for public facilities, economic development, and housing. Larger counties are eligible to participate in the U.S. Department of Housing and Urban Development's (HUD) urban counties program.[74]

State aid generally refers to grants of money to counties either for general purposes or for special programs. State law authorizes such grants.

Grants to Counties

Grants for resurfacing and other road and bridge projects are available through the Local Maintenance and Improvement Grants Program at the Georgia Department of Transportation. A minimum of 10 percent to 20 percent of state motor fuel tax revenues are dedicated to funding the program each year.[75] The funds are made available to counties based on a ratio of the county public road mileage and population to total public road mileage and population in the state.

The state is authorized to make grants to counties for water pollution control projects, whether qualified for federal aid or not. In addition, the state is empowered to grant funds to assist in the construction of solid waste handling systems. Further, the state is authorized to establish an assistance fund for matching federal and county funds to acquire land for recreational purposes and to improve, expand, develop, or construct outdoor recreational facilities, if approved by the federal government. Such funds cannot finance more than 25 percent of the cost, and to be eligible, the county must fund at least 25 percent of the cost.[76]

The state is empowered to make grants to counties to assist in the construction and modernization of publicly owned and operated medical and auxiliary medical facilities, mental retardation centers, and mental health centers when such projects have been approved for federal grants. Generally, state aid may not exceed one-third of the cost.[77]

Counties and Municipalities: Consolidation Improvement Grants

The state is empowered to grant funds and other assistance to two or more counties or municipalities or any combination thereof for a program in which the state participates when the local governments are able and willing to provide for the consolidation, combination, merger, or joint administration of the program to reduce its cost or simplify its administration.[78] However, funds have not been appropriated for such grants in recent years.

Counties are authorized by the state constitution and general law to enter into contracts with other counties and municipalities for the purpose of sharing ad valorem tax proceeds and other revenues for the development and operation of regional facilities, including business and industrial parks, conference centers, convention centers, airports, athletic facilities, recreation facilities, and jails or correctional facilities.[79]

Borrowed Revenue

Counties may borrow funds to meet operating expenses and to finance capital expenditures. Commonly used instruments include tax anticipation notes for annual temporary loans payable by December 31 from general county funds. These instruments are typically considered sources of short-term revenue to pay for maintenance and operation expenditures early in the year and until property tax receipts are collected later in the year. Other borrowing mechanisms include general obligation bonds, certificates of participation, installment purchase agreements, and revenue bonds. Bonds, certificates, and installment contracts are repaid from either general county funds or a particular source of revenue.

General obligation bonds are paid by the county that issues them, and the funds to repay them are derived from specific taxes levied by the county. They are backed by the full faith and credit of the county. Revenue bonds are repaid solely from specific revenue generated by public works facilities purchased or constructed with the bonds and, by law, are not debts of the county. The borrowing of funds is subject to numerous legal restrictions, procedures, and requirements, including prior voter approval of general obligation bonds to be paid from general county funds. Voter approval is not required for temporary loans, revenue bonds, certificates of participation, or installment purchase agreements.[80] Borrowing is discussed more fully in Chapter 21.

Other Revenues

Other possible revenue sources include leases, parking lots and garages, and public concessions.

EVALUATIVE CRITERIA

Revenue and taxation decisions are complex political decisions, and those involved in making these decisions are well aware that individual members of the taxpaying public do not want to bear more than their fair share of the revenue burden.[81] Decisions determining fair share, or how to distribute the revenue burden in a community, represent the most important choices made by a governing authority. Two general approaches come into play in decisions about revenue sources: benefits-received approach and ability-to-pay approach.

The benefits-received approach implies that the revenue burden should be allocated according to the benefits received from public services. User fees and charges are nontax revenue sources that directly reflect this approach. Although this approach has wide appeal in a society with a market economy, one in which consumers pay for the benefits received from private goods and services, there are problems associated with its application in the public sector. In the delivery of many county services (e.g., sheriff, roads, and recreation), it is impossible to measure the benefits received by specific county residents. Governmental services usually produce general benefits for the entire community, making the benefits-received approach difficult to apply in financing the delivery of public services.

The ability-to-pay approach underlies most local government revenue systems and their heavy reliance on taxes. Under this approach, the tax burden is distributed according to some indication of taxpayer ability to bear the burden, usually income, property, or some other indicator of wealth. The ability-to-pay approach allows for some redistribution of affluence in society, a value associated with tax system design, but is inconsistent with the benefits-received approach.

In making decisions to increase existing tax rates or to adopt new revenue sources, the following criteria warrant careful consideration:

- Equity

- Balance

- Ease of administration

Equity

Equity implies a fundamental concern for the fairness of the distribution of the revenue burden in a community. The equity issue has two components—horizontal equity and vertical equity.

Horizontal equity involves equal treatment of taxpayers who have equal ability to pay taxes. If two taxpaying units are essentially equivalent in all respects but one unit pays significantly more tax, the tax system lacks horizontal equity. With regard to the property tax, for example, when owners of homes of equivalent market value pay different property tax amounts (because of different assessed valuations), the principle of horizontal equity is violated. Vertical equity, on the other hand, involves unequal treatment of taxpayers who have unequal or different capabilities to pay taxes. Although there are no clear guidelines, "most would argue that those with more capacity ought to pay more taxes."[82] With regard to the income tax, for example, when lower-income individuals pay a higher income tax amount and/or percentage than do individuals with higher income, the principle of vertical equity is challenged.

Vertical equity involves the relationship between income and taxes actually paid (effective rate). The nominal or statutory tax rate is the rate legally defined as applicable to the tax base. The effective tax rate is different, reflecting the actual fiscal impact on the taxpayer. The effective rate is usually calculated by dividing the tax paid by a relevant measure of affluence, usually income. Thus, vertical equity reflects an understanding that statutory tax rates affect individual taxpayers according to their unique financial conditions. With this in mind, a tax can be classified in one of three equity categories reflecting three different revenue burden distributions:[83]

1. Regressive—a tax with effective rates that are lower for individuals or families with high affluence than they are for those with low affluence
2. Progressive—a tax with effective rates that are higher for individuals or families with high affluence than they are for those with low affluence
3. Proportional—a tax with effective rates that do not change across individuals or families with different affluence levels

Balance

Revenue must be maintained at a steady flow from year to year to support the continuous and uninterrupted provision of needed public services. Some revenues such as the sales tax and income tax are elastic, meaning that their yields are highly responsive to changes in economic activity. In periods of economic growth or high inflation, for example, revenue yields would rise at roughly the same rate as inflation. Likewise, revenue yields would decrease during recessions, reflecting the slowdown in economic activity.

Although it is desirable for tax systems to include elastic revenues, stable revenue sources are also important. The yields from stable revenue sources such as property taxes and user fees and charges will not fluctuate automatically with changes in the economy. Yields from these sources change only when the tax rate is altered. One important exception has been the significant devaluation of real property in some parts of Georgia due to the severe recession. Typically, property values remain stable, slowly increasing over time. Fortunately, economic recovery should result in the property tax base slowly rising in value once again. It is important, then, for county revenue systems to maintain a balance of both stable and elastic revenue sources so that counties can adequately support their operations no matter what the state of the economy.[84]

Ease of Administration

Just as equity and balance are important considerations, the collectability of the revenue and the ease of administration warrant careful attention as well. The goal of administration is to extract desired revenues while minimizing the costs of revenue collection. Revenue collection involves both administrative costs (the costs to the government of collecting the tax) and compliance costs (the costs to the taxpayer of complying with the tax law). These two types of costs vary significantly from one revenue source to another, showing that revenue collection requires effort by both the taxpayer and the collecting government.

While the property tax involves relatively high administrative costs, nonproperty tax revenue involves high compliance costs. In administering the property tax, the government maintains parcel records, assesses the value of property, calculates individual tax liability, and distributes tax bills to property owners. The taxpayer is simply responsible for paying the bill. And in many cases, this task is handled by the bank through an escrow account. Since the taxpayer is minimally involved in the process, the compliance costs are low while the administrative costs to the collecting agency are extremely high.

On the other hand, nonproperty taxes are essentially taxpayer administered, relying to a large extent on voluntary compliance. The individual or firm maintains records of taxable transactions, tabulates the tax base, calculates liability, and makes the payment. The county conducts private audits to ensure an acceptable level of compliance. In such voluntary systems, administrative costs are minimized and the taxpayer bears the bulk of total collection costs.

REVENUE PATTERNS

Local governments in the United States operate in an intergovernmental system. They generate revenues from their own sources as authorized by their state governments and receive intergovernmental revenues in the form of federal and state aid. A small amount of funds are also transferred between local governments pursuant to interlocal agreements, but these funds usually make up less than 1 percent of total local revenues for Georgia county governments. Over the past decade and a half, the amount of revenue derived from intergovernmental revenues for Georgia counties has grown, accounting for 7.6 percent of revenues in 2007 com-

Table 18-1. *Revenue Yield, by Source, 1990, 2000, and 2007*

Revenue sources	1990			2000			2007		
	1,000s of 2007 dollars	Per capita 2007 dollars	Percent of Total	1,000s of 2007 dollars	Per capita 2007 dollars	Percent of Total	1,000s of 2007 dollars	Per capita 2007 dollars	Percent of Total
Own-source revenue (OSR)									
Property tax	2,027,489	311	42.50	3,144,356	382	34.06	3,695,910	387	42.94
Local option sales tax	371,991	57	7.80	948,246	115	10.27	875,689	92	10.17
Special purpose sales tax	662,507	102	13.89	1,043,428	127	11.30	1,324,211	139	15.39
Excise and selective use tax	69,141	11	1.45	140,002	17	1.52	125,293	13	1.46
Licenses, permits, and fees	110,744	17	2.32	264,981	32	2.87	224,081	23	2.60
Service charges	705,185	108	14.78	1,817,626	221	19.69	753,640	79	8.76
Other revenue	580,529	89	12.17	1,258,833	153	13.64	952,440	100	11.06
Total OSR	4,527,585	695	94.90	8,617,473	1,047	93.35	7,951,564	833	92.38
Intergovernmental revenue (IGR)									
Federal	42,349	7	0.89	159,839	19	1.73	183,686	19	2.13
State	155,680	24	3.26	403,334	49	4.37	403,186	19	4.68
Local	45,474	7	0.95	50,970	6	0.55	69,389	7	0.81
Total IGR	243,503	37	5.10	614,142	75	6.65	656,261	69	7.62
Total revenue	4,771,089	733	100.00	9,231,615	1,122	100.00	8,607,825	902	100.00

Source: Georgia Department of Community Affairs; Tax and Expenditure Data Center, Carl Vinson Institute of Government.

Note: Figures have been adjusted for inflation using the U.S. Bureau of Economic Analysis price index for state and local government purchases of goods and services. All figures are in constant 2007 dollars.

pared with 5.1 percent in 1990 (Table 18-1).[85] Own-source revenues continue to provide more than 90 percent of total county funding.

The two dominant county revenue sources are property and sales taxes, which when combined account for more than two-thirds of all county revenues. Generating nearly $3.7 billion in 2007, the property tax continues to be the mainstay of county revenue despite revenue system diversification that began three decades ago. While the amount of revenue produced by the property tax dropped as a percentage of the total from 1990 to 2000, its growth in dollars collected has been steady, and rising property values in the mid 2000s propelled it back to its historical proportion of 42 percent to 43 percent of total revenue. Most property tax revenue comes from taxes on real and personal property (82.1 percent), with significantly smaller amounts coming from taxes on motor vehicles (7.4 percent), public utilities (3.3 percent), intangibles (2.7 percent), mobile homes (0.3 percent), and railroad equipment (less than 0.1 percent). During the 1990s and early 2000s, some diversification continued, especially in fees and charges for services.

The amount of revenue from sales taxes ($2.2 billion) accounted for 27 percent of total revenue compared with 23.1 percent in 1990. Much of this growth has been in the adoption of the SPLOST used to fund capital needs. In 2007, 150 of Georgia's 159 counties collected $1.3 billion in SPLOST revenues compared with only $744 million ($1.04 billion constant 2007 dollars) collected in 127 counties seven years earlier. The LOST has been a significant source of general revenue for counties since 1975, with 148 counties receiving $876 million in LOST revenue in 2007. State and local governments suffered a reduction in sales tax revenues from 2008 to 2010. Complete county data from the Department of Community Affairs were unavailable at press time, but for the 67 counties that had submitted data for 2008, sales tax collections were flat, with only a 1 percent increase from $1.043 billion to $1.053 billion. A significant decline in sales tax revenues began in 2009 and continued in 2010. Recovery of this revenue source is expected in late 2010 and 2011.

In addition to these two major revenue sources, counties receive revenue from excise and special-use taxes (e.g., alcoholic beverage, insurance premiums, hotel-motel, and franchise payments); licenses, permits, and fees (e.g., business licenses and occupation taxes, alcoholic beverage licenses, and building permits); and service charges (e.g., ambulance, parks and recreation, and garbage and trash collection). Counties also derived $952 million in other revenues, with much of this other revenue coming from interest earnings, fines, forfeitures, and court fees.

NOTES

1. Robert L. Bland, *A Revenue Guide for Local Government* (Washington, DC: International City Management Association, 1989), 17. See also James J. Gosling, *Budgetary Politics in American Governments* (New York: Longman, 1992), 159.

2. Portions of this chapter are drawn from Betty J. Hudson and J. Devereux Weeks, *County and Municipal Revenue Sources in Georgia*, 3rd ed. (Athens: Carl Vinson Institute of Government, University of Georgia, 1997).

3. See U.S. Advisory Commission on Intergovernmental Relations (ACIR), *Local Revenue Diversification: Income, Sales Taxes and User Charges*, Report A-47 (Washington, DC: ACIR, 1974); *Principles of a High Quality State Revenue System* (Cambridge, MA: Lincoln Institute of Land Policy and the National Conference of State Legislatures, no date).

4. Georgia Department of Community Affairs, *Georgia Local Government Finance Highlights* 2009 (www.dca.state.ga.us).

5. Ibid.

6. OFFICIAL CODE OF GEORGIA ANNOTATED (O.C.G.A.) §48-5-7(a).

7. O.C.G.A. tit. 48, ch. 5, art. 5A; GA. COMP. R. & REGS. 560-11-2-.56(2)(d).

8. GA. CONST. art. VII, §1, ¶3(d), (e)(1); O.C.G.A. §§48-5-7, 48-5-7.2, 48-5-7.3, 48-5-7.4.

9. GA. CONST. art. VII, §1, ¶3(c); O.C.G.A. §§48-5-7, 48-5-7.1.

10. GA. CONST. art. VII, §1, ¶3(e)(2); O.C.G.A. §48-5-7.5.

11. GA. CONST. art. VII, §1, ¶3(c)(2), (e)(1), (f); O.C.G.A. §§48-5-7, 48-5-7.1, 48-5-7.4.

12. GA. CONST. art. VII, §1, ¶3(g); O.C.G.A. tit. 48, ch. 5, arts. 11, 12.

13. O.C.G.A. §§48-5-44, 48-5-47.1, 48-5-48. Local homestead exemptions are found in local acts of the General Assembly.

14. O.C.G.A. §48-5-273.

15. O.C.G.A. §48-5-32.1.

16. O.C.G.A. tit. 48, ch. 6, art. 3.

17. O.C.G.A. tit. 48, ch.6, art. 1.

18. O.C.G.A. tit. 48, ch. 8, art. 2.

19. The counties of Bulloch, Chattooga, Colquitt, Habersham, Houston, Mitchell, Rabun, and Towns dedicate their LOST to schools via local constitutional amendment.

20. O.C.G.A. §§48-8-87, 48-8-50.

21. O.C.G.A. §§48-8-3, 48-8-82.

22. O.C.C.A §48-8-89.

23. O.C.G.A. tit. 48, ch. 8, art 3.

24. O.C.G.A. §48-8-110.

25. O.C.G.A. §48-8-111.

26. O.C.G.A. §§48-8-111, 48-8-112, 48-8-115. See also O.C.G.A. §48-8-111.1. A consolidated government that levies this special local option sales and use tax is not subject to the five-year limitation on imposition of this tax. Consolidated governments are also exempt from the requirements to contract with cities on capital outlay projects or to operate projects jointly with a city.

27. O.C.G.A. §§48-8-112, 21-2-540.

28. O.C.G.A. §§48-8-6(b), 48-8-112, 48-8-121.
29. O.C.G.A. tit. 48, ch. 8, art. 5.
30. Ga. Const. art. VIII, §6, ¶ 4; O.C.G.A. tit. 48, ch. 8, art. 3, pt 2.
31. 1978 Op. Att'y Gen. No. 85-18.
32. O.C.G.A. tit. 48, ch. 8, art. 2A.
33. O.C.G.A. §§3-4-80, 3-6-60.
34. O.C.G.A. §3-5-80.
35. O.C.G.A. §3-4-131.
36. O.C.G.A. tit. 36, ch. 18; §36-76-3.
37. Ga. Const. art. IX, §4, ¶1(c); O.C.G.A. §§33-8-8.1, 33-8-8.2.
38. O.C.G.A. §33-8-8.3.
39. Ga. Const. art. IX, §4, ¶1(b).
40. O.C.G.A. §48-13-10.
41. Greater Atlanta Home Builders Association v. DeKalb County, U.S. District Court, Case No. 1:00-CV-1290-GET, *aff'd without opinion* 11th Circuit Court of Appeals, 37 Fed. Appx. 980 (May 30, 2002); O.C.G.A. §48-13-9.
42. O.C.G.A. §§48-13-5, 48-13-10(e).
43. O.C.GA. §§48-13-9(c), 48-13-10(g).
44. O.C.G.A. §48-13-6.
45. O.C.G.A. tit. 48, ch. 13, art. 1.
46. O.C.G.A. §§7-1-758, 7-1-958, 48-6-93, 48-13-16.
47. O.C.G.A. §48-6-90 et seq.
48. O.C.G.A. §48-13-51 (h).
49. O.C.G.A. §48-13-51(a)(1)(D), (2).
50. O.C.G.A. §48-51-13(2).
51. O.C.G.A. §48-13-51(a)(3).
52. O.C.G.A. tit. 48, ch. 13, art. 3.
53. O.C.G.A. §48-13-51.
54. Ibid.
55. O.C.G.A. §48-13-56.
56. O.C.G.A. §48-13-56.1.
57. O.C.G.A. tit. 48, ch. 13, art. 5.
58. O.C.G.A. tit. 15, chs. 6, 7, 9, 10; ch. 21, arts. 1, 3, 5, 6; tit. 40, ch. 6, art. 14; §27-1-14.
59. O.C.G.A. §36-80-3; tit. 36, ch. 83.
60. Ga. Const. art. IX, §§2, 3; O.C.G.A. §36-70-24.
61. O.C.G.A. §46-5-134.
62. Ga. Const. art. IX, §2, ¶3(12); O.C.GA. tit. 8, ch. 2; §§36-13-6, 48-13-8, 48-13-9.
63. Ga. Const. art. IX, §4, ¶1(b)(1).
64. O.C.G.A. §§3-4-50, 3-5-40–3-5-43, 3-6-40.
65. O.C.G.A. tit. 36, ch. 71.
66. O.C.G.A. §40-2-33.
67. O.C.G.A. §§3-2-33, 3-2-34, 3-2-35, 3-10-1, 3-10-11.
68. O.C.G.A. §16-13-49.

69. Hill v. Clayton County Board of Commissioners, 283 Ga. App. 15 (2006). See O.C.G.A. §16-13-48.1; Chatham County v. Kiley, 249 Ga. 110, 111 (1)(1982). For state drug fund money, see O.C.G.A. §16-13-49(u)(4)(D)(iii).
70. O.C.G.A. §16-12-32.
71. O.C.G.A. §16-14-7.
72. O.C.G.A. §12-8-2.
73. O.C.G.A. §17-5-52.
74. 42 UNITED STATES CODE ANNOTATED (U.S.C.A.) §5301 et seq.; O.C.G.A. §50-8-8.
75. O.C.G.A. §32-5-27(d).
76. O.C.G.A. §§12-5-32–12-5-34, 12-5-37, 12-8-37.1, 12-3-8.
77. O.C.G.A. tit. 31, ch. 7, art. 3.
78. O.C.G.A. §36-80-6.
79. GA. CONST. art. IX, §4, ¶4; O.C.G.A. tit. 36, ch. 73.
80. GA. CONST. art. IX, §§5, 6; tit. 36, ch. 82, arts. 1, 2, 3; §§36-80-2, 36-80-10–36-80-14, 36-60-13, 36-60-15.
81. This section relies heavily on chapters 6 and 9 in John L. Mikesell, *Fiscal Administration: Analysis and Applications for the Public Sector*, 3rd ed. (Belmont, CA: Brooks/Cole, 1991).
82. Ibid., 154.
83. Ibid., glossary.
84. See Sanford M. Groves, *Financial Trend Monitoring System: A Practitioner's Workbook* (Washington, DC: International City Management Association, 1980), 21–25; Bland, *Revenue Guide for Local Government*, ch. 2.
85. Financial data from the *Survey of Georgia Local Government Finance* conducted annually by the Georgia Department of Community Affairs are used in this analysis. Data on general revenue categories for fiscal years 1990, 2000, and 2007 are presented in Table 1; data on specific revenue sources are presented in the text only. Data on the number of counties receiving sales tax revenue came from the Georgia Department of Revenue, *Statistical Report* (Atlanta: Georgia Department of Community Affairs 2008).

19

Paul Glick, Sabrina Wiley Cape, Richard W. Campbell, and Patti Lee

Operations Budgeting

The operating budget is the most important document that a county will produce.[1] It is "the only document that summarizes the entire array of public programs to be undertaken by county governments."[2] The budget drives the other financial management systems and becomes the most important tool by which a local government's goals are accomplished and objectives are met. Counties in Georgia are required to prepare an operating budget each year. A capital budget, which covers proposed expenditures for items with a life of more than one year, is not an annual requirement. (Capital budgets are discussed in Chapter 20.) However, for each capital projects fund in the capital budget, counties are required to adopt and operate under a project-length balanced budget.

The annual operating budget (in this chapter, referred to as the budget) is not only a plan that guides the operations of county government and its divisions; it is also a political document. In a democratic society, government officials have an obligation to efficiently execute the will of the people. Citizens likewise have a right to oversee and check the policy and administrative decisions of their representatives and appointed public servants. The budget serves both of these democratic aims. It is an important management tool, providing information essential to improving the efficiency of program operations. And, as an accountability document, the budget provides information that citizens can use in assessing county activities and operations.

Described as a "wish book with price tags attached," the budget reflects the commitment of resources to the implementation of proposed policies and programs. The budget, then, is the product of a complex process of resolving conflicting needs and wants. It also is an essential component of a responsive and responsible county government.

The claim that "each local government's budgeting process is unique ... the product of geographical, historical, economic, political, and social factors peculiar to that jurisdiction" certainly applies to counties in Georgia.[3] No one would argue, for example, that Fulton, Gwinnett, Clarke, Taliaferro, and Quitman Counties confront the same issues or that their budgets or budget processes are or should be the same. However, county budget processes in Georgia do reflect important features and values associated with budget decision making generally. This chapter reviews state legal requirements relating to county budgeting and financial disclosure, describes the process of county budgeting, explores the multiple purposes served as the budget is formed and administered, and discusses selected policies intended to guide the operating budget process.[4]

STATE LEGAL REQUIREMENTS

Counties are creations of the state, and the state of Georgia has a vested interest in the financial well-being of all 159 counties.[5] Prior to 1980, there were no general state statutory or constitutional requirements related to budget development or the disclosure of financial information. In that year, the General Assembly enacted the local government Financial Management Standards Act (FMSA) requiring all counties to adopt an annual balanced budget and to provide for regular audits.[6] Subsequently, the General Assembly enacted two important local government budgeting laws. In 1997, it directed the state Department of Community Affairs to create a uniform chart of accounts for the state's local governments (see Chapter 16 for a more detailed discussion of the uniform chart of accounts),[7] and in 1998, it amended the 1980 budget law expanding and clarifying state requirements related to local government budgeting.[8]

The budget law, as amended, imposes the following requirements on counties:

- Establish an official fiscal year for the county's operations.[9] There is no prescribed fiscal year, but most begin on either January 1 or July 1.

- Adopt a balanced budget and provide for a regular audit.

- Prepare a proposed budget for submission to the county commission.[10] The budget proposal must include anticipated revenues by source and expected expenditures by function.

- Adopt project budgets, rather than annual budgets, for major capital projects. An annual budget corresponds with a county's fiscal year, but a project budget is adopted for the project period, without regard to the fiscal year. Normally, the issuance of general obligation bonds or the special purpose local option sales tax (SPLOST) has funded major capital projects. Prior to this change in the law, counties were required by state law to adopt annual budgets for each project. For example, if a county were to build a new jail over a three-year period, it would need to estimate the costs that would occur in each of the three years. If the project were not completed on time, many of the same costs would be budgeted in more than one different fiscal year. Under the law, however, counties can budget the total cost of the project in the year in which the project began, with no additional budget action required in the later years of the project, unless the total budget is increased.

- Limit the requirements for adopting budgets. Counties now only need to adopt annual budgets for the general fund, each special revenue fund, and each debt service fund. Counties are not required to adopt budgets for other funds such as water and sewer. However, a county may—and is encouraged to—adopt annual budgets for all of its other funds.

- Notify the public that the budget proposal is available for public review.[11]

- Conduct a public hearing at least one week prior to the adoption of the budget resolution or ordinance, notice of which must be published at least seven days before the hearing.[12]

- Adopt a budget resolution or ordinance, which can contain dollar amounts different from the amounts contained in the proposed budget.[13] Notice of the meeting at which the budget ordinance or resolution is to be adopted must be advertised at least seven days before the meeting.[14]

- Adopt budget amendments by ordinance or resolution.[15] Formerly, it was not always clear at a commission meeting when a commission was actually amending the budget. For example, when a county commissioner moved to buy a new fire truck and the commission voted "yes," had the budget been amended? Under the new law, county commissioners are required to amend the budget through a more formal process (that is, by approving an ordinance or resolution).

- Provide for an audit[16] of the financial affairs and transactions of all funds and activities in accordance with generally accepted governmental auditing standards (GAAP).[17] The audit report must contain financial statements prepared in conformity with

GAAP and the opinion of the auditor regarding the statements and must disclose any apparent material violation of state or local law. Counties with populations of more than 1,500 persons or expenditures of $300,000 or more must be audited each fiscal year, while all other counties must be audited at least once every two fiscal years.[18]

- Submit a copy of the audit report to the Georgia state auditor within 180 days after the close of the fiscal year, or the close of each second fiscal year in the case of counties not required to be audited annually.[19]

- Submit a copy of the final budget and audit to the Carl Vinson Institute of Government annually to be posted on its Web site.[20]

The budget law also clarifies the legal level of budgetary control. The level of control is the level of budget detail that the county commission must adopt in its budgets; overspending at this level would result in a violation of the law.[21] The law establishes the legal level of control at the departmental level within each fund, unless a more detailed level of control is established by resolution or ordinance of the commissioners.[22]

When the legal level of control is the department, transfers of appropriations within any fund below the departmental level require only the approval of the budget officer.[23] However, the law does not define the term department. Therefore, the county commission must make departmental allocations clear within the budget (see Table 19-1).

If the county commissioners keep the department as the legal level of control, only the county commission can transfer budget amounts between departments within each fund. For example, in Table 19-1, if the county commission had a need to spend more than the $2 million in the Public Works Department, the commission would have to amend the budget. If the county spends more on any department than the budget allows without first amending the budget, it is breaking the law.

STAGES OF THE COUNTY BUDGETARY PROCESS

The county budgetary process is divided into four stages: preparation, adoption, execution, and auditing. Although the way the budget document develops through these four stages is simple, the total process is complex.[24] It involves many different actors such as the chief administrative officer, the commissioners, the clerk to the commissioners, the department heads, the constitutional officers (i.e., sheriff, superior court clerk, tax commissioner, and probate judge), other county and state elected officers who receive funding through the county (i.e., magistrate judge, state court judge, solicitor general, district attorney, and superior court judge), and others, who change roles from one stage to the next.

"The budget" is really two budgets. The first budget, or legislative budget, is a request for funds. The legislative budget is the focus of concern during the first two stages of the process (i.e., preparation and adoption). A budget request is prepared by the constitutional officers, other county and state elected officers who receive funding through the county, department heads, and other staff for action by the board. Once the response to the funding request is completed by the adoption of an appropriation resolution or ordinance, the budget becomes a plan that each county department, constitutional officer, and other county and state elected officers receiving funding through the county are authorized to undertake. This second budget, or management budget, is critical to the final two stages in the process (i.e., execution and auditing). This is the budget that the administrative officers must execute, making sure that spending does not exceed limits. It also serves the audit function, providing a foundation for the county's financial accounting structure.[25]

Preparation

Budget preparation begins with the creation of a budget request. In many counties, the clerk of the commission (that is, the clerk of the board of county commissioners or the clerk of the sole commissioner) is designated as the budget officer and prepares the budget under the supervision of the chairman of the board of commissioners or a designated budget committee. In such cases, the commission and/or budget committee retains ultimate responsibility, and the clerk of the commission assumes the day-to-day responsibilities associated with budget preparation. In

Table 19-1. *Sample General Fund Allocations, by Department*

Department	Amount
General government	$1 million
Sheriff	$3 million
Tax commissioner	$1 million
Finance	$1 million
Public works	$2 million
Parks and recreation	$1 million
Total budget	$9 million

those counties in which there is a county administrator or manager, that person is usually designated as ultimately responsible for budget preparation and submission. These counties often also have either a director of finance or budget director who assumes the day-to-day responsibility for budget preparation. The budget officer (whether the clerk, administrator, or manager) is also responsible for coordinating the work of a centralized budget and finance staff as well as the budget activities of the constitutional officers, other county and state elected officers who receive funding through the county, department heads, and their staffs.

To ensure that the budget is ready and in place when the fiscal year begins, it is necessary to establish a plan for developing the budget early in the process. First, the budget officer distributes a budget calendar to all participants. The budget calendar is a schedule of the various actions or steps that are necessary to prepare, review, and finally adopt a budget. It gives a specific timetable and assigns responsibility for each action. Table 19-2 presents a suggested budget calendar based on a January 1 fiscal year. Preparation of the budget request is time consuming and should begin about four to six months before the start of the county's fiscal year.

Once the budget participants know who is responsible for what and by when, the next step is to estimate the amount of revenue that will be available. Since counties cannot spend more dollars than they collect, the designated budget officer carefully estimates the amount of revenue the county can expect from each revenue source. Revenue collections in previous years serve as a basis for the forecast. For the purpose of estimating the property tax, the previous year's millage rate is applied, but once the budget is adopted a new millage rate will be set in order to generate revenues to cover expenditures.

Department heads play an important role in budget preparation. Working with members of their staff, they prepare and submit budget requests to the person responsible for day-to-day budget activities. The constitutional officers, other county and state elected officers who receive funding through the county, and department heads should prepare realistic requests that reflect constraints confronting the county in a particular fiscal year. They must provide accurate numbers to support their request and articulate and "sell" their respective programs.[26] In order to assist the constitutional officers, other county and state elected officers who receive funding through the county, and department heads, the budget officer issues guidelines indicating the limits within which budget requests should be prepared. The guidelines contain information such as the following:[27]

Table 19-2. *Suggested Budget Calendar (January 1 Fiscal Year)*

Due Date	Budget Steps	Day-to-Day Responsibility
September 1	Budget calendar is prepared.	Budget officer*
September 1	Budget preparation forms are printed and ready for distribution.	Budget officer
September 15	Budget information for current year and for prior years is entered on forms for each department. Budget request forms and instructions are then distributed to departments.	Budget officer
October 1	Revenue estimates for the next budget year are completed.	Budget officer
October 15	Expenditure estimates are made and are returned to the budget officer.	Department heads
November 15	a. Budget requests are summarized.	a. Budget officer
	b. Requests are analyzed and adjusted.	b. Budget officer
	c. Proposed expenditure plan is assembled.	c. Budget officer
	d. Proposed revenue program is prepared.	d. Budget officer
November 22	Proposed budget for next budget year is submitted to the board of commissioners.	Budget officer
November 30	Proposed budget is reviewed.	Governing authority
December 1	Public hearing is advertised.	Budget officer
December 8	Public hearing on budget is held.	Governing authority
December 15	Board's review of proposed budget is completed. Revisions are made to the budget.	Governing authority
December 24	Budget adoption meeting is advertised.	Budget officer
December 31	The budget is adopted. The appropriation ordinance and the revenue ordinance are adopted.	Governing authority
January 1	Monthly or quarterly allotment schedules for departments are prepared. Budget accounts are created. The adopted budget is entered into these accounts.	Budget officer

*The budget officer can be any one of the following: county administrator, manager, clerk of the commission, finance officer, budget officer, or a commissioner.

- Revenue estimates
- Planned changes in the level of service delivery
- A review of current year operations
- An analysis of general economic conditions expected for the coming year
- Assumptions to be made about wage rates and other prices
- Conditions under which additional personnel can be requested and the number of personnel who may be promoted
- Planned productivity gains
- Instructions for completing the forms

In addition, the budget officer prepares and distributes budget request forms to all county departments, constitutional officers, and other elected state and county officers who receive funding through the county. These forms ensure consistency and uniformity in the information submitted in departmental requests, thereby facilitating the review process by the person or committee responsible for budget preparation. Two commonly used forms are the budget expenditure request form and the personal services cost explanation form:[28]

1. *Budget expenditure request form.* This form shows the details of a department's budget request. It usually lists expenditures by line item and activity within a department. It includes actual expenditures from the preceding two or three years, the current year's budgeted expenditures, the budget request for the next fiscal year, and information regarding the extent to which the request is an increase or decrease in the current budget.

2. *Personal services cost explanation form.* This form shows the basis for a department's request for funds to pay personnel costs in the next fiscal year. It usually includes cost data related to current salaries, salary increases, overtime, social security, and new employees.

The budget officer reviews departmental requests and prepares an integrated budget for submission to the governing authority. Although this review can include formal hearings in which the constitutional officers, other county and state elected officers who receive funding through the county, and department heads defend and justify their requests publicly, the process is usually informal, with considerable day-to-day interaction as the budget officer and the department heads resolve specific details.

Once the review is completed, the budget is presented to the governing authority, usually six weeks before the beginning of the fiscal year. When the budget is submitted to the governing authority, a copy must be placed in a public location convenient to all residents. In addition, availability of the budget must be advertised the same week that the budget is made public.[29]

The budget document submitted to the commissioners should include (1) a budget message, (2) a budget summary, and (3) detailed budget requests.

Budget Message

The budget message describes the significant features of the proposed budget; identifies the differences between the proposed budget and the current budget and explains the reasons for these differences; discusses new programs contained in the budget; identifies and explains the need for additional revenue sources; identifies major accomplishments achieved during the year; and identifies public needs that were recognized as important but could not be addressed in the proposed budget.

Budget Summary

The budget summary shows estimated revenues by major source and requested expenditures by departments and activity. It also presents a detailed schedule, by department, of funds requested for capital expenditures.

Detailed Budget Requests

This portion of the proposed budget provides detailed expenditure data by major expenditure item (object code) for each department. It also includes expenses, which are not charged to specific departments (i.e., bond redemption, judgments, and losses, etc.). Finally, it contains revenue estimates by major and minor revenue sources.

Adoption

The second stage of the budgetary process, adoption, is the responsibility of the county commissioners. The adoption stage provides an opportunity to review the performance of county operations and to assess the quality and level of services delivered. Review of the proposed budget normally takes four to six weeks. Although a budget or finance committee often conducts a major part of the review, budget adoption requires formal action by the board.

The commissioners are required by state statute to conduct a public hearing to consider the budget.[30] This hearing provides citizens and various community interest groups an opportunity to present their views on various aspects of the proposed budget. The county commission can also request that the budget officer, the constitutional officers, other county and state elected officers who receive funding through the county, and/or department heads come before it to explain and discuss specific elements in the budget request. Although not required, the county commission can conduct more than one public hearing.[31]

After required hearings are held and any changes are made, the budget is ready for adoption. The commissioners must take two actions in order to adopt the budget:

1. It must enact a revenue resolution or ordinance establishing the tax levy.
2. It must enact a budget resolution or ordinance appropriating funds to departments.

With adoption, the budget is no longer a proposal or a request for funds. The so-called legislative budget has become the management budget. This budget guides the implementation of the commissioners' policies and programs and serves as a benchmark for making judgments about performance.

Execution

The third stage in the budgetary process, the execution stage, has been referred to as the "action phase of budgeting," when plans contained in the budget are actually put into operation.[32] While there is inevitably "a push and pull between flexibility and control,"[33] historically, budget execution has been viewed as a way of maintaining control over the use of resources, as county governments put into practice the various policies and programs authorized in their budgets. In a democracy, where the power of the purse rests with legislative bodies, managerial controls must be established to ensure that actual spending does not exceed appropriations and that resources are expended only for those purposes intended by the legislative body.

Fund Accounting

The most important component of a management control system is the accounting structure employed to record and report a county's financial transactions. Accounting systems vary significantly from one county to another. (See Chapter 16 for an explanation of basis of accounting.) Many counties, especially the most populated, employ integrated computer-based financial management systems, but many others continue to rely on bookkeepers. No matter how basic or sophisticated the system of budget execution, accounting for the resources appropriated by the board of commissioners remains a fundamental need.

Unlike accounting in profit organizations (where the corporate organization itself is a single, accountable entity), governmental accounting involves the use of multiple funds, reflecting the existence of multiple accounting entities.[34] Fund accounting has evolved in the public sector to keep track of revenue from many different sources that is designated for a variety of specific purposes and activities. Most county services and administrative activities (i.e., law enforcement, fire, public works, and financial administration) are supported by tax revenue and are accounted for in the general fund. However, appropriations designated for debt service and revenue generated by specific revenue sources for a specified purpose must be accounted for separately in other governmental funds.

Counties also engage in activities that are self-supporting, which are funded by fees and charges rather than general tax revenue (e.g., water and sewer, utilities, mass transit, golf courses, etc.). Financial transactions and financial reports related to these activities must be kept separate so that the "profitability" of the enterprise can be determined. They are accounted for in proprietary funds.

The Governmental Accounting Standard Board suggests that counties employ 11 generic fund types that fall under three fund categories. These fund types are described in some detail in Chapter 16.[35]

Budgetary Accounting and Preauditing

Budgetary accounts and preaudits are as important to a management control system as the use of fund accounting. Budgetary accounts are established for each activity and line item contained in the adopted budget. The budgetary expenditure accounts, referred to as appropriations, contain resources that the county is authorized to expend during the fiscal year.

The appropriations balance is reduced routinely as expenditures are made. In fact, prior to expending funds, it must be determined that the appropriations balance is sufficient to cover the expenditure. This control technique is referred to as the preaudit function. Generally accepted accounting principles, reflecting this concern for control, require that yearly financial reports compare budgeted revenues and budgeted expenditures with actual revenues and actual expenditures.

Auditing

The final stage of the budgetary process involves a retrospective examination of the process of budget execution. Auditing represents an attempt to check and evaluate county operations within a given fiscal year. Audits provide feedback to the governing authority and other county officials on the integrity of financial transactions and formal reporting, on the efficiency of program operations, and on the effectiveness of county policies and programs.

The three types of audits are financial audits, performance audits, and program audits. As noted in the section on state legal requirements, counties are required to have a financial audit prepared. An independent accounting firm usually performs the financial audit in the months immediately following the fiscal year end. This audit must be prepared according to generally accepted governmental auditing standards and must contain the required basic financial statements. The audited financial statements are collectively referred to as the "annual financial report."

The annual financial report also includes a letter from the auditor containing its judgment about whether or not the financial statements are a fair representation of the county's financial position, the results of its operations, and cash flows of its proprietary funds (funds that are self-sustaining, usually through charges and fees).

Because performance audits and program audits are not required by state statute, most counties do not conduct these audits. Those counties that do usually have an in-house staff of management analysts. Performance audits are also referred to as efficiency audits and represent attempts to measure the level of activity performed in specific divisions and departments. Performance audits focus on workload measures; information such as numbers of assaults investigated per shift, books loaned per week, and building permits issued per month is recorded. These workload measures allow management to monitor changes in the level of effort and the effect of these changes on performance.

Program audits focus on results rather than level of activity or workload measures. These audits require the skills associated with evaluation research and represent an attempt to assess the effectiveness of program operations. Effectiveness is defined as the extent to which the results of program operations are consistent with the program's goals and objectives. In order to make a judgment about effectiveness, it is necessary to measure the effect that the program actually has on the community. Assessing program impact produces information that allows the county to decide whether the results from specific programs are worth the investment or whether community resources might be better used to pursue other policies and programs.

Overlap of Budgeting Stages

The four stages of budgeting—preparation, adoption, execution, and auditing—overlap significantly. For example, while the budget request for FY 2011 is being prepared, the budget for FY 2010 is being executed (and perhaps amended), and the audit for FY 2009 is being conducted. During the subsequent phase, the governing authority reviews the budget request for FY 2011, considers the audit report for FY 2009, and makes decisions concerning any necessary budget amendments for FY 2010—all in the same time period. The situation is further complicated because the county's fiscal year may be different from those of the state (July 1–June 30) and federal (October 1–September 30) governments. When local funds must be budgeted to match federal or state funds, discrepancies in fiscal years can confound the county budget process.

BUDGET VALUES AND BUDGET FORMATS

Three values pervade the county budgetary process—control, management, and planning[36]—regardless of the budget practice or procedure a local government uses. Each value is reflected in a specific budget format that provides a framework within which budgetary decisions are made and budgetary data presented. The three most common budget formats are line-item budgets, performance budgets, and program budgets. All budget decisions require information, which will vary with the format. The format chosen by a particular jurisdiction will largely depend on the extent to which budget decision makers are concerned with controlling the use of public resources (line item) and/or making judgments about how efficiently (performance) and effectively (program) those resources are used. Stronger executive leadership is important if counties are to achieve greater administrative efficiency and responsiveness to their citizens.[37]

Line-Item Budgets

Control-oriented budgets frequently take the form of very detailed line-item descriptions of authorized expenditures. The focus in the budgetary process is on line items, or objects of expenditure (e.g., personnel, pencils, gasoline). Originally, budgets were designed primarily to give elected officials more control over how public money was spent. They were intended to reduce the potential for corruption and waste in county government. Although this format achieves its objective of control, it also creates a relatively inflexible financial management system that may not allow administrators enough leeway to make minor adjustments when unanticipated problems or opportunities arise. For this reason, a strict line-item budget usually is not preferred. Rather, less restrictive line-item formats are found in county budgets today. Table 19-3 shows a simplified example of a line-item budget reflecting a strong control orientation.

Performance Budgets

Management is another focus of public budgets, often reflected in the use of performance budgets. Like performance audits, performance budgets are more concerned with efficiency than with control over expenditure decisions. In such budgets, workload data and performance indicators are provided to illustrate the efficiency of the services described. Table 19-4 presents a simplified example of a performance budget format.

Program Budgets

Focusing on broad overall functions rather than on agencies or specific tasks, the program budget emphasizes planning. As the example in Table 19-5 shows, a program budget is concerned with programs rather than with departments or objects of expenditure. Sometimes, however, additional detail in program budgets is desirable to specify how program

Table 19-3. *Example of Line-Item Budget Format*

Item	Budget
Salaries—governing authority	$11,000
Wages and salaries—other personnel	38,400
Per diem	2,250
Payroll taxes	8,500
Health insurance	6,700
Life insurance	5,800
Postage	900
Utilities	2,900
Gasoline and motor oil	1,300
Telephone service—local	2,175
Telephone service—long distance	300
Debt service	13,850
Total	$214,100

funds are to be allocated to departments and objects of expenditure. Many program budgets do contain line-item detail (see Table 19-6).

Budgetary Trends

State law does not require that Georgia counties follow any prescribed budget format. Rather, a county usually selects a format that reflects the primary focus of its budget and the level of financial detail that county officials want to include. The National Association of Counties has expressed the concern that because line-item budgets "merely state what each department and other administrative units plan to buy, [they] fail to inform the taxpayer what he is really receiving for his money [and tend to] 'hamper' as much as aid the deliberative processes of county government."[38] While it is true that county commissions or the governing authority are central to the budget process and that they must exercise

Table 19-4. *Example of Performance Budget Format (Sanitation Services Program Only)*

Service	Budget
Refuse Collection	
1. Personal services	$3,500
2. Contractual services	500
3. Supplies and materials	500
4. Capital outlay	1,000
Total	$5,500
Performance Statistics	———
Residential Collections	
Pickups per week from residences:	1,000
Tons of refuse collected per year:	375
Cost of collection per ton:	$8
Cost per dwelling = pickup per year:	$3
Total annual cost:	$3,000
Commercial Collections	
Commercial stops—two pickups per week:	100
Tons of refuse collected per year:	250
Cost of collections per ton:	$8
Cost per stop per year:	$20
Total annual cost:	$2,000

Source: Adapted from Arthur A. Mendonsa, *Simplified Financial Management in Local Government* (Athens: Institute of Government, Institute of Community and Area Development, and Center for Continuing Education, University of Georgia, 1969), 164, 167.

Table 19-5. *Example of a Simple Program Budget Format*

Program	Budget
General administration	$28,000
Public safety	21,000
Water services	110,500
Sanitation services	17,000
Roads, streets, and bridges	14,300
Recreation services	2,000
Total	$192,800

control through the use of the line-item format, the view that county budget decisions can benefit from other kinds of information has gained some acceptance over the years.

Local governments, especially larger jurisdictions, increasingly are using more sophisticated results-oriented budget formats. For example, several counties across Georgia, including Gwinnett County and Athens–Clarke County, use performance measures as part of the budget process. However, the line-item budget remains one of the more commonly used formats.[39]

The lack of appropriate measures of performance has hampered budget reform and the use of results-oriented budgeting. However, one

Table 19-6. *Example of a Detailed Program Budget Format (Public Safety Only)*

Program	Item	Budget
Public Safety	Salaries—Police	$18,000
	Uniforms—Police	700
	Gasoline and oil—Police	2,400
	Vehicle maintenance—Police	500
	Telephone—Police	700
	Operating supplies—Police	400
	Salaries—Fire	15,000
	Uniforms—Fire	600
	Total	$51,900

study of county governments found that analytic competency and political support can lead to increased use of performance measurement in budgeting, which can result in more efficient, effective, and accountable government.[40]

BUDGET-RELATED POLICIES

County commissioners must address many important questions as they assume their budget-making responsibilities. A few of these questions are presented below. A prudent board of commissioners is one that develops agreed-upon responses to such recurrent questions and, further, formalizes its responses in policy statements intended to guide future actions.

Must the Budget Balance?

Georgia law requires counties to adopt balanced budgets.[41] When the budget is balanced, revenues must equal expenditures. However, there are two scenarios in which revenues and expenditures need not be equal: (1) when the county is trying to accumulate resources, usually for cash-flow purposes, for capital items, or for unforeseen emergencies; or (2) when the county has incurred a deficit fund balance (i.e., actual expenditures have exceeded revenues) in prior years and wishes to eliminate this problem. In Georgia, this second option is not allowable unless the county has an adequate unreserved fund balance (i.e., the accumulated difference between revenues and expenditures over the life of the fund) from the previous year to cover the difference between revenues and expenditures in the proposed budget.

How Much Should a Fund Balance Be?

Fund balance can refer to "reserves" or "rainy day" funds, but accountants define fund balance as the difference between the assets and the liabilities on the balance sheet or the difference between revenues and expenditures since the fund (e.g., the general fund) was created. Accounting rules allow counties to reserve portions of fund balance. When a portion of fund balance is reserved, it is not available to spend. Reserves usually result from legal restrictions. The portion of fund balance that is not reserved, or the unreserved fund balance, is what is available to spend in the subsequent year.

Although this question is one of the most frequently asked by local government elected officials, there is no easy answer to the question regarding size of fund balance. There are situations in which a very high balance could present a problem. Like businesses, counties must have adequate resources to meet their payrolls and pay their bills. Counties use fund balances to meet these cash-flow needs; businesses refer to such resources as "equity" or "retained earnings." But there is also a significant difference between counties and businesses. Because businesses operate to make a profit; they can never have too much equity. By contrast, counties operate to provide social and essential services. Therefore, if a fund balance becomes too large, a county can be criticized for taxing its residents and businesses beyond what it needs for current operations. Adopting a financial policy that explains why a certain fund balance is being maintained will help a county's position if a taxpayer were to sue the county for levying excess property taxes.

Although some taxpayers might question the need for any fund balance at all, there are some convincing arguments that support maintaining adequate fund balances. The primary argument is that fund balances need to be maintained to ensure adequate cash flow. If a county relies heavily on property taxes (as opposed to sales taxes) to finance its operations, cash-flow problems can result. For example, some counties operate within a calendar fiscal year (January–December) but do not receive their property taxes until November or December. Therefore, the year is almost over before the property taxes are available to spend. Counties can either maintain an adequate fund balance to cover cash-flow requirements during the year or borrow money for this purpose (usually through the issuance of tax anticipation notes). The more conservative approach would be to accumulate adequate fund balance to cover cash flow problems and thereby avoid interest costs associated with borrowing money.

Some counties accumulate fund balances to cover contingencies not provided for in the budget that require expenditures. Contingency funds are used for emergencies such as flooding caused by excess rainfall, the explosion of a gas main on a county road, or the collapse of a county bridge. Some counties include separate contingency accounts in their budget; others use fund balance for this purpose.

Many counties across the United States maintain fund balances equal to the equivalent of one to three months of operations. For example, if a county's expenditure budget is $12 million, the policy might be to maintain a fund balance of $1 million (i.e., one-twelfth of $12 million). Only in extreme cases (i.e., in which cash-flow problems require larger fund balances) do county fund balances exceed three months of operations. Again, there is no "right answer" as to how much a county's fund balance should be.

Do Appropriations Lapse at the End of the Fiscal Year?

When a portion of a county's adopted budget remains unspent at the end of the year, what happens to that amount? Georgia law does not appear to address this issue specifically. Generally, governing authorities use one of three financial policies to address this question. Under the most common policy, any unspent appropriations lapse at the end of the fiscal year and are not carried forward to the subsequent year. Any outstanding encumbrances (e.g., purchase orders outstanding) at year's end must therefore be reappropriated in the subsequent year, usually through a budget amendment, thereby increasing the budget. The county commission must reappropriate the amount of encumbrances; however, it has detailed information about the encumbrances that must be carried forward because they have been outlined in the previous year's budget.

Another policy stipulates that if any part of an appropriation is encumbered, that portion is added (i.e., carried forward) to the subsequent year's budget automatically. When a county adopts this policy, the commission need not take any legal action regarding encumbered appropriations that are carried forward. Some county commissions adopt this financial policy because they see no need to formally approve a carryover of items budgeted in the previous year.

A third policy approach allows all unencumbered appropriations (i.e., any portion of an appropriation that has not been charged with expenditures) to be carried forward. This policy makes it possible for department directors to accumulate appropriations from year to year, but keeping track of the budget can be complicated. Few counties use this policy. Generally, it is recommended only for capital projects.

NOTES

1. Portions of this chapter are drawn from Ronald B. Hoskins, "Budgeting," in *Handbook for Georgia Mayors and Councilmembers*, 2nd ed., ed. J. Devereux Weeks (Athens: Carl Vinson Institute of Government, University of Georgia, 1984), and Arthur A. Mendonsa, *Simplified Financial Management in Local Government* (Athens: Institute of Government, Institute of Community and Area Development, and Georgia Center for Continuing Education, University of Georgia, 1969).
2. John V. Witherspoon, "Budgeting," in *Guide to County Organization and Management* (Washington, DC: National Association of Counties, 1968), 171.
3. Lon Sprecher, "Operating Budgets," in *Local Government Finance: Concepts and Practices*, ed. John E. Peterson and Dennis R. Strachota (Chicago: Government Finance Officers Association, 1991), 45.
4. For a more detailed discussion of local government budgeting, see Robert L. Bland and Irene S. Rubin, *Budgeting: A Guide for Local Governments* (Washington, DC: International City/County Management Association, 1997), and Roy T. Meyers, ed., *Handbook of Government Budgeting* (San Francisco: Jossey-Bass,

1998). With regard to recent improvements in local government budgeting and financial management, see Roland Calia, Salomon Guajardo, and Judd Metzgar, "Best Practices in Budgeting: Putting NACSLB Practices into Action," *Government Finance Review* 16 (April 2000): 9–17.

5. For a thorough and useful summary of state legal requirements related to local government budgeting, which is updated annually after each session of the Georgia General Assembly, see Paul Hardy, Betty J. Hudson, Myra Byrd, Richard W. Campbell, and Paul E. Glick, *Compliance Auditing in Georgia Counties and Municipalities: A Practical Guide to State Laws for Auditors and Local Government Officials* (Athens: Carl Vinson Institute of Government, University of Georgia, 2010), 141.

6. OFFICIAL CODE OF GEORGIA ANNOTATED (O.C.G.A.) tit. 36, ch. 81.

7. O.C.G.A. §36-81-3(e). Also see *Uniform Chart of Accounts for Local Governments in Georgia*, 2nd ed. (Atlanta: Georgia Department of Community Affairs, 2001). See the DCA's Web site (www.dca.ga.gov) for more information.

8. O.C.G.A. §§36-81-2, 36-81-3, 36-81-5.

9. O.C.G.A. §36-81-3(a).

10. O.C.G.A. §36-81-5(a).

11. O.C.G.A. §36-81-5(e).

12. O.C.G.A. §36-81-5(g).

13. O.C.G.A. §§36-81-3(b)(3), 36-81-6(a).

14. O.C.G.A. §36-81-6(a).

15. O.C.G.A. §36-81-3(d).

16. Guidelines for audit preparation are contained in *State and Local Government Committee, Audit and Accounting Guide: Audits of State and Local Governmental Units* (New York: American Institute of Certified Public Accountants, 2002).

17. Although subject to change, generally accepted accounting principles (GAAP) represent the consensus at any given time as to how the financial accounting process should operate and how financial statements should be prepared. The authoritative GAAP statement is found in *National Council on Governmental Accounting, Governmental Accounting and Financial Reporting Principles* (Chicago: Municipal Finance Officers Association, 1979). More recently, the Governmental Accounting Standards Board has been created, and the Government Finance Officers Association publishes a monthly newsletter on accounting, auditing, and financial reporting titled the *GAAFR Review.*

18. O.C.G.A. §36-81-7(a)(1), (2).

19. O.C.G.A. §36-81-7(d)(1).

20. O.C.G.A. §36-80-21.

21. O.C.G.A. §36-81-2(14).

22. O.C.G.A. §36-81-5(b).

23. O.C.G.A. §§36-81-2(14), 36-81-3(d)(2).

24. For an insightful discussion of the intricacies and complexities of the budgetary process generally, see Aaron Wildavsky, *Politics of the Budgetary Process*, 3rd ed. (Boston: Little, Brown and Co., 1979). For a discussion of the local government process, see Witherspoon, 45–64.

25. This distinction between legislative and management budgets comes from Robert N. Anthony and David W. Young, *Management Control in Nonprofit Organizations* (Homewood, IL: Richard D. Irwin, 1984), 357–59.

26. Witherspoon, 56.

27. Anthony and Young, 366.
28. Jack Rabin, W. Bartley Hildreth, and Gerald Miller, "Budgeting: Formulation and Execution," in *Public Budgeting Laboratory* (Athens: Carl Vinson Institute of Government, University of Georgia, 1996).
29. O.C.G.A. §36-81-5.
30. O.C.G.A. §36-81-5(f).
31. O.C.G.A. §36-81-5(h).
32. Robert D. Lee Jr. and Ronald W. Johnson, *Public Budgeting Systems*, 2nd ed. (Baltimore: University Park Press, 1977), 209.
33. Witherspoon, 61.
34. For two basic introductions to governmental accounting, see Leo Herbert, Larry N. Kellough, and Alan Walter Steiss, *Governmental Accounting and Control* (Monterey, CA: Brooks/Cole, 1984), and Paul E. Glick, *A Public Manager's Guide to Government Accounting and Financial Reporting* (Chicago: Government Finance Officers Association, 1990).
35. National Council on Governmental Accounting, 9.
36. These values are discussed in some detail in Allen Schick, "The Road to PPB: The Stages of Budgetary Reform," *Public Administration Review* 26 (December 1966): 243–58.
37. Beverly A. Cigler, "County Governance in the 1990s," *State and Local Government Review* 27 (Winter 1995): 55–70. On the role of executive leadership more generally, see National Commission of the State and Local Public Service, *Hard Truths/Tough Choices: An Agenda for State and Local Reform* (Albany: Nelson A. Rockefeller Institute of Government, State University of New York, 1993).
38. Witherspoon, 172.
39. Daniel E. O'Toole and Brian Stipak, "Budgeting and Productivity Revisited: The Local Government Picture," *Public Productivity Review* 12 (Fall 1988): 1–12.
40. Xiaohu Wang, "Performance Measurement in Budgeting: A Study of County Governments," *Public Budgeting and Finance* 20 (Fall 2000): 102–18. Also see Joni Leithe, *Implementing Performance Measurement in Government* (Chicago: Government Finance Officers Association, 1997), and David N. Ammons, ed., *Accountability for Performance: Measurement and Monitoring in Local Government* (Washington, DC: International City/County Management Association, 1995).
41. O.C.G.A. §36-81-3(b)(1).

20

Sabrina Wiley Cape, Richard W. Campbell,
Paul E. Glick, and Patti Lee

Capital Improvements Planning

A capital budget involves different criteria and a longer time frame than does an operating budget. As discussed in Chapter 19, the annual operating budget describes costs incurred in the normal operations of county departments responsible for delivering services that benefit the citizenry in the current fiscal year, and these operating costs are financed out of current-year revenues. Capital costs, on the other hand, usually are incurred in the acquisition of equipment and in the construction of facilities and infrastructure that may benefit residents of the county well into the future. Since capital purchases involve long-term benefits, they are classified as capital improvements and may be funded through the issuance of bonds, proceeds of the special purpose local option sales tax (SPLOST), or other forms of borrowing (see Chapter 21). Capital budget decisions, then, are made separately and usually are handled in a multiyear capital improvements plan (CIP).

The CIP outlines a recommended schedule of public improvements to be accomplished over a multiyear period, usually four to six years. In the same manner as the annual operating budgetary process, the CIP is developed with a calendar, instructions and guidelines, and standardized forms. Each department submits a capital projects request, with justification and cost estimates. The governing authority assesses the requests based upon a ranking of projects submitted by the departments and, when the assessment is complete, acts on the proposed capital improvements plan.[1]

While capital budgets and CIPs are important elements of sound financial management, historically they were not widely used in Georgia counties. However, a recent survey of county officials conducted by the Georgia Department of Community Affairs (DCA) revealed that 44.7 percent of the counties surveyed prepared a capital budget in 2008, a 17 percent increase from the 27.7 percent of counties using capital budgets in 2000.[2] This finding would seem to indicate that many Georgia county officials have come to recognize the capital budget and CIP as essential policy tools for communicating the county's long-term infrastructure needs to the public.

The purpose of this chapter is to emphasize the importance of long-range capital planning to the financial future of Georgia counties, to outline the steps involved in the process of developing a capital budget and CIP, and to review financial policy issues that county commissioners need to address as they plan for the future of their county's investment in capital assets.

THE CAPITAL IMPROVEMENTS PLAN

A discussion of capital budgeting should begin by first distinguishing between the terms "capital improvements plan" and "capital budget." Typically, the CIP is a plan identifying needed capital expenditures projected for some period of time into the future. The capital budget is the first year (i.e., the most current year) of the CIP and normally is incorporated into the annual operating budget. It provides resources for specific facilities, improvements, and equipment. The relationship of the CIP and the capital budget is important. The CIP identifies the capital needs, and the capital budget indicates which capital needs will be completed in the current year's operating budget.

A CIP indicates which capital assets to purchase, construct, renovate, or repair, presented in order of priorities; the estimated cost of the capital assets; the year in which the required capital expenditures should occur; and the method that will be used to finance the cost of the capital assets. Usually a CIP will improve a county's capital asset purchase and replacement program. Benefits from developing a CIP include the following:

- *Providing for orderly comprehensive replacement of capital facilities and equipment.* The lack of a coordinated process for considering and approving capital projects can result in undisciplined, uncoordinated approval of capital projects. Such ad hoc procedures inevitably waste public resources, fail to consider available information, and sometimes result in poor project timing. Optimal results require an orderly process that considers all projects at the same time and produces a planning document that considers available financing sources and reasonable schedules for project completion.

- *Ensuring continuity*. Changes in county commissions can affect continuity. A capital improvements plan, however, will allow county personnel to continue to purchase, replace, and/or construct capital assets in an orderly manner.

- *Assisting with long-range fiscal planning*. Counties that do not engage in long-term financial planning may be unaware of how county capital needs will accumulate over future years. Consequently, they may defer needed maintenance on buildings and equipment and delay capital replacement projects in order to balance the current year's operating budget. The CIP process can help identify financial imbalances and begin the steps necessary to assure sound, long-term operations and capital financing strategies.

- *Planning and timing projects adequately*. Using a CIP can help governing authorities avoid installing capital facilities only to discover later that the facilities need to be changed or replaced. Good planning can ensure that efforts are coordinated and costly duplications avoided.

- *Enhancing the county's bond rating*. Investors and bond-rating agencies stress the value of a CIP for a county seeking to borrow funds. The absence of rational, long-term planning can prevent a county from receiving a favorable credit rating from the rating agency. A poor credit rating can result in a higher interest rate on bond issues sold by counties that do not document and disclose their long-term capital financing needs and plans.

- *Providing the county a public relations tool*. Most capital programming processes offer the public a chance to raise questions and offer opinions. Typically, this opportunity is received favorably by civic groups as an important link between county government and its constituents and as representing good business practices and management. The press also appreciates receiving background information on capital projects presented clearly in an organized document. Many county commissioners find that by providing opportunities for public input early in the capital planning process they can effectively defuse volatile opposition to specific projects later on. For example, with regard to a SPLOST referendum, having a CIP in place can help build public support and confidence in the proposed capital projects.

What has prevented more counties in Georgia from using the mechanism of capital budgets and CIPs in the past? First of all, capital items are expensive. It is not uncommon to defer certain capital costs to subsequent years in order to balance the operating budget. Because they are central players in the annual operating budget process, county commissioners sometimes find it hard to see beyond the end of the current operating budget year.

Politics may also play a role. The deferment of major capital costs to subsequent years (i.e., the decision *not* to invest in capital), while possibly a good political decision, may be a bad financial decision (i.e., the maintenance costs incurred on an asset not replaced can become excessive). It is important, then, that county commissioners recognize the significance of a capital improvements plan. The adoption of a CIP provides the opportunity for the orderly replacement of capital assets within the financial capacity of the county.

THE CIP PROCESS

The CIP process is as important as the plan itself. In other words, many observers of local government operations believe that the capital improvements plan is as much process as it is product. As with any process, there are clearly definable steps necessary for its completion. Some of the more important steps in a typical CIP process are listed and discussed here.

Step 1. Prepare a CIP Calendar

The CIP calendar is a very useful document for developing and monitoring the CIP process. Like the operating budget calendar, a CIP calendar is simply a chronological list of the tasks that need to be completed in the CIP process. The calendar may include the county personnel responsible for completing those tasks. By regularly consulting it, whoever is responsible for coordinating the capital improvements plan can determine at any point in the CIP process whether or not it is on schedule.

Step 2. Assign Staff to Coordinate the CIP

Practice and experience have shown that a centralized organization for staffing the CIP process works best. A county department or, in the case of smaller counties, a single individual (such as the county clerk or county administrator/manager) should be responsible for coordinating the entire CIP preparation process. This assignment need not include any decision-making or resource-allocating responsibilities; rather, it entails completing technical and procedural tasks. The staff of the regional commission can also be a resource in this process.

Step 3. Establish CIP Policies

The primary role of county commissioners in the CIP process is to articulate the policies that guide the process. Following are some of the CIP policy issues that county commissioners will address: What are capital projects? What is the length of the CIP? What criteria are used to prioritize capital projects? How much of the CIP is funded each year in the operating budget? For accounting purposes, how many capital project funds will be maintained?

Defining Capital Projects. Capital expenditures are different from operating expenditures primarily because of the costs and estimated useful lives associated with capital assets. Capital assets generally are more costly than current assets, and county commissioners often consider them "big ticket" items. In order for counties to classify an item as capital, its cost should be large enough to justify special attention. Generally, this cost amount is classified as a capital asset threshold. The level of the threshold depends primarily on the size of the county. In larger counties, a CIP may not include a purchase unless it costs $30,000 or more. In a large county, items costing less than the threshold may be purchased from the operating budget without causing the operating budget much stress. However, in some smaller counties, an item costing $5,000 warrants special attention and may be capital in nature. Finally, for an asset to be considered capital, it should have an extended useful life, usually at least two years. With the issuance of the Governmental Accounting Standards Board Statement 34 (commonly referred to as GASB Statement 34), many counties, along with their independent auditor, evaluated whether it would be beneficial to increase their existing dollar thresholds of what constitutes a capital asset and a capital project.

Length of the CIP. Although a CIP legitimately may encompass any number of years, the most commonly used time period is 5 years, the current year (that portion incorporated into the operating budget) plus 4 years projected into the future. Time and experience indicate that these are the most realistic and manageable periods to use. A 5-year period projected into the future provides a realistic opportunity to adequately plan and prepare for most capital needs as they arise. A period of time much longer than that has proven to be less useful as a planning tool. Cost estimates for projects to be funded 20 years in the future tend to be less accurate and therefore less useful than 5-year estimates. However, for environmental improvements, such as water and sewer systems, a CIP of 20 years may be appropriate. Anything less than 5 years generally is considered too short a time in which to recognize the need for, much less to plan and build, a major capital facility.

Although set up on a multiyear basis, a CIP should be reviewed annually. An annual review of the CIP guarantees that a regular reassessment of county capital needs will be accomplished. Additions to and deletions from the CIP may be made during this formal review process to ensure that the CIP best reflects the county's current capital needs. Even if no changes in the CIP are made, an annual review confirms that those projects in the CIP are still legitimate capital needs of the county. Each department director and constitutional officer should participate actively in the annual review process.

Establishing Criteria for Prioritizing Capital Projects. Ranking requested capital projects in order of priority is perhaps the most important and one of the more difficult tasks involved in the completion of the CIP. After the department directors and constitutional officers indicate their proposed capital items by cost and fiscal year, the total cost of all capital needs requested is determined and compared with the resources available. Unfortunately, most of the time, adequate funding is not available for all requested projects. Therefore, these capital items must be weighed and ranked to determine which will receive funding in the current year and which will be deferred to subsequent years.

Decision makers will be faced with many "apples versus oranges" kinds of decisions. For example, should the county purchase a computer for the tax assessor's office, or should the county resurface two miles of paved roads? Is it better to build a garage used to repair public works vehicles or replace a heating system in the county courthouse? At issue, then, will be which project has the highest priority. The choice is subjective; there is no objective formula available. However, in order to address these kinds of choices, a county commission needs to adopt a policy that will incorporate evaluation criteria in the priority-setting process.

Evaluation criteria can focus the county commission's judgment in a consistent, rational way. They are not intended to replace basic decision making but to provide a rational basis for deciding which projects in the CIP to fund. Ideally, the evaluation criteria policy should be established by the county commission and then be refined by the county administration before adoption. The criteria used by each county will vary, based upon each county's needs and priorities.

Examples of evaluation criteria in the CIP prioritization process could include any or all of the following:

- Mandatory project—The project will fulfill a judge's order that a county build a new facility.

- Maintenance project—The project is necessary to preserve an asset such as the county courthouse roof.

- Project improves efficiency—A new computer system could substantially reduce the amount of time spent on tax billing.

- Project provides a new service—A newly established senior citizen program requires building renovations to house it.

- Policy area project—Purchasing two passenger vans will enable the county to fulfill its policy of transporting senior citizens to obtain medical treatment.

- Extent of usage—A new walking trail that will be used by a great percentage of the county's residents could warrant higher priority than projects affecting fewer people.

- Project's expected useful life—Certain long-lasting equipment could receive a higher priority rating than shorter-lived equipment.

- Effect of project on operation and maintenance costs—A new lighting system could provide better lighting in the county courthouse at reduced electrical costs.

- Availability of state/federal grants—Some equipment could be grant funded.

- Elimination of hazards—Adding a stoplight to a county road will allow for better traffic control and reduce traffic accidents.

- Prior commitments—Only one-third of a construction contract that the county signed has been completed.

Often, numerical values are added to criteria to provide an objective evaluation. However, this priority-setting process should be considered a "first cut" with additional analysis required.

Allocating Operating Budget Resources for Capital Items. Some counties have adopted policies that indicate what percentage of the operating budget they try to allocate for capital items. The allocation does not include those resources necessary to build additional buildings or major additions or renovations to buildings, all of which normally are financed from either locally approved general obligation bonds, revenue bonds (i.e., for enterprise fund projects), or SPLOST.

To determine an applicable amount of the operating budget to allocate to capital, county commissioners should review the percentage of general fund expenditures incurred in previous years (e.g., for the last five years). As past experience is reviewed, care must be taken to ensure that unusual capital expenditures (such as large equipment purchases resulting from opening a new building) have not occurred, thereby distorting the percentages. This analysis, along with projected capital needs, should provide a basis for establishing a CIP funding policy. There is no "right answer" to how much of the operating budget should be allocated to capital because circumstances can differ in each county.

In addition to general fund resources, other types of funding are available for capital projects. Alternative funding sources include bonds, grants, SPLOST, special assessments, and leases.

Step 4. Develop Data-Gathering Forms

The perfect form to be used to gather CIP data does not exist. The purpose of CIP forms is to collect the information necessary to encourage and facilitate systematic thought and rational decision making in the CIP process. Most counties find that, in developing their capital planning efforts, it helps to keep the initial forms used during the first two or three years simple. If additional information is required, supplemental forms and ultimately revisions in subsequent years' capital documents can be added. The following elements consistently appear in most CIP forms: project name, description, and location; submitting department or office; estimated project costs, with sufficient data to support the estimate (e.g., square feet); estimated cost and financing presented by year; financing sources; and a site location map, as applicable.

Step 5. Solicit Project Requests and Proposals

Instructions from the county commission chair and/or administrator or manager that encourage realistic capital spending and prudent investment of the county's resources generally will result in responsible requests for funding. Soliciting requests for project proposals to include in the CIP might begin with a staff meeting. Usually the personnel responsible for the operating budget are also responsible for the CIP. These persons could include department directors, supervisors, and constitutional officers. During this meeting, personnel responsible for the CIP distribute the CIP forms and explain the process and timetable. Everyone receives instructions at the same time, and questions and concerns can be covered with everyone involved in the CIP process. Topics normally addressed at these meetings include general financial and long-term outlook, policies that affect operations and capital planning, current work in progress, current year's timetable, problems encountered in the previous year and how they will be addressed, explanation of forms and instructions, description of a properly completed request packet, and where to go for help.

Step 6. Evaluate Requested Projects

Who should evaluate the requested projects is an important question. In smaller counties, county commissioners might participate in this process. In other counties, a committee could be formed to review the requested projects as they relate to the established criteria. Another option is for each committee member to evaluate capital requests against one specific criterion. As mentioned earlier, the criteria usually are assigned numeric values that allow for an objective rating, and this rating process would be a first cut with necessary additional reviews.

Step 7. Develop Funding Plan

After the higher priority projects have been determined, the CIP coordinating unit described in Step 2 should evaluate the county's ability to finance requested projects. As already discussed, the amount of the operating budget allocated to capital outlay will affect the amount of capital projects that can be completed. Obviously, larger construction and renovation projects need to be funded from sources other than the operating budget.

The CIP will only be as effective as the plan for financing the proposed projects. The county's ability to finance the CIP generally depends on the level of recurring future operating expenditures, the current level of bonded indebtedness, and the county's legal debt limit. Many projects proposed in the CIP will have an ongoing impact on the county's operating budget. For example, a new facility would result in increased costs for supplies, maintenance, utilities, and personal services. Calculating the operating costs associated with capital projects is a critical step in the CIP process. Analysis of the debt structure of a county is one of the most important parts of the financial analysis of the CIP process. When determining the most appropriate method for funding a capital project, factors to consider include

- Is the financing option legally available?
- Is the financing option politically acceptable?
- Is the financing option administratively feasible?

The two major funding sources are general obligation bonds and SPLOST proceeds. In 2008, DCA reported that almost all of the state's counties (155) were using SPLOST to fund capital projects.[3] Other funding alternatives, which are quite limited, include the use of a capital lease and federal grants for capital outlay. Figure 20-1 shows a sample page from a CIP, which emphasizes cost estimation and the identification of funding alternatives.

Step 8. Provide for Public Input

Opportunities for public input can be provided at various stages of the capital programming process. At some point, the entire CIP, including its timing, could be subjected to public review. In preparing the CIP, county staff members and the county commissioners should be conscious of the need to present the CIP to the public. The following opportunities for public review and input might be considered:

- Accept public input at the outset of the process. Ask department heads, supervisors, and constitutional officers to attend a public hearing before completing their forms so that ideas from the public are incorporated into their submissions.

- Provide for public review of the proposals as submitted to the county commissioners by the county administrator/manager or other responsible CIP official. Other methods such as public hearings, government television channels, and civic group presentations could be used to solicit public input.

- Schedule public review after consideration by the county commissioners and before final adoption.

Step 9. Provide for Adoption by County Commissioners

After the capital document is presented to the county commissioners and reviewed in public, the procedures should provide for a method of adoption. Characteristically, the CIP is adopted as a planning instrument, and the capital budget is adopted separately as a specific authorization in the operating budget. Since 1998, local governments are required to adopt and operate under a project-length balanced budget for each capital projects fund in use by the government.[4]

Depending on how the CIP is integrated into the operating budget, the capital budget usually constitutes approval to proceed with procurement and other administrative actions necessary to implement the first year of the capital program.[5]

Figure 20-1. *CIP Example*

GWINNETT COUNTY, GEORGIA
CAPITAL IMPROVEMENT PROGRAM (modified)

PROJECT: Gwinnett Environmental and Heritage Center – F-0498

DEPARTMENT: Community Services

DESCRIPTION: The Environmental and Heritage Center will incorporate a facility for environmental education, with hands-on exhibits, teaching labs, and classrooms. The site will also provide passive recreational activities such as trails. Phase I completion includes a unique playground adjacent to the building.

JUSTIFICATION: The facility is needed to maximize classroom and family educational efforts on water resources and management, our natural environment, such as animal and plant life, and to provide a trail system that exposes visitors to historical and natural features such as wetlands.

O & M IMPACT: O & M is estimated to be $750,000–$1,000,000 per year. Facility will require full-time and part-time staffing as well as contractual services.

Financing Method	Prior Years	2008	2009	2010	2011	2012	2013	Totals
SPLOST	21,779	1,000						22,779
IR–Dividend[1]	1,795							1,795
Trans In-Stormwater	25	25	25	25	25	25	25	175
Contrib–Private Source	122							122
Other-Misc.	31							31
Totals	23,752	1,025	25	25	25	25	25	24,902
Project Cost								
Construction	12,737							12,737
Land	3,817	1,000						4,817
Equipment/Furnishings	3,816	25	25	25	25	25	25	3,966
Professional Services	3,380							3,380
50,000,000[2]	1							1
Totals	23,751	1,025	25	25	25	25	25	24,901

[1] Interest revenue/dividend.
[2] Represents spending from prior year.

Source: Randy Colvin, Gwinnett County, Financial Services.
Note: Numbers are in thousands of dollars.

NOTES

1. For a detailed discussion of the selection and evaluation of capital projects, see J. Richard Aronson and Eli Schwartz, "Capital Budgeting," in *Management Policies in Local Government Finance*, ed. J. Richard Aronson and Eli Schwartz (Washington, DC: International City/County Management Association, 1987), 400–421.

2. Georgia Department of Community Affairs, *2009 Government Management Indicators Survey* (Atlanta: DCA, 2009).

3. Ibid.

4. Official Code of Georgia Annotated (O.C.G.A.) §36-81-3(b)(2). For a brief summary of this provision, see Paul T. Hardy, Betty J. Hudson, Myra Byrd, Richard W. Campbell, and Paul E. Glick, *Compliance Auditing in Georgia Counties and Municipalities: A Practical Guide to State Laws for Auditors and Local Government Officials* (Athens: Carl Vinson Institute of Government, University of Georgia, 2010), 79–80.

5. For a more detailed description of capital budgeting, see "Planning and Budgeting for Capital Improvements," in *Budgeting: A Guide for Local Governments*, ed. Robert L. Bland and Irene S. Rubin (Washington DC: International City/County Management Association, 1997), 167–95.

21

James P. Monacell, Paul T. Hardy,
Paula S. Sanford, and Wes Clarke

County Indebtedness

Unlike individuals and businesses, counties have special restrictions on borrowing money. In general, counties may only borrow money when it can be paid back within the calendar year, unless they receive voter approval. However, there are exceptions. This chapter will discuss how counties borrow in both the short term and the long term.

ROLE OF DEBT

Counties sometimes borrow in order to cover temporary shortfalls in revenues over expenses but usually to fund capital improvements. Long-lived capital improvements are financed with long-term indebtedness for several reasons. Spreading the costs of debt service over the useful life of facilities ensures that the taxpayers or ratepayers who receive the benefit of the facilities over that term bear the corresponding expense. Raising funds immediately for needed facilities would impose a one-time burden only on current citizens. Building reserves over a period of time in order to allow facilities to be paid for without debt would, again, burden citizens who do not receive the benefit of the facilities and in fact would defer the availability and use of facilities for the citizens who would be paying for them.

Because debt imposes a long-term burden on future commissions, taxpayers, and ratepayers, indebtedness should not be incurred lightly. Commissioners should make indebtedness decisions only after staff and experts have made recommendations regarding the proper form and structuring of such indebtedness, comprehensively taking into consideration the anticipated revenues and future needs for capital and operating expenditures. A debt obligation must be considered not individually but in terms of the aggregate debt service of all obligations over time.

TEMPORARY LOANS

The Georgia Constitution authorizes counties to incur temporary loans, which are repayable on or before December 31 of the year in which the loans were made. Such loans are commonly known as tax anticipation notes, or TANs.[1] Most ad valorem taxes are received by the county only once per year, yet the county must pay its expenses throughout the year. TANs allow a county to even out its revenues during the course of a year.

Although they ordinarily are used to fund temporary deficiencies in operating expenditures, TANs are sometimes used to fund a capital project when permanent funding of some kind is expected before the end of the calendar year.[2] Temporary borrowing in anticipation of permanent funding of a capital project may not be prudent if contingencies could arise that might derail the permanent funding.

TANs for either operating expenses or capital expenditures may be incurred when

1. the aggregate outstanding amount of all such temporary loans does not exceed 75 percent of the county's total gross income from taxes of all types collected in the preceding calendar year,

2. such loans would mature on or before December 31 of the calendar year in which they are incurred,

3. no similar loan remains unpaid from a previous calendar year, or

4. the aggregate amount of such loans outstanding does not exceed the total anticipated revenues of the county for the current calendar year.[3]

TYPES OF LONG-TERM INDEBTEDNESS

Reflecting the seriousness of long-term indebtedness, such borrowing by counties is restricted and must be obtained in strict conformity with provisions of Georgia law governing its issuance. A county may not simply go to a bank and "get a loan."

The Georgia Constitution requires that the county not incur any new debt without receiving approval by a majority of the voters.[4] The form of long-term indebtedness incurred by counties pursuant to the referendum procedure is known as general obligation debt. Upon issuing general obligation debt, a county legally commits all of its available resources and taxing power to its repayment.

There are, however, limited exceptions to the referendum requirement such as the issuance of revenue debt, the incurrence of lease-purchase obligations and certificates of participation, and authority and agency borrowings (described later in this chapter). However, any borrowing on behalf of the county must meet the requirements applicable to indebtedness in one of the allowable categories.

The most common form of long-term debt is a bond. A bond is a single security, typically with a face value of $5,000, while a bond issue represents the selling of multiple bonds at one time. The face value of a bond means that the government agrees to pay the bond holder that amount of money when the bond matures. Furthermore, governments typically agree to pay an explicit interest rate on the bond, which occurs semiannually.[5] The county's finance director will work with a financial advisor who specializes in bonds to establish an explicit interest rate that they predict will closely match the current market interest rate when the bonds are finally sold.

When developing a bond issue, a county must prepare several important documents: the official statement, bond resolution, bond indenture, and notice of sale if the bond will be sold through competitive bidding. These documents provide information to investors about the bond issue so that they can evaluate the bond's risk and interest income potential as well as authorize the issuance of the bond. The documents include information such as the bond issue's or government's credit rating (if there is one), the amount of bonds to be issued, and their maturity date and explicit interest rate.[6]

GENERAL OBLIGATIONS

General obligations are debts (usually, but not necessarily, in the form of bonds) made by a county representing its full faith and credit and backed by its ad valorem taxing power. A general obligation can be issued for any purpose for which ad valorem taxes may be levied.[7] However, the total of outstanding long-term general obligation debt incurred by a county may not exceed 10 percent of the assessed value of all taxable property within the county.[8] Every general obligation debt must have a term not in excess of 30 years. Before incurring the debt, the board of commissioners must provide for the assessment and collection of an annual ad valorem tax sufficient to pay into a sinking fund an amount equal to the principal and interest.[9]

As previously mentioned, a new general obligation for financing must be authorized by a referendum election. In order to meet this requirement, the county commission must adopt a resolution calling for a special election to be conducted on one of the dates prescribed by statute for such elections. The call for election must be published for not less than 30 days prior to the election in the official county newspaper and include a statement of the question of whether debt shall be incurred by the county in a particular amount and for a particular purpose, the amount of principal to be paid each year, and the interest rate or maximum interest rate to be applicable.[10] If debt is to be authorized for several purposes, separate ballot questions must be voted upon, unless the several purposes constitute one project.[11]

General obligation debt can be "refunded" (refinanced) without the necessity of an additional voter referendum. A refunding generally is undertaken in order to take advantage of lower interest rates. However, if the amounts of debt service payable will be increased through refinancing, a referendum is required.[12]

SPLOST DEBT

A special form of general obligation debt may be authorized when a county 1 percent special purpose local option sales tax (SPLOST) referendum question includes the following optional language: "If the imposition of the tax is approved by the voters, such vote shall also constitute approval of the issuance of general obligation debt of the county for the above purpose [specified for the use of the SPLOST]."[13] When a successful SPLOST referendum includes the debt language on the ballot, SPLOST general obligation debt can be issued without further voter approval. Such SPLOST debt is repayable first from the SPLOST receipts, although it is also backed by an assessment of ad valorem taxes, which would have to actually be collected to the extent that SPLOST receipts are not sufficient to repay the debt.[14] The county commission must determine that the SPLOST receipts alone are expected to be sufficient to pay the debt service,[15] and the terms of the SPLOST debt cannot extend beyond the term of the current SPLOST. Proceeds derived from SPLOST debt must be used to pay for projects that are authorized through the SPLOST ballot for the expenditure of SPLOST monies. The notice published for the SPLOST election must set out the specifics for any debt proposed to be issued, including the maximum principal and interest to be due in each year.[16]

The ballot language authorizing the incurrence of debt to fund SPLOST projects is sometimes not included in a SPLOST referendum question. Failure to include the debt language may reflect a concern on the part of county officials that voters who would support the imposition of a SPLOST may not support debt. However, since any such debt actually incurred must be repaid from the anticipated SPLOST receipts, the SPLOST imposes no new obligation on the taxpayer. SPLOST debt frequently can be obtained on very favorable terms due to the dual repayment sources: the SPLOST itself and the full faith and credit obligation of the county to pay any deficiency in the funding of debt service through SPLOST receipts. SPLOST debt that is authorized need not be issued, but if the commission decides to issue it, proceeds of the issuance will allow the county to begin SPLOST projects quickly after the SPLOST is approved by the voters and will result in the completion of the promised facilities sooner. Without such borrowing, work on the SPLOST-authorized facilities can begin only after sufficient funding for the project has been collected through the tax or after the project is funded by lease-purchase or certificate of participation arrangements discussed later in this chapter.[17]

A referendum for the imposition or reimposition of a SPLOST can authorize not only the incurrence of SPLOST general obligation debt but also the expenditure of SPLOST tax receipts to pay the debt service on previously incurred general obligation debt. The effect of implementing such a plan is to move the burden of payment of debt service of previously incurred general obligation debt from property tax millage to SPLOST collections.

COUNTY REVENUE DEBT

Counties have the ability to issue revenue debt for a variety of potentially revenue-producing undertakings such as transportation facilities, water and sewer systems, solid waste operations, libraries, sports facilities, exhibition facilities, parking, and jails.[18] Revenue debt to be issued for projects other than electric generating and distribution systems does not require a voter referendum.[19] Revenue debt cannot be issued for a term in excess of 40 years.[20]

The revenues used to pay revenue debt must be derived from an enterprise fund receiving the fees, charges, or other amounts resulting from the operation of one or more such undertakings described in the Revenue Bond Law. Revenue debt represents no call on the full faith and credit and taxing power of the county but must be repayable solely from revenues of undertakings for which such debt can be issued and that are pledged for that purpose.[21] Consequently, revenue debt can only be used when the financial undertakings will be self-sustaining from the revenues pledged. However, the Revenue Bond Law allows a number of like or unlike undertakings to be combined, and by such method, counties may use revenues from an established profitable undertaking to support a new or unprofitable undertaking.[22]

When revenue bonds have been authorized and validated through the required superior court proceedings but have not yet been issued, the Revenue Bond Law authorizes counties to borrow through "interim receipts," commonly known as bond anticipation notes. Bond anticipation notes are used to obtain an advance of funds for the acquisition or construction of an undertaking and are payable from the proceeds of the bonds when issued. A bond anticipation note may be useful, for example, when a facility must be completed prior to obtaining permanent financing on favorable terms through the issuance of revenue bonds.[23]

FINANCING THROUGH AN AUTHORITY

A county may have the services of a subordinate governmental authority with power to issue revenue debt on the county's behalf. The powers of particular authorities are sometimes unique and are frequently limited. Legal counsel will need to determine whether an authority may finance any particular purpose for the county and under what circumstances. For example, there are numerous jurisdiction-specific authorities created by constitutional amendments prior to 1983 that may have continuing power to assist with county financings.[24] On the other hand, development authorities are available in every county. Pursuant to the Development Authorities Law, a development authority may finance a wide range of projects affecting trade, commerce, and industry so long as the projects are not operated by a county.[25] When legally permissible, the county and an appropriate authority can enter into an intergovernmental contract and engage in an indirect county-backed form of financing, sometimes known as a contract revenue bond, without a voter referendum, even if the facilities financed would not pay for themselves when the revenues derived from the county are not considered.

This type of contract revenue bond may be particularly useful in situations in which a facility or utility system to be financed is not expected, at least initially, to produce revenue sufficient to repay the debt. A county and an authority would enter into an intergovernmental contract for the provision of services for the use of the facility. The contract may be for a term of up to 50 years, and both the county and the authority must have express power under law to undertake the type of facility or provide the type of service specified in the contract.[26] If such a contract may be entered into, the authority may be empowered by its governing legislation to issue its revenue debt to finance the capital assets the county requires and to pledge the county's obligations under the intergovernmental contract as partial or full support for the indebtedness. Such a contract constitutes the full faith and credit obligation of the county.[27]

REDEVELOPMENT PROJECT FINANCING

Counties have powers to undertake redevelopment projects under the Urban Redevelopment Law.[28] Counties that have authorized the use of the Redevelopment Powers Law by local law and referendum have additional powers including the power to create tax allocation districts (TADs).[29] Any project that is the subject of a proper redevelopment plan in a designated redevelopment area pursuant to provisions of either the Urban Redevelopment Law or the Redevelopment Powers Law may be undertaken and financed by its revenue debt.[30] Projects may include facilities of the county in appropriate circumstances.

Counties themselves may issue revenue bonds for projects approved under these redevelopment laws or, except in the case of tax allocation bonds, may authorize redevelopment agencies to issue such bonds.[31] Because such agencies are distinct political bodies, they may enter into intergovernmental contracts with the county. This affords the opportunity to use the contract revenue bond technique discussed earlier in this chapter.[32] An urban redevelopment agency may be activated for any county pursuant to the provisions of the Urban Redevelopment Law or the Redevelopment Powers Law, when applicable. A redevelopment agency has the powers authorized for urban redevelopment agencies plus the additional powers under the Redevelopment Powers Law.[33]

Counties may issue tax allocation bonds repayable from increments of ad valorem taxes above a baseline value established in a tax allocation district.[34] This power is available only in counties that have adopted the Redevelopment Powers Law by virtue of a local act of the General Assembly and a voter referendum approving the local law. Tax allocation bonds are typically used to finance public infrastructure undertaken to spur private development.

SPECIAL DISTRICT DEBT

A county commission can establish districts within the county and issue general obligation bonds or revenue debt payable from the ad valorem taxes or revenues generated within that district alone.[35] A general obligation bond to be issued for such a district requires a voter referendum of the voters in the district. Revenue bonds issued for such a district would be payable by the designated revenues generated within the district. The district-debt technique may be useful if only a portion of the county will benefit from the financed facilities (for example, when a water system serves only a portion of the county).

LEASE-PURCHASE FINANCING

Counties are empowered to enter into multiyear lease, purchase, and lease-purchase contracts for property to be acquired.[36] There are two principal conditions imposed upon such multiyear contracts. First, the contract must state the total obligation due in each calendar year. Second, although the contract can provide for automatic renewal unless the county takes some positive action, the obligation of the county to make payments must terminate absolutely and without further obligation at the close of each calendar year.[37] Typical contracts provide that if the contract is not renewed, the county will forfeit the property financed and may be liable for the stated obligations for the last year for which the contract was renewed.

A lease-purchase or installment sale contract may be used as financing. In such a case, the contract will allocate a portion of the county's payments to principal and a portion to interest. If the payments are made in full, the contract should provide that the county will own the asset when all of the county's payments are completed. A vendor or third party usually acquires the property and makes the property available to the county in return for periodic payments corresponding to principal and interest. The principal amount of the contract will be the acquisition and/or construction costs of the property, and interest will be determined by agreement with the party providing the financing based on market conditions. The term of the contract will be set by the parties, with consideration given to the useful life of the property financed and the sources of repayment.[38]

A county must make an annual appropriation in the county budget for payments expected to be due with respect to the contract during each fiscal year. Should the county fail to make an appropriation or should it take affirmative action under the terms of the contract not to renew at the end of the calendar year (a "non-appropriation"), the property financed may be forfeited to the party providing the financing.[39] Failure of the county to complete the contract could not only result in it losing the property but also prevent the county from obtaining similar credit in the future. Because of the risk of non-appropriation, lenders normally provide lease-purchase financing only for facilities that they regard as essential to county operations.

Lease-purchase financing must be for the full cost or value of the property subject to the contract. A county cannot have "equity" in the property at the outset of the contract. Georgia law prohibits a county from giving away or forfeiting county property; if the county had equity in the property at the outset of a lease-purchase contract and did not renew the contract after the first year, such a forfeiture would occur.[40] The county may improperly create such equity, for example, if it pays for and does not finance a portion of the cost of the property financed or if the county contributes the real property that it already owns in a lease-purchase to finance improvements to that real property. Legal counsel may be able to assist in structuring around these equity issues by narrowing the scope of the property made part of the lease-purchase or by reallocating borrowed funds to a different project.

There are several other limitations on lease-purchase financing. Without a court order, property cannot be financed if it has been the subject of a failed referendum within the last four years.[41] For example, if the voters did not approve a SPLOST to build a new jail, the county may not use lease-purchase financing to build a jail for four years unless a court orders the county to build a new jail.

Another limitation to lease-purchase financing is that the total principal amount of lease-purchase financing, when added to outstanding general obligation debt, cannot exceed 10 percent of the assessed valuation of all taxable property in the county.[42] Additional limitations apply for real estate financing. A public hearing must be held prior to entering into a real estate lease-purchase contract.[43] The average annual payments of real estate lease-purchase financings cannot exceed 7½ percent of the governmental fund revenues of the county for the calendar year preceding the year of the closing (plus any SPLOST receipts dedicated to such purpose).[44] Further, unless that real property was approved as a project to be funded in the county's last SPLOST referendum, such real property may not be the subject of lease-purchase financing if it would push the total principal amount of such financings over $25,000,000.[45]

CERTIFICATES OF PARTICIPATION

Certificates of participation (COPs) are a variety of lease-purchase contract and are subject to all of the same rules. Typically, in order to accomplish a COP transaction, a trustee issues securities that represent percentage interests in the right to receive payments from the county under the lease-purchase contract. COPs typically are sold through investment bankers in the bond market, and similar documentation to that applicable to a bond issue is used. Like many bond issues, COPs may be insured, and the county may be required to take on continuing information disclosure obligations.

BOND VALIDATION

General obligation bonds, SPLOST bonds, county revenue bonds, and tax allocation bonds must be validated through a superior court proceeding prior to their issuance.[46] Validation procedures establish that the bonds and their security are valid and incontestable. Tax anticipation notes, lease-purchases, certificates of participation, and redevelopment agency revenue bonds are not subject to validation.

TAX-EXEMPT INDEBTEDNESS

Counties frequently can incur their indebtedness on a "tax-exempt basis." This means that the lender or bondholder will not pay federal or Georgia income taxes on interest paid by the county and as a result, will accept a lower interest rate.

This tax exemption on interest paid by counties is not automatic or always available but depends upon the compliance by the county with various requirements of the Internal Revenue Code, including the nature and use of the assets financed, among other requirements.[47] Expert bond counsel is typically engaged for the county to consult regarding the qualification of tax exemption and to issue legal opinions upon which both the county and the investor can rely.

CREDIT QUALITY

Much like an individual's credit score, a county's credit quality represents the perceived ability of the county to repay its debt on time and in full. Therefore, the better the perceived credit quality, the lower the interest rates the investors will require in order to lend money (e.g., purchase bonds). For general obligation bonds, the credit quality is based on the county itself whereas the credit quality for revenue bonds is based on the project's revenue-raising potential.

Bond ratings are an industry standard method for assessing the credit quality of a county or project and are needed in order to attract nonlocal or institutional investors.[48] Credit rating companies use several factors in determining a credit rating, the most important of which are the economic situation of the issuer, current debt, financial administration and soundness of the county, and the general government situation, which includes the adequacy of the government's power to raise revenue, intergovernmental relations, and provision of services.[49] Not all counties may want to obtain a credit rating for three reasons: (1) the government may anticipate receiving a poor rating; (2) the issue may be marketed locally, so investors will already be familiar with the quality of the issue; and (3) the amount of debt to be issued may be so small that the cost and effort expended to obtain a rating would not be worth the interest savings gained from having one.[50]

For bond issues that would be perceived as having poor credit quality, the issuer can purchase bond insurance or obtain a letter of credit in order to reduce interest costs and increase the issue's marketability. However, counties should use credit enhancements only if their cost is less than the interest savings over the life of the bond.[51]

MARKETING COUNTY INDEBTEDNESS

As described in this chapter, there are several types of authorized county debt. Such indebtedness can take the form of loans, notes, bonds, and certificates of participation. The indebtedness can be either "tax-exempt" or "taxable." Georgia law generally does not dictate the financial arrangements under which indebtedness is incurred, although there are detailed requirements for the legal procedures involved.[52] Debt can be incurred by negotiation or competitive bid, either directly with a financial institution or through an investment bank, as determined by the county commission or its ordinances. However, given the responsibility of commissioners to their constituents and the complexity of the financial markets, independent financial advice from financial advisers or investment bankers frequently is obtained prior to the incurrence of debt in order to ensure that both the financial structure is sound and the cost of borrowing is favorable.

NOTES

1. Ga. Const. art. IX, §5, ¶5; O.C.G.A. §36-80-2.
2. City of Bremen v. Regions Bank, 274 Ga. 733, 559 S.E.2d 440 (2002).
3. Ga. Const. art. IX, §5, ¶5.
4. Ga. Const. art. IX, §5, ¶1(a).

5. B. J. Reed and J. W. Swain, *Public Finance Administration*, 2nd ed. (Thousand Oaks, CA: Sage Publications, 1997).
6. P. A. Leonard, "Debt Management," in *Management Policies in Local Government Finance*, 5th ed., ed. J. R. Aronson and E. Schwartz (Washington, DC: International City/County Management Association, 2004).
7. O.C.G.A. §48-5-220.
8. Ga. Const. art. IX, §5 ¶1 (excepted from the 10 percent debt limitation and referendum requirements are certain federal loans and debt to pay for ad valorem property tax valuation and equalization programs); Ga. Const. art. IX, §5, ¶4.
9. Ga. Const. art. IX, §5, ¶6.
10. O.C.G.A. §§21-2-540, 36-82-1.
11. Rea v. City of LaFayette, 130 Ga. 771, 61 S.E. 707 (1908); Purdue v. O'Kelley et al., 280 Ga. 732, 632 S.E.2d 110 (2006).
12. Ga. Const. art. IX, §5, ¶3.
13. O.C.G.A. §48-8-111(c)(2).
14. O.C.G.A. §48-8-111(e)(2).
15. O.C.G.A. §48-8-121(c).
16. O.C.G.A. §48-8-111(b).
17. Text under heading "Lease-Purchase Financing."
18. O.C.G.A. §§36-82-61(4), 36-82-62.
19. See O.C.G.A. §36-82-61(4)(c)(iv).
20. O.C.G.A. §36-82-64.
21. O.C.G.A. §36-82-66.
22. O.C.G.A. §36-82-61(4) (defines "undertakings" for which revenue bonds may be issued as certain projects or any combination thereof).
23. O.C.G.A. §36-82-64.
24. "Lapse on Continuation of Local Constitutional Amendments Under the Constitution of 1981," 21 Ga. St. Bar J. 78 (1984).
25. O.C.G.A. §36-62-7.
26. Ga. Const. art. IX, §3, ¶1.
27. Nations v. Downtown Development Authority, 256 Ga. 158, 345 S.E.2d 581 (1986); Building Authority of Fulton County v. State of Georgia, 253 Ga. 242, 321 S.E. 2d 97 (1984).
28. O.C.G.A. Chapter 36-61.
29. O.C.G.A. Chapter 36-44.
30. O.C.G.A. §§36-44-5(a)(9), 36-61-12(g).
31. Ibid.
32. Ga. Const. art. IX, §3, ¶1.
33. O.C.G.A. tit. 36, chs. 44 and 61.
34. O.C.G.A. §36-44-14.
35. Ga. Const. art. IX, §2, ¶6; art. IX, §5, ¶2; O.C.G.A. §36-82-60 et seq.
36. O.C.G.A. §36-60-13; Bauerband v. Jackson County, 278 Ga. 222, 598 S.E. 2d 444 (2004).
37. O.C.G.A. §36-60-13.
38. Ibid.

39. O.C.G.A. §36-60-13(a)(4) (title to property remains in vendor until fully paid for by county), §36-60-13(b)(1) (contract may provide for automatic termination in the event that appropriated or otherwise obligated funds are not available to satisfy county's obligations under the contract), §36-60-15 (county may accept title to property subject to such a contract and is authorized to transfer title back to the vendor in the event the contract is not fully consummated).
40. McElmurray v. Richmond Co., 223 Ga. 440, 156 S.E.2d 53 (1967).
41. O.C.G.A. §36-60-13(f).
42. O.C.G.A. §36-60-13(e).
43. O.C.G.A. §36-60-13(g).
44. O.C.G.A. §36-60-13(h)(1)(A).
45. O.C.G.A. §36-60-13(h)(1)(B).
46. O.C.G.A. tit. 36, ch. 82, arts. 2 and 3 (validation process for bonds).
47. I.R.C. §103, 140-150.
48. Leonard, "Debt Management."
49. Reed and Swain, *Public Finance Administration*.
50. Leonard, "Debt Management."
51. Ibid.
52. O.C.G.A. §36-82-250(4) (requiring use of an independent financial advisor in connection with the adoption of an interest rate management plan).

Intergovernmental Relations

22

Harry W. Hayes and Betty J. Hudson

Intergovernmental Cooperation and Service Delivery Strategies

Intergovernmental cooperation is an arrangement between two or more governments for accomplishing common goals, providing a service, or solving a mutual problem. A number of methods are available to Georgia communities for coordinating intergovernmental service delivery:

- Informal cooperation
- Mutual aid agreements
- Formal agreements

Each community must review thoroughly its own situation and determine which method or methods offer the most logical and acceptable conditions for providing the type of government desired by citizens.

ALTERNATIVE METHODS OF COOPERATION

Informal Cooperation

Informal cooperation refers to simple cooperative actions or agreements that are voluntary and require no structural change in the participating local governments. An example of informal, interlocal cooperation is the casual exchange of information over the telephone between county and city clerks. Another example would be the occasional or one-time loan of equipment by one government to another.

Mutual Aid Agreements

Mutual aid agreements are usually based on a "you help us, we'll help you" relationship in which two or more governmental units provide supplemental emergency services. These agreements, which must be in writing, are usually for police, fire, emergency management (civil defense), and riot control situations.[1] Legislation in this service area, the Georgia Mutual Aid Act, authorizes local law enforcement agencies, fire departments, and emergency medical services to cooperate with and render assistance to other such local agencies when they request help in a local emergency.[2] Counties are authorized to develop emergency management mutual aid agreements with other counties and municipalities for reciprocal aid and assistance.[3] Counties are also authorized to enter into mutual aid resource pacts with other counties, municipalities, and specified jurisdictions for the purpose of providing fire services and other emergency response.[4] In order to facilitate interstate cooperation, particularly for Georgia counties that border neighboring states, Georgia counties and cities are authorized to enter into agreements with public agencies outside Georgia to perform any governmental service, activity, or undertaking that each agency is otherwise authorized by law to perform.[5]

Formal Agreements

Formal agreements include joint service agreements and service contracts. As a general rule, governmental functions and services that readily lend themselves to some kind of formal agreement have one or more of the following characteristics:

- Cost-benefits that are easily defined

- Mutual benefits to the participating governments

- A noncontroversial nature

Through joint service agreements, two or more local governments mutually perform a particular function or service. Often such agreements involve joint acquisition, construction, ownership, and maintenance of property; joint employment of personnel; or other similar cooperative activity. Under joint service agreements, local governments share ownership and control. Services that are amenable to being provided under joint service agreements include code enforcement and planning.

Service contracts, while similar to joint service agreements, have some distinguishing features. Under a service contract one unit of government is selling a service to another unit. Although the terms of the contract must be agreeable to the parties, the government supplying the service usually controls the administration of the service. Typical contract services include office space, water supply and treatment, sewage disposal, and fire protection. Other functions and services may also be adaptable to contractual arrangements. For example, several public service activities—jail, communications, and records—readily fall into such service contract agreements.[6]

SERVICE DELIVERY STRATEGIES

The intent of the Service Delivery Strategy law[7] is "to provide a flexible framework within which local governments in each county can develop a service delivery system that is both efficient and responsive to citizens in their county." In recognition of the unique characteristics of each county throughout the state, the legislation does not mandate a specific outcome for the delivery of services in every county but rather grants discretion to counties and cities. Local governments are required to develop service delivery systems that reduce unnecessary duplication, promote cooperation, eliminate funding inequities, and minimize interjurisdictional land-use disputes.[8] The service delivery strategy in each county must be adopted by resolutions by the county, all cities with populations of more than 9,000, the city that serves as the county seat, and 50 percent or more of all other cities with populations of more than 500 within the county. All 159 counties have strategies on file with the Department of Community Affairs (DCA).[9]

What Is a Service Delivery Strategy?

Pursuant to the Service Delivery Strategy law, local governments must carefully scrutinize the services they currently provide in order to identify overlap or gaps in service provision, examine the existing method of funding those services, and develop a reasoned approach to allocating the delivery and funding of the services among the various local governments and authorities in each county. A service delivery strategy is intended to be a concise action plan, backed up by the appropriate ordinances and intergovernmental agreements, for providing local government services and minimizing land-use conflicts. While the law does not dictate specific service delivery and land-use planning arrangements within any given county, it does require every strategy to include four basic components and meet six criteria.

Components of a Service Delivery Strategy

Each strategy must identify all services presently provided in the county by cities, counties, and authorities; assign which local government will be responsible for providing a specific service in which area of the county; describe how all services will be funded; and identify all intergovernmental contracts, ordinances, and resolutions to be used in implementing the strategy, including existing contracts.[10]

Identification of Services

Each strategy must list all local government services provided or primarily funded by the county, each city, and each authority within the county and describe the geographic area in which the identified services are provided by each jurisdiction. State law does not specify the services that should be included in a county's strategy; however, all services provided by a county or its cities must be included.

Assignment of Service Delivery Arrangements

The strategy must assign the local government or authority that will provide each service, identify the geographic areas of the county in which each service will be provided, and describe any services that will be provided by a local government to any area outside its geographical boundaries. If a local government is providing the service outside its geographic boundaries, the strategy must include a map delineating the areas served extraterritorially by any service provider. The law does not preclude cities and counties from offering the same services but does encourage local governments to provide services in the most efficient manner possible. If a county's service delivery strategy assigns two or more local governments within the same county the responsibility to provide identical services within the same geographic area, the strategy must explain this duplication of services, including any overriding benefits or insurmountable problems that affect continuing the arrangement. If a city or county decides to either add a new service or drop an existing service after the strategy is adopted, an update to the service delivery strategy must be negotiated with all parties to the original strategy.

Funding Sources

The strategy must describe the source of revenue each local government will use to fund each service it will provide within the county (e.g., countywide revenues, unincorporated area revenues, municipal revenues, enterprise funds, or some combination).

Legal Mechanisms for Implementation

Finally, the strategy must identify the mechanisms, if any, to be used to implement the service delivery strategy, including but not limited to intergovernmental agreements, ordinances, resolutions, and local acts of the General Assembly.

Criteria

In assigning and implementing service delivery responsibilities, the following requirements must be met:

- The strategy should eliminate duplication of services or explain their continued existence.

- Jurisdictions charging water and sewer rate differentials to customers outside their boundaries must be able to justify such differentials.

- Services provided primarily for unincorporated areas must be funded by revenues derived exclusively from the unincorporated areas.

- Conflicts in land-use plans within a county (that is, between the county and its cities) must be eliminated.

- Provision of extraterritorial water and sewer services by any jurisdiction must be consistent with land-use plans.

Elimination of Duplication

When two local governments provide or offer the same service in overlapping areas, the service delivery strategy must (1) identify the steps to eliminate unnecessary competition and duplication of services and the time frame in which such steps will be taken or (2) explain the reasons for continuing the existing overlap or duplication of service. For example, if a city water department and a county water authority both have excess water capacity and have extended water lines in order to serve the same area of the county immediately adjacent to the city's jurisdictional boundaries, the services are considered to be duplications. However, if a city provides a service at a higher level than the base level of service provided by the county throughout the geographic area of the county, the service is not considered to be a duplication. Thus, city maintenance of its own police department to patrol within the city, in addition to sheriff department patrols of the entire county, is not viewed as a duplication of services.

Although the service delivery strategy law permits a county and the cities within it to adopt a strategy that makes no changes to the existing service delivery arrangement within the county, the water and sewer rate equity and the tax equity criteria may require changes in how those services are funded.

Elimination of Double Taxation

The strategy must ensure that the cost of any service provided by a county primarily for the benefit of the county's unincorporated area (e.g., fire service or solid waste collection) is borne by the residents, individuals, and property owners who benefit from the service. Funding for such service must come either from special service districts created by the county in which property taxes, insurance premium taxes, assessments, or user fees are levied or imposed or through any other mechanism agreed upon by the affected parties that will eliminate double taxation of municipal property owners. If the county and one or more cities jointly fund a countywide service, the strategy must ensure that the county share of such funding is borne by the residents, individuals, and property owners in the unincorporated area who benefit from the service.

Determining which county services should be paid for out of the general fund and which services should be paid from revenue sources derived from the unincorporated area has been one of the more difficult issues facing counties and their cities in reaching service delivery agreements. Some county services are made available countywide to all residents and in many instances, to nonresidents. Such services include public health, county roads, the county courts and jail, and the operation of the offices of the county constitutional officers. Countywide revenues such as property taxes should be allocated to those services from the county's general fund. The General Assembly addressed this issue by specifically providing that county constitutional officers (i.e., sheriff, superior court clerk, probate judge, and tax commissioner) and the services they provide are not included in the local government services that must be addressed in service delivery agreements.[11] Moreover, the attorney general has said that the costs of the operations of the county constitutional officers "are not to be included in the deliberations of local government officials when formulating agreements between counties and cities regarding the delivery of local government services."[12]

Elimination of Arbitrary Water and Sewer Differentials

The strategy must ensure that water or sewer fees charged to customers located outside the geographic boundaries of a service provider are not arbitrarily higher than the fees charged to customers inside its boundaries. If a local government believes a rate differential is arbitrary and disputes the reasonableness of such water and sewer rate differentials, the law provides a detailed process for that local government to challenge the arbitrary rate differentials on behalf of its residents. If it is determined that the water and sewer rates charged to a local government's outside customers are arbitrary, the strategy may provide for a phased-in adjustment of rates.

Compatible Land-Use Plans

Local governments within the same county must identify any incompatibilities or conflicts in their land-use plans and either amend their land-use plans so that they are compatible and nonconflicting or adopt a single land-use plan for the entire county. This provision is intended to protect citizens who reside near the boundaries of one local government's jurisdiction from undesirable and incompatible land uses (such as industrial operations, large commercial centers, high-density residential development, and offensive agricultural operations) being allowed to locate nearby in areas under the control of another local government.

Extraterritorial Water and Sewer Service Consistent with Land-Use Plans

The provision of extraterritorial water and sewer services by any jurisdiction must be consistent with all applicable land-use plans and ordinances. Under the state comprehensive planning act, all counties and cities must prepare a comprehensive plan, including a land-use element which, in many cases, is implemented by way of a zoning ordinance, subdivision regulations, or other land development controls. This requirement for consistency is designed to ensure that a government proposing to extend its water or sewer lines into the jurisdiction of another government does not violate the other government's comprehensive plan.

Dispute Resolution

If a county and the cities within it are unable to reach agreement on a service delivery strategy, the law requires them to attempt to resolve their differences through some method of alternative dispute resolution. If alternative dispute resolution is unsuccessful, the neutral party is required to prepare a report and provide it to each local government within the county. The report is considered a public record. The cost of alternative dispute resolution is shared by the disputing parties on a pro rata basis according to population. The county's share is based upon the unincorporated population of the county.[13] If the county and the affected cities fail to complete a service delivery strategy, the county or any affected municipality may file a petition in superior court in the county seeking mandatory mediation on any unresolved items. The cost of mediation is to be shared by the disputing parties based on population.[14]

Verification by the Department of Community Affairs

The department may only verify that the county has adopted a strategy and that the strategy meets the requirements of the act. The law specifically states that DCA shall neither approve nor disapprove the specific elements or outcomes of the strategy. As long as the strategy meets the required criteria, local governments have complete discretion to develop their own arrangements.[15] Any city or authority that is located or operates in more than one county must be included in a department-verified strategy for each county in which the city or authority is located or operating.[16]

Sanctions for Noncompliance

No state-administered financial assistance, grants, loans, or permits can be issued to any local government or authority that is not included in a DCA-verified service delivery strategy. In addition, projects that are inconsistent with a strategy are ineligible for state funding and permits. Examples of state funding, grants, and permits that counties could lose by failing to reach or update a service delivery strategy include Local Maintenance and Improvement Grants, Georgia Environmental Finance Authority water and sewer loans, recreation grants, Community Development Block Grants, and water withdrawal, wastewater treatment, and solid waste disposal facility permits. Each state agency is required to make certain that any projects under consideration for funding or permit approval are consistent with the service delivery strategies of the applicable counties.[17] If a county and cities are participating in court-directed mandatory mediation, the court is authorized to suspend sanctions pending the outcome of mediation.[18]

Strategy Updates

Local governments are encouraged to keep their service delivery strategies accurate and up to date and should complete periodic updates. DCA has developed a series of forms for counties and affected cities to use in submitting, extending, or revising their service delivery strategies. These forms may be downloaded from DCA's Web site (www.dca.ga.gov). Counties are required to review and completely update their approved service delivery strategies under six conditions:

1. When the county updates its comprehensive plans, at least every 10 years
2. Whenever necessary in order to change service delivery or revenue distribution arrangements
3. When necessary due to changes in revenue distribution arrangements
4. When local governments are created, abolished, or consolidated (including first-time cross-county annexations by cities)
5. When the existing service delivery strategy expires
6. When the county and affected cities agree to revise the strategy[19]

A county and its cities may fail to be in compliance with the requirements of the Services Delivery Strategy law in the following circumstances:

1. The service delivery strategy is not formally adopted by all required governments.
2. The strategy does not address all required components and criteria, leaving DCA unable to verify the strategy.
3. The strategy is not updated as required.

DCA maintains an online database that allows local governments to check the status of their service delivery agreements. Other publications that can help counties and cities understand this law, such as *Charting a Course for Cooperation and Collaboration*, are available through DCA.

NOTES

1. OFFICIAL CODE OF GEORGIA ANNOTATED (O.C.G.A.) §36-10-1.
2. O.C.G.A. tit. 36, ch. 69. See also O.C.G.A. §§38-3-29, 38-3-30 in regard to local mutual aid arrangements.
3. O.C.G.A. §38-3-29.
4. O.C.G.A. tit. 25, ch. 6.
5. O.C.G.A. tit. 36, ch. 69A.
6. See O.C.G.A. §42-5-53 concerning county correctional institutions and §§15-7-80–15-7-85 concerning the provision of municipal court services by counties.
7. O.C.G.A. tit. 36, ch. 70, art. 2. See Association County Commissioners of Georgia, Georgia Municipal Association, Georgia Department of Community Affairs, and Carl Vinson Institute of Government, *Charting a Course for Cooperation and Collaboration* (Atlanta: Georgia Department of Community Affairs, 1997).
8. O.C.G.A. §36-70-20.
9. O.C.G.A. §36-70-25(a), (b).
10. O.C.G.A. §36-70-23.
11. O.C.G.A. §36-70-2(5.2).
12. 2002 Op. Att'y Gen. No. U2002-2.
13. O.C.G.A. §36-70-25.1(b), (c).
14. O.C.G.A. §36-70-25.1(d).
15. O.C.G.A. §36-70-26.
16. O.C.G.A. §36-70-27(a).
17. O.C.G.A. §36-70-27.
18. O.C.G.A. §36-70-25.1(d)(2).
19. O.C.G.A. §36-70-28.

23

Paul T. Hardy, Betty J. Hudson, and Harry W. Hayes

Extraterritorial Powers, Annexation, Merger, and Consolidation

Counties do not exist in a vacuum, so it is necessary for them to maintain effective relations with all levels of government. Perhaps the most crucial relationship, however, is that between a county and the city or cities located within it. As discussed in the previous chapter, both formal and informal agreements are available to local governments in dealing with the questions of who will provide services to county and city residents and how such services will be funded.

This chapter addresses the following issues in county-city relations:

- Extraterritorial powers

- Annexation

- Merger of governmental functions (functional consolidation)

- Consolidation of governments (governmental consolidation)

EXTRATERRITORIAL POWERS

Counties and municipalities are authorized by the Georgia Constitution, several general statutes, and local acts to carry out certain functions beyond their geographical boundaries. For example, most city charters authorize cities to extend water and sewer services "within and without the boundaries of the municipality," and the Georgia Supreme Court has determined that such provisions are sufficient for cities to provide extra-territorial services without first entering into a contract with the county.[1] The Georgia Constitution authorizes counties to exercise specified powers and provide certain specified services within the boundaries of a municipality or within another county only through a contract with the municipality or other county. Counties are also permitted to exercise the power of eminent domain extraterritorially for purposes of acquiring property for an airport, but only with the consent of the county, city, or other political subdivision where the property is located.[2]

A grant of extraterritorial power to counties and municipalities is contained in the Revenue Bond Law.[3] This act provides that a county or municipality may issue bonds to finance revenue-producing undertakings, which may be located within or outside the county or municipality, and may collect fees for services furnished.[4] The term "undertaking" is defined to include the following:

- Causeways, tunnels, viaducts, bridges, and other crossings

- Highways, parkways, airports, docks, piers, wharves, terminals, and other facilities

- Water supply and sewage and solid waste disposal systems

- Dormitories, laboratories, and libraries

- Golf courses, tennis courts, parks, swimming pools, athletic fields, and educational, athletic, and exhibition buildings

- Public parking areas

- Sea wall and beach erosion protection systems

- Jails[5]

Another area of extraterritorial power involves urban redevelopment. Under the Georgia Urban Redevelopment Law, counties and municipalities may exercise redevelopment powers as far as five miles beyond their boundaries. However, the powers cannot be exercised within the territorial boundaries of a municipality or another county without its consent.[6]

ANNEXATION

Through annexation, a municipality can bring the residential, business, and vacant properties adjacent to its boundaries into the city limits. By so doing, all or some of a county's urban, commercial, or undeveloped areas may be brought under the jurisdiction of a city. In theory, annexation can be appropriate in order to provide municipal services for developing areas on the city fringe. However, county commissioners should be aware that there may be significant negative consequences to county residents whenever annexation occurs. These consequences may include revenue losses by the county and county school system, disruptions in or inadequate delivery of services, and the undermining of land-use plans that have been developed with unincorporated residents' input and support.

No annexation can become effective until any county objections recognized by law are resolved according to the dispute resolution process in place in state statute.[7] The dispute resolution process calls for an independent panel of arbitrators to hear the county objection and issue findings and binding recommendations, if any. Counties may by majority vote object to annexation "because of a material increase in burden upon the county directly related to . . . the proposed change in zoning or land use, proposed increase in density, and infrastructure demands related to the proposed change in zoning or land use."[8] The proposed change in zoning or land use must result in a substantial change in the intensity or type of allowable use or significantly increase the cost or decrease the useful life of county infrastructure. Further, it must differ substantially from existing uses suggested by the county's land-use plan or those permitted for the property.[9] If no objection is raised, a municipality may proceed with the annexation but may not change the zoning or land-use plan relating to the annexed property to a more intense density for one year without approval by the county.[10]

All annexations, except those by local act of the General Assembly, become effective on the first day of the month following the month in which all requirements for that type of annexation are completed.[11] Annexations by charter amendment become effective on either the date that the local act becomes effective or on such later date as provided in the local law, except that the annexation becomes effective for ad valorem tax purposes on December 31 of the year of annexation.[12]

A municipality is required to give written notice of a proposed annexation to the governing authority of the county in which the area proposed for annexation is located. The notice must be given within five business days of accepting an application or petition for annexation or adopting a resolution for a referendum or, for an annexation by local act, at the time the notice of intent is published. A map or other description sufficient to identify the area must be included with the notice.[13] Counties have 30 days to file an objection. Municipalities are required to submit a request for preclearance under Section 5 of the federal Voting Rights Act for each annexation at the time of annexation to the U.S. Department of Justice and must also provide a copy of the request to the Georgia Department of Community Affairs.[14]

A city may only annex into an adjoining county for the first time if the county governing authority agrees to the annexation. If the county disapproves the annexation, the city may challenge the disapproval in superior court.[15]

There are four basic methods for accomplishing annexation in Georgia: charter amendment, 100 percent method, 60 percent method, and referendum method.

Charter Amendment

The traditional and still frequently used method of municipal annexation is by General Assembly amendment to the city charter, expanding corporate boundaries.[16] The General Assembly has imposed the requirement that any annexation of this type must be approved by the voters of the affected area if the area is more than 50 percent residential or if the population of the area is more than 3 percent of the existing population of the city or 500 persons.[17]

100 Percent Method

Municipalities may annex contiguous unincorporated areas by ordinance if all owners (with certain exceptions) of the land to be annexed sign written annexation applications.[18] For the purposes of this method, "contiguous" is defined as an area that directly abuts the city boundary or that would abut the boundary if it were not separated by land owned by the city or state, the width of a street or right-of-way, a creek or river, or a railroad or other utility right-of-way. The abutting area must be at least the lesser of either one-eighth of the aggregate external boundary or 50 feet of the area to be annexed. In addition, the entire parcel of land owned by the person seeking annexation must be annexed (i.e., the land cannot be subdivided in order to meet the requirements), and annexed parcels must be of sufficient size to meet the annexing city's minimum size requirements for construction of a building or structure. This design prevents "spoke" annexations, with the exception that municipally owned land that is separated by the length of a street or right-of-way, creek or river, or railroad or utility right-of-way may be annexed by such a spoke annexation.[19]

60 Percent Method

Municipalities with a population of 200 or more may annex by ordinance contiguous unincorporated areas upon the signed application of no fewer than 60 percent of the voters and no fewer than 60 percent of the landowners in the area to be annexed. For the purposes of this method, "contiguous" is defined as an area of which one-eighth of the aggregate external boundary directly abuts the municipal boundary or would abut the boundary if it were not separated by land owned by the city or state, the width of a street or right-of-way, a creek or river, or a railroad or other utility right-of-way. Land cannot be subdivided in order to meet this requirement. A municipality is required to prepare a plan for servicing the area to be annexed and to hold a public hearing before annexing it.[20]

Referendum Method

Municipalities may annex adjacent or contiguous "urban" areas by resolution if a majority of the voters therein who vote in the election favor annexation. A municipality must prepare a plan for servicing an area to be annexed and hold a public hearing prior to a referendum to ratify or reject the annexation resolution. The area to be annexed must meet the legal definition of an area developed for urban purposes.[21]

Unincorporated Islands

Cities are prohibited from annexing or deannexing any property if it would result in the creation of new unincorporated islands. A simplified process permits a city to annex all or any part of an existing unincorporated island contiguous to the existing city limits without the consent of the residents or landowners.[22]

Deannexation

Cities are authorized to deannex by ordinance any area or areas contiguous to the corporate limits. An identification of the property deannexed must be filed with the Department of Community Affairs and the county in which the property is located. The county must agree to the deannexation.[23]

FUNCTIONAL CONSOLIDATION

Merger of county and municipal governmental services under one government is often referred to as functional consolidation. One governmental entity may pay the other for providing a service. Ordinarily, the consolidated service is under the primary control of the governmental unit charged with providing the service. Alternatively, the county and city may contract for an exchange of merged services. For example, the county might provide parks and recreation for the entire county while the city furnishes human resources management.

Some counties and cities have merged tax-collecting and building inspection functions. Performing such functions separately, in both county and city, creates duplication of staff, records, equipment, and office space. Merging functions promotes more efficient performance of the service and is more convenient for the public. When there is such a merger, the costs are prorated between the governments involved.

GOVERNMENTAL CONSOLIDATION

Structural Reorganization

As of October 2009, Georgia had seven consolidated governments, more than any other state in the country (see Figures 23-1 and 23-2). The most comprehensive approach to solving county-city problems is total consolidation of county and city governments into a single new government.[24] This type of government is also sometimes referred to as a unified government. The new consolidated government is assigned both county and municipal functions. Reorganization of this type requires the following:

- Establishment of a single legislative body representing and responsible to all segments of the county population

- Establishment of one administrative office to direct government business

- Merger of existing county and city departments and offices into one departmental system

Decisions involved in the reorganization, especially the question of jobs and responsibilities of current personnel under the new government, require careful evaluation. The status of the county elective offices, commonly referred to as county constitutional officers (e.g., judge of the probate court, clerk of the superior court, sheriff, and tax commissioner), under a reorganized government involves constitutional questions, but it is clear that governmental consolidation can have only minimal, if any, effect on the status of these offices.

Service Districts

In order to accommodate the urbanized areas of the county and at the same time avoid placing an excessive tax burden on low-density areas, a consolidated government often includes the creation of at least two types of service districts: (1) a general service district encompassing

Figure 23-1. *Consolidated Governments in Georgia Counties, 2009*

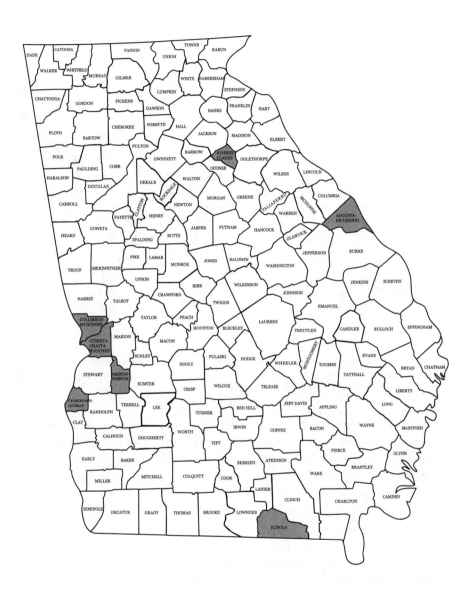

Source: Carl Vinson Institute of Government, University of Georgia, 2009.

Figure 23-2. Consolidated Governments

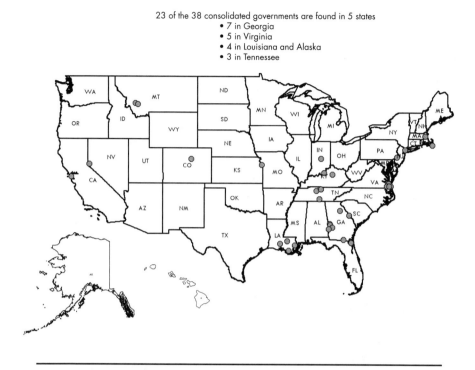

23 of the 38 consolidated governments are found in 5 states
- 7 in Georgia
- 5 in Virginia
- 4 in Louisiana and Alaska
- 3 in Tennessee

Source: Adapted from data from the National Association of Counties. Prepared by the Carl Vinson Institute of Government, University of Georgia, 2010.

the entire county, with taxes levied for functions of countywide benefit, and (2) an urban service district in which taxes or fees are levied for municipal-type services of primary benefit only to persons within that district. As the need arises, the urban services district may be extended to take in new areas.

Functions for which taxes could be levied by the general service district might include general administration, courts, public health, libraries, welfare, recreation, inspections, and certain public works functions of countywide application. Examples of urban services include local street maintenance, refuse collection, and animal control.

The state constitution authorizes the General Assembly to provide by local law for the consolidation of a county and a city.[25] In addition, the General Assembly is authorized to provide by general law for city-county consolidation.[26]

Methods of Consolidation

Four methods have been documented in creating consolidation charters in Georgia. The legislatively initiated local charter method begins with creation of a charter commission by local act of the General Assembly. Under this method, the charter commission is authorized to prepare the charter and either required to submit the charter for legislative adoption[27] or empowered to submit the charter directly to the voters.[28] A second method is the legislatively created charter method, whereby the General Assembly enacts the charter as local law without involvement of a local charter commission.[29] In the third method, the local citizen initiative, a citizen charter commission is formed without specific authorization from the legislature. This commission prepares the consolidation charter and submits it to the local legislative delegation for enactment by the General Assembly.[30] The fourth method is the local government–instituted charter commission wherein the county and city or cities create a joint charter commission that prepares a consolidation charter and submits the charter to the county and city governing authorities for approval and then to the General Assembly for enactment.[31]

Regardless of the method used in creating the consolidation charter, a consolidation cannot become effective unless approved separately by a majority of the voters voting on the issue in the entire county and by a majority of the voters voting on the issue in the city. If a majority of the voters of a city containing less than 10 percent of the population of the county do not approve consolidation, that city would not be included in the consolidation.[32]

Advantages and Disadvantages of Consolidation

Some of the advantages that have been identified for governmental consolidation include the following:

- Taxpayers pay only for benefits received.

- Issues of responsibility between two governments are eliminated as well as intergovernmental disputes involving issues such as annexation, tax equity, service delivery, and tax revenue distribution.

- There is unified responsibility for community problems and it is easier for citizens to deal with one government rather than two.

- One government means greater efficiency in performing governmental functions.

- There is one stop for economic development. Business and industry may be more willing to locate in an area where there is only one layer of government regulation.

- A consolidated government may be perceived as more progressive than having two layers of government.

Disadvantages to consolidation may include the following:

- Costs of producing services may go up.

- Costs of services to some taxpayers may increase.

- Jobs may be abolished in order for improvement in efficiency and economy to be realized.

- Bigger may not always better. A single government may be less responsive to public demands.

- Transition costs may be high in the initial years following consolidation. For example, benefits and pay scales for the employees of the higher-paying government are typically extended to all employees of the consolidated government, thereby increasing personnel costs.

Full governmental consolidation is often a lengthy process involving legal, fiscal, and political considerations.

NOTES

1. Coweta County v. City of Newnan, 253 Ga. 457, 320 S.E.2d 747 (1984).
2. GA. CONST. art. IX, §2, ¶3; OFFICIAL CODE OF GEORGIA ANNOTATED (O.C.G.A.) §6-3-22; City Council of Augusta v. Garrison, 68 Ga. App. 150, 22 S.E.2d 412 (1942); Collier v. City of Atlanta, 178 Ga. 575, 173 S.E. 853 (1933); Ball v. Peavy, 210 Ga. 575, 82 S.E.2d 143 (1954); R. Perry Sentell Jr., *Additional Studies in Georgia Local Government Law* (Charlottesville, VA: Michie Company, 1983), ch. 9.
3. O.C.G.A. tit. 36, ch. 82, art. 3.
4. O.C.G.A. §36-82-62.
5. O.C.G.A. §36-82-61(4).
6. O.C.G.A. §36-61-2(2).
7. O.C.G.A. §§36-36-11, 36-36-110–36-36-119.
8. O.C.G.A. §36-36-113(a).
9. O.C.G.A. §36-36-113(d).
10. O.C.G.A. §36-36-112.
11. O.C.G.A. §36-36-2(a).
12. O.C.G.A. §36-36-2(b).
13. O.C.G.A. §§36-36-6, 28-1-14.1.
14. O.C.G.A. §36-36-3(f).

15. O.C.G.A. §36-36-23(b), (d).

16. R. Perry Sentell Jr., *Studies in Georgia Local Government Law*, 3rd ed. (Charlottesville, VA: Michie Company, 1977), 489, 490. The boundaries of a municipality may not be changed except by local act or by such other methods as may be provided by general law. Whenever a local act of the General Assembly deannexes property, it cannot be annexed by the municipality from which it was deannexed under any general law method for a period of three years. O.C.G.A. §36-35-2.

17. O.C.G.A. §36-36-16.

18. O.C.G.A. tit. 36, ch. 36, art. 2.

19. O.C.G.A. §36-36-20.

20. O.C.G.A. tit. 36, ch. 36, art. 3.

21. O.C.G.A. tit. 36, ch. 36, art. 4.

22. O.C.G.A. §36-36-92.

23. O.C.G.A. §36-36-22.

24. GA. CONST. art. IX, §3, ¶2.

25. GA. CONST. art. IX, §3, ¶2(a).

26. GA. CONST. art. IX, §3, ¶2(b). See O.C.G.A. tit. 36, ch. 68.

27. Ga. Laws 1999, 3518 (Hawkinsville–Pulaski County, ref. failed).

28. Ga. Laws 2004, 4811 (Cusseta–Chattahoochee County).

29. Ga. Laws 1995, 3648 (Augusta–Richmond County).

30. Ga. Laws 1990, 3560 (Athens–Clarke County).

31. Recent consolidation efforts by the City of Rome and Floyd County and the City of Albany and Dougherty County each used this method.

32. O.C.G.A. §36-60-16.

24

Ross King, Richard M. Gold, Kevin R. Doran, and
Kathleen Bowen

State and Federal Relations

Running a county government in the 21st century is more complex and demanding than ever before. Citizens want top-of-the-line services delivered effectively and efficiently, superior quality of life, and a clean and healthy environment. At the same time, they want to receive tax relief at the federal, state, and local levels of government. The ideal 21st-century county official must therefore be smart, innovative, and politically astute. County commissioners need to be able to work well with their counterparts in municipalities and other counties as well as with officials in federal and state government. Understanding, developing, and maintaining effective intergovernmental relationships can determine whether a county meets its future goals.

County commissioners should strive to develop good working relationships with their state legislators and members of Congress. To foster these relationships, counties and county interests are represented at both the federal and state levels by professional organizations, including the National Association of Counties and, in the state of Georgia, the Association County Commissioners of Georgia.

At the federal level, the National Association of Counties (NACo) serves Georgia counties and their peers across the nation. NACo was created in 1935 to give county officials a strong voice in the nation's capital and continues to fulfill that role. Membership is voluntary, and dues are based on population. NACo's membership includes counties from across the United States and represents three-quarters of all counties and over 85 percent of the nation's population.[1] NACo describes itself in the following way:

NACo is based on Capitol Hill in Washington, D.C., and is a full-service organization that provides an extensive line of services including legislative, research, and technical as well as public affairs assistance to its members. The association acts as a liaison with other levels of government, works to improve public understanding of counties, serves as a national advocate for counties and provides them with resources to help them find innovative methods to meet the challenges they face.[2]

At the state level, the Association County Commissioners of Georgia (ACCG) represents Georgia's 159 counties. ACCG is a Georgia non-profit corporation, begun in 1914 in Athens with 19 charter member counties. ACCG's mission is to serve as the consensus-building, training, membership services, civic engagement, and legislative advocacy organization for Georgia's county governments. ACCG brings Georgia counties together on matters of public policy that have special impact on local governments.

In order to properly develop membership consensus, both NACo and ACCG utilize a policy development process that draws upon the active participation of each organization's membership—rural, suburban, and urban county government officials from both the elected and appointed ranks. Once formally adopted by the memberships, these platforms are the basis for the lobbying work of the organizations' professional staff, elected board of managers, and statewide membership.

ACCG considers the policy development process to be one of its core responsibilities. The association's policy system has six standing committees: General County Government, Economic Development and Transportation, Health and Human Services, Public Safety and the Courts, Revenue and Finance, and Natural Resources and Environment. This process is officially initiated with the appointment of committee officers and members by the ACCG president. Both elected and appointed county government officials are encouraged to actively participate in this policy process. Deliberations at committee meetings are open, and a free exchange of ideas is encouraged. Each committee sets its agenda following the appointment process in May of each year. The level of detail in the agenda dictates the frequency of meetings throughout the summer and early fall. Committees finalize their work typically by early September. The recommendations from all six committees are then distributed to the entire ACCG membership in draft form for review prior to the Legislative Leadership Conference (typically conducted in early October). Before the Legislative Leadership Conference in the fall, the ACCG Policy Council considers comments from the general membership and resolves any incongruities from the recommendations received from the six policy committees. The proposed county platform is then presented to the full association membership at the Legislative Leadership Conference. Each county, having an equal vote, votes to adopt or reject the policy recommendations that are developed. The county platform is the result of that final vote.[3]

RELATIONS WITH STATE GOVERNMENT

The Legislature

The Georgia General Assembly convenes annually on the second Monday in January for its 40-day legislative session to adopt the state budget and to address legislation and resolutions introduced each session. State legislators are elected for a two-year term of office, a period known as a biennium. The first session is held in odd-numbered years, and the concluding session of the biennium, in even years. Legislative matters pending at the end of the first session can be carried over to the second. Any business still pending at the end of the second session dies, however.[4] Should important matters arise between regular legislative sessions, the governor may call the General Assembly back into special session. In recent decades, most special sessions have been called to deal with legislative and congressional reapportionment or with state budget crises. To convene a special session, the governor issues an executive proclamation stating the subjects to be considered. The decision to call a special session is not subject to review by the courts, and there is no limit as to how many subjects may be included in the proclamation.[5]

All legislation introduced in the Georgia General Assembly is classified as either a bill or a resolution. The word bill refers to proposed legislation. A resolution is similar to a bill but may not have the force of law, depending on the subject matter and intent of the legislature. A bill becomes an act, law, or statute when it passes both houses in identical form and is signed by the governor, becomes law without the governor's signature, or is passed despite the governor's veto.[6]

The effective date for a general bill passed at a regular session of the General Assembly is the following July 1, unless a specific date was provided for in the legislation. Often, a general bill will specify that it shall become effective upon approval of the governor or upon its becoming law without approval (see Figure 24-1).[7]

Figure 24-1. *How a Bill Becomes Law*

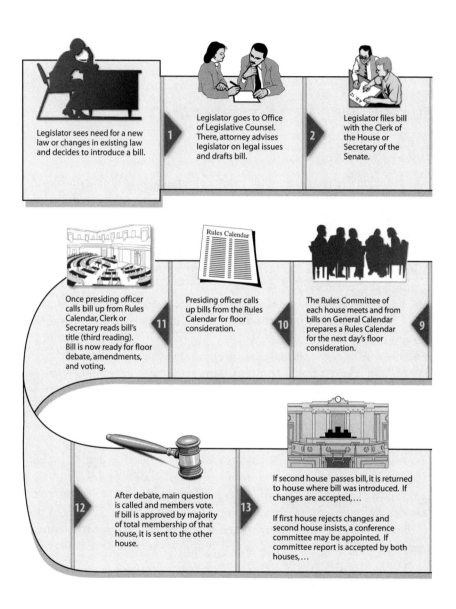

Legislator sees need for a new law or changes in existing law and decides to introduce a bill. **1**

Legislator goes to Office of Legislative Counsel. There, attorney advises legislator on legal issues and drafts bill. **2**

Legislator files bill with the Clerk of the House or Secretary of the Senate.

Once presiding officer calls bill up from Rules Calendar, Clerk or Secretary reads bill's title (third reading). Bill is now ready for floor debate, amendments, and voting. **11**

Presiding officer calls up bills from the Rules Calendar for floor consideration. **10**

The Rules Committee of each house meets and from bills on General Calendar prepares a Rules Calendar for the next day's floor consideration. **9**

After debate, main question is called and members vote. If bill is approved by majority of total membership of that house, it is sent to the other house. **12**

If second house passes bill, it is returned to house where bill was introduced. If changes are accepted,... **13**

If first house rejects changes and second house insists, a conference committee may be appointed. If committee report is accepted by both houses,...

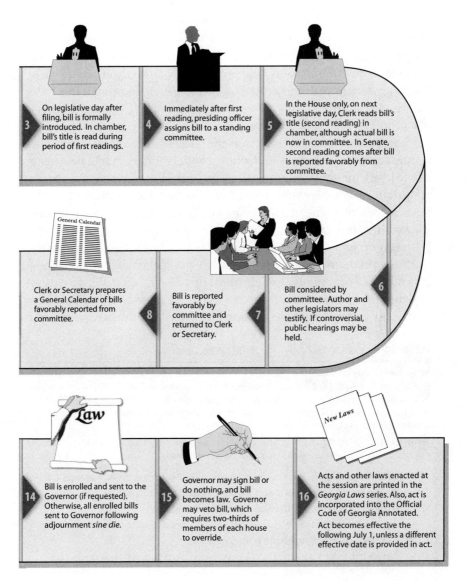

On legislative day after filing, bill is formally introduced. In chamber, bill's title is read during period of first readings. **3**

Immediately after first reading, presiding officer assigns bill to a standing committee. **4**

In the House only, on next legislative day, Clerk reads bill's title (second reading) in chamber, although actual bill is now in committee. In Senate, second reading comes after bill is reported favorably from committee. **5**

General Calendar

Clerk or Secretary prepares a General Calendar of bills favorably reported from committee. **8**

Bill is reported favorably by committee and returned to Clerk or Secretary. **7**

Bill considered by committee. Author and other legislators may testify. If controversial, public hearings may be held. **6**

Law

Bill is enrolled and sent to the Governor (if requested). Otherwise, all enrolled bills sent to Governor following adjournment *sine die*. **14**

Governor may sign bill or do nothing, and bill becomes law. Governor may veto bill, which requires two-thirds of members of each house to override. **15**

New Laws

Acts and other laws enacted at the session are printed in the *Georgia Laws* series. Also, act is incorporated into the Official Code of Georgia Annotated.

Act becomes effective the following July 1, unless a different effective date is provided in act. **16**

Many bills that are introduced ultimately have an impact (fiscal or otherwise) on county governments. Counties must often provide mandated services that are solely funded by local property taxes and other local revenues. In other cases, required services may be funded by combined financial commitments from both state and local governments. These services include criminal prosecution and punishment, indigent legal defense, mental health/mental retardation and substance abuse care, environmental management, cooperative extension service, and transportation infrastructure. It is therefore very important that state legislators hear from county commissioners regarding the potential effect of a proposed bill on the county.

Legislation is often introduced as the result of a specific issue raised by a state legislator's constituents. County commissioners should be among a state legislator's most important constituents. Whether a county's needs at the state level are legislative or financial, county commissioners should not underestimate the benefits of having an effective working relationship with state legislators. While ACCG will communicate counties' positions on issues, it is vitally important that legislators hear directly from the voters in their home districts, especially county commissioners and other community leaders (see Table 24-1). Being able to clearly explain a situation and why it needs a legislative remedy will increase the chances of getting desired legislation introduced and adopted, especially

Table 24-1. *Effective Lobbying at the State Level*

Input from county commissions and staff can broaden the scope of information that legislators typically receive. As ACCG advises, "Remember to develop an ongoing rapport with members of your legislative delegation. Remind your legislators that county officials and ACCG/NACo are among the very few sources of information where a legislator can learn about the impact of legislation on an entire community."

When speaking to legislators about issues, always remember that your presentation matters and can be quite influential as long as you remember a few key rules:

- Be brief and succinct. Don't tell them how to build a watch; tell them what time it is.
- Stay on point. Don't clutter the message with extraneous information.
- Maintain lots of contacts. Develop and utilize networks.
- Public opinion affects legislative opinion. Set your priorities accordingly.
- Honesty is not the best policy: It is the only policy.
- Remember, today's opponent may be tomorrow's ally. You might be angry, but act professionally; otherwise, you will diminish your effectiveness. Don't burn bridges.
- Thank your legislators for the good things they do. Complaints not balanced by appreciation can wear thin over time. Take time to say thank you.
- Use the golden rule as your guide. Treat your legislators as you would like to be treated when it comes to issues of public importance.

Sources: Lobbying the Legislature (ACCG); NACo Lobbying Techniques (NACo).

if commissioners have maintained ongoing communication and a good working relationship with their legislative delegation.

During each session, the General Assembly considers many bills that are referred to as local legislation. A local act is a legislative measure that applies to a specific county, city, or special district named in the act. Such acts are commonly used to alter forms of government, create local authorities or special districts, create cities, change city boundaries, and make other changes that apply only to the political subdivision named in the act.[8]

Perhaps the General Assembly's single most important function each session is to authorize funding for all agencies and programs of state government. Although appropriations acts are passed in the same way as legislative statutes, there are differences. For one thing, statutes continue in effect until repealed, amended, or overruled as unconstitutional. Appropriations acts, however, are valid only during the fiscal year for which they are enacted. A second difference is that, unlike statutes, appropriation acts are not incorporated into the Official Code of Georgia Annotated (O.C.G.A.).[9]

According to Georgia's constitution, "the General Assembly shall annually appropriate those state and federal funds necessary to operate all various departments and agencies." No money can be drawn from the state treasury unless appropriated by law. Every appropriation must expire at the end of the fiscal year for which it was enacted.[10]

In Georgia, the budgetary process leading to a general appropriations act is a year-round process involving both executive and legislative branches (see Table 24-2). During the fall, the governor meets with state agency heads to give them a chance to explain their budget request for the coming fiscal year. Prior to the legislative session, department heads also present their budget requests before the appropriations committees of the House and Senate. The constitution requires the governor to present to the General Assembly within five days of its convening each year an annual budget message, a detailed report on the financial condition of the state, and the draft of a general appropriations act for the next fiscal year.[11]

Once the legislature enacts a new state budget, the governor has extensive authority in its implementation, with broad powers and responsibilities over how state agencies spend their funds. Many observers of state government consider budgetary power to be the governor's single most important power. To help with this responsibility, a full-time agency, the Office of Planning and Budget, exists within the governor's office.[12]

Table 24-2. *The Budget Cycle in Georgia*

Activity	Date
Budget request instructions to agencies	June
Agencies prepare budget requests	July
Budget requests submitted to Office of Planning and Budget (OPB)	September
OPB analyzes requests	October–November
OPB presents initial recommendations to the governor	November
Governor meets with agency heads on budget	November–December
Final budget decisions	December–January
Budget document sent to General Assembly	January
Legislative appropriations process	January–March
Appropriations bill to governor for action	February–April
Operating budget instructions to agencies	April
Agencies prepare annual operating budgets	April
Operating budgets approved by OPB	May–June
OPB monitors allotments and expenditures	July

   The Internet is an excellent resource for researching various legislative issues. There are numerous Web sites specific to Georgia issues, law, and regulations. As a service to ACCG members, the organization's Web site (www.accg.org) tracks key issues and has links to many state government entities, including www.georgia.gov, which is perhaps the most comprehensive link to virtually all aspects of Georgia state government. It links to the governor's office and allows access to daily legislative activity and legislation being considered by the Georgia General Assembly as well as to archives containing bills that were considered in previous sessions. It also links to regional, county, and municipal Web sites as well as state regulatory agency sites.

The Executive Branch

The links to Georgia's regulatory agencies, which are a part of the executive branch of state government, can be especially helpful to county commissioners and their staff. Local officials should not only work with state legislators but also understand how state regulatory agencies and their governing boards operate. Since these boards typically meet monthly to create policies, promulgate rules, and take actions that can affect the operations of a county, it is crucial for county commissioners and key appointed county staff to know and communicate with appropriate state agency personnel and board members.

Administrative and regulatory agencies are created to address specific issue areas (such as the environment, transportation, and health care), and in many instances, their charge is to interpret how the laws passed by the legislative branch are to be implemented. In other words, the legislature may delegate to regulators the power to create the criteria that will allow a law to go from theory into practice, of course staying within the bounds established in law by legislators. If regulatory agencies exceed their rule-making authority, new rules and regulations may face possible court challenges.

State boards, such as those overseeing the Department of Transportation, the Department of Natural Resources, the Department of Community Affairs, and the Department of Community Health, regularly take actions that have the force of law and that affect local government significantly. Most state agency board members are political appointees who do not answer directly to a voting constituency. Commissioners and county government staff should regularly give input to state agency board members regarding issues that may impact counties.

RELATIONS WITH THE FEDERAL GOVERNMENT

Unfunded Mandates, Devolution, and Preemption

During the past three decades, there have been significant reductions in federal program assistance (fiscal and technical) for local governments that negatively impact the relationship between federal, state, and local governments. Further eroding successful intergovernmental relations are the adoption of new unfunded federal mandates, the establishment of devolution as a federal policy, and the increased federal preemption of local home rule.

Unfunded mandates are directives from one level of government—federal or state—to another level of government (typically local). Local governments begin to feel the full impact of these mandates when federal revenue sharing and other federal grant-in-aid programs are either eliminated or drastically cut. Measures have been taken to provide for closer federal agency scrutiny of the fiscal impacts of proposed federal legislation and regulations in order to restrict the adoption of new unfunded mandates.[13] Over the past decade, responsibility for public programs that were federally mandated and federally funded has increasingly been returned to state and local governments. This process is known as federal government devolution. In principle, devolution signified a return to the original spirit and intent of the U.S. Constitution, returning responsibility for public programs to states and communities, since local government is the level of government closest to the people. In practice, however, devolution has meant passing the responsibility for operating public programs and, inadvertently or not, the responsibility to fund such programs to local governments. While home rule is vital to local governments, it is difficult for counties and municipalities to assume additional financial responsibilities for programs devolved from higher levels of government. Counties have worked to limit the devolution phenomenon whenever it has presented local responsibility for programs without the necessary funding.

How preemption works can best be seen through the process of national legislation and federal court decisions taking precedence over "traditional" local authority and decision making. The Religious Land Use and Institutionalized Persons Act is an example of the federal legislative system taking actions that are detrimental to the local land-use decision-making process.[14] This act limits the ability of local governments to proscribe the siting of religious organization facilities and thus preempts local input into a local land-use matter.

With the federal government actively involved in the passage of legislation that affects local governments and with the ability of local governments to seek annual federal appropriations assistance, it is imperative that local officials maintain contact with congressional delegation members. Although it is more difficult to maintain the same level of communication with Congress and the federal executive branch than it is with state government, maintaining contact at the federal level is vital. Utilizing the lobbying service of NACo is one means of keeping current with the issues under consideration in Washington, D.C. In addition, through Web sites such as www.naco.org or thomas.loc.gov, local officials can keep abreast of information on federal government issues. Whether visiting members of Congress in their district offices in Georgia or in Washington, local officials should follow several important guidelines (see Table 24-3).

How Congress Can Help: Financial Assistance

Through the federal appropriations process, Congress directs funding to numerous county and local governments for a wide variety of projects. There are several opportunities that local governments could pursue.

Commerce, Justice, and Science

The Commerce, Justice, and Science appropriations bill is a broad-based bill that funds many different federal departments and agencies.

Table 24-3. *How to Communicate with Congressional Offices*

Before meeting with your U.S. senator, representative, or his or her staff, it is important to have a thorough understanding of the major aspects of any issue, project, or financial request for which you are seeking assistance. If possible, bring background material and a brief white paper outlining the request. Prepare answers to potential questions if you are seeking financial assistance. Be prepared to explain the alternatives that have been examined, the level of support the project enjoys, and the resources the county will contribute. If you are instead communicating a specific position about an issue that needs a federal legislative remedy, you should thoroughly understand the issue in order to be able to communicate what the local impact will be if your position is (or is not) supported at the federal government level.

Understanding how a congressional office functions and having strong relationships with key staff is vital. Generally, the Washington, D.C., office has legislative staff, and the district and state offices have staff who focus on constituent services, such as helping with federal benefits and assistance with federal agencies.

For purposes of acquiring federal appropriations, county officials should interact with the Washington, D.C., staff. The Washington office of a House member typically includes 8 to 10 people, and a senator's office can have as many as 30 staff members, depending on the size of the state. The Washington staff typically consists of a chief of staff, legislative director, several legislative assistants, legislative correspondent, press secretary, scheduler, and staff assistant. The chief of staff oversees both the administrative and political operations of the office. The legislative director monitors the legislative schedule and works to implement the member's overall agenda. Legislative assistants each focus on a set of specific policy issues (e.g., health care, defense, environment, etc.). Legislative correspondents respond to constituent inquiries on policy matters. The press secretary oversees communication between the member and the media and public. The scheduler prepares a daily minute-by-minute schedule for the member and establishes the travel arrangements. The staff assistant performs general support duties.

Maintaining contact with the district offices of congressional members is also beneficial. These offices maintain daily contact with the Washington, D.C., office and are the local "eyes and ears" for members of Congress. The district offices typically concentrate on specific constituent services that members of Congress can assist with at the federal level, such as tracking down missing federal assistance payments—like Social Security checks for example. In addition, the offices maintain staff members who regularly attend policy issue meetings within the member's district. These staff members are very close to their congressional member and typically accompany him or her on travels within the district.

When meeting in Washington, D.C., be flexible. Every effort will be made to arrange a meeting between a county official and the particular member of Congress or the Senate. Unfortunately, due to the unpredictable congressional schedule, you may find yourself meeting with staff only—and sometimes in a hallway—but take advantage of the opportunity. Meeting with staff can, in many cases, be as important as meeting with your U.S. senator or representative. The representative or senator will be fully apprised of your visit and issues of concern. Congressional staff members play a vital role in the process, and members are heavily dependent upon them for input and advice.

After the meeting, follow up with a brief note. In the note, review the topics discussed and outline next steps. Also use the note as an opportunity to answer any questions that were left unanswered during the meeting. Finally, thank the legislator and staff for their time and attention.

The most applicable sections for counties are the Justice Department accounts covering areas such as violent crime reduction, community-oriented policing services, and juvenile justice. Through the Bureau of Justice Enforcement, the Commerce, Justice, and Science bill funds programs to address violent crime. Competition for these funds is fierce and often requires an innovative approach to reducing violent crime. The community-oriented policing services program has traditionally helped communities meet their law enforcement needs by providing law enforcement equipment, mobile emergency communication systems, 911 infrastructure, and public safety programs. Any funds secured in this account through a congressional earmark would be in addition to funds secured through the discretionary grant application process. In the past, the Commerce, Justice, and Science bill has included funding for specific juvenile justice programs around the nation that include after-school programs, innovative partnerships, and many juvenile rehabilitation programs.

Energy and Water

Included in the Energy and Water appropriations bill is funding for the Army Corps of Engineers. These funds are most often directed toward the maintenance of water systems and waterways. The corps is involved in many projects, including harbor deepening, seawall construction and restoration, ecosystem restoration, and shore protection. As with other federal programs, the corps requires specific authorization from Congress to proceed on such projects, which generally means that a project takes two years to initiate: one year to secure congressional authorization and a second year to secure funding. The other main account within this bill is the Energy Efficiency and Renewable Energy account under the Department of Energy. This account funds projects that enhance the nation's energy productivity through means such as biomass and biorefinery systems; solar, wind, and hydropower technologies; weatherization activities; and enhanced green building technologies.

Interior and Environment

Several accounts in the Interior and Environment bill are important to counties, but one in particular is much more popular than the others. Each year, the Interior and Environment bill has included funding for wastewater and storm water infrastructure needs in the State and Tribal Assistance Grant account, which is under the jurisdiction of the Environmental Protection Agency. This account has become highly competitive in the past few years and is typically one of the most requested sources of federal appropriations funding.

Labor, Health and Human Services, and Education

The Labor, Health and Human Services, and Education Departments appropriation bill is the largest of the annual domestic appropriations bills and provides some opportunities that warrant consideration. Within the Department of Labor, funds are routinely set aside for local job training and other workforce demonstrations that may involve activities such as youth employment, worker retraining, welfare-to-work, or reemployment efforts aimed at reducing recidivism. Within the Department of Health and Human Services, funds are available for the construction and renovation of health care facilities, which can encompass capital expenditures related to a wide variety of facilities such as counseling centers and public clinics. There are also opportunities to seek funds for demonstrating innovative proposals to provide improved health services to county residents. In the Department of Education, identified funds can frequently be obtained for a variety of educational undertakings, including distance-learning activities and after-school children's programs. Counties may be interested in pursuing such opportunities in conjunction with area schools or as part of a separate adult education effort.

Transportation and Housing and Urban Development

Each year, Congress must approve a transportation appropriations bill that funds the activities of federal transportation agencies as well as investments in local transportation infrastructure, including buses, intelligent transportation systems, ferry boats and ferry terminal facilities, airports, railways, and roads and bridges. Funding for buses and bus facilities is a common element in federal action plans for counties. Because the funds can be used to acquire buses, shuttle buses, and bus-related facilities, many specific projects are identified in this account. Every local government can use this funding to offset local funding currently obligated for this purpose. Securing an individual line item for a project in the appropriations bill under this account would complement any pending grant applications in the U.S. Department of Transportation.

Intelligent transportation systems programs have also become popular in the past several years, with many counties seeking funds for signal coordination and prioritization as well as installation of variable message signs. Intelligent transportation systems are designed to apply high-technology solutions to the everyday problems of traffic. Examples include the use of remotely controlled traffic signals to direct the flow of traffic during heavy congestion and the use of variable message signs alerting motorists and residents to changes in traffic patterns, as in the case of hurricane evacuations.

Another notable account funds road, highway, and bridge projects. The Transportation, Community, and System Preservation account funds projects that increase transportation efficiency, minimize environmental impacts, and encourage community development while providing a sustainable transportation infrastructure in order to reduce the need for future investments.

In addition to transportation, the bill includes funding for Economic Development Initiative grants. These grants fund project such as land acquisition for public use and the rehabilitation and/or construction of parks, community centers, and museums. There must be a demonstrated overall economic development component to the projects funded. Typically these grants are directed toward locations that are underdeveloped or economically distressed or to projects that benefit low- and moderate-income persons.

Annual Federal Appropriations Process

Each year, Congress passes and the president signs 12 appropriations bills that make up the federal budget. For each of these, several steps must be taken before the legislation becomes law (see Table 24-4).

Even though the process should be completed by September 30, the end of the fiscal year, there are relatively few deadlines imposed on Congress to force compliance. In short, it is a dynamic and fluid series of events that change each year and vary among the 12 appropriations committee subcommittees. In some years, the process extends into October, possibly even December. It is important to note, however, that in an election year the process generally follows the earlier dates, leaving members of Congress more time to campaign.

Presidential Budget Submission. The president initiates the appropriations process by submitting his budget to the Congress on the first Monday in February. The president's budget is the result of months of discussions between the federal agencies and the Office of Management and Budget and reflects the president's views on federal revenues and expenditures.

Subcommittee Hearings (House and Senate). Shortly after the president submits a budget, staff members of the 12 appropriation subcommittees, in both the House and Senate, begin to closely review the document for

Table 24-4. *The Federal Appropriations Process*

Activity	Approximate Date
Presidential budget submission	Early February
Subcommittee hearings (House and Senate)	February–April
Budget resolution	By April 15
Subcommittee allocations	April–May
Subcommittee approval (House and Senate)	April–July
Full committee approval (House and Senate)	May–July
House passage	June–September
Senate passage	June–September
House-Senate conference committee meeting	September
House passage of conference report	September
Senate passage of conference report	September
Presidential signature (if vetoed, the process repeats)	By September 30 (but may be extended)

changes in budget or policy. After reviewing the president's budget, each subcommittee holds a series of hearings to gather input from the federal agencies and the public. The number and length of hearings varies with each subcommittee. Some limit hearings to as little as two weeks while others conduct hearings for months. These hearings often take place February through April.

Budget Resolution (House and Senate). According to the Congressional Budget and Impoundment Act of 1974, as amended, the Congress should pass a budget resolution by April 15, which establishes aggregate revenue and expenditure levels for the federal government. The act prohibits House or Senate consideration of any revenue or appropriations bill until the budget resolution is adopted by the Congress, or May 15, whichever is earlier.

Subcommittee Allocations or 302(b)s (House and Senate). Following adoption of the budget resolution, the appropriations committee allocates the budget among the 12 subcommittees. The overall amount of spending is referred to as the 302(a), which references §302(a) of the 1974 act. The amount allocated to each of the subcommittees is referred to as the 302(b), which references §302(b) of the 1974 act. In April or May, the full appropriations committee meets to approve allocation of the 302(b) levels.

Subcommittee Approval (House and Senate). After subcommittee hearings are held, the staff reviews the testimony presented and prepares recommendations to the subcommittee chairperson. Following discussions with the staff, the chairperson presents his or her recommendations, known as the Chairman's Mark, to the subcommittee at a meeting known as a markup. The subcommittee members offer amendments to the Chairman's Mark and give approval to the document. The subcommittee markup often takes place April through July.

Full Committee Approval (House and Senate). Following approval by the subcommittee, the bill and its accompanying report are drafted and printed for distribution to the members of the committee. The entire committee thereafter meets to discuss the subcommittee's version of the bill and make changes as desired. The full committee markup often takes place May through July.

Full House and Senate Approval. Once the appropriations committees have approved the legislation, it is forwarded to the full House or Senate for consideration by the entire body. By tradition, the House considers the bill first and sends the measure to the Senate, where the entire text is deleted and replaced with that approved by the Senate appropriations committee. Approval by the chambers often takes place June through September.

House-Senate Conference Committee. Following approval of a bill by the House and Senate, a committee is appointed to negotiate the differences between the two versions. The negotiators, known as conferees, are usually the members of the appropriations subcommittee in which the measure originated. Upon reaching agreement, the final bill, known as the conference report, is drafted. Conference committees usually meet in September.

Full House and Senate Approval of the Conference Report. After approval by the conference committee, the conference report is sent to the House and Senate for final approval. Debate on the conference report is conducted under very narrow rules allowing for virtually no amendments. Passage of the conference report by the House and Senate often takes place in September.

Presidential Signature. Once the House and Senate each approve an identical conference report, it is forwarded to the president to be signed into law, usually in September or October.

Maintaining a strong federal and state government relationship is vitally important. Whether seeking legislative remedies, regulatory relief, appropriations assistance, or some other matter, the reality will always remain that county governments must strive to work with federal and state governments. There are numerous ways to succeed in this task, including becoming involved in professional organizations such as ACCG and NACo. Those county officials who strive to maintain relationships with the state and federal government will ultimately benefit.

NOTES

1. NACo overview at www.naco.org.
2. Ibid.
3. 2009 ACCG County Platform.
4. Edwin L. Jackson, Mary E. Stakes, and Paul T. Hardy, *Handbook for Georgia Legislators*, 12th ed. (Athens: Carl Vinson Institute of Government, University of Georgia, 2001), 59.
5. Ibid., 61–62.
6. Ibid., 101.
7. Ibid., 193–94.
8. Ibid., 109.
9. Ibid., 134.
10. Ibid., 135.
11. Ibid., 138.
12. Ibid., 139.
13. 2 UNITED STATES CODE ANNOTATED (U.S.C.A.) §1501 et seq., Pub. L. 104-4. A national initiative was undertaken in the early 1990s by NACo, with strong support from organizations such as ACCG, to drastically curtail adoption of new unfunded mandates. This initiative culminated with the approval of the Unfunded Mandates Reform Act of 1995.
14. Religious Land Use and Institutionalized Persons Act of 2000, 42 U.S.C.A. §2000cc et seq.

PART 6

Public Access and Media Relations

25

Kelly J. L. Pridgen

Open Meetings and Open Records

Georgia's open meetings law[1] and open records law[2] are commonly referred to as the "sunshine laws." The open meetings law requires that the public have notice and access to meetings of commissioners as well as those of other governmental boards, committees, and authorities. The open records law establishes the procedure for providing county and other governmental agency records to anyone requesting to see them. The sunshine laws give citizens and noncitizens alike the opportunity to learn about how government operates, how tax dollars are spent, and how decisions that affect their daily lives are made. This access to county government is key to fostering public trust in the actions of county commissioners.

OPEN MEETINGS

Who Must Comply with the Open Meetings Act?

Georgia's open meetings law applies to meetings of the governing authority of "agencies," such as the county (i.e., the board of commissioners or the sole commissioner),[3] and committees established by the board of commissioners on which a member of the board serves.[4] The open meetings law also applies to the governing body of every county department, agency, board, bureau, commission, authority, or similar body.[5] Meetings of the planning and zoning board, the zoning board of appeals, the personnel review board, the merit system board, the board of tax assessors,[6] the board of equalization,[7] the water and sewer authority, the development authority, the hospital authority, the housing authority, and the recreation authority must also follow the requirements of the open meetings law.

What Meetings Must Be Open?

In general, whenever a quorum of the board of commissioners or other board gathers at a designated time to conduct or discuss public or official business, it is considered to be a meeting that must be open to the public and comply with the other requirements of the open meetings law.[8] This mandate applies to gatherings at which any public matter, official business, or policy is discussed or presented, including work sessions—even if no final action is taken. A quorum of commissioners may attend social gatherings without violating the open meetings law so long as no county business or other public matter is discussed.

Requirements of the Open Meetings Law

The county must provide the public with advance notice of meetings and agenda as well as allow access to the meeting and to a written summary and minutes.

Notice of Meeting

- *Notice for regular meetings.* Notice of the time, place, and dates of regular meetings (e.g., the board's monthly meeting) must be made available to the general public and be posted in a conspicuous place at the regular meeting place of the board of commissioners.[9]

- *Notice for special meetings.* For any meetings that are not conducted at the regular meeting place or time, the county must post the time, place, and date of the meeting for at least 24 hours at the regular meeting location and give written or oral notice at least 24 hours in advance of the meeting to the legal organ of the county or a newspaper with equal circulation.[10] In counties in which a legal organ is published less than four times per week, the time, place, and date of the meeting must be posted for at least 24 hours at the regular meeting location and, upon written request from broadcast or print media in the county, notice must be provided to the requesting media 24 hours in advance of the meeting. The media outlet, in turn, must make the information available to the public upon inquiry.[11]

- *Notice for emergency meetings.* When special circumstances occur, the county may hold a meeting with less than 24 hours' notice, if the county provides notice of the time, date, and location of the meeting and an agenda to the legal organ.[12] The legal organ is responsible for making information available to members of the public upon request.

A Meeting Agenda

An agenda of all matters expected to come before the board must be made available upon request and must be posted at the meeting site.[13] The agenda must be available and posted as far in advance as is practicable during the two weeks prior to the meeting.[14] If a particular issue is not included on the posted agenda, then it may only be considered if it is deemed necessary by the board.[15]

Public Access to the Meeting

Members of the public must be allowed access to the meeting.[16] If attendance at a meeting is larger than the meeting room can accommodate, then the commissioners should move the meeting to a larger meeting room, if available.[17]

Public Recording of the Meeting

Members of the public may make audio or video recordings of the meeting.[18]

A Meeting Summary

A written summary of the subjects and a list of the officials attending the meeting must be prepared and made available within two business days of the meeting.[19]

Minutes of a Meeting

The minutes must, at a minimum, contain the names of the commissioners present at the meeting, a description of each motion or other proposal made, and a record of all votes.[20] For emergency meetings (i.e., meetings with less than 24 hours' notice), the minutes must describe the notice given and the reason for the emergency.[21] Contracts, maps, and other documents that were approved in the meeting may be included in the minutes or incorporated by reference.[22]

When an Emergency or Disaster Affects Compliance with the Open Meetings Law

If the governor or other authorized state official declares an emergency or disaster that renders it impossible or imprudent to hold a meeting at the regular time and place, meetings may be called by the chairman or any two commissioners. To the extent made necessary by the emergency, the commissioners are not required to comply with "time consuming procedures and formalities prescribed by law," according to the Georgia Emergency Management Act of 1981.[23]

Exemption from Open Meetings Law Requirements

The General Assembly has created special exemptions to the open meetings law. Some gatherings are not considered meetings and are therefore not subject to any requirements; other gatherings may be conducted in a closed meeting but are still subject to certain requirements.

There are two types of gatherings that are not considered meetings subject to the requirements of the open meetings law (i.e., the county is not required to publish notices, post an agenda, or prepare a written summary or minutes). First, when a quorum of the board of commissioners inspects county facilities under its jurisdiction (such as fire departments, the courthouse annex, and the water treatment plant), it is not subject to the open meetings law so long as other county business or any other public matter is not discussed.[24] However, if a quorum of the board is present and members begin to discuss or conduct other county business during such an inspection, they are in violation of the open meetings law. Second, when commissioners meet with "other government officials" (e.g., members of the Department of Transportation or Department of Revenue) at a location outside their county,[25] the gathering is not considered a meeting so long as no final action is taken.[26] This exemption to the open meetings law hinges upon meeting with an official or officials from another government agency. However, retreats or meetings located outside the county that only members and employees of the county attend must comply with the requirements of the open meetings law.

County commissioners may close an open meeting to discuss certain topics in an executive session. As explained later in this chapter, there are special procedural requirements that commissioners must follow to legally conduct an executive session. The following meetings relevant to county commissioners may be conducted in closed or executive sessions.

Meetings with the County's Attorney to Discuss Pending or Potential Lawsuits

The attorney-client privilege allows the board to meet with its attorney to discuss pending or potential lawsuits or claims against or by the county in a closed meeting.[27] Two things must be considered before closing a meeting pursuant to the attorney-client privilege. First, the attorney representing the county in the pending or potential lawsuit must be present. Second, a lawsuit by or against the county must already be filed, or there must be a potential lawsuit. A mere threat to take legal action against the county is not enough to close a meeting to discuss a potential lawsuit.[28] In order to determine whether a threat to sue the county is a potential lawsuit that may be discussed in an executive session, commissioners should ask the following questions:

1. Is there a formal demand letter or something else in writing that presents a claim against the county and indicates a sincere intent to sue?

2. Is there previous or preexisting litigation between the county and the other party or proof of ongoing litigation on similar claims?

3. Is there proof that the other party has hired an attorney and expressed an intent to sue?[29]

Additionally, the meeting may not be closed to receive legal advice on whether a topic may be discussed in a closed meeting.[30]

Meetings to Discuss Tax Matters Made Confidential by State Law

Only tax matters that are required to be confidential by a state statute or appellate court case may be discussed in executive session.[31]

Meetings to Discuss the Future Purchase or Condemnation of Real Estate

Commissioners may close a meeting to discuss the purchase of real estate by the county.[32] The exception applies only when the county acquires property—not when it sells property. Additionally, it applies only when the county is purchasing real property. The exemption does not apply when the county purchases personal property, such as vehicles, equipment, or supplies.

Meetings to Deliberate on the Employment, Appointment, or Dismissal of a County Employee or Officer

Commissioners may close the portion of the meeting during which they are deliberating on hiring, appointing, compensating, disciplining, or dismissing an employee.[33] However, any portion of a meeting during which the board receives evidence or hears arguments involving disciplinary actions must be open.[34]Additionally, all votes on personnel matters must be taken in public.[35]

Because executive sessions are the exception, not the rule, if there is any doubt whether a topic may be discussed in a closed meeting, the county attorney should be consulted. If doubt remains, the meeting should be open.

Procedures for Properly Conducting an Executive Session

In creating special exemptions to the open meetings law, the General Assembly also established certain requirements for conducting executive sessions.

- *Precede with an open meeting.* All executive sessions must evolve directly from a properly advertised open meeting.

- *Vote to close the meeting.* The board, in a properly advertised open meeting, must vote to close the meeting.[36] The reasons for closing the meeting and the results of the vote must be entered into the minutes of the open meeting.[37]

- *Allow only relevant attendees.* If a session is closed, it must be closed to everyone not affiliated with the county or the business being conducted.[38]

- *Discuss only legally exempt topics.* Only matters that are legally exempt from the open meetings law may be discussed at the executive session.[39] If someone attempts to bring up a nonexempt topic, the chairman should rule that person out of order. If the nonexempt discussion continues, the chairman should adjourn the meeting immediately.

- *Vote on matters discussed in executive session, generally in an open forum.* The open meetings law specifically requires any vote on a personnel matter to be taken in public.[40] Although the Georgia Court of Appeals found that voting on whether to accept or reject a settlement offer in a pending lawsuit during an executive session was appropriate under the attorney-client exception to the open meetings law,[41] many counties vote in an open meeting to ratify any action discussed in a closed meeting to avoid any issue with the open meetings law.

- *Prepare minutes.* Minutes must be prepared for the open meeting that precedes the executive session and must reflect the names of the commissioners present and the names of commissioners who voted to close the meeting as well as the specific reason for closing the meeting.[42] Minutes of a closed meeting may be taken but are required only for land acquisitions.[43] In the case of executive sessions held to discuss land acquisition, minutes must be taken as in an open meeting, except that the county may delay releasing the portion of the minutes that would disclose the identity of the real estate until the property has been purchased or the county decides not to purchase it.[44]

- *Sign affidavit.* At the end of the closed meeting, the chairperson or presiding officer must sign a notarized affidavit stating, under oath, that only legally exempt topics were discussed and providing the legal authority for the exemption.[45] The affidavit must be included with the minutes from the open meeting.[46]

Consequences of Noncompliance with Open Meetings Laws

In addition to the district attorney or solicitor, the attorney general is authorized to file a criminal action against individuals who violate the open meetings law.[47] Anyone who knowingly violates the open meetings law may be found guilty of a misdemeanor and fined up to $500.[48] If the chairman or commissioner signs an executive session affidavit containing false information, he or she may be convicted of a felony and fined $1,000 and/or imprisoned for up to five years.[49]

The attorney general or any other person, firm, or corporation may bring a civil action in superior court to require the county to obey the open meetings law.[50] Such lawsuits must be filed within 90 days of the date that the alleged violation of the open meetings law occurred.[51] However, for zoning decisions, the action must be brought within 30 days.[52] If challenged successfully, any resolution, ordinance, rule, regulation, or other official action made or adopted at a meeting that does not comply with the law will not be binding.[53]

The county may be required to pay the complaining party's attorney's fees, unless the county can show that it acted with substantial justification in not complying with the open meetings law.[54] Further, participation in a meeting that is held in violation of the open meetings act may be grounds for recall.[55]

Making Open Meetings Work

The open meetings law provides county commissioners with a tool that encourages public participation in county government. It is a prime opportunity for county commissioners to show their citizens how their tax dollars are spent. Following are some steps that county commissioners can take to avoid problems with implementing the open meetings law while furthering the purpose of the law in their county.

For Local Officials

- *Update meeting procedures and policies.* Make sure that local ordinances and policies regarding meetings are consistent with the new changes in the open meetings law.

- *Understand the law.* Ask the county attorney to review the open meetings law requirements. Consider periodic seminars conducted by the county attorney for the board of commissioners and other county boards and committees. Make sure that all members of the board and key staff understand the requirements of the open meetings law, particularly the exemptions. This step could prevent an unintentional introduction of a nonexempt topic during an executive session.

- *Foster compliance by other boards and committees.* Make sure that other county boards are aware of their responsibilities under the open meetings law. Send them a copy of any meetings ordinances that apply. Oftentimes, committees and other boards incorrectly assume that only the board of commissioners is subject to the open meetings law.

- *Avoid closed meetings.* Always begin with the assumption that an issue should be discussed in an open meeting. Executive sessions are only for those narrowly defined circumstances that are spelled out in the law. If the topic seems to be in a gray area, then it should be discussed in an open meeting. Do not risk going into executive session to discuss topics that are not clearly exempt from the law.

- *Create an executive session procedure.* Although not required, some local governments have adopted policies regarding closed meetings such as using a preestablished motion to go into executive session, requiring all members (rather than just the chairman or mayor) to sign an executive session affidavit, using a preestablished resolution upon coming out of an executive session that certifies that the meeting was devoted to exempt topics, and authorizing the chairman or mayor to execute the executive session affidavit.

For Citizens and the Media

- *Furnish advance notice of meetings.* Notify the local media, and post meeting notices at the meeting site as soon as a meeting is scheduled. Although it is not required by the open meetings law, counties can further public awareness of meetings by posting meeting notices and agendas on the county Web site or through the government access channel, if available.

- *Post the agenda early.* Post the agenda at the meeting site and on the county Web site as soon as it is prepared.

- *Provide adequate meeting space.* Make sure the meeting room adequately accommodates the audience. In addition to providing enough seating, the room should be arranged so that the audience may see and hear the meeting. Offer members of the press a table or other designated area, if available, where they can hear and see the meeting.

- *Distribute meeting material.* At the meeting, make available copies of the agenda and other meeting material that may be of interest to those attending.

- *Offer a media workbook.* Provide press members with their own meeting workbooks, similar to those provided to the commissioners and manager, which contain copies of contracts, resolutions, ordinances, and other requests to be considered at the meeting. Although not required, this gesture can establish a positive relationship with the local media. Oftentimes, the media's perceived violations of the open meetings and open records law could be lessened by willingly and voluntarily providing information up front.

- *Televise meetings.* Consider broadcasting meetings on the government access cable channel or making footage available through the county Web site.

OPEN RECORDS

Who Must Comply with the Open Records Law?

Georgia's open records law applies to anyone who possesses records of the county, including all county departments, agencies, boards, bureaus, commissions, authorities, and other similar bodies.[56] Further, it applies to companies, individuals, and other entities that do business with or have contracts with the county to provide services for the county.[57] Generally, the county employee or official who maintains the records is the records custodian, who actually responds to requests for county records. For example, if an individual requested commission meeting minutes, the county clerk would be the likely records custodian to handle the request. If an individual requested personnel records, the personnel director or his or her designee would likely be the records custodian.

Public Records That Are Subject to Disclosure

All documents, papers, letters, maps, books, tapes, photographs, computer-based or computer-generated information, or similar material prepared and maintained or received in the course of the operation of the county are public records subject to disclosure unless they fall within one of the legal exemptions to the open records law.[58] Handwritten notes, e-mails, calendars, internet "cookies" (information that is downloaded to your computer when you visit Web sites), and text messages are public records subject to disclosure under the open records law.

Records That Are Legally Exempt from Disclosure

Some records are not required ever to be disclosed, while other records may be withheld from disclosure only temporarily. Most of the exemptions to the open records law merely permit the county to withhold records; in other words, although records are exempt, the county may release them. However, certain records must be kept confidential and may not be released. This section discusses some of the exemptions most relevant to county commissioners.

Records That Must Be Kept Confidential

In addition to medical records,[59] the following records must not be released except under specific circumstances:

- *Information that could lead to identity theft.* Social security numbers, mother's birth name, credit card, debit card, bank account, account and utility account passwords and numbers, financial data, insurance data, or medical information must be redacted from all records before they are released.[60] If technically feasible and not cost prohibitive, month and day of birth must be redacted.[61] However, it should be noted that for certain requests, information pertaining to the following may be released:

    Individual or representative. An individual or his or her legal representative may obtain records containing social security numbers, mother's birth name, credit card, debit card, bank account, account or utility account passwords and numbers, financial data, insurance data, or medical information.[62]

    News media. A news media representative may obtain a social security number and day and month of birth (except those of nonelected public employees, including county employees, teachers and employees of the public school system).[63]

    Government employees. A government employee may obtain records containing social security numbers, mother's birth name, credit card, debit card, bank account, financial data, insurance data, or medical information if he or she is doing so for administrative or law enforcement purposes.[64]

Deceased individuals. Any individual may obtain day and month of birth and mother's birth name of a deceased individual.[65]

Credit reporting agencies. Consumer reporting agencies may obtain credit and payment information.[66]

Fraudulent requests. If the records custodian believes that a fraudulent request has been made, he or she must apply to the superior court for a protective order to protect the records.[67]

- *Confidential tax matters.* Tax matters made confidential by state law such as certain occupation tax records, taxpayer depreciation schedules, and taxpayer accounting records must not be released.[68]

- *Trade secrets.* Trade secrets and certain proprietary information protected by the Georgia Trade Secrets Act of 1990 may not be released.[69]

- *Federal government.* Records specifically required by the federal government to be kept confidential may not be released.[70]

- *Cable and video service provider financial information.* Financial statements providing the aggregate amount of the provider's gross revenues that specifically identify subscriber, advertising, and home shopping services revenues for the county, the amount of the franchise fee payment due to the county, and any business records made available to the county for auditing purposes from cable and video service providers that have a state franchise agreement must not be released.[71] It should be noted that this exemption does not apply to records given to the county by these providers through a local cable or video franchise agreement.

Records That Are Temporarily Exempt from Disclosure

The following records may be (but are not required to be) withheld for a specific period of time.

- *Investigation of complaints against county employees.* Records containing materials from investigations of complaints against public officers or employees or relating to the suspension or termination of a public officer or employee are not subject to disclosure until 10 days after the investigation is complete.[72]

- *Appointment of the executive head.* Records that would identify all of the applicants for the position of executive head of an agency (such as county manager or county administrator) may be withheld until three finalists are selected, unless the public has had access to the application and interview process.[73] Fourteen days prior to the final decision, the names and application materials of the three finalists must be released, unless the applicant no longer seeks the position.[74] However, the county may be required to provide information regarding the number of applicants and the race and gender of those applicants.[75]

- *Land acquisition.* Real estate appraisals, engineering or feasibility estimates, or other records relating to the acquisition of real property may be withheld only until the transaction has been completed or terminated.[76]

- *Pending bids and proposals.* On construction projects, the engineer's cost estimates and competing bids and proposals may be withheld until such time as the final award of the contract is made or the project is abandoned.[77]

- *Attorney-client privilege.* Records subject to the attorney-client privilege (i.e., records pertaining to the requesting or giving of legal advice concerning pending or potential litigation, settlement, administrative proceedings, or other judicial actions in which the county is involved) may be withheld on pending litigation.[78]

- *Pending violations.* Records of law enforcement, prosecution, or regulatory agencies in any pending investigation, other than the initial incident report, may be withheld until the prosecution or any direct litigation is final or terminated.[79]

Records That May Be Withheld

Certain records—including records of confidential evaluations relating to the appointment or hiring of a public officer or employee[80] and attorney work product[81]—may be (but are not required to be) withheld from disclosure.

- *Carpooling.* The names, addresses, telephone numbers, hours of employment, or any other information that would reveal the identity of an individual who participates in or has expressed an interest in participating in car pools, van pools, bus pools, or other provision of transit routes may be withheld.[82]

- *Fire alarms and security systems.* Records that would reveal the names, addresses, telephone numbers, security codes, e-mail addresses, or any other data or information collected, developed, or received by the county in connection with the installation, service, maintenance, operation, sale, or lease of a burglar alarm system, fire alarm system, or other electronic security system may be withheld.[83]

- *Neighborhood watch and public safety programs.* Records that would reveal the names, home addresses, telephone numbers, security codes, e-mail addresses, or any other data or information developed, collected, or received by the county in connection with a neighborhood watch or public safety notification program may be withheld.[84]

- *Invasion of privacy.* Records of which disclosure would be an "invasion of privacy" according to Georgia case law may be withheld.[85]

- *Law enforcement, prosecutors, judges, teachers, and school employees.* Records that would reveal the home address, telephone number, social security number, insurance, medical information, or family members of law enforcement officers, firefighters, judges, emergency medical technicians and paramedics, correctional employees, prosecutors, Georgia Bureau of Investigation forensic scientists, nonelected public employees, including county employees, public school teachers, and employees of public schools, may be withheld.[86]

- *Confidential source.* Records compiled for law enforcement purposes that would disclose the identity of a confidential source and endanger the life or physical safety of any person or that would disclose the existence of a confidential surveillance or investigation may be withheld.[87]

- *Accident reports.* Georgia Uniform Motor Vehicle Accident Reports may be withheld unless the person requesting the accident report is named in the report, represents someone named in the report, or files a statement of need.[88] Additionally, other governmental agencies may acquire accident reports without filing a statement of need if they are obtaining the accident report in conjunction with an ongoing administrative, criminal, or tax investigation.[89]

- *Computer programs or software.* Although the data and information stored on computers are public records, citizens may not copy licensed computer programs and software.[90]

Response to an Open Records Request

The open records law requires that all public records, except those legally exempted from disclosure, must be open for personal inspection by any individual at a reasonable time and place[91]—usually within three business days from the receipt of the request.[92] The person who typically responds to the request is the person who is in control of the documents or the records custodian. However, the time to respond to the request begins once the request is received by the county, not the records custodian. The county must respond within three business days of receiving the request[93] by doing the following:

- *Determine whether the county has the requested documents.* The county is not required to prepare any reports, summaries, or compilations that are not in existence at the time of the request.[94] However, requests may be made for documents that do not currently exist but will exist in the future.[95] For example, if an individual requested copies of minutes of future meetings, the county would be obliged to provide copies of the minutes as they come into existence.

- *Determine whether the requested documents are subject to an exemption to the Open Records Law.* The records custodian should give careful consideration before determining that a record is not subject to disclosure. Remember, the rule is that the record is open; the exceptions for not having to release a document are very narrow. As will be explained, failure to provide an open record is a crime.[96] However, a records custodian will not be held liable if he or she is sued for releasing a record in error in good faith reliance that it was subject to the open records law.[97] Once it has been determined that all or part[98] of a document falls under one of the legal exemptions, the county must provide, in writing, the specific legal authority exempting such record from disclosure by code section, subsection, and paragraph.[99] Upon the discovery of an error in designating an exemption, the county has only one opportunity to amend or supplement the designation.[100] Such a correction or amendment must be made within five days of the discovery of the error or within five days of the institution of an action to enforce the act, whichever is sooner.[101] If a requested document contains both open and exempt information, the records custodian must still release the document but may redact or mark out the exempt information.[102]

- *Provide an estimate of any copying or administrative charges for responding to the request.* The records custodian must notify the party making the request of the estimated charge prior to fulfilling the request.[103] Where fees are specifically authorized by law, those fees shall apply.[104] If there are no fees provided by law, then the county may collect a uniform copying fee of up to 25 cents per page.[105] Reasonable charges for search, retrieval, and other direct administrative costs may be collected.[106] However, the hourly charge shall not exceed the salary of the lowest-paid full-time employee with the requisite skill and knowledge to perform the request.[107] There may be no charge for the first 15 minutes of work.[108] For records made available through electronic means, the agency may charge the actual cost of the computer disk or other types of removable media and for other administrative costs directly attributable to providing access,[109] unless it is information from a geographic information system. Counties may establish license fees or other fees for providing information from the geographic information system to recover a reasonable portion of the cost to the taxpayers associated with building and maintaining the system.[110]

- *Provide inspection and copying of the requested documents, if available.* If the records or documents cannot be made available within three business days of receipt of the request by the county, a written description of the records, along with a timetable for inspection and copying, must be provided within three days. When requested, records that are maintained by computer shall be made available when practicable by electronic means, including Internet access, subject to reasonable security restrictions. The records custodian must supervise the copying and may adopt and enforce reasonable rules governing the work.[111] The copying must be done in the room where the records, documents, or instruments are kept by law.[112] The records custodian must also use the most economical means available in responding to the request.[113] When a person has requested copies and does not pay, the county is authorized to collect the charges in any manner authorized by law for the collection of taxes, fees, or assessments owed to the county,[114] so long as an estimate for the charges was provided to the requesting party before the records custodian fulfilled the request.[115] When requests are made by other agencies, the procedures and copying fees do not apply if they are sought in conjunction with an ongoing administrative, criminal, or tax investigation.[116] Even records otherwise exempt from public disclosure may be released to the requesting agency.[117]

Penalties and Fines for Failure to Comply with the Open Records Law

In addition to the district attorney or solicitor-general, the attorney general is authorized to file a criminal action against individuals who violate the open records law.[118] Anyone who knowingly and willfully violates the open records law, either by refusing access or failing to provide documents within the requisite time, may be found guilty of a misdemeanor and may be subject to a fine not to exceed $100.[119]

As with the open meetings law, the attorney general or any other person, firm, or corporation may bring a civil action in superior court to require the county records custodian to release records.[120]

The county may be required to pay the complaining party's attorney's fees if the records custodian acted without substantial justification in denying an open records request.[121]

County Actions to Make Records More Accessible to the Public

Actions include the following:

* *Understand the law.* Make sure that all members of the board of commissioners and all employees understand the basics of open records law (particularly the deadlines and the penalties for noncompliance) as well as when it is necessary to contact the county manager or attorney in responding to a request. Often, requests are made to frontline employees, such as receptionists. Because the three-day response period begins when the county rather than the records custodian receives the request, it is very important that anyone within the county who may potentially receive a request be aware of his or her duties under the law in addition to any county policy or procedure on responding to requests.

- *Update and implement open records policies.* Adopt and disseminate a policy on responding to open records requests. Educate employees on the policy requirements and stress the importance of delivering open records requests to the appropriate person in a timely manner.

- *Encourage other county officials, boards, and committees to comply.* Make sure that other county boards, committees, departments, and elected officers are aware of their responsibilities under the open records law. Send them a copy of any policy or forms for use in responding to requests. Other boards and county officers frequently incorrectly assume that only the board of commissioners is subject to the open records law.

- *Designate records custodians.* Designate the appropriate individuals as records custodians to handle open records requests for each department. Make sure that a backup plan is in place in case the designated custodian is out of the office or unavailable to respond to requests.

- *Deal with incorrect requests.* Instruct county staff on how to handle requests that are made to the wrong department or phrased incorrectly. For example, if a citizen requests tax records from the board of commissioners, the staff member should immediately forward that request to the correct county department. The time to respond to a request begins once the county receives the request, so even though the citizen may have given the request to the incorrect department, the request is nevertheless considered delivered. If a requestor asks for a record under the Freedom of Information Act, which is a federal law applicable to federal records, treat it as a request under Georgia's open records law.

- *Provide records through the county Web site.* Providing citizens with the option of accessing records through the county's Web site makes getting information easier for citizens and saves staff time. Examples of records that counties post online include meeting schedules, agendas, minutes, ordinances, budget items, and audit information. Thought should be given to the type and format of records that will be made available electronically. For example, posting of original documents could lead to alteration of records by outside parties. In order to protect the integrity of documents that are posted online, consider converting them into PDFs or a similar format. The open records law requires that, when practicable, records must be made available electronically when requested.[122] If your county does not yet have a Web site, weigh the cost to the taxpayers of providing this access against the time and money that could be saved by not having to photocopy requested records.

- *Provide quality "citizen service."* Emphasize to county employees the importance of good customer service. Almost all of the information contained in county records belongs to the public. Make sure that county employees understand that, regardless of the attitude of the party requesting the documents, these are public records and, as public employees, they are required to assist the requestor. The requestor should not be considered an adversary.

- *Increase availability of records by placing them in a central location.* Show citizens the valuable services that they receive for their tax dollars by looking for ways to make records more accessible. For instance, copies of regularly requested records, such as meeting minutes, the code of ordinances, or the county budget, could be placed in the public library.

- *Make copying easier.* Consider making a coin-operated copy machine available to those citizens who prefer to make their own copies. This option may be more economical for the requestor and at the same time allow county staff to continue with their other duties.

- *Limit exemptions.* Always begin with the assumption that a record is subject to disclosure. The exemptions to the open records law are very narrow. Do not try to restrict access to records that do not clearly fit within an exemption. The risk for criminal penalties[123] and lawsuits[124] is much greater if you fail to release an open record than if you release a record that is exempt. Reliance on the open records law is a defense if you are sued because you released a record that you believed, in good faith, was required under the open records law.[125]

- *Request legal review.* Not all requests need legal review. Discuss in advance with the county attorney the situations in which he or she should be consulted to review records requests. Also, identify who will provide legal review of records if the county attorney is out of town or otherwise unavailable. Be sure that all designated records custodians, including the county officers, are familiar with the procedure.

- *Make a written record of oral open records requests.* Although the person receiving the open records request on behalf of the county may ask that open records requests be made in writing, he or she may not require them to be in writing.[126] Most requestors will readily provide a written request for two reasons: (1) it protects them from misunderstanding the request and (2) it helps focus the request in order to avoid excessive charges (for example, when the request is for something other than meeting minutes, agendas, or ordinances). A written request also becomes an identifiable record, triggering the three-business-day time period. To simplify the process, a county could provide the requestor with a basic request form if he or she appears at the courthouse in person, or the form could be mailed, faxed, e-mailed, or posted on the county's Web site. County staff receiving the request should use a standard form for recording requests not received in writing.

- *Create a records inventory for quicker access.* Make an inventory of the county's paper and electronic records. Within three business days of a request, the requested records should be found and any relevant exemptions identified. Remember, claimed exemptions may only be amended or corrected one time.[127] An inventory will allow for quicker access to records as well as complete and accurate responses to requests.

- *Implement or update the county records retention plan.* State law requires counties to have a records retention plan.[128] This plan should be created with input from department heads, records custodians, and IT staff and should include both paper and electronic records. The Georgia Department of Archives provides a retention schedule for local government records that can be used to determine the length of time required to keep certain records. This schedule is updated on a regular basis and is available at sos.georgia.gov/archives/who_are_we/rims/default.htm. Once a policy has been adopted, all county employees should familiarize themselves with and follow the records retention plan.

- *Prepare timetable when records are not immediately available.* If the requested records cannot be processed within three days of receiving the request, politely advise the requestor that the records are not confidential but cannot be provided until a certain date. Be sure to explain why they cannot be obtained quickly. Remember that the law also requires that you provide a written notification to the requestor describing the records as well as a timetable for their release within three business days.[129]

- *Seek reimbursement of cost uniformly.* Apply the open records policy regarding cost reimbursement for copying and supervising records requests equally. Do not charge some citizens but not others for copies and administrative time unless the policy provides that no charge is imposed for minimal amounts of copying. The copying and administrative charges authorized by the open records law are not to be used to discourage frequent or unpleasant requestors. Rather, they are designed to ease the cost of providing access to public records to the taxpayers, who ultimately pay the cost of compliance beyond what is collected in fees from the requestor.

- *Avoid bureaucratic traps.* If a requested record is available at the time of the request, do not make the requestor wait three business days merely because the law allows it. The law does not require that the county wait the three-business-day window to respond; it merely allows the county three business days to process those requests that cannot be filled immediately.

- *Avoid using legal technicalities.* Resist taking advantage of technicalities and loopholes in the law. Trying to work around the law is the surest way to guarantee that new changes will be made that will make it even tougher for county officials to comply efficiently with the open records law. When faced with a "gray" area or a loophole, remember that the General Assembly and the courts are available to clear up the issue. Be assured that the courts have made it clear that they will always lean toward making access easier or records more open.

For more information on this topic, see the Georgia's Open Meetings and Open Records Laws Guide for County Officials available from the Association County Commissioners of Georgia.

NOTES

1. OFFICIAL CODE OF GEORGIA ANNOTATED (O.C.G.A.) §50-14-1 et seq.
2. O.C.G.A. §50-18-70 et seq.
3. O.C.G.A. §50-14-1(a)(1)(B).
4. See O.C.G.A. §50-14-1(a)(2).
5. O.C.G.A. §50-14-1(a)(1)(C), (D).
6. See 1995 Op. Att'y Gen. No. U95-22.
7. See Bryan County Board of Equalization v. Bryan County Board of Tax Assessors, 253 Ga. App. 831 (2002); 1995 Op. Att'y Gen. No. U95-22.
8. O.C.G.A. §50-14-1(a)(2).
9. O.C.G.A. §50-14-1(d).
10. Ibid.
11. Ibid.
12. Ibid.
13. O.C.G.A. §50-14-1(e)(1).
14. Ibid.
15. Ibid.
16. O.C.G.A. §50-14-1(c).
17. Maxwell v. Carney, 273 Ga. 864 (2001).
18. O.C.G.A. §50-14-1(c).
19. O.C.G.A. §50-14-1(e)(2).
20. Ibid.
21. O.C.G.A. §50-14-1(d).
22. O.C.G.A. §§36-1-25, 36-10-1.
23. O.C.G.A. §§38-3-54, 38-3-55.
24. O.C.G.A. §50-14-1(a)(2).
25. Ibid.
26. Ibid.
27. O.C.G.A. §50-14-2(1).
28. The Claxton Enterprise v. Evans County Board of Commissioners, 249 Ga. App. 870 (2001); Decatur County v. Bainbridge Post Searchlight, Inc., 280 Ga. 706 (2006).
29. Ibid.
30. O.C.G.A. §50-14-2(1).
31. O.C.G.A. §50-14-2(2); 1995 Op. Att'y. Gen. No. U95-22.
32. O.C.G.A. §50-14-3(4); Johnson v. Board of Commissioners, Bibb County et al., 302 Ga. App. 266 (2010).
33. O.C.G.A. §50-14-3(6).
34. O.C.G.A. §50-14-3(6); Moon v. Terrell County, 249 Ga. App. 567 (2001).
35. Ibid.
36. O.C.G.A. §50-14-4(a).
37. Ibid.
38. See Jersawitz v. Fortson, 213 Ga. App. 796 (1994); 1998 Op. Att'y Gen. No. U98-3.

39. See O.C.G.A. §50-14-4(b).
40. O.C.G.A. §50-14-3(6).
41. Schoen v. Cherokee County, 242 Ga. App. 501 (2000). But see 1998 Op. Att'y Gen. No. U98-3.
42. O.C.G.A. §50-14-4(a); Moon v. Terrell County, 249 Ga. App. 567 (2001).
43. O.C.G.A. §50-14-3(4).
44. Ibid.
45. O.C.G.A. §50-14-4(b).
46. Ibid.
47. O.C.G.A. §50-14-5(a).
48. O.C.G.A. §50-14-6.
49. O.C.G.A. §16-10-71.
50. O.C.G.A. §50-14-5(a).
51. O.C.G.A. §50-14-1(b). See Guthrie v. Dalton City School District, 213 Ga. App. 849 (1994); Walker v. City of Warner Robbins, 262 Ga. 551 (1992); Anti-Landfill Corporation, Inc. v. North American Metal Company, LLC et al., 299 Ga. App. 509 (2009).
52. O.C.G.A. §§50-14-1(b), 5-3-20. See Hollberg v. Spalding County, 281 Ga. App. 768 (2006).
53. Ibid.
54. O.C.G.A. §50-14-5(b); Evans County Board of Commissioners v. Claxton Enterprise, 255 Ga. App. 656 (2002); Slaughter v. Brown, 269 Ga. App. 211 (2004).
55. See O.C.G.A. §21-4-3(7); Davis v. Shavers, 263 Ga. 785 (1994).
56. O.C.G.A. §50-18-70(a).
57. Ibid. See Hackworth v. Board of Education for the City of Atlanta, 214 Ga. App. 17 (1994).
58. O.C.G.A. §50-18-70(a).
59. O.C.G.A. §50-18-72(a)(2).
60. O.C.G.A. §50-18-72(a)(11.3)(A).
61. Ibid.
62. O.C.G.A. §50-18-72(a)(11.3)(A), (B)(v).
63. O.C.G.A. §50-18-72(a)(11.3)(A).
64. O.C.G.A. §50-18-72(a)(11.3)(B)(ii), (iii), (viii), (ix).
65. O.C.G.A. §50-18-72(a)(11.3)(B)(vi).
66. O.C.G.A. §50-18-72(a)(11.3)(B)(vii).
67. O.C.G.A. §50-18-72(a)(11.3)(D).
68. O.C.G.A. §§50-18-72(e)(3), 48-13-15(a), 48-5-314(a).
69. O.C.G.A. §§50-18-72(b)(1), 10-1-760 et seq.; Theragenics Corp. v. Georgia Department of Natural Resources, 244 Ga. App. 829 (2000).
70. O.C.G.A. §50-18-72(a)(1).
71. O.C.G.A. §36-76-6(d).
72. O.C.G.A. §50-18-72(a)(5).
73. O.C.G.A. §50-18-72(a)(7).
74. Ibid.
75. Ibid.

76. O.C.G.A. §50-18-72(a)(6)(A).
77. O.C.G.A. §50-18-72(a)(6)(B).
78. O.C.G.A. §50-18-72(e)(1).
79. O.C.G.A. §50-18-72(a)(4).
80. O.C.G.A. §50-18-72(a)(5).
81. O.C.G.A. §50-18-72(e)(2). Note that just because an attorney is involved does not automatically make any records related to his or her involvement exempt as work products. See Fulton DeKalb Hospital Authority v. Miller and Billips, 293 Ga. App. 601 (2008).
82. O.C.G.A. §50-18-72(a)(14).
83. O.C.G.A. §50-18-72(a)(11.2).
84. Ibid.
85. O.C.G.A. §50-18-72(a)(2). See Fincher v. State, 231 Ga. App. 49 (1998); Dortch v. Atlanta Journal and Atlanta Constitution, 261 Ga. 350 (1991).
86. O.C.G.A. §50-18-72(a)(13), (13.1).
87. O.C.G.A. §50-18-72(a)(3).
88. O.C.G.A. §50-18-72(a)(4.1).
89. O.C.G.A. §§50-18-77, 50-18-72(a)(4.1)(k).
90. O.C.G.A. §50-18-72(f)(2).
91. O.C.G.A. §50-18-70(b).
92. O.C.G.A. §50-18-70(f).
93. O.C.G.A. §50-18-72(h); Athens Newspapers, LLC v. Unified Government of Athens–Clarke County, 284 Ga. 192 (2008).
94. O.C.G.A. §50-18-70(d).
95. Howard v. Sumter Free Press, Inc., 272 Ga. 521 (2000).
96. O.C.G.A. §50-18-74(a).
97. O.C.G.A. §50-18-73(c).
98. O.C.G.A. §50-18-72(g).
99. O.C.G.A. §50-18-72(h).
100. Ibid.
101. Ibid.
102. See O.C.G.A. §50-18-72(g).
103. O.C.G.A. §50-18-71.2.
104. O.C.G.A. §50-18-71(b).
105. O.C.G.A. §50-18-71(c).
106. O.C.G.A. §50-18-71(d).
107. Ibid.
108. Ibid.
109. O.C.G.A. §50-18-71(f).
110. O.C.G.A. §50-29-2(b).
111. O.C.G.A. §50-18-71(a).
112. Ibid.
113. O.C.G.A. §50-18-71(e).
114. O.C.G.A. §50-18-71(g).
115. O.C.G.A. §50-18-71.2.

116. O.C.G.A. §50-18-77.
117. Ibid.
118. O.C.G.A. §50-18-73(a).
119. O.C.G.A. §50-18-74(a).
120. O.C.G.A. §50-18-73(a).
121. O.C.G.A. §50-18-73(b).
122. O.C.G.A. §50-18-70(g).
123. O.C.G.A. §50-18-74.
124. O.C.G.A. §50-18-73.
125. O.C.G.A. §50-18-73(c).
126. Howard v. Sumter Free Press, Inc., 272 Ga. 521 (2000).
127. O.C.G.A. §50-18-72(h).
128. O.C.G.A. §50-18-99.
129. O.C.G.A. §50-18-70(f).

26

James F. Grubiak

Meetings Procedure, Organization, and Public Participation

During meetings of the county governing authority, decisions are made that formally set county programs in motion and authorize the expenditure of county funds.[1] The legislative and executive powers and duties of a county governing authority are joint powers and duties and may be exercised only as a group in meetings of the board. Individual members do not have the authority to act independently unless so authorized by statute.[2]

Properly organized and conducted meetings provide the structure through which a board of commissioners or sole commissioner (i.e., the county governing authority) may debate an issue and come to a decision. A meeting that is well organized will be more productive, more efficient, and above all, more businesslike than a meeting that is unorganized or poorly organized.[3]

RULES OF PROCEDURE

Thomas Jefferson was instrumental in disseminating rules of procedure or parliamentary law throughout the United States with publication of the first American book on parliamentary law in 1801. In 1876, Henry Martyn Robert published *Robert's Rules of Order*, which became and has remained the standard parliamentary law guidebook for a variety of organizations, including governmental bodies at the federal, state, and local levels.[4]

There are several important principles that are typically represented in any adopted rules of procedure. The most important are the following:

- The purpose of parliamentary procedure is to facilitate the transaction of business and to promote cooperation and harmony.
- All members of the deliberative body have equal rights, privileges, and obligations.
- Majority vote decides.
- The rights of the minority must be protected.
- All members of the body have a right to full and free discussion of every proposition presented for a decision.
- All members have the right to know the meaning of the question before the board and what its effect will be.
- All meetings must be characterized by fairness and good faith.[5]

The overall principles of parliamentary procedure are often more important than the specific rules. On occasion, observing the technicalities of parliamentary procedure may be necessary if business is to be accomplished fairly. In other instances, however, the rules can be relaxed, and the meeting can proceed more informally. Generally, the presiding officer is the best judge of these situations. An effective chairman knows when to apply the rules strictly and when to take a more relaxed approach.[6]

Before a commissioner (especially the chairman) can understand and be thoroughly familiar with the rules of procedure applicable to meetings of the governing authority, he or she must first determine which rules of procedure apply or have been adopted, if any. Generally, there are two circumstances that might apply with respect to the existence of rules of procedure. First, the county enabling act (that is, the local act of the General Assembly that created the county's form of government) may provide for specific rules of procedure such as *Robert's Rules of Order*. Second, the enabling act may be silent on the matter, in which case the governing authority may use a standard guide to parliamentary procedure such as *Robert's Rules*, or the commissioners may design their own rules of procedure. Note that failure to follow rules of procedure is not necessarily fatal to a decision made by the commissioners. Unless certain rules of procedure are specified by a local act of the General Assembly, the courts ordinarily will not annul or invalidate an otherwise properly enacted ordinance, even if the rules of procedure are not faithfully observed.[7]

For those counties that have the discretion to adopt their own rules or that choose to supplant procedures specified in the county enabling act by way of home rule,[8] a model ordinance providing simplified rules along with a guide to parliamentary procedure is available from Association County Commissioners of Georgia (ACCG).[9] It is highly recommended that all counties adopt some form of parliamentary procedure by ordinance or resolution if the county's enabling act does not specify procedures.

It is critical that the county attorney be directly involved in the adoption of any meetings procedures or rules of order because defective procedures could negate decisions made by the governing authority at a meeting. In addition to avoiding conflicts between any adopted procedures and requirements of local enabling acts, those counties that have adopted zoning ordinances should ensure that any adopted procedures do not conflict with adopted procedures for conducting meetings and hearings related to adopted zoning ordinances.[10]

WHAT CAN A COMMISSIONER DO TO PREPARE FOR MEETINGS?

A commissioner who comes to meetings unprepared may prolong the meeting and create an unfavorable impression on the media and public. A commissioner should know the issues and his or her position on them.

Prior to each meeting, a commissioner should do the following:

1. Study the data, reports, and memoranda that accompany the agenda
2. Review his or her own research and observations on the issues as well as pertinent county resolutions or ordinances
3. Review alternative solutions to each problem
4. Choose what seems to be the best solution, determine what positions others are likely to take, and consider where and how much he or she is willing to compromise
5. Be ready to argue effectively for his or her position

HOW ARE MEETINGS CONDUCTED?

The governing authority and its presiding officer can ensure that governing authority meetings are carried out in an orderly and dignified fashion. Certain organizational matters may be addressed in a county's enabling act. If they are not, a county may adopt an ordinance addressing a variety of organizational issues such as preparation of agendas, use of consent agendas, order of business, procedures for amending agendas, decorum, abstentions, public hearings, and related matters. A model meetings organization ordinance addressing these issues is available from ACCG.[11]

Open Meetings

Regardless of the legal basis for organizing and conducting meetings, many critical matters related to meetings of county officials and staff are addressed in the state open meetings law and must be accommodated.[12] The Georgia "sunshine" law stipulates that all meetings, except those expressly exempted by law, are to be open to the public.[13] A meeting is defined as a gathering of a quorum of the members of the governing authority or of any committee of its members, pursuant to a schedule of, or call or notice, at which any public matter, county business, or county policy is to be discussed or at which official action is to be taken.[14] Furthermore, the act states that no resolution, rule, regulation, ordinance, or other official action is binding unless made in accordance with the open meetings act.[15] It is unlawful for any governing authority member to conduct or participate in a meeting not in accordance with the act.[16] See Chapter 25 of this handbook and the handbook on open meetings and records published by ACCG for more detailed information on requirements of the Open Meetings Act.[17]

When and Where Meetings Are Held

Under Georgia law, all official business of the county must take place at the county site, more commonly referred to as the county seat. That is, the decision-making process of the commissioners, including deliberation and voting on any issue before the board, must occur in the county courthouse or other administrative offices of the county governing authority within the boundaries of the county seat.[18] An exception applies during an emergency or disaster of natural or manmade causes. In such an event, the county may meet anywhere inside or outside the county boundaries as necessary to conduct county business.[19] Notwithstanding the foregoing, committee meetings, public hearings, and the like may be held outside the county seat because such bodies are advisory or administrative in nature and are not authorized to make final decisions for the county.

Although the public must be allowed access to meetings, the county governing authority is not required to provide a meeting place large enough to accommodate all members of the public.[20] Nonetheless, meetings must be accessible to persons with disabilities as required by federal law.[21]

Meetings must be held in accordance with a regular schedule, and the governing authority must prescribe the time, place, and dates of regular meetings.[22] Oftentimes, the county enabling act specifies how many regular meetings will be held by the governing authority each month as well as the day and time of each meeting. Although commissioners must meet at least at the times and on the days specified in the enabling act, nothing in current law bars them from holding additional regularly scheduled or special meetings. The additional meetings can be at whatever time and day the commissioners choose as long as proper notice is given.[23]

The Agenda

Well-run meetings are not a result of chance; rather, they are the result of thorough and careful planning. Careful planning is especially important for those meetings that are likely to be divisive. Members of the board and other officers should submit agenda items for upcoming meetings well in advance of the meeting in order to allow staff sufficient time to gather information and properly prepare it for the board's consideration. The clerk may be directed to contact members of the board or other officers to solicit agenda items.[24]

A formal, written agenda, typically following the official order of business, must be prepared in advance of each meeting. An agenda provides an outline of items to be considered and may list them in order of priority. The agenda must include all items that are expected to be considered at a particular meeting.[25] It may also briefly state what action is requested of the governing authority as well as any previous action taken by it. As a courtesy, and to ensure responsible consideration of the issues coming before the commissioners, the agenda—together with appropriate data, reports, and memoranda—should be provided to each commission member at least one day before the meeting. A copy of the agenda and accompanying materials might also be sent to the local media in time for publication before each meeting. Furthermore, state law requires that the agenda be made available to the public and be posted at the meeting site.[26]

Although state law allows commissioners to add necessary items to the agenda after it is posted, last-minute additions to the agenda that introduce items that members may not have had time to study should be avoided.[27] As a rule, commissioners should establish a deadline for submitting requests or communications for inclusion in the agenda. Any item received after the deadline should be held over for the next meeting unless a majority of governing authority members present at the meeting vote to add it to the agenda.

Consent Agendas

Consent agendas can be useful when commissioners have a great deal of business to consider. The consent agenda typically includes items that require a decision but that are not controversial. Items on a consent agenda are considered as a group, without debate or amendment. Individual items can, however, be removed from the consent agenda at a meeting and put back on the regular agenda for consideration whenever a commissioner objects to a specific item on the consent agenda.[28]

Order of Business

Meetings should follow an order of business formally included in its rules of procedure. The governing authority should not depart from this order except in unusual cases and then only by majority vote. An order of business makes it easier to prepare the agenda and minutes. A suggested order of business for regular meetings follows (other types of meetings should follow procedures adapted to their special needs):

1. *Call to order.* The presiding officer announces the beginning of the meeting. The name of each member is called, and his or her presence or absence is recorded by the clerk. The presiding officer then determines if a quorum is present.

2. *Minutes.* The minutes of the previous meeting are read, followed by suggestions from members for corrections. The minutes are then approved with corrections, if any.

3. *Administrative-fiscal matters.* This category of business includes advertising for bids and awarding contracts, budgetary and appropriation matters, tax rates and fee schedules, and personnel matters.

4. *Reports.* Reports from committees, department heads, or the administrator or manager (if one is employed) are given.

5. *Old business.* Items of business unfinished prior to adjournment of the previous meeting are completed or continued. For example, proposed resolutions or ordinances that must be read two or more times before enactment are read at this time.

6. *New business.* Subjects and proposed resolutions or ordinances not previously presented to the governing authority are discussed.

7. *Appearances/public comment.* Individual citizens and representatives of groups, associations, and businesses appear in order to make statements, raise issues, present petitions, or otherwise address the commissioners. Although not required, procedures may be adopted requiring citizens to provide advance notice of the topic they wish to address.

8. *Adjournment.* When there is no further business, the presiding officer adjourns the meeting.

Quorum

A specific number of commissioners must be present at a meeting in order for it to be considered valid. This number is called the quorum. Requiring a quorum to conduct business and ultimately make decisions helps guarantee that the will of the majority of the commissioners prevails and the rights of the minority are protected.[29] The quorum for conducting business may be specifically stated in county enabling acts. If not, the quorum consists of a majority of the positions on the board. Until a quorum is present, there can be no meeting.[30]

Voting

The underlying principle of any deliberative body, including boards of commissioners, is the concept of majority vote. That is, more than half of the members in attendance must agree on an issue before it becomes effective.[31] Note, however, that county enabling acts may specify otherwise. For example, some enabling acts provide that a majority of the members of the board is necessary in order to pass a resolution or enact an ordinance. In certain instances, more than a simple majority vote is required to pass a measure, but governmental boards cannot limit their own powers by adopting a rule requiring more than a simple majority vote.[32] However, the General Assembly may condition approval of certain acts by a local government upon attaining a "super majority" (for example, a two-thirds or three-fourths vote of the members).

Unless specified in a county's enabling act, roll-call votes are not required. The only exception is a vote on whether or not to go into executive session (i.e., a meeting that is closed to the public). Those votes must be roll-call votes.[33] Whenever a roll-call vote is held, the name of each person for or against a proposal must be recorded. If a roll-call vote is not held, then the vote is recorded as "all voted in favor" or "four voted in favor and one opposed," for example. It is presumed that all who are present at a meeting have voted in the affirmative unless the minutes reflect a negative vote or an abstention.[34]

Abstentions

Although a member of a board of commissioners may refrain from voting, commissioners are under a strong obligation to vote on all motions because decision making is one of the primary discretionary duties of the office to which they were elected. A public officer should abstain from voting only when he or she has a conflict of interest between his or her own interests and those of the county.[35]

Meeting Summary

Minutes do not become official until approved at the next subsequent meeting of the commissioners. However, state law requires that a summary of each meeting be prepared and made available to the public within two days of any meeting. The summary must describe the subjects considered at the meeting and which commissioners were present at the meeting.[36]

Minutes

The record of a meeting is called the minutes. All actions taken by the county must be fully and accurately recorded in the minutes. The minutes are intended to be a nonbiased account of the business accomplished at the meeting. As such, the minutes should neither show any member's individual bias nor record verbatim what each member said. The minutes should never be used as a forum in which to comment on something said or done at the meeting. Effective minutes succinctly summarize what happened at the meeting in a straightforward narrative style. Although the specific form and content of the minutes may vary, the minutes should follow the arrangement of items on the agenda of the meeting.[37]

At a minimum, the minutes must include names of commissioners present at the meeting, a description of each proposal or motion made, and a record of all votes.[38] In the event of a called meeting with less than 24 hours' notice, the minutes must reflect the reason or special circumstances that led to holding the meeting with less than 24 hours' notice.[39]

If a board goes into an executive session to discuss an exempt topic, the minutes of the meeting must also record the vote for this decision and indicate the reason for closing the meeting to the public.[40] An affidavit by the presiding officer certifying that the executive session was limited to exempt topics must also be included in the minutes of the open meeting.[41] Generally, however, minutes need not be kept of executive sessions.[42] If they are, they should be kept in a confidential file. The exception is for executive sessions convened to discuss the acquisition of real estate. In such instances, minutes must be taken, but that portion of the minutes dealing with the real estate can remain confidential until the property in question is acquired or the project is abandoned.[43]

The official minutes of the meetings of a county governing authority must be maintained in the offices of the county governing authority. Any documents related to official actions of the commissioners, such as contracts or maps, may be either included in the minute book or incorporated by reference to a specific central location or locations where such documents are stored.[44]

Decorum

During all meetings, members are expected to behave with dignity and conduct themselves in a professional and respectful manner. All remarks should be directed to the chair and not to individual commissioners, staff, or citizens in attendance. A commissioner should not speak at a meeting until recognized by the chair, and all remarks should be addressed to the motion or agenda item being discussed. Personal remarks are inappropriate and should be ruled out of order by the chair.[45]

WHICH OFFICIALS PARTICIPATE IN MEETINGS?

In addition to the presiding officer and the commissioners, several appointed officials perform tasks vital to the conduct of meetings. They are the clerk of the governing authority, the administrator or manager (if any), and the county attorney.

Presiding Officer

The presiding officer of a county governing authority is the chairperson of the board or the sole commissioner when the said official is the governing authority. The chair of a board of commissioners is normally a member of the governing authority. However, depending on the county's enabling act, the chairperson may or may not have the power to vote and introduce motions. In some counties, the chair's only responsibility relative to the other board members is to preside over meetings. In this situation, the chairperson votes and makes motions like any other member of the board. In other counties, the chair votes only in the case of a tie or to veto actions by the board as a whole. Generally, the situation depends on whether or not the chairperson is elected to represent the entire county or a district within the county. In cases in which the chair represents a district, it is unlikely that the county enabling act would deprive the chairperson of the power to vote or make motions that would benefit his or her district.[46]

The performance of the presiding officer is the key to effective, businesslike meetings. He or she ensures that meetings are orderly and conducted in conformity with the rules of procedure and that they progress at an appropriate pace. At the same time, the presiding officer is responsible for ensuring that governing authority members and citizens have ample opportunity to express their views. In order to be an effective presiding officer, the chair must

- have a sense of fair play;
- use good manners;
- maintain decorum, even under tense situations;
- act quickly to restore order if a disturbance occurs;
- preserve each participant's right to speak without interruption;
- limit discussion to questions on the floor;
- disallow attacks on members or their motives;
- insist that all remarks be addressed to the chair;
- exercise self-control and not be drawn into verbal battles; and
- maintain dignity and composure.[47]

Other Members of the Governing Authority

Commissioners (i.e., the other members of a board of commissioners) share with the presiding officer the responsibility for properly conducted meetings. This responsibility includes having respect for one another's views. It also requires willingness to compromise, whenever possible, for the good of the county.

Commissioners must use their best judgment on how much time to spend examining a problem before reaching a decision. Actions of a governing authority should be deliberate, and the possible consequences should be carefully weighed. Members will probably never know as much as they would like to about the consequences of various actions. However, failure to make a decision or take action can create as many problems as a decision made too quickly. Moreover, commissioners should not allow a vocal minority that chooses to attend a particular meeting to unduly determine the outcome of a decision. Commissioners must exercise discretion and act for the good of the majority of the citizens.[48]

Clerk of the Governing Authority

Duties of the clerk of the governing authority (county clerk) differ significantly from county to county. They may include recording the governing authority's official actions, preparing and distributing the agenda, bookkeeping and maintaining other records, preparing and processing correspondence and reports, and managing the governing authority office, and in some counties, preparing the budget.

Administrator or Manager

Whether referred to as an administrator or manager, this officer plays a significant part in preparing for business to be considered at governing authority meetings. He or she is called upon to obtain facts and develop alternatives, make recommendations to the governing authority, and carry out policy decisions. This officer's role in meetings is determined largely by the governing authority. A good relationship between the governing authority and the administrator or manager can result in a smooth linkage of policy making to policy execution. Such a relationship can also improve the effectiveness of governing authority members and reduce the amount of time they must spend on county matters.

County Attorney

The county attorney advises the governing authority on its powers and duties under the law. He or she is usually required to attend meetings in order to provide immediate legal advice and keep abreast of county programs and problems. Upon request, the county attorney prepares resolutions or ordinances, local acts to be introduced to the legislature, contracts, and other legal documents. He or she also advises other county officers on official legal matters and represents the county in court and may serve as parliamentarian to the governing authority. The county attorney may also provide legal advice pertaining to pending or potential litigation or other judicial actions in an executive session. He or she must be in attendance at any executive session in order to invoke the attorney-client privilege.[49]

Every county should have an attorney who is accessible to county officials at all times. This person does not need to be a full-time officer but should advise the commissioners regarding the deliberations and decisions of the governing authority.[50]

WHAT ARE THE VARIOUS TYPES OF MEETINGS?

As a rule, governing authorities may hold regular meetings, pre-meeting work sessions, executive sessions, special meetings, committee meetings, and public hearings.

Regular Meetings

Regular meetings are official meetings held periodically to consider county business, make policy decisions, approve contracts, establish budgets, and levy taxes, among other things. Many of these matters are effectuated by the enactment of resolutions or ordinances at regular meetings. The time and frequency of meetings are usually specified in enabling acts passed by the legislature, in county resolutions or ordinances, or a combination of the foregoing. For example, a county enabling act may specify one regular meeting per month. The commissioners may, by resolution or ordinance, establish additional regular meeting dates in addition to the one required by law.

Pre-Meeting Work Sessions

Pre-meeting work sessions can facilitate decision making by providing commissioners the opportunity to discuss issues with staff in advance of regular meetings, finalize agendas, or create consent agendas. Note, however, that pre-meeting work sessions are considered meetings for the purposes of the Open Meetings Act. Therefore, work sessions are subject to the same notice requirements as any regularly scheduled meeting addressing county business.

Executive Sessions

Governing authority meetings that are closed to the public often are referred to as executive sessions. Such meetings may only be held for very limited purposes expressly authorized by law and by observing procedures specified in the law.[51] For example, a board of commissioners may go into executive session in order to discuss the acquisition of real estate or when discussing certain personnel actions. Only persons necessary to the discussion may attend executive sessions. They may include the members of the governing authority, county clerk, manager or administrator, and county attorney. Generally, if a private citizen is in attendance, the commissioners cannot meet in executive session.[52] There is some authority, however, for including necessary parties in the discussion, even if they are private citizens.[53] See Chapter 25 of this handbook for further details regarding under what condition executive sessions may be held.

Special Meetings

These meetings are usually convened in order to discuss and vote on one or a limited number of issues. Often these matters directly affect a certain group of citizens, many of whom will attend the meeting to argue for or against a proposed action. For example, some counties schedule special meetings for the limited purpose of considering rezonings. Holding a special meeting on a controversial subject is a good way to avoid a prolonged regular meeting and to focus the staff's and elected officials' attention on the matter at hand.

Committee Meetings

Much of the work of the county governing authority may be done through committees. In essence, county commissioners have the power to provide for a division of labor by creating committees to perform investigations, take evidence, make reports on pending or contemplated actions, and for other purposes relating to their legislative function. A county's enabling legislation may include provisions for this power, but in the absence of authorizing language, committees may still be created as needed.

Committees are instrumentalities of the governing authority. Commissioners may accept or reject the advice and recommendations given by a committee to the governing authority, but the governing authority may not delegate its powers to a committee. It has to make its own decision, albeit with input from the committee. If the governing authority adopts or ratifies the recommendations of the committee, they become the act of the governing authority.[54] Be mindful that committee meetings are subject to the requirements of the open meetings laws in the same manner as meetings of the full board.

Public Hearings

Public hearings allow citizens to express opinions on matters of public concern. Hearings may be held immediately prior to, during, or following a meeting of the governing authority or at other places and times that the governing authority determines. Generally, no official action is taken during a public hearing. Some hearings, such as those for zoning decisions,[55] adoption of a budget,[56] setting property tax millage,[57] adopting development impact fees,[58] or implementing business and occupation taxes,[59] are required by law. Hearings, whether required or voluntary, are called by the governing authority in order to gather facts related to proposed action, gauge public opinion, or permit citizens to "blow off steam." Merely giving citizens an opportunity to express their opinions may not eliminate the problem or resolve the issue at hand, but it does allow county officials to demonstrate their concern for citizens' views. For some hearings, like those regarding zoning decisions, policies and procedures for calling and conducting hearings must be officially adopted by the governing authority and be made available to the public.[60]

PUBLIC PARTICIPATION

Virtually all meetings of the county governing authority as well as all meetings of committees, boards, and commissions of the county are, by law, open to the public. That is, the public must at all times be afforded access to such meetings, and visual and sound recording must be permitted during the meetings.[61]

Citizen Comments and Input at Meetings

Although access is guaranteed by state law, citizens do not have a right to participate in the deliberations of a county governing authority as it conducts its meetings. The exception would be if the meeting is a public hearing.

Most counties do, however, provide for some form of citizen input and remarks at meetings, although the approach varies greatly from county to county. In some counties, citizens are allowed to comment on any matter of business before the commissioners without restriction. In others, a specific time on the agenda is set aside for all public remarks. Members of the public who wish to address the commissioners may be required to submit their name and the topic of their comments to the county clerk or manager a specified number of days prior to the meeting. Some counties may allow, by majority vote, public comment on any agenda item while the matter is being considered by the commissioners. Commissioners may allow citizens to speak to an issue but limit the amount of time made available to each citizen.[62] However, with respect to comments by citizens in zoning proceedings, state law provides that the opponents and the proponents of a zoning decision have equal time to present their case, and that time shall be no less than 10 minutes per side.[63]

Potential problems to do with accommodating citizen input and keeping order can best be avoided by having a set of clearly defined written rules or procedures that cover citizen participation, including decorum. These rules or procedures should be readily available for distribution to citizens and the media.

Encouraging Citizen Attendance

Meetings of the county governing authority offer an excellent opportunity for citizens to hear from and speak to their elected representatives. In order to encourage greater citizen participation, consider the following steps:

1. *Provide adequate notice of meeting.* Printing the time and location in the legal notice section of the local newspaper is not enough. Publish the agenda in the newspaper. Post the agenda on the county Web site and public buildings and through the government access channel, if available. Take advantage of free time that must be provided by radio and television stations for public service announcements.

2. *Schedule and situate meetings for maximum attendance.* Weekday evenings are usually most convenient. Arrange for adequate parking.

3. *Furnish a congenial setting for meetings.* The meeting room should be well maintained, dignified, adequately lighted, at a comfortable temperature, and large enough to accommodate the public. There should be good acoustics or a public address system and adequate seating provided for citizens. Governing authority members should face the audience and one another; a semicircular arrangement is effective. The clerk, attorney, and other county officials should be seated where they can best assist in the conduct of the meeting.

4. *Schedule business for maximum participation.* Scheduling subjects of greatest public interest early in the meeting is usually a good idea.

5. *Distribute the agenda and other information.* As citizens enter the meeting room, they should be given a copy of the agenda. A seating chart of governing authority members and the respective areas they represent, a simple organization chart of the county government, and a list of the names of the chief administrative officers are also helpful.

6. *Use visual aids for presentations.* Topics often can be presented visually for greater clarity. Zoning change requests, budget presentations, and reports, for example, can be made more informative

and interesting through the use of visual aids such as maps, charts, and PowerPoint presentations.

7. *Assist the news media.* Media reporters should be seated at a table where they can easily see and hear the proceedings. Upon entering the meeting room, they should be given a copy of the agenda. Data, reports, and memoranda sent with the agenda to governing authority members prior to the meeting should also be available for reporters.

Opening Ceremonies

Many counties open their meetings with the pledge of allegiance. If this is the procedure, the American flag should be prominently and correctly displayed. The presiding officer may lead the pledge, or prominent citizens or representatives of local civic organizations may be invited to do so.[64] An opening ceremony may also provide an opportunity for commissioners to recognize effective employees of the county, significant events taking place in the county, or accomplishments of citizens. Resolutions or certificates may be presented to acknowledge such achievements. Family members of the honorees may also be invited to attend.

Citizen Decorum

Citizens who attend meetings or comment on agenda items at a meeting do not have the right to interrupt or heckle commissioners, staff, or other citizens who have been granted an opportunity to address the commissioners.[65] Citizens should be held to the same standards of decorum that apply to the commissioners. That is, inappropriate or offensive remarks and personal attacks should not be allowed. Inappropriate behavior can be ruled out of order. If a citizen becomes abusive or disrupts the meeting, the presiding officer may recess the meeting or have a deputy or other law enforcement officer remove the disruptive person from the meeting, if necessary, in order to restore order. A person who knowingly commits any act that prevents or disrupts a lawful meeting may be found guilty of a misdemeanor.[66]

NOTES

1. Portions of this chapter are drawn from chapter 2 of the *Handbook for Councilmen in Council-Manager Cities*, 3rd ed. (New York: National Municipal League, 1976); "City Council Meetings," in *Handbook for Georgia Mayors and Councilmembers*, 2nd ed., ed. J. Devereux Weeks and Emily Honigberg (Athens: Carl Vinson Institute of Government, University of Georgia, 1984), 15–23; chapter 5 of the *Handbook for Virginia Mayors and Councilmen*, ed. J.

Devereux Weeks (Richmond and Charlottesville: Virginia Municipal League and Bureau of Public Administration, University of Virginia, 1963); and Elizabeth M. Lee, "Planning and Conducting City Council Meetings," *Management Information Service* 2, no. 5–9: 8–11.

2. See, generally, McQuillin Mun Corp. §13.07 (3rd ed.); *Sturgis Standard Code of Parliamentary Procedure*, 2nd ed. (New York: McGraw-Hill, 1966), 239.
3. See, for example, the foreword to *Meetings, Organization and Public Access for Counties*, 3rd ed. (Atlanta: Association County Commissioners of Georgia, 1999).
4. *New Robert's Rules of Order* (New York: Merriam-Webster, 1994), 10–11.
5. *Sturgis Standard Code of Parliamentary Procedure*, 8–11.
6. *New Robert's Rules of Order*, 2.
7. South Georgia Power v. Baumann, 169 Ga. 649 (1929).
8. GA. CONST. art. IX, §2, ¶1(b)(1).
9. *Parliamentary Procedure for Counties: A Guide and Model Ordinance*, 2nd ed. (Atlanta: Association County Commissioners of Georgia, 1994).
10. OFFICIAL CODE OF GEORGIA ANNOTATED (O.C.G.A.) §36-66-5.
11. *Meetings, Organization and Public Access for Counties.*
12. O.C.G.A. §50-14-1 et seq.
13. O.C.G.A. §§50-14-1(b), 50-14-2, 50-14-3.
14. O.C.G.A. §50-14-1(a)(2).
15. O.C.G.A. §50-14-1(b).
16. O.C.G.A. §50-14-6.
17. *Georgia's Open Meetings and Open Records Laws: A Guide for County Commissioners* (Atlanta: Association County Commissioners of Georgia, 2010).
18. Brewster v. Houston County, 235 Ga. 68 (1975). See Jackson v. Gasses, 230 Ga. 712 (1973); O.C.G.A. §36-4-1 et seq.; Dozier et al. v. Norris et al., 241 Ga. 230 (1978); Op. Att'y Gen. No. U83-47.
19. O.C.G.A. §§38-3-54, 38-3-55.
20. *Maxwell v. Carney*, 273 Ga. 864 (2001); see, generally, McQuillin Mun Corp. §13.07.20 (3rd ed.).
21. Americans with Disabilities Act, 42 UNITED STATES CODE ANNOTATED (U.S.C.A.) §12101 et seq.
22. O.C.G.A. §50-14-1(d).
23. Ibid.
24. *New Robert's Rules of Order*, 184.
25. O.C.G.A. §50-14-1(e)(1).
26. Ibid.
27. Ibid.
28. *New Robert's Rules of Order*, 189.
29. Ibid., 11.
30. *Sturgis Standard Code of Parliamentary Procedure*, 237; O.C.G.A. §1-3-1(d)(5).
31. *New Robert's Rules of Order*, 11.
32. *Sturgis Standard Code of Parliamentary Procedure*, 240.
33. Moon v. Terrell County et al., 249 Ga. App. 567 (2001).
34. O.C.G.A. §50-14-1(e)(2).

35. *Sturgis Standard Code of Parliamentary Procedure*, 241. Note, however, that abstaining from voting may not be sufficient to overcome the conflict. See Department of Transportation et al. v. Brooks et al., 254 Ga. 303 (1985) and Op. Att'y Gen. No. 92-15; but see also Dick et al. v. Williams et al., 215 Ga. App. 629 (1994).

36. O.C.G.A. §50-14-1(e)(2).

37. *New Robert's Rules of Order*, 218; *Sturgis Standard Code of Parliamentary Procedure*, 238.

38. O.C.G.A. §50-14-1(e)(2).

39. O.C.G.A. §50-14-1(d).

40. O.C.G.A. §50-14-4(a).

41. O.C.G.A. §50-14-4(b).

42. Op. Att'y Gen. Nos. U88-30, U98-3.

43. O.C.G.A. §50-14-3(4).

44. O.C.G.A. §36-1-25.

45. *New Robert's Rules of Order*, 260.

46. Palmer v. Claxton, 206 Ga. 860 (1950); Gostin v. Brooks, 89 Ga. 244 (1892); see, generally, McQuillin Mun Corp. §13.25.10 (3rd ed.) and Sands & Libonati Loc Govt Law §11.09.

47. *New Robert's Rules of Order*, 272.

48. City of Smyrna et al. v. R. L. Ruff, Sr. et al., 240 Ga. 250 (1977); Bozik v. Cobb County, 240 Ga. 537 (1978).

49. O.C.G.A. §50-14-2(1); The Claxton Enterprise v. Evans County Board of Commissioners, 249 Ga. App. 870 (2001).

50. As of May 2010, 17 counties had full-time employees serving as county attorneys. The remainder retained private attorneys to serve as county attorneys on a contractual basis.

51. O.C.G.A. §§50-14-2, 50-14-3, 50-14-4.

52. Jersawitz v. Fortson, 213 Ga. App. 796 (1994); Moon v. Terrell County, 249 Ga. App. 567 (2001).

53. Op. Att'y Gen. No. U98-3 (1998).

54. See, generally, McQuillin Mun Corp. §13.51 (3rd ed.) and Sands & Libonati Loc Govt Law §11.13.

55. O.C.G.A. §§36-66-4, 36-66-5.

56. O.C.G.A. §36-81-5(f).

57. O.C.G.A. §48-5-32.1.

58. O.C.G.A. §36-71-6.

59. O.C.G.A. §§48-13-6(c), 48-13-28.

60. O.C.G.A. §36-66-5; Tilley Properties, Inc. v. Bartow County, 261 Ga. 153 (1991).

61. O.C.G.A. §50-14-1(c).

62. See, generally, McQuillin Mun Corp. §§13.07, 13.07.10 (3rd ed.).

63. O.C.G.A. §36-66-5(a).

64. *New Robert's Rules of Order*, 188.

65. *Sturgis Standard Code of Parliamentary Procedure*, 242.

66. O.C.G.A. §16-11-34.

27

Beth Brown and R. Terry Hadaway

Communicating with Constituents

Thirty years ago, communication was much simpler than it is today. Major television networks and large newspapers dominated the American media landscape, and cable television and the Internet did not exist. People did not demand, nor did they have, instant access to information. Today, the communications industry is a very different business. In addition to receiving information through traditional media outlets, people can now get instant updates through computers, cell phones, and handheld devices. Never in history have county officials had so many opportunities to reach members of their communities as quickly as they can today.

At the same time, people have far greater control over how, when, and where they find and receive information. County commissioners must diversify their approach to communications in order to successfully engage citizens in decision making and increase awareness of local government programs and services. In order to reach constituents, commissioners can use a mix of traditional media relations, Web sites and electronic communications, community forums, public relations campaigns, and other outreach strategies. The effectiveness of a particular method depends on several factors: who the intended audience is, what the message is, when recipients need to know the information, and why they need it.

MEDIA RELATIONS

While the approaches and delivery strategies of newspapers, television networks, radio stations, and magazines continue to evolve as a result of electronic communications, these media outlets still serve as primary sources of information. The more comfortable a commissioner is in working with reporters, editors, and broadcasters, the more likely he or she will benefit from news coverage that is accurate and balanced.

Given the inevitability of news media attention, county commissioners should be aware of five factors affecting a commission's relationship with the news media:

1. The media's mandate to function as a watchdog of government is one of the oldest principles of journalism, and one that is taken very seriously. The media look more closely at government processes than they do any other topic and have far greater access to information concerning the decisions made by government than any other entity they cover.

2. The media shape public opinion about the commission and individual commissioners. Reporters are information conduits for their audiences—the people whose lives are affected by activities and decisions of local government.

3. Reporters expect to have access to decision makers and government leaders. County commissioners should strive to be responsive and accessible to the news media. Public information officers and others in county government can assist a commissioner in preparing a response to a media inquiry, but they cannot substitute for the commissioner.

4. Working with the media involves some risk. At some point, a commissioner is likely to be misquoted or misrepresented. On the other hand, refusing to work with the news media practically guarantees unsatisfactory news coverage. Direct interaction with the media will help ensure that a commissioner's perspective is considered.

5. A proactive approach to media relations is far better than a reactive one. Commissioners should establish relationships with local reporters and reach out to them with accurate, firsthand information before issues become controversial. A reporter who is familiar with a commissioner's positions is more likely to be comfortable contacting that commissioner as a source.

INTERVIEW TIPS AND TECHNIQUES

Responsiveness is the primary rule when working with the media. Reporters work under tight deadlines and can cover issues with varying degrees of depth, depending on the type of media. When a reporter requests an interview, a commissioner should be sure to know the reporter's deadline and understand the subject and angle of the article (see Table 27-1). The following are some other tips for handling media interviews:

Be prepared. Once the topic of an interview has been determined, a commissioner should identify three to five key points that he or she wants to communicate. Remember that a reporter will use only a few seconds or a quote or two from the interview, so give simple, clear, and concise answers and try to repeat key points several times during the interview.

Anticipate questions. Consider the issue that the reporter is covering, anticipate difficult questions, and prepare answers for those questions. It may be helpful for a commissioner to speak with others in the government who can provide additional information on the issue so that he or she is comfortable answering questions about that issue. A commissioner may also want to set up an interview with the reporter and have a county expert present in order to help answer the reporter's questions.

Don't use jargon or acronyms. Government officials tend to use their own set of jargon and acronyms for many programs and services, but using jargon can make it difficult for reporters and the public to understand government processes and decisions. Try to avoid using "government-speak" during an interview, and clearly define terms or acronyms that a reporter may find unfamiliar. In this way, the reporter— and ultimately the public—will better understand county government and any specific issues discussed in the interview.

Say what you can or explain why you can't. In some situations, such as law enforcement investigations, pending lawsuits and items discussed in executive sessions, a commissioner may be limited in how much information he or she can provide to the media. Whenever confidential information or pending lawsuits are involved, the county attorney should be consulted before the interview to determine what can and what cannot be discussed in order to better prepare the commissioner to answer the questions. Explain why the question can't be answered, and provide a reasonable timeline for when additional information will be released. Never answer a question by saying "no comment"; this response only signals to a reporter that there is something to hide.

Maximize the opportunity. Reporters are often assigned to cover many different topics. As a representative of local government, a county commissioner has an opportunity to help educate them beyond the topic at hand. Help them make connections to other programs and services, and provide them with additional information and resources by e-mail or by pointing them to the county's Web site.

Ask a follow-up question. At the end of an interview, ask the reporter a question about the topic discussed in order to ensure that the key message has been identified. If not, take the opportunity to repeat the primary points, offer additional insight, or recommend other contacts who can provide similar perspectives that support a specific position.

Remember, a news interview is an opportunity to reach people in the community and provide them with information that they want and need to hear. Initiate contact with a reporter rather than wait to be contacted. Establishing a relationship with local reporters and understanding the environment in which they work can help a county commissioner be more comfortable in dealing with the media.

Table 27-1. *What to Expect from Media Outlets*

Newspaper	• Deadlines are based on the publication, which may be daily or weekly.
	• Interviews typically are conducted on site (at a speech or event location) or over the phone.
	• Reporters usually have some time for limited research.
	• Reporters prefer to have supporting information e-mailed or faxed.
	• Reporters like photo opportunities that will support a story, but they will need lead time.
	• Several quotations may be used; an interviewee's background is referenced for additional information.
Television	• Deadline is usually the same day (reporters often get assignments that morning and work on short deadlines, especially for midday news).
	• Reporters do not have much time for research and typically look for quick facts.
	• Visual elements are needed as support for stories (the more visual, the more coverage).
	• A station may send satellite crews or just a reporter with a camera to get the story.
	• Reporters may pull stories on regional or national issues from satellite telecasts and then look for local angles.
	• A reporter may spend 15 minutes interviewing a subject but use only 30 seconds of actual footage.

Table 27-1. *What to Expect from Media Outlets (continued).*

Radio	<ul><li>Stations vary greatly in size and format.</li><li>Stations pick up much of their news coverage from print and television media.</li><li>Interviews are almost always conducted by phone.</li><li>Reporters usually working under short deadlines will not have much time for research.</li><li>Stories can be recorded live or used later as an edited tape.</li><li>Sound bites are critical since there is no visual support.</li></ul>
Magazine	<ul><li>Outlet provides best opportunity for in-depth coverage on an issue.</li><li>Many agendas are set months in advance.</li><li>Staff or freelance reporters may be used.</li><li>Reporters usually start with a telephone interview and follow up with field visit.</li><li>Reporters have time to cover more than one angle and can use many sources.</li></ul>
Internet	<ul><li>Most media outlets also have Web sites where they provide additional information on an issue or links for more information.</li><li>News stories can be distributed immediately through Internet capabilities.</li></ul>

County commissioners will face decisions that the media will scrutinize and will be asked questions that they would rather not answer. Prepare for those times, and answer the tough questions with honesty and sincerity.

WEB SITES AND ELECTRONIC COMMUNICATIONS

According to the Internet and American Life Project conducted by the Pew Research Center, more than 77 percent of American adults use the Internet.[1] Furthermore, more than 59 percent say they use the Internet to visit local, state, or federal government Web sites. These findings underscore the importance of developing and maintaining a Web site for your county that provides information about your local government.

A well-designed Web site can make it faster and easier for constituents to find information and thereby reduce the number of phone calls to county offices, saving personnel time and money. Newcomers can learn how to file for a homestead exemption, register a vehicle, identify the utilities that serve the jurisdiction, and find other county contact information for services of interest to them. Business owners can find out how to register their businesses for occupation tax purposes, determine permitting requirements, and in some cases even identify opportunities to bid on county business. From communicating information on county events and recreational programming to providing e-services such as paying property taxes and traffic citations online, local government Web sites are becoming primary sources of information for more and more people. Information made available on the county Web site should be considered an open record.[2]

Web sites also promote transparency in government. Many county Web sites post county commission agendas and minutes from meetings as well as other official county information such as budget documents. Some counties even provide live feeds or recorded coverage of commission meetings. With the increased demand for information from the public, county officials should seek to provide as much information online as possible.

In addition, a well-designed Web site can attract residential and business interest in a community by showcasing high-quality services, cultural and recreational opportunities, workforce preparedness, and other assets. Business leaders who are considering investing in or relocating to a community or families who are deciding where to purchase a home require information for comparison purposes. The county that does not have a Web site that allows for quick comparisons to other counties is at a competitive disadvantage.

E-COMMUNICATIONS AND SOCIAL MEDIA

Many counties are turning to electronic communications in order to connect with citizens in their community, especially as the size and distribution of traditional media shrink. With e-communications, a county is able to control the distribution of information and the perspectives presented. People can sign up to receive county e-newsletters, public safety notifications, emergency alerts, and other information directly from their county government. E-communications provide an opportunity to directly engage constituents and reach them quickly and easily with a variety of information.

Some local governments are exploring other social media opportunities such as Facebook and Twitter. More than 300 million Americans regularly use Facebook, and more than 65 million of them access this service through a mobile device.[3] These social media sites are not just for the younger generation; the fastest-growing demographic of Facebook users are people aged 35 and older.[4]

County governments may use these social media networks to communicate with citizens on a regular basis or only in emergency situations. Furthermore, these social media platforms provide good opportunities for local officials to keep constituents informed about their activities. Engaging in social media networking may not be right for every community. As with all forms of communication, counties and their elected officials should evaluate the distribution tools that work best for their constituents and develop policies for their use.

GOVERNMENT-COMMUNITY INTERACTION

Many other methods of communication are available to local governments. Every county employee is a customer service representative for local government. Most customers are residents of the community and interact with people in both work and personal settings. County employees should be encouraged to be advocates for local government programs and services and should be provided with information when changes are implemented so that they can help to spread the word.

Other ways to communicate with citizens include volunteering to speak to local civic associations, the local chamber of commerce, homeowners associations, or other community groups. Members of these organizations are the activists in any community. A county commissioner can use these speaking opportunities to further his or her message or encourage public input on an important issue.

Public involvement is another important communications tool. When dealing with a major change or issue that is generating controversy, consider forming a stakeholders group representing multiple interests, and work with these constituents to develop a resolution. People are not always going to agree, but working together can take the heat out of a debate. Each side is able to listen to the other's perspective, which may yield a surprising middle-ground position. Such efforts show that the commission is open to hearing multiple viewpoints. Failure to incorporate ideas from stakeholder groups into the decision-making process may result in negative public feedback.

PUBLIC RELATIONS CAMPAIGNS

Public relations campaigns are designed to increase awareness about a specific issue, and they employ a variety of communications methods in order to distribute information. These campaigns seek to move people from awareness to action. Considerations involved in creating such campaigns include determining who the target audience is, what the key messages are, which distribution channels will be used in order to get information to the target audience, and what the desired result will be.

For example, water supply is a major concern for many local governments, especially in times of drought. An effective public relations campaign might be to inform homeowners about ways in which they can reduce their outdoor water use and thereby contribute to the larger effort of conserving water and extending the water supply.

In this example, homeowners are the target audience. Key messages might include recommending hours during which residents should water their lawns and gardens and providing information about drought friendly garden plans and other landscaping tips to reduce water use. In terms of distribution channels, a county might consider including this information in water bills, publishing informative articles in the local newspaper, sponsoring events or workshops with local gardening centers, installing drought friendly landscaping with signage in a local park, or other creative ways to encourage public support. The underlying goal of the campaign is to change water-use habits in order to conserve water in the community.

Before developing a campaign, a local government should explore what is already available in order to save both time and financial resources. Other counties, state and federal agencies, and organizations like the Association County Commissioners of Georgia may have public relations campaigns that can be modified or used in order to address issues in a particular community. Also, commissioners should be aware that public relations campaigns may not be used to promote or oppose candidates or issues to be voted on in a referendum.[5]

Today's county officials have more opportunity than ever before to interact with constituents and involve community members in local government. Incorporating a variety of communications strategies ensures that information has the greatest reach.

NOTES

1. www.pewinternet.org. Accessed April 22, 2010.
2. www.insidefacebook.com. Accessed April 22, 2010.
3. mashable.com/2009/07/07/facebook-users-older. Accessed April 22, 2010.
4. OFFICIAL CODE OF GEORGIA ANNOTATED (O.C.G.A.) §50-18-70 et seq.
5. O.C.G.A. §21-5-30.2.

Index

The notations n, t, and f refer to note, table, and figure, respectively.

public hearings, 551–52
regular, 550
special meetings, 551
voting, 545
Memorandum of understanding,
development incentives, 276
Mental illness and mental retardation
judge of the probate court, 69
regional planning/community service
boards, 86
Mental illness/health, 362, 363
Merger of governmental functions, 487–88
Merit or civil service system, 58
Merit systems, 151
Metropolitan North Georgia Water
Planning District, 235
Millage rates, 399
Ministerial duties, 115
Edmond v. Lincoln County, 116
official immunity, 116–17
sovereign immunity, 116–17
Minutes of board meetings, 118–19
Misappropriating property, 136
Misdemeanors, violations of ordinances, 31
Misrepresenting the truth, 136
Mobile source control program, 231
Modified accrual basis of accounting,
386–87
Motor vehicles
accident report confidentiality, 527–28
accidents
liability issues, 114, 117
county responsibility, 117
county repair shops, 316–17
emission control, 229
fueling stations, 317
parking, county roads, 285, 286
tag collection fees, 411
Motor vehicles/equipment purchase and
maintenance, 316–17
Mutual Aid Act, 474
Mutual aid agreements, for service delivery,
474

Name-clearing hearings, 59
liberty interests, 154–56
other aspects, 156
procedural requirements, 155
when required, 155
National Association of Counties (NACo)
congressional lobbying, 504
communications tips, 505t
federal issues, 504

functions described, 495–96
on line-item budgets, 437
membership, 495
National Civic League, 16
National Clean Diesel Campaign, 231
National Commission for Accreditation
of Park and Recreation Agencies
(CAPRA), park and recreation
standards, 326
National Environmental Policy Act, 252
National Fire Protection Association
Standards, 339
National Flood Insurance Program, 246
National Incident Management System
(NIMS), 79
National Oceanographic and Atmospheric
Administration, 253
National Park Service, 251
National Pollutant Discharge Elimination
System (NPDES), 237
vehicle fleet maintenance, 317
National Sex Offender Registry, 95
Natural resources
comprehensive planning, 211–12
impact of sprawl, 217–18
overview, 225–26
regional planning, 219
vital areas in planning, 211
See also Department of Natural
Resources
Neglect of duties, 135
Negligence
county property, 114
Edmond v. Lincoln County, 116
federal civil rights claims, 110
operation of county vehicles, 117
supervision of employees, 111–12
Nepotism, ethics code guidelines, 127
News media. *See* Media; Media relations
New Source Review program, 230
9-1-1 authority, 193
9-1-1 emergency services. *See* Emergency
9-1-1 services
1983 actions, 108
employee claims, 157
Non-appropriation risk, 464–65
Nonpoint source pollution, 239–40
Nonproperty taxes, compliance costs, 417
Nontax revenue, 409–14
"No personal profit" rule, 129
NPDES. *See* National Pollutant Discharge
Elimination System
Nuisance complaints, animal control, 350